# THE OPERA COMPANION

George Martin has been a member of the Metropolitan Opera
Association and a director of the Metropolitan Opera Guild.
His books include


VERDI: HIS MUSIC, LIFE AND TIMES


A COMPANION TO TWENTIETH-CENTURY OPERA


THE RED SHIRT AND THE CROSS OF SAVOY
(the story of Italy's Risorgimento, 1748-1871)

# THE OPERA
# COMPANION

## BY GEORGE MARTIN

DRAWINGS BY EVERETT RAYMOND KINSTLER

*John Murray*

First published in Great Britain 1962 by Macmillan Publishers Ltd.
This paperback edition first published in Great Britain 1984 by
John Murray (Publishers) Ltd, 50 Albemarle Street, London W1X 4BD
by arrangement with Dodd, Mead & Company, New York

Reprinted 1985, 1988, 1990, 1991, 1992, 1994

Printed in Great Britain at the University Press, Cambridge

British Library Cataloguing in Publication Data
Martin, George, 1926 –
    The opera companion
    1. Opera
    I. Title
    782.1    ML1700

ISBN 0-7195-4110-7

Acknowledgement is made to the following for permission to use selections from their copyrighted publications indicated below:

W. H. Auden: From *Some Reflections on Music and Opera* by W. H. Auden in the *Partisan Review*, January-February, 1952.

Bell Telephone Laboratories and O. J. Murphy: From *Measurements of Orchestral Pitch* by O. J. Murphy in the *Journal of the Acoustical Society of America*, Vol. 12, #3, January, 1941.

John Calder, Ltd.: From *Life of Rossini* by Stendahl, translated by Richard Coe. Copyright 1957 by John Calder, Ltd.
From *Rome, Naples and Florence* by Stendahl, translated by Richard Coe. Copyright 1959 by John Calder, Ltd.

Doubleday and Company: From *George Balanchine's Complete Stories of the Great Ballets* by George Balanchine. Copyright 1954 by Doubleday & Company, Inc. Reprinted by permission.

A. M. Heath and Company, Ltd.: From *The Memoirs of Beniamino Gigli*. Copyright 1957 by Beniamino Gigli.

Houghton Mifflin Company: From *Looking for a Bluebird* by Joseph Wechsberg. Copyright 1944, 1945 by Joseph Wechsberg.

Edwin F. Kalmus: From *Treatise on Instrumentation* by Hector Berlioz, translated by Theodore Front. Copyright 1948 by Edwin F. Kalmus.

Pierre Key Publishing Corporation: From *This Business of Singing* by Pierre Key. Copyright 1937 by Pierre Key Publishing Corporation.

Lincoln Kirstein: From *Blast at Ballet* by Lincoln Kirstein. Copyright 1938 by Lincoln Kirstein.
From *Glossary* by Lincoln Kirstein in *Dance Perspectives No. 1*. Copyright 1958.

Alfred A. Knopf, Inc.: From *The Life of Richard Wagner* by Ernest Newman. Copyright 1941, 1946 by Alfred A. Knopf, Inc.
From *The Wagner Operas* by Ernest Newman. Copyright 1949 by Alfred A. Knopf, Inc.
From *The Story of the Metropolitan Opera* by Irving Kolodin. Copyright 1936, 1953 by Irving Kolodin.

Macmillan & Company, Ltd. and St. Martin's Press, Inc.: From *Grove's Dictionary of Music and Musicians* edited by Eric Bloom. Copyright 1954 by St. Martin's Press, Inc.

# CONTENTS

PART III   THE SYNOPSES                                197

THE OPERAS

    Catalogue of all operas mentioned in the text and many others giving the composer, librettist, date and place of first performance and for some operas the theatre. Part I, Operas with first performances from 1597 through 1939; Part II, Operas with first performances from 1939 through 1959; Part III, the operas of Mozart, Verdi, Wagner and Puccini listed in order of production.

    Basic operatic Italian.

# PREFACE

I have designed this book rather differently from most of the traditional opera guides that are now available. I have made no attempt at "completeness" with a synopsis of every opera now in the repertory nor have I tried to expose with a thirty or forty page critique all the subtleties of any one opera. Rather I have tried, particularly in the short chapters and Glossary that make up Part I and II of the book, to provide any reader with the information necessary to go to any opera and find it at least interesting if not enjoyable.

By information I mean such simple things as the definition of a baritone or a "lirico spinto," an explanation of how a singer makes a noise and an orchestra tunes, and some history of such diverse things as the claque and the castrati. I also mean some rather more complicated things such as the why and how of an overture, the sounds of an orchestra, and the structure of a melody.

I hope that these chapters and the Glossary will provide the casual operagoer with a background for opera such as he already has for the theatre. Most persons through greater exposure and education have a far better idea of what a play can do and how the playwright goes about it. This background gives them a greater tolerance for slight successes or even failures. We have all been to plays that we felt did not succeed but which we still found interesting because we understood the problem and enjoyed watching the playwright work at it. One reason the opera repertory has been so static may be that the casual operagoer has lost this background and now can only clutch at the acknowledged and isolated masterworks.

A background, however, implies something to which to refer, and so I have included in Part III synopses of forty-seven operas. Again, in them I have departed from the usual procedure in that I have not quoted musical excerpts. Today so few persons can read music at sight that it is almost a snobbism to quote it, and in the taxi or subway on the way to the opera no one has a piano at hand to pick out the notes. Instead of the musical phrase I have emphasized the key words that can be heard and understood in performance. Thus in Act II of *Tosca* I think the casual operagoer is better served if he is alerted to Tosca's "quanto" (how much) and "il prezzo" (your price), than if he is given the music or words of the first line of Scarpia's answering aria. Those words are lost in a rush of sound, and the few notes torn out of the phrase and without harmony are meaningless. This reflects my belief that for most casual operagoers a performance is primarily a theatrical rather than a musical experience, a reason, possibly, why Puccini with his superb sense of theatre is more popular than Wagner.

Everywhere throughout the book I have attempted to foresee and answer the casual operagoer's question. This has involved me with Authorities, written and oral, who are irritating persons because they hedge and shuffle. But this is inevitable in opera, an art in which each performance starts a new tradition while the old one never dies. At times, however, I sympathized with the Greek boy caught yelling down the crack in the rock at Delphi: "Doesn't anyone down there know anything for sure?"

But of course I could not foresee every question and, like the Authorities, I too have hedged or ignored those I could not answer. Still I trust the book will be a start for most operagoers.

GEORGE MARTIN

*New York City*

# PART ONE

# The Casual Operagoer's Guide

---

"Simply to hear anyone speak of an opera, or to be in the theatre, or to hear singing is enough to make me beside myself!"

*MOZART*

(*In a letter to his father, October 11, 1777.*)

# I·

## THE OVERTURE, THE PRELUDE
## AND THREE CHORDS

---

All artists want to arrest the attention of the audience before beginning the work at hand. A flourish or fanfare is one method; clearing the throat is another. Opera developed the overture.

As early as the seventeenth century there were divergent styles, the French and the Italian, and cross words about which was better in theory and practice. The French preferred their overtures in three parts: slow, slow and quick. The Italians agreed on the three parts but wanted them quick, slower and quick. They argued that a big audience needed a big noise to arrest its attention and that the French slow opening was always confused with continued tuning of the instruments.

At first composers did not tie into the overture any of the music of the opera that followed. It was enough to set the mood, merry or sad, and, if merry, to be sufficiently noisy to cover the arrival of late-comers. Naturally, as one merry overture was rather like another and none was musically tied to any particular opera, composers stole tunes from themselves and each other and even switched whole overtures from opera to opera as needed. One of the last and most famous examples of this is Rossini's overture to *Il Barbiere di Siviglia*. He wrote it first for *Aureliano in Palmira* (Milan, 1813), a serious but unsuccessful opera about some incredibly virtuous Romans and the Queen of Persia. Then two years later he used it again for *Elisabetta, Regina d'Inghilterra* (Naples, 1815), a highly successful drama about England's Virgin Queen. Finally, less than four and a half months later, he used it to open *Il Barbiere* (Rome, 1816). He could do this partly because the operas were given in different cities and there were no victrola records, radios and "international" artists to spread the music with the speed of today, and partly because the overture, quite by chance, fit its final resting place.

But inevitably composers less carefree than Rossini wondered about the purpose of the overture. Clearly, if it was to arrest attention, it should do so appropriately; and did not this mean setting the mood and preparing the audience psychologically for the opera that followed? Otherwise, attention was not arrested, but misled. Granted the purpose, how did the composer set about it?

Mozart's overtures show him trying first one way, then another. The overture to *Die Entfuehrung aus dem Serail* (5 min.) is in the traditional Italian style—quick, slower, quick—but to these tempi Mozart has added music from the opera and an orchestration of it that is unique to the opera. Thus, the quick themes are Turkish music, the slow one the Spanish noble sighing for his lady kept captive by the Pasha; and, throughout, Mozart has scored the Turkish music with a delightful excess of triangle, cymbals and drums. Before the curtain rises, the audience knows it will hear a silly Turkish story with a dash of Spanish sentiment. It is a completely effective overture.

But alas for those who look for neat arguments. In his overture to *Le Nozze di Figaro* (4 min.), Mozart threw aside all methods and wrote the thing itself—the perfect overture. In it he quotes no themes or arias from the opera, has no contrasting slower section, scores it in a usual fashion and employs no special rhythms. Yet somehow he captured the essence of the opera with its surface comedy of manners and undertones of virility and passion.

It is easier to see some of what he did in the overtures to others of his operas. The overture to *Così fan tutte* (4 min.) reflects in its speed and scoring for woodwinds the shimmering atmosphere of the bay of Naples and its artificial society. It also quotes from the opera the music to which its moral and title is sung. For the overture to *Don Giovanni* (7 min.) Mozart quoted some of the statue's music and composed a new theme which, although Don Giovanni never sings it in the opera, is a fine characterization of him. And in the overture to *Die Zauber-floete* (7 min.) Mozart creates a spiritual atmosphere that he introduces and interrupts with a rhythmic pattern suggesting a knocking on the closed door of the mysteries. All of these procedures were in general use in Mozart's time and still are today.

Mozart's contemporary, Gluck, also experimented with the overture and sometimes moved directly into the first scene without a break. This, of course, has the advantage of not losing the audience's attention while it applauds, comments and looks around the house. Gluck also used music from the opera that followed and, particularly in the operas he wrote for Paris, developed the idea of treating the themes symphonically. Thus if Gluck had written the overture to *Die Entfuehrung,* he might have presented the Turkish and Spanish themes as in conflict (rather than merely contrasting), with the Spanish theme emerging at the end triumphant. The danger in such symphonic treatment is that it takes time to work out, and some of Gluck's overtures run for more than ten minutes. The themes must be presented, contrasted, combined and ultimately resolved. If the composer does this too fast, the audience simply does not grasp it. And if he does it too successfully, the overture is no longer an introduction but a separate masterpiece, leaving the opera merely an unnecessary gloss.

This is not an irrelevant, theoretical problem: it is exactly what happened to Beethoven in trying to write an overture for his opera, *Fidelio.* He composed four in the following order: "Leonora #2" (1805), "Leonora #3" (1806), "Leonora #1" (1807), and the *Fidelio* overture (1814). (Leonora is the heroine's real name; Fidelio her assumed name. The curious numbering represents a scholar's argument over the date of composition; some claim that "#1" was done in 1805 before "#2." "Leonora #1" is relatively unimportant. "Leonoras #2" and "#3" are both symphonic masterpieces, and both appear regularly in the concert hall. Both, coming from the same opera, have much the same music but are differently developed, which is in itself a fascinating study of genius. Most critics find "Leonora #3" even greater than "#2.")

*Fidelio* is a rescue opera. The faithful wife disguised as a man finally locates her missing husband in the deepest dungeon of a state prison. The brutal warden is about to kill him for personal reasons when the wife reveals her identity, threatens to die with the husband and tries to delay the murder until the good governor, who is on his way, can arrive. The evil warden is about to kill both husband and wife when the governor's arrival is announced by a trumpet call.

Beethoven's problem, as he fully recognized, was that in "Leonora #2" and "#3" (13 min.) he had superbly presented the conflict, built up the tension, resolved it with the trumpet call and left the opera nothing to do. When the curtain finally went up and revealed a girl ironing the family linen while her swain tried to talk of love, the effect was ludicrous or, even worse, boring. The momentous overture staggered the pacing of the opera beyond recovery. Beethoven's fourth effort, the *Fidelio* overture (6 min.), is much shorter, less developed and without the trumpet call. It suggests a story of tension and conflict that is to be taken seriously, and it leaves the telling of it to the opera.

There is still another hassle over "Leonora #3" in which everyone can take sides. The second and last act of *Fidelio* has two scenes: the first, in the dungeon, has the trumpet call; the second is one of general rejoicing, freeing of prisoners and praising of the faithful wife. Some producers, supported by critics, insert "Leonora #3" between the two scenes. One critic claims this is "its true setting"; another replies it "destroys the dramatic balance of the whole act."

Some of Wagner's overtures, or preludes as he called them when the curtain rose without a break, are so grand that they, too, almost fall into the *Fidelio* trap. The prelude to *Die Meistersinger* (9 min.), for example, is a complete symphonic capitulation of the opera. First, the Mastersingers are presented from their good side, foursquared and disciplined; then Walter's themes and the unformed Prizesong swirl around romantically and are followed by the Mastersingers, presented this time from their worst side, picayune and pedantic; finally, Wagner fuses the best of both into an art inspired by the young and new and disciplined by the old and trained. It is superb; but it causes Wagner trouble. He moves directly into the church scene; but the audience, misled by concert versions of the prelude and desiring to release its excitement after the tremendous orchestral climax, starts to applaud, and a smattering of appreciative handclaps crashes into the chorale. Having a chorale was a stroke of genius, for solo voices would have sounded minuscule after the prelude, and it also was a supremely logical way of slowing down the pace so that it can be built up again. But it leaves the stage director with an almost bare stage and four minutes of miming to work out for a tenor, so that in solving his musical problem, Wagner created a theatrical one. And here, after the prelude, Wagner often loses the bulk of his audience for as much as ten minutes, or until the apprentices come in. (At the next performance look around and gage the attentiveness of the audience at this point.)

The opera *Die Meistersinger* is a masterpiece; and partly because it is so long, the effect of the prelude is dissipated and the opera makes its own point as though for the first time. But *Tannhaeuser,* for which Wagner wrote a similar symphonic overture (15 min.), does not come off so well; much of it after the overture seems windy and inept.

Wagner, like Mozart, tried all kinds of overtures. In *Lohengrin* he has a prelude (9 min.) built up of Lohengrin's themes, but he does not treat them dramatically with conflict and resolution. There is no suggestion of Elsa's death or of Ortrud; Wagner merely establishes a mystical mood as the prelude slowly swells to a climax and then fades away. One result is that when the curtain parts, the sound of the human voice is arresting, not disappointing. As a piece of music it is not nearly so impressive as the prelude to *Die Meistersinger,* but as a prelude to an opera it may be more successful.

Verdi's preludes are all very much shorter than Wagner's and are so tied to their operas that they can have no independent existence. The overture to *La Forza del Destino,* a sort of costume drama whoop-de-doo, is almost the only exception, although he wrote a longer, formal overture for *Aida,* which he discarded in favor of a short prelude. Typically in *Rigoletto,* for example, he suggests the tragic turn of the opera by quoting the music of Monterone's curse, and then, as the curtain rises, presents the Duke's court with its tinselly dance music; the tension and contrast of the opera, which no audience fails to grasp, has been superbly set in a matter of minutes, with the first act well under way and the resolution of the conflict left for the opera. He does the same thing in *La Traviata* where, of course, his prelude to Act IV is justly considered a miracle of mood. But in all of them he uses music from the opera and merely sets the pace and mood.

Meanwhile, hundreds of lesser composers frankly threw up their hands at the overture and invented the potpourri, a succession of the opera's arias and numbers strung together, played fortissimo and offered as a dividend to the audience on the hopeful theory that repetition makes the heart grow fonder. This worked well for the satire or the simple, sentimental show, whose only object was a gentle emotion recollected with tranquillity. But even such a gay composer as Sullivan, Gilbert's other half, discovered when they began to reach for something more serious in *The Yeomen of the Guard* that he had to wrestle with the problem of the overture and do something more than just string the numbers together. Art has a way of imposing its own requirements.

The adventurous composers, however, continued their experiments on other lines, one of which led to the abolishment of the overture. Wagner's few bars of introduction to *Die Walkuere* merely depict the storm from which Siegmund, seconds later, will find shelter in Hunding's hut. Verdi's *Otello* also begins with a storm, into which he and Boito, the librettist, worked the chorus with such skill that the curtain can rise on the first note. Richard Strauss' *Salome* and *Elektra* both start directly.

This is the fashion today. No one now is absolutely certain why an overture was ever needed; possibly the lack of a rheostat to dim the house candles made it necessary. Most composers, except when being deliberately nostalgic, start off directly with the opera after a few bars of the simplest sort of mood setting, often no more than three or four chords.

Whether the overture or the shorter prelude will survive at all is a question to which every première gives a new answer. But there are several things to note about it. First, it is clinging with tenacity and some success to comic and chamber operas. The reverse of this is that it is most successfully omitted when the opera begins with some grand scene of agitation which stuns the gabbling audience into attention— thus, the storm scenes, the escaped prisoner in *Tosca* or the tense and maddened crowd in *Turandot.* These agitated scenes come naturally to dramas, particularly those about wild and passionate individuals who are the title roles; they come far less easily into comedies, which depend much more frequently on building situations. Mozart's *Le Nozze di Figaro,* for example, begins with Susannah trying on a hat while Figaro measures the room for placing the bed, a cause for agitation, but one that in the beginning is concealed from the audience *and* Figaro. There are, of course, as always in opera, exceptions so glaring that they destroy any theory, and Verdi in his comic opera, *Falstaff,* whips the audience into the first scene between Falstaff and Dr. Caius after only seven bars of allegro vivace. But here there is a tension self-explanatory to the audience: Falstaff deliberately and arrogantly ignores Dr. Caius' outraged greeting. Puccini's *Gianni Schicchi* has no such visible and obvious tension. It opens with relatives praying around a dead man's bed and takes thirty-one bars of allegro slowing down to largo to start the opera. Thus the dramatic structure of the first scene may be the decisive factor in a composer's mind when he decides against an overture.

Of course, another factor never to be underestimated is the tantalizing and infuriating vision hanging before every composer of Mozart's overtures leading a fine double life in the concert hall and the opera house.

# II·

## MELODY, ARIA AND RECITATIVE

The casual operagoer waits through the recitative for the aria he knows and likes; then he wakes up, pays attention, responds emotionally, and at its end subsides till another favorite and familiar aria comes along. Operagoing for him is like island hopping in the Pacific—small, luxuriant explosions of Paradise separated by long stretches of flat, dull water. Happily, each time he goes again to the same opera, the islands are larger and the water less. The knowledge that this *will* happen and that eventually the entire opera will be "terra firma" is what turns ordinary, safety-first businessmen into excited operagoers.

Memory has a large share in this. The succession of notes which on first hearing seem confused and unrelated becomes on repetition a melody: the listener's mind has then successfully organized the notes into patterns, although the patterns need not necessarily give him pleasure. Little is known about how the mind organizes the patterns and perhaps even less about why some patterns please and others do not, but it is clear that much of the organizing is psychophysical—the listener's mind projects onto the music its own bodily experiences. Thus the lady who talks of the waltz "with the swoop and glide" is not half so silly as the critic who sprains his tongue to avoid such phrases.

To everyone a rising scale seems a defiance of the law of gravity, and the higher the note, the greater seems the strain necessary to produce and maintain it. A descending scale, on the other hand, releases tension and gives a feeling of coming to rest. Listening to a soprano work her way slowly up the scale raises the same feeling of tension in a listener as does watching a weightlifter go from thighs, to chest, to straight up. On stage the corpse of Hamlet or Juliet is visibly laid out, and in the pit the music corresponds: a funeral march or "miserere" invariably proceeds horizontally with only minute changes up and down in the melody. This corresponds to the incalculably strong sense in every man that the vertical represents life and the horizontal death.

The very words with which all the world describes music is evidence that the mind projects its bodily experience onto the notes. "Up and "down" the scale is wholly inaccurate. The singer tightens his vocal cords, the violinist's finger shortens the string, the pianist's hand moves east, west, north or south, but no one's cord, finger or hand moves up and down. The scale is not a ladder but a series of relationships: this string vibrates faster than that, or is under a greater tension, or is shorter. In the same way tempo (*See* Glossary) is relative: how fast is presto, how slow lento? The standard by which anyone answers, when evasion is no longer possible, seems to be the speed at which he normally walks. Obviously, this varies tremendously, but it is not surprising that much of the world finds the New York City Ballet exhausting because its tempos seem so unremittingly fast.

Apparently, the mind associates "up" the scale with the effort needed to defy the law of gravity because it knows it is easier to lie down than to stand up, to be silent than to sing, to produce a low note than a high note, and it organizes the notes to some extent in terms of the energy it knows is required to produce them in a throat. For, no matter what he may take up later, man's first instrument in time and use is his voice, and he knows that it takes more energy to tighten his vocal cords to produce a higher note. This concept he transfers to a violin or piano, even though on these no increase in energy is required for a higher note. The voice is the fundamental instrument of the world, and a response to any instrument depends to some extent on the body's experience with its vocal cords.

The mind's ability to organize a pattern of notes is inextricably linked with its response to the notes. Like the chicken and the egg, no one knows which comes first. But clearly the listener's body reacts to a high note sympathetically and sets up tensions in its own throat and chest reflecting those it recognizes in the singer. In the same way, a ballerina watching another inevitably tends to mirror the dancer's motions. This sympathetic muscular response is one reason why opera lovers, alone and in private, croak into song with the victrola, why automobile drivers alone on a long trip will bellow along with the radio, and why unsophisticated Italian audiences at the opera frequently join right in with the singers. The response is in the throat; the ear is merely a conduit.

The composer's job is to organize the notes and the tensions they represent into patterns that, as Robert Erickson says in *The Structure of Music,* "move toward and away from points of relative tension and relative rest." When this is done successfully, the listener's mind, depending on its abilities, recognizes a melody. No one, of course, can tell a composer how to write a good melody, but there are some simple rules, perhaps all too obvious, which the operagoer can apply to what he is hearing for the first time so that he can possibly thereby recognize a melody faster and more intelligently.

1. Tonic accent: The highest note of a series all of the same volume and duration will seem to be accented. It is demonstrable in a physics laboratory that it is not, but the listener's mind will have it so. As an example, sing a scale up and down or the opening notes of "Frère Jacques." Top notes, therefore, even without emphasis, tend to be the climax or fulcrums of patterns, and a good composer is chary of sprinkling them around indiscriminately. With emphasis, of course, they dominate the pattern. Likewise, the lowest note in a series receives what is sometimes called "reversed tonic accent."

2. Agogic accent: A note of the same pitch and volume as its neighbors but held longer will seem accented. Again demonstrably not so, but the mind insists on it. Erickson says of this: "Our ears and minds always try to organize sounds into accent patterns. When we hear a clock making 'tick-tock' we are organizing the sound into such an accent pattern. The fact that if we try we can hear the same clock going 'tock-tick' proves that our minds do the organizing." Or repeat "East Pole" several times quickly, and notice the mind, out of habit, suddenly snap the unsual sound into "Police."

3. Steps or skips up or down: If the notes proceed up the scale one by one as in "Frère Jacques," the feeling is one of relative calm. If they jump up three, four or more at a time, the feeling is angular and tense. Try to remain sitting and relaxed while singing vigorously, "Stand Up, Stand Up for Jesus." Thus in *Don Giovanni* when Donna Anna recognizes her father's murderer and swears vengeance, she covers an octave in two jumps. But when talking to her fiancé, for whom she does not show much affection, after two moves she is still on the starting note. Mozart made fun of these excited jumps in *Così fan tutte* where he has the inconstant Fiordiligi protest her constancy in jumps of an octave and a half.

4. Momentum: Any series of notes which proceeds in one direction develops a momentum, and the note on which the pattern turns will seem accented and will gather the tension of the pattern. This is in ad-

dition to being the highest or lowest note in the series. Try "Frère Jacques" and notice how the accent on "nez" of "sonnez le matina" survives in spite of the heavy accent on "son" which precedes it. Or consider either of the turns in "Drink to Me Only with Thine Eyes."

5. Repetition and sequence: Repetition occurs when the phrase or pattern of notes is repeated exactly, as in "Frère Jacques." Sequence is more dynamic and is repetition of the phrase but starting on a note higher or lower than before. The "dormez-vous" of "Frère Jacques" is in sequence. Omitting the last note of the phrase is merely a variation to heighten the tension and expectancy. The Liebestod of *Tristan und Isolde* is almost entirely rising sequences with only slight variations of the opening eight-note pattern. "Un bel dì vedremo" from *Madama Butterfly* is an example of descending sequences.

Now, bearing all this in mind, look at the Welsh folk song, "All Through the Night" ("Sleep, my love, and peace attend thee"). You do not have to be able to read music to see the patterns.

Sleep, my love, and peace attend thee, all through the night;
Guardian angels God will lend thee, all through the night;
Soft the drowsy hours are creeping, hill and dale in slumber sleeping;
Love alone his watch is keeping, all through the night.

The first three notes in measures 1 and 2 come down the scale in identical steps (not skips because it is a lullaby) except that those in measure 2, being in sequence, start a note higher. The dot after the first note means that it is held longer, so that the rhythm is a slow "tuum-ti-tum-tum." This rhythmic pattern, labeled A, repeats exactly in measure 5, although the notes move up instead of down, and repeats partially in the second and third notes of measure 3. Measures 6, 7 and 8 have identical patterns, labeled B, in descending sequence. Notice that the composer, whoever he may have been, was careful to use his top note (*) in each line only once, although he achieved a second and different accent in the first and third lines, which are identical, by holding the first note (‡) of measures 3 and 11 twice as long as its predecessor and longer than any other of the notes in the song, with the exception of the ending in measures 4 and 12.

A good singer raises all these relationships in the listener's subconscious by his "phrasing." A phrase is generally three or four patterns, but it may be fewer, which when taken together form a unit. It is seldom longer than what a singer can accomplish in one breath. Again, this seems to be psychophysical: the duration of a breath and the rhythm of breathing are fundamental units by which the mind organizes.

In the folk song the phrase is four measures, and a good singer should be able to sing the entire verse in four breaths (the first line is repeated). Some singers sneak in a quick breath before measure 3, but it must be almost instantaneous or it will force the "all through the night" refrain into nagging prominence. Breathing anywhere else, of course, destroys the phrasing altogether.

A simple aria or song can be as few as two or three phrases, and in putting them together the composer has exactly the same objective as in a pattern: to work towards and away from "points of relative tension and relative rest." He hopes the whole will be more than merely the sum of its parts, and he applies the same general rules in constructing it. Thus in the folksong the composer uses his top note in measure 6 of line 2 only once, and the top notes in lines 1 and 3 now are subordinate accents in the overall picture, which builds up slowly to a climax and then quietly declines—a pattern well suited to a lullaby.

This kind of patterned structure is not peculiar to music; it occurs in every sort of activity to which conscious thought is applied. For example, consider the Lord's Prayer as it has come down from the Elizabethan times in the Anglican prayer book. If printed as though written by some modern poet, its structure becomes immediately apparent.

| | | APPROX. NO. OF SYLLABLES |
|---:|:---|:---:|
| Our | Father | 1 |
| who art | in heaven | 2 |
| Hallowed be Thy Name | Thy kingdom come | 4 |
| Thy will be done on earth | as it is in heaven | 6 |
| Give us this day our daily bread | And forgive us our trespasses | 8 |
| As we forgive those | who trespass against us | 5 |
| And lead us not into temptation | But deliver us from evil | 8 |
| For Thine is the kingdom | And the power and the glory | 6 |
| for ever | and ever | 3 |
| A | men | 1 |

This patterned structure also frequently occurs unconsciously. Anyone who has ever waited in line for a chest X ray will recognize the musicality of the phrase, "Take a deep breath. Hold it. All right, next."

In organizing his phrases into a song or aria, the composer can use or recreate any number of forms, most of which involve some repetition. The form of the folk song is ABA; the last line or section repeats the first. Actually, of course, because the first line of "All Through the Night" is repeated before advancing to B, the form is AABA, but this is no more than a species of the great genus ABA: theme, contrasting theme and repeat of the first theme. Composers, a wild and antisocial lot, do not stick to the forms recognized by society; rather, as need and inspiration hit them, they vary the forms in unique and wonderful ways so that there are headless arias, truncated phrases, formless songs and sometimes, alas, endless recitative. The only test is: does it succeed? But the composers are not so free as they or their audiences believe. Although in this century the forms supposedly have been abolished, still they rule us from their graves, and there are at least three basic forms in terms of which most arias can be analyzed and grasped. The most common of these is the ABA form. It is the constant framework of today's popular song and the cliché of the musical comedy.

There are several obvious advantages to an ABA form: it is neat and gives a feeling of balance; the last section, being a repeat, can be slightly varied for greater brilliance and the audience, having just heard the simpler version, will get the point; and finally, the middle section is ripe for a contrast in either melody, harmony or rhythm. In the history of opera it has always been a popular form. In the eighteenth century it was, by custom, almost the only form allowed and was called a "da Capo" aria (*See* Glossary). Every sort of situation or song was cast into the form, whether suitable for it or not.

Gluck's "Che farò senza Euridice" (what shall I do without Euridice) from *Orfeo* is an example of this form only slightly varied. It is ABACA, with C being only a brief interjection and the final A being considerably more brilliant than the preceding ones. The highest note, taken twice and held twice as long as most, is reserved for the final A. Other examples, some more perfect than "Che farò," are "Casta Diva" from *Norma,* "Salut! demeure chaste" from *Faust,* Micaela's prayer in Act III of *Carmen,* and a recent example, Baby Doe's final aria in *The Ballad of Baby Doe* (1956).

There are disadvantages, however, to the ABA form, and the examples suggest some of them. It is static. The singer in the final A is expressing exactly what he did before; his position has not changed. Hence, inasmuch as the deity so seldom answers, it is perfect for operatic prayers. It is also good for the end of scenes and acts, when the action should be stopped. Mozart closes Act I of *Le Nozze di Figaro* with "Non piu andrai," a perfect ABACA (technically called a rondo). By the final A the audience has a real sense of drawing to a close. But it is not good for arias which advance the action, such as question-and-answer arias: "What am I going to do now? I'm going to kill that man." Obviously it is ludicrous for the tenor, after making the decision, to go back and repeat the question (unless he is Hamlet). Thus there is an area in which the form AB can succeed where ABA cannot.

At its simplest the AB form is "Frère Jacques" or "Barbara Allen"; in both the A is the rising sequence and the B the descending. It is a far less artful form, and in opera in all periods when a folk element, simplicity, or drama, as opposed to singing, is on the rise, the AB form is apt to accompany it. Thus Verdi in his peasant mind and passionate heart heard many of his most famous arias in AB form. "La Donna è mobile" from *Rigoletto* is one, as is almost the entire of *Il Trovatore;* and in *La Traviata* Verdi has Alfredo declare his love in AB form but sing the preceding drinking song, a set number, in ABA form.

Perhaps nowhere more than here is the difference between eighteenth- and nineteenth-century opera more apparent. Gluck has Orfeo wonder what he will do without Euridice in an ABA aria and then in the following recitative decide he will commit suicide. Verdi would have (this is easy when the man is dead) put the decision into the aria itself, an AB form. The effect of the two is quite different. Gluck achieves an extraordinary intensity through the very restraint and balance of the form. But the aria ends and the opera proceeds rather like a counterpane with the stitching between arias very visible. Verdi's form achieves intensity through its passion and pace. Hanslick, the great Viennese critic, complained of *Il Trovatore* that the situations were shot onto the stage as if from a pistol.

Because it does not repeat the first section, the AB form is clearly better for ballads or arias that have a number of stanzas. Thus the sophistication of the libretto may influence the composer's choice of form, or within the same opera the peasants may get a chorus in AB form while the Countess expresses herself in an ABA aria.

Of course many arias do not fit neatly into the schoolroom forms, and it is possible to waste hours arranging and rearranging the alphabet in order to come up with something of no significance. It is enough to recognize that one of the basic forms of song is statement, development and restatement, or phrased differently, theme, contrast and repeat of theme; and to recognize that another basic form is statement and answer, or theme and contrast; and finally, to recognize that the difference between them is intrinsic and that a good AB aria does not become a good ABA aria merely by repeating the first part.

The last of the basic forms is simple A, probably the most difficult to bring off successfully as the audience must be persuaded that it has heard the beginning, middle and end of an entity, the aria, without any of the props of repetition or of obvious musical or emotional divisions in the structure. One of the most famous of such arias is Don José's "Flower Song" in Act II of *Carmen*. The layman cannot reproduce the melody as he can the "Habanera" or "Toreador" songs, and yet in the opera house he recognizes it to be the musical climax of the first two acts and often reserves his greatest applause for it. It has patterns in rising and descending sequence and these, together with some secret magic of Bizet, are more than enough.

A much earlier example is "Che puro ciel" from Gluck's *Orfeo* in which Orfeo exclaims on the beauty of the Elysian Fields. The orchestral accompaniment with oboe "obbligato" (*See* Glossary) repeats, but the voice line does not. Certain rhythmic patterns do reoccur, however, and the general line of the aria is one of slow rise and then rather quick descent. Most vocal scores, particularly the older ones, labeled the song "quasi recitative" rather than "aria," indicating that no matter what Gluck may have considered it later editors were puzzled by it. Modern editors might be less so, because since Wagner the simple A form of aria has been the most fashionable. Modern operas whose arias are mostly in AB or ABA form are said to be old hat and written by moles burrowing in the dust of the last century.

As a form, the A depends far more on the pattern of notes than the phrase made up of several patterns. This gives the composer great freedom or a "plastic" line, as the critics never tire of saying. What they mean is that the composer can fit his patterns exactly to the words and that the form itself does not impose any requirements or restrictions on the music. Obviously, in an ABA form the words must divide in some way that gives a sense of balance, such as the folk song, or the musical divisions will be thrown off. The same, but to a somewhat lesser extent, is true of the AB form. In the old days it was assumed that a libretto would be in verse form with line and stanza divisions; today many librettos are straight prose.

Naturally, prose in the A form is very close to recitative, and sometimes it requires an audience of considerable musical sophistication to hear any pattern or melody at all. An extreme example of this is Debussy's *Pelléas et Mélisande,* which on first or even fourth hearing sounds to many ears like no more than a continual murmur sparked by an occasional hiccup. And it would be no more than that except that Debussy's gift for orchestral coloring and tiny patterns—just a turn of notes, a change in rhythm or even a silence—was so great that for many he succeeded in creating a unique, magical world. So far, no other composer using the same technique has been able to achieve a like success, and argument arises occasionally whether the technique can be used in any but a very special case, for Debussy's libretto, although in prose, was extremely poetic.

But even in recitative much can be done with patterns if the composer repeats even just a little. Puccini was a master at this. The first half of the opening act of *La Bohème* has no aria and yet it seems to sparkle with melody. The patterns often run to three or four measures in length so that they become a phrase, but one independent of its neighbors, and the succession of patterns never builds into an aria. Puccini, however, is careful to provide a feeling of continuity in more subtle ways. First, he keeps the rhythm fairly constant in ⅜ time, a rollicking tempo of "tum-ti-tum" and one which, by falling naturally into first a long then a short note, provides a succession of natural accents. Changes in the rhythmic pattern are usually brief and introduced by the orchestra as a tiny prelude to a new character appearing on stage or a new bit of stage action. Next, the orchestra introduces most of the patterns while the singers are silent; and then, after the audience has had a chance to grasp it, Puccini repeats the pattern but this time gives snatches of it to the various singers. The result is conversation between three or four singers which seems melodic and yet is extraordinarily free and varied.

The technique has great pace and historically is rooted in "opera buffa," so that it is not surprising that Puccini had success with it in the comic parts of *La Bohème* and in *Gianni Schicchi*. The technique is also constantly used today by other composers who, alas, lack Puccini's genius for the melodic mosaic with the result that the audience often feels it is getting endless recitative. The difficulty is aggravated by a change in fashion of librettos, which began with Wagner. Puccini's librettos, which compared to those of Wagner or Richard Strauss were painfully old fashioned, were carefully worked towards points of lyrical effusion or, as suggested above, were comic. But today, in this ideological century, librettists want to deal with ideas, and the ideas frequently arrive on stage as rather talky dramas. *Wozzeck* is a brilliant exception. Just one of its many virtues is its brevity—fifteen tiny scenes that run barely more than two hours and into which is compressed the tragedy of a man and the responsibility of the world. Most of its kind run more than three hours, or, being in one act, have no break and exhaust the audience in seventy-five or ninety minutes.

This sort of conversational drama is a problem for opera. W. H. Auden, the librettist for Stravinsky's *The Rake's Progress,* stated his view in *Reflections on Music and Opera:*

"A good libretto plot is a melodrama in both the strict and the conventional sense of the word; it offers as many opportunities as possible for the characters to be swept off their feet by placing them in situations which are too tragic or too fantastic for 'words.' No good opera plot can be sensible for people do not sing when they are feeling sensible.

"The theory of 'Music-drama' presupposes a libretto in which there is not one sensible moment or one sensible remark: this is not only very difficult to manage, though Wagner managed it, but also extremely exhausting on both the singers and the audience, neither of whom may relax for an instant.

"In a libretto where there are any sensible passages, i.e. conversation, not song, the theory becomes absurd. If, for furthering the action, it becomes necessary for one character to say to another 'Run upstairs and fetch me a handkerchief,' then there is nothing in the words, apart from their rhythm, to make one musical setting more apt than another. Wherever the choice of notes is arbitrary, the only solution is a convention, e.g. 'recitativo secco.' " In this convention the singer delivers the words very fast, accompanied only by a harpsichord or the lowest strings.

It is hard to poke holes in Auden's argument. Wagner did not altogether "manage it," and the most boring sections of his operas are invariably the "sensible" ones; Erda, Fricka or Gurnemanz, for example, are constant offenders. Even Verdi's melodic genius staggered under the political discussion in *Don Carlo*.

The great advantage of "recitativo secco" over the music drama's constant orchestral accompaniment is that it moves so very much faster. The next situation for a lyrical effusion is set up often in a matter of seconds as opposed to minutes. The disadvantage is that the stitching between the arias is perfectly plain and, in these days, distressing to those unfamiliar with the convention. Also, being a stop-and-go technique, it is a drag on the momentum of the opera. Mozart used it constantly in the beginning of his acts, but for the finales he orchestrated throughout.

Composers constantly experiment with the problem, and each première offers a new solution. The variants, possible and tried, are legion. Even in the eighteenth century, in addition to "recitativo secco," there was "recitativo accompagnato," in which the full orchestra accompanied the singer. Mozart used both, often beginning his great dramatic arias with a page of "recitativo accompagnato," which leads more smoothly into song. From these developed the technique of constant orchestral accompaniment, which has become the prevailing fashion today. In the nineteenth century Massenet, disliking spoken dialogue, had the singers in *Manon* talk over the simplest chords held generally on the strings. These sections, however, are always the first to be cut, with confusion resulting in the development of the story. Bizet, on the other hand, composed *Carmen* as a series of numbers connected by spoken dialogue; the recitatives were added after his death—a debatable act, for the opera moves more slowly. But except in France the recitatives are used, perhaps to cover the linguistic failings of the singers. Puccini's technique was described above: it was a traditional Italian response to the problem. But other Italians were not so successful, however lovely their arias. Richard Strauss has many dull spots, almost always where the words get too important. Auden complains that the Marschallin's monologue in Act I of *Der Rosenkavalier* "is so full of interesting detail that the voice line is hampered in trying to follow everything."

Of composers writing today, perhaps the most skillful in handling conversation is Poulenc. In his *Les Dialogues de Carmélites* (1957), the totally different *Les Mamelles de Tirésias* (1947) or the monologue on the telephone for soprano, *La Voix Humaine* (1958), he combines a strong melodic gift with extraordinary orchestral sensitivity. For him the various instruments do not create part of a general sound; rather, each creates a unique sound, which he varies constantly, and thus achieves accents for the conversation. Stravinsky, on the other hand, in *The Rake's Progress* (1951) deliberately returned to the harpsichord and "recitativo secco." This took most operagoers by surprise, but the opera has been very successful everywhere but at the Metropolitan. Pizzetti successfully dodged the problem in his *Murder in the Cathedral* (1958), which was a typical twentieth-century libretto but cast in a most untypical form. The drama, written by T. S. Eliot as a festival play, made no pretense of presenting characters. The tempters and knights have no names and do not need them; they are ideas. They do not have to fuss with "handkerchiefs" and Pizzetti never has to face the problem of recitative. The opera, however, has an oratorio quality to it that is unsuitable for most subjects.

Perhaps the most interesting recent experiment, because the most fundamental, occurs in Prokofiev's *War and Peace* (1942). Here in successive scenes, both running less than ten minutes, he presents the same situation in two quite different ways—one boldly experimental, the other traditionally operatic—a demonstration of ability like his "Classical Symphony." Both scenes present councils of war: the first, Napoleon and his marshals at the Battle of Borodino; then Kutuzof and his generals in a peasant hut deciding to abandon Moscow. Napoleon is presented on a hill surrounded by his marshals and aides-de-camp; in the distance cavalry clatter by and cannon boom. The scene is superbly cinematic and created for glorious technicolor.

Prokofiev attempted to translate it directly onto the stage without re-writing it for opera. There are nineteen short speeches of which Napoleon has eight, including the two longest. Aides dash in with reports and out with orders. There is much talk of divisions, reserves and bastions. The scene ends with a live cannonball plopping at Napoleon's feet, which he calmly rolls down the hill.

It is a magnificent effort to expand opera into an area where only Verdi's *Simon Boccanegra,* with its political council scene, had trespassed before. This is war as Tolstoy saw it—not the troops running around the back of the stage with a banner. But the scene does not quite come off. While it may succeed as a spectacle, it fails as music, perhaps because, after all, it is only movie music.

Prokofiev handled the Kutuzov council traditionally. Many officers are present, but there are only four speeches of which Kutuzov has two, and the libretto is so constructed that it produces two lyrical effusions. The first is an aria by General Raievsky who argues that Russia lives in her men and therefore they should abandon the city. This, as befits a subordinate, is a simple aria based on a single rising phrase; it leads directly into Kutuzov's hymn to Moscow, which is in ABA form and closes the scene. Musically it is very successful; and yet . . . and yet, the mind keeps returning to Napoleon on that hill.

The frontier at present for the composers seems to be in the area of conversation and recitative. The audience wants an intellectual libretto with a well-constructed plot in which the characters are psychologically true and in which all the groundwork is laid for future happenings. Circumstance and coincidence are in bad repute. Inevitably this throws the emphasis onto the drama and recitative at the expense of the aria. Composers recognizing that recitative is often dull are casting around for new conventions and techniques for advancing the action. Prokofiev attempted to use movie techniques; others have actually used slides, such as Moore in *The Ballad of Baby Doe* and Kurka in *The Good Soldier Schweik,* although in both of these the slides were merely atmospheric. But perhaps actual movies or new instruments with electronic sound or Berg and Schoenberg's technique of the half-sung word will be the solution and start of a new convention that today's operagoers will accept as readily as the eighteenth century did its "recitativo secco." Meanwhile, the paradox of the decade is that recitative, which most laymen consider the least interesting part of opera, is undergoing the most interesting experimentation.

# III·

## THE OPERATIC VOICE AS AN ARTISTIC INSTRUMENT

In the end a person must like the human voice as an instrument to like opera. No amount of preparation, study, comfortable seats, or alcoholic drugs in the intermission can make it otherwise enjoyable.

As an instrument the voice has its limitations. It cannot "roll" like a drum; it cannot, like an organ, sustain a note indefinitely; compared to a piano, its range is limited; unlike a flute, which once tuned cannot go flat, it can wobble flat or sharp for an act, an aria or even a note.

Perhaps its most intriguing limitation is its mystery. It is the oldest instrument in the world in any culture. Every person born has played it. Yet no one really knows much about it. Violinists can watch slow-motion movies of Heifetz's fingers. The violin teacher can say, "See, like this." The singing teacher can only plead helplessly, "Listen." No one can tell another, or knows himself, exactly how to adjust the vocal cords to sing the note A—and is it different for an A in a scale, in a trill or in a chorale? No one knows.

This mystery undoubtedly contributes to the intensely personal quality of a singer and his career. He quite literally plays on himself. Consider what may be the physiological effects for a tenor of living at the top of his lungs for thirty years. Even practice must be done on the one instrument. A violinist can do scales on an old violin and then for performance turn to his Stradivarius. But the singer, like the ballerina, is given one instrument at birth. Thereafter, if he is wise, he prays that neither his petulance nor poor teaching will destroy it. For a poor teacher can destroy a voice beyond repair.

### RANGE

The human voice has a range of about five and one-half octaves, or from C below the bass staff to F above the treble staff. The piano extends more than an octave on either end.

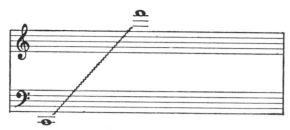

Actually, a singer's range for noise is not much greater than a layman's. Many businessmen can gurgle a low C, but it takes a bass to sing it. Sometimes a baritone will sing a bass role and all will be well except for a few of the very lowest notes. These will sound—the baritone standing very still with his jaw on his chest—but they will not project or "sing." The difference is immediately apparent. At the other end of the scale, when a soprano cannot reach and "sing" the note, it comes out as a screech. In straining for high notes, everyone—singers, housewives and businessmen—tends to sing louder and louder, because for high notes the vocal cords must be held tauter and it therefore takes more of a physical effort to cause them to vibrate. (*See* Chap. IV, "The Operatic Voice as a Mechanical Instrument.")

In opera, singers are classified by range: soprano, tenor and so on. This is another way of saying that a singer is classified by the roles he sings. The classification is helpful but not binding. Both basses and baritones, for example, sing Don Giovanni, generally considered a baritone role, and Boris Godunov, a bass role. The only sure classification is "male" and "female" voice, for occasionally a singer will start as a baritone and then switch to tenor e.g. Lauritz Melchior, Jean de Reszke, Enrico Caruso, or drop from tenor to baritone e.g. Leonard Warren.

This is possible because the difference in range may be small. Many baritones can sing all the notes in a tenor role. What matters far more than the occasional high or low note is the "tessitura" of the role. This Italian word means "web" or "frame"—where the average notes of the role fall within the singer's range. Said differently, the role "lies" high or low. The "tessitura" is all important to a singer, for a slight strain, unimportant in a single aria, can be exhausting over three hours of singing. Some roles are known for their "grueling" (critics love the phrase) tessitura. One such is the Princess in *Turandot*.

The operatic voice has six classifications three each for men and women. Taking them in descending order:

SOPRANO: The highest female voice. The normal range is two octaves rising from middle C. However, for emphasis or to show off, singers and complaisant composers frequently do more. Mozart wrote several high F's in *Die Entfuehrung*, and all sopranos, if they can, put in high E flats in the Mad Scene of *Lucia di Lammermoor*.

MEZZO-SOPRANO: The middle female voice. (Italian: mezzo—middle) Its range is two octaves from A with an occasional high B flat. Mezzos have a shorter range than sopranos, as they lack the extra top notes. In most operas the female lead is a soprano. However, Carmen, Azucena and Dalila are all mezzos.

CONTRALTO: The lowest female voice. Its range is two octaves from F below middle C to F an octave and a half above. It is very like the mezzo-soprano, and probably the old-fashioned way of speaking of "high" and "low" voice was sufficient and sensible. Ulrica in *Un Ballo in Maschera* and La Cieca in *La Gioconda* are contraltos.

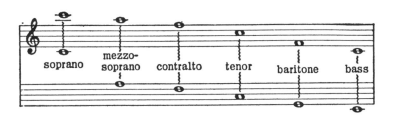

TENOR: The highest male voice. Its range is from C below middle C to C above; but very few sound well above A.

BARITONE: The middle male voice. Its range is from G an octave and a half below middle C to F above. The tenor is generally the lover or hero, and the baritone or bass, the villain. However, Don Giovanni, Rigoletto, Figaro and Simon Boccanegra are all "good" baritones, morals aside.

BASS: The lowest male voice. Its range is from E almost two octaves below middle C to middle C. Some basses can sing to low C. Mozart in *Die Entfuehrung* asks Osmin to hold a low D for seven measures—which is too long for any faking.

All six types of voice appear in *La Gioconda*. Ponchielli, a careful music teacher, provided six leading roles, one for each. He gave each at least one solo and several duets and trios in various combinations. For the less studious he provided a suicide, a murder, an attempted poisoning, a corker of a private party and a booming shipboard explosion.

## FURTHER CLASSIFICATIONS

Sopranos are sometimes further divided into lyric, dramatic and coloratura, but these divisions are very general and many sopranos fit in two categories. The terms are also used to describe roles, as, "Mimi is a lyric role."

LYRIC SOPRANO: A voice with a light, innocent quality. The role is usually graceful, charming and a little sentimental, e.g. Mimi in *La Bohème,* Gilda in *Rigoletto,* Marguerite in *Faust* or Micaela in *Carmen.*

DRAMATIC SOPRANO: A powerful voice with soaring notes, big leaps and great declamatory ability, e.g. Donna Anna in *Don Giovanni,* Leonora in *La Forza del Destino,* Salome or Elektra in their operas, Santuzza in *Cavalleria Rusticana* and almost any of the great Wagnerian roles.

COLORATURA SOPRANO: An acrobatic voice able to manipulate endless runs, trills and turns i.e. "coloratura" e.g. Lucia in *Lucia di Lammermoor,* Olympia in *Les Contes d'Hoffmann* or the title role in *Lakmé.*

The difficulty with these terms is that critics and singing teachers think in them, but composers do not. Violetta in *La Traviata* is mostly lyric, but "Sempre libera," the finale to the first act, requires a coloratura's agility. Aida is mostly dramatic until her last scene when, the struggle over, she turns lyric. A singer like Maria Callas is good in all departments.

The Italians, considering themselves experts in the field, draw even finer distinctions in types of voice and role. The four types most frequently cited and often used by critics are "leggiero," "lirico," "lirico spinto" and "drammatico." The last is identical with its English counterpart. "Leggiero" is a very light voice or role, "lirico" a little heavier and "lirico spinto" heavier yet. The very light voices are apt to be right for comic roles, such as Zerlina in *Don Giovanni* or Papagena in *Der Zauberfloete.* Mimi in *La Bohème* is a "lirico" role; Tosca is "lirico spinto." Violetta in *La Traviata* and Gilda in *Rigoletto* are "lirico"; Aida is "lirico spinto."

MEZZO-SOPRANO and CONTRALTO: They have no subdivision. The quality of voice, deep and full-toned, by its nature makes them dramatic rather than lyric.

LYRIC TENOR: A voice with high, bright tones and an easy, flowing style. Alfredo in *La Traviata* and Rodolfo in *La Bohème* are lyric tenor roles. Gigli (1890–1957), one of the great lyric tenors, sang publicly for forty-one years until 1955. This is a long career for a singer, and he ascribed his good fortune in part to his refusal to sing dramatic roles, such as Otello, for which his voice was ill suited.

DRAMATIC TENOR: A voice corresponding to the dramatic soprano with ringing tones and full resonance. In Germany the singer is called the "heldentenor," the "hero-tenor." Lauritz Melchior was one. Otello is the great dramatic role in Italian opera.

Again the Italians have finer distinctions; they add to the four given above for sopranos a "tenore robusto" for the heaviest roles. "Leggiero" roles are Almaviva in *Il Barbiere di Siviglia* and Don Ottavio in *Don Giovanni;* "lirico" roles, Alfredo in *La Traviata* and Rodolfo in *La Bohème;* "lirico spinto" roles, Cavaradossi in *Tosca* and Don Carlo, Parsifal and Lohengrin in their operas; "drammatico" roles, Radames in *Aida* and Andrea Chenier and Tannhaeuser in their operas; and "robusto" roles, Otello, Siegfried and Tristan in their operas. But again good tenors generally overlap three of the five categories, so that the classifications "light" or "heavy" and "lyric" or "dramatic" are about all that have much meaning.

BARITONE: There are no subdivisions. Some of the roles sometimes sung by basses are Escamillo in *Carmen,* Wotan in *The Ring* and Don Giovanni.

BASSO CANTANTE: A high bass voice with as many lyric qualities as

a bass can have. A smooth style is important. Roles are Méphistophélès in *Faust,* King Philip in *Don Carlo,* Sparafucile in *Rigoletto* and the title role in *Boris Godunov.* Ezio Pinza was one.

BASSO BUFFO: A bass specializing in comic roles, such as Dr. Bartolo in *Il Barbiere di Siviglia.* Buffo roles require agility, and in a sense a basso buffo is the coloratura of the basses. Other roles are Melitone in *La Forza del Destino* and the title role in *Don Pasquale.*

BASSO PROFUNDO: The lowest bass voice, powerful and sonorous. It should be capable of tremendous dignity and solemnity, e.g. Sarastro in *Der Zauberfloete,* Grand Inquisitor in *Don Carlo* or King Marke in *Tristan und Isolde.* Osmin in *Die Entfuehrung aus dem Serail* is unusual in that it is a comic role.

## COLOR AND CONTRAST

Color and contrast are the glory of the human voice, not just in opera but in all types of singing. But it is especially true of opera because opera is by nature dramatic.

Color is partly the inherent tone of the voice and partly what the singer can do with the God-given tone. All voices have some color. The ideal is a voice with lots of color. To say a singer has a "white" tone or voice is to say that while it may be on pitch it has no roundness, no depth, no color.

Any roomful of persons will furnish examples of voices with varying depth and tone. Office lawyers, perhaps because they are forever trying to drain the confusing, emotional content out of words, are apt to have thin, dry, "white" voices. Courtroom lawyers, who in front of a jury try to pour emotional content into words, are apt to have full, resonant voices. Persons talking constantly to the deaf through machines drain their voices of resonance because a full, round tone blurs in the machine. A nervous person testifying in court, getting married, or at a cocktail party, is apt to lose the full quality of his voice because his throat tightens. (The physical reasons for the qualities of a voice are discussed in Chap. IV, "The Operatic Voice as a Mechanical Instrument.")

Color is easier to demonstrate than define. Consider the right voice for Carmen, all sex, spitting and red roses; for Butterfly, innocence, sweetness and white cherry blossoms. There is more to the difference than just acting; a singer colors (or tries to color) his voice for a certain role or aria. In the case of *Carmen* the singer of Carmen is aided by being a mezzo-soprano. The lower female voice tends to be richer, fuller than the high voice—which is why Carmen and Dalila are mezzos.

Singers are not good talkers and have trouble explaining how they color their tones. The best Caruso could do, for example, in explaining to Mr. Pierre Key in *This Business of Singing,* was to say:

"I keep my voices in a sort of drawer. When I am to sing Radames, I take out of one drawer my Radames voice. It is heavy and dramatic in fibre. For Nemorino, in *L'Elisir d'Amore,* I turn to another drawer in that cabinet for a lighter quality of voice. And during the day when I have a performance I try to keep in the mood of the character I am singing that evening, so that my voice as well as my thoughts will be in keeping with what I am to do on the stage. An artist does not sing Vasco di Gama's music in *L'Africana* with the same weight of tone he uses for that of Lionel in *Marta.* He approaches a song that is not operatic with consideration of the style demanded; and he suits his tones to fit. To adopt one weight and general color of voice for every piece of music is to be mechanical, inartistic, and vocally limited."

"Amen" to the conclusion; but the world is still waiting for a clear explanation of how a singer colors his tones. Probably no full explanation is possible because, as Caruso's remarks suggest, the process is not wholly mechanical—not just singing from the front of the mouth, off the lips or from the top of the throat. A great deal of the technique is artistic and in the realm of magic; the singer so immerses himself in the role that the correct color begins to come before he steps onto the stage.

Coloring is not limited simply to roles. Even within a single aria an artist can give incredible variety and meaning to the words by coloring. Consider the Countess' aria "Dove Sono" in *Le Nozze di Figaro.* It divides obviously in two parts: first, at a slow, sad pace, she regrets that the Count no longer seems to love her; second, hopefully, she wonders if someday his love for her will revive. No singer misses the color change here.

But there is much more, and without going through the entire aria consider just the opening twelve bars. The first phrase, "dove sono" (where are they [those happy moments of love]), is two bars. The singer's color is—somehow—lamenting mystification. But the next phrase, "i bei momenti" (those happy moments), also two bars, should have a little different color. On "bei" the tone should brighten as though the memory manages for a note to bring back some of the happiness. Even the vowels—da Ponte was a great librettist—assist the singer. "Dove sono" is all lamenting "O's." But "bei" (pron. bay.ee) introduces a vowel sound associated more with happiness.

The next phrase describes the "moments" as "di dolcezza e di piacer" (of sweetness and pleasure), and the singer's color must show that these joys were innocent and pure.

Mozart then, musically, starts the tune over again. The first phrase, "dove andaro" (where have they gone), is two bars. The coloring is the same as before with possibly a slight shade of indignation, for the next phrase is "i giuramenti" (the vows). Here the singer's color must suggest solemnity. For the Countess the vows still have meaning. And so on.

The changes are, of course, extremely subtle, but this is the area that separates the artists from the mere singers—the area where the more you listen, the more you hear. The ability to sing like this is what excites opera fanatics to rave about this or that singer's interpretation. But the difficulty of it and the experience of life required explain why great artists are so infrequent. And great listeners, too.

Coloring is in itself a form of contrast, but the composer has other tools on which to rely. The first and most obvious form of contrast is the male against the female voice. In *Turandot* Puccini has the Princess explain in an aria why she hates men: years before, a lovely Princess, Louling, had been captured, raped and killed—by a man. The aria is long (but not too long) and the high voice creates an atmosphere wholly feminine and narcissistic. When the Prince, the tenor, bursts in impetuously—"no, no"—his male voice shatters the tonal texture like a rock coming through glass.

This sort of contrast is common to theater, but where opera can do more than the theater is in the combination of contrasting voices. Two famous examples of this are the quartets in *La Bohème* and *Rigoletto*. In Act III of *La Bohème* Musetta and Marcello brawl with each other and part while Mimi and Rodolfo agree to live together until the spring. The quartet in the last act of *Rigoletto* is more complicated. Instead of contrasting two couples, Verdi combines four individuals: the Duke flatters Maddalena with gay insincerity; Maddalena refuses him but finds him attractive; Gilda sees that her student lover, the Duke, is merely a libertine; Rigoletto urges Gilda to forget the Duke and promises himself revenge on his daughter's seducer.

Contrast is not only in the voices. Frequently the orchestra comments on, or clarifies, the action. This is Wagner's trademark and, especially in *The Ring,* the overriding principle of construction. Siegfried's Funeral March in *Goetterdaemmerung,* for example, reviews by musical reference the preceding operas. Likewise in Verdi's *Otello* at the very end as Otello dies, he gasps out his last words, "un bacio" (a kiss), while the orchestra repeats the love duet music from Act I.

A superb example of contrast and color in voices is Act III, scene 1, of Verdi's *Don Carlo.* Although it is a romantic opera, Verdi constructed the scene with classic symmetry. It opens with a monologue for bass voice. King Phillip broods that Elizabeth, the Queen, has never loved him. Next there is a duet for two bass voices in which the King asks the Grand Inquisitor if he must sacrifice his son, Don Carlo, for political reasons. The Grand Inquisitor replies that God did not hesitate to sacrifice His son. Tonal coloring is vital here, as both voices have the same range. The Inquisitor must be proud, icy and compassionless. The King must be proud, bitter and troubled. Then follows a duet for bass and soprano in which the King accuses the Queen of consorting with Don Carlo. She denies it and faints. Rodrigo and Eboli enter to assist her, and there is a quartet for bass, baritone, soprano and mezzo-soprano—each expressing totally different thoughts on the situation.

Now Verdi starts subtracting voices. The men go out, and there is a duet for two sopranos, high and low voice, in which Eboli reveals that in fact she has been consorting with the King. She begs the Queen's forgiveness. Again, color between the two soprano voices is vital. Finally Eboli remains alone—solo for mezzo-soprano. She laments her fatal gift of beauty and resolves to serve her Queen by saving Don Carlo.

The scene is one of the greatest in opera. Even when badly performed, it makes an impression; but when great artists sing the roles and the nuances begin to come across the footlights, the impression is overpowering. And, as one last footnote to Verdi's virtuosity, notice that he did not use a tenor.

## SOME SINS AND TESTS OF SINGING

Caruso scornfully scored the singer's greatest sin: "To adopt one weight and general color of voice for every piece of music . . ."

Other sins are:

SCOOPING: This occurs when the singer, instead of hitting the note squarely on pitch, slides into it from below. If exaggerated, it gives a sort of coyote quality to the aria.

FLATTING: This is singing just under the note. Some singers have trouble hearing the note exactly. Some hear it well enough but cannot adjust the vocal cords accurately. It is apt to be a sign of exhaustion: tired singers may sing flat.

SHARPING: This is singing just above the note. It is rarer than flatting and is apt to be a first-act trouble, as it frequently results from nerves and tension.

FOCUS: To sing a note perfectly on pitch the singer must vibrate his larynx at exactly the necessary number of cycles per second. For middle C it is 523.251. Some "spread" is inevitable and unnoticeable; but if his voice wanders from 515 to 530, then his focus is not good. The spread may be too little and too inconsistent to be sharp or flat, and yet the voice will not generate the same excitement as one that "bores" in at exactly the same frequency as the orchestra or another singer with the same note. The effect of poor focus or a spread is exactly the same as that of a radio tuned just off the wave length: the sound is dull and fuzzy although apparently accurate.

TREMOLO: This is the shaky effect some singers have. It is a sliding rapidly on and off the note—an actual change in pitch. Some (very few) think it a fine effect, reflecting great intensity. But to most ears it sounds as though the singer is about to give out. The word is frequently used interchangeably with "vibrato" (*See* Glossary).

VIBRATO: This is the rapid reiteration of the same note. It is generally unconscious and represents a failure in breath control. Sometimes it is useful as an effect for portraying great emotion. (*See* Chap. VI for vibrato and tremolo as orchestral effects.)

Opera fanatics are the most infuriatingly opinionated of all connoisseurs, and they positively create opportunities for the more humble to ask their opinion about how a singer is doing. For them the more innocent the questioner, the better. What is the poor, literal-minded stockbroker to think when he hears a red-faced, supposed authority with pursed lip and blazing eye thunder, "Terrible! I didn't think she'd be able to finish the aria." The soprano's every step, every note now become an agony of fearful anticipation. It is worse than watching his child in the jumping class of the horse show. As the curtain drops he gasps his relief to his other neighbor. "La Diva," that one snorts, "has never sung better."

The first rule is to discount whatever any enthusiast, critics included, announces during the performance or six weeks thereafter. Then apply some of the following tests:

In all types of voice the top and bottom notes go bad first, either because of a cold or old age. If the singer is just glancing at the top notes instead of holding them, or if the notes sound thin and shrieky without any body, it is not good. An old or tiring singer also is apt to have trouble focusing his voice.

In all operas there are quiet, hushed moments when the singer should be able to float a note out over the orchestra and seem to hold it there. If at such moments he cannot pick up the audience's attention almost visibly and suspend it, breathless, with the note, he is not good. Sopranos particularly should be able to do this.

An old or tiring singer saves himself for the big aria—a form of cheating. One way of doing it is to speak rather than really sing the lesser moments; it takes less physical effort. The singer covers up by appearing to stress the words' meaning. The tone, however, will not have the body or roundness of a truly sung note. Likewise, shouting ejaculations at moments of stress is not real emphasis but a blind. Suspect any performance in which only the purple passages are purple.

An old or tiring singer also tends to overact. In spite of the cartoons, opera is not, or should not be, an art of the broad, physical gesture. The tenor who continually twirls his cape or the soprano who flutters around with endless facial responses is probably deliberately distracting attention from vocal inadequacies.

In sopranos, listen for the trills. Many cannot do them at all; many no longer can when tired. A trill ought to be perfectly clear; any confusion as to whether it was a trill or just a wobble is not good. This is part of the general rule that every note should sound. A run or turn in which only the last, held note sounds is poor. Each note in a scale should seem a pearl of equal size and color, perfectly beaded.

The voice should have some of the same quality throughout. If the low notes sound like a different person singing, it is not good. In sopranos, listen for the point at which she seems to pass from her low to her high voice. If there is an audible "break" in quality of tone, it is not good.

In all voices, but particularly in the bass and baritone, which are the least agile, listen for rhythm. When the rhythm is perfect, the most extraordinary things happen: every note sounds, diction is pure and seemingly effortless, the words seems to set the pace instead of being "sung" to a melody, and the scene leaps alive. Sloppy diction inevitably involves sloppy rhythm and vice versa.

Listen to the quality of the note from the moment of attack (*See* Glossary). Good singers lay notes out, one alongside another, like perfect bars of gold—gold from beginning to end. Bad singers will have a split second at the beginning when the note has a slightly different quality—dross and then gold. It may be breathy, or produced with a slight catch, or merely slow in getting started, but the singer will not give the same impression of precision and power.

Listen to how the singer releases the note. If he lets go with a physical spasm that sounds like a grunt or a tiny shout, it is not good; the note should cut off cleanly. Tenors, particularly on high notes, are apt to have trouble with this.

And one last test which is emphatically NO test at all—the amount of applause. Everyone wants the beginner to succeed: her husband bought the flowers, her brother started the applause, and she has twenty relatives in the audience who lent her money for singing lessons. As for the old men and divas, opera fans are far, far more loyal than their baseball cousins, and they resolutely close their ears to the sound of an idol disintegrating before them. It is hard to be angry about this, for it is based on real affection. Even for past revelations there is present gratitude: a thing of beauty is a joy forever.

# IV·

## THE OPERATIC VOICE AS A
## MECHANICAL INSTRUMENT

So much is still unknown about the voice and its production that this chapter must begin with a warning: it sets forth nothing more than the presently popular conception of how a singer makes sound. There are many other conceptions; each has a score of singing teachers prepared to die for it. At the moment, however, most are more or less happy with the following ideas.

The voice as an instrument has three parts: the lungs, the larynx and the cavities of the throat, mouth, nose and head. Compared to an organ, the lungs are the bellows, the larynx the reed, and the cavities the cylindrical tube. Compared to a violin, the lungs are the arm pulling the bow, the larynx the string that is caused to vibrate, and the cavities the violin's belly and back (the wood box).

To sing requires a great deal more breath than to speak, and every teacher starts with breathing exercises. Suetonius, the Roman historian, reports that Nero, for example, would lie flat on the floor with lead weights on his chest, apparently on the same theory that baseball players now swing two bats when approaching the plate. Some nineteen hundred years later Queena Mario, a Metropolitan diva, starts her "School of Singing" with a month of breathing exercises to be done flat on the floor and designed to develop the back muscles that control the diaphragm. Such exercises can be costly. When Kirsten Flagstad began at thirty-eight to study Isolde for the first time, her back muscles and lungs developed to such an extent that she split all her dresses.

Without a good supply of breath there can, of course, be no singing at all. As an example of the sort of supply that can be developed, there is the famous story by an eyewitness of the bass Lablache (1794–1858; *See* Glossary). At dinner one day he "sang a long note from piano to forte and back to piano; then drank a glass of wine without having breathed; then sang a chromatic scale up the octave in trills, still in the same breath; and finally blew out a candle with his mouth open." Needless to say, few singers today can emulate the feat.

Breath is controlled by the diaphragm and to a far lesser extent, particularly in men, by the muscles around the ribs. The diaphragm drops, allowing the lungs to expand and fill with air, or pushes up, collapsing the lungs and squeezing the air out. Clearly perfect control is necessary to maintain a steady pressure, and without a steady pressure, the most extraordinary sounds come out. Listen to anyone try to sustain an even note while jumping, bending or lifting a weight —which is why singers do not swoop around stage or bend much in the middle.

Good breath control is achieved only when the singer has learned to control his muscles without tensing them, just as the layman uses his hand most effectively if each finger and the wrist are not stiffened. The tensed muscle in any part of the body soon begins to shake involuntarily and quickly is exhausted. Worse still, tenseness in one muscle leads by chain reaction to tenseness in others, so that disaster accelerates for the singer having a bad night. Or as confidence comes, each act may improve. The irony of it, repeated endlessly in life, is that the great singer may accomplish the most difficult passage, and half the audience, seeing how relaxed he looks, will think it was nothing.

The larynx is located in the Adam's apple, so called because a piece of the first apple is supposed to have stuck there and because, by making it possible to talk, it is still the cause of a good deal of sinning. It is a muscular box in which two cartilages, the vocal cords, stretch across the only opening, the glottis, that leads from the lungs to the mouth. The cords are roughly half an inch in length for a man and less for a woman or child. They can separate or close. On the intake of air, they are wide apart; on exhaling, they can be apart or stretched across the opening, where, as the air goes by, they will vibrate. If they are tight and the space is narrow, they will vibrate fast and produce a high note; if loose and open, slowly and a low note.

A loud tone is produced not by vibrating faster (which would raise the pitch) but by stronger air pressure making the amplitude of the vibration greater, i.e. the "swing" of the same number of vibrations a second is now wider. This is like a child's swing or a ball on an elastic: the farther away it is pushed, the quicker it returns. For higher notes, more air pressure is required to vibrate the cords, as they are tauter. This is the reason why, when trying for high notes, everyone sings loudly; for a low note the effort is not necessary. The agility of a voice depends on the speed with which the cords will answer the mind's signals. It is a complete mystery how the mind knows at what tension to stretch the cords in order to reproduce a note. As Scholes (*See* Glossary) points out, "This is the equivalent of a violinist turning the pegs of his instrument without sounding the strings, then starting to play and finding the strings perfectly tuned."

Sometimes singers have a "breathy" quality to their tone. This occurs when air escapes from the lungs and through the glottis before the vocal cords get in position to sound the note. Kirsten Flagstad suffered in the beginning with this, and in her biography she reports that when her teacher succeeded in getting her to close the cords between notes, she discovered that her voice had grown to three times its size—presumably because she was working her wind supply more efficiently.

Apparently, there is no difference between a singer's larynx and that of a layman. After Tamagno, the tenor who created Otello, died, a commission of doctors and scientists performed an autopsy on his larynx. To their disappointment, it was just like anyone else's.

The cavities of nose, throat, mouth and head are the resonating chamber, or the equivalent of a sounding board, for the larynx. The vocal cords by themselves would probably be inaudible, just as the tuning fork or piano without a sounding board is only a faint sound. The cavities are all the open spaces above the Adam's apple. There are several down the front of the face—the nose, the sinuses, the roof and front of the mouth; further back there are the throat and passages leading into the head. Medically speaking, any cavity is a sinus.

The cords in the larynx vibrate and in turn start the air above them vibrating at the same rate. This "column of air," as singers call it, vibrates in the cavities, and it is at this point that singing teachers begin to run for their weapons. It is supposed to be physically impossible to direct the "column of air" into some cavities and not into others. Yet most persons *feel* they can do just that; they can sing the same note in the front of their mouth or the back, and their ear tells them the sound is quite different. Further, they can put a twang or nasal sound in or out at will. Roughly speaking, the Italian style of singing makes more use of the cavities in the front of the face. This gives a bright tone. Singers sometimes call this "mask" placement. The German style (and to some extent the average American voice) makes greater use of the throat and head cavities. This often gives the tone a more "covered" quality. The effect is variously described as "hooded," "hooty," "tubey" or "hollow." Elisabeth Schwartzkopf tends to have this sort of tone; Renata Tebaldi, the other. A good singer can, to some extent, switch back and forth and "cover" his tone when he feels the dramatic situation requires it. Maria Callas is particularly good at this.

In ensemble singing the blend is better if all the voices have the same placement; otherwise, those placed to the front tend to predominate. This can be turned to artistic advantage, for it allows a voice to stand out for a few bars without increasing its volume and disturbing the balance. Likewise, a singer with a strong "cutting" quality to his voice is resounding it from the front of his mouth and teeth.

Of course, to a large extent the tone of any voice is determined by the way God made the singer's head—brains as well as cavities. Scholes reports that certain Australian natives are supposed to have very small sinuses and hence voices without much resonance. But again, it is a mystery why some sinuses do well and others poorly.

The cavities, however, have a still more important role to play. Voices vary tremendously; any operagoer can recognize Tucker or del Monaco, yet few can tell good violins apart. The difference seems at least in part to lie in the fact that the cavities reinforce certain of the vibrations and not all of them.

Each note, the operagoer will remember from his physics course, consists of a number of different vibrations. If a string is plucked, it will vibrate over its full length; each half will also vibrate, and each third, and so on. Each of these additional and simultaneous vibrations also gives off a note, although most ears cannot distinguish them. These additional notes or overtones have a definite relation to the fundamental note and to each other. Taking the note G as the fundamental note, its first twelve overtones are:

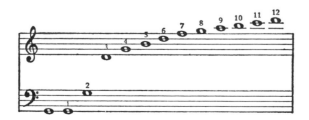

If on a piano the damper pedal is depressed so that the strings are free of the dampers and then a note is sung into the strings, the string of that note and also the strings for the overtones of that note will vibrate sympathetically, and at least some of the overtones will be audible. (If you cannot hear the strings of the overtones vibrating, place sawdust or fuzz on the strings and, if you are on the correct strings, you can see it jiggle as the strings vibrate.)

These overtones (sometimes called harmonics or partials) are the only notes that a valveless brass instrument like a bugle can play. All bugle calls, for example, fit on notes 2, 3, 4 and 5. Taps is 223,234, etc. The notes are sounded by inducing the column of air in the bugle to vibrate in two halves, three thirds, etc. The bugle is based on a fundamental note, which does not sound: i.e., the column of air never vibrates as a whole; it vibrates only in fractions. If it changed its fundamental note, it would have a new series of overtones. Thus a trumpet, a sort of bugle with valves, can play an ~ntire scale by having the three valves change the fundamental note by opening up additional lengths of tube. In all the trumpet is able to have seven fundamental notes, and thereby, on their overtones, it can play a complete chromatic scale.

The cavities in a singer's head pick up these overtones and reinforce certain of them. Again it is a mystery why some sinuses seem to prefer this overtone to that, but they do have preferences, and those determine, at least in part, the distinctive quality of a voice. Some persons believe that cavities reinforcing particularly the upper overtones produce a bright voice; those favoring the lower overtones, a full voice; and those favoring all equally, a very smooth voice. But others argue that the second and fourth overtones impart clearness and brilliance, while the odd-numbered give a hollow, nasal quality.

Not every singer or speaker can sound a pure fundamental note. If it wavers in pitch, however slightly, it may introduce two or three new sets of overtones, some of which, reinforced by sympathetic cavities, clash with the fundamental tone. This produces an ugly sound.

But the margin for a good tone is even slimmer. In the last forty years it has been clear that every vowel sound consists of two fundamental notes—consonants are little more than ways of starting and stopping vowel sounds—and that the combination of the two notes is different for each vowel. To the untrained ear, of course, the two notes sound as one. A man can produce two fundamental notes at once because the tongue subconsciously divides the mouth into two different cavities and the air vibrating within each cavity produces separate notes. This means that the larynx with its vocal cords is not necessary for speech but merely adds power. And this is true because people without any vocal cords can still whisper. The reason the notes stay approximately the same for a man, woman or child, regardless of their differing cavities, is that the notes are determined not by the cavity alone, a variable, but by the relation between it and the size of the mouth, another variable; the two variables when taken together produce, always, a constant. Thus it has been possible to make a machine rather like an organ that reproduces the two notes and hence the vowel, a true talking machine.

Whispering is a way to test the truth of the assertion that vowels are composed of two notes of absolute pitch, although most ears will be able to hear only the combined note. Whisper the vowel sounds "oo" and "ee." Both sound on a note, and it is impossible to make either sound on the other's note. In fact, with each vowel two notes sound, so there are two sets of overtones, of which the cavities will reinforce some. If they select conflicting overtones, the voice will be ugly; if the same ones, the voice will be pure; if different but agreeably so, the voice will seem rich. The combinations can, considering the number of cavities, be endless.

Probably the layman cannot hear the two notes in a vowel sound, but a singer can, whether he recognizes the scientific fact or not. Thus, Queena Mario in her lessons emphasizes that good notes have both a high and a low to them, a rich body. This is generally particularly noticeable in high soprano notes, although not in the very highest. In tenors this is at least partly the reason for the "baritone" quality of many of the most famous, such as Caruso or Melchior. Their top notes sounded full and rounded, not like just the top half of a chord. In performance, of course, it all passes quickly, but thirty minutes at a singing lesson will convince most ears that there are two notes.

The fact that each vowel sound has two notes of absolute pitch raises the question at once of what happens when the composer asks a singer to sing "ee" on some note that is not one of "ee's" two notes. If the requested note or any of its overtones falls on one of the notes of "ee," the singer should be able to do it; but if it does not, then he must fake the vowel sound. This means that perfect pronunciation is often impossible in song. It is also, of course, a reason why some translations "sing" so poorly.

Another home test to show that the vowels have absolute pitch is to play a recorded aria at ascending speeds and to listen to the sound of the vowel change as the pitch of the note changes.

Vowel sounds, of course, vary with language, and those languages that have impure vowel sounds or diphthongs are more difficult to sing. In this respect French and Italian are easier than English or German. Many English vowel sounds tend to be diphthongs: the common word "why" is "i" and "e"; "prune," "oo" and "eh"; "foil," "oi-ill"; and "fear," "ee-ur."

With the mechanism of singing so complicated and mysterious, it is not surprising that there are many theories of voice production. Probably all have some truth, and the differences, so black and white to singing teachers, are only gray and matters of emphasis.

One theory, more popular at the beginning of the century than now, involves "registers"—head, throat and chest register. It may have evolved as an effort to explain the change in timbre of a soprano's voice as she descends the scale or to explain why, depending on where she is in the scale, her head, throat or chest seems to be vibrating. Certainly it feels as though the voice moves from the head to the chest, and there is a clear crossover point as sopranos go up or down. A noticeable "break" at this point is today considered very poor, and sopranos work hard to develop an even scale. Lotte Lehmann says of the method of one of her teachers, "We had exercise sheets with the three vocal registers, chest voice, middle register and head voice, printed in different colors. The voice fairly leaped audibly from one register to another, a thing I couldn't agree with, for to me a steady flow of tone was the highest possible aim."

Bernard Shaw, too, had some comments on the theory of vocal registers, which he cast in the form—or maybe it was true—of research done by his mother's singing teacher in Dublin: "In his search for the secret of 'bel canto' (*See* Glossary) he had gone to all the teachers within his reach. They told him that there was a voice in the head, a voice in the throat, and a voice in the chest. He dissected birds, and with the connivance of medical friends, human subjects, in his search for these three organs. He then told the teachers authoritatively that the three voices were fabulous and that the voice was produced by a single instrument called the larynx. They replied that musical art had nothing to do with anatomy, and that for a musician to practice dissection was unheard of and disgusting . . ."

Another theory, claiming like its competitors to have the true secret of "bel canto," involves the use of two membranes located just above the true vocal cords and called the "false" vocal cords. They are what are first constricted and then released in a cough. Some singers, in spite of a slight coughing sound, use these to control the air supply when attacking the first note of a phrase. This method is called the "Coup de Glotte" or "Blow of the Glottis," although the method's adherents would prefer it to be called the "Caresse de Glotte." This style of singing greatly emphasizes the larynx as the source of all tone. It considers that the conscious use of the resonating cavities is not good singing because it is essentially uncontrolled and was forced on the singer by the increasing size and role of the opera orchestra during the last century.

With so little known about the voice, it is not surprising that a great deal of mumbo jumbo has grown up about its care. Most singers have a host of superstitions and gypsy remedies for its ills. Mme. Mathilde Marchesi advised Nellie Melba, "A singer never washes her head. She cleans it with tonic. She cleans it with a fine tooth comb. But she never washes it." Presumably the purpose of this was to avoid a head cold; but why did Mme. Marchesi think riding horseback would injure the vocal cords?

The common cold is the great enemy of all singers. If it is a head cold and mucus clogs the nose and head cavities, the effect on the sound is at once apparent. The cavities may not reinforce the usual overtones, may even select discordant ones, and in any event, the volume of tone will be greatly reduced. The effort of singing at all therefore greatly increases.

A throat cold is even more serious. If the vocal cords get inflamed, they may become impossible to control or, at very best, sluggish, so that it becomes a physical impossibility for the singer to do any rapid passages. Or the cords may grow so inflamed that they will not close at all (laryngitis), and the singer can only whisper.

The terrifying thing for the singer is that the inflamation, if aggravated, may permanently damage the cord. It could, for example, change the required adjustment for some note or produce a slightly different sound that the cavities did not pick up and reinforce.

To avoid irritating their throats in any way, some singers go to great lengths. The usual rules are to abjure smoking as a constant irritant of the cords and a threat to the wind supply. Drinking and heavy eating are bad because they knot the intestines, and then the diaphragm cannot work as easily. Suetonius reports that Nero, to help his diaphragm, used to clear his stomach by forced vomiting and enemas. Singers also like to avoid parties where the smoke of others gets in their throats or where they have to talk over other voices. Queena Mario estimated, for example, that a late party in a smoke-filled room costs even the nonsmoking singer several days of enforced idleness. After a long performance or before it, some singers talk in whispers. After one particularly hard season, Marcella Sembrich retired to her villa in Switzerland and whispered for a month.

On the other hand, just to keep everything uncertain, Caruso smoked; but as an envious colleague remarked, he had "the bellows of an ox and a constitution of iron."

Flagstad remarked about her voice in *The Flagstad Manuscript* that she never coddled it or fussed about colds. Even in the coldest weather she walked with her collar open and without a scarf. And she felt that perhaps because of this her voice continued strong and sure.

This is an era of outdoor types, and Marjorie Lawrence would approve the same philosophy. But both suffered with colds. Flagstad, in her first year at the Metropolitan in 1935, had laryngitis which affected her hearing, and for a while she sang without being able to hear the orchestra at all. As she observed dryly, if she had lacked a good sense of pitch, she could not have done it.

Years later, in her last season at the Metropolitan (1952), while singing in *Alceste,* she again caught cold. She could barely speak before breakfast, and even after, her voice sounded buried and heavy. To raise it she went in the bathroom and yelled. Because she did not want the neighbors to hear her croaking like a sea lion she turned on all the faucets. She estimated she was able to raise her voice about one tone every half hour.

For his colds Caruso used a spray of ether and iodoform. According to Mrs. Caruso, it "was not a cure but had the property of restoring the voice for a period of three hours." She described in *Enrico Caruso* how one evening Tettrazini, with a cold and in a panic before a concert, called on Caruso. He sat her down in all her finery on the edge of the tub and sprayed her throat. "As he sprayed, she [Tettrazini] had to pant quickly and not stop for a moment or the ether would have gone down into her lungs and anesthetized her. This spray acted something like a varnish or coat of shellac over the vocal cords."

Medically, iodoform is an antiseptic, a sort of mouthwash, and ether, besides anesthetizing the irritated vocal cords, is a stimulant like alcohol.

Another time when he suffered from a cold, Caruso put balsam of Bengué in his nose and all over his head and neck. It worked; but pity the poor soprano! Bengué contains menthol, which will contract the mucous membranes.

Most singers try to avoid singing early in the morning. The vocal cords, like any muscle, seem to "wake up" stiff. Beniamino Gigli complained of a regular matinal catarrh which kept him hoarse for several hours. But he ingenuously admitted, "Quite apart from this, I would rather sleep late than sing early. There is nothing of the lark about me. . . ." Marjorie Lawrence, on the other hand, suggests that the test for a good or bad voice for a performance in the evening is to leap out of bed in the morning and try for a high C.

Before the performance there are all sorts of rituals and superstitions. Many singers like a glass of champagne. The idea is charming, and the carbonation seems to clear the throat and nose. Maria Jeritza favored pineapple juice. Melba had an apple or an omelette with water. Fruit has the same antiseptic effect as champagne. Caruso had the most extended routine. Regularly "before singing he filled his mouth with salt water which he seemed to inhale into his lungs and then spat out. A pinch of snuff to clear the nostrils, a wine glass of whiskey followed by a glass of charged water and finally a quarter of an apple. In every costume he carried two little bottles of warm salt water." And every morning, regardless of whether he had a performance that day or not, Caruso spent a half hour with a steam inhalator.

Following each of her performances, Mary Garden drank a glass of milk with ten drops of iodine in it. Probably the effect was purely psychological—a doctor once told her it was a good thing after an exertion and a tonic for the nervous system. But it is just possible she knew that persons living in the center of continents tend to goiter because sea air containing iodine does not blow over the unpicked vegetables; that she considered Paris and Chicago, where she sang most, to be the center of continents; and that she took iodine in this way to prevent goiter.

Sometimes a singer will get what is called a "misplaced larynx." This is particularly apt to happen to mezzo-sopranos and contraltos, who "chest" their low notes. "Chesting" is singing the low notes all in the throat without face or head resonance. The effect on a single note is often thrilling; on successive notes it begins to sound ragged and uncontrolled. The difficulty seems to be that the larynx tends to drop slightly on low notes (you can feel it on the Adam's apple) and to rise slightly for high ones. The danger is that if the larynx gets used to "sagging" rather than to being properly placed for the note, it loses the ability to get in position for the highest notes. Snobs are always predicting that this or that mezzo will soon be out: "Listen to how she's chesting her low notes." Exercises, however, can solve the problem, although it may take a season. A misplaced larnyx is a danger for all singers. Coloraturas who suddenly sing an unusual number of lyric roles are apt to increase the number of their coloratura exercises as a balance. Besides the loss of top notes, signs of a misplaced larynx are an inability to sing softly and a breathy quality on pianissimos.

The most tragic thing that can happen to a singer is to develop a nodule, sometimes called a polyp. A nodule is a tiny growth, often no bigger than a pin point, on some part of the vocal cord. It can be on top, on the edge or on the underneath side. The last is by far the hardest to remove. It prevents the cords from vibrating properly. Sometimes it will affect just one note; sometimes several or even most of the singer's range. The voice becomes harsh and raspy like that of a cheerleader or baseball fan, both of whom also develop nodules. It can come from excessive use of the voice, or singing over a cold, and in spite of the greatest care. With sopranos it is most apt to affect the range between C and F sharp on the upper half of the staff.

One of the most famous—because it was ultimately happy—examples of a nodule involved Lucrezia Bori. In 1915 she was well started on a brilliant career and was one of the leading sopranos at the Metropolitan when it became evident that she was developing a nodule. She gave up singing altogether for four years while she had an operation, at first thought to be unsuccessful, to remove the nodule. But she returned to the operatic stage at Monte Carlo in 1919 and to the Metropolitan in 1921, from whence she retired in 1936. Unfortunately, most singers are usually not so lucky, and the operation takes some of the sheen off the voice, or possibly they don't attend to it soon enough, and the nodule gets too large.

The voice is also subject to an ailment called "hysterical aphonia," a form of shock induced by fear and reducing the singer to whispers.

The voice is completely gone; the larynx will not respond to the mind's directions. This completely irrational ailment once attacked a French tenor who was making his debut at the Metropolitan. He already had an established reputation in Europe and apparently had nothing to fear, and he was in good voice; but, suddenly, ten minutes before curtain time, he discovered he could speak only in whispers. The best cure for hysterical aphonia is a severe jolt. The house doctor announced that he had a liquid that would do the trick. In fact it was sterile water. He injected the entire capsule into the man's buttock through a large syringe and a blunt needle. He had trouble getting it in. The agony of the injection unlocked the tenor's voice and, after sniffing some heated menthol, he went on stage. As was expected, he was a success and stayed at the Metropolitan for a goodly number of years.

# V.

## THE CASTRATI

The castrati would be no more than an interesting footnote for scholars except that their position in opera is so inescapable: they were the best singers the world has ever heard. For more than 150 years (1650–1800) they dominated opera at a time when, with the exception of music in the church, opera was synonymous with serious music. Their contemporaries—sober, critical men —have left accounts of their feats that strike modern ears as incredible; and yet there are so many accounts from so many sides, all in agreement, that they must be accepted. They tell of tremendous skill in bravura singing, trills, scales and jumps; of extraordinary volume and control of it; and, above all, in the best of them, of an ability to express noble sentiments and pathos. The music the castrati have left behind them bears out the accounts. The coloratura (*See* Glossary) is beyond the skill of most singers of today, and whereas now in *Lucia di Lammermoor* the soprano competes with a flute, in Handel's operas the male soprano competes with a trumpet.

It is hard today when there are so many competing forms of entertainment to realize the position of opera and the castrati in the seventeenth and eighteenth centuries. There were, of course, no radio, television or movies; but there were also no symphony concerts or instrumentalists. Whatever it might be in private—flutes, recorders or violas—music in public was opera or the church. It was universally accepted, except in France, that Italian opera was the best and Italian singers the best. Thus Handel (1685–1759), a German writing for a London audience, composed thirty-seven operas, all in Italian, for which he employed Italian singers. To find them he had to travel no farther than Germany, where every little principality and palatinate had its court opera and troupe of Italian singers of which at least two or three were sure to be castrati.

The kind of opera that the castrati favored and that favored them was "opera seria," a form now extinct but which from 1650 to 1750 reigned unchallenged. During that time, of course, it went through various evolutions, but in general an "opera seria" was a succession of long arias set in a mythological or historical story, sung in Italian, and culminating in a happy ending. Its audience was aristocratic and it glorified the aristocratic virtues of chivalry, mercy, courage and "noblesse oblige." Its opposite, "opera buffa," which developed later, dealt with the next-door neighbor and such everyday sentiments as avarice, cowardice and each man for himself. "Opere serie" were usually far more episodic than dramatic, and the scenes, instead of advancing the action, were designed to allow the singer to display the various sides of the character: rage, jealousy, sorrow. The music was frequently only sketched and the singer was expected to improvise trills and runs and to embellish the aria. At this the castrati were supreme, and they dominated the musical world as conductors do today or as Liszt and Paganini did in the nineteenth century.

"Opere serie" are seldom performed today. The convention is foreign to audiences trained to enjoy the suspense thrillers of Puccini and Bizet or the orchestrations of Wagner and Strauss. And there is no good solution to the problem of casting the castrato roles. Probably the Mozart audiences could bridge the difference most easily. Mozart wrote several "opere serie," of which the greatest is *Idomeneo,* his favorite of his own operas. But the opera closest to "opera seria" and still in the general repertory is Gluck's *Orfeo*. It is of course the first of Gluck's "reform" operas by which he and his librettist, Calzabigi, hoped to do away with the conventions and clichés that were choking "opera seria." In its extended use of the orchestra, ballet and chorus and, more particularly, in its simplicity of style, it is not typical. But in its static scenes—each designed to trigger Orfeo into an aria of despair, hope, pleading or sorrow—and in its language and happy ending, its parentage is clearly visible. The role of Orfeo was first taken by Guadagni, a male alto, who was a good actor (he had lessons from Garrick) but a singer without much technique and not likely, therefore, to insert his own embellishments on the arias. He was undoubtedly picked for this reason, and he made a great success of the role, particularly in London.

The exact origins of the castrati are unknown, but their existence is inextricably entwined in the development of church music. By dictum of St. Paul (I Cor. 14:34) women are to keep silent in church. Most Christian churches and particularly the Roman Catholic Church have until recently interpreted this, to the despair of their choirmasters, to mean that women cannot sing in choirs. As long as church music was

Gregorian chant, the interdiction was not so serious, but when it began to add higher voices, the only possible voices could be those of boys, falsettists or castrati.

Boys are an unprofitable investment of time and training because they no sooner get adept than their voices change. Falsettists generally cannot go higher than the alto range, and their tone is forced and unpleasant. For a brief time in the sixteenth century, however, a group of singers known as Spanish falsettists managed by a secret technique to extend their range through the soprano register. Little is known about them, and their secret is lost. Apparently, most of them actually did come from Spain and, as far as can be determined, actually did sing falsetto, although some scholars have offered evidence suggesting that at least some of them were, in fact, castrati. The records of the Vatican show that the Spanish falsettists began to die out about 1625 and to be replaced by acknowledged castrati.

The Church's attitude towards the castrati was thoroughly equivocal. It threatened with excommunication anyone known to have been connected with such an operation. But on the other hand, even the Pope's private chapel employed castrati. There were also civil penalties, but these seem almost never to have been enforced. The Church also fulminated against women on the stage. The result was, of course, that it helped to create the demand for the castrati and thus insured the supply.

The confused attitude of the Church and the latent threat of civil punishment contributed to the secrecy with which the operation was performed and have made it almost impossible to find out anything definite about it or the children subjected to it. Naturally, no one connected with such an operation spoke much of it, and generally a castrato voice was the result of an "accident," "an attack by a pig" or "necessitated for reasons of health." The boys seem mostly to have come from very poor families in the region of Apulia, the heel of Italy; the parents apparently hoped the children would support them in their old age.

The exact operation is in dispute. Angus Heriot, a dispassionate scholar, has a footnote in his book, *The Castrati in Opera,* in which he paraphrases an earlier description of the operation and makes some observations on it: "The child, often drugged with opium or some other narcotic, was placed in a very hot bath for some time, until it was in a state of virtual insensibility. Then the ducts leading to the testicles were severed, so that the latter in course of time shrivelled and disappeared. Eunuchs of this type were known in ancient times as 'Thlibiae' or 'Thlasiae,' in contradistinction to eunuchs proper who had been subject to full castration. The latter operation does not seem ever to have been practised in the case of castrato singers."

Others argue that such an operation would simply render the boy infertile without affecting his other masculine characteristics and thus fail to prevent the thickening of his vocal chords. They insist the operation was a full castration or shearing off of the testicles. The two views exist unreconciled.

There were several superstitions of the time about the operation. One was that if it were performed in damp weather, the boy would have a squeaky voice. Thus an injudicious reference to the weather was a fine way to insult a castrato. It was also supposed that the later a boy was castrated, the lower his voice would be.

Some of the male sopranos apparently were such naturally rather than by any operation: they were simply undeveloped. And, no distinction was made between them and the castrati whose name they shared. One natural castrato once strained for a high note during a performance and, to his horror, compressed years of adolescent development into a single instant—to the complete ruin of his career.

The practice of castration strikes most modern sensibilities as barbaric, chiefly because it was inflicted on those under the age of consent. In spite of tales to the contrary, it seems to have had no direct effect on the man's health. The castrato lived as long as his neighbor; he was neither necessarily fatter nor thinner; he had the same sexual desires, gratified in the same way. Indeed, as Heriot points out, "they were of course much in demand by the opposite sex, for their embraces could not lead to awkward consequences." The difficulties unquestionably were psychological. Heriot exhumed pathetic evidence of this from the records of the Neapolitan conservatories, where young singers, castrati and others, were trained: opposite the names of many of the castrati was the cryptic entry, "he ran away." It seldom appeared opposite the names of the other boys, although in fact they were treated more roughly.

The difficulties, of course, did not end with boarding school. Because there was perfectly audible evidence of infertility, the Church forbade the castrati to marry, on the ground that the only purpose of marriage was to procreate. Some castrati, however, did marry; and one, Tenducci, even claimed to have produced two children. The extraordinary thing about the children is that, at the time, most persons in London who knew Mr. and Mrs. Tenducci accepted them as his. Tenducci's explanation was that the surgeon had missed a duct during the operation. This is the only instance recorded of possible fertility.

Probably the "difference" accounted for much of the success of the castrati. Each must have looked at his future and decided that the best life could only be in singing, and therefore he would become a great singer. Also, of course, the conservatories got the boys young and worked them hard. The rewards were great and obvious. Many castrati became extremely rich and influential, retiring with honor to a villa or to teach in a conservatory.

The most astounding career of all was that of Farinelli, the greatest of the castrati and, according to many, the greatest singer of all time. He was born in 1705. His real name was Carlo Broschi, but he was always called Farinelli. Among castrati he is almost unique in that he came from the nobility; and just why his father should have had him castrated is unknown. He made his debut in Naples in 1720 in the first work by Metastasio, perhaps the greatest librettist who ever lived. Thereafter, the two became great friends and corresponded for more than sixty years, addressing each other as "dear twin" in memory of their joint debut before the world.

In 1722 he went to Rome, where occurred the famous incident recounted by Dr. Burney (*See* Glossary): "He was seventeen when he left that city [Naples] to go to Rome, where during the run of an opera, there was a struggle every night between him and a famous player on the trumpet, in a song accompanied by that instrument; this, at first, seemed amicable and merely sportive, till the audience began to interest themselves in the contest, and to take different sides: after severally swelling a note, in which each manifested the power of his lungs, and tried to rival the other in brilliancy and force, they had both a swell and shake [trill] together, by thirds, which was continued so long, while the audience eagerly waited the event, that both seemed to be exhausted; and, in fact, the trumpeter, wholly spent, gave it up, thinking, however, his antagonist as much tired as himself, and that it would be a drawn battle; when Farinelli, with a smile on his countenance, shewing he had only been sporting with him all that time, broke out all at once in the same breath, with fresh vigour, and not only swelled and shook the note, but ran the most rapid and difficult divisions, and was at last silenced only by the acclamations of the audience. From this period may be dated that superiority which he ever maintained over all his contemporaries."

Dr. Burney also reported an incident that exhibited Farinelli's success with pathos. He was singing in a pasticcio, "Artaserse." "Senesino (another castrato) had the part of a furious tyrant, and Farinelli that of an unfortunate hero in chains; but in the course of the first air, the captive so softened the heart of the tyrant, that Senesino, forgetting his stage-character, ran to Farinelli and embraced him in his own." And at the rehearsal for this opera, which was being given in London, the orchestra was so staggered by Farinelli's virtuosity that it forgot to play. Farinelli had such a success in London that Hogarth even put a squib about him in "The Rake's Progress" (Plate 2) where he shows a crowd worshipping at a statue of Farinelli and a woman screaming, "One God, One Farinelli."

Farinelli's next conquest was Spain. The King, Philip V, was a melancholic who moped around the court unshaven and weeping. Even worse, he refused to attend to the business of state, and the Queen and ministers were in despair. The Queen, for a large fee, persuaded Farinelli to come and sing for the King. She managed the debut with the greatest care so that the King first heard the voice, as if by accident rather than medical design, in the next room. The plot succeeded, and thereafter Farinelli sang every night for Philip, who brightened up, shaved regularly and attended to the business of state. Dr. Burney reports that Farinelli sang the same four songs every evening for nine years, at the end of which the King died happy. It is not certain whether he sang *only* those four songs or whether they were merely part of a larger program. The titles of two of them are known. They are both from "Artaserse" by Hasse: "Pallido i sole" and "E pur questo dolce amplesso." But even if he sang the same four songs every evening, it is important to remember that he would have improvised on the arias so that there would have been some variety.

The new king, Ferdinand VI, kept Farinelli on, and his influence became, if possible, even greater. He managed the music at court, imported horses for breeding, and arranged irrigation systems. His influence has been compared to that of Rasputin, with the difference being that Farinelli seems to have made himself loved by everyone, an extraordinary feat at a Spanish court. Ferdinand died in 1759 and his half brother Charles, King of Naples, succeeded him. Charles presumably wanted to start a fresh administration and asked Farinelli to leave Spain. The singer retired to a villa outside Bologna, where he received all sorts of guests, including Casanova and Dr. Burney, and in general played the grand old man until he died in 1782. The grave has been lost, but the villa still exists.

Hindsight can see that even in 1782, the year of Farinelli's death, the history of opera was turning away from the castrati; to their contemporaries, of course, they seemed as supreme as ever. But in 1782 Paisiello produced his *Il Barbiere di Siviglia,* which ran continuously, somewhere, for thirty-three years until Rossini's opera with the same name and subject displaced it. Its fantastic success reflected the increasing stature of comic opera. Also in 1782 Mozart produced his *Die Entfuehrung aus dem Serail,* which was not only comic but in German, something inconceivable to Handel fifty years earlier. Only in France had serious composers resisted the triumph of the castrati in Italian opera and attempted to write in the vernacular.

For many years, of course, there had been comic operas, operas in the various Italian dialects, German "singspiels" and English ballad operas. But no one had taken them seriously. They were interludes between the acts of the real thing, "opera seria," or rustic efforts for fairs and fetes; but they were not for the theater. The castrati even occasionally sang in comic operas, but this was generally in women's roles because at that moment or at that place women were banned from the stage. But they did not dominate comic opera as they did "opera seria" with its mythological and historical stories. Comic opera was far more apt to be about the neighbor next door, which meant realism, and realism and the castrati were inevitably at odds.

Mozart's operas are indicative of the change that was coming. In 1781 he wrote *Idomeneo,* an "opera seria" requiring a castrato. Ten years later, on commission and perhaps not recognizing the changing times himself, he wrote *La Clemenza di Tito,* another "opera seria" requiring a castrato. But between he wrote *Die Entfuehrung, Le Nozze di Figaro, Don Giovanni, Così fan tutte* and *Die Zauberfloete,* two German operas and three which, although in Italian, were not "opera seria" in any way. Mozart, of course, did not consider himself a pioneer, and almost all Italians, castrato or not, did not consider him at all. Mozart's operas came to Italy very late; the first full productions of *Don Giovanni* and *Le Nozze* were in 1811, or twenty years after

Mozart's death. *Die Entfuehrung* had its Italian premiere in 1935 [*sic*]!

In Italy the great composers continued to write "opera seria," but even there the emphasis was changing. Rossini, for example, wrote several, but his best work and the one of which he was proudest was *Il Barbiere di Siviglia*. But even more important perhaps than his comic genius was his insistence that the arias be sung as written. The greatest glory and tradition of the castrati was their ability to extemporize on an aria, like jazz artists of today. Such an approach inevitably glorifies the performer at the expense of the composer. Rossini is supposed to have had a furious disagreement with Velluti, one of the most distinguished of the castrati, over his interpretation of his arias in *Aureliano in Palmira* and to have sworn never to let a singer depart from the written notes again. Velluti in turn swore never to appear in another Rossini opera. Later he did, and in the end the two became great friends; but over the years Rossini won his point.

Contemporary accounts suggest that it was well taken. As early as 1742 one outraged operagoer was complaining, "The Presumption of some Singers is not to be borne with, who expect that a whole *Orchestra* should stop in the midst of a well-regulated Movement, to wait for their ill-grounded Caprices, learned by Heart, carried from one Theatre to another, and perhaps stolen from some applauded female Singer, who had better Luck than Skill, and whose Errors were excused in regard to her sex . . . The study of the Singers of the present Times consists in terminating the Cadence of the first Part with an overflowing of Passages and Divisions at Pleasure, and the Orchestra waits; in that of the second the Dose is increased, and the Orchestra grows tired; but on the last Cadence, the Threat is set going, like a Weather-cock in a whirlwind, and the Orchestra yawns."

The vanity of some of the castrati extended even beyond the aria. Marchesi (1754–1829) is supposed to have refused to sing unless he could make his entrance on horseback or coming downhill and wearing a helmet of multicolored plumes at least six feet high. Further, a fanfare was to announce his entrance, and his first aria was to be one of his favorites, no matter what the dramatic situation or the part he was singing. The old court aristocracies indulged this sort of behavior more easily than the more serious-minded audience that was developing from the bourgeoisie.

As the audience changed, so did the subject matter of the operas. Napoleon's marshals, the new Kings of Naples and Spain, and the rising bankers and tradesmen were not interested in operas glorifying heredity, tradition and "noblesse oblige." They had none, and the opera librettos gradually turned away from the "opera seria" stories to the more domestic tragedies of *Norma* and *Lucia di Lammermoor*. Probably one of the last years in which operas were written especially for royal celebrations was 1825, when Spohr, Spontini and Rossini each wrote one. All three were failures. Rossini's was for the coronation of Charles X of France; the others for petty German princes.

Napoleon is frequently credited with having extinguished the castrati, and in a sense he did, but indirectly. He himself evidently greatly enjoyed their singing, as he invited Crescentini (1762–1846) to come to Paris and for six years the singer performed regularly at the Tuileries court theater. But Italy under the Napoleonic occupation and regimes had strong, centralized governments, and for the first time the old civil laws began to be enforced. Also, beginning in about 1798, Heriot shows that the conservatories lost a great part of their enrollment, castrato and other, undoubtedly because of the general fever and excitement pro and con Napoleon and the reform that swept up and down Italy for many years. *Tosca* gives a hint of the excited atmosphere in Rome.

The effect of the turmoil was to reduce greatly the number of trained singers and especially the number of castrati, who at one time in the eighteenth century, it has been estimated, accounted for 70 per cent of the male opera singers. Most of the older castrati retired about 1810, and Velluti (1781–1861) was almost their only successor. All the contemporary accounts at this time lament the decline in singing. The last opera composed especially for a castrato seems to have been Meyerbeer's *Il Crociato in Egitto,* done for Velluti in 1824. Twenty years later a castrato sang in London. He was the first in fifteen years. Velluti was the last of the operatic castrati, and he gradually retired in the 1830's to his farm near Venice, where he experimented with advanced agricultural theories and methods.

In the Church the castrati continued considerably longer, or possibly the Church was merely performing an humanitarian service in giving them a job and a home. One of the last of these was Domenico Mustafa (1829–1912), who was director of Papal music. Emma Calvé was so impressed by his technique that she look lessons from him and apparently learned how to produce certain high, floating notes that elude the sopranos of today. The very last castrato of all was Alessandro Moreschi (1858–1922). There is some disagreement about whether Moreschi was a true castrato or a congenital eunuch. But whatever the medical fact, he was musically a male soprano in the direct tradition of the castrati. He had a public career and performed at the funerals of Victor Emmanuel II and Umberto I. He retired in 1913.

Moreschi has a unique niche in musical history because of recordings he made which still occasionally come on the market or can be heard over the radio. His technique is not exceptional, and it is always difficult on old records (these were recorded in 1902 and 1903) to be sure what the true tone and timbre of the voice may be. Clearly he is a soprano and not a falsettist. His tone is stronger than a boy's but without a woman's fullness or body. It has something of a boy's unearthly quality, and on some notes it is pleasing; on others it is whiny or raspy. But his technique is faulty even on the simple, religious songs he sings, and so he is not a good example, however interesting, of the kind of singing and tone that made the best castrati so famous.

# VI·

## SOUNDS OF THE ORCHESTRA

One of the hardest things to do in the opera house is to hear, really hear, the sounds of the orchestra. All day long sounds assault our ears which, unlike our eyes, have no lids to close when tired or surfeited. The ear's only defense in the street, office or home is to beg the mind to block out the sounds—which the mind usually does, except when the sound is of a tap dripping or a neighbor's dog barking. So defenseless is the ear and so adept has the mind become at blocking out sounds that much of what we might like to hear, we do not, simply out of habit.

The habit is harder to overcome in the opera house than in the concert hall because of the additional distraction of what is happening on the stage. The human mind, unlike the dog's, gives precedence to what the eye sees over what the ear hears, and when the visual image is exciting, the mind hardly notices what it hears. Unfortunately, the reverse is not true. When one of Wagner's heroines stands immobile for twenty minutes, a depressing visual image, the mind usually has long since turned off the ear, an act about as foolish as boring a hole in the last lifeboat.

But to be saved takes some energy and experience. The energy needed is to be able to wipe the day's aural slate clean—not always so easy—and really listen to the squeaks and bumps that come up from the orchestra pit. The experience needed is some knowledge of the instruments of the orchestra: how they look and sound, and how composers thought of them.

Berlioz, for example, thought this about the clarinet and Weber's scoring for it in *Der Freischuetz:* "There is no other wind instrument which can produce a tone, let it swell, decrease and die away as beautifully as the clarinet. Hence its invaluable ability to render distant sounds, an echo, the reverberation of an echo, or the charm of the twilight. I know no more admirable example of such shading than the dreamy melody of the clarinet, accompanied by the tremolo of the strings, in the Allegro of the *Freischuetz* overture. Is this not the lonely maiden, the blond betrothed of the huntsman, with her eyes raised to heaven uttering her tender plaint, amidst the rustling noise of the deep forest shaken by the storm?—O Weber!" (O Berlioz!) The passage begins about five minutes into the overture, or at measure 96.

No one can instill into an operagoer the energy to listen, and the experience can only be offered. But didactic talk is always boring, and this chapter offers every prospect of being the most boring in the book. Take warning: there is no easy way to talk about instruments of the orchestra, one after another, without sounding like a catalogue. But at least it is all gathered here in one place, so that it may be easily skipped. Therefore, be it clearly understood: the following discussion will prove an unmitigated and wearisome bore to anyone for whom opera is not already a serious addiction or who cannot discover in himself a hankering after the vice.

The discussion is in two parts: first, the sound and shape of the more important instruments are described and operas listed in which they can be heard; and second, one opera, *Carmen,* is analyzed in terms of its instrumentation—which instrument Bizet chose to use at a particular moment, together with some speculations on why.

## I. THE INSTRUMENTS

The opera orchestra, like any other, divides into four groups: strings, brass, woodwinds and percussion. These are defined in the Glossary. Depending on the composer, period and type of opera, the number of instruments required may vary anywhere from one hundred fifty to three or four. A large, well-endowed opera house will have at its command for Wagner or Richard Strauss an orchestra of about the following:

| *Strings* | *Brass* | *Woodwinds* | *Percussion* |
|---|---|---|---|
| 16 first violins | 4 trumpets | 2 piccolos | 2 prs. of kettledrums |
| 16 second violins | 8 French horns | 3 flutes | 1 bass drum |
| 12 violas | 4 trombones | 3 clarinets | 1 snare drum |
| 12 cellos | 3 tubas | 2 bass clarinets | 1 pr. of cymbals |
| 8 doublebasses | | 4 oboes | 1 triangle |
| ——— | | 1 English horn | and such others as |
| 6 harps | | 3 bassoons | tambourine, bells, |
| | | | chimes, etc. |

The instruments within a group are listed by range, with those playing the higher notes first; because many overlap, however, the real difference is often more in quality than in pitch.

Some of the players, particularly in the percussion and woodwind groups, play two instruments, so that there are generally more instruments represented than men in the pit. Most players own their own instruments. The Metropolitan Opera, for example, provides only percussion instruments, but even then many drummers use their own drums.

An eighteenth-century opera or comic opera might require only the following:

| *Strings* | *Brass* | *Woodwinds* | *Percussion* |
|---|---|---|---|
| 9 first violins | 2 trumpets | 2 flutes | 1 pr. of kettledrums |
| 8 second violins | 2 French horns | 2 clarinets | 1 pr. of cymbals |
| 6 violas | | 2 oboes | 1 triangle |
| 7 cellos | | 2 bassoons | |
| 6 doublebasses | | | |

As can easily be seen, the strings outnumber the other instruments by more than two to one. When playing for an eighteenth-century opera, the orchestra frequently rearranges its seating so that the brass and woodwinds, being so many fewer, combine to form one group opposed to the strings rather than preserving a separate identity. The orchestra then will give off a noticeably different "balance" of sound —far more "stringy." This is partly because the development of valves and mechanical perfection of the brass and woodwinds was still in the future. Mozart's horn could play considerably fewer notes than Richard Strauss'.

Because the strings form the general sound against which the other instruments contrast, this discussion leaves them to the end and begins with the instruments producing the more special sounds. And because this *is* a catalogue and it may be of interest, the approximate price of each instrument—except the strings, which vary widely—is indicated at the end of the description of the instrument.

## THE WOODWINDS

THE PICCOLO: It plays the highest notes the orchestra possesses. The full name is "flauto piccolo," and old treatises sometimes still refer to

PICCOLO

it as the small flute. It is about thirteen inches long and, like a regular flute, is played out to the side of the face. Its range is an octave higher than a flute, or three octaves beginning at the C above middle C. Its lower notes are indistinguishable from those of a flute, which it overlaps; its top notes are brilliant, penetrating and rather shrill. It is seldom used as a solo instrument but is reserved for special situations requiring brilliance or for comic effects. It is usually played as a secondary instrument by one or two of the flutists.

*Carmen,* Act I: The introduction to the chorus of the boys is a solo for two piccolos, which continue thereafter to dominate the chorus.

*Rigoletto,* Act IV: The lightning in the storm. This is true of almost any storm, e.g. *Der Fliegende Hollaender.*

*Die Walkuere,* Act III: The glitter in the fire music. The harps play the same pattern underneath.

And, of course, piccolos are constantly in military bands on and off stage in order to penetrate the heavy brass and open air, e.g. "Stars and Stripes" by Sousa.

FLUTE

THE FLUTE: Supposedly the modern flute is the direct descendant of Pan's pipe, the "syrinx," made of reeds. Later, and until the beginning of the nineteenth century, most flutes were made of boxwood, which still produces the sweetest tone but absorbs moisture too easily. Today most flutes are made of silver. The flute's range is three octaves rising from middle C. Each octave, roughly speaking, has a slightly different quality to it. The lowest is thick, breathy and, because the overtones do not sound, an almost pure tone of the note sounded; the middle octave is sweet, mellow and rather pastoral and is the one most persons recognize immediately as the flute; the high octave is bright and beginning to get shrill like a piccolo. Except for the special effects of the piccolo, the flute is the top of the woodwind section, and its highest octave is often used to give a sharp edge to the tones of the clarinets, oboes and bassoons.

Berlioz contrasted the particular quality of a flute with other instruments in his famous description of the flute solo in Gluck's *Orfeo:* "When listening to the D-minor melody of the pantomime in the Elysian Fields scene in *Orfeo,* one is immediately convinced that only a flute could play this melody appropriately. An oboe would be too child-like, and its tone not sufficiently clear. The English horn is too low. A clarinet would doubtless have been more suitable, but it would have been too strong for some of the passages. . . . Moreover, Gluck's melody is conceived in such a way that the flute can follow every impulse of this eternal grief, still imbued with the passions of earthly life. The voice starts almost inaudible, seemingly afraid to be overheard; then it sighs softly and rises to the expression of reproach, of deep pain, to the cry of a heart torn by incurable wounds; gradually it sinks back into a plaint, a sigh and the sorrowful murmur of a resigned soul."

Berlioz's opinions, set forth in his *Treatise on Instrumentation,* are particularly interesting because he consistently derived his inspiration from the character of the instruments. He did not, as many do, compose first at the piano (which he could not play) and then merely distribute the notes among the orchestra according to range.

*Orfeo,* Act II: Second pantomime ballet in Elysian Fields. Flute solo centering in the middle octave over light string accompaniment.

*Carmen,* Act II: Duet for flutes introducing the first aria of the act, Carmen's "les tringles des sistres"; mostly at the top of the middle octave.

*Carmen,* Act III: Entr'acte played as the Prelude to Act III. The flute, at the top of the middle octave, has the melody at first alone and then supported by a clarinet. Later the melody shifts to an English horn supported by a bassoon. The flute, mostly at the top of the lowest octave, also introduces the first chorus, immediately after the curtain rises.

*Rigoletto,* Act II: The introduction to Gilda's aria, "Caro nome," immediately after the Duke leaves, has a solo flute in rising runs, and then two flutes introduce the melody.

*Aida,* Act III: Immediately after the priests depart and as Aida enters, three flutes sound the melody associated with her over very light strings.

*Die Zauberfloete:* Inevitably in this opera, *The Magic Flute,* the instrument itself plays a leading part. Indeed, Mozart's problem was how to avoid dissipating its unique quality before the opera's climax, the trial by fire and water. His solution was brilliant: first, he introduced a red herring for the audience's attention, Papageno's bells, which he reserved exclusively for Papageno, and around which he built two lengthy scenes; second, he used the flute as part of the general accompaniment for every character, even Monostatos, so that its tone never became a symbol for Tamino, having to "enter" whenever he entered or whenever Pamina thought of him. Thus, he could husband its effect as a solo instrument for any scene he selected. In fact, he gave it two solos: one in the finale to Act I when Tamino plays and the animals creep in to listen—and even this he constantly interrupted with Tamino's voice—and the other, this time uninterrupted, in the finale to Act II as the climax of the opera.

CLARINET

THE CLARINET: Like the flute, the clarinet is twenty-six inches long and cylindrical for most of its length; in the last six inches it becomes conical. But, unlike the flute, it is closed at one end with a reed. It generally is made of African blackwood or granadilla, either of which allows a greater expression and build-up of tone than metal or other woods. The clarinet's ability to increase and decrease its tone is unequaled by any of the other woodwinds. Its range is from E below middle C to C three octaves above. Like the flute it has a different sound in different "registers." The lowest, the first octave, produces a vibrant, hollow tone good for scenes of horror; the next, a short register of six notes, sounds dull and is avoided if possible; the third, the medium or clarinet register, is the general area of play and has a clear, full tone; and finally the highest register, the last octave, has a clear, hard, even tart quality and is generally used for filling out massive harmonies.

Most composers seem to have felt that the clarinet was a peculiarly feminine instrument. Even in marches for the parade ground, its softer, sweeter tone is used to contrast with the raucous brass. In opera it frequently haunts or suggests the prima donna in all her moods. Prokofiev in *Peter and the Wolf* scores it typically in its low register for the cat and directs it be played "con eleganza." Berlioz felt that only frivolous gaiety or artless joy could not be expressed by the clarinet.

*Der Freischuetz,* Overture: Described above.

*La Traviata,* Act II: It sounds while Violetta writes her note to Alfredo after the departure of Germont père and before Alfredo's return.

*Tosca,* Act III: It introduces Cavaradossi's aria as he tries to write the letter.

*La Bohème,* Act I: As Mimi knocks and enters, she is accompanied by the clarinet over quiet strings.

*Tristan und Isolde,* Act II: As Isolde listens to the horns to see if the hunters have disappeared, the clarinet representing her desire rises above the rustling of the wind in the leaves, a tremolo (*See* p. 78) on the strings.

*Goetterdaemmerung,* Act I: Interval between Scenes 2 and 3. As Bruennhilde waits anxiously for Siegfried, there is a solo passage for two clarinets.

*Il Trovatore,* Act II Scene 2: The Count's aria, close to the beginning of the act, has a triplet accompanying figure for the clarinet in its low register.

*Faust,* Act III (Garden Scene): There is a long run as the curtain rises.

*Faust,* Act V (Prison Scene Prelude): Clarinet solo over string accompaniment.

THE BASS CLARINET: It is a variation of the clarinet and sounds an octave lower. It is longer than the regular clarinet, and the bell hooks around and up like a saxophone. The mouthpiece fits into a metal tube which hooks into the top of the wooden tube. It gives a low, hollow sound.

 *Aida,* Act IV Scene 1: Immediately after Radames is brought in, the clarinet mostly in its lower range introduces Amneris' appeal to him. It continues throughout it and Radames' reply with a triplet figure.

*Tristan und Isolde,* Act II: It introduces and accompanies Marke's monologue after he has discovered Tristan with Isolde.

*Tannhaeuser,* Act III: It sounds occasionally as a solo instrument during Elisabeth's prayer and the orchestral close of it.

*Simon Boccanegra,* Act I Scene 2: It has the solo melody as the Doge prepares to curse Paolo and it continues throughout the curse with a stabbing, triplet accompaniment.

OBOE, ENGLISH HORN

THE OBOE: Unlike those of the clarinet and flute, the oboe's tube is conical, although from the balcony the difference is not noticeable. The oboe appears identical to the clarinet except that in place of a mouthpiece two reeds, bound back to back, rise directly from the tube. The oboe's range is from B below middle C to A two and a half octaves above. Thus, it has a shorter range than the clarinet, lacking the four or five notes on either end. Its effective range is considerably less, being only an octave and a half starting at the G above middle C, or roughly corresponding to the medium or clarinet register of the clarinet. The oboist's breath-control problem is quite different from that of other wind players, as he needs only a small, even stream of air passing through the reeds. As a result, oboists are apt to look as if they are about to explode, and traditionally they are supposed to be in a constant state of frustration because they can never empty their lungs.

The sound is distinctive, particularly at the start of the note, which has a fuzzy or tart squeak to it. But, in spite of this, the tone has a tender quality, and it often carries the melody. Richard Strauss liked the oboe's "thick and impudent low tones" and its "thin and bleating" high ones, which he felt were good for comic effects.

*Orfeo,* Act II: The accompaniment to Orfeo's aria, "Che puro ciel," is an oboe "obbligato" (*See* Glossary) expressing a sense of serene wonder.

*Cavalleria Rusticana:* Lola's single aria has an oboe accompaniment with a marvelous air of insinuating impudence.

*Aida,* Act III: The introduction to Aida's aria, "O patria mia," and later when she first suggests to Radames that they flee.

*La Traviata,* Act IV: The oboe introduces and responds to Violetta's first aria, "Addio del passato."

*Faust,* Act I: Close to the beginning, after Faust's thrice-repeated "rien," he goes to the window. As he opens it and the first light enters the room, the oboe has a solo over quiet strings. Later it has another solo with the offstage chorus.

THE ENGLISH HORN: It is neither a horn nor English, having received its name by a series of historical accidents. It is an alto oboe, with a range five notes lower than the regular oboe, and is usually played by the second or third oboist. It is larger than the oboe and has as a mouthpiece a small pipe holding the two reeds. Its depth of tone gives it a plaintive quality, less piercing and more veiled than that of the oboe; the sound is not so spry. It is best for melancholy, dreamy, rather distant melodies. Berlioz felt that it had "no equal among the instruments for reviving images and sentiments of the past."

*Carmen,* Act II: The English horn introduces and is the solo instrument throughout Don José's Flower Song.

*Tannhaeuser,* Act I Scene 3: The shepherd's pipe. The melody is unusually gay for the instrument.

*Tristan und Isolde,* Act III Scene 1: The shepherd's pipe almost immediately after the curtain rises. The droopy melody perfectly fits the quality of the instrument.

BASSOON

THE BASSOON: The name comes from the Italian "bassone" (big bass), and the instrument is the bass of the woodwinds. It is a long, slightly conical tube folded back on itself. The double-reed mouthpiece on a long hook comes out the top, against which the bottom has been folded back; as a result, it looks as though it came out of the middle of a single tube. The bassoon's range is four octaves from a B flat below the bass clef to C two octaves above middle C. It is usually made of maple or rosewood and folded back, it stands about four feet high; unfolded, it would be almost eight and one-half feet. The tube tapers over the eight feet from three-sixteenths of an inch at the reed to about one and seven-eighths inches at the bell.

Its tone is not very strong or brilliant and sounds like a soft, liquid hoot. It can be very comic, even grotesque. Its highest tones sound pained.

*Carmen,* Act II: The entr'acte preceding Act II begins with a solo for two bassoons. Then after the higher woodwinds and strings have exchanged phrases several times, the clarinet repeats the bassoon's melody while the bassoons tiptoe up and down the scale underneath.

*Il Trovatore,* Act IV: Two bassoons and two clarinets open the act.
*L'Elisir d'Amore,* Act II Scene 2: A bassoon has the solo melody introducing the tenor's aria, "Una Furtiva lagrima."

The woodwinds, producing a common hollow, liquid sound, often play together as a group. The entr'acte in *Carmen* preceding Act III is an example. The solo flute has the melody over a harp accompaniment; the solo clarinet repeats it, again over the harp and with the flute in a descant above; then the English horn and bassoon, over the harp and light strings, take up the first phrase of the melody and are answered by the flute and clarinet together repeating the phrase. The same thing is done with another phrase, and then the instruments in this order—clarinet, English horn, second flute, first flute—drop off in turn as each repeats a small pattern of notes. Likewise at the end of the entr'acte preceding Act II, the woodwinds, flute, oboe, clarinet and bassoon drop off in turn as each repeats a phrase.

This is the classic style of orchestration, very clear and presupposing an ear able to hear the difference in tone between the instruments. If the ear cannot differentiate, some of the effect is lost. Its clarity is its unique fingerprint, inherited from eighteenth-century chamber music. In the romantic style and particularly in Wagner each instrument is used to add its peculiar splash of color in building up the general orchestral sound. Group relationships are a looser tie. The result is a magnificent wash of sound in which the listener immerses himself without trying, or being able, to identify its components. No one not a specialist can hear what the clarinets or oboes are doing in the *Die Walkuere* Fire Music or can pick out the rhythm of the triangle. The clarity of the individual instruments has been sacrificed for a new sound. But Wagner could also write magnificently for the individual instruments, as when in *Lohengrin,* Act II Scene 2, Elsa emerges on the balcony. For three minutes he uses only woodwinds over a few simple horn chords, extracting every conceivable shade and nuance. Here perhaps even more than in Bizet or Mozart, because there is no action on the stage, it is important to hear the sound.

## THE BRASS

THE TRUMPET: It is a cylindrical tube of drawn brass fifty-three inches long and wound once around on itself; it ends in a small bell and has a cup-shaped mouthpiece. The shapes of the tube, bell and mouthpiece all contribute directly to the trumpet's bright tone. Conical tubes, big bells and funnel-shaped mouthpieces, as in French horns, produce a somber, mellow sound. The trumpet's range is from E below middle C to a B flat almost two octaves above. Soft tones are hard to produce and are usually restricted to the middle of the range.

TRUMPET

Its tone is particularly brilliant and martial. It can also make an extremely sarcastic "blaaaat" sound or, with a mute inserted in the bell, an ironic wail.

*Carmen,* Act I Prelude: It combines with a clarinet, bassoon and cello to introduce the Carmen or Fate theme.

*Carmen,* Act I: The change of guard and the boys' chorus.

*Aida,* Act I: The first aria, "Celeste Aida," has a trumpet and trombone introduction.

*Aida,* Act III: Radames' first aria, "Pur ti riveggo."

*Die Walkuere,* Act I: Siegmund's sword theme.

*Die Walkuere,* Act II: Bruennhilde's war cry.

*La Bohème,* Act II: Three trumpets playing in thirds open the act. Later they repeat the same melody, only muted.

*Tristan und Isolde,* Act II: In the closing bars, after Melot wounds Tristan, the trumpet cuts through the sound of the other instruments.

THE FRENCH HORN: The horn was originally the horn of an animal, the conical, curved shape of which is still the shape of today's horn. Held up to the lips, it curls out, once around, and out under the elbow. With all the additional crooks for the valves, which open additional lengths of tube, the horn, if unraveled, would measure eleven feet eight and one-half inches. In addition to its conical tube it has a funnel-shaped mouthpiece and ends in a large bell. Its range is from two octaves below middle C to an octave and a half above it. It is the most difficult to play of all the instruments, and some charity is allowed to the player when he bobbles a note.

Its tone is the mellowest in the orchestra, and a combination of horns gives a rich, majestic harmony. Because of its mellow quality it blends better than almost any other instrument except the strings and is constantly used to fill in the harmony below the melody or to provide an unobtrusive rhythmic beat. Richard Strauss called it the "faithful horn."

FRENCH HORN

*Tristan und Isolde,* Act II Scene 1: As the curtain rises, the hunting horns for which Bragaene listens are heard slowly disappearing into the woods.

*Tannhaeuser,* Act I Scene 3: The Landgrave enters to an extended series of horn calls.

*Der Freischuetz,* Overture: In the adagio introduction, measure 10, there is a passage for four horns which is often said to mark the beginning of the Romantic period in nineteenth-century music.

*Carmen,* Act I: Micaela's and Don José's duet.

*Carmen,* Act III: A typical echo effect closes Micaela's aria, which is colored throughout by the horn.

*Tosca,* Act III: Opening phrases.

*Faust,* Act III (Garden Scene): Opening phrases.

THE TROMBONES: The trombone resembles the trumpet rather than the horn in that it has a cylindrical tube, small bell and cup-shaped mouthpiece. There are soprano, alto, tenor and bass trombones, but by far the most common is the tenor, with a tube 107 inches long. Its range is about two and one-half octaves from the E below the bass clef to the B flat above middle C. Although there is a valve trombone, its tone is less pleasing and it has never displaced the slide trombone. On the other hand it is far more agile and can play a true legato (*See*

Glossary), which the slide trombone cannot, for the movement of the player's arm, however swift, takes appreciable time, and the notes inevitably have a slight staccato (*See* Glossary) quality. Verdi, however, used valve trombones in *Otello*.

Its tone varies with the degrees of loudness. Very loud, it is menacing and terrifying. Less loud, it is commanding and majestic. Very quiet, it is gloomy and mournful. Berlioz imagined he could hear "strange monsters uttering groans of repressed rage from gruesome darkness."

TROMBONE

The trombone usually appears as the cap to the climax, and there are no well-known operatic trombone solos. But in Wagner's *Ring* they accompany Wotan as an almost continuous symbol of proud power. They also are the dominant instrument in music for the Walkuere.

*Aida,* Act I Scene 2: After Radames enters but before he sings, the trombones open and dominate Ramfis' prayer. They stop with him and do not sound with Radames although he sings the same melody.

The brasses like the woodwinds, but less frequently, sometimes play as a group, emphasizing their special sound. The quality of their tone, however, limits them generally to short passages in hunting, martial or ceremonial scenes. For the grand climax they are invariably joined by the other instruments, particularly the strings. *Aida,* an opera in which all the men are either generals, kings or archbishops, can sound, if badly performed, like Sunday afternoon at the bandstand.

THE TUBA: The bass of the brass instruments. It exists in many varieties with differing number of valves and shapes. It began to appear in the opera orchestra about 1860, and Wagner in his *Ring* used it regularly. It is apt to play the "oomp" of "oomp-pah-pah," and it has no famous solos.

TUBA

## THE PERCUSSION

The percussion instruments are the most variable in the orchestra. Anything that makes a noise, for want of a better home, can creep in here, although technically it may not fit the definition. George Antheil's *Ballet Mécanique,* for example, is generally said to be scored exclusively for percussion although it requires a small airplane propeller and two electric doorbells, large and small. The bells conceivably can qualify; the propeller cannot.

Percussion instruments divide into two groups: those that produce notes of definite pitch and those that do not. Of those that do, by far the most important are:

THE KETTLEDRUMS OR TIMPANI (Italian): These are metal shells, generally of copper, covered by skin at the open end and struck by a stick with a sponge or felt head. The tighter the skin, the higher the note produced; and when the drummer puts his ear directly over the skin, scratches it with his finger, and then twists the screws around the edge, he is tuning the drum. The size of the shell also determines the pitch: the smaller ones sound higher notes. The average diameter is about twenty-eight inches.

It would be convenient to be able to say that a shell shaped as a perfect hemisphere gave the noblest sound, but there is argument over it. French and American drums tend to be perfect hemispheres; German and English shells, to be deeper; and Italian shells, deeper still. Russian drums have almost flat bottoms. There is also disagreement over the sticks and heads—rigid hickory or whippy malacca, wool or felt. The English and Germans favor light sticks with small, wool heads; the Americans, hickory sticks with felt heads. There *are* sticks with whalebone handles, wooden grips and sponge heads.

The kettledrums are an Eastern instrument brought to Europe by the returning crusaders. For many years thereafter they were the cavalry drums of Central Europe; one drum was slung on each side of the horse. In the East they were slung on camels. Henry VIII introduced the drum into England in 1542. Being an avid musician, he sent to Vienna in order to get a pair of authentic Hussar drums.

**KETTLEDRUMS**
**(TIMPANI)**

*Aida,* Act II Scene 1: Shortly after Aida enters, Amneris turns to her with feigned affection and consoles her for the Ethiopian defeat. After Amneris' first two phrases, and also after the fourth, the kettledrums have five quick but individual notes.

*Tosca,* Act I: The kettledrums are used throughout the opera—so much, some say, that they lose their effect. In Act I they are most easily distinguished in the second exchange between Cavaradossi and Angelotti, particularly when Cavaradossi describes the well in the garden as Angelotti is about to run off.

*Tosca,* Act II: As Scarpia dies and Tosca gasps, "e morto" (he is dead).

*Tosca,* Act III: With bass drum just before Cavaradossi is shot.

*Faust,* Act IV: At the death of Valentine, leading into a short "a cappella" (*see* Glossary) requiem.

*Lohengrin*, Act III: After Lohengrin kills Friedrich.

*Die Walkuere*, Act III: After Bruennhilde asks what her punishment will be, and leading into Wotan's announcement that she must sleep until awakened by a man.

Other percussion instruments of definite pitch are bells, the xylophone, the glockenspiel and the celesta. The last three are defined in the Glossary.

Of the instruments that do not produce a sound of definite pitch, the most important that need description are the bass and snare drums.

THE BASS DRUM: This is capable of giving the loudest noise in the orchestra; it is also effective as one of the quietest. It is usually about three feet in diameter and sits on a cradle. It consists of two skins stretched over either end of a short cylinder. The Russians, however, sometimes use a bass drum with only one skin stretched on a wide, shallow cylinder. It looks like a regular bass drum cut in half. Most persons do not realize that a bass drum is bass in relation to a tenor drum, i.e. within its own group, and not in relation to the entire orchestra. Several instruments can sound lower than the drum's indefinite pitch. The stick generally has a felt head.

*Aida*, Act IV Scene 1: The priests offstage recite three charges against Radames, and to each he refuses to answer. A quiet roll on the bass drum marks each silence.

*Tosca*, Act II: The bass drum sounds three times with a gong as Tosca places the candles by Scarpia's head.

SNARE DRUM

THE SNARE DRUM: It is sometimes called a side drum because when marching it is slung to the side of the body. It consists of two skins stretched over either end of a short cylinder about two feet in diameter. Over the bottom skin, snares (strings) or wires are stretched, and these give the tone a sharp quality, almost a rattle. They can be loosened, and the drum then sounds like any other. The sticks are wooden, and the technique consists almost entirely of rolls, which are achieved by having each stick in turn hit the drum twice, very fast. It is infuriatingly difficult to do well.

*Carmen,* Entr'acte preceding Act II: A light, short, repeated roll accompanies all but the middle of the entr'acte.

*Tosca,* Act II: A roll on two drums off stage interrupts Scarpia's pursuit of Tosca. Another closes the act.

*Faust,* Act II (The Fair, Kermesse): Snare-drum roll, over which there is a cornet solo with horn accompaniment. The cornet is slightly smaller than the trumpet and has a brighter, brassier sound.

*Faust,* Act V, Prison Scene: At the end of the trio. Several bars later Marguerite dies at the stroke of the gong.

Other instruments that do not produce a sound of definite pitch are the triangle, cymbals and tambourine, all of which are defined in the Glossary, and such others as the whip, ratchet and wood blocks.

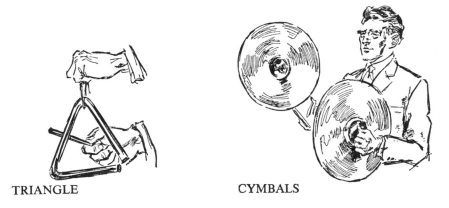

TRIANGLE          CYMBALS

## THE STRINGS

The strings, as the term is generally used, consist only of the violin family; the harp is distinguished because it is plucked rather than bowed. Of the strings, and indeed of all the instruments in the orchestra, the violin is unequaled for purity of tone, range, agility, richness and flexibility of sound. But its virtues to a large extent are common to all the strings which as a family have certain clear advantages over the woodwinds and brass: the string player need never stop to draw breath; he can if needed play chords; and finally, he has two methods of sounding his instrument, bowing and plucking the string. The sound is quite different.

The violin family consists of the violin, the viola, the cello or violoncello, and the doublebass. The instruments grow larger and the strings therefore longer as the range descends. The violin and viola are held by the left hand and snuggled into the shoulder and chin. The cello is played sitting with the instrument between the legs. The doublebass is played standing.

VIOLIN

THE VIOLIN: Its range is from G below middle C to E four octaves above it. The instrument itself is a work of art requiring nearly sixty separate pieces of wood, not including the "fittings." The greatest violinmakers were both Italians from Cremona—Amati (1596–1684) and Stradivari (c. 1644–1737). The modern bow came later and is credited to the Frenchman, François Tourte (1747–1835).

The violin in opera is seldom used as a solo instrument except at the most intense moments, and then the danger is always that it will either sound too thin or, if accompanied, not be noticed. Puccini in *La Bohème,* Act I, has a solo violin passage at the moment when Rodolfo tells his friends that he will remain in the garret to finish his article. The other strings merely hold notes underneath; but, even so, the solo passes unnoticed, probably because it does not, at that particular moment, have any point to make.

The violins usually play as a group; sometimes, however, they may be divided into first and second violins or even further so that they play six-, eight- or ten-part harmony. Add to this the combinations and divisions possible within and with the other members of the family, and clearly the variety and richness of sounds possible for the strings are greater than that of any other group in the orchestra.

*Tannhaeuser,* Act I Scene 2: Venus appeals to Tannhaeuser to remain with her as a solo violin plays a short series of phrases ending in a series of very high trills. Clearly Wagner was trying for a sound of unique intensity.

*Les Contes d'Hoffmann,* Act III: The evil Dr. Miracle accompanies Antonia with a solo violin passage as she sings herself to death.

*La Traviata,* Act IV Prelude: The first violins have a unison solo with string and wind accompaniment.

*Carmen,* Act I: Micaela's entrance is introduced by a skittering phrase for the first violins in a unison solo.

THE VIOLA: It is tuned a fifth lower than the violin, and its range is from C below middle C to an A more than two octaves above it. Throughout its tone it has a sad and somber quality; the low notes in particular have a husky sound. Most nonmusicians have trouble distinguishing its sound from that of violins; this is partly, however, because most composers do not use it individually but merely as a bass for the violins.

*Tosca,* Act II: It can most easily be heard in the offstage Gavotte (*See* Glossary) close to the beginning of the act, which is scored for flute, viola and harp.

*Faust,* Act IV: The violas have a solo tremolo (*See* below, p. 78) during the duel; they sound before each of Faust's first three thrusts at Valentine. The fourth and fatal thrust is preceded first by a tremolo on the cellos and doublebass and then by one on the violas.

THE CELLO: The strings of the cello sound an octave lower than those of the viola. The cello's range, therefore, is from the C two octaves below middle C to an E an octave and a half above it. Its tone is firm but rather melancholic, and it frequently is given tender, languishing melodies or religious passages. It was Toscanini's instrument.

*La Traviata,* Act I Prelude: The cellos topped by a clarinet and bassoon pick up the violins' melody and carry it to the end of the Prelude while the violins step around above.

*Rigoletto,* Act II: Sparafucile enters and converses with Rigoletto to a melody carried by a single cello and single doublebass, both muted.

CELLO

*Carmen,* Act IV: After Escamillo leads in Carmen, he tells her that if she truly loves him, within the hour she will have cause to be proud of him. It is Escamillo's proudest and tenderest moment, his offering of his courage to her. The cellos have the melody and the bass; the violas weave around them.

*Tristan und Isolde,* Prelude: The cellos have the opening phrase, repeated twice, and then the first long phrase above the general orchestra.

*Tosca,* Act III: During Cavaradossi's exchange with the jailor leading to his aria. For eleven measures four cellos are the only orchestral sound; then, after two measures of general sound, they continue, joined by two solo violins.

*Tannhaeuser,* Act III: The cello sings "The Evening Star" after Wolfram.

*Die Walkuere,* Act I: A solo cello has the melody immediately after Siegmund drinks the water given him by Sieglinde.

THE DOUBLEBASS: It is about six feet tall and is the bass for the string section. Consequently, it and the bassoon frequently play together. Its range is from three octaves below middle C to the D just above it. It generally doubles the cello's notes an octave lower. Because of the weight of its strings which must be bowed hard to be set vibrating, it is not agile. Koussevitzky played the doublebass. In the jazz combo it is treated as a percussion instrument and slapped or plucked rather than bowed. Composers find it particularly suitable for expressing gloom, awe or preoccupation.

*Otello,* Act IV: Otello enters the chamber to murder Desdemona to one of the rare solos for doublebass.

*Aida,* Act IV Scene 1: The priests enter to a solo for muted doublebass.

*La Traviata,* Act I Prelude: The doublebasses have the "oomp" of the "oomp-pah-pah" while the cellos above them have the melody.

*La Bohème,* Act I: Immediately after Colline falls down the stairs and while Rodolfo asks if he is dead, the doublebass holds a long note.

DOUBLEBASS

There seems to be no variation of sound that the string family cannot produce. It can be forceful or yielding, gay or sad, abandoned or restrained; it is both the slave and king of the orchestra. Part of its variety springs from the number of ways possible to set a string in motion. The possibilities exist for all the stringed instruments, although on the doublebass or cello with thick strings some of them are difficult if not impossible. Some of the more common techniques in addition to regular bowing are:

*Pizzicato:* When the string is plucked rather than bowed. It makes a "plink" sound like a guitar. It is constantly used for tiptoeing effects, either serious or comic, or merely for musical reasons, such as a contrasted ending to a long sweep on the violins. One of the most famous examples is J. Strauss, Jr.'s, *Pizzicato Polka.*

*La Bohème,* Act I: Just as and after the four friends bid the landlord, Benoit, goodnight and then prepare to leave for the Café Momus;

for all strings.

*La Bohème,* Act III: Soon after the beginning of the act as the women separate and go their different ways; for violins.

*Carmen,* Act II: When Carmen dances for Don José.

*Faust,* Act IV: Méphistophélès' serenade.

*The Tremolo:* The rapid reiteration of the same note or two notes on adjacent strings; the bow looks as though it were merely quivering. It expresses agitation, terror, excitement or just general intensity; on higher notes it becomes ethereal and seraphic. (*See* Glossary for confusion between tremolo and vibrato in singing.)

*La Traviata,* Act IV: Violetta reads her letter from Germont père over a string tremolo. Verdi has another just at the moment when she thinks she is getting well but actually is about to die.

*Die Walkuere,* Act I Prelude: The storm is set forth on the double-basses and cellos marching up and down while the other strings with a tremolo imitate the driving rain and wind.

*Die Walkuere,* Act I Scene 3: Siegmund's call to his father, Walse, soon after Hunding and Sieglinde retire, is set off by an agitated tremolo.

*La Bohème,* Act IV: As the friends exchange insults before the duel; and as Mimi and Musetta enter.

*Carmen,* Act I Prelude: The Carmen or Fate theme is introduced over a string tremolo.

*Faust,* Act II (The Fair, Kermesse): As Méphistophélès reads the palms of Valentine and Siebel.

*The Vibrato:* The rocking of the left hand and finger that presses on the string. It is always one of the first actions parodied by laymen poking fun at soulful violinists who claim that a vibrato makes the tone richer and sweeter. Presumably it changes, ever so slightly, the length of the string and thus varies the overtones. Lack of vibrato is said to produce a very dry tone—some call it a "white" tone.

*Sul ponticello:* Literally, on the bridge. This is bowing the string close to the bridge. It produces a buzzy, rather metallic sound which is supposed to induce goosepimples. The effect, however, is so subtle that most operagoers who get their goosepimples from the bassdrum never notice it. Also since the bow's proximity to the bridge is relative, it is often hard to tell whether the violins are attempting and failing, or ignoring, the score's direction. Prokofiev requires it in *Peter and the Wolf* for a string tremolo after the wolf swallows the duck. It is indicated in three places in *Tosca:*

*Tosca,* Act I: Just after Tosca enters and, in her fourth phrase, accuses Cavaradossi of talking to a lady, there are two measures, beginning on her word, "donna." Then, as she leaves him, beginning with her final word, "neri," there are two more.

*Tosca,* Act II: When Scarpia tells Spoletta to have the execution "come Palmieri" (like Palmieri's), he says, after explaining, "Va." Then Tosca has a short phrase. Scarpia sets the hour of execution at four A.M. and Spoletta repeats "come Palmieri." These last two phrases are over strings sul ponticello.

Some other effects which are not necessarily peculiar to the strings but most often turn up there are:

*The Trill:* The rapid alteration of the note with one immediately higher. This raises a feeling of emphasis and expectation if continued for any length of time.

*Il Trovatore,* Act II Scene 1: The lead-off note of the Anvil chorus is a trill.

*Carmen,* Act II: There is a rare trill for woodwinds without strings at the end of Carmen's song at the beginning of the act.

*Simon Boccanegra,* Act I Scene 2: As Boccanegra turns to begin his curse of Paolo.

*Lohengrin,* Act III: As the Prelude ends, Wagner uses a trill to raise the curtain.

*Goetterdaemmerung,* Act III: As the Rhinemaidens rise to the surface of the river, and throughout their scene with Siegfried as they swim about.

*Mutes:* A mute for the strings is a small wooden or steel comb fitted over the bridge of the instrument to reduce the volume of sound and to give a veiled tone. Mutes often, but not necessarily, are put on the entire string section at the same time. The brass also have mutes which are stuck into the bells. Drums can be muted by covering the surface in part or completely with a cloth.

Mutes are put on and off the strings so frequently that it is rare to find an isolated passage where the contrast is evident. One of the clues to a muted string, besides reduced volume, is a lack of bite on the attack (*See* Glossary) of each note; muted strings always sound smooth and somewhat devitalized.

*Tristan und Isolde,* Act III: Before the Liebestod, as Marke and Brangaene talk over the unconscious Isolde, the Liebestod theme is played by the first violins muted; they continue muted for the first phrases of the Liebestod itself.

*Rigoletto,* Act II: The cello and doublebass on the melody under Rigoletto's conversation with Sparafucile.

*Tosca,* Act I: As the kneeling Sacristan sings his Angelus.

*Faust,* Act III: Faust and Marguerite's duet, "O nuit d'amour," close to the end of the act.

The last instrument is the harp, which does not fit into any group. Orchestral scores show it next to the percussion.

HARP

THE HARP: It is an ancient instrument and generally associated with the angels and their cause. According to painters and illustrators, Hell hears only brass instruments, particularly trombones; but Heaven has the harp. Ireland had it for a number of years as its national symbol, and for a time in Wales it was a man's only possession that could not be seized for debt.

It is made of wood, generally sycamore, and the strings are usually catgut, except for the longest which are wire. It has forty-seven strings and seven pedals, which are so arranged that the player at his option can raise every string either a whole or a half tone and thus play all the notes in every scale. Its range is from three octaves below middle C to F four above. The low notes are not much used; some say because harpists are too lazy to reach for the long strings. The low notes have a veiled, mysterious quality, and the high, a bright, characteristically liquid sound. The harp blends particularly well with the brass.

Most persons expect the harpist to be a lady. This harks back to the early Victorian age when the ladies of fashion decided they looked particularly graceful reaching the harp strings and the instrument became a parlor fad. When the ladies grew old and decayed, the husbands sold the harps, and the new generation went on to the piano.

*Cavalleria Rusticana,* Prelude: Turiddu's song to Lola, sung behind the curtain, has a harp accompaniment.

*Il Trovatore,* Act I Scene 2: Manrico's offstage serenade.

*Lucia di Lammermoor,* Act I Scene 2: The introduction to this scene of Lucia by the fountain is a harp solo over light accompaniment.

*Die Walkuere,* Act I Scene 3: When the door blows open and lets Spring into Hunding's hut and Sieglende's heart, it comes accompanied by a harp.

*La Bohème,* Act III: As the act opens at the gate to Paris at dawn, the harp has the melody first with the flute, then alone, then again with the flute.

*Aida,* Act I Scene 2: From the beginning of the scene until the dance of the Priestesses only the harp sounds.

*Aida,* Act II Scene 1: The harp opens the scene together with a trumpet which sounds every other measure.

# VII·

## SOUNDS OF THE ORCHESTRA (*Cont.*)

---

### II. THE SCORING FOR *CARMEN*

Bizet's scoring for *Carmen,* considering that it appeared after Wagner's operas were beginning to be performed regularly, is unusual in its simplicity and clarity. *La Bohème* is far more heavily scored, particularly in the first act, and possibly some of its notes are superfluous: they look logical on paper but add nothing unique to the sound. Certainly this is true of Richard Strauss. Bizet's scoring is the reverse: every note sounds, and the essence of each instrument is distilled. If Puccini tried to apply what he learned from Wagner, Bizet harked back directly to Mozart.

Bizet's orchestra for *Carmen* has no exotic instruments except the castanets and tambourine, both of which Carmen introduces on stage. But there are no tubas, bass clarinets, contrabassoons or anvils. Verdi requires bagpipes and mandolins for *Otello,* and Puccini in *Tosca* requires, in addition to a full-sized orchestra, an organ, a celesta, a gong, church and sheep bells, rifles and cannon. He even indicated in the score exactly where the Sacristan's tic should twitch.

It is not possible to know exactly why Bizet scored the opera as he did; no letter has been found in an attic in which he explains to an uncomprehending friend just why he used the triangle here or the horn there. So what follows is fashioning theory after the fact; but such speculation is not idle if it sharpens the operagoer's perception and helps him to savor the sound.

Further, although Bizet added arias and even the character of Micaela long after he began to work on the score, it is not false to the result to telescope the fits and starts into one creative spasm.

Before he began, Bizet must have counted four main characters: Carmen, Don José, Micaela and Escamillo. How was he going to distinguish them in the orchestra? For Carmen he used violins, played mostly in their lower range and with great incision. For Micaela he used the violins played sweetly and largely in their higher range. He also for Micaela added the French horn, giving a noble, mellow quality to her sound. For Escamillo, courageous and untroubled, he used the trumpets, horns and trombones. For Don José, the most complicated character and the only one to develop throughout the opera, he used the whole orchestra with some emphasis on the wood-winds. Don José is apt, when talking to another character, to adopt his or her orchestral coloring, which is psychologically correct, because he is pulled in opposite ways by Carmen and Micaela. He does not, how-ever, lack courage and stands up to Escamillo in the fight in Act III. This is the only time his music has trombones except when, imme-diately after the fight, he turns on Carmen, "Je te tiens" (I hold you). No wonder she hesitates: it is a new Don José.

The pattern of instruments is good. The brass, which tend the soonest to become monotonous, support the character onstage the least; the more versatile violins and woodwinds support the char-acters onstage the most. Micaela's appearances are mostly alone or with Don José when her horn can make its effect and not be lost in the ensemble. The woodwinds are free to be used as solo instruments in the entr'actes.

The Prelude begins with the orchestra all out in bullfight music with typical scoring: melody in the woodwinds and violins over a rhythm provided by the brass, bass strings and percussion. The second section is the toreador song with the entire string family carrying the melody which, after the previous agitation, contributes to its smooth effect. The trumpets and trombones provide the rhythm and a sense of swag-ger: Escamillo is introduced. The bullfight music repeats, and then suddenly comes Carmen's motif or the Fate theme: Dah, dee, dee, dee, dah, boomp, boomp. The tune is played on a clarinet, a bassoon, a trumpet and the cellos; the boomps on horns, harps, doublebass and kettledrums. The cellos give a darker, more somber color than the violins could, and this is increased by the hollow sound of the low-voiced woodwinds. The trumpet is unexpected and does not occur later in Act I when the theme reappears. Probably it is here because, after the noise of the bullfight music—with its triangle, cymbals and full orchestra—Bizet wanted to give the theme more body, so that it would not seem unimportant or pale. Richard Strauss thought it gave the sound a fine "demonic" quality.

The first act opens on the square in Seville, and the woodwinds—first the flutes and then the clarinets—rise like shimmering vapor off the hot streets. Micaela makes her entrance preceded by the first violins in a timid, hesitant phrase.

The guard changes, as it must, on a trumpet call. But why did Bizet score the boys' chorus for piccolos rather than flutes? Probably because the boys are squeaky, little boys and the piccolo has a squeaky, shrill sound. The comic effect is musically built into the scene.

As the cigarette girls come out for their midday break, the woodwinds continue to suggest the heat. The smoking is going to be a slow drag not a quick puff. This also serves as a foil for Carmen, who appears to an agitated theme—the Fate music now raised from the cellos to the violins and played more than twice as fast. In Carmen's Habanera (*See* Glossary) the violins dominate the orchestral sound for the first time.

Micaela enters, and while she delivers her message to Don José, the horn sounds an unobtrusive but constant accompaniment, along with light strings and woodwinds. Then when he begins to sing, the horn has a rocking phrase which continues for most of their duet. Bizet also gives the harp, demurely mute during the Habanera, a running figure underneath the violins, which gives the aria a sense of pace or flow.

After the fight in the factory, and when Carmen is bound and left in Don José's custody, she sets out to lure him from duty's path with the Seguidilla (*See* Glossary). In it she promises she will meet him at the Inn of Lillas Pasta near the ramparts. Like the Habanera the Seguidilla has a predominantly string accompaniment, but a flute introduces it and continues throughout. Flutes also introduce Carmen's song at the Inn in Act II and the smugglers' sextet in Act III; and the entr'acte before Act III has a flute solo. All these scenes take place either on the edge of town or in the mountains, places that represent freedom and fun to Carmen. Bizet clearly intends the flute, by its pastoral quality, to characterize her as a wild one who dislikes the fetters and toil of the city.

The entr'acte preceding Act II, with its light roll on the snare drum, suggests the military—obviously Don José, the Conquering Hero, released from prison and come to get his reward. But then why is the little tune, which he later sings as he approaches the Inn, carried by the bassoons with that rather comic sound? Perhaps because Bizet, knowing how the reception will turn out, is being sardonic about Don José's expectations.

At the Inn, Escamillo sings the Toreador Song with full orchestra but especially with four horns, two trumpets and three trombones—

a great deal of brass for someone not even a Vicomte. Carmen, however, does more damage with just castanets and the lightest pizzicato accompaniment on the strings into which two trumpets begin to sound. Bizet had courage to score the dance so lightly. It is one extreme. Richard Strauss in *Salome* took the other.

Bizet kept the distinctive sound of the English horn to introduce Don José's Flower Song. It is the first time in the opera that it sounds alone, and it repeats the Carmen or Fate theme but with its own peculiarly mournful timbre. By saving it for here, Bizet achieved a real aural impact; everyone's attention is alerted and focused on the most important aria of the opera. In it Don José, by revealing to Carmen just how much he loves her, gives her the tool to destroy him.

The entr'acte preceding Act III, set in the mountains, is a bit of pure pastoral sound scored for flutes, oboe, English horn, clarinets and bassoons, with harps, horns and very light string accompaniment. This is night in the Spanish mountains; it has a cool, clear quality to it. Verdi's night on the Nile in *Aida* is heavy and tropical, full of crickets, toads and night noises, all created by a single flute, violins, violas and cellos. It is a bit of virtuoso scoring that those who would dismiss him as a mere organ-grinder would do well to consider. Wagner's night in Nuremberg, during and ending Act II of *Die Meistersinger,* is again different. It could only be in a small town. The closing bars are scored for flute, clarinet, bassoon, horns and strings.

Carmen's Card Scene is to string accompaniment, except that the trumpets and trombones underneath knot into softly shifting chords of disaster. Rabid symbolists insist on identifying them as Escamillo, but more likely Bizet was simply after the harsh, hollow sound, which he increased by adding an occasional touch of bassoon, oboe or clarinet.

Michaela's aria is dominated by the horns, which fade in and out of the night against a background of soft chords on the woodwinds and violins. Notice how Bizet avoids overdoing the sentiment by *not* using the harp.

The entr'acte preceding Act IV is interesting mainly because of its use of the tambourine and triangle as rhythm instruments, which with their uncertain pitch add to the feeling of confused, spontaneous excitement.

More interesting in Act IV are Escamillo's brief remarks to Carmen. He states that if she loves him, when he is in the arena, she will have cause to be proud of him. Amidst the excitement the quiet moment is arresting and beautiful. It is all that is best in Escamillo, and the music makes it so. No brass instrument sounds; the cellos have the melody and its bass, while the violas weave around them. Carmen answers in kind but with the addition of the higher-pitched violins. Why did Bizet here abandon his pattern of brass for Escamillo? Undoubtedly because the cellos have a warmth that even the horn cannot match and, following the parade to the arena in which the brass had a prominent part, the cellos make the point better.

Except for the final chords, the opera ends with Don José's voice, broken and uncomprehending, over a tremolo for strings. Bizet, like most operagoers, probably was satisfied that in the end the most expressive instrument was not in the orchestra but on stage: the human voice.

# VIII·

## TUNING A—THE PROBLEM OF PITCH

Before the opera begins, the orchestra tunes—which is a practical beginning of the performance and is symbolic of an agreement between all the instrumentalists and singers backstage that this note or pitch will be the fundamental pitch for the performance; all the other notes, up and down, will be determined by reference to it. All orchestras and bands tune to the A above middle C on the piano, which is called "tuning A." But there is not always agreement even now about the pitch—the high or low of the sound—of tuning A. In 1879 Adelina Patti refused to sing at Covent Garden in London until the orchestra tuned down to the French A, and as recently as 1958 singers at the Vienna Staatsoper complained of being forced to strain their voices because the orchestra was tuning high.

Any disagreement on the pitch of tuning A at once raises the fundamental question of sound and its symbol. Sound in music is the result of the vibration of a body, such as a string, a reed, or a column of air enclosed in a tube. The pitch of a sound, i.e. whether it is high or low, depends on the number of vibrations or cycles made by the body in a second. The symbol of the sound is the note which the composer puts in the score and by which he asks the performer to reproduce a sound of a certain pitch. When Mozart in 1780 inked in tuning A in a score, he heard in his mind a sound resulting from a string that was vibrating at a rate of 422 cycles per second. This is known from an accurate copy of the tuning fork used to tune his piano. Any orchestra intending to play Mozart should, therefore, tune to an A of 422 cps. But none does; rather, each of them tunes to an A of approximately 440 cps, which is almost a half tone higher, a perfectly audible increase in pitch.

Such a large increase presents a special problem to the singer because he cannot make any *mechanical* adjustment to his voice that will raise the pitch. The string player can tighten his string, and the wind-instrument player can change (slightly) the length of the vibrating columns of air. But the singer simply has to sing higher, not just for one note but for the entire aria or opera. This makes the Queen of

Night's arias in *Die Zauberfloete* even more difficult to sing today than when Mozart wrote them.

The problem for singers is further aggravated by two curious and constant phenomena that cannot be explained but which always occur. The first is that any orchestra, after it works into the symphony or opera, drifts slightly up in pitch—at most about 2.5 cps in the course of an hour. The second is that whenever the music gets particularly dramatic or emotional, both singers and orchestra rise still higher in pitch. This means that at the end of an act—for example, when Andrea Chenier and Madeleine mount the tumbril for the guillotine—the singer must sing considerably sharper than at the beginning of the act. It also is one reason why any singer making a debut or under some other emotional strain is apt to sing sharp.

The best way of seeing what a rise in pitch can mean is to examine a tuning chart for a piano, which shows the number of cycles per second at which each string should vibrate.

Each column is an octave. The notes are numbered starting with the lowest note, A. There are twelve notes in all—seven white, five black —from one A to the next. Each higher A is always double the number of cycles per second of the preceding A. The fifth A, or forty-nineth key up on the piano, is tuning A at 440 cps. Mozart's A of 422 cps is clearly far closer to the piano's G sharp, or A flat, than to its tuning A. If the orchestra tunes to 448 cps, as did the La Scala orchestra from 1941 to 1950, the difference is 26 cps, or a half tone. This is a sufficiently large difference to change the key in which the aria or symphony is played from that in which Mozart heard and intended it to be played.

The number of cycles per second, 440, of tuning A in itself is a compromise. There never has been any absolute value accepted by musicians everywhere or even in one country. Handel's personal tuning fork which he had in London sounds an A of 423 cps; and yet the organ at Trinity College, Cambridge, had an A of 395. Most organs, however, were apt to be very high, some sounding an A of more than 500 cps. Bach frequently scored the organ and woodwind accompaniments to his cantatas in different keys, relying on the different pitches that would be used to have them sound, in fact, in the same key. In general, however, the eighteenth-century pitch was lower than 440, so that today most of the performances of the operas of Mozart, Gluck, Handel and even Beethoven are pitched too high for historical accuracy.

# FREQUENCY OF THE TONES OF THE USUAL EQUALLY TEMPERED SCALE, ARRANGED BY CORRESPONDING PIANO KEY NUMBERS AND BASED ON THE A OF 440 CYCLES PER SECOND

| Note Name | Key No. | Freq. cps | Key No. | Freq. cps | Key No. | Freq. cps | Key No. | Freq. cps | Key No. | Freq. cps | Key No. | Freq. cps | Key No. | Freq. cps | Key No. | Freq. cps | Note Name |
|---|---|---|---|---|---|---|---|---|---|---|---|---|---|---|---|---|---|
| A | 1 | 27.500 | 13 | 55.000 | 25 | 110.000 | 37 | 220.000 | 49 | 440.000 | 61 | 880.000 | 73 | 1760.000 | 85 | 3520.000 | A |
| A♯—B♭ | 2 | 29.135 | 14 | 58.270 | 26 | 116.541 | 38 | 233.082 | 50 | 466.164 | 62 | 932.328 | 74 | 1864.655 | 86 | 3729.310 | A♯—B♭ |
| B | 3 | 30.868 | 15 | 61.735 | 27 | 123.471 | 39 | 246.942 | 51 | 493.883 | 63 | 987.767 | 75 | 1975.533 | 87 | 3951.066 | B |
| C | 4 | 32.703 | 16 | 65.406 | 28 | 130.813 | 40 | 261.626 | 52 | 523.251 | 64 | 1046.502 | 76 | 2093.005 | 88 | 4186.009 | C |
| C♯—D♭ | 5 | 34.648 | 17 | 69.296 | 29 | 138.591 | 41 | 277.183 | 53 | 554.365 | 65 | 1108.731 | 77 | 2217.461 | | | C♯—D♭ |
| D | 6 | 36.708 | 18 | 73.416 | 30 | 146.832 | 42 | 293.665 | 54 | 587.330 | 66 | 1174.659 | 78 | 2349.318 | | | D |
| D♯—E♭ | 7 | 38.891 | 19 | 77.782 | 31 | 155.563 | 43 | 311.127 | 55 | 622.254 | 67 | 1244.508 | 79 | 2489.016 | | | D♯—E♭ |
| E | 8 | 41.203 | 20 | 82.407 | 32 | 164.814 | 44 | 329.628 | 56 | 659.255 | 68 | 1318.510 | 80 | 2637.021 | | | E |
| F | 9 | 43.654 | 21 | 87.307 | 33 | 174.614 | 45 | 349.228 | 57 | 698.456 | 69 | 1396.913 | 81 | 2793.826 | | | F |
| F♯—G♭ | 10 | 46.249 | 22 | 92.499 | 34 | 184.997 | 46 | 369.994 | 58 | 739.989 | 70 | 1479.978 | 82 | 2959.955 | | | F♯—G♭ |
| G | 11 | 48.999 | 23 | 97.999 | 35 | 195.998 | 47 | 391.995 | 59 | 783.991 | 71 | 1567.982 | 83 | 3135.964 | | | G |
| G♯—A♭ | 12 | 51.913 | 24 | 103.826 | 36 | 207.652 | 48 | 415.305 | 60 | 830.609 | 72 | 1661.219 | 84 | 3322.438 | | | G♯—A♭ |

But in the early nineteenth century the pitch of tuning A began to rise everywhere. One reason was the development of the symphony orchestra and the gradual perfection of the woodwind and brass instruments. The conductor traditionally liked to tune high in the hope that the audience would be impressed with the sound of his orchestra: slightly sharp notes sound brilliant; flat ones sound dull. Manufacturers of instruments likewise pushed the tone up because it made the instruments sound more brilliant. Military bands, particularly, tuned very high. By the middle of the century, British orchestras were tuning to an A of 453 cps, Viennese to an A of 456, and American to an A of 457.

The differences caused all sorts of trouble. Wagner, on behalf of his singers, complained to the British in 1877 about the height of their pitch; and brass and woodwind players, with their limited mechanical adjustments, found that the instrument that was in tune in Vienna was hopelessly out of tune in Paris. Everyone complained that the situation was getting out of hand, but it was already beyond the powers of individuals to correct.

Finally, in 1858 the French Government appointed a commission to report on the disparity of pitches and to make recommendations. On the commission were Auber, Berlioz, Halévy, Meyerbeer, Rossini, Thomas, two physicists and four government officials. The commission's report in 1859 listed the various pitches being used in Europe and showed how the pitch had risen in four of the leading cities.

The report then recommended that A be set at 435 cps, and the Government promulgated such a decree. Most of France, Germany, Austria and some of Italy followed the recommendations; unfortunately Great Britain did not, and by 1879 when Patti refused to sing, tuning A at Covent Garden had reached 455 cps.

In 1885 the Austrian Government sponsored an international conference which also adopted 435 cps as the standard pitch. Further, it recommended that all wind instruments be manufactured so that they sounded an A of 435 cps at 75° F. This was important because wind instruments rise in pitch as they warm up, but they rise at different rates depending on the material of the instrument walls, the volume of the air inside to be heated by the player's breath, and the temperature in the opera house or concert hall. Of equal importance was the recommendation that the oboe be displaced as the tuning instrument of the orchestra by a tuning fork kept in motion by electricity. There

| City | | No. of cps of tuning A |
|------|--|------------------------|
| Lille | | 452 |
| Paris | Grand Opera | 448 |
| | Opera-Italien | 448 |
| Marseilles | | 447 |
| Bordeaux | | 443 |
| Toulouse | Theatre | 442.5 |
| | Conservatoire | 437 |
| Brussels | Musique des gindes | 455.5 |
| London | Philharmonic Society | 455.5 |
| | piano with instruments | 452.5 |
| | piano to accompany voice | 434 |
| Berlin | | 451.5 |
| St. Petersburg | | 451.5 |
| Prague | | 449.7 |
| Leipzig | | 448.7 |
| Munich | | 448.1 |
| The Hague | | 446.2 |
| Pest | | 446 |
| Turin )<br>Wurtemberg)<br>Weimar ) | | 444.7 |
| Brunswick | | 443.5 |
| Gotha | | 443.2 |
| Stuttgart | | 443 |
| Dresden | | 441 |
| Carlsruhe | | 435 |
| Paris | 1700 | 404 |
| | 1858 | 448 |
| Berlin | 1752 | 421.9 |
| | 1858 | 451.7 |
| Turin | 1845 | 440 |
| | 1858 | 444.7 |
| Milan | 1845 | 446.5 |
| | 1856 | 450.3 |

are several reasons why the oboe is a poor tuning instrument. First, the player can spread the pitch over as much as 5 cps simply by the pressure of his breath and lips, and second, the oboe has thick ebonite walls that retain the heat of the breath better than, for example, the metallic, thin-walled flute. The oboe, therefore, takes considerably longer to reach an equilibrium of losing interior heat to the exterior and colder opera house; and only when the point of equilibrium is reached is there certainty of pitch. The recommendation that electricity be used to keep the tuning fork in motion was a further effort to eliminate all the variables and to get a note of exact pitch independent of temperature, sounding boxes and a player's memory of the pitch. Once again, unfortunately, Great Britain did not take part in the conference.

The United States developed its standard pitch independently, although many of the musical groups and manufacturers followed the Vienna recommendation of 435 cps. In 1925 the associated music industries of the country compromised on 440 cps and adopted it as the standard pitch for manufacturers. In 1936 the American Standards Association confirmed 440 as the standard pitch; thus, 440 became to all intents the "official" United States pitch. In 1937 the Federal Government began broadcasting the tone over short-wave cycles so that any manufacturer or musician could check his tuning exactly. The International Organization for Standardization adopted 440 cps as standard pitch in 1955 when it was approved by seventeen member nations, among which were France, Austria, Italy, Switzerland, the United Kingdom, the U.S.S.R., Sweden, Norway, Denmark, the Netherlands and Spain. The United States was not a member of the conference but sent a message urging the adoption of 440 cps.

This pitch is still too high for purists and singers; the latter would probably prefer a standard pitch of 435 cps, and the purists dream of hearing each composition at the pitch at which the composer imagined it. This can be achieved with string quartets and unaccompanied singing. But any further changes of standard pitch are unlikely. The cost always strikes the manufacturers as prohibitive, for it does not lead to any increase whatsoever in sales; the change strikes the scientists as perverse as 440 cps happens to be easy to reproduce electrically, while some of the other possible pitches would require more complicated machinery. Indeed, what uniformity there is now on 440 cps seems a miracle of international co-operation.

Of course declaring an international standard and observing it are quite different. There are always periodic rumors that this orchestra or that conductor is tuning high, presumably to appear more brilliant. The rumors are difficult to pin down. The only true test involves considerable equipment that the average concert or operagoer does not have. One gentleman, however—Mr. O. J. Murphy of the Bell Telephone Laboratories—ran a series of tests (750 observations) on broadcast music from September, 1939, to January, 1940, to discover how closely the performing musicians were keeping to the standard pitch. He placed an electric filter on his radio that passed the cycles per second ranging from 420 to 460 and included only the note A. This was compared with a standard oscillator, which in turn was checked regularly with the National Bureau of Standards' signal.

Murphy discovered that 70 per cent of the musical groups tuned to, and stayed within, a spread of 439 to 443 cps. He further reported:

"Semi-permanently tuned instruments such as pianos and organs showed almost no variation in pitch during the course of a given performance and a relatively narrow range of variation from instrument to instrument. Orchestras showed as much as 2 cps random variation during the performance of a given selection, this variation generally being due to different instruments in the group successively sounding A; super-imposed on this random variation was a definite upward trend of pitch as the concert progressed, sometimes amounting to 2.5 cps in the course of an hour. Symphony orchestras averaged more than one cycle per second higher in pitch than either light concert orchestras or dance bands, the mean values being 441.8, 440.6 and 440.4, respectively. String groups were consistently higher in pitch than any other class studied and showed a wide spread in the observed values. Miscellaneous solo instruments such as harp, guitar, violin, cello, etc., showed the widest variation in pitch but the average value of all these instruments taken together was 441.5 cps. Brass bands showed an average value of 441.4 cps. . . .

"In nearly all cases where symphony orchestras and solo instruments combined in the performance of concertos, the orchestra tended to adapt its pitch to that of the solo instrument, usually dropping slightly for piano and nearly always rising considerably for violin or cello. After the performance of a concerto the orchestra frequently returned to approximately its original pitch for subsequent selections. The effect of retuning during intermission was also observable in most cases, the orchestra usually returning to approximately the pitch with which they began the performance after having drifted upward during the first half of the concert. The tendency of the pitch to rise during the course of an orchestral performance was almost universal."

When he tested singers, Murphy discovered: "Some few measurements were made on singers with orchestral accompaniment. No significant difference was observed in orchestral pitch between vocal and non-vocal selections, but the moment-to-moment variation in the singer's pitch was found to be so great that the results seemed of questionable value and are, therefore, not included here."

Most orchestras today probably intend to tune to 440 cps. Some, like that of the Metropolitan Opera when in New York, tune directly to an electronic tuner. At the Metropolitan the tuner is placed at the conductor's feet and, before the opera begins, the audience can see the first violinist bend over to turn it on; then, as the orchestra tunes, the audience can hear an electronic note sounding at 440 cps. When the tuner is broken, as during the 1959–60 season, the orchestra tunes to the oboe. The Boston Symphony tunes to an A of 444 cps played by an oboe at the beginning of a concert. If there is a soloist who cannot or will not tune that high, the orchestra tunes down to his pitch. Tuning to the oboe, of course, is really tuning to the oboist's memory of 444 cps, and most musical groups do tune to the oboist's (or violinist's) memory; that memory, however, may recently have been refreshed by a tuning fork in the wings. Where there is a piano or an organ, as Murphy points out, the musicians tune to that. There is an indestructible rumor that in piano concertos the piano is tuned a little sharp so that it will sound more brilliant on its entrance and so that it can allow the strings leeway to rise in pitch as the concert progresses. While this may be so—as yet no responsible person has offered evidence of it—frequent tunings, both visible and audible to the concertgoer, seem to belie it, as do Murphy's observations.

What there is now that there has never been before is an absolute standard against which tuning can be checked and to which disgruntled singers can appeal. The National Bureau of Standards broadcasts the 440-cps tone continuously over certain short-wave bands—2.5, 5, 10, 15 and 25 MG—from its stations WWV (Beltsville, Maryland) and WWVH (Hawaii). The tone can be heard over the entire United States and much of the world. The B.B.C. has a similar service. The tone is combined with a time signal so that there is a "beep" imposed on it every second, but it is a perfectly loud, clear tone available to all manufacturers, musicians or anyone that wants to test his piano or victrola. This is a far cry from the pitchpipes of the seventeenth century which were nothing more than adjustable whistles or even the tuning forks of more recent times.

# IX·

## THE CLAQUE

The claque would be like the Loch Ness Monster, there yesterday and tomorrow but never today, except that it un-questionably exists in some form or other in almost every opera house. Its history is ancient and, as institutions go, honorable. Indeed, although it distresses some to say it, much can be said in favor of claques.

The modern claque is of French origin. The word comes from the verb "claquer," to clap the hands, and means any group of professional applauders holding itself out for hire. It can be hired by the artist, or the opera house, or even some aficionado who desires to compliment some diva. The price is not high, largely because the claqueurs, the members of the claque, are opera lovers who are happy to applaud for the price of admission. One New York claqueur described his fellows as "grave, thoughtful men who have reached the age of discretion."

The largest and one of the earliest claques was organized by the Emperor Nero. The Roman historian Suetonius in his *De Vita Caesarum* characterized Nero's voice as "neither loud nor clear" and unkindly intimated that Nero's claque was born of necessity.

Nero made his debut at Naples, and almost immediately after he opened his mouth, the theater rocked in a violent earthquake. He refused, however, to consider the convulsion of nature as a criticism of his art and persevered to the end of his aria. His claque consisted of five thousand young men from the lowest class who were specially trained in three kinds of applause: "bombi," like the humming of bees; "imbrices," like the rattle of rain on the roof; and "testae," like the tinkling of porcelain jugs clashed together. The men were divided into groups and strategically placed around the theater. They were well known for their fine heads of hair, stylish clothes and rings, which they wore on their left hands. The leaders of the groups drew large salaries.

Nero did not, however, rely exclusively on the claque for applause. Suetonius grudgingly admits that he did not "omit any of those expedients which artists in music adopt, for the preservation and improvement of their voices. He would lie upon his back with a sheet of lead upon his breast, clear his stomach and bowels by vomits and enemas, and forbear the eating of fruits, or food prejudicial to the voice."

The claque in France is supposed to have begun in 1820, when a certain M. Sauton opened an office for the hiring of claques. He called his business "L'Assurance des Succès Dramatiques." In the next thirty years the claque developed into an extremely complex organization. M. Sauton or his successors would rent out for the evening a claque consisting of the leader, the "chef de claque"; the ordinary applauders who, because they sat under the chandelier at the opera, were sometimes known as the "chevaliers du lustre"; and a series of specialists. These were the "rieur," who specialized in guffaws at comic sallies (the "rieuse" giggled); the "pleureuse," who arrived with tear-compelling fumes trapped in a smelling-salts bottle and with numerous handkerchiefs; the "bisseur," who called out "bis" or "encore"; the "commissaire," who discussed the good points of the production during intermissions; and the "chatouilleur," who endeavored to keep the audience in a good humor with jokes to his neighbors.

This was the high point of the claque as an organization. At no other time and in no other city, with the possible exception of Vienna, has the claque achieved such stature. The chef de claque was sometimes consulted about new productions. He was admitted to dress rehearsals, he studied the score, and he placed his men with care. And then the claque was expected to do its job: to launch a new production or a new actress, or to revive the popularity of one that (or who) was slipping.

Oscar Thompson in *The International Cyclopedia of Music and Musicians* quotes a letter to show how seriously a chef de claque at this time took his work. It seems that Mme. Rachel, the celebrated actress, had complained that at the second performance of her play the applause had dwindled noticeably. The scolded chef de claque replied with a letter as follows:

"I cannot remain under the obloquy of a reproach from such lips as yours! At the first representation, I led the attack in person thirty-three times. We had three acclamations, four hilarities, two thrilling movements, four renewals of applause, and two indefinite explosions." He then went on to say that his men were positively exhausted with fatigue and had told him that they could not do so much again. "So," he wrote, "I applied for the manuscript and, having profoundly studied the piece, I was obliged to make up my mind for the second representation to certain curtailments, in the interest of my men."

But however amusing or admirable the Paris claque might be as an organization, its artistic ideals were lamentable. It was strictly for hire, and throughout much of the nineteenth century in Paris those who controlled the opera houses and large purses were men of almost no taste or discrimination. The claques reflected this in their choice of personnel and behavior at the performances.

In Italy, too, the claque never developed any artistic stature but verged constantly on bad taste, judgment and manners. Scholes, in *The Oxford Companion to Music,* quotes an Italian correspondent of the London *Musical Times,* who set out the fees demanded by Italian claqueurs in 1919. The list is indicative of the Italian approach: so much for an entrance, regardless of whether applause then is appropriate. Otello's entrance in Verdi's opera, for example, is completely spoiled if applause covers his first, clarion notes. The list does indicate, however, how much harder it is for the men to win applause from an audience.

| | |
|---|---|
| For applause on entrance, if a gentleman | 25 lire |
| For applause on entrance, if a lady | 15 lire |
| Ordinary applause during performance, each | 10 lire |
| Insistent applause during performance, each | 15 lire |
| Still more insistent applause | 17 lire |
| For interruptions with "Bene!" or "Bravo!" | 5 lire |
| For a "Bis" at any cost | 50 lire |
| Wild enthusiasm—— | a special sum to be arranged |

A Viennese or New York claqueur would recoil in horror from perpetrating "interruptions" or "wild enthusiasm."

The claque supposedly came to New York in 1910, when the Metropolitan opened its season with Gluck's *Armide,* an opera never performed in the city before. Fremstad had the lead; the tenor was Caruso; the conductor, Toscanini; and the producer, Gatti-Casazza. Faced with wholly unfamiliar music, the audience sat on its hands.

Gatti, according to the story, was in despair; Caruso, unnerved. Gatti consulted the tenor, Alessandro Bonci, who suggested that his valet, who knew every note of every opera, including *Armide,* be authorized to form a claque. And so *Armide* was saved for that season and even repeated in the next.

This charming story with so many names and the valet is surely untrue, but no matter. It is true that Caruso spent about $8,000 a season distributing tickets to friends and acquaintances and that he had in every contract the right to buy fifty seats to each of his own performances. But with Caruso this is generally considered to reflect an excess of generosity and fellow-feeling, rather than a Neronic insatiability for applause. His widow, also his biographer, states that he never employed the claque.

Some in New York viewed the advent of the claque with alarm. Walter Damrosch, writing *My Musical Life* in 1923, complained with Germanic indignation of the claques "maintained by some of the singers and conductors who, in rivalry with each other, foolishly spend their money in the hiring of twenty to fifty husky men, under a well-trained leader, who stand at the side of the balconies and family circle and clap with the machine-like regularity of a steel hammer in an iron foundry in order to produce so and so many recalls after an act." At that time the claque at the Metropolitan was led by Schol, an umbrella maker by day.

In recent years the operatic claque with the best taste and judgment was undoubtedly the one operating at the Vienna Staatsoper during the 1920's. It consisted of a group of some thirty or forty regulars, many of whom were music students. Its applause was for hire but only if, in the opinion of the leader, the performance merited it; otherwise the fee was returned. Likewise, applause was never withheld after a superior performance because the artist was not a client.

Joseph Wechsberg, a member of the claque in its great days, has described how it worked in several chapters of *Looking for a Bluebird*. The leader was a dedicated opera lover named Schostal who came from a family of Moravian textile merchants. His relatives considered him quite lost after he became interested in opera and never saw or communicated with him thereafter except once a year, when they sent him enough cloth (always blue serge) to make one suit.

Schostal always sat behind a marble pillar in the fourth balcony, where the acoustics were perfect. From there he could not see the stage, but he was perfectly placed to direct the claqueurs in the rest of the balcony. His claque was a cosmopolitan group and included at one time, in addition to the regular Viennese, two Frenchmen, a Czech, a Chinese, an Ethiopian prince and an American pianist from Ohio.

Impecunious opera lovers in Vienna longed to get in the claque, and a vacancy was immediately filled by some member's friend who had been waiting for years. Admission was by examination. Schostal and the applicant would repair to some café, and over beer Schostal at the piano would play arias, entrances and recitatives and the applicant would have to identify the opera, act and scene. If he passed, he would be tried out first on the "light" operas. This meant Wagner, where applause is confined almost entirely to the end of the act.

The French and Italian operas were much more difficult to handle. Wechsberg, for example, describes the second act of *Carmen* as a claqueur's nightmare: "You start working right after Carmen's gypsy song, 'Les tringles des sistres tintaient,' and you applaud after her dance with the castanets. Then Escamillo enters (applause), sings his famous 'Couplets' (applause), and leaves (more applause). By that time the public is likely to applaud spontaneously after each number —the quintet, Don José's offstage 'a cappella' [*See* Glossary] song, Carmen's dance for Don José, and the tenor's famous 'la fleur que tu m'avais jetée.' The trouble is that the enthusiastic listeners are apt to break into 'wild' applause in the wrong places, such as in the middle of an aria after an effective high C. In Vienna, where opera was a way of life and even the small boys discussed opera as they discuss baseball in this country [U.S.A.], 'wild' applause was considered heresy and one of the claque's functions was to influence public acclaim into orderly channels."

Members of the claque received nothing for their efforts except the ticket to the balcony. Schostal, of course, charged a fee and kept the balance. This dedicated man apparently had dreams of building a world-wide claque cartel with himself as head, traveling from house to house giving instructions, administering and listening. It was with real regret he dismissed the American pianist from Ohio whose nerve had failed twice on a particularly difficult bit of timing in a quiet house. Schostal had been training him to be the leader at the Metropolitan.

Claques at the Metropolitan surged again into the news in 1954 when General Manager Bing announced that for a time the number of standees would be cut in half, or down to one hundred. He did not elucidate further than to say there had been complaints from other patrons of excessive applause and interruptions from the standees. It was generally thought at the time that claques hired by competing artists were attempting to outdo each other. At the Metropolitan, claqueurs frequently stand down near the stage from whence a "bravo" will roll easily throughout the house.

The announcement flushed some letters and an article, which revealed that the cost of a small claque, six or eight, ranged from twenty-five to one hundred dollars a performance, the Saturday afternoon performance, which is broadcast, being the most expensive. A chef de claque named John Bennet, who came from the Bronx, managed the business details and distributed the tickets, which were always for standing room. The claqueurs, mostly older men, were given nothing more than the ticket, and one in an anonymous letter even claimed that he was never given any instructions.

The claqueurs to a man blamed the interruptions and blatant "bravos" on fan clubs of certain artists. These were composed, said the claqueurs, of wild-eyed adolescents who knew nothing about opera. The true claqueur, so the argument ran, confined himself to an occasional, perfectly placed "bravo"; he might start a splatter of applause but he never overextended it; he always applauded the conductor as an act of professional courtesy; and he never, no never, interrupted an aria with applause.

But before dissolving all criticism in a surge of emotion for these white-haired, old music lovers, so courteous and eager to applaud, it must be recorded that each year a resentful Ezio Pinza paid their leader fifty dollars to be let alone—which is not art at all but blackmail.

The argument for the claque, assuming that the group is directed by an artist not a thug, is that it is professional. It teaches the audience when and when not to applaud. It recognizes a superior performance and creates a atmosphere in which the fragile beginnings of a good performance can wax into an exciting one. The fan clubs, on the other hand, with their interruptions prevent the performance from gaining momentum. Only the claque, which attends regularly and appropriates the best positions in the balcony and standing room, can discipline the fan club.

Fan clubs are not new. As far back as 1726 in London, according to Dr. Burney (*See* Glossary), "The violence of party . . . for the two singers Cuzzoni and Faustina, was so great that when the admirers of one began to applaud, those of the other were sure to hiss; on which account operas ceased for some time in London." Today violence against a singer is most unusual, but at the close of a Maria Callas performance of *Norma* at the Metropolitan in 1956, someone in the balcony threw down a bouquet of carrots and onions that hit the stage with an expressive thud. More usual and in the same year were the fifty-foot paper banners reading "Bravo del Monaco, il Re di tenore."

Possibly the greatest commotion caused by any fan club was at the farewell performance at the Metropolitan of Geraldine Farrar. She had announced she was retiring, and everyone knew she meant it. Her last appearance was in Leoncavallo's *Zaza* on April 22, 1922. Banners hung from the boxes, balloons floated over the orchestra, and between acts onstage the Gerryflappers invested their Queen with crown and scepter. In return, backstage after the opera and her farewell speech, Farrar distributed all her costumes and props to delighted and weeping girls. Then, through cheering crowds and dressed entirely in clothing stitched by her devoted admirers, she drove away from opera forever. But even claqueurs are not immune to sentiment and would agree that this was well done.

The claque in its present or some other subdued form will undoubtedly continue. The desire for applause is universal among performers; the claque is not a western aberration. The Kabuki theater in Japan has its "omuko-san" or, "honorouble shouter of cries from the gallery." The "shouters" form a club or, as the Japanese put it, "a craft" and have free seats in the gallery. The favorite cry is "matte imashita," or "I was waiting for you!"

It is possible that good performances of opera or theater cannot exist without applause unless the work, like *Parsifal,* pretends or achieves religious significance. Inevitably both the artist and manager occasionally want a claque, and so neither is prepared to kill it, even if that were possible. Certainly to do so would require concerted action.

# X·

## BALLET IN OPERA

Ballet and opera are true "kissing cousins" in that the salutation, while acknowledging a common ancestor in the court spectacle, at best exaggerates what is no more than cautious friendship and at worst conceals a virulent hostility. Each art is the specialization at the cost of the other of some part of the court spectacles that flourished throughout Europe in the seventeenth century. *Mercurio e Marte* (*Mercury and Mars*) is a typical example.

This extravaganza with music by Monteverdi was performed in Parma on December 21, 1628, to celebrate the marriage of Margherita of Tuscany to Odoardo, Duke of Parma. Its final scene—after a great many others, including an equestrian ballet ridden by the Duke and his College of Nobles—is described by Alan Yorke-Long in *Music at Court:* "The seven cavaliers, who included the Duke, were liberated from sea monsters by Mercury and Mars, whereupon the enraged Neptune flooded the arena to the depth of two feet, to the terror of the audience, who feared the theatre would collapse with the weight of the 4,000 spectators, the water and the machines. A pack of monsters appeared, who surrounded Galatea's island, and a grand Naumachia ensued, until suddenly the sky opened and Jove descended in an enormous machine with a hundred attendants. After bidding the combat cease, he flung down Discord into the sea, proclaiming that nothing should interrupt the felicity of the Ducal pair."

Clearly, *Mercurio e Marte* foreshadowed as much as it realized. Both the dancing master and singing teacher must have gleefully rubbed their hands as they contemplated new and greater opportunities for their students. But in time, as the spectacle receded and each art grew more specialized, it became increasingly difficult to rejoin them in a unified piece. Emphasis can, for example, turn Gluck's *Orfeo* into opera, ballet or spectacle. *Orfeo* is ripe for each, and it should fuse all three, but it is rare to find a singer who can move or a ballerina who will stand still.

For ballet by definition is movement. George Balanchine says of it in his *Complete Stories of the Great Ballets:* "What ballet does is to take movements we're all familiar with—running and jumping, turning, and balancing, lifting and holding—and mold attitudes that underlie these actions into a spectacle that entertains." As an example Balanchine suggests Broadway at Times Square: "A talented choreographer can . . . by showing us special patterns of movement and behavior, entertain us with a character ballet, make us laugh or make us sad. He makes order out of what seems to us crowded and chaotic, makes what is fleeting and transitory permanently interesting."

Roughly, there are three types of ballet—story, mood and pure movement—and endless possible gradations and combinations of them. Thus out of the Times Square hurly-burly the choreographer can make a story ballet—girl, separated from boy, finds him; a mood ballet—the lonely man in the crowd; or simply pure movement where, as Balanchine says, "the music provides the plot the dancers move to." This might be a line of people crossing the street, scrambling with another line coming out of a subway exit, separating, and then crossing against the light. The emphasis would be on the line *as* a line, without comments about urban society or the individuals in the line.

But the line, whether of the people crossing the street or merely of the dancer's body, must be always in motion, however slow; complete repose can only be momentary and for contrast. This is the mechanical explanation of ballet's five basic positions, in all of which the feet and legs are turned out in order to give the dancer freedom of movement in every direction. The positions make the best use of the hip joint, the pivot of every movement of the leg, by allowing the thighbone to rotate more freely in the socket. The turned-out positions also have an aesthetic justification, in that most ballet is danced on a stage, and the movements to be seen and appreciated by the audience must be made on a plane more or less perpendicular to the audience's sight lines. If the dancer raises his leg directly towards the audience, it sees only the sole of his shoe; if sideways, it sees the length of his leg. Thus Doris Humphrey in *The Art of Making Dances* states bluntly that in her opinion "these circular stages are highly injurious to the dance . . . [which] is at its best from only one direction."

Of the three types of ballet—story, mood and pure movement—the best choreographers today are most interested in the last. This is unfortunate for opera, because pure movement is the most difficult with which to combine. There are a number of reasons for this. Pure-movement ballets presuppose an unobstructed view of the body: no props or costumes—only leotards (*See* Glossary) or at most shirts and tights, an impossible contrast with the overdressed characters of most operas. And in order to see the body clearly the lighting must be high, very high by operatic standards. Then because dancing and dancing alone is to hold the eye, there must be space for movement: no scenery, banners or sopranos cluttering the stage. Finally, and worst of all, pure movement, being the negation of story and mood, tends, if at all extended, to dissipate the dramatic effect the opera has so carefully nurtured. These are staggering demands to impose on operas, particularly those of the nineteenth century, which involve blood, thunder and assassins on a darkened stage and in which story and mood are all-important. The attempts to combine the two arts have not always been fortunate, and Alan Yorke-Long, an opera man, describes ballet as "the idolized and overweening art of the Twentieth Century." Lincoln Kirstein, a ballet man, blasts opera-ballet: "The sources [of it], to say nothing of the actual statement, have all the vitality of habitat groups in the Museum of Natural History or photographs of Holland and Norway in the *National Geographic Magazine.*"

The opportunity for ballet in opera usually appears in one of four ways or in some combination of them: as illustration, where the dancer mimes the singer's part; as a divertissement or interlude in the opera and completely independent of its action; as an integral part, where the opera's effect or action can be completed only with ballet; and, lastly, as the decisive element, where the opera progresses only through the action of the ballet. Often unsuccessful ballets in opera result from the choreographer's or composer's failing or refusing to come to terms with the ballet's function in the opera.

Ballet as illustration, without any life of its own and as merely a mirror image of the singer's text, is the least important of the forms of ballet in opera. Neither composers nor choreographers take kindly to it as it is essentially redundant: either the song or dance should speak for itself. But there was a famous Diaghilev production of Rimsky-Korsakov's *Le Coq d'Or* in which the chorus and singers were stationary while the ballet danced the action. But it was not how Rimsky-Korsakov imagined his opera, and recent productions have not repeated the experiment. Bartok's *Bluebeard's Castle,* a two-character opera, has been done this way; and in Sir Thomas Beecham's famous movie (1950) of *The Tales of Hoffman,* Moira Shearer danced Olympia, the mechanical doll, while a coloratura warbled on the sound track.

The typical ballet divertissement occurs when one of the operatic characters gives a party and entertains his guests, such as Prince Orlofsky in *Die Fledermaus,* Alvise in *La Gioconda* or Flora in *La Traviata.* The composer may or may not have indicated whether the ballet is to be one of mood or story. In *La Gioconda* it is to be a Dance of the Hours—dawn, noon, evening, night—but the choreographer can determine whether it is to be a story or mood ballet. In *La Traviata* the chorus in the background sings of a haughty maid who requires her matador lover to kill five bulls in one afternoon, and the ballet, if given, should follow the words. But it almost never does, and the audience is frequently left wondering why there was a sudden explosion of Spanish music in the middle of Flora's Paris party. In *Die Fledermaus* the ballet is inserted by the producer, so there is no indication at all from the composer. Usually there is a "pas de deux" to a Strauss concert waltz. Balanchine describes a "pas de deux" as "a kind of romance. The man is tender and admiring as he lifts the woman and supports her in order to display her beauty, while she, in her reliance on his strength and assurance, admires him in return." The man's strength and lateral leaps make her speed and brilliance all the more feminine.

The essence of the divertissement is that it can be cut out without any loss to the opera; the danger is that frequently producers and balletomanes think it can be added without any damage. The Paris audience and Opera have traditionally demanded that ballets be inserted in all operas, and most composers, however unwillingly, have complied. Verdi, for example, added ballets for the Paris productions of *Macbeth, Il Trovatore* and *Otello;* but as might be expected, the music is inferior and the ballets are almost never given. Wagner, however, refused and touched off the greatest operatic scandal of the nineteenth century.

When his *Tannhaeuser* was announced for the Paris Opera in 1861, sixteen years after its Dresden premiere, everyone knew that there was an extended ballet in it—the Venusburg scene which opens the first act. This might have been sufficient except that the Jockey Club, a retreat of aristocratic young bloods and old bones, liked to linger over its dinner and arrive in time for Act II. As its representative explained to the management which then explained to Wagner, "Les Jockeys," who supported a large number of ballerinas, expected to be given the opportunity to applaud their favorites without hurrying their meal. Wagner refused—a froufrou ballet in the midst of a thirteenth-century contest of song was ludicrous—and the price of tickets for the first performance soared.

Actually, nothing happened the first night. And the second performance, held the following week, with Emperor Louis Napoleon and Eugenie present, started well. Then suddenly as Act II began, a storm of whistles, catcalls and boos rippled round the house and continued right to the end of the performance even though the Emperor and Eugenie by remaining visibly supported Wagner. At the third performance the noise was, if anything, worse, and Wagner withdrew the opera.

The Princess Metternich, wife of the Austrian Ambassador and friend of Wagner, chilled some of the self-satisfaction by remarking where she knew it would be repeated that in Vienna, where there was a preguillotine aristocracy, no Marquis or Duke would think of hooting from his box for a ballet in *Fidelio*.

Ballet ceases to be a mere divertissement and becomes an integral part of opera when it completes the stage action and heightens the drama, as in the final scene of *Un Ballo in Maschera*. There everyone is masked and the anonymous, costumed dancers swirl around the king, first concealing and then revealing him to the assassins; the greater the gaiety of the dancers, the more sinister and desperate seem the assassins. The constant movement heightens the tension by suggesting how easy escape would be, how uncertain the assassins will find the king, and most of all by symbolizing his life. The instant he is struck, the dancing hesitates, dwindles and stops, as though life itself were movement. The voice and orchestra can only suggest this; ballet can make it visible.

A different use of ballet, but one still integral to the opera, occurs in *Samson et Dalila*. In the Bacchanal Saint Saens wants to characterize the entire Philistine nation as depraved and licentious. It is the first time any but a few of its leaders have appeared, and as the opera is already in its last scene, he must do it quickly. Ballet by posture and gesture can do it quicker and better than the voice. Old Praetorius, a composer and novelist in the early seventeenth century, who accused the ancient waltz of causing "innumerable murders and miscarriages," would literally have no words for the Bacchanal.

Ballets as characterizations appear throughout opera and many like the Polovtsian dances from *Prince Igor* have been pulled from opera into the ballet repertory. Tchaikovsky's *Eugene Onegin* is particularly interesting as an example of Russian dancing, for in Act I the peasants dance; in Act II the middle-class gentry, and in Act III St. Petersburg society. As the social scale rises, the dances get less and less energetic, true to the general rule that the folk hop and jump while the gentry glide. And of course for anyone with three eyes in his head, in the finale to Act I of *Don Giovanni* Mozart put all three types of social dancing on the stage at once.

Ballet can be even more than an integral part of an opera, and in Gluck's *Orfeo* it is coequal with song and a leading element: the opera's action advances through the ballet. Thus the scene in which the Furies block Orfeo's descent into Hades becomes a dialogue of song and gesture. And in the Elysian Fields the dancers not only create the dreamlike atmosphere but they and they alone unite Euridice and Orfeo who, because of his pledge not to look at his wife's face until they regain the earth's surface, cannot search for her. Without good ballet the opera staggers along badly out of balance.

It is indicative of many of the problems of ballet in opera that to find an opera in which ballet is coequal with song it is necessary to go as far back as Gluck (1714–87), who died before the French Revolution and was possibly one of the last composers to whom court patronage and the court spectacle seemed natural and inevitable even though performed in a public opera house. During the nineteenth century opera turned steadily away from simple mythological or historical stories which ballet could tell, and as new instruments were invented and old improved, the orchestra became the coequal of the singer. Meanwhile in western Europe and especially in France, the ballet corps became almost exclusively feminine—all the steps and turns were designed to show off the ballerina—so that inevitably in opera the emphasis shifted to ballet as divertissement. Sometimes the men were even replaced by women in men's clothing. The only country where this trend was emphatically *not* true was Russia and is one reason why the most interesting and vigorous ballets in opera during the nineteenth century are apt to be Russian and why Diaghilev's appearance in Paris in 1909 with a troupe of Russian dancers and Nijinski stunned all of western Europe and started a revolution in western dancing.

Opera has not kept pace with the revolution in ballet and rarely shows even faint signs of doing so. In Puccini's operas, for example, there is no place or part to which dancing can contribute, except possibly in his last opera, *Turandot* (1926), with its surging crowds and the three court officers, Ping, Pang and Pong. Richard Strauss used ballet rarely and in *Salome*, awkwardly. Possibly the most natural use of it occurs in Schoenberg's *Moses und Aron,* an opera written in 1932 but which had its first complete stage performance only in 1957. In the scene of the Golden Calf Schoenberg uses ballet to express the successive steps of disintegration of the Israelites as they grow tired of waiting for Moses to come down from the mountain with the word of God. The opera is quite different from anything in the present repertory except *Wozzeck* (1921). True to the twentieth century it is very ideological. The conflict is between Moses and Aaron—Moses, who understands the spirit of the word of God but lacks the power to communicate it, and Aaron, who has power over words but no comprehension of their spirit. Aaron, of course, gets the people into trouble.

It is likely that before there can be any real rapprochement between ballet and opera, a new twentieth-century style of writing opera, perhaps like that employed in *Wozzeck* and *Moses und Aron,* will have to develop. The Metropolitan Opera tried in 1935, by joining forces with the Kirstein-Balanchine American Ballet, to make use of the most imaginative choreographer available. The agreement was that Balanchine would do the opera ballets and also present his own repertory. The collaboration lasted only three years and ended in noisy, thrilling disaster. It left the Metropolitan looking stuffy, cheap and badly managed. The opera house, for example, on the ground of expense, refused ever to let the ballet rehearse *The Bartered Bride* dances with the orchestra; it also failed to inform the ballet of cuts in the orchestral score, so that in the first performance when the orchestra finished, the dancers were still hopping. The American Ballet hardly appeared much better. It thoroughly confused its appearance with the Second Coming and demonstrated with regularity that it knew nothing about opera (nineteenth-century style) and cared less. Even so, something was achieved: Balanchine's dances for *Carmen* have not been equaled. Irving Kolodin, an opera critic, observed: "Balanchine could have made a fresh and vital thing of the danced portions of a Metropolitan production; but the production itself would have to be fresh and vital before such a departure could be regarded as an adjunct rather than an intrusion."

But even with new productions it is doubtful if the Metropolitan audience of 1935–38 could have accepted Balanchine's ideas. He had a background of working with Diaghilev, Picasso, Cocteau and Stravinsky, the ultimately successful avant garde of the beginning of the century; but the opera audience had no such background. When Balanchine offered his production of Gluck's *Orfeo* in 1936, the time and place were different but the situation was not unlike Paris in 1861. The production lasted two performances. It was never repeated.

The singers were put in the orchestra pit and the entire stage was given to the dancers. Over the objections of Balanchine, who wanted a tenor, the role of Orfeo was sung by a contralto, traditional opera casting; but the part was danced by a man. Kirstein explained the concept: "We saw Hell as a concentration-camp with flying military slave-drivers lashing forced labor; the Elysian Fields as an ether dream, a dessicated bone-dry limbo of suspended animation, and Paradise as the eternity we know from a Planetarium arrayed on the astronomical patterns of contemporary celestial science. The movement was danced and mimed in some of Balanchine's most accomplished erotic patterns, touching and electric encounters, and noble plastic groups. Attic vase drawings, themselves, and not polite dancing-school scarf dances, in his love-knots and amorous garlands had really come to life. Pavel Tchelitchev's scenery and costumes, which in tonality and atmosphere recalled Massacio, Piero della Francesca, and our everyday work-clothes, clad pseudo-Eleusinian mysteries equal in dignity and grandeur to Gluck's superb score."

Olin Downes, music critic for the *New York Times,* called it "the most inept and unhappy spectacle this writer has ever seen in the celebrated lyric theatre. It is absurd as an interpretation of the opera. It is ugly and futile, impudent and meddlesome, wholly ineffective in performance. There is no genuine relation whatever between the style of the pantomime and the style of the opera . . . so far as the stage and the choreography are concerned, [it all] is plain bad—bad and dull . . ."

When the screams of outrage died away, Edward Johnson, the manager of the Opera, gave a polite interview in which he never mentioned the American Ballet by name. He talked briefly about the difficulties and economics of running an opera house and remarked in effect that the ballets in opera should be modest, unobtrusive and traditional. Kirstein published a pamphlet, *Blast at Ballet* (1938), in which, while scorching everyone in sight, he burned up more fresh ideas and theories than most men can hoard in a lifetime. Balanchine went on twelve years later to produce what many consider his masterwork, *Orpheus,* with music specially composed by Stravinsky.

There are numerous theories about who and what went wrong. It seems clear that Balanchine was, whether he intended to or not, offering a revolutionary concept of what opera is and how to give it. This inevitably implied rough criticism of the Metropolitan, its management and patrons, and aroused an unnecessarily personal, blind response. The failure also seems to indicate, in view of Balanchine's unquestioned later success with Stravinsky's music, that a choreographer cannot beget a twentieth-century masterpiece by raping an eighteenth-century opera. And it suggests that twentieth-century ballet will not return to the opera house until it can accompany twentieth-century opera as an equal, not merely as a divertissement.

The conflict between ballet and opera, movement and singing, is not new, although many balletomanes, enjoying the fruits of their revolution, try to claim that it is and blame opera for its creation. But almost two hundred years ago Dr. Burney (*See* Glossary) observed of the French Opera: "They still lay great stress on dancing and decoration; but how few subjects fit for music will admit dancing in the texture of the drama? And as to singing and dancing at the same time, if equally good, they must distract and divide the attention in such a manner as to make it impossible to enjoy either: it would be eating two costly dishes, or drinking of two exquisite wines at once—they reciprocally destroy the effect of each other. When music is really good, and well performed, the hearer of taste wants no adjunct or additional provocative to stimulate attention."

# XI·

## THE EMERGENCE OF OPERA AS A
## FORM OF PUBLIC ENTERTAINMENT

Opera, like any other form of art, reversed the human experience and existed before it was conceived and born; only years after the event did historians name and catalogue it. Any date marking its birth, therefore, is unsatisfactory because it requires a bloated emphasis on some part of the frame, which pulls the picture off balance. Two dates are generally mentioned and are convenient, if artificial, pegs on which to hang a little history. They are 1597, when a group of gentlemen scholars produced a musical drama in Florence, and 1637, when the first public opera house opened in Venice.

Besides the problem of dates, there is the problem of definition. What is an opera? The word itself, according to Grout in *A Short History of Opera,* was used for the first time in its present sense in 1639. It means, literally, a "work" and is a shortened form of the Italian "opera in musica," "a work of music." The word came into general use very slowly throughout the next two hundred years. Meanwhile, an opera was called a "favola" (fable), a "tragedia" or a "dramma." Mozart, as late as 1787, called *Don Giovanni* a "dramma giocoso," a comic drama.

What is common to all these terms and the works they describe and is absent from the medieval church pageant or the Renaissance court entertainment is a concentration on the main character for his own sake and on the music. In a medieval pageant about Daniel in the Lions' Den, for example, Daniel as a person never comes to life; he is merely a prop to illustrate the lesson for the day. The music, sometimes charming, is incidental. Opera shifted the emphasis to Daniel and the music. Often there was no lesson. Opera set out merely to tell a dramatic story about persons in terms of music.

The definition is clearly relative. Stories can be more or less dramatic, the music more or less important. *Tristan und Isolde* is more operatic than *Il Trovatore,* which is more operatic than *Die Fleder-*

*maus.* Drawing the line is very difficult; knowing when it has been crossed is easier. *Die Fledermaus* is operetta (*See* Glossary).

The first of the two dates mentioned above, 1597, marks the year that the first opera, or what is considered the first opera, was produced. It was the work of a group of friends in Florence, most of whom were nobles and amateur poets and musicians; at least two, however, were professional musicians and attached to the Medici court. The friends used to meet at the house of Jacopo Corsi. There they discussed the role of music in Greek drama which as true sons of the Renaissance they desired to resurrect and emulate. But they were looking back rather than ahead, and that partially explains why they eventually lost control of the revolution they sparked.

No one knew (or knows) exactly how the Greeks used music in their drama, so the Florentine friends had scope for their experiments. It was evident, however, that the Greeks constructed their dramas by alternating scenes and choral odes: scenes in which characters came into conflict advanced the action while choral odes reflected on it. The Florentines, therefore, took Greek mythological stories and had the characters in scenes declaim at each other in lengthy recitative, stopping only for an occasional choral comment. No words or phrases were repeated, and the accompaniment, in order not to interfere with the noble poetry, was extremely light—a harpsichord, a lute or lyre, or some combination.

Probably the friends tried a scene first this way, then that, until in 1597 they produced their first work, *Dafne,* with music by Peri. The music is lost, but the libretto was published in 1600 and—evidence of the work's success—again in 1604. The friends first produced it privately at Corsi's house and—imagine the excitement—in the presence of "Don Giovanni Medici and some of the principal gentlemen of the city." Later it was repeated at Corsi's, this time before the Grand Duchess and two Cardinals; and in 1599 it was done at the Palazzo Pitti.

The significance of the experiment and the succeeding works in the same style was twofold. It emphasized the identification of a character, secular and dramatic: the soprano voice was no longer a nameless, ethereal descant over a choir; it was Ariadne—there she was, wailing over Theseus, the villain! Further, it endeavored to enhance the character's unique identity and feelings through music.

The friends achieved this new emphasis by inventing a new style of writing for the voice. At that time vocal music, whether for the church or home, was mostly choral, like a madrigal, with voices weaving in and out and building up a complex web of sound. It could be very beautiful, but it was not apt for telling a dramatic story on stage. For one thing, the words got lost. What the Florentines invented was a kind of recitative—a solo voice over chords which by their rhythm and pitch emphasized the words.

The courts at Florence and its neighboring Duchies, seeking entertainment and having musicians in their service, seized on the new form. Thus Peri's second opera, *Euridice* (the music exists), was produced in the Palazzo Pitti in 1600 for the wedding of Henry IV of France and Marie de Medici. Another opera, *Il Rapimento di Cefalo,* by Caccini, was performed during the same festivities at the Palazzo Vecchio. Apparently the royal couple liked opera, for they invited the librettist of the three operas, Rinuccini, to come to Paris. Further, in 1608 at Rouen the first libretto in translation, *Le Ravissement de Cefale,* was published to celebrate the birth of the second royal son. Without royal patronage opera might not have survived its infant years.

The place of music in Greek drama remained a mystery, but the Florentine friends (sometimes called the "camerata" because they met in a room—Italian, "camera," room) had stumbled upon opera. They thought, however, they were merely using music to enhance poetry; and they were probably not altogether happy at the turn their discovery began to take, for very soon the music began to dominate the poetry. It is typical of the Florentine point of view that they eschewed word repetition and frowned on Caccini who, in order to show off his daughter's good voice, began to add a few little trills and runs to the more emotional moments. But the Florentine idea of resurrecting Greek drama was essentially sterile and of interest only to scholars or at best to the most educated class.

Art forms, however, have a life independent of their creators, and professional musicians, who cared less for Greek drama than for music, began to experiment with the new form. Almost at once melody began to creep into the long recitatives, and it was the melody the people repeated. The combination of noble sentiments with melody produced the first popular aria to "sweep" all Italy. It was Ariadne's Lament (Italian, Arianna) from Monteverdi's opera, *Arianna,* produced in 1608 at the Court Theatre in Mantua. Rinuccini again was the librettist. Every Italian with a voice, a lute or harpsichord performed the Lament and wept with Ariadne. The aria is just as moving today (it has been recorded), and the text could come out of any modern Italian opera:

| | |
|---|---|
| Lasciatemi morire! | Leave me to die! |
| E chi volete voi che mi conforte | Who will comfort me |
| in così dura sorte, | in this hard fate, |
| in così gran martire? | in this great martyrdom? |

A contemporary report of one of the performances of *Arianna* insists that "none of those present remained unmoved. There was not one lady who did not shed a compassionate tear over the touching sound of the music." Unfortunately, the *Lamento d'Arianna* is all that survives of the opera, although it was revived in Venice in 1639 to inaugurate one of the public opera houses and was considered greatly superior to the more "modern" works.

The new form or style, opera, seemed to have unlimited possibilities. Anything could be done with it. In its flexibility and comparatively late origin, opera is like the novel, about which literary purists complain that it is neither epic, nor lyric poetry, nor essay, nor dialogue, nor history. So, too, the detractors of opera complain that it is neither purely choral, nor symphonic, nor terpsichorean. But, like the novel (*Don Quixote*, 1605), opera seemed to coalesce some of the times' changing political, artistic, and urban currents into a new, satisfying form.

The court entertainments at the turn of the century fit into none of the modern categories of opera, ballet, spectacle, theater or parade. They were some of each with medieval trappings that were fast becoming obsolete, such as the ballets on horseback, tourneys or ceremonials in which the courtiers paid homage to the monarch. They were extravaganzas—opportunities for princely display—to impress visiting dignitaries and to set the standard of taste and beauty for the local gentry. Often the entire court took part in them. At Padua five balconies and a stage were built around an open field for alternating tourneys and operas. It was all preceded by a dance which, according to a contemporary, was for "eighty Padovan ladies of surpassing beauty and majestic manners, who because of the excellency of their noble bearing and the luxury of their adornments, seemed to be worthy of being invited to the wedding of a goddess." At Parma the Duke entertained his friends with a court ballet in which he and his equally splendid brothers danced as Sunbeams while their sisters circled round them as Stars.

This sort of thing the new form by absorption and refinement began to replace. And considering the communications of the times, it spread quickly. Rome had what historians call an opera in 1606, Mantua in 1607, Bologna in 1610 and Viterbo in 1616. It took *La Bohème,* for example, more than two years to reach Paris and New York in 1898.

Of the early opera composers Monteverdi (1567–1643) was the greatest. Indeed he is the first great name in opera. Yet one of the curiosities of his fame is that for almost two hundred years, beginning about 1650, he was completely forgotten. Mozart probably never heard of him. Then about 1850 scholars began to discover manuscripts, run down references and publish his works. Bach had a similar eclipse but for a shorter time.

Monteverdi's career spanned the revolution in music that gave birth to opera and established it firmly in Venice as a form of public entertainment. Before 1637 opera or the extravaganza was a private affair. The great man had in his service musicians, stage architects and painters, and they were quite literally his servants. Just as he might give a dinner, the great man gave an entertainment. It reflected his personality in the choice and manner of production and audience invited. If he enjoyed spectacles, masques or ballets, he might build a private theater. Often these were very splendid like the Teatro Farnese at Parma seating five thousand, or the theater in the Palazzo Barberini in Rome, which held three thousand. If he had no private theater, then his architects would build a temporary one at the end of the hall or put up stands and a stage in the gardens. The musicians were expected to compose and perform on order, not only on the great occasions, but from day to day. Thus, soon after Monteverdi started work as a violist and singer at the ducal court of Mantua, the music-loving Duke took him along on a military campaign against the Turks in Hungary. It lasted a year. Later he took Monteverdi to Flanders. When the Duke's son married in 1608, the Duke staged an opera festival in celebration, and one of the operas was *Arianna.* But when in 1612 the Duke died and the son succeeded, Monteverdi was abruptly dismissed.

Before 1612, however, Monteverdi had composed two works which clearly were headed towards opera in today's sense. These were

*Arianna,* described before, and its predecessor, *La Favola d' Orfeo,* first produced in 1607 and the earliest work still occasionally presented as an opera today. In it Monteverdi took the Florentine idea of recitative, pointed it up with melodic emphasis and added a larger supporting orchestra which allowed a greater variety of sound. Typically for the first thirty years of the opera's existence it was produced privately at musical societies or court theaters. But it was repeated outside of Mantua, and the idea of a favola's being a work independent of a particular court or wedding or visiting dignitary was thereby strengthened. This concept had to develop before a public theater was possible.

After being forced to leave Mantua, Monteverdi, a widower aged forty-five with two sons and unemployed, returned to his father's house in Cremona. It must have been hard, and his father probably grumbled that banking was the only business for sensible men: look at those Medici in Florence! But a year later Monteverdi was elected musical director of St. Mark's in Venice, a post he held until his death in 1643. His reputation unquestionably earned him the post, but it was such a good post for him that it seems today as if the Gods must have been at work. Besides the courts only the Church offered steady work to musicians; and better than the courts, it was less susceptible to seasonal changes because of succession. It could, however, be very autocratic. In Rome in 1644 the austere Pope Innocent X set his face against comic opera, and it simply had to decamp and develop in Naples. But Venice, being a Republic and politically as well as geographically distant from the Vatican, was able to offer Monteverdi the benefits of a church post without some of its disadvantages. Venice in the seventeenth century offered its artists greater freedom of expression than any other city in Europe. Here Monteverdi came to spend the last thirty years of his life and to write his greatest music.

Naturally, most of what he wrote was for the Church. But he did not abandon dramatic, secular works or the style he was developing. Venice had no court, so on occasion he would compose an entertainment for one of the neighboring Duchies, generally Parma or, after a while, Mantua again. One of these was the extravaganza, *Mercurio e Marte,* described on p. 102 and composed in 1628 to celebrate the Duke of Parma's wedding. Earlier in 1624 for a private production in Venice he composed a dramatic cantata or ballet to a sung narration, *Il Combattimento di Tancredi e Clorinda.* A narrator recounts how a Christian knight fights and kills a Saracen warrior only to discover it is the Saracen maid he loves. The dancers mime the action—the fight, the pause, the renewed fight and the tragic discovery. In it Monteverdi used for the first time two effects associated ever since with dramatic music, particularly opera, the tremolo and pizzicato on the stringed instruments (*See* pp. 77 and 78).

Monteverdi, reaching his seventieth year, must have watched the opening of the first public opera house with the greatest interest. It was the Teatro San Cassiano, named after the parish it adorned and built in 1637 by a nobleman who immediately rented it to an impresario to manage at his own risk. The idea of a public opera house was new, and there must have been many who doubted; but by 1641 so successful was the San Cassiano, three more just like it had opened in Venice, the last brashly calling itself the "Teatro Novissimo."

In the six years remaining in his life Monteverdi wrote four operas, all for the public theaters. Two are lost; of the others, one, *Il ritorno d' Ulisse* (1641), has been described as "an improvisation of genius, a vast sketch in which certain parts have been worked out, and others scarcely outlined." The last, *L' Incoronazione di Poppea* (1642), is a finished masterpiece, an incredible achievement for a man in his seventy-fifth year. It is often said that musical genius is the first to show itself: Mozart composed at five. Verdi, who produced *Falstaff* at eighty, and Monteverdi, with *Poppea,* suggest it may be the last to grow tired.

*Poppea* was the first opera on an historical subject rather than on one from mythology, the Bible or some pastoral idyll. As such it represents a further humanization of the form. It recounts how Poppea, desiring to be Empress, successfully schemes to have Nero divorce Octavia against the advice of his noble friend, Seneca. There is a sub-plot about the courtship of a witty page and a maid of honor. The orchestration is fuller and the songs shorter than in his earlier operas; the action is rapid and the characters clear-cut. The work has a startling modern quality about it, perhaps because it is one of the first operas to be free of the courtly background. Indeed its subject, with its unkind view of royal behavior, would have been impossible for a court opera.

Court opera, of course, did not come to an abrupt end everywhere merely because the Venetians had reportedly gone crazy over some new fad. In Vienna in 1666 the Hapsburg Emperor, Leopold I, in order to celebrate his marriage to a Princess of Spain, staged a series of festivities that were easily THE social event of the seventeenth century. The climax was an opera, *Il Pomo d'oro*, having a prologue and five acts with apparently sixty-two scenes and requiring twenty-four sets. Most of the music was by the court opera composer, the court ballet composer, and even Leopold, who composed the aria for the ninth scene of the second act. The opera ended with a grand ballet and all the courtiers and performers paying homage to the new Empress. The production, more spectacle than opera, took place in a covered theater, seating two thousand, specially erected in the main square of the Imperial palace. The stage was strong enough to support an army of Athenians with ladders and two elephants assaulting a fortress of Mars, and the machinery could manage a descent from the heavens by the Goddess Pallas in a chariot of clouds.

The public theaters in Venice could neither afford such magnificent sets nor hire the armies of stagehands needed to man the machines necessary to achieve such effects. They did the best they could, but inevitably the scenery was de-emphasized. This benefited the music, which received more attention. It is a general rule, only rarely proved by exception, that the more spectacular the scenery, the worse the music.

One result of the success of the public opera houses in Venice was that they stamped the new, emerging form as one in which music via singing rather than music via ballet or spectacle would dominate. This was, of course, also partly the result of the Italian predilection for the human voice. Monteverdi, for all his orchestral experiments and innovations, never composed a piece for orchestra alone. Further, the public opera houses, by cutting the ties to the courts, established the new form as one independent of courtly events and persons and with an integrity and stature of its own. *Il Pomo d'oro*, episodic and filled with references to the Hapsburgs, would be impossible to revive without a complete rewriting; but not so *Poppea*. The public opera houses also tied opera to the cities; it became an urban art. Esterhazy could build his fabulous palace and theater in 1766, employ Haydn to compose for it, and throw the performances open to all free of charge; yet, although wondering and admiring visitors came to this first festival on a country estate, it always remained outside the main stream of opera.

None of this, of course, was obvious when Monteverdi died in 1643. The public theaters might have continued for twenty years and then failed. Certainly many persons expected it. But during the seventeenth century the Venetians developed a frenzy for opera that was unique. Soon after 1650 public theaters opened in Rome, Florence, Genoa, Modena and Bologna; but by then the Venetians were supporting four continuously and often, during Carnival season, many more. In all, between 1637 and 1700 more than 350 operas were produced in Venice in seventeen theaters, of which nine were newly constructed public opera houses. One still exists as a movie house under the name Teatro Malibran. In the last twenty years of the century, according to Grout, Venice with a population of 125,000 supported six opera companies with seasons running from twelve to thirty weeks. The common folk paid nightly; wealthy families rented boxes by the season.

It is impossible to account for what happened in Venice. For some mysterious combination of politics, geography and culture, the city had a musical explosion. A hundred years later the good Dr. Burney (*See* Glossary) surmised with delightfully Anglo-Saxon reasoning that perhaps it was because the Venetians, by reason of living on small islands, could not go for rides or long walks.

Opera as a form developed more slowly in other countries, keeping —in France particularly—some peculiar characteristics. But always throughout the seventeenth century as a constant goad and example to the rest of Europe were the Venetians, plainly having a marvelous time. It must have irritated the people in the North; plainly it intrigued their travelers, because everyone on arriving in Venice went straight to the opera and then wrote a long letter home. Thus the Venetian form of opera, rather than the Florentine or Viennese, became the basis of today's form. And, although fashions change with each half century, the concept has remained fundamentally the same.

# XII·

## A HISTORY OF OPERA IN TERMS
## OF PERSONS AND HOUSES

---

### I. SEVENTEENTH AND EIGHTEENTH CENTURIES

The modern opera house, like the theater, developed out of the Renaissance stage, and it is possible to argue that since 1650 there have been no new developments, only refinements. By then the concept of an auditorium with balconies, a stage set off by an arch, a rising curtain (it used to drop) and a pit for the musicians was accepted, and architects, designers, poets and composers all conceived their works in those terms. The spotlight, allowing a completely black stage and house and freeing the artist by complete isolation from every material and human frame, is sometimes cited as the only new development. Some do not like to admit it, but often the most intense communication between artist and audience is achieved in night clubs with the only stage a spotlight.

The Renaissance audience attended a social rather than a theatrical or musical event. They were all the invited guests or the court of some great man who wished to honor a friend or impress an enemy by putting on an extravaganza. Dynastic weddings were often scheduled for Carnival, between Christmas and Lent, and the festivities would last for weeks. The feeling of a social event was intensified by the entertainment being given in the great man's house or private theater. Further, as there was no dimming of the houselights, each man could see his neighbor or his heart's delight among the ladies. Seating the audience was important, and Nicola Sabbatini (1574–1654), in his *Manual for Constructing Theatrical Scenes and Machines,* had some observations on it, along with those on the windlass and the pulley:

"The accommodating of an audience is a matter of much importance and trouble. Yet, at these performances there is never a lack of willing helpers, especially those who seek the job of showing ladies to their seats. Were the performances given daily, there would still be plenty of those. You must take care, however, to select for this purpose, persons of years of discretion, so that no suspicion or scandal arise. The ladies are to be placed in the orchestra, or as we say, in the third of the hall nearest the stage, taking care to place the least important in the first rows nearest the parapet and proceeding in the other rows according to rank. Care should be taken always to place the most beautiful ladies in the middle so that those who are acting and striving to please, gaining inspiration from this lovely prospect, perform more gaily, with greater assurance, and with greater zest.

"The more elderly ladies should be seated in the last rows on account of the proximity of the men, so that every shadow of scandal may be avoided. Those who are responsible for seating the men should be persons of authority and, if possible, should be acquainted with all or at least part of them. In giving them the seats, it will be necessary to see that the common or less cultivated persons are set on the tiers and at the sides, since the machines give a less perfect appearance in these places, and because such people do not observe them minutely. The persons of culture and taste should be seated on the floor of the hall, as near the middle as possible, in the second or third rows. They will have the greatest pleasure there, since in such a position all the parts of the scenery and the machines are displayed in their perfection, and they will not be able to see the defects which are sometimes discerned by those on the steps or at the sides."

The emphasis on the best seat from which to see the scenery was typical of the Renaissance, which reveled in perspective. The royal or great man's box was always in the center and raised so that it would be level with the horizon line on stage. The laws of perspective had been discovered and used in painting for almost a hundred years before being used on the stage. But by 1545 when Sebastiano Serlio (1475–1554) published his book, *Architettura,* and discussed the construction of scenery, perspective was the wonder of the stage, even more than of painting because the illusion was more perfect. When the curtain dropped, the audience wanted to gasp at the street disappearing into the distance with the houses getting smaller and smaller. At first the scenes conformed to conventions. There was a Tragic Scene set on a street with houses. Serlio wrote, "In this setting the houses must be those of great persons, because amorous adventures, sudden accidents, and violent and cruel deaths such as we read of in ancient and modern tragedies alike have always taken place in the houses of lords, dukes, grand princes, and particularly kings." Serlio's rising excitement over the unfortunate kings did not mean the Comic Scene was devoid of interest. In a somewhat curious grouping it had "houses appropriate to private persons, as citizens, lawyers, merchants, parasites and other similar persons. Above all, the scene should have its house of the procuress, its tavern, and its church."

The houses were important because they gave an unparalleled opportunity for perspective. Serlio particularly recommended balconies and cornices because they formed projecting corners or "an open portico with arches in the modern style leading to another house." The street scene, with its attempt at complete illusion, was the start of a magic the theater still dispenses to happily credulous audiences.

At first there was only the one scene, and the play, musical intermezzo or dances would all be before it. The houses to the front were apt to be either made of, or reinforced with, wood. Sabbatini, a stage designer coming a hundred years after Serlio when the stage painter had supplanted the architect, observed wearily: "Boards, of course, require more time and money, but they are less apt to be damaged by those behind the scene, especially the thick-headed ones." Apparently sometimes when the curtain dropped, there were tears and gaps in the scenery; and this was a scandal.

By 1638 when Sabbatini wrote his Manual, the curtain everywhere began to be raised because, in his words, it "produces its effect with greater speed and without confusion and fright, that often occurs when part of the curtain sometimes falls on the audience." But it went up just once, at the beginning of a performance. Thereafter the audience expected many scenes, all changed before its eyes and very fast. This was part of the wonder of the theater. The backstage was never revealed, and, if all went well, in a sort of cinematic fade out and in, the new scene would be set. Sets were carefully designed so that walls would slide away revealing others, which meant that doors for entrances and exits had often to be lined up two or three thick. The changes did not always go smoothly; there were many cords to get tangled, pulleys to jam. Sabbatini pleaded for only "worthy and sincere men" backstage, but evidently often, then as now, the most delicate conception was spoiled by some dunderhead.

Out of such sour experience Sabbatini suggested a few ruses to gain the extra seconds needed: "We ordinarily use various tricks to distract attention. For example, some confidential person is sent to the rear of the hall, who, watching for the time when the scene should be changed, feigns to make a noise with another person also in the know, or else (although this might occasion much disturbance) pretends that some of the beams supporting the seats are in danger of breaking, or with the sounding of a trumpet, a drum, or some other instrument draws attention from the stage. At that very moment the change of scene is made without anyone seeing it. Obviously, care must be taken not to reveal this stratagem to any save those responsible for carrying it out.

"Of such devices the best in my opinion is that of the trumpet or other instrument since the pretense of a brawl or the collapse of the tiers brings many dangers resulting in great confusion not easily calmed down."

The machines to which Sabbatini refers were stage machinery designed to produce certain effects, such as causing a Hell to appear or a Cloud with a Goddess to descend slowly to the stage. The effects could be infinitely complicated and varied: for clouds alone there were vertical, diagonal, expanding, horizontal and triple clouds. Clouds and the heavens seemed to have an endless fascination for the court audience and probably were the most popular effects except for the "Glory," a special machine for bringing down goddesses or revealing a figure within a cloud. At the Hapsburg court in Vienna in 1666 the Prologue of *Il Pomo d'oro* ended with clouds rolling away and revealing a symbolical Glory of Austria on a winged horse surrounded by Cupid and Hymen, each on its own individual, movable cloud and all three caroling away. A chorus of eight, representing the provinces and possessions of Austria, assisted them from the stage floor. The casting of these was Spain and Sardinia, male sopranos; Italy and Bohemia, male altos; Hungary and America, tenors; and Germany and Austria, basses.

The lighting at this time was done mostly by chandeliers with either candles or oil lamps. Each had a disadvantage. If the performance was long, the body heat of the audience was apt to cause the candles to droop, and then the wax dripped. If the décolletage was low, the ladies preferred oil. But oil smelt bad, particularly if a lamp burnt out, and perfumes were often used to cover the smell. The auditorium was almost as light as the stage and, with the machines and movable scenery, there was not much room backstage for special lighting effects. Hell fire was produced generally by men underneath the stage who threw resin into the torches. This flared in a small explosion, through which Orfeo was expected to walk. The courage of the early performers seems very large. Occasionally everything burnt to the ground.

It was against this background that the first public opera house opened in Venice in 1637. It was immediately successful, and some musical reasons for its success have been suggested in Chap. XI. A political reason probably was that it was a Republic. There was no court around which to gyrate, and so there was no sudden break with tradition or competition with a ruling house. Then, like Florence or other political states that were independent of the Church, Venice had a more secular culture, making it easier for the Venetians to break with the older forms of music and public behavior. The Church in Rome, for example, never could decide what its position on the theater and opera was to be, with the result that Rome for three hundred years played a small part in Italian music—except, of course, for church music. Probably for the same reasons the first public opera house in Germany opened in Republican Hamburg, the only German city before the nineteenth century to develop a tradition of German opera and to withstand, at least for a while, the deluge of Italian singers and composers imported by the German Princes and Archbishops. It is indicative of the strength and primacy of the Italian influence that the first German opera, *Dafne,* by Heinrich Schuetz, used the same mythological subject as its Italian counterpart and was produced in 1627 at a castle in Saxony to celebrate the wedding of the local Princess.

The public opera houses could not afford such magnificent sets nor hire the armies of stagehands needed to man the machines for a proper *Glory.* They did the best they could, but inevitably the scenery became less and the music more important. But just the fact of a public opera house changed public behavior. The gentleman might expect his lady to sit with other Ladies in Waiting at a court function, but he certainly did not expect her to sit anywhere but in his box in a public theater. The family box developed as a social center. The ushers, no longer picked with the care suggested by Sabbatini, were not social equals or acquaintances, and scandal whisked round the house. The scenery perhaps was not as good, but the show was just as exciting.

An Englishman, F. M. Misson, has described in *A New Voyage to Italy* (fourth edition 1714) what going to the opera in Venice was like at the turn of the century. The book is a series of letters to a friend back home. The friend was interested in opera. Misson confessed that he was not, but he dutifully went in order to be able to compare for his friend the Venetian with the Paris opera, which at that time was being given at the Palais Royal. At this time there were seven public opera houses in Venice and only one in Paris.

"It is undeniable Matter of Fact, that the Ornaments and Decorations of these, here, fall extremely short of the others [Paris]. The Habits are poor, there are no Dances, and commonly no fine Machines, nor any fine Illuminations; only some Candles here and there, which deserve not to be mentioned. Whoever says the contrary, must be either a Fool or blind.

". . . I find a certain Confusion and Unpleasantness in several Parts of their Singing in those Opera's: They dwell many times longer on one Quavering, than in singing Four whole Lines; and oftentimes they run so fast, that 'tis hard to tell whether they Sing or Speak, or whether they do neither of the Two and both together . . . I must confess their excessive Quaverings agrees not with me, tho' it requires a great deal of Practice and Trouble to attain it; and tho' 'tis extremely grateful to the Ears of those People. The Symphony is much smaller than at Paris; but perhaps, it is never the worse for that. There is also one Thing which charms them . . . I mean those unhappy Men who basely suffer themselves to be maimed that they may have the finer Voices. The silly Figure! which, in my Opinion, such a mutilated Fellow makes, who sometimes acts the Bully, and sometimes the Passionate Lover, with his Effeminate Voice, and withered Chin is such a thing to be endured. It is impossible that such Persons can have that Vigour and Fire, which is necessary for the Beauty of Action; and indeed, there is nothing more cold and languid than the manner after which they act their Parts.

"Some time after they have begun either an Opera or a comedy, they commonly open the Doors for some Gondoliers or Watermen, especially those that belong to the Nobles, who make a considerable Body at Venice, and are very necessary Persons. Their Office on this Occasion is to applaud the Actors by clapping their Hands, and shouting like Madmen. I won't neither express, nor make you conceive what Terms they use, when they congratulate the Women; who receive also other Applauses, by Sonnets made for them, and printed, which sometimes fly about the whole Theatre. Before I finish this Article, I must tell you, that these Theatres belong to some Noblemen, who get considerable by them, tho' they continue no longer than the Carnival lasts."

The Paris Opéra, with which Misson was comparing the Venetian, had developed very differently. The first opera house was built in

Paris as late as 1671. Before then opera had been an exclusive, court function and, like all court spectacles, had relied heavily on scenery and ballet to offset the dullness of the music. This was partly because Louis XIV (born, 1638; King, 1643–1715) preferred dancing to singing, which struck him and many of his countrymen as a poor substitute for the real thing, classic French drama. Even today French opera relies heavily on scenic effects—it is always "a charming picture" —and seldom employs the word repetition that comes so naturally to Italian opera.

The opera began to move from the French court in 1669, when Louis granted to a certain Abbé Perrin a royal letters patent, originally for twelve years, to form an "Académie Royale de Musique" to present public performances of "opera and drama with music and in French verse." Thus started the state-subsidized background for public opera production so typically French and so different from the Venetian. The terms of the letters also laid the cornerstone of the tradition at the Paris Opéra of opera in French regardless of the libretto's original language. The letters defined opera as "a play in verse set to music and sung, accompanied by dances, machines and decorations," and this emphasis on the drama and spectacle rather than on the music has continued. But even though the Opéra had left Versailles for Paris, the ties to the court, at least in the beginning, remained close. Louis granted his nobles a special dispensation allowing them to appear as singers and dancers even though the performances would be before a paying public. And the rehearsals or possibly private performances of the first opera publicly produced, *Pomone,* by Cambert in 1671, took place at a Marquis' palace.

Two years later in 1671 Perrin delegated his rights to Lully (1632–87) who, although born an Italian, became the first great French opera composer. He exercised his monopoly to the exclusion of any competitor, and this stunted the development of opera in France. Lully's method of working was to take a story of either Greek or Roman mythology, submit it to Louis XIV for approval, plot out the decorations and the dances, send it to the Academy to have the poetry manufactured, and then write the music. Those who think the music should come first find Lully's operas depressing. Misson was only one of many to report that French opera excelled in costumes, dances and stage machinery but not in music.

After Lully died in 1687 (*See* Glossary under Baton), the Paris

Opéra went into a decline. A group of Italians had come and were successfully presenting Italian "opera buffa" (*See* Glossary) for which they had been granted a monopoly. But in 1697 they made fun of the King's mistress Madame de Maintenon, in *La Fausse Prude* and were banished from Paris for twenty-one years. Immediately a group of French comedians began giving comedies and satires with music and spoken dialogue. This annoyed both the Comédie-Française, which had the monopoly of speaking French on the stage, and the Opéra, which had the monopoly of singing it. By intrigue and patronage the comedians persevered until 1715, when they legitimized themselves by buying at an auction conducted by the failing Opéra the right to sing on the stage. Thereafter the only threat to the comedians, who now styled their product "opéra comique," was the troupe of Italians that returned after twenty-one years claiming the monopoly on "opera buffa," which clearly was being infringed by "opéra comique." This conflict was finally solved by a merger in 1762 from which descends the present-day Opéra-Comique. The Italian repertory, however, continued with other companies, and from about 1660 to 1876, with only occasional breaks, there was always an Italian company giving seasons in Paris.

But although the music at the Paris Opéra may have been out of the main stream and uninteresting, French society, which frequented the Opéra, was fascinating, and the guide books of the eighteenth century all dwell at length on opera in Paris, how to go to it, how much to pay and where to promenade. Perhaps the most amusing is John Millard's *A Gentleman's Guide in His Tour Through France* (1770), which includes in its title the following statement: "Wrote by An Officer Who lately travelled on a Principle which he most sincerely recommends to his Countrymen, viz. Not to spend more Money in the Country of our natural Enemy, than is requisite to support, with Decency, the Character of an ENGLISHMAN."

Before getting to the opera, Millard carefully explains the exchange rate for money and cautions all travelers: "No coin of a former reign will pass in this king's time, all the coins being called in upon the demise of their kings. Travellers should therefore be careful not to receive any old coin in change, as they will meet with great difficulty in getting it off again."

Then he proceeds with the necessary information: "There are three theatres in Paris; that of the Opéra in the palace of the Thuilleries;

that of the French comedians, in the Fauxbourg St. Germaines; and that of the Italian comedians, Rue Maucoufeil.

"The operas are performed four times a week in winter; Sundays, Tuesdays, Thursdays, and Saturdays; and three times a week in summer. The price is a pistole in the balconies, seven livres ten sols in the first boxes and the amphitheatre, four livres in the second boxes, and forty sols in the pit." (This last was standing room; the pit in Paris did not get seats until 1794.)

"The decorations of this theatre [Thuilleries] are magnificent, and the scenery beautiful, though but little can be said in favour of the singing and music.

"Friday is the best day for the French Opera in the summer, and Saturday in the winter.

"The gardens of the Thuilleries are frequented by the best company in the evenings." (The opera let out between seven and eight in the evening, and the entire audience then would promenade in the gardens. In Dr. Burney's opinion it formed "an assembly not to be met with in any other part of the world.")

"The gardens of the Palais Royal, by the best company, from twelve at noon till dinner time.

"The Luxembourg gardens are most frequented in an evening."

So that if the tourist were seen in the wrong garden, it was not because Millard had not warned him. In fact Millard was full of warnings about the nasty French: "Most of the French houses are without a necessary, and where there are any, they are commonly on the tops of the houses; so I suppose they count it less trouble to drop their daizy at the door, than like Christians, mount to the place destined for that purpose, which is often six or seven stories high."

In Vienna the opera did not break loose from the court until 1740 when Maria Theresa (1717–80) came to the throne and needed money to defend her province of Silesia against the Prussians. Under her father, Charles VI (born, 1685; Emperor, 1711–40), the court had enjoyed "The Golden Age of Baroque Opera." This was more of *Il Pomo d'oro*—scenic extravaganzas, always in Italian and generally with Italian singers, poets and stage directors—because Charles felt, quite correctly, that they were the best. Perhaps the most famous of these Baroque Operas was *Angelica vincitrice di Alcina,* by Fux (1660–1741), one of the few Austrians to excel in the Italian style. In the opera's second act the stage parted to reveal a large sheet of sparkling water over which opposing flotillas of gold-painted ships sailed to join battle. Charles, a great patron of the arts, genuinely liked opera and deliberately kept it a court function and private, although he invited thousands of guests. But it was not open to the public and in no way dependent on its favor. Indeed, at one time the local Viennese complained to the Emperor that they had no theater. One was built, but opera was forbidden in it.

Maria Theresa herself was an accomplished singer and fond o music, but Silesia came first. She refused to finance Baroque Opera out of her household accounts, but she was willing, and even eager, to have opera in Vienna, so she encouraged courtiers and impresarios to put on seasons. But when it had to pay for itself, it was a struggle. One crisis was surmounted by a public lottery; but even more successful, because continuing, were faro tables, run by permission of the Empress in the rooms off the theater. These provided a steady and sizable income. Baroque Opera, however, with its enormously expensive scenery and machines was through. As a result the music got more attention and improved, preparing the way for Gluck and Mozart. By the time Dr. Burney visited Vienna in 1772 there were two theaters in Vienna which were open alternately except on Sunday or a festival. He saw an opera by Salieri (*See* Glossary) and felt that the price of admission was not high, although the Emperor and his family attended in the royal box, and the seats in the pit had backs to them. Part of the front part of the pit was railed off and called the amphitheater; the seats there were twice as expensive. The boxes were all let by the season to the principal families, so there was no great choice of seats for the visitors. In the Brussels Opera House at this time, where the boxes were also let to subscribers, a group of seats in the pit were railed off and reserved for strangers who might otherwise be unable to get a good seat.

The smaller German Principalities longed for the splendor of Baroque Vienna and refused to imitate Maria Theresa's economies. In 1753, according to Alan Yorke-Long in *Music at Court,* at the Saxon capital of Dresden "at the twelfth performance of *Solimano* [by Hasse] the Court ladies were still hiring Swiss Guards to keep their places in the theatre, to watch the elephants and camels in the Turkish triumph, and to marvel at [the] last scene of the Turkish camp by the Tigris at night, with ships sailing on the river and the gardens of Babylon hanging dizzily in the distance. For *Ezio* [by Hasse] in 1755 the great scene-designer Servandoni was fetched specially from Paris, and in the Roman triumph, which took twenty-five minutes to pass on the stage, four hundred soldiers and more than a hundred horses from the royal stable were deployed." Then in 1756 Frederick the Great of Prussia pounced on Dresden, and the music-loving ladies and their King had to flee to friendly courts. When the Saxon King returned to his capital in 1763, he had learned nothing in seven years. He repaired the opera house and began again.

Everywhere in Germany opera was Italian. Republican Hamburg, which had started so bravely with its municipal opera house in 1678 and had seen some 280 German operas produced in seventy-two years, finally, after 1738, had nothing but Italian opera. Even Frederick the Great, playing the flute at *Sans Souci* and forging the German nation, would have nothing but Italian opera at Berlin. There were many reasons for this. Chief among them unquestionably was the Thirty Years War (1618–48), which decimated Germany and from which, many historians feel, the country has never recovered. It is estimated that the population of Magdeburg, for example, by the end of the war had dropped from thirty-five thousand to five thousand. Twenty thousand died in 1631 when the Imperial Hapsburg troops sacked the city. Even today Germans from one section or city frequently exhibit an astounding partisan ill will to those of another, and this is probably a residue of the War in which princes shifted their alliances so often that sooner or later everyone was stabbed in the back. It took the exhausted German people almost one hundred and fifty years to regain the ground lost and to produce a native culture.

Another reason was that musical life then was international. It was controlled and supported with a few exceptions by the royal families and leading nobles, all of whom were related and knew each other. It was possible in 1674 to have an opera, *La Lanterna di Diogene,* containing an aria by Viennese Emperor Leopold I and which was, as Loewenberg reports in *Annals of Opera,* "a satirical opera 'a clef,' each of the twenty-six characters representing members of the European high society, from Leopold I, Louis XIV, Charles XI of Sweden down to various Dukes, Counts and Ambassadors. The twenty-seventh character 'Tirreo Eunuco' was politely described . . . as an 'incerta persona.' " This sort of thing would have been impossible in the nineteenth century, say with Verdi or Wagner.

Lastly, secular music in the seventeenth and eighteenth centuries was opera, and the Italians were the best at it. Farinelli (1705–82; *See* Chap. V, "The Castrati") and other singers dominated the musical imagination of the eighteenth century just as, with the rise of instrumental music, Liszt, Paganini and other virtuosos did in the nineteenth. The present century has seen still another shift in fashion with the dominance of the conductor—Toscanini, Bruno Walter and others. Some say the future belongs to the engineer controlling the sounds of electronic instruments.

In Italy in the eighteenth century the center of operatic activity shifted from Venice to Naples, where a school of outstanding composers arose specializing in two styles: "opera seria" and "opera buffa." "Opera seria" was on a grand scale with historical or mythological themes; it was a close cousin to the Viennese Baroque opera except that the music was of greater importance and the scenery of less. The aria, generally sung by a castrato, was the crux of every scene, and over the years it became extremely stylized, so that for any situation there was a certain type of aria that was appropriate. The singer was expected to embellish the aria with extemporaneous runs, trills and flourishes, and this—more than the drama, scenery or composed music—was what excited the audience. Thus the composer wrote a vehicle for a particular singer rather than searching his soul in nineteenth-century romantic style to produce an immortal masterpiece. Grout, in *A Short History of Opera,* reports that forty leading composers in the eighteenth century wrote fifty operas each: Verdi wrote twenty six, Wagner thirteen, and Puccini twelve. There was no repertory as today. The audience wanted new music each year, although it was perfectly willing to have the same librettos used over and over; for example, Mozart's was the seventh setting of Metastasio's *La Clemenza di Tito.* The scores of the operas were almost never published and, in any event, were extremely sketchy. Only the favorite arias might be published and, as there was no copyright, the composer was far less interested in preserving his old work for posterity than in receiving a commission for a new one, which he could complete in four to six weeks.

One result of this approach to opera, so different from today's, was that no one really listened much; opera was still a social rather than a musical event. A Frenchman, De Brosses, writing in 1740 described what went on at Rome: "The ladies hold, as it were, at homes in their boxes, where those spectators who are of their acquaintance come to call on them. I have told you that everyone must rent a box. As they are playing at four theatres this winter, we have combined to hire four boxes, at a price of twenty sequins each for the four; and once there I can make myself perfectly at home. We quiz the house to pick out our acquaintance, and if we will, we exchange visits. The taste they have here for the play and for music is demonstrated far more by their presence than by the attention they pay. Once the first scenes are past, during which the silence is but relative, even in the pit, it becomes ill-bred to listen save in the most interesting passages. The principal boxes are handsomely furnished and lighted with chandeliers. Sometimes there is play, more often talk, seated in a complete circle as is their custom, and not as in France, where the ladies add to the show by placing themselves in a row in the front of each box; so you will see that in spite of the splendour of the house and the decoration of each box, the total effect is much less fine than with us."

Besides visiting in the opera, the Romans also played cards and chess. In Milan the diversion was faro. Florence offered hot suppers served in the boxes. At Turin each box had a room off it with a fireplace and all the conveniences for refreshments and cards. At Venice the boxes could be closed off from the theater by a shutter.

All travelers reported that the gabble and noise were deafening except during two or three favorite arias which, greeted with wild applause, were repeated. One visitor, Lalande, estimated that the typical Milanese spent a quarter of his life at the opera. It is not surprising then that the archduke's box in Milan had attached to it not only a private sitting room but also a bedroom.

"Opera seria" generally occupied the main theater of the town to the exclusion of "opera buffa." It had the grand heritage, the social appeal and the support of royalty and the aristocracy, even if it lacked the attention of its audience. "Opera buffa," on the other hand, was generally performed in the second or third theater without any of the réclame of "opera seria"; and yet by about 1780 it was slowly becoming clear that "opera buffa" had greater vitality than "opera seria." There were several reasons why. The smaller theater made it easier for the singer to make contact with his audience, and it is in the nature of comedy to come downstage, place one foot on the prompter's box and talk directly to the audience. This was far more likely to hold the audience's attention than the distant symbolical dramas of "opera seria." Further, comedy meant everyday realism in which the rising middle class was far more interested than it was in the mythological and historical characters in which the aristocracy saw itself. The lawyer or the shopkeeper knew all about misers and spendthrift nephews; and he cared nothing about Paris, Helen and the golden apple, even if he knew of them. So for a composer the fun and excitement of such an audience made up for the lack of prestige. The result was that, beginning about 1733 with Pergolesi's *La Serva Padrona,* the oldest opera still in the general repertory, a series of outstanding composers— among them Paisiello, Piccini and Cimarosa—turned out "opere buffe." These were taken by touring Neapolitan companies all over the world, and no visitor came to Italy, especially Naples, without seeing an "opera buffa" and then writing a detailed description home. The operas were often very close to pure theater, with only the simplest tunes and a great deal of horseplay, and they derived much of their tradition from straight acting. Naples had a playhouse, which was described by an Englishman, Samuel Sharp, in a letter from Naples in 1765 that is a masterpiece of Anglo-Saxon disdain:

"The playhouse is hardly better than a cellar, and is really very much known by that name, being usually called the 'Cantina' [cellar]. You descend from the street down ten steps into the pit, which holds seventy or eighty people, when crowded, each of which pays a carline, that is, four pence halfpenny, for his admittance. There is a gallery round the pit, which is formed by partitions, into ten or twelve boxes. These boxes holding four persons conveniently, let for eight carlines. Under these discouragements it will not be difficult to conceive, that the scenes, the dresses, the actors, and the decorations of the house, must be very indifferent: It will not, however, be so easy to imagine the shabbiness of the audience, which chiefly consists of men in dirty caps and waistcoats, in the pit, for the boxes are generally empty. All the Italian Gentlemen and Ladies are very indelicate in the article of spitting before them, never making use of a handkerchief, or seeking a corner for that purpose; but in the 'Cantina' their nastiness is offensive to the last degree, not only spitting all about them, but also on every part of the wall, so that it is impossible to avoid soiling your clothes. This habit is carried by some to such excess, that I cannot but ascribe the leanness of many *Neapolitans,* and the swallowness of their complexions, to the abundance of this evacuation."

Needless to say, progress or change does not necessarily enter through the cellar, but "opera buffa" largely did. It was allowed in the grand theaters generally only as intermezzos between the acts of an "opera seria," and in town after town it supported itself in a way that "opera seria" never did. The result was that it was constantly and rudely reminded that it ought to be short and amusing or moving, a discipline all composers and forms need.

The opera houses throughout Europe at this time supported themselves in every conceivable way, some of which foreshadow the methods of today. Thus, according to Sharp, at Turin a group of forty gentlemen underwrote the season. At Milan and Vienna there were faro tables. At Naples an impresario leased the theater from the King and was probably the only Italian to win Sharp's sympathy: "The Impresario, or manager, is bound to very hard terms, so that his profits are inconsiderable, and sometimes he is a loser. The theatre being a part of the palace, the King reserves for himself, Officers of State, and Train, fifteen boxes; nor does the King pay the manager one farthing, whereas the late King used to present him annually with four thousand ducats. The junto deputed by his Majesty to supervise the Opera, reserve to themselves the right of nominating singers and dancers, which obligates the manager sometimes to pay them an extortionate price. Another disadvantage he lyes under, is, the frequent delay of payment for the boxes, and a manager must not take the liberty to compel persons of quality to pay their just debts."

On the whole, Sharp felt that the Neapolitan kings had not contributed much to the opera, and he concluded with one last jab: "I must not omit a foolish singularity, in relation to the women dancers at Naples, that in consequence of an order from court, in the late King's time, they all wear black drawers. I presume it was from some conceit on the subject of modesty, but it appears very odd and ridiculous."

But in spite of the black drawers as the eighteenth century entered its last quarter, all of Europe except France still considered Italian opera supreme and Naples its fount. Its conservatories trained the best singers; its composers were the most admired; and young composers, including Mozart, struggled to get there. In faraway Berlin Frederick the Great, now old and crotchety, would still have nothing but Italian operas with Italian singers. He could decide because he supported the opera: in Berlin anyone decently dressed was admitted to the pit gratis. The Elector of Cologne, a somewhat gayer personality, had "opera buffa" in his palace entirely at his own expense but available only to his guests and courtiers. Hamburg, the only German city with a tradition of German opera, by 1772 had no opera at all. Outside of France, all was Italian opera. Then came the French Revolution, and in twenty years the complexions of Europe and music had completely changed.

# XIII·

## A HISTORY OF OPERA IN TERMS
## OF PERSONS AND HOUSES (*Cont.*)

---

### II. NINETEENTH AND TWENTIETH CENTURIES

The French Revolution, from the Bastille in 1789 through
its backwash leading up to Waterloo in 1815, affected
musicians as much as politicians and soldiers—perhaps more, because
in music there was no concluding Congress of Vienna settling bounda-
ries, indemnities and dynasties. At the political Congress the waltz
delivered the minuet a coup de grâce, and for musicians the revolution went right on.

For them, however, it did not make life better; and for most it probably made it much worse. Under the old order the aristocracy and
courts supported the musicians by employing them as servants. There
was an order to life, and while the artistic temperament might rage
at being a servant—a social inferior ordered to play and not to play—
it at least got fed. After the Revolution, as the surviving aristocracy
retrenched and regrouped to fight legislative battles, the musicians
without any patron starved, unaided even by good copyright laws for
almost a hundred years. It was only during this period that the concept
of an artist or musician as a Bohemian arose.

The old order could work well. Haydn, who lived to see the new,
started in 1761 at twenty-nine with Prince Esterhazy. He wore livery
and a wig and each day inquired "whether His Highness shall be
pleased to order a performance of the orchestra." Five years later he
became the head musician whose duties included conducting the orchestra, directing operatic productions, performing chamber music and
above all composing all types of music for the Prince's festivities. He
also composed on his own time for courts and musical groups all over
Europe. He became, while still eating at the servants' table at Esterhazy, a European celebrity. This never struck him as incongruous or
demeaning: "I have associated with emperors, kings, and many great
lords, and they have told me many flattering things. But I wouldn't
want to become familiar with such persons; I prefer to associate with

persons of my own class." In his own class he included Mozart. Haydn was too kind to say it: the merely very rich and very social are usually very boring.

In 1790 Prince Esterhazy reduced the number of his musicians and retired his famous musical director on full pay. Haydn was fifty-eight and still vigorous. After a short stay in Vienna, he left for London, where he wrote his most famous symphonies. He was lionized by society and, figuratively speaking, stepped into the nineteenth century as an artist independent artistically and financially, for his concerts and compositions sold well. At the time this probably was possible only in London, always more middle-class than Paris or Vienna.

While Haydn was away, his young friend Mozart, in Vienna, died. Mozart's biographers conjecture about the actual disease, but they are in no doubt about his condition, brought on by "excessive work, continual fatigue and profound misery." Like Haydn, Mozart had served a great man, the Archbishop of Salzburg. But unlike Haydn, Mozart, proud and passionate, found the position galling and the Archbishop intolerable. He quit and, as he was unable to attach himself to another great man, tried to conquer Vienna as a free artist. But it was too soon. The position was not yet recognized; public concerts were the exception not the rule; he had no steady access to the court theaters or orchestras; he had to waste time and energy being his own business manager, agent and copyist; and he had to provide for a family. It was too much. Even Beethoven, no man's servant, twenty-five years later regularly received stipends from four of the Viennese aristocracy.

Rossini (1792–1868) was one of the first composers to succeed without a patron and purely on the commercial success of his operas. But it was a frenetic undertaking. He wrote thirty-eight operas in nineteen years, from 1810 to 1829, when he was thirty-six. He lived until 1868, but in those last thirty-nine years he never wrote another opera and composed only a few songs and two religious pieces. His biographers speculate on the comparative importance of various reasons without any help from Rossini, who deliberately refused to explain. The reasons generally given are: he felt his music was out of touch with the times; he felt the art of singing had declined with the disappearance of the castrati; he believed the administration at the Paris Opéra, preferring Meyerbeer, would give his operas only the most slovenly productions; he had "nerves" and physical ailments that probably were venereal in origin. Whatever the proper balance in the reasons, he was used up. And considering the system under which he had succeeded it was not surprising.

Italy in 1810, when Rossini started, was a mass of small states, some no bigger than cities and all dominated either by the Napoleonic French or by the Austrians, the Bourbon French and the Church. Napoleon had conducted two Italian campaigns; the Austrians and Bourbons, aided by Lord Nelson in Naples, had retaliated; and, in the seesaw battle, the structure of Italian society had been destroyed. The aristocrats who survived began to save what they could. The tottering courts continued subsidies to singers and theaters as a public gesture but only on a reduced scale and without taking on new commitments. In Milan the Austrians forbade gambling at La Scala, the theater's greatest source of revenue. King Ferdinand in Naples likewise closed the tables at the San Carlo. Suddenly, throughout Italy, particularly in the smaller towns, the theaters, singers and composers were thrown completely on their own.

Stendahl, a contemporary, in his *Life of Rossini* (1824), has given an account of how theatrical society in the smaller towns organized itself:

"A *contractor*—usually the wealthiest burgher of some petty township, for this particular office carries with it considerable social prestige and not a few other advantages, although it frequently turns out to be financially ruinous!—undertakes to run the theatre in the town whose leading citizen he has the honour to be; so to start with, he forms a company, which consists invariably of: a *prima-donna,* a *tenore,* a *basso cantante,* a *basso buffo,* a second (female), and a third (male) *buffo* singer. Next, the *impresario* engages a maestro (composer) to write an original opera for him, having always due regard, in the setting of his *arias,* to the particular characteristics of the voices of the singers who are to perform them. The *impresario* then purchases a text (the *libretto:* always in verse), which may cost him anything from sixty to eighty francs, the author being usually some wretched *abbé* parasitically attached to one of the wealthier households in the neighborhood . . . Next, the *impresario* . . . proceeds to hand over all the business management of the theatre to his agent, who is usually a lawyer, and in fact the same arch-scoundrel who manages his personal business in private life; while *he* (the impresario) is more properly occupied in falling in love with the *prima donna;* at which point, the great question which arises to tickle the curiosity of the entire neighborhood, is whether or not he will offer her his arm in public.

"Thus 'organized,' the company eventually gives its first performance, but not without previously having survived a whole month of
utterly burlesque intrigues, thus furnishing an inexhaustible supply of
gossip to entertain the entire countryside. This *prima recita* is the
greatest public happening in all the long, dull existence of the town
concerned—so momentous indeed, that I can think of nothing in
Paris which could offer anything like an adequate comparison. For
three weeks on end, eight or ten thousand persons will argue the merits
and defects of the opera with all the powers of sustained concentration
with which heaven has seen fit to endow them, and above all, with the
maximum force of which their lungs are capable. This *première,* unless
blasted at the very outset by some scandal of positively catastrophic
dimensions, would normally be followed by some thirty or forty others,
at the conclusion of which, the company disbands."

Stendahl meant that the same opera was repeated, generally every
night except Friday, some thirty times. Then a new opera might take
its place. There were three operas plus some ballets presented during
the average large town's carnival season. Those who could afford it
went every night. Rich families took a box for the season. Small
wonder that, except for the first performance, the audience paid no
attention except to its favorite arias. It visited, played cards, negotiated
business deals and, above all, talked; the opera house was the social
center of the town. Stendahl thought thirty performances was "about
the number of times that it is profitable to listen to an opera of average
competence." Of course singers at the time were still expected to improvise embellishments on the arias, particularly on the encore, so
that no performance was an exact duplication of its predecessor. But
Stendahl himself recommended at least four or five minutes of whispered conversation to release the tension of the soul between arias. He
scorned the French audiences for their "fundamental illusion that
*every note is meant to be listened to"* and insisted that the most moving passages could make their best effect only if they followed something more pedestrian.

Tradition in Italy required the opera houses to put on at least one
new opera each season and the composer to conduct the first three performances of it. He did this seated at the harpsichord, not standing
prominently as now. After the third performance, he would generally
move on to another town and opera. He had no royalties or copyrights

in his work, and the opera belonged to the impresario for two years, after which it became public property. The composer could only hope for another commission to start the cycle again. For *Il Barbiere di Siviglia* Rossini received about $500 and, as a gift from the impresario so that he should look well in the pit, a nut-brown suit with gilt buttons.

Rossini sometimes composed four operas a year, and in 1812 he did five. In the last five years when he was in Paris where they took the productions of a genius more seriously and paid more for them, he composed only one a year. So that in his "Italian" period he composed thirty-three operas in fourteen years. Inevitably every note was not worth listening to, and many, like the overture to *Il Barbiere,* which had been used for two other operas, had been heard before. This method was part of a style and atmosphere of opera that Wagner and others, brooding twenty years over a masterpiece, hurried out of favor, but it produced *Il Barbiere,* unquestionably the world's most popular comic opera.

Opera in England at the time was produced essentially in the same style only with more money and respectability. No one there lost his head merely over a sublime duet, and since there was only one operatic center, London, it was less hectic. Covent Garden, the chief theater, was rebuilt after a fire in 1809 by a syndicate that appealed for funds to the public but especially to the "nobility and gentry." The ground lease was held by the Duke of Bedford, and the syndicate included Dukes, Earls and Marquis. With the house built, the aristocrats then let it to a series of impresarios who put on seasons of opera, plays or musicals. It became a permanent opera house only in 1847. An impresario might turn a profit, go broke or, if he were lucky, be bailed out by a Duke, but the theater's existence did not depend on public or government support. The syndicate was perfectly willing to have the house stand idle till another impresario came along. Throughout this period and until 1911 the dominant color of the interior was green, and until the advent of gas in the 1870's it was lit by candles, 270 of them a night, burning in forty glass chandeliers. The auditorium remained lit throughout the performance, and the audience moved around and talked except during the favorite arias. Encores were sung, and roles were frequently altered to suit favorite singers. An extreme instance of this occurred in 1847 when a contralto, Mme. Alboni, sang the baritone role of Charles V in Verdi's *Ernani*. At this time singing was popular as a parlor art, and the audience as a whole was probably more knowledgeable about singing technique than at any time since. The dramatic side of the performance was at a nadir. Adelina Patti even had a clause in her contract excusing her from attending rehearsals.

Queen Victoria and Albert were fond of opera and went frequently. When she arrived late, the performance stopped for the National Anthem. But, according to Harold Rosenthal, the historian of the house, she personally persuaded the management to play it only at the beginning and end of each season. The Queen herself was an amateur singer, taught by the great bass Lablache (*See* Glossary and p. 34). The repertory consisted almost entirely of Italian operas—by Rossini, Donizetti and Bellini—except for Meyerbeer, whose stage effects were popular. His operas, however, were sung in Italian, the reigning language, and the theater was called The Royal Italian Opera House. When Berlioz, a French composer, conducted the première of his *Benvenuto Cellini* in 1853, a claque hissed and hooted throughout the entire performance. Even the presence of Victoria, Albert and the blind King of Hanover and his Queen did not stop them. Berlioz and others blamed the Italians living in London, who had probably been organized by musicians and singers who wanted nothing but Italian opera. Berlioz's French effort, though on an Italian subject, was unacceptable, and he withdrew the opera. The policy of opera sung in its original language did not start until 1889.

BERLIOZ

French opera in Stendahl's time, at least according to him, was a miserable affair: "Most of the seats at the *Grand Opera* are taken, either by members of the lower orders, or else by gaping provincials freshly disembarked from the stage-coaches—the two classes of mortals who are *by instinct* admirers of anything expensive. Add a sprinkling of newly-arrived English landed gentry (in the boxes), and a score or so of licentious rakes (in the balcony) who have paid to stare at the 'corps de ballet': this, together with the annual subsidy of 600,-000 francs voted by the Government, represents the total sum of support which the *Grand Opera* receives in Paris." This description could fit almost any period including the present at the "Grand Opera," for its brilliant periods have been few and not very bright.

By the middle of the century the low standards of opera composition and production affected composers everywhere. Many, like Berlioz, turned to other forms of music; and after the death of Donizetti, of the great ones, only Verdi and Wagner, both born in 1813, continued to write primarily for the theater. Although the same age, Verdi was a success almost a generation before Wagner; so, in operatic history, he precedes. The careers, operas, virtues and failings of the two men are so different that comparison is almost meaningless, although the partisans of each continue to fight with loaded definitions of greatness. It is true that Verdi, unlike Wagner, did not revolutionize the opera orchestra, design a theater, or theorize about music drama. It may even be true, as Ernest Newman, the great Wagnerian declared, that Verdi was not "a front-rank musician." Much depends on taste and the definitions. But it is indisputable that no musician in the last four hundred years writing in any form—operatic, symphonic or other—has communicated so directly to so many persons for so many years. Musicians and listeners whose experience is predominantly symphonic forget this.

Verdi's achievement was to pull into the theater the great mass of people everywhere. Under him opera became popular with all classes and conditions of men. D'Annunzio, in a memorial ode, said of him, "Pianse e amo per tutti" (he wept and loved for all). More than any other composer Verdi gave opera the right and ability to survive in a democratic age and prevented it from becoming like polo, an interesting but irrelevant aberration of the rich and idle.

The production of opera in this period hit bottom. Wagner at Cologne complained bitterly of a performance of *Die Zauberfloete,* in which the Queen of Night sang always in brightest daylight; and Stendahl in Paris grieved over trees that threw shadows on the sky. In their own ways, the best composers attempted to do something about it. In France Berlioz, who either could not or would not conform to the required low standards of the "Grand Opera," wrote articles on behalf of Gluck, Weber and Beethoven and kept alive a more dramatic and musical concept of opera. In Italy Verdi demanded more rehearsals, withheld his operas from La Scala and other houses that gave sloppy productions, and supervised as many of the productions as he could.

In Germany Wagner attacked head on. He wrote during his life (1813–83) thirteen operas, ten of which are still given regularly. No other composer has such a high percentage of living works, and it reflects Wagner's conviction that *"every note was meant to be listened to."* To achieve his aim, he worked for years on the librettos and music, often stopping work on one opera to complete another. But this was not enough. The audience and singers, in his opinion, had acquired such bad habits that they had to be completely retrained. Verdi in 1847 had required 150 rehearsals of a duet in *Macbeth* and, unheard of, a dress rehearsal. But Wagner for the first Bayreuth Festival required two summers of training, and one of the tenors worked with special training for eighteen months. To house it all, Wagner created a special theater. That a poor composer, continually in debt, should have achieved this is one of the incredible facts of the nineteenth century. And it does not take away from Wagner's tenacity to say that he could not have achieved it without King Ludwig of Bavaria. The composer and his patron are in the direct line of operatic tradition.

Exactly when Wagner first began to ruminate on his plan to reform opera by performances in a Festival Theatre is unknown, but as early as 1850, in a letter to a friend, he revealed what would develop in 1876 into the first Bayreuth Festival. He wrote that he would like to erect a simple, wood theater in a field near Zurich and to give three performances of his opera (not yet composed, but he had been working on a libretto called *Siegfried's Death*) to an audience consisting mostly of impresarios, who could see how opera was to be produced. After the third performance he proposed in an airy gesture to burn the score. Singers and orchestra were to be "the best to be found anywhere" and would be "invited" to donate their services to him for six weeks. Newspapers would, of course, carry the advertisements and, to quote Ernest Newman from *The Life of Richard Wagner,* "The problem of expense was to be solved in the simplest way imaginable. Some rich man or other was to provide 10,000 thalers for the building."

Twelve years later in 1862 he published *The Ring* poem, the libretto for his four operas, and in the preface he again—this time in greater detail—outlined his hopes for its production. It was above all to be "free of all the influences of the regular repertory of our existing theatres." He hoped to find some German town without a theater and with a public unsoiled by current operatic taste. The financing was still vague. Perhaps "an association of art-loving well-to-do men and women" could raise the money by subscription. Even better would be for some German Prince to pay the bill. At that time Wagner had not yet met the Prince who would support him to his goal, but he existed in Ludwig, heir to the Bavarian throne.

When in 1864 Ludwig, only eighteen and a half, suddenly succeeded to the throne, he summoned Wagner to Munich and began an association that would last the rest of the composer's life. Ludwig was a serious, sensitive, intense young man, sadly out of sympathy with his court and statesmen. As he grew older he spent continually less time in Munich and more in the mountains, which he loved. Eventually, in 1886 at forty-one, he was the victim of a political plot in which four doctors declared him insane and incapable of recovering, although they had not examined him personally and had never even been in his presence. But on their testimony a commission, accompanied by asylum warders, set out for his castle to arrest him. The King knew that once incarcerated he would never be released or permitted to see or talk to friends again, and he drowned himself in Starnberg Lake.

But before this unhappy end the King and Wagner created at Bayreuth a Festival Theatre which, probably more than any other deed, influenced the development of music and opera in the following hundred years. Beginning in 1864 the King rescued Wagner financially and socially many times and for no reward. Few men, musicians or otherwise, have been so unattractive as Wagner in their personal relations, and accounts of his behavior, while at first rather deliciously appalling, end in being merely sickening. It is part of Ludwig's glory that, like the Deity, he could see through the bad in the man to the good.

By 1871 Wagner had settled on Bayreuth as the town, and he began to raise money to build the theater. The original plan was that for a large fee persons would be "invited" to become Patrons, and only Patrons would be "invited" to attend the performances. But this plan was compromised almost at once. First, it became possible for persons to combine to take up a Patron's subscription and finally, by the time of the first Festival in 1876, to buy a ticket. Friends assisted, and

Wagner Societies were started in many German cities. But even when Wagner came to conduct a benefit concert, the money raised barely covered expenses. There was no ground swell for Wagner among the German people. What they thought of him was reflected in a court decision that to compare Bismarck to Wagner was legally punishable as an "insult" to Bismarck, "since Richard Wagner is universally re-garded as a man suffering from megalomania."

The intellectual class did no better. An appeal to 3,946 German book and music dealers raised nothing—not one cent. An appeal to eighty-one German theaters to give benefits for the Festival Fund was ignored by seventy-eight of them; the other three refused.

The rich and powerful did well enough to get their names on the published list of Patrons, but most subscribed only enough to assure themselves of several good seats if the productions ever came off. They bought their seats—and that was all. Many of the German Princes re-fused to do even that much, and both the Sultan of Turkey and the Khedive of Egypt, who made real contributions, appeared in the un-likely role of supporter of "Holy German Art."

By 1873 only a third of the money needed had been raised and the possible donors were exhausted. Bayreuth itself had contributed the site; Ludwig had made the largest single gift; and the shell of the theater was rising. But there were no singers, orchestra, or stage equip-ment and no way of getting any without either cash or solid financial backing; and at any bank Wagner was a bad risk.

Wagner appealed to the King, and Ludwig responded by lending Wagner the money to complete the theater and to produce the operas. Wagner was to repay the loan out of receipts from the performances, the Patrons' contributions and benefit concerts. Wagner was informed through the King's secretary that this was the end: the King could do no more. But the following year Wagner had nothing left with which to hire the singers and orchestra and once again appealed to Ludwig. The King abrogated the agreement in Wagner's favor and, in New-man's words, "at considerable inconvenience to himself . . . saved Bayreuth."

The theater, when finished, reflected Wagner's theories of opera pro-duction and differed from the usual horseshoe-shaped opera house with a royal box in the center. It was long and thin like a concert hall with the orchestra out of sight in a pit sunk under the lip of the stage so that the audience looked directly at the singers onstage without any glare from the orchestra's desk lights or distraction from the weaving back and arms of the conductor. The orchestra floor rose sharply and the rows of seats curved, so that every seat had a head-on, unobstructed view of the stage. To modern eyes the rise and curve resembles the end of a stadium. There were no boxes or balconies except for a small gallery at the rear for Wagner's family and royalty. Neither were there any billiard rooms, gaming tables or grand foyers, and the restaurant was in a separate building. The theater was lit by gas, which could be dimmed so that the auditorium was much darker than the stage.

Wagner from the first intended the Festival to be an experience not an event. One of the attractions for him of Bayreuth was that the audience would have to assemble well in advance. It could not rush in at the last minute or later from home or office or rush out before the curtain to catch a train. In every detail of his planning he deliberately fostered an atmosphere of intense absorption, even of dedication. As he had explained earlier in a letter to the King, he did not want "the lounging opera public, accustomed solely to the trivial, but only those who hitherto have remained aloof from these shallow entertainments."

The first season at Bayreuth, the summer of 1876, consisted of three cycles of *The Ring. Das Rheingold* and *Die Walkuere* had been first presented in 1869 and 1870 in Munich, but *Siegfried* and *Goetterdaemmerung* were presented for the first time. The singers were the best Wagner could lure to Bayreuth and, with one or two exceptions, were probably the best that could be had. Many came at a financial sacrifice to be part of what they felt was a great musical event. The members of the orchestra for the rehearsals during the summer of 1875 refused to accept anything more than their expenses. The performances were an artistic success, and the musicians and impresarios who came left impressed. There were, however, some typical Wagnerian disappointments. The dragon for *Siegfried* had been ordered from London, and while the head and body arrived in time for the performance, the neck was delayed in the mails.

Financially the Festival produced a staggering deficit and a pack of creditors baying for their money. The deficit was beyond anything Wagner could handle, and the King not only had to forgo repayment on the first loan but to make another almost as large. But he had seen some of the performances and felt it was worth it. Wagner, however, as the months passed, began to despair that the example would have no effect on opera in Germany or elsewhere: the singers would resume their habits, and the old round of trivial performances before a gabbling audience would begin again.

He was partly correct. No opera house built after Bayreuth followed his theories of construction. Even after World War II, when many of the German houses were rebuilt, they followed the older Italian plan of balconies or boxes in a horseshoe or circular shape, perhaps modified but plainly a variation of the Italian style rather than of Bayreuth.

The explanation does not lie in acoustics, for those of Bayreuth are considered to be among the best in the world. Every opera house built or rebuilt since 1876 has had its own peculiar reasons for rejecting the Bayreuth design, but one reason generally applicable may be that Wagner at Bayreuth created something outside the main stream of opera. There the operas are given uncut and, as he intended, in a Festival atmosphere. The audience, often come from a great distance, gathers in the early afternoon. After the first act there is an intermission of more than an hour, during which arrangements are made for dinner. At the second intermission, again more than an hour, dinner is served at a restaurant in a building separate from the theater. All this is done in what is essentially a country town, where space is cheap.

But since 1637 when the first public opera house opened in Venice, opera has been an urban art, supported in each city by the music lovers and society of that city. Sometimes they work with, and sometimes against, each other, but their combined support, taste and behavior set the tone of the house. For them the opera house has always been a place of glamour and excitement—a mixture of a clubhouse, social parade and musical temple. At Bayreuth Wagner exorcised the clubhouse and social parade into other buildings, leaving the temple inviolate. But this is impossible, even if desirable, in a city opera house where the audience gathers after the day's work and is eager to be home by midnight. Inevitably the socializing invades the temple, and boxes and narrow balconies which hang from the side walls and from which the audience looks across at itself provide a cozier, more social tone than does the more isolated intensity of concert hall design in which each person sees only the blank, back of the head in front of him.

Such anonymity is deliberately fostered by the concert hall and rightly so, but most opera houses cannot be so one-sided. In the concert hall all the music is essentially serious; there is no tradition and perhaps no possibility of comic symphony interrupted by laughter and happy whispering in the audience. Opera, on the other hand, has a tradition of "opera buffa" and a series of great masterpieces, which include all five of Mozart's best-known operas. It is curious but understandable that serious music tends to fragmentize its audience into isolated individuals, each responding within himself directly to it. After a successful performance of a great serious work the audience disperses, each man hugging himself, silent and alone. A comic opera, on the other hand, tends to meld the audience into a unit; it laughs together and after the curtain it goes out in groups, chattering and enthusiastic. Wagner never wrote a comic opera. *Die Meistersinger,* his closest approach, is a romance, and the character of Beckmesser is more of a sarcasm than a humor. The theater that Wagner designed for his operas was eminently suitable for serious, tragic and even religious works. It is less good for the comedies and Mozart.

But aside from his theories of design, Wagner's success at Bayreuth had an immediate effect on the opera world. Cumulatively it cannot be overestimated. Beginning in 1882 there began to be Festivals almost every year, and each member of the audience, deeply impressed, returned to his own city and started to agitate for Wagner's operas done in the Bayreuth style, even to the point of copying the scenery exactly as the Metropolitan did for the American première of *Die Walkuere.* The operas were soon being produced everywhere, and every opera house wanted a singer or conductor trained by Wagner at Bayreuth. It

was not until about 1890, according to Bruno Walter, that the conductor's name began to appear regularly on the program, and at first he was listed as the "musical director." Before then, the singers dominated the performance; but Wagner, with his emphasis on the orchestra and a production equally good in all departments of orchestra, singing, scenery and lighting, shifted the emphasis inevitably from the singer to the conductor, the co-ordinator. There were many who did not like the new style and who complained that the "Bayreuth Bark" was not singing at all; but they were soon swamped by the musicians and a new audience that was developing for Wagner and claiming to feel more intensely about music than the Italians ever did. For seven years, from 1884 to 1891, the Metropolitan produced all its operas, even *Aida,* in German. This was not a success, and thereafter the Metropolitan adhered to its policy of presenting each opera in its original language. In 1889 Covent Garden adopted the same policy and dropped the *Italian* out of its name, becoming merely *The Royal Opera House.* Such was the pressure of the new German opera; the extraordinary fad for Wagner, which lasted almost fifty years, had begun.

Changing social habits and a nonmusical invention also aided Wagner's reforms and changed the atmosphere of the opera house. About 1875 all the theaters began to replace candles with gas; the Metropolitan in 1883 was built with a large gas chandelier. A half-darkened auditorium became the rule. Soon after, electric lights, introduced at Covent Garden in 1892 and at the Metropolitan in 1893, made it possible for the first time to extinguish the house lights altogether. The effect of this was far-reaching. Most persons find it unnatural, even difficult, to hold an animated, social conversation in the dark, and the chattering during the performance dwindled to what it is now. This is a benefit of the darkness. A loss is that no one now can follow the libretto. The Italians used to follow all performances in the libretto, even those in Italian, and particularly those of new operas. When Toscanini, for the première at Turin in 1897 of *Tristan und Isolde,* had all the lights turned off, the audience rioted: how were they to know what was going on? And the lights were left half on. But the darkness has made it more difficult for a new opera to win an audience and has been a reason for the ever-narrowing repertory of well-known operas, a phenomenon unknown in any century but this.

In general, the invention of the electric light aided the musical rather than the social audience to dominate the opera house, which helped raise the standards of performance. Artistically it has greatly aided an opera such as *Tristan und Isolde* but probably hurt one like *Il Barbiere di Siviglia*. A good performance of a comedy benefits from the momentum the audience gains in seeing itself laugh. Night-club entertainers with a comic flair play in a full or half light and never in the isolated spotlight; that is for the soulful chanteuse.

The change in social mores allowing a lady to smoke and drink also had an effect on the opera house. Before the turn of the century at Covent Garden there was only one very small refreshment bar and smoking was not allowed in the foyers. This was not a problem because the ladies did not smoke and the men wanted to associate with the ladies who received in their boxes during the intermission. At the Metropolitan there was no refreshment bar, but the inaugural program announced in the smallest type "parties desiring ices can be supplied by the waiter, in corridor." There was no foyer at all on the grand tier floor until 1903, which was also the year the décor of the house was changed from ivory and pinkish orange to its present red and gold. With the introduction of the restaurant and long bar on the grand tier floor new habits developed. The hostess no longer received in her box; she took a table at "Sherry's Metropolitan" and in the intermissions crushed her guests into an undersized restaurant with a kitchen the size of a postage stamp, all miraculously clinging onto the corner of the building. The corner is not even a right angle, and to be able to get a table became more of a badge than to sit in a box. Again it was not all clear gain. The music lovers go out of their minds as society returns late after the curtain has gone up. But opera has never been exactly like a string quartet—four players and an audience with one end in mind.

Another nonmusical influence was the egalitarian effect of democracy and its tax structure. Beginning about 1890 society in London began to loose its grip on the opera house as a new audience infiltrated the balconies and less desirable boxes. Many of these were sober, serious Germans who came to hear Wagner. *Lohengrin* was given every year except one from 1875 to 1905. Nellie Melba, who sang Italian and French opera, observed sadly in her *Melodies and Memories* that when she reopened Covent Garden after World War I, she felt all the old society had disappeared. The change in New York was more gradual but just as clear. In both cities the members of society who were truly interested in music began to play a direct part in opera production; they hired an administrator to work for them and no longer let the building to an impresario. The society that was not interested slowly dropped out. The result was a further emphasis on the music and less on star singers and freak productions.

But this, too, was not all clear gain: money and backing were lost. In 1925 the regular Saturday night performance at Covent Garden, which has its season in the summer, was abolished because of society's new habit of the country weekend. And in 1931 George V, whose favorite opera according to Melba was *Rigoletto,* could not take the Royal Box because of economies in the Civil List. Ironically when the good King died in 1936 and the Court went into mourning with much of London's social season canceled or curtailed, the opera had a sudden burst of popularity. But it was ephemeral, whereas the government's entertainment tax was eternal and a real burden on opera houses. Indirectly the opera houses also felt the income taxes on both the audience and the artists. Also union wage scales appeared and opera expenses soared without any commensurate saving possible: a chorus is a chorus is a chorus.

Out of the confusion and hard times emerged a fascinating document of opera that revealed just what most administrators want most to keep secret to avoid endless suggestions and haggling from the audience. It is a report of the London Opera Syndicate, which put on three seasons of opera at Covent Garden during the twenties. The report concerns the eight-week season of 1925 with a repertory of fifteen operas. Two of these, *Elektra* and *Andrea Chenier,* were uniquely expensive and do not figure in the report. The Syndicate needed to sell 94 per cent of Covent Garden to break even; it sold an average of 78 per cent.

The report includes a tabulation of three columns, which it presents as follows:

1. The order of popularity of the operas, gauged by the average booking per performance.

2. The order of costliness.

3. The order of financial results, beginning with the most profitable (or least unprofitable).

| *1* | *2* | *3* |
|---|---|---|
| Tosca | Rosenkavalier | Tosca |
| Rosenkavalier | Meistersinger | Rigoletto |
| Meistersinger | Walkuere | Butterfly |
| Fedora | Tristan | Lucia |
| Tristan | Lohengrin | Fedora |
| Aida | Fedora | Meistersinger |
| Rigoletto | Aida | Il Barbiere |
| Lucia | Tosca | Tristan |
| Lohengrin | Der Fliegende | Rosenkavalier |
| Il Barbiere | Hollaender | Aida |
| Walkuere | Lucia | Der Fliegende |
| Butterfly | Il Barbiere | Hollaender |
| Der Fliegende | Butterfly | Lohengrin |
| Hollaender | Rigoletto | Walkuere |

The report continues:

"The average loss on the last six operas in column 3 was nearly five times as great as the average loss on the first five in the same column.

"The average booking for the German season was seven and a half per cent better than for the Italian. On the other hand the average cost of the German productions was twenty per cent higher, and as a result the loss on this part of the repertoire was twice as great as on the other.

"The soloists accounted for thirty per cent of the total expenses, the orchestra for twenty-one per cent, and the chorus and ballet fourteen per cent.

"The orchestra for the German operas cost about seventy-five per cent more than for the Italian, the chorus forty per cent more, the soloists very little more.

"The more ambitious operas musically speaking are the most unprofitable."

Consider again what the report states: the average loss on the last six operas, of which five can be called Wagnerian, was nearly FIVE times as great as the loss on the first five, all typical Italian operas. Small wonder that the Wagnerian operas have never entered the repertories of the smaller houses of the world and that after 1945, when governments and citizens were poor and taxes great, even the largest houses pared their Wagner repertory. But there were also other reasons. Wagner's operas, particularly *The Ring, Tristan und Isolde* and *Parsifal,* require powerful voices, and these did not exist. When in the 1959–60 season at the Metropolitan the Tristan scheduled for a performance was ill, he and two others each sang an act. The newspapers in commenting on the performance reported that there were only fifteen tenors in the world who could sing Tristan. Many operagoers would say that there were none. Sometimes this is ascribed to poor diet during the war years in every country but the United States, a reason that American singers thereafter suddenly flooded the world's stages.

Perhaps even more important is that there is only one Bayreuth where the operas are given uncut—which true Wagnerites insist make them seem shorter—and where the intermissions are sufficiently long to rest the tall and the fat who fit so uncomfortably into most operahouse seats. Most important, in the opinion of Ernest Newman, is that most of the other performances given are inferior to those at Bayreuth —so much so that Wagner would have forbidden them. This probably reflects directly the cost of production.

To some extent in the history of opera Wagner must bear the blame for this. He created such awesome, gigantic and inspiring, but unwieldy, masterworks that the average opera house or company cannot handle them. In *The Ring* he created a whole new world, complete in its own terms, as did Michelangelo on the Sistine ceiling. But like that masterpiece *The Ring* can be seen in toto only in the town of its origin; elsewhere it appears only in faint, blurred reproductions.

Since World War II the Wagner fad has come to an abrupt end, which suggests that, quite aside from great singers, the opera audience is looking for something different. When the soprano Birgit Nilsson singlehandedly revived the glories of *Tristan und Isolde* at the Metropolitan in 1959–60, she lured out of retirement all sorts of opera fanatics who came, often miles and at great inconvenice, to hear their favorite work well sung. Most of these good people had one other thing in common: they were over forty. But when the Metropolitan the previous season put on Berg's *Wozzeck* and to its great surprise sold out every performance after the first, who filled the house? Unfortunately only an inexperienced, amateur pollster seems to have asked the question. He went around the house talking to everyone he could and asked why they were there. Over and above the subscribers and standees, the audience—the additional 10 per cent or so that makes a sold-out house—seemed to be a new and different audience. The people were not regular operagoers; they found most operas boring, old-fashioned, poorly staged and with ridiculous librettos. They went mostly to the theater, favoring such playwrights as Miller, Williams, Anouilh and Giraudoux. They had taste; they adored Mozart. *Wozzeck,* so they said, spoke to them. These people were all under forty; their operatic lives came during and after World War II. Is there an operatic revolution in the offing? This is the sort of question that does well over brandy.

Drinking men often say that the present century is more like the eighteenth than the nineteenth, and there may be truth in it, allowing a time lag for the conservatism of opera. In Mozart's time the world was breaking up; the political and social order and even religion were under a philosophical attack that soon came to blows. Men could be and were "wiped out" financially and spiritually. Part of humanity's answer to such times is to laugh, and Mozart did this brilliantly in all his operas. In the nineteenth century the world stabilized again. No banks failed much. The Crimean and Franco-Prussian wars were upsetting, but more to pride than to life or spirit, and people worried about themselves, their pride and their salvation. In most of Wagner's operas redemption and salvation are important themes. Today the young operagoer jocularly understates his view of the world with the remark: "Salvation! I've got to provide for the children first." This may be part of the appeal of *Wozzeck;* it concerns survival rather than salvation. It may explain the greatly increased popularity of Mozart's *Così fan tutte,* with its laughter at the conventions of life.

It is worth a trip to the opera house these days to look at the audience and wonder who they are, why they come, how social patterns are changing, where the real power lies, and what *they* want. Does any of it make sense—all that noise and screeching? And what's going to happen next?

PART TWO

# Glossary

---

"I had always imagined that Cliché was a suburb of Paris, until I discovered it to be a street in Oxford."

*PHILIP GUEDALLA*

(*Some Historians.*)

HECTOR BERLIOZ, AFTER GUSTAVE DORÉ

# A GLOSSARY OF OPERATIC TERMS AND MISCELLANEA

The symbols and abbreviations used are mostly self-explanatory or familiar.

Languages are abbreviated thus: Fr. for French, Ger. for German, It. for Italian and Sp. for Spanish; others, where occurring, are spelt out.

Names of operas (and only names of operas), whether discussed elsewhere or not, are printed in italics.

Terms consisting of two or more words are entered as though spelt as one. Thus, A CAPPELLA is entered as though spelt ACAPPELLA. Proper names are listed by last names.

"q.v." is short for the Latin "quod vide," which means "which see" and signifies that there is an entry in the Glossary under the word immediately preceding the symbol.

"i.e." is short for the Latin "id est," which means "that is (to say)."

"e.g." is short for the Latin "exempli gratia," which means "for instance," i.e. one example out of many.

"Lit." is short for "literally."

*"See"* signifies that there is related information to be found in the Glossary or as indicated elsewhere under the word or chapter immediately following the symbol.

Many other words and terms are defined elsewhere in the book and may be discovered by referring to the Index.


**Absolute Pitch**—An ability possessed by some to recognize or sing any given note, i.e., a sound of so many vibrations a second. It is a feat of memory and can be learned although, of course, most musicians have it to some degree naturally. Wagner, however, lacked it; Mozart had it.

**A Cappella**—(It.) A direction that a choral work is to be sung unaccompanied. "Cappella" means "chapel," and the direction is therefore "as in the chapel" or "in the church style." The term may originate in the tradition of the Sistine Chapel, for which, it is said, no instrumentalists have ever been engaged. A cappella singing in opera is rare, but examples are Don José's entrance in Act II of *Carmen,* the requiem for Valentin in Act IV of *Faust,* and the "Gran Dio" chorus in the Act I finale of *Macbeth.* For the orchestra to have to sound the note for the latter, generally on the horns, is an indictment of the singers' ability to stay on pitch or of the musical director's taste. *Tannhaeuser,* with the shepherd and the pilgrims, has more a cappella singing than most operas.

**Adagio**—(It.) Lit., "at your ease" or "leisurely." A direction for the tempo (q.v.) of a piece, e.g., the Prelude to Act I of *La Traviata,* the Prelude to Act I of *Lohengrin* and Lohengrin's farewell to the swan.

**Ad Lib**—(Latin.) A contraction of "ad libitum," or "at will." A direction allowing the performer, according to the context, to (1) vary the rhythm; (2) drop out or include the part of some voice or instrument; (3) drop out or include some part of the music, such as a repeat or a cadenza; and (4) insert a cadenza at the place indicated.

**Alfresco**—(It.) Lit., to (in) the fresh (air). Any performance is alfresco when given out-of-doors.

**Allegro**—(It.) Lit., "Cheerful," i.e., lively, bright. A direction for the tempo (q.v.) of a piece, e.g., the Anvil Chorus or "Di quella pira" in *Il Trovatore,* "Madamina" in *Don Giovanni,* or the Toreador Song in *Carmen,* which is directed to be taken allegro moderato.

**Amphora**—A Greek jug. A term used by the critic Ernest Newman to describe certain tenors. He liked to quote the definition given in the classical dictionaries: "A two-handled, big-bellied vessel, usually of clay, with a longish or shortish neck and a mouth proportioned to the size, sometimes resting firmly on a foot, but often ending in a blunt point . . ."

**Andante**—(It.) Lit., "going," but slowly rather than fast. A direction for the tempo (q.v.) of a piece, e.g., "La ci darem la mano" in *Don Giovanni,* "Voi che sapete" in *Le Nozze di Figaro,* the Miserere in *Il Trovatore,* or the fourth-act quartet in *Rigoletto.*

**Aria**—(It.) The aria used to be a definite form of vocal solo with strict rules for its composition. In Handel's time there were as many as fifteen types of arias. This sort of classification has disappeared, with the possible exception of an "aria buffa," a comic aria. Today an aria is any lyrical vocal solo with instrumental accompaniment that is extended enough to be a piece in itself. *See* Chap. II, "Melody, Aria and Recitative."

**Arietta**—(It.) A short and simple aria. The term is used more by critics than composers, who are more likely to call the number a song or canzonetta, e.g., "Le Veau d'or" in Act II of *Faust*. Often they are buried in larger ensembles, such as Manrico's song from the tower in the Miserere in Act IV of *Il Trovatore*. "The Evening Star" in *Tannhaeuser* is an arietta, although Wagner would flinch at the Italian term.

**Arioso**—(It.) As a type of vocal piece it falls between recitative and aria. It usually is a short, melodic phrase ending recitative, but it can be any lyric strain that is not developed into an aria. As a style of singing it is rather declamatory. There is an example in Gluck's *Orfeo* beginning nine measures after the end of "Che faro," the interval between being eight bars of recitative. Another is Violetta's impassioned farewell to Alfredo in Act II Scene 1, of *La Traviata*.

**A Tempo**—(It.) A direction to resume the original tempo (q.v.) of a piece after it has been temporarily varied.

**Attack**—The beginning of a note or piece by a performer. It should be prompt and decisive. The fainthearted "slip in."

**Ave Maria**—(Latin.) Lit., "Hail, Mary . . ." A prayer used in the Roman Catholic Church and directed to the Virgin. The most famous operatic setting of it is Desdemona's prayer in Verdi's *Otello*.

**Baccelli, Giovanna Zanerini** (?–1801)—A ballerina who made a great career in London and at the Paris Opera. In London when she danced in a benefit in 1781, the House of Commons adjourned so members could attend. In Paris where she was the mistress of the Third Duke of Dorset, the British Ambassador, she delighted the public by appearing regularly after he was made a Knight of the Garter with a blue ribbon on her forehead inscribed *"Honi soit qui mal y pense."*

**Ballabile**—(It.) Lit., "danceable." Any piece suitable for dancing. In opera it usually appears in its plural. "ballabili," and means the series of dances in the opera. Verdi wrote five ballabili for the Paris production of *Otello*. In ballet terminology it applies only to dances executed by the chorus.

**Ballad Opera**—A form of English opera which flourished for about twelve years, 1728–1740. There was spoken dialogue in the vernacular interspersed with simple songs which were new words set to old, familiar music, i.e., ballads. The most famous was the first: John Gay's

*The Beggar's Opera*. Later English composers imitated Gay's style, but since they composed new music, their operas are not, strictly speaking, "Ballad Operas." The most famous modern opera of this latter kind is Kurt Weill's *Die Dreigroschenoper* (*The Threepenny Opera*) based on John Gay's libretto.

**Band**—The word is used loosely in any of three meanings: (1) any group of players, regardless of types of instruments represented, (2) any group that plays martial music, and (3) any group in which all the instruments are of the same family, i.e., a brass band, a wind band or a string band. *See* ELASTIC BAND.

**Barbershop**—A style of singing, heavy on sentiment and chromatics (q.v.). It is much favored by amateur male quartets and appears occasionally in modern opera as a satiric form.

**Barcarolle**—(Fr.) A song or instrumental imitation of a song in the style of those supposedly sung by Venetian gondoliers. The tempo is ⁶⁄₈ and generally languid and lilting. The most famous operatic barcarolle is Offenbach's in *Les Contes D' Hoffmann*.

**Barrel Organ**—As an instrument it is an automatic organ with pins on a barrel turned by hand to "play" the pipes. It is not a hurdy-gurdy (q.v.). As a style of playing the piano it is rhythmic like boogie-woogie without being so insistent.

**Basso**—(It.) The Italian equivalent of "bass" and frequently used to describe a singer with that range.

**Baton**—(Fr.) A short stick, generally fifteen to twenty-eight inches long and of wood, held by a conductor so that the performers may more easily follow his directions for time and expression. At various times in the past conductors have favored rolled paper, a violin bow, or a staff beat upon the floor. The last may have gone out of fashion after the great Lully's experience with it. He was conducting a Te Deum for the quick recovery of the sick Louis XIV and, in thumping, he hit his foot, which developed an abscess from which he died. Lully composed "Au clair de la lune."

**Bel Canto**—(It.) Lit., "beautiful song." The term is loosely used and today to say that a singer has bel canto qualities or mastered the art of bel canto may mean merely that he is a good singer—beautiful tone, good phrasing, even breath control, a pianissimo, etc. Sometimes it is used to describe a singer who confines himself to lyric rather than dramatic roles. Historically it refers to the art of singing and training for singing that flourished in Italy throughout the seventeenth and eighteenth centuries. The emphasis then was on the voice as an instrument. The difference of approach can be seen in part by a comparison of Donizetti's flutelike mad scene for Lucia in *Lucia di Lammermoor* and Verdi's directions that Lady Macbeth in her mad scene (the sleepwalking scene) in *Macbeth* was not to sing but to gasp, sob and whisper.

**Berceuse**—(Fr.) A cradlesong or lullaby. The most famous operatic berceuse is from *Jocelyn* by Godard. The opera survives only in its aria, which is beautiful.

**Bis**—(Latin.) Lit., "twice." The French use it as an exclamation of applause as English-speaking people use the French word, "encore."

**Blue Note**—The flattened note that is characteristic of jazz. It is generally the third or seventh in the scale.

**Bohemian**—This term for mad, gay artists living on poetry, music and air comes from the mistaken notion at one time prevalent in Europe that the gypsy came from Bohemia. Actually, on evidence of *The Bartered Bride,* the Bohemians are just as interested in good marriages, i.e. doweries, as are any other solid citizens. The term arose only in the years after the French Revolution when the artist's relations to society went through a complete change. Nothing replaced the court or aristocratic patron except the uncultured and unsympathetic state bureaucracy dominated by middle-class business interests. Only those artists who were fantastically successful or were sycophants could survive. The rest, starving, huddled together in their Latin Quarters and protested by wearing outlandish clothes and beards and by joining revolutionary movements, e.g., Wagner, who nearly starved in Paris and fled Dresden only a step ahead of the police after the failure of the 1848 revolution.

**Bolero**—(Sp.) A dance in ¾ time and lively (Ravel's "Bolero" is an exception to the general rule). The dancer usually accompanies himself with castanets. It may be danced by a couple.

**Brass**—A collective name for instruments made of metal and played by blowing through a cup- or funnel-shaped mouthpiece into a column of air. The player's lip, stretched across the mouthpiece, acts as a reed, and by changing the tautness of his lip and the air pressure thereon, the player can change the pitch of the note. On some instruments further notes are possible because of valves, but the principle remains basic. Typical brass are the bugle, trumpet, horn, trombone and tuba. *See* PERCUSSION, STRINGS and WOODWINDS.

**Bravo**—(It.) Lit., "well done." An exclamation of applause. It is especially appropriate at Italian operas. The merely chic never applaud. The cognoscenti make it an opportunity for drawing distinctions: "bravo" for the man, "brava" for the woman and, if they are feeling generous, "bravi" for all the performers.

Pronunciation gives further opportunity for distinction. If feeling Italian or keeping up with them, roll the "r" hard, hit the first syllable and say the word twice swiftly. This is especially charming in ladies. If being homespun, thud both syllables evenly in a flat tone. The singers prefer both ways. Never attempt "bravissimo." This is overboard, and you are revealed a Rube.

**Brindisi**—(It.) Lit., "a toast." A song in which someone's health is drunk; a drinking song. Typical examples occur in Act I of *La Traviata* and in *Cavalleria Rusticana.*

**Brio**—(It.) *See* CON BRIO.

**Buffo**—(It.) Lit., a "whiff" or a "puff." It is used as an adjective meaning "comic." Thus a basso buffo is a bass specializing in comic parts. Opera buffa—comic opera—is the same word. A "buffone" is a comic, a jester. Rigoletto refers to himself as a "buffone."

**Burney, Dr. Charles** (1726–1814)—An Englishman of great charm and learning. He was a friend of Johnson, Reynolds and Garrick. He wrote an invaluable "History of Music" for which, in order to gather facts and form conclusions, he traveled throughout France, Italy, Austria, Germany and the Low Countries, wining, dining and talking to everyone and anyone who knew anything about music. His "History" is still in print. His account of his travels, also still in print, is equally charming and informative.

**Cabaletta**—(It.) The final section of an extended aria or duet that has a cabaletta. It generally is short, quick and brilliant. It was very popular in early nineteenth-century opera. The final section of Elvira's aria, "Ernani involami," in *Ernani* is an example of a conventional cabaletta as distinguished from Violetta's "Sempre libera" in *La Traviata,* which has more dramatic reason and force. "Jumpy" is a good word to describe a cabaletta. Some critics say the word derives from "cavallo," a horse, and that a characteristic of a cabaletta is a fast triplet accompaniment sounding like the hoofbeats of a galloping horse. The word is an invention of the public and critics, and composers never so designated the music. Stravinsky in his score for *The Rake's Progress* (1951) may have been the first composer to use the word.

**Cachucha**—(Sp.) A dance from Andalusia. It is in ¾ time, is danced by a single performer and resembles a bolero (q.v.). Originally the tune was sung with guitar accompaniment.

**Cadenza**—(It.) A brilliant passage in a vocal (or instrumental) solo designed to show off the voice. The word means "cadence" or "close," and originally a cadenza was an ornamental closing of the song which the singer improvised anew each time. Today singers in *Lucia di Lammermoor,* for example, prepare their cadenzas beforehand in order, presumably, to give a greater appearance of spontaneity. Cadenzas are no longer in fashion and occur mostly in the operas of the early nineteenth century or earlier.

**Calliope**—A pipe organ in which the tone is produced by steam rather than by wind under pressure.

**Callithumpian Concert**—*See* CHARIVARI.

**Can Belto**—A pun on bel canto (q.v.). Generally it is said of Italian tenors with ranging top tones and not much else—as, "he sure can belto."

**Can-Can**—A French music-hall dance popular in Paris at the end of the nineteenth century. The most famous operatic can-cans are by Offenbach. The definition of a can-can given by Scholes (q.v.) is intriguing: "A boisterous and latterly indecorous dance, of the quadrille order, dating from about 1840 and then exploited in Paris for the benefit of such British and American visitors as were willing to pay well to be shocked. Its exact nature is unknown to any one connected with this Companion" ("Oxford Companion to Music," ninth edition).

**Canon**—A strict form of musical imitation. A "round" like Frère Jacques is a simple canon. Each voice in turn must repeat exactly the subject or tune introduced by the first voice. A famous and very apt canon occurs just before the duel in Tchaikovsky's *Eugene Onegin* as a sort of musical counterpart to the Dueling Code by which Lensky and Onegin are trapped. Another, equally famous, occurs in Act I of *Fidelio.*

**Cantata**—(It.) A vocal piece on a religious subject. It generally is lyrical rather than dramatic and is performed without action or scenery. In early days cantatas were often very short. Today they frequently are long enough to be short oratorios. Originally the word meant any piece that was sung as opposed to being played (sonata). Tosca sings a cantata off stage before Queen Caroline early in Act II of *Tosca*.

**Carmagnole**—(Fr.) A catchy song and dance popular during the Reign of Terror in Paris. It is said to have been sung particularly often at executions. Giordano uses it in Act III of *Andrea Chenier*.

**Cavatina**—(It.) A short song of any sort. Really another term for arietta. Mozart in *Le Nozze di Figaro* called Figaro's first aria, "Se vuol ballare," a cavatina. Others are the Countess' first aria, "Porgi Amor," in Act II and Barbarina's aria in Act IV.

**Cecilia, Saint**—For Christians, the traditional patron saint of music. Her day is November 22. Throughout the seventeenth, eighteenth and nineteenth centuries, musicians celebrated her and gave her name to choral societies, music halls and clubs. Then research, in spite of everyone's best endeavors, began to indicate that she had no connection with music at all. (This was after St. Paul's Cathedral, London, accepted a stained glass window memorializing her role in music.) Musicians tend to blame artists for the mistake, as the latter in their paintings were always thrusting musical instruments into the Saint's hands. She was a Sicilian and was martyred about 176 A.D.

**Chaconne**—An old Spanish dance. It is usually in ¾ time, slow and dignified. French opera in the early eighteenth century was apt to end with a Chaconne, e.g., Gluck's *Orfeo* (1762).

**Chamber Opera**—Any opera requiring only a small cast—often without any chorus—and a small orchestra. Britten's *The Turn of the Screw* (1954) is typical with a cast of seven, no chorus, and a thirteen-man orchestra playing eighteen instruments. Just across some indefinable line, and regular opera, is R. Strauss' *Ariadne auf Naxos* with a cast of fifteen or more, depending on how the roles are doubled, and an orchestra of about thirty-five playing seventeen instruments. Chamber opera has had a vogue recently because of the high cost of producing opera.

**Charivari**—(Fr.) Violent music—noise—made with all sorts of instruments. Sometimes a charivari is given to a person currently in public disfavor as a mock serenade. Every country has some term for it. In the U.S.A. it is "shivaree" and is given to a newly married couple on their wedding night. It is also called "callithumpian concert," "katzenmusik" and "scampanata" in the U.S.A., Germany and Italy, respectively.

**Chromatics**—On a piano there are thirteen notes from middle C to and including the C next above or below. Eight of these are white notes and form the diatonic scale in the key of C. This is the scale a stockbroker or any nonmusician will finally sing if put under great pressure. It is the most familiar scale, and music from about 1600 to 1850 restricted itself almost exclusively to those eight fundamental notes. Caution: only in the key of C are the eight notes all white; in other keys the scale is still composed of eight notes, but some of these will be black. Always there will be five notes not in the scale as sung, i.e., the diatonic scale. To the nonmusician they sound like "in-between" notes; they are the chromatics. Wagner was one of the first to use them extensively, particularly in *Tristan und Isolde,* and their use loosens the feeling of firmness of rigidity that arises from sticking to the fundamental eight notes. It also contributes greatly to the feeling in *Tristan* of being awash in a sea of sound, endlessly rising and falling. *See* SCALE and KEY.

**Clashpans**—An old name for cymbals.

**Coda**—(It.) Lit., "tail." A term describing any passage, whether long or short, added to the end of a song or orchestral piece to give it a greater feeling of finality. It is usually brilliant and fast; often it is based on a foregoing theme.

**Coloratura**—Vocal runs, trills, and other ornaments added to make the effect of the passage more brilliant and to show off the singer's technique. A coloratura soprano is one who specializes in this style. *See* Chap. III, "The Operatic Voice as an Artistic Instrument," p. 25. The word is fake Italian but universally used.

**Coltello**—(It.) Lit., "knife." Enthusiastic Italians used to applaud the castrati (q.v.) by crying out, "Eviva il coltello"—"Hurrah for the knife."

**Con Brio**—(It.) Lit., "with spirit." A direction to singers or a description of a style of singing. Verdi directed the tenor in *Rigoletto* to sing "la donna è mobile" con brio. As a description of a particular singer or style it means a voice bright and full of life.

**Comprimario, -a**—(It.) In opera, a term used to describe a role of importance though not a leading role, or to describe the singer who specializes in such roles. Martha in *Faust,* Goro in *Butterfly* and Mime in *Das Rheingold* are typical comprimario roles with difficult cues and requiring excellent timing and pitch; hence they are often assigned to veteran but fading singers.

**Cork Opera**—A minstrel show—because burnt cork is used to blacken the face.

**Cortège**—(Fr.) Lit., "procession"; and the music suitable thereto is generally a rather slow, stately march (q.v.). It is not necessarily a funeral procession nor, in spite of journalistic use, available only to dead heads of state and military heroes. Delibes in his ballet "Sylvia" has a grand "Marche et Cortège de Bacchus" and a cortege of sailors and workers.

**Countertenor**—A very high, male voice, not falsetto. It has a peculiar quality—a "hollow" sound, some think. Its range is a fifth higher than a tenor's or similar to an alto. It is very rare. Alfred Deller, an English countertenor, for example, discovered that he could not find any teacher to instruct him as none knew enough about the voice.

**Couplet**—(Fr.) A stanza of a poem for which the music repeats for each stanza, e.g., the Toreador Song in Act II of *Carmen,* which is sometimes called the Couplets.

**Cravatentenor**—(Ger.) A tenor who sings as though his necktie were too tight.

**Crescendo**—(It.) Increasing, swelling in loudness. Rossini employed it as a device so often he was called by some "Signor Crescendo." Probably the longest crescendo occurs in Ravel's "Bolero."

**Cymbals**—Metal platters that are struck either together or with an instrument. They appeared in Western music in the early nineteenth century. The construction of the best cymbals is one of the well-guarded secrets of the world. The composition of the metal is known only to a Turkish family, Zildjian, which has been making cymbals for generations. Recently a branch of it set up business in the U.S.A.

**Czardas**—(Hungarian). A national dance, alternating between fiery passion and languid melancholy. The word has no connection or association with the Russian "czar" but is derived from the Hungarian word "tcharda," meaning tavern.

**Da Capo**—(It.) Lit., "from the head." A direction in a piece for the performer to start again from the beginning. Thus in a typical da capo aria the last section, usually the third, is a repetition of the first, and the score shows only the first two and a da capo sign, D.C.

**Dead March**—A march for funerals. The most famous is Handel's from his oratorio "Saul." The British Royal Marine Corps of Drums and the U. S. Marine Drum and Bugle Corps strike a tempo of about seventy steps a minute. The U. S. Army bands vary between sixty and eighty, and the French "Marche de la Légion Étrangère" is paced between seventy and eighty. The French proverbially march faster than the British. *See* MARCH.

**Décor**—(Fr.) Generally used to mean only the scenery; but sometimes it also includes the stage direction.

**Decrescendo**—(It.) Decreasing, lessening the loudness. "Diminuendo" means the same. Both are opposites of crescendo (q.v.).

**Diatonic**—(Read SCALES first). This is the most common of all scales. On the piano, starting at middle C, the scale consists of the eight white notes from C to the next C above. The distinctive feature of the scale lies in the ratios between the fourth note, E, and the first, C, and the fifth note, F, and C. The ratio of a "fourth" is 4:3; the ratio of a "fifth" is 3:2. These ratios have been particularly pleasing to the human ear, and the scale is built around them. Any song in the diatonic key (q.v.) of C is apt to use the notes C, F and E most frequently. *See* WHOLE-TONE SCALE and CHROMATICS.

**Dies Irae**—(Latin.) Lit., "Days of Wrath." The second part of the Mass for the Dead (Requiem, q.v.). The words are by Thomas of Celano, a friend of St. Francis of Assisi.The plainsong tune is by an unknown composer. It has been used by many later composers for its dramatic connotation, e.g., Saint Saens, "Danse Macabre." Others have written new music, e.g., Verdi, "Requiem."

**Diminuendo**—(It.) *See* DECRESCENDO.

**Ditty**—A short, simple song. Some say the word derives from the French "dite," a thing spoken, and is in the tradition of the French Opéra-Comique style of spoken dialogue. Hence, in a ditty the melody is apt to be simple and the words important, spoken as much as sung.

**Diva**—(It.) Goddess. A term applied to a reigning soprano. If there are several, each will consider herself to be the "prima diva" of the company or the season.

**Do**—(It.) The name given by Italians and many others to middle C on the piano. The entire scale, starting with C or Do, is:

| | | |
|---|---|---|
| C | Do | doe |
| D | Re | ray |
| E | Mi | me |
| F | Fa | fah |
| G | Sol | soul |
| A | La | lah |
| B | Ti | tee |
| C | Do | doe |

**Doctor of Music**—The highest academic degree awarded in England and the United States for work in music. Usual abbreviations are D.Mus., Mus.D. or Mus.Doc.

**Elastic Band**—This is the nub of a tired pun involving any performer who is out of time and tune with the orchestra. It can be put any number of ways, e.g., "He thinks the orchestra is an elastic band."

**Encore**—(Fr.) Lit., "again." Since about 1700 English audiences have expressed approval of a performance by calling "encore." Strictly, the term probably is a request to repeat the work just completed. It has come to mean, however, just "more of the same" or even just "something more." It also has come to mean the work performed in answer to the cry. Thus, "as an encore, she sang . . ." Before 1700 the English cried "altra volta" or "ancora," both Italian phrases.

**Entr'acte**—(Fr.) Lit., "between the acts." Originally it was a piece of music played between the acts of a play or opera. Later it came to mean, also, the period between the acts, i.e., the intermission.

**Euterpe**—In Greek mythology there were nine Muses. Euterpe was the Muse of lyric poetry and, because the poems were frequently sung, she was also, but only incidentally, the Muse of music, which had no patroness of its own. However much they may say they do not care, this lack of recognition on Olympus secretly irritates musicians. For the musicians' bad luck with their Christian patroness, *See* CECILIA, SAINT.

**Evirato**—(It.) Lit., "unmanned." Another term for castrato; the plural is "evirati." *See* Chap. V, "The Castrati."

**Fa**—(It.) *See* Do.

**Fabliau**—(Fr.) Lit., "a fable." A troubadour ballad form used for stories rather than love songs. Massenet wrote a rather imperfect one for Manon to sing as an alternative to a Gavotte (q.v.) in Act III of *Manon*.

**Fandango**—(Sp.) A lively dance in triple time (q.v.). Generally it is danced by one couple, accompanied by castanets, tambourine and guitar, with other instruments ad lib (q.v.). One characteristic is the sudden stop, at which the dancers have to hold their positions until the music resumes. Mozart has a fandango in Act III of *Le Nozze di Figaro*. Sometimes the dance alternates with vocal couplets (q.v.).

**Fanfare**—A fancy root-a-toot-toot on the trumpets. It is said to derive from a Spanish word "fanfarria" meaning "noisy arrogance." A "flourish" is an Elizabethan English word meaning the same thing. Composers sometimes write fanfares for instruments other than trumpets. In *Tannhaeuser*, Act I, Wagner has a series of horn calls, or a fanfare for horns, announce the Landgrave, and Massenet in Act III of *Manon* has what amounts to a fanfare for the voice for Manon as she promenades on the Cours-la-Reine.

**Farandole**—A street dance of Southern France and the Basque Country. The dancers form a line holding hands. Then the leader, always a bachelor, winds the chain in and around and about the town. It is not very adaptable to opera, but Gounod has one in *Mireille* and Bizet has one in his incidental music for *L'Arlésienne*. It is in lively, triple time. "Grove's" (q.v.) reports, "The Farandole has occasionally been used for less innocent purposes than that of a mere dance: in 1815 General Ramel was murdered at Toulouse by the infuriated populace, who made use of their national dance to surround and butcher him."

**Farinelli** (1705–82)—Probably the most famous singer of all time. He was a castrato, male soprano. For details of his extraordinary career, *See* Chap. V, "The Castrati."

**Fiasco**—(It.) A failure, a flop. Two of the most famous operatic fiascos were the premières of *La Traviata* and *Madama Butterfly*. The word arrives at its meaning through a bit of glass history. A fiasco is the bulb-shaped Italian wine bottle set in a straw basket. Originally these were odd-shaped because of some defect in the blowing. Hence the word's secondary meaning of a failure. Its opposite is furore (q.v.). If a première was a disaster, Rossini would send his mother a picture of a fiasco without any comment.

**Fioritura**—(It.) The Italian word for coloratura (q.v.). Lit., it means "flowering" and refers to the embellishments singers added to arias. It frequently appears in plural form, "fioriture."

**Flat**—To sing flat is to be always a little bit under the note. More than a little is not singing.

**Flourish**—*See* FANFARE.

**Forlana**—(It.) Sometimes, furlana. An old Italian dance. It is supposed to be particularly popular among gondoliers. It is lively and in triple time (q.v.). Ponchielli has one in the first act finale of *La Gioconda.*

**Forte, Fortissimo**—(It.) Lit., "strong," "most strong." It is a direction to the performer to play loud or most loudly. It is written "f" and "ff." Mezzo forte, written "mf," is a direction to play or sing "half loud." The opposite of f. is piano (q.v.). *See* Più.

**Fugue**—It is a form of vocal or instrumental composition. It begins like a "round" but then becomes much more complicated as it introduces new themes and develops old ones. Each voice starts or "enters" in succession with the same phrase; then—roughly speaking—comes a "development" section in which first one voice then another is prominent; and at the end all join in a grand statement of the original phrase or, depending on the mood of the piece, trail away to a single voice. It is a natural form for an opera finale as it winds all the parts together into a last chorus. Verdi used it in *Macbeth* and *Falstaff* as a finale, and Wagner used it to close Act II of *Die Meistersinger.* Musicologists talk about the subject, the answer, the development and the countersubject, but most persons only can hear the first theme and recognize it again at the end, while losing it completely in the middle.

**Furiant**—A Bohemian dance in ¾ time, very fast and with changing rhythm. It has no connection with the word "fury." Smetana has one in *The Bartered Bride.*

**Furore**—(It.) Lit., "fury" or "frenzy." A term used to describe the frantic cheering at a success or the work itself. It is the opposite of fiasco (q.v.).

**Galop**—A very quick, spirited dance in ¾ time. It was originally German. One characteristic was a constant change of step or hop. The galops most frequently played today are by Offenbach.

**Gavotte**—(Fr.) An old French dance form, lively but dignified. Beginning with Louis XIV, it was popular at the French Court. One characteristic was that the dancers lifted their feet rather than shuffled them. Puccini uses one as a background to Act II in *Tosca,* where an offstage orchestra is playing at the reception for Queen Caroline. Massenet has Manon sing one in Act III of *Manon,* and Giordano has the aristocrats dance one in Act I of *Andrea Chenier.*

**Gibus**—An opera hat; from the name of the inventor in Paris in the nineteenth century. It also sometimes appears as an adjective as "a gibus-hat." Pronounced "shjee.boo." There is a tempest in a thimble about when to wear it. The London rule seems to be only with black tie; the New York rule, only with white tie. The opera hat, which collapses, is made of nonshiny silk. There is also a "silk top hat," which is made of shiny silk, and to wear this to the opera with black or white tie is quite, quite wrong.

**Giraffe**—An old-style upright grand piano in which the strings, instead of stretching out horizontally from the keyboard, rise vertically.

**Glockenspiel**—(Ger.) Lit., "chime-bells." A musical instrument of flat, steel bars struck with a hammer. It can be laid out flat like a xylophone (wood bars) or be mounted, as in bands, on a lyre. It is

Papageno's instrument in *Die Zauberfloete,* but in Mozart's time there were actual bells, not bars. It is scored for dances in *Die Meistersinger, Prince Igor,* and *La Gioconda.*

**Grand Opera**—An imprecise term most often used to refer to nineteenth-century French opera, Meyerbeer especially, which favored extravagant gestures, strong situations and huge ensemble scenes.

**Green Room**—A name given to a room backstage in which the performers can receive and entertain friends and admirers before and after the performance. In the seventeenth and eighteenth centuries the rooms were attractively decorated, and there might be several in one theater assigned to the performers according to salary. Today such rooms are rare and performers receive in their dressing rooms or the manager's office, so that the term is now applied to any room that is the scene of adulation or commiseration after a performance. The Glyndebourne Opera House, however, has a very fine green room. The term was originally theatrical and appeared first in London c. 1670. No one knows its exact origin. Presumably the first such room was decorated in green. Green-room gossip is stage gossip.

**Grove's**—This is the shorthand title of "Grove's Dictionary of Music and Musicians" which in its fifth edition, published by Macmillan & Co. Ltd. in 1954, ran to nine volumes. It is the most complete reference work in English on music. As in the encyclopedias the articles are written by contributors and vary in style and accuracy, but the standard is high. It is "Grove's" because the first edition in 1878 was planned and edited by Sir George Grove. *See* THOMPSON, OSCAR, and SCHOLES, PERCY.

**Habanera**—(Sp.) It was originally an African dance, which went to Cuba (Havana-Habana) and from there to Spain, where it became very popular. The most famous operatic habanera is in *Carmen,* Act I. It is generally accompanied by a song and danced by two dancers of opposing sex. Thus when Carmen sings and dances it alone, it is hard for the men not to join her. "Grove's" (q.v.) reports "The dance, if well done, can be extremely graceful, but even in its most classic form is bound to be indecent, vividly recalling the 'danse du ventre' of the Algerian café."

**Hanway, Jonas** (1712–86)—Said to have been the first man in London to make a practice of carrying an umbrella in the streets. He was a traveler and had thrilling adventures in Persia. *See* MORNINGTON, EARL OF.

**Head Voice**—An imprecise term used by singers to differentiate between those notes which, when sung, seem to vibrate more in the head than the chest. It is always the top of the singer's range. *See* Chap. IV, "The Operatic Voice as a Mechanical Instrument," p. 40.

**Hemidemisemiquaver**—The name for a "sixty-fourth" note in writing music. It is the very, very shortest note in musical notation that has an entity of its own. It is the quickest note. Hence the *New York Times* employs it as a title of a section of one-sentence announcements and reviews of musical events.

**Hurdy-Gurdy**—A term commonly but mistakenly applied to any instrument turned by a handle. A true hurdy-gurdy is a kind of mechanical violin. One hand turns a rosined wheel that is set in the instrument near the bridge and that rubs on the strings from underneath; this acts as a bow. The other hand, by playing a keyboard alongside the neck of the violin, changes the length of the strings. The instrument had a vogue in French high society about 1750. In the next century it became a favorite of street musicians, and when they abandoned it for the barrel organ (q.v.), they or their public apparently transferred the old name to the new instrument. Donizetti wrote hurdy-gurdy accompaniments for two Savoyard songs in *Linda di Chamounix* (1842).

**Ilgenfritz, McNair**—A Philadelphian, opera lover and amateur composer who died in the early 1950's with the delightful idea of trying to seduce the Metropolitan from beyond the grave. He bequeathed to it a rumored $150,000 if it would produce one of his operas. There was a one-act work that might have cost about a fifth of the bequest. But the Metropolitan turned it down—which really proves nothing about the Metropolitan's virtue.

**Imbroglio**—(It.) Lit., "mix-up," "confusion." In opera it defines a situation in which instruments and voices are scored to produce confusion. Two examples are the ballroom scene in *Don Giovanni* and the street fight in *Die Meistersinger*.

**Impresario**—(It.) From "impresa" meaning "undertaking." Generally, anyone who undertakes or manages a business involving contracts with artists. More specifically, the director of a traveling ballet or opera company.

**Instrumentation**—The study or knowledge of what is practical or sounds well in writing for individual instruments. It is different from orchestration (q.v.). Berlioz's famous "Treatise on Instrumentation" is frequently incorrectly stated to be on orchestration.

**Intendant**—The administrative director of an opera house or theater in German-speaking countries, although the word seems originally to have been French.

**Intermezzo**—(It.) Lit., "in the middle." In opera it is an instrumental passage indicating the passing of time. The most famous example occurs in *Cavalleria Rusticana* when the villagers are all in church. Others, more often played as a prelude to an act, are Puccini's in *Manon Lescaut* and Leoncavallo's in *I Pagliacci*.

**Janissary Music**—A term for the effect produced by heavy use of a triangle, cymbal and base drum, all of which were originally Turkish instruments used by the Janissaries, the Sultan's bodyguard. Mozart's overture to *Die Entfuehrung aus dem Serail* is an example.

**Katzenmusik**—(Ger.) Lit., "cat music." *See* CHARIVARI.

**Keen**—An Irish funeral song accompanied by wailing. Also, to mourn thus.

**Key**—The scale is the basis of traditional music. There are many kinds of scales, but the most familiar is one of eight notes, called the diatonic scale. (*See* TWELVE-TONE and CHROMATICS.) A scale can be in different keys depending on the note on which it starts. The diatonic scale in the key of C begins on any C on the piano and runs on the white notes to the next C. If it began on D, in order to have the same relation between the notes as in the key of C and thus to remain a diatonic scale, it would have to use two black notes. It then is the diatonic scale in the key of D, and the black notes to be used are indicated by sharp signs (♯) at the beginning of each line of music. This is called the key signature.

**La**—(It.) *See* DO.

**Lablache, Luigi** (1794–1858)—One of the most famous operatic bassos of all time. As a young boy he ran away from the Neapolitan Conservatory five times to join opera companies but was always dragged back. After the fifth time the Conservatory built a theater. Lablache was tall, handsome and in his later years enormously fat. He was one of the thirty-two torchbearers at Beethoven's funeral. He was born and died in Naples. He had an international career and was particularly popular in London, where he instructed Queen Victoria in singing. For an account of his breath control, see Chap. IV, "The Operatic Voice as a Mechanical Instrument," p. 34.

**La Donna Im-mobile**—A hoary bilingual pun on Verdi's "la donna è mobile" invariably made by Anglo-Saxons who speak no Italian and are at their first Wagner opera.

**La Marseillaise**—The national anthem of France by popular acclaim rather than legislative fiat. It was written by Rouget de Lisle in 1792 at Strasbourg before the Reign of Terror and when France was being threatened by Austria. It became very popular in Marseille and volunteer troops from that city took it to Paris where it became known as "La Marseillaise"—"the thing those fellows up from Marseille are always singing." These same volunteer troops took part in the sack of the Tuileries Palace, and the song became associated with the Republicans. Actually its author was a Royalist who was later imprisoned and almost executed. In his original version De Lisle included a symphonic passage that is always omitted. The song appears in several operas—perhaps most naturally in Act IV of *Andrea Chenier.*

**Largo**—(It.) Lit., "broad." A direction to play or sing in a broad, stately style. Often this means slowly, but the direction itself is for style, not pace—although this is increasingly less true. The most famous "Largo" is Handel's. Few seem to realize that it is not an instrumental piece but an aria, "Ombra mai fu," from the opera *Serse,* in which the singer merely thanks a tree for providing him with shade. Caruso made a splendid recording of it. It is usually taken too slowly. Verdi directs the Count di Luna's aria, "Il balen," in Act II Scene 2 of *Il Trovatore* to be sung largo; and Wagner directs the march to which Elsa first appears on her way to the church in Act II of *Lohengrin* to be played "largo e solenne."

**Legato**—(It.) Lit., "tied" or "connected." A direction to sing or play so that the voice or instrument moves smoothly from one note to the next, not necessarily its neighbor. Sometimes it is used as an adjective, i.e. "a legato style." Its opposite is staccato (q.v.).

**Leitmotiv**—(Ger.) Lit., "leading theme." A term invented by a German critic to describe a short phrase of notes or harmony associated with a particular character in Wagner's operas. Actually the musical theory of motive had been used before Wagner but not so extensively or as a system.

**Leotard**—The skintight practice garment that is almost the badge of the dancer. It may also be the foundation for a costume. The name is derived from that of Jules Leotard, a famous French trapeze artist of the nineteenth century.

**Libretto**—(It.) Lit., "little book." The words or the text of an opera or oratorio.

**Lied**—(Ger.) A song. The plural is Lieder. In *Die Meistersinger* the Preislied is the Prize (-winning) Song.

**Longueurs**—(Fr.) Lit., "the long places," i.e. the dull spots in an opera.

**Maestri Sostitutti**—(It.) Lit., "substitute conductors"; in the United States called "assistant conductors." In the opera house they are the work horses of the musical staff, leading the offstage chorus or band and giving cues or the pitch to some singer onstage. At the Metropolitan seven are needed in the first act of *Tosca* to cue in the bells, the canon, entering chorus, and singers. The job is not easy. The offstage chorus must sing slightly sharp (q.v.) and ahead of the beat for its sound to reach the audience on pitch and in time.

**Maestro**—(It.) Lit., "master." One who is learned or skilled in any art or science. It is used as a courtesy title for musicians.

**March**—Music for the troops, generally in ¾ time. Originally the word referred simply to the drum rhythm. The U. S. Army and Marine Corps bands march at 120 steps to the minute; the British Army at 108; the French Army at 120 for the infantry and 144–50 for the "Chasseurs." Marches occur throughout opera and next to the waltz (q.v.) are probably the most frequently used rhythm. The most extended and probably the most famous is the triumphal march in Act II of *Aida. See* DEAD MARCH.

**Mario** (1810–83)—One of most famous tenors of all time. His voice seems to have been very sweet and only moderately trained. But he was exceedingly handsome and his costumes were always dazzling. He favored tights as he considered he had good-looking legs. He is known only by his given name, Mario, because being a noble and the son of a famous general he did not dare sign his family name to anything so demeaning as a contract; thus, he signed only "Mario." The family name of which he was so solicitous was Candia. His other given names were Giovanni and Matteo.

**Mass**—(Latin, Missa; It., Messa; Fr. and Ger., Messe.) Some say the word is derived from the phrase, "Ite, missa est (ecclesia)"— "Depart, the congregation is dismissed." This is said in the Roman Catholic Church to those persons not permitted to take part in the communion service. The Mass itself takes place during the consecration of the elements in the communion service. The divisions of the musical mass are Kyrie, Gloria, Credo, Sanctus and Agnus Dei. These are the pàrts of the communion service that remain constant throughout the entire church year.

**Mazurka**—A Polish dance. It is generally danced by four, eight or twelve couples. It has strong accents—the men frequently stamp or click their heels—and pride of bearing is important.

**Meistersinger**—(Ger.) The word is both singular and plural. In Germany some artisans formed guilds in various cities to preserve and continue the art of song. As such they were successors of the Minnesinger (q.v.) but unlike them were not nobles. The rules of the Meistersinger were set out in a "Tabulatur." Wagner in *Die Meistersinger* has one of the Meistersinger explain the rules. The songs were mostly on biblical subjects. Critics have characterized the melodies as "uninspired." The guilds originated about the fourteenth century in Mainz, flourished throughout the fifteenth and sixteenth centuries and declined thereafter. The last one became defunct in 1839 in Ulm. The most famous Meistersinger, even without Wagner's opera, was Hans Sachs of Nuernberg (1494–1576), who wrote some five thousand songs.

**Melba, Nellie** (1861–1931)—A famous Australian soprano and one of the first Dames of the British Empire. Her maiden name was Mitchell. She created her stage name out of Melbourne near which she was born. In her memoirs she describes the origin of Peach Melba. One day at the turn of the century, when Edward VII was still King, she was lunching alone at the Savoy Hotel in London. She was debating what to have for dessert when there arrived "a little silver dish which was uncovered before me with a message that Mr. Escoffier [the great French Chef] had prepared it specially for me." She tasted, was delighted, and inquired the name of the dessert. Word came back that it had no name but that Mr. Escoffier would like to honor her by christening it "Pêche Melba." She accepted. All this was in the lifetime of many but two World Wars ago. Escoffier was such a great chef that gourmet clubs still have Escoffier dinners as something very extra special.

**Melodrama**—In opera, melodrama means speaking against a musical background. Recitative is sung. Beethoven's grave-digging scene in *Fidelio* is an example; another is where Violetta reads the letter aloud in the last act of *La Traviata*. Technically, where one person speaks it is "monodrama"; where two, "duodrama."

**Messa di Voce**—(It.) Lit., the "placing of the voice." The term means, however, the art of increasing and decreasing the loudness of a note. It must not be confused with "mezza voce" (q.v.).

**Metastasio** (1698–1782)—He is the greatest librettist—if numbers be all—as some of his librettos were set sixty or seventy times, and some composers even used one libretto twice. He was the court poet in Vienna. He started life as a grocer's son. When he was eleven, he stood on the street corner and improvised verses. A rich man heard him and was so impressed that he adopted the boy and had him educated. Later the old man left his protégé a fortune. Metastasio's next sponsor was a singer called "La Romanina." His first opera text was for her. She was older than he, and when she died, she bequeathed her fortune to him. But he renounced the bequest in favor of her husband.

**Mezza Voce**—(It.) Lit., "half voice." A direction to sing quietly. Sometimes used as "he has a good mezza voce."

**Mi**—(It.) *See* Do.

**Mime**—Acting without speech. When it is done to music, it almost inevitably becomes ballet. Pantomime, by adding the Greek prefix "pan," meaning "all," should mean that the entire performance is mimed, but people and critics sometimes use it incorrectly to refer to a phrase or small section of the performance.

**Minnesinger**—(Ger.) The word is both singular and plural. The Minnesinger were the German equivalent of the troubadours of the twelfth and thirteenth centuries in the Mediterranean countries. They were always nobles and were distinguished from their Latin colleagues by a more chaste conception of love. It is said that only a German like Tannhaeuser would have preferred Elisabeth to Venus. Wagner's opera *Tannhaeuser* is an example of the sort of grand poetical contests the Minnesinger held.

**Minuet**—Originally a French dance form it became popular all over Europe and England in the eighteenth century. It is in ¾ time. It is in contrasting sections: the first and the third are alike; the second, called the "trio" (originally for three instruments), is generally more lyric. It was a dance of dignity and grace. In *Don Giovanni* Mozart has the Don and other nobles dance a minuet at the ball. Puccini has a dancing master instruct Manon in one in Act II of *Manon Lescaut*.

**Mise en Scène**—(Fr.) Lit., "placed in the scene." The French term for the staging, scenery and stage direction.

**Miserere**—(Latin) The opening word of the Fifty-first Psalm (Fiftieth in Roman Catholic numbering), which reads, "Miserere mei, Domine . . ." (Have mercy upon me, O God). In Roman Catholic churches it is said or sung as part of the burial service. In opera a "miserere" is generally a musical setting of the mood rather than the actual text of the psalm. Thus in Act IV of *Il Trovatore* the monks pray for mercy for a soul that is about to depart.

**Morbidezza**—(It.) Lit., "delicacy" or "gentleness." Hence the direction to singers, con morbidezza, does not mean "with morbidity" but "with gentleness." Critics are apt to use the word or some form of it to describe the sort of melody Puccini wrote or the style singers use for his arias.

**Mornington, Earl of** (1735–81)—Noted for daring to walk through the London streets openly carrying his violin case in spite of the jeering mob. Scholes (q.v.) observes, "There was courage in this family, for one of his sons was the famous Duke of Wellington."

**Music Drama**—This is a term much used by critics writing about Wagner and his musical heirs to distinguish their style from that of "opera" composers. And so used, both terms, opera and music drama, are relative. Opera implies an emphasis on the aria—stopping the action to allow a lyrical effusion and casting it into a specific musical form, like the rondo or canon; music drama implies melodic recitative in which words are not repeated, songs are not in verses, and the drama is not sacrificed to create musical forms. The distinction breaks down on many works, e.g. Verdi's *Otello* or *Don Carlo,* Wagner's *Die Meistersinger,* and the term is less frequently used than fifty years ago.

**Noodling**—Instrumentalists' slang for sloppy playing.

**Number**—In opera a generic term of which aria, duet, chorus, etc., are the species. A number is any musical entity capable of standing alone with a beginning and an end and giving a sense of completeness. Many operas have been composed as a succession of numbers connected by spoken dialogue or recitative. The term may have started because in old scores the arias, duets, etc., were actually numbered in the order in which they came.

**Obbligato**—(It.) Lit., "obligatory." The word is in danger today, through ignorant use, of coming to mean its opposite, ad libitum (q.v.). It is a direction in a score (q.v.) that the particular instrument or part must be played or sung as written. Thus, the flute obbligato in Gluck's *Orfeo* was to be played exactly as he wrote it and not as some impresario or instrumentalist thought might produce applause.

**Oeuvre**—(Fr.) Lit., "work." In a plural sense it means all the works of one composer: Debussy's oeuvre. A "chef d'oeuvre" is a chief work or masterpiece. An "hors d'oeuvre" is something created by a chef "outside" his "oeuvre" which is the dinner or the meat course.

**Opera**—There is no good definition of the word, and the variety of the form precludes one. About the best that can be said is that opera is a staged drama in which the accompanying music is more than, or as important as, the words or actions of the drama. "Staged" can be defined as the employment of any costume, action or prop that sets the singers apart from the audience so that the audience, instead of being in the drama, is merely watching it. Thus a choir in a processional is separate from the congregation and part of the drama; but, having reached its stall, it merges with the congregation for long periods of the service while the minister or priest conducts the drama. "Drama" can be defined as a presentation of anything about which a God, man, or animal does, or can feel strongly, or is trying to persuade an audience that he does. Thus a man asleep can be high drama if he is having a nightmare or if a rattlesnake is about to bite him. In this last it is the audience that feels strongly. But someone on stage or off must care about what is happening. Nothing is more unoperatic than some church music which merely fills voids in the service and about which no one cares. When the music is not more than, or as important as, the words or actions, the performance becomes ballet or mime or a play with musical accompaniment.

The word "opera," according to Grout in his *Short History of Opera,* was not used in its present sense before 1639 when Cavalli presented his *Le Nozze di Teti e Peleo* at Venice as an "opera scenica." It means, literally, a "work," and it is a shortened form of the Italian "opera in musica," a "work of music." It is not a plural of the Latin word "opus." For many years, what today is called an opera was a "favola" (fable), "tragedia" or simply "dramma."

**Opera Buffa**—(It.) In French, opéra bouffe. Lit., "comic opera." Any opera that is funny, and is meant to be, is an opera buffa. Historically the style developed first in Italy in the eighteenth century and was opposed to opera seria (q.v.). Then the latter, roughly speaking, began to stagnate, and composers did their "serious" operas in the comic style. Opera buffa composers, for example, taught the opera seria composers how to make a concerted finale rather than just ending with an aria. Mozart composed in both styles and then successfully merged them in *Don Giovanni* and *Le Nozze di Figaro*.

**Opéra-Comique**—(Fr.) This term does NOT mean "comic opera." It identifies a building in Paris where (in theory) operas are produced with spoken dialogue rather than recitative. The latter are produced (in theory) at L'Opéra (The Opera). Again the term identifies a building. The division arose in the eighteenth century. It has no meaning today other than to designate two theaters, the managements of which agree between themselves as to which operas will be produced where. Both *La Bohème* and *La Traviata* are done at the Opéra-Comique. Neither is comic nor uses spoken dialogue.

**Opera Seria**—(It.) "Serious" opera as opposed to opera buffa (q.v.). Its subject was usually mythological or, at very least, historical whereas opera buffa laughed at everyday maid, mistress and miser. Opera seria died at the close of the eighteenth century. One of the very last was Mozart's *La Clemenza di Tito* (1791), composed for the coronation of Leopold II of Bohemia.

**Operetta**—Lit., a short opera. The line between opera buffa (q.v.) and operetta is sufficiently thin to be indistinguishable to most eyes. Those claiming clear vision report that operetta implies spoken dialogue and a sentimental, nostalgic plot, whereas opera buffa implies recitative, is wittier and more hardboiled. Operetta today except for subject matter is probably synonymous with musical comedy. The same work is apt to be premièred as a musical comedy and revised as an operetta.

**Opus**—(Latin.) Lit., "a work." A term used with a number by composers and their publishers to identify a composition: Opus 1, Opus 2, etc. There is constant confusion as to whether the numbering is by date of composition or publication. The work need not necessarily be music: Berlioz's Op. 10 is his "Treatise on Instrumentation" (q.v.). Massenet who was very superstitious had an Op. 12b but no Op. 13. Operas being clearly identified by name generally do not have an "opus number." *Der Rosenkavalier,* however, is Op. 59 of Richard Strauss. Where the composer is publishing a series of very short pieces, he may combine them into one Opus with identifying numbers, as Op. 10 No. 7.

**Oratorio**—A dramatic composition for soloists, chorus and orchestra. The libretto is usually a text from the Scriptures or based on some incident described therein. It differs from opera most in being performed without scenery or costumes and with an Earnest Air. The line between it and opera can be very thin. Saint-Saens, for example, started his *Samson et Dalila* as an oratorio and then switched it to an opera at the suggestion of his assistant.

**Orchestration**—The writing or scoring (*See* SCORE) for groups of instruments. It of course, depends on a knowledge of what effects are possible for instruments in combination. *See* INSTRUMENTATION.

**Overture**—All artists want to get the audience's attention before beginning the work at hand. A trumpet flourish (*See* FANFARE) is one method. Opera developed the overture. If the overture is short and there is no break, it is a prelude (q.v.). Today the trend seems to be away from overtures, and most operas begin with a few chords. *See* Chap. I, "The Overture, the Prelude and Three Chords."

**Pasticcio**—(It.) *See* PASTICHE.

**Pastiche**—(Fr.) In Italian, pasticcio. Lit., a "pie." A composition in which favorite operatic selections are strung together like a medley without any regard for their original purpose or effect. Sometimes new words are set to the music. It can also mean a composition worked on by many composers so that there are many styles instead of one unifying style.

**Patter Song**—Any song or aria in which part of the effect and humor lies in the character's uttering as many words as possible in the shortest time. Examples run throughout opera—Rossini, *Il Barbiere di Siviglia,* "Largo al Factotum"; Mozart, *Don Giovanni,* "Madamina"; and, of course, every Gilbert and Sullivan opera.

**Patti, Adelina** (1843–1919)—She was probably the most famous soprano of the second half of the nineteenth century. Her rendition of "Home Sweet Home," from the opera *Clari,* shrank strong men to weeping boys. She was essentially a coloratura (q.v.), but she also sang dramatic roles.

**Pedro**—Dom Pedro II de Alcántara (1825–91) was the second and last Emperor of Brazil. He was a music lover and in 1857 tried to lure Wagner to Rio de Janeiro. One time he registered at a hotel in Bayreuth simply as "Pedro," and when asked by the clerk to fill in his "occupation," he wrote "Emperor." He was a genial man, much loved by his subjects, who deposed him in 1889 but solicitously granted him a pension. In history he is known as Dom Pedro the

Magnanimous.

**Pentatonic Scale**—(Read SCALES first.) In this scale the fundamental difference in pitch from C to C an octave above is divided into five intervals or five notes. Obviously, some of the intervals are larger than those in scales having more notes or more rungs to the ladder. This means the difference in pitch, high or low, between the notes is easier to hear; thus the pentatonic scale is apt to be the first that primitive people develop. Folk songs often use the pentatonic scale. On the piano the black notes form a pentatonic scale.

**Percussion**—A collective name for instruments played by striking a surface that resounds. By this common definition a piano is a percussion instrument, but the term usually is taken to include only drums, bells, gongs, triangles, castanets and other such instruments. Some drums and even some cymbals can be tuned to sound a particular note, but most percussion instruments are of indefinite pitch. *See* BRASS, STRINGS and WOODWINDS.

**Piano, Pianissimo**—(It.) Lit., "soft" and "most soft." It is a direction to the performer and is written "p" and "pp." Sometimes composers to ensure obedience to their wishes write "pppp." Its opposite is forte (q.v.). *See* PIU.

**Piccini, Nicola** (1728–1800)—One of the most famous opera composers of the eighteenth century. He was born in Bari, Italy, but lived mostly in Paris where his adherents and those of Gluck fought verbally and physically. Piccini, a kind and peaceable man, took no interest in the squabble and on Gluck's death in 1787 he attempted to found by subscription an annual concert in memory of his opponent. The plan failed for lack of subscribers. Piccini's last years were pathetic. His pensions were cut off, although he had many dependents, and he was kicked from pillar to post by smalltime politicians treading the waves of the revolution. No opera of his is now being given. In style they were melodic rather than dramatic like Gluck's. Piccini gave Marie Antoinette singing lessons; Gluck gave her lessons on the clavichord.

**Più**—(It.) Lit., "more." A qualifying word in directions to the performer, e.g. più forte, louder.

**Pizzicato**—(It.) Lit., "plucked." A direction to string players to pluck the string rather than bow it. It gives a "plink" effect to the note.

**Polka**—A Bohemian or Czech dance. Not a Polish dance. It originated about 1830 and swept over Europe like an epidemic. It arrived in the U.S.A. in 1844 just when Polk was running for president. There were jokes. The most famous operatic polka occurs in Act I of Smetana's *The Bartered Bride.*

**Polonaise**—(Fr.) This French word is used even by Poles to describe a Polish dance. It is in ¾ time and is stately and dignified. It is more of a processional than a dance. Polonaises occur in Act III of *Eugene Onegin* and the "Polish" act of *Boris Godunov.*

**Ponticello**—(It.) The bridge of a stringed instrument over which the strings pass.

**Portamento**—(It.) Lit., "carrying." A direction to the performer, either singer or string player, to move from one note to the next very smoothly. It is more than legato (q.v.) because the performer must sound, however briefly, all the notes between the two that are written. This gives a slide effect. The trombone is the only brass or wind instrument that can achieve it.

**Pot-pourri**—(Fr.) Lit., "rotten-pot." The term refers to the jar used to keep rose leaves and spices. It is used to describe a composition stringing favorite melodies of an opera together without working out any development or connecting links.

**Prelude**—In opera it is a short introduction to any act and leads directly into the act without a formal ending. The term is not very exact and overlaps with overture (q.v.). An example of the confusion is Wagner's Prelude to *Die Meistersinger.* He named it a prelude, and the curtain rises without break. But it runs for more than ten minutes and is a complete symphonic outline of the entire opera, which puts it squarely in the developing tradition of the overture. For concert performances many operatic preludes are rounded off with a few chords added either by the composer or someone else. *See* Chap. I, "The Overture, the Prelude and Three Chords."

**Practicable**—Italian and sometimes other scores and librettos refer to practicable doors or windows in the scenery. This means one that will open. A curious example occurs in Verdi's *I Lombardi* in which the Valley of Jehoshaphat is to be "dotted with practicable hills."

**Presto**—(It.) Lit., "quick." A direction to the performer. No direction asks for quicker tempo (q.v.) except prestissimo. In *Don Giovanni* Mozart directs the "Champagne Aria," "Fin ch'han dal vino," to be sung presto.

**Prima Donna**—(It.) Lit., "first lady." Properly speaking there is no plural. It is used to denote the principal soprano in an opera company. If there is any possibility of confusion, the admirers refer to the object of their adoration as "prima donna assoluta." Because of the extraordinary behavior of some of the objects, however, the term has developed derisive connotations. Historically there was a matching term, "primo uomo" (first man), which referred to the leading castrato (q.v.) in the company. This has dropped out of use except for caustic comment.

**Prix de Rome**—A prize of four years of study in Rome offered to composers by the Academy of Fine Arts, a branch of the Institut de France. The winner lives in the Villa Medici of the Académie de France, founded by Louis XIV in 1666, which is one of the sights in Rome. The competition is frequently cited both for and against state support of the arts. Berlioz's struggles, successful on the fifth attempt, to write a piece bad enough to win are both ludicrous and tragic. And when the judges decided that Ravel, after winning a second prize four years before, no longer was good enough to qualify for the competition, there was a national scandal followed by resignations and new appointments. The list of winners who were never heard of again is very long, but some of the others are 1819, Halévy; 1830, Berlioz; 1832, Thomas; 1839, Gounod; 1857, Bizet; 1863, Massenet; 1884, Debussy (with "L'Enfant Prodigue"); and 1887, Charpentier. Belgium and the United States have similar but less famous Prix de Rome.

**Probe**—*See* REHEARSAL.

**Puns**—Punning, the witty use of a word in two incongruous senses, is not possible strictly in musical terms. The closest approach to it is achieved by Mozart in *Le Nozze di Figaro*. Figaro complains that all women deceive their husbands, and Mozart scores several toots on the horns (traditionally cuckolds sprouted horns). Offenbach in *Orpheus in the Underworld* has Orpheus play the violin concerto that Euridice claims drove her from their home. It is a beautiful, souped-up version of the even more beautiful lament for Euridice that Gluck gives to his Orfeo. The contrast of the contexts is humorous. But usually musical jokes consist of illustration, such as Wagner's scoring of Beckmesser's aches and pains in Act III of *Die Meistersinger*.

**Quartet**—Any composition, movement or aria for four performers; or the four artists themselves. Additional numbers are quintet—five performers; sextet—six; septet—seven; and octet—eight.

**Quintet**—*See* QUARTET.

**Ranz des Vaches**—(Fr.) The name given to a type of horn call or song used by Swiss peasants to call in the cattle. The term means "cow procession." It was said that the sound of a ranz des vaches would produce waves of homesickness in any Swiss peasant unlucky enough to hear it while in a foreign country. Foreign princes who hired Swiss mercenaries were reported to have standing orders to inflict death on anyone playing it within earshot of their troops. Rossini has a typical one just after the storm in his overture to *William Tell*. For some reason, it is a music-box favorite.

**Rataplan**—A made-up word to imitate the sound of a drum. Operatic composers wrote "rataplan" numbers in which chorus, cannons and concubines whooped it up in army camps. The most famous of such scenes are in Donizetti's *La Fille du Régiment*, Meyerbeer's *Les Huguenots*, and Verdi's *La Forza del Destino*.

**Re**—(It.) *See* Do.

**Recitative**—(It. recitativo; Fr., récitatif; Ger., recitativ). The term used to describe the declamatory links between arias and set numbers in an opera or oratorio. *See* Chap. II, "Melody, Aria and Recitative."

**Régisseur**—(Fr.) The producer or director responsible for the entire production of an opera. The term is somewhat complimentary and reserved for only the greatest directors like Max Reinhardt who manage to put their quickening stamp on every aspect of the production. Another famous régisseur was Alfred Roller, who worked with Mahler of the Vienna Staatsoper; together they set many of the standards and traditions of today.

**Rehearsal**—(It., prova; Fr., répétition; Ger., probe.) The practice session in which the artist hopefully perfects his part before the public performance.

**Répétiteur**—(Fr.) Lit., "repeater." In the opera house, the man who teaches the singer his part. He also sometimes cues or prompts the singer in actual performance from the wings or the prompter's box. It is one of the traditional training grounds for young conductors.

**Requiem**—The first word in the Roman Catholic Mass for the Dead and generally used to denote the entire Mass. The opening sentence is, "Requiem aeternam dona eis, Domine" (Give them eternal rest, O Lord). In the Church it is sung annually on All Souls Day (November 2) and such other times as may be appropriate. Almost all composers have written Requiem Masses, including Berlioz, Mozart and Verdi.

**Rescue Opera**—A term used to describe a type of French opera that was very popular during and after the French Revolution. In it one paragon of virtue saves another after overcoming the most fearful trials and tribulations. Many of the stories, arising out of the Revolution, were supposedly based on fact. The most famous example is Beethoven's *Fidelio* (1805).

**Ricordi**—An Italian publishing house in Milan founded in 1808. It was run by members of the family for four generations. Among others it published Rossini, Bellini, Donizetti, Verdi and Puccini. During an air raid in World War II the building, housing more than 300,000 engraved plates of musical publications, was demolished and the plates were completely destroyed.

**Ritornello**—(It.) Lit., "little return." The instrumental passage that closes an aria or leads to the next verse. Typically it repeats the closing phrases that were sung. Sometimes, but incorrectly, it refers to the orchestral introduction to the first verse of an aria.

**Rubato**—(It.) Lit., "robbed." Often the term appears as "tempo rubato." It is used to describe exceedingly slight variations in tempo within a phrase. The nonmusician probably cannot fix the changes, but the phrase seems full of "life." Excessive rubato degenerates into romantic playing or singing and robs the composition of its basic tempo so that, thereafter, changes in tempo seem willful and aimless rather than purposeful and exciting.

**Salieri, Antonio** (1750–1825)—An Italian composer at the Austrian court. He was a friend of Gluck and Haydn and a teacher of Beethoven and Schubert. The only musician he seems to have disliked is Mozart. However, the dislike did NOT extend to poisoning Mozart—although Pushkin wrote a play and Rimsky-Korsakov an opera on this subject.

**Savoy Operas**—These are the operas of Gilbert and Sullivan, most of which were produced at the Savoy Theatre in London by D'Oyly Carte. The producer's performers continued after his death in the D'Oyly Carte Opera Company, which still tours (with younger replacements) and considers itself the one true prophet of Gilbert and Sullivan. A member of this troupe or even a worshipper of its art is frequently called a "Savoyard."

**Scales**—A scale is the fundamental frame of music. Accept as fact that to all ears there is some special relationship between a sound vibrating at a certain number of cycles per second and a sound vibrating at double or half that number, or a relationship of 2:1. Any two such sounds or notes form the outer limits of a scale. The scale itself is the progression of notes from one sound vibrating at, say, 261.626 cps (middle C on a piano) to the sound vibrating at 523.51 cps (C an octave above middle C). (*See* the chart on p. 89.) Obviously, the distance from C to C can be traversed in any number of steps, or notes, just as a ladder can have any number of rungs spaced close together, far apart, or unequally. The most common scales are pentatonic (q.v.), whole-tone (q.v.), diatonic (q.v.), and twelve-tone (q.v.). The pentatonic scale has five notes; the whole-tone, seven; the diatonic, eight; and the twelve-tone, twelve. The diatonic is the most common. A composer may select any scale he wishes; some make up new scales, but the difficulty with this is that many instruments will be unable to sound the new and different notes, i.e. the holes on the flute would have to be differently spaced.

**Scaria, Emil** (1838–86)—A famous Austrian bass-baritone who created the role of Gurnemanz in *Parsifal* at Bayreuth. He died insane. One of the first signs of his insanity appeared at a performance as Wotan in *Die Walkuere*. In the third act he suddenly did everything backward: he entered from the right instead of the left, cringing instead of imperious, and transposing all the high notes an octave down and the low notes an octave up. The next day he did not know what he had done. But thereafter he was prone to forget whole pages of the score and had a special prompter assigned to him. His last performance was in *Tannhaeuser,* during the second act of which he suddenly whispered to the Elisabeth, "What opera is it we are singing?" and had to be led from the stage.

**Scena**—(It.) In opera, the musical divisions of the act as opposed to geographical divisions, i.e. changes of locale. Thus a scena is something like a number, except that it includes the character's entrance and exit, the build-up, and the denouement as well as the aria, quartet or whatever.

**Schmalz**—(Ger.) A term, with derogatory connotations, for any composition that has immediate popular appeal. It comes from "Schmiss und Schmalz," a Viennese expression for snappy rhythm and lush melody.

**Scholes, Percy** (1877–1958)—The author of "The Oxford Companion to Music," which went through eight editions in less than sixteen years and entered its ninth in 1955, a record for a work of musical reference. Scholes' entries were witty, honest and detailed. His book is one of the best one-volume reference books on music available. His name is pronounced "Skoals."

**Score**—The musical notation of a particular composition. "Score" and "full score" are synonymous and include every part to be performed. These are set out on a staff (q.v.), starting generally with the voices and working down through the wind instruments to the horns, strings and percussion. This is what the conductor uses. The violinist uses just the violin part, separately printed; the clarinetist, the clarinet part; and so on. A "vocal" score of an opera or other choral work will show the vocal parts set out in full, but the orchestral parts are reduced to a piano version. A "piano" score reduces both vocal and orchestral parts to a piano version. "Scoring" has two meanings: copying out the notes in musical notation and the art of orchestrating.

**Schwellton**—(Ger.) The art of swelling the voice from soft to loud and contracting it to soft on the same note. It is the same as the Italian "messa di voce."

**Seguidilla**—(Sp.) An old Spanish dance. It can be either fast or slow, but it is usually fast, in a minor key, and accompanied by castanets, guitar or voice. Bizet in the first act of *Carmen* has a seguidilla to which Carmen seduces Don José.

**Septet**—*See* QUARTET.

**Serenade**—Lit., "evening" music, from the Fr. "soir" or the It. "sera." Generally, the term applies to any music to be played in the evening in the open air. Specifically, it connotes a lover singing to his mistress on a balcony or at a window while he accompanies himself on any sort of an instrument (other than a wind instrument). The perfect example is Mozart's serenade in Act II of *Don Giovanni,* "Deh vieni alla finestra . . ." (Hey, come to the window . . .). Others are Wagner's for Backmesser in Act II of *Die Meistersinger* and Gounod's for Méphistophélès in Act IV of *Faust.* In order, the instrument specified is a mandolin, lute, and guitar.

**Sestet**—A fancy word for sextet (q.v.) and used only by pedants or persons frightfully kinked about sex.

**Sextet**—*See* QUARTET.

**Shake**—*See* TRILL.

**Shanty**—A sailor's work song. It means just that, and to describe a composition as a sea shanty is as redundant as to call a man a sea sailor. "Blow the Man Down" is a shanty.

**Sharp**—To sing sharp is to sing a little bit above the note. It is the opposite of flat (q.v.).

**Singspiel**—(Ger.) A term of musical history used to describe a type of German opera in which there was spoken dialogue interspersed with songs, all in the vernacular. It was popular at the end of the eighteenth century. Mozart's *Die Entfuehrung aus dem Serail* and *Die Zauberfloete* are in singspiel style but are of so much more musical interest that they form, as they have been described, "the apotheosis of singspiel." In a typical singspiel the folk sang songs and the gentlefolk arias. Today the term is sometimes used loosely to describe any opera or operetta with spoken dialogue.

**Soap Opera**—Scholes (q.v.) describes it: "This term (known to every American reader of this book and included here for the enlightenment of puzzled British readers) is applied to any broadcast daily-continued story designed to reduce the more sentimental part of the female population to pleasurable tears of sympathy and, concurrently, to keep bright in their memories the merits of some manufacturer's special product (originally soap). Certain popular masterpieces of this kind were reported in 1946 to have already run for ten or fifteen years and the total number of daily listeners was then computed at twenty millions."

**Sol**—(It.) *See* Do.

**Solo**—(It.) Lit., "alone." A composition for single instrument or voice. *See* QUARTET.

**Sonata**—Originally this distinguished a composition for instruments from one for voices, a cantata (q.v.). Later it came to mean a particular form of instrumental composition.

**Soubrette**—(Fr.) The lady's maid in comic operas. It was a standardized character, pert and coquettish. It has come to mean any role of that type. A typical soubrette part is Adele in *Die Fledermaus* or Despina in *Così fan tutte*. Susanna in *Le Nozze di Figaro* is the greatest of these roles because of the depth Mozart gave to it.

**Staccato**—(It.) Lit., "detached." A direction to sound notes in such a way that each stands entirely separate with a moment (however short) of silence before and after it. It is the opposite of legato (q.v.). It is not the same as pizzicato (q.v.) where the string is plucked rather than bowed as it is here.

**Staff**—The series of five horizontal lines on which notes are written. A sound of so many vibrations per second is indicated by placing a note on a certain line or space on the staff.

**Stretto**—(It.) Lit., "drawn together." In opera it is used in two senses: either to describe the quickening of the actual tempo (q.v.), or the succession of accents at the end of an aria, or the finale of the act, though the tempo may remain the same; or, on the other hand, to describe that part of the aria or finale in which the accents succeed each other more rapidly. The quickening of accents produces a sense of tension or excitement.

**Strings**—A collective name for instruments which sound when a bow, formed of string or hair, is pulled across thin wires or gut which are stretched taut. Some instruments—such as the piano, harp and guitar—also have taut strings or wires, but these are caused to vibrate by striking or plucking rather than by bowing. Typical string instruments are the violin, viola, cello and double bass. *See* BRASS, PERCUSSION and WOODWINDS.

**Swan Song**—An artist's last performance or the last composition of any musician, poet or other creative artist. It refers to the ancient belief that a swan sang its most beautiful song just before it died. Today the reference is confusing as the most common and semidomesticated swan (Cygnus olor) is mute, but the whooper swan (Cygnus musicus) has a loud, resonant honk. It is a mystery why any poet thought it beautiful, and the gift of song probably was attributed gratuitously to the serene and graceful bird whose pure white plumage symbolized faultlessness or excellence. References to the swan song appear as early as Chaucer; and Ben Jonson called Shakespeare the Swan of Avon. Rossini was sometimes called the Swan of Pesaro.

**Tambourine**—A small drum. One end is open, the other covered with parchment. Set in the hoop are pairs of metal plates that "jingle." It is one of the most ancient of all instruments and is thought to be the instrument with which Miriam and her maidens celebrated the victory of the Israelites over the Egyptians. Bizet uses it in *Carmen,* and stage directors frequently have Carmen accompany herself with one in the opening aria of Act II.

**Tarantella**—(It.) A dance of Southern Italy; very fast. There is a spider near the port of Taranto in the heel of Italy called the tarantula. Its bite was for hundreds of years thought to be poisonous and its victims developed violent contortions and froth at the mouth. The only known cure was the furious and exhausting dance, the tarantella.

Musicians made a good thing of it until the doctors demonstrated that the tarantula's bite was comparatively harmless. Verdi has a chorus and ballet in *La Forza del Destino* for which he indicates tempo di tarantella.

**Taylor, John** (1703–70)—Itinerant oculist. He operated on Bach and Handel, both of whom died blind, and many considered him a quack. He was the oculist to George II, his son to George III and his grandson to George IV.

**Te Deum Laudamus**—(Latin). A very ancient Christian hymn incorporated into the liturgy of most of the sects as the supreme expression of thanksgiving. As such, it is constantly being used by church Christians to celebrate a victory in war. Many composers have set it. In opera Puccini, at the close of the first act of *Tosca,* has Scarpia express his lust for Tosca against a background of a Te Deum celebrating the supposed Austrian-Bourbon victory over Napoleon at Marengo.

**Tempo**—(It.) The speed at which a composition is to be performed. Composers indicate this in either of two ways, or sometimes in both. The older method is by word (in decreasing order of speed): presto, allegro, andante, adagio and largo. (*See* each listed separately.) But, of course, one man's presto is another's andante. So composers attempted to tie the speed to something more definite by stating that in the particular piece a note of certain time value, i.e. an eighth or a quarter, etc., would be sounded so many times a minute. But even this is no more than a general indication leaving room for interpretation. The plural of the word is tempi, and often critics remark on a conductor's "tempi," meaning choice of speeds, as good or bad.

**Tessitura**—(It.) Lit., "web" or "texture." The word describes the average level of a singer's part, i.e., it "lies" high or low. It is very different from "range" which, because of an occasional high or low note, may be extended, while the tessitura is limited.

**Thompson, Oscar**—The editor for many years of "The International Cyclopedia of Music and Musicians," published in an eighth edition by Dodd, Mead and Co. in 1958. This is the largest one-volume reference book on music available. It falls between "Grove's" (q.v.) and Scholes (q.v.). Like the former it is written by contributors, none of whom can match the wit and style of Scholes. But the articles are often longer and more complete than Scholes and often include a catalogue of each composer's work. Some of the opera synopses, however, are inaccurate. The "Cyclopedia" *is* one volume and with thin paper, but do not try to lift it off a high shelf while standing on a ladder.

**Ti**—(It.) *See* Do.

**Tremolo**—(It.) The word is now thoroughly confused with vibrato. There are two effects: one, the rapid iteration of one note without varying the pitch, and two, the rapid alternation of two notes varying in pitch. The first is more difficult to do on purpose. Probably originally the first (no varying of pitch) was a tremolo and the second a vibrato. And this is how instrumentalists, as opposed to singers, are apt to use the terms. But today it is necessary when hearing anyone use either term to ask him exactly which effect he means.

**Trill**—It is the same thing as a shake, which is the older word. It is the most important of all the ornaments a singer can apply to his song. For almost two hundred years (1650–1850) a singer without a shake was simply of no account. Dr. Burney (q.v.) reported, "The Italians call a bad shake, or no shake at all, but a quivering on the same note, 'tosse da capra,' a goat's cough . . . Those who have a good shake, like persons with a fine set of teeth, are too ambitious of letting you know it." There are many variations of trills. The simplest is the rapid alternation of adjacent notes. The trill is the result of intent; the vibrato or tremolo often is not. For the confusion over these last terms, *See* TREMOLO.

**Trio**—A composition for three instruments or three voices of the performers themselves. *See* QUARTET.

**Triple Time**—Any rhythm which has three beats to a measure, i.e. oomp-pah-pah. It can be a waltz or not depending on how the beats are accented.

**Tutti**—(It.) Lit., "all." A term describing those sections of a composition where the chorus or instrumental group, without the soloist, performs. It can also be a direction in the score (q.v.) for the group to begin. Often the soloist is not excluded by the direction.

**Twelve-Tone** music, row, scale, system or technique—(Read SCALE first.) These are terms used to describe music based on a scale of twelve notes as opposed to the traditional one of eight, the diatonic scale. (*See* CHROMATICS and KEY.) The theory, greatly oversimplified, is that if all twelve notes of the scale are treated as being of equal importance, then the composer has the maximum freedom to move from one to the next. Some twelve-tone composers adopted a system of sounding all twelve notes in an arbitrary order, the row. The order had to be maintained, but the notes could be sounded in order forwards, backwards or inverted, i.e. the high ones low and the low high. The notes could also be in different octaves. Those favoring the system and scale claim that music will thereby develop a new vocabulary and a new vitality. Those disliking the system say that its appeal is to the mind and eye, not the ear. It is sometimes called "atonal" music, a confusing term because it means "without tone" and yet is used to describe something that has tone, although the tone is unanchored in a system of scales by key. The most successful opera using twelve-tone techniques is Berg's *Wozzeck.*

**Tzigane**—(Fr.) A gypsy.

**Uproar**—A veritable Methuselah of puns; on the word "opera."

**Vamp**—As a verb it means to extemporize the bass accompaniment until the performer is ready to begin. At its least artistic, vamping consists of nothing more than oomp-pah-pah while the singer catches his breath.

**Verismo**—(It.) A term used to describe the naturalistic or realistic style of opera that flourished in Italy at the turn of the century. Its hallmarks were violence, passion and sensationalism. Its chief proponents were Mascagni, Leoncavallo and, to a lesser extent, Puccini. The style never caught on in other countries to quite the same extent. In Germany one of the best veristic operas was D'Albert's *Tiefland;* in France, Massenet's *La Navarraise.*

**Vibrato**—(It.) *See* TREMOLO.

**Virtuoso**—Any performer with exceptional technical or mechanical skill in his art. The word has changed its meaning gradually and to-day an artist apparently can be a virtuoso without being a fine "interpreter." This distinction was unknown a hundred fifty years ago.

**Vocal Score**—*See* SCORE.

**Waltz**—Together with the march (q.v.), one of the most common rhythms in opera. It is really both a rhythm and a dance, for triple time existed long before the waltz as a dance developed from the folk dances of southern Germany. The Austrians, beginning with the Congress of Vienna in 1815, adopted the waltz as a national dance and with Johann Strauss, Sr. and Jr., captivated the world with the Viennese melody and beat. The French waltz developed a slower tempo. So excited did the Viennese become over waltzing that according to reports there were chambres d'accouchement off the dance halls where a lady could drop her child almost without missing a turn. Sociologically the waltz was important because the great public dance halls drew no social distinctions, which hastened the end of the minuet and court dances. In the finale to Act I of *Don Giovanni,* Leporello and Masseto, at the bottom of the social scale, dance a waltz; the nobles dance a minuet.

**Whole-Tone Scale**—(Read SCALES first.) In this scale the rungs of the ladder—the interval between each note—are equally spaced. In the most common scale, the diatonic, two intervals are only half as large as the others, C D E *F* G A B *C,* or do-re-me-*fa*-sol-la-ti-*do.* The italicized note is only a semitone above its predecessor. A whole-tone scale in order to cover the same rise in pitch from do to do, or C to C, can have only seven notes as opposed to the diatonic scale's eight. Because the intervals between all the notes are the same, they have no distinctive relations such as the notes just above or below the semitones in the diatonic scale. This gives any composition using a whole-tone scale a vague, indefinite feeling. Debussy was particularly fond of it and in his piano works and *Pelléas et Mélisande* made extensive use of it. On the piano a whole-tone scale is C, D, E, F♯, G♯, A♯, C. (*See* chart on p. 89.)

**Woodwinds**—A collective name for all the instruments played by blowing directly, with or without a reed, into a column of air enclosed in a tube with holes in it. The fingers opening and closing the holes change the length of the vibrating column of air and hence the pitch of the note. The term includes instruments made of metal, e.g. the saxophone and flute, but constructed on the same principle. Typical woodwinds are the piccolo, flute, clarinet, oboe, bassoon and saxophone. *See* BRASS, STRINGS and PERCUSSION.

**Zarzuela**—(Sp.) A Spanish form of opera buffa or revue in which anything from ladies' fashions to political crises is satirized. The operas are generally one act with spoken dialogue. A famous zarzuela is *La Gran Via* (The High Road) by Valverde. It was first produced in 1886.

# PART THREE

# The Synopses

---

In France . . . nothing which has once been generally approved may ever be allowed to fade *gradually* into the background. On every single count it is necessary to give *battle*. As a good Frenchman, I am resolved and adamant that what I admired yesterday, I shall continue to admire today; for if not, what should I find to talk about tomorrow? So-and-so's opera is a recognized *masterpiece;* it therefore is, and will remain, "exquisite"; and if (incidentally) it bores me to tears, the fault lies exclusively in *myself*. Even before we were ten years old, we had had to learn the hard lessons of life from the family retainer who used to put our hair in curlers: "There is no way of being beautiful, young Master, without *suffering* for it first!"

*STENDHAL*
*Life of Rossini*

# SYNOPSES

---

The synopses that follow are arranged by composer and thereunder by date of production. The composers are in order of birth date.

The form of the synopses varies slightly to reflect the composer's method of composition. Mozart wrote numbers, arias and duets, etc., connected by recitative. The arias in the synopses are numbered just as they are in the score, and the recitative is indicated by being indented. The same form of synopsis is used where the numbers are connected by spoken dialogue. The later composers blurred the numbers into the recitative, and in their operas the synopsis indicates where each worked his way to a resting point for a lyrical effusion. In all operas, but particularly in Wagner, the musical scenes are indicated, although there may be no change of geographical locale. But the musical scenes are the blocks out of which the composer built the act, and the operagoer may more effectively grasp the whole if he sees the parts. Other variations are slight and self-explanatory.

Each synopsis attempts to present an uncut version of the opera while indicating where the usual cuts are made. Some operas, however, exist in versions dating from the first, second or third production or even performance. The synopses give the version the operagoer is likely to hear, while merely indicating others. Differences of interest only to scholars are generally ignored.

The indicated timings are, of course, averages. An opera, particularly by Mozart or Wagner, can gain or lose twenty minutes depending on the conductor. And tempos on recordings are apt to be faster than those of an actual performance. This is particularly true of ballets.

The scenic descriptions are in every instance taken from the score. This may raise a confusion, however, for many opera houses have accustomed operagoers to watching Violetta renounce Alfredo in a garden rather than in a room, and there is hardly an opera that at some time has not had a scene transferred indoors or outdoors or done with lights or without lights, and each new attempt gives the operagoer a chance to fulminate or rhapsodize as he will. But the composer set the scene as indicated in these synopses.

Lastly, the words indicated are those which an operagoer is most likely to be able to pick up at a performance or off a record. Pronunciations differ; orchestras play more or less loudly; and composers sometimes do not arrange to have important words heard. The words selected for each opera represent a compromise of words that can, and words that ought to, be heard. The indicated pronunciation is intended merely as a beacon for those at sea in a foreign language and is not a demonstration of the pure Tuscan tongue or the clarity of French from the Loire Valley.

## THE OPERAS

# ORFEO

Opera in three acts. First performed at Vienna on October 5, 1762. Revised version performed at Paris on August 2, 1774. Music by C. W. Gluck. Libretto by R. Calzabigi.

### PRINCIPAL CHARACTERS

| | | |
|---|---|---|
| Orfeo | contralto | or.FAY.oh |
| Amor, God of Love | soprano | ah.MORE |
| A Happy Shade | soprano | |
| Euridice | soprano | eh.oor.eh.DEE.che (Sometimes the first syllable is merged into the second.) |

The action takes place in Greece and Hades during antiquity.

*Orfeo* as one of the oldest operas still presented is particularly interesting for the vestiges it exhibits of eighteenth-century opera. In 1762 when Gluck and his librettist, Calzabigi, first produced it in Vienna, opera was traditionally either "opera buffa" or "opera seria," literally comic or serious opera. For the first, Gluck (1714–87) had a slight talent which showed itself best in a series of French comic operas he composed and produced shortly before *Orfeo*. For the traditions and conventions of the second, "opera seria," he had, as he aged, constantly less sympathy; yet in this tradition are all his most famous operas.

An "opera seria" was generally on a classical subject and always in Italian with a happy ending. Primarily, it was a vehicle for the singers to display their techniques. The best singers of the time were the castrati and, as regards technique, they have never been equaled. Their greatest glory was improvising florid runs and trills on an aria which they might repeat two or three times while the dramatic continuity of the opera expired. The singing thus became an end in itself rather than the means of expressing the drama, and an eighteenth-century opera seria might strike an audience of today as more of a concert in curious clothes than an opera.

Gluck and Calzabigi set out to redress the balance between singing and drama, to make the singing once again express the emotions of the characters. They were reformers but working within the tradition of the time. *Orfeo* has a classical subject, a happy ending tacked on and is in Italian; the title role required a castrato, a male alto. In its use of ballet and final homage to the God of Love, it reflected an old tradition of court opera, the "licenza," in which the performers and sometimes the courtiers paid homage to the admiring sovereign. The music and text, in their symmetrical structure of verse and answering verse, aria and chorus, were typical of the eighteenth century. But the human interest and dramatic intensity were new. Guadagni, the castrato, was famous as an actor and undoubtedly emphasized the dramatic side of the role as well as the vocal. Gluck's great achievement in the opera was that the successfully re-emphasized the drama without sacrificing the beauties of the voice.

GLUCK

The casting of the title role is a problem: there are no more castrati. When Gluck produced the opera in Paris in 1774, he rewrote the part for a tenor and also added an old-fashioned display aria for him, totally out of style with the rest of the opera. But this reworking of the role for a tenor has never been accepted as satisfactory. A musical reason may be that the particular quality of a tenor voice is unsuited to the kind of melodies Gluck wrote for Orfeo. These are mostly simple, serene and with little strain or push to them. The tenor voice, being the top of the male range, seems peculiarly suited for arias with a feeling of agitation, strain or push. Sometimes a baritone is used, and he sings the notes as originally written but an octave lower. Berlioz in 1859 in Paris revised the score and for the first time cast a contralto, a woman, as Orfeo. This casting has been favored since. An argument for it is that the contralto quality most closely resembles that of a male alto.

Because of the casting problem, two existing versions by the composer, and the ease with which arias can be excised or inserted, the opera is produced in versions, and a poor production may well reflect poor editing rather than a poor performance. The opera's title is variously listed as *Orfeo, Orfeo ed Euridice* or *Orfeo, ed Euridice.*

The opera begins a few days after Euridice's death from snakebite. She was wandering in the fields one morning when a man named Aristeus attempted to force her. She broke lose from him and in her flight stepped on a snake, which bit her.

## OVERTURE (3 min.)

It is peculiarly heavy-footed and not so effective an introduction to the opera as the opening measures of Act I which follow.

## ACT I (Euridice's Tomb—31 min.)

**chorus** *Chorus:* They mourn Euridice. Through the lament Orfeo intones his wife's name. Finally he asks the mourners to hang garlands **ballet and chorus** on her tomb. This is done to a ballet at the end of which the chorus returns briefly to its lament and then at Orfeo's request, leaves him.

*Orfeo:* He starts an aria; musically it is in three identical verses, each **aria** of which is followed by a differing recitative. The verses are a formal lament: Thus do I call my love, thus seek her, thus mourn her. The recitatives are his more personal comment on each verse: I call her, but only an Echo answers; I seek her, but find only her name carved on the trees. The third recitative becomes rugged and assertive: I will go to the Underworld and bring her back.

*Amor:* He arrives to urge on Orfeo and to offer help. In an aria he **aria** says: take your lyre, tame the furies with your music and win her back. He implies that the Gods will help Orfeo, but he imposes a condition: Orfeo must not look at Euridice before getting back aboveground or he will forfeit her life. (In the legend he explicitly forbids Orfeo to tell Euridice about the condition. This is only implicit in the **aria** opera.) Then in another, livelier aria Amor urges Orfeo to persevere and endure all the trials.

*Orfeo:* He worries whether he will be able to do it—not look at

Euridice! And she won't understand. But he dismisses these fears and starts at once for the entrance to the Underworld. (Here comes the bravura aria Gluck wrote for the tenor in the Paris production. It is generally cut. In it Orfeo sings: I bo-o-o-o-o-ldly go-o-o-o-o.)

## ACT II (45 min.)

### SCENE 1 (The Furies—15 min.)

(Sometimes the first scene of this act is played as the second scene of Act I. This makes the first act the longest, which is good for audience psychology and posteriors; but Gluck's calculated contrast between the entrance to Hades with its Furies, and the Elysian Fields with its Happy Shades, is dissipated by the intermission.)

**chorus, ballet and chorus**     *The Furies:* They wonder who dares invade their domain. There is a short ballet, and then the Furies wonder again. This time they threaten the unknown intruder with Cerberus, the watchdog.

*Orfeo:* His appeal to the Furies is in three verses—musically each is different. The Chorus answers each verse. The answers are musically **solo with chorus**     similar, only growing more and more quiet. He begs the Furies to be merciful and let him pass. He calls to them: "Furie, Larve" (Furies and Spectres). They refuse by shouting: "No." He begs pity for a tortured soul.

*The Furies:* They reply that there is only death and grief in the Underworld.

*Orfeo:* He appeals again, saying he knows what Hell is; he has one within him.

*The Furies:* They are moved to the beginnings of pity.

*Orfeo:* In his third appeal he explains his own Hell: his love has died and now he is slowly dying of love.

*The Furies:* They are overcome, and quietly now they tell each other to let him pass. (Orfeo can now continue further into the Underworld, **ballet**     which perhaps makes the best dramatic sense, or he can wait while the Furies do their demoniac dance which can, without good stage business, be awkward.) The Dance of the Furies.

SCENE 2 (The Elysian Fields—30 min.)

**ballet and flute solo**     The scene opens with a lengthy ballet. It is in three sections, the middle one of which is the famous flute passage. (*See* Chap. 6, Sounds of the Orchestra, Instruments, p. 60.)

*The Shades:* The chorus, led by a happy shade, describes how here all **chorus**     earthly desires, fears and sadness are gone, leaving rest and content. (Sometimes the solo happy shade is sung by Euridice. Dramatically, it is better not so; she should be at least a little unhappy at her separation from Orfeo. The part is usually sung by one or divided between two shades.) The chorus goes out.

**aria and oboe obbligato**     *Orfeo:* Alone, he sings: "Che puro ciel . . ." (how pure a light). But without Euridice all the beauty and peace are nothing. The aria is accompanied by an oboe "obbligato" (*See* Glossary).

*The Shades:* They are drawn by his song and say that Euridice will be **chorus and ballet**     returned to him. There is a short ballet while one of the shades goes to get her. Orfeo then repeats his appeal in a very brief recitative and the chorus repeats its promise. Then Orfeo, his back to Euridice, grasps her hand and together they start the journey back to the surface of the world.

Vocabulary, Act II

| | | |
|---|---|---|
| furie | foo.ryay | furies |
| larve | lar.vay | spectres |
| che puro ciel | kay poor.oh chell | how pure a sky |

## ACT III (45 min.)

SCENE 1 (The Journey Back—30 min.)

*Orfeo and Euridice:* He hurries her up the path. At first she is barely **recitative**     aware of where she is or that it is Orfeo. But life comes slowly back to her and she begs him to look—just one look—at her. Orfeo tries to hurry her on, but finally she refuses to go another step: he does not love her; she'd rather be dead again amongst the shades.

Unable to evade the issue, Orfeo stops. He urges her to have faith, **duet**     but she repeats she would rather die than live again unloved. Together both suggest death is preferable to the pain in their hearts.

**recitative**    *Euridice and Orfeo:* She is unconvinced. Orfeo has changed. He has secrets; he won't look at her.

**aria**    She starts a lengthy and more vigorous aria in which she longs to be back in the Elysian Fields. Life with its pain is a deception. Orfeo, in what are almost asides, despairs of convincing her.

Euridice says she will go no further. Finally she says "Tu addio . . ." (farewell). Orfeo turns, and grasps her, as she dies again. He can hardly believe it. Then he realizes "Son io, Son io" (I am the one [who killed her]).

He sings "Che faro senza Euridice . . ." (what shall I do with-
**aria**    out Euridice . . .)? The aria is in three short verses which are not quite identical, although each begins with the same phrase. (An artist can make them of such increasing intensity that the last is too painful and, as Orfeo then reflects, only suicide is conceivable, to join Euridice in death.)

*Amor:* He stops Orfeo from stabbing himself and revives Euridice, saying that Orfeo's love, by failing the condition, is proven so great that Euridice is his reward.

(At this point some productions end with a trio of Amor, Orfeo and Euridice. Others use the trio to end the opera after a chorus and ballet in praise of Love and its God or end with the ballet following the trio.
**chorus and ballet**    The choice is not vital. The remainder of the opera [15 min.] is entirely ballet with an occasional chorus interjection, all representing an eighteenth-century idealization of antiquity. This generally involves a scene change to some acropolis or vale in Arcady. Depending on the merits of the ballet, the final scene seems either stilted and dated or charming and a good conclusion to the story which is, after all, a myth.)

### Vocabulary, Act III

| | | |
|---|---|---|
| tu addio | two ah.dee.oh | you farewell |
| son io | son ee.oh | I am the one |
| | | (who killed her) |
| che faro | kay far.OH | what shall I do |
| senza Euridice | sen.tsah Euridice | without Euridice |

# DIE ENTFUEHRUNG AUS DEM SERAIL

## (The Abduction from the Seraglio)

Opera in three acts. First performed in Vienna on July 16, 1782. Music by W. A. Mozart. Libretto by G. Stephanie after C. F. Bretzner's libretto for an opera on the same subject by J. André, which was first produced in Berlin on May 25, 1781.

### PRINCIPAL CHARACTERS

| | |
|---|---|
| Belmonte, a Spanish nobleman | tenor |
| Osmin, overseer for the Pasha | bass |
| Pedrillo, servant of Belmonte | tenor |
| Pasha Selim | speaking part |
| Constanza, loved by Belmonte | soprano |
| Blonde, maid of Constanza | soprano |

The action takes place in Turkey during the sixteenth century at the country palace of the Pasha.

Historically the opera is not an opera—because to Mozart's contemporaries in Vienna the language of opera was traditionally Italian —but a "singspiel," which meant it was supposed to be a popular piece that the common, German-speaking Austrians could enjoy: no Italian recitative, no carefully constructed finales, just little numbers. The difficulty with this was Mozart. As Sir Donald Tovey explains, "Mozart and Gluck are the two great reformers of opera, and the way in which Mozart reformed it is a most disconcerting lesson for Earnest Persons. He reformed it because, though, as all Italians averred throughout most of the nineteenth century, his genius was melancholy, he was an inveterate comedian and sinfully fond of music."

It never occurred to Mozart, unlike Sir Arthur Sullivan, that he was "above" the music-hall plot, or that he had to be serious, or that he had to be always comic. Instead, he lavished his music equally on the silly and the serious, entrancing his audience and driving musicologists to study "singspiel" as an unexpected basis of modern opera.

Turkey, the Ottoman Empire, was a fad in Vienna at the end of the eighteenth century. The threat of political domination receded when the Turks failed to take Vienna in 1687. Slowly thereafter the customs and dress of the Turks began to be intriguing rather than terrifying. All the composers, even Beethoven, wrote "Turkish" pieces and operas. At first the Turks were portrayed as cruel and lecherous, but gradually as time and fear passed, the "noble" Turk replaced his evil predecessor. The Pasha Selim in Mozart's opera is unbelievably noble. However, he is best known for being Mozart's only leading character who does not sing a note.

MOZART

In the opera, Belmonte is a Spaniard whose beloved, Constanza, was captured by pirates and sold, together with her servants, Blonde and Pedrillo, into slavery. Belmonte has traced them to Turkey, where they were bought by Pasha Selim, a rich and generous Turk, who has himself fallen in love with Constanza.

### OVERTURE (5 min.)

It is in ABA form (*See* Chap. II, *"Melody, Aria and Recitative,"* p. 14) with either end being spirited and martial in the Viennese idea of "Turkish" style. The middle section is in the minor and reflects the sighs and sadness of the captives and Belmonte. (The Turks introduced the triangle into Western music, and in the last measures Mozart rattles one for all its worth.)

### ACT I (35 min.)

The square in front of Selim's summer palace on the seashore. It is afternoon.

**aria**    No. 1 (2 min.)—*Belmonte:* He rhapsodizes on the thought of seeing Constanza again.

He wonders how he can get in the palace. Osmin, the Pasha's overseer and watchdog of the harem, comes out. He is enormously fat, ill-humored and suspicious. He leans a ladder against a tree, teeters up it and begins picking figs.

No. 2 (8 min.)—*Osmin; Osmin and Belmonte:* Deliberately ignoring Belmonte, Osmin lugubriously philosophizes on married love. If you **aria** have a good wife, he suggests, shower her with kisses, lock her up from your neighbor and, above all, beware of youthful serenaders and moonlit nights. Between each verse Belmonte tried to speak to him, but Osmin ignores him. Finally, Belmonte breaks through: **duet** "ist das des Bassa Selim Haus" (is that Pasha Selim's house)? Osmin allows it is and that he, Osmin, works there. Belmonte then asks him if he knows Pedrillo. At once Osmin flies into a rage: Pedrillo's head belongs atop a pole. He tells Belmonte to go to the "Teufel" (devil) and threatens to hit him. Belmonte, surprised and confused, withdraws.

Osmin mutters against Pedrillo, a foreigner with easy, sly ways. Pedrillo enters and attempts to be polite, but Osmin cuts him off short.

No. 3 (5 min.)—*Osmin:* He accuses Pedrillo of always thinking of **aria** girls and snooping around the harem. Osmin promises to catch him someday: "ich hab auch verstand" (I have also understood). Then in a fast coda he gleefully describes how he'll mangle, strangle, rip and tear Pedrillo to pieces. He goes out irate but happy.

(Mozart wrote his father about this aria: "Osmin's rage becomes comical with its accompaniment of Turkish music . . . as [it] gradually increases, the [coda] comes just when the aria seems at an end. It is in a totally different measure and key, which is bound to be very effective. For just as a man in such a towering rage forgets himself, so must the music too forget itself.")

Belmonte returns. Pedrillo delightedly informs him that Constanza is true to him. The Pasha, a perfect gentleman, has not forced himself on Constanza. Blonde, however, has been given to Osmin, and Pedrillo can't bear even to think of it. But all is not lost. He has found favor by being such a good gardener. He will introduce Belmonte to the Pasha as an architect, as the Pasha is mad for buildings and gardening. The Pasha, at the moment, is out yachting with Constanza, but he will return shortly. Pedrillo goes off to meet him.

**aria** No. 4 (5 min.)—*Belmonte:* He is beside himself with excitement. He can barely breathe. His heart pounds, he insists (the orchestra beats lightly): "klopft mein liebevolles Herz" (beats my loving heart). The ghastly separation will be over: "War es ein Traum" (was it a dream)?

(The aria, in two verses, has a particularly lovely accompaniment. Mozart wrote his father: "Would you like to know how I have expressed it? And even indicated the throbbing of his heart? By the two violins playing octaves . . . you feel the trembling, the faltering, you see how his throbbing heart begins to swell: this I have expressed by a Crescendo. You hear the whispering and the sighing, which I have indicated by the first violins and the mutes playing in unison.")

The Pasha and Constanza pull up to shore in his yacht, followed by a boat full of Janissaries who disembark first and sing the Pasha and Constanza ashore.

**chorus** No. 5 (2 min.)—*Janissaries:* (The Chorus, Mozart wrote, can be described as lively, short and written to please the Viennese.)

The Janissaries leave, and Selim asks if Constanza is ready to love him. In a bravura aria she explains that she can never love him. He paces back and forth, bored.

**aria** No. 6 (5 min.)—*Constanza:* She wails that she loves another. Her days of joy are over and turned to despair. Tears fill her eyes.

The Pasha grudgingly allows her one more day to forget her grief. But as soon as she has gone in, he admits he wants her love freely given, not forced. Pedrillo comes up with Belmonte, a famous architect, and the Pasha rather absently agrees to attach him to the household. Then he goes in. Belmonte is ecstatic. Now he will see Constanza. He and Pedrillo start to enter, but Osmin's bulging stomach blocks the way. He is furious that the Pasha has hired another foreigner, a friend of Pedrillo.

**trio** No. 7 (2 min.)—*Osmin, Pedrillo and Belmonte:* The three tussle and push. Osmin blusters: "Marsch, fort" (march off, quickly). They insist, "Platz, fort" (move aside, quickly), and in the end they win.

(Again, to his father Mozart explained: "I wind up with a great deal of noise, which is always appropriate at the end of an act.")

Vocabulary, Act I

| | | |
|---|---|---|
| ist das des Bassa Selim Haus | ist das des Bah.sah Say.lim house | is that Pasha Selim's house |
| Teufel | TOY.fel | devil |
| ich hab auch verstand | ish hahb owk fair.shtahnt | I have also understood |
| Herz | hairts | heart |
| war es ein traum | var es eye'n trowm | was it a dream |
| marsch, fort | marsh fort | march off, quickly |
| platz, fort | plats fort | move aside, quickly |

## ACT II (48 min.; with cut, 43)

A garden in Pasha Selim's palace. The sun is just setting. To the back are the buildings of the harem and on one side are Osmin's quarters.

No. 8 (4 min.)—*Blonde:* She warns Osmin to stop bullying her. Eu-
**aria**    ropean girls, she explains, are won by tenderness and kindness. (Her last run rises, or should, to three successive high E's, which makes casting the part difficult.)

    Osmin blusters that in Turkey she should behave like a Turk. He commands her to love him. Blonde replies that she is English and never will be a slave. She also threatens to scratch out his eyes. Even worse, she threatens to tell all the Turkish women what their rights are and how men ought to treat them. Osmin blanches at the thought of such a revolution.

No. 9 (3 min.)—*Osmin and Blonde:* Osmin insists that she'll soon learn who's boss. Impressively he slowly descends the scale to low E flat. Blonde chatters her defiance and, unimpressed, descends her scale
**duet**    to a low A flat. Osmin is outraged. "Oh Englander" (on Englishmen), he mutters as he wonders how they could breed such insolent women. She orders him out. He starts to object, but her threats of physical violence terrify him and he goes.

    Constanza wanders out in the garden. She knows nothing yet about Belmonte.

No. 10 (6 min.)—*Constanza:* She longs for Belmonte. "Traurigkeit" (sadness) surrounds her. She sighs to the breezes, but there is no relief
**aria**    for her "bitten schmerz" (bitter grief). Soon, like the rose about to wither, she must die.

    Blonde tries to encourage her but Constanza will not be con-soled. Blonde spies Selim Pasha coming and sneaks off so that he won't send her to Osmin. Selim asks Constanza if the end of day has influenced her heart. Tomorrow, he reminds her, she must return his love. Proudly, Constanza refuses him. She will die first. But before death there are tortures, he suggests.

**No. 11 (8 min.)**—*Constanza:* She now launches into her great aria, "Martern Aller Artern." It is the most difficult coloratura aria Mozart **aria** wrote and requires, in addition, great dramatic ability. It is constructed like a concerto with an orchestral introduction and four solo instruments, flute, oboe, violin and cello. It completely stalls the plot, and purists have always wanted it cut, particularly if the soprano is going to make a mess of it. But it is a musical masterpiece.

In the aria, Constanza defies his tortures. "Der Tod" (death) will set her free.

Constanza sweeps out, followed by Selim who is impressed. Pedrillo and Blonde enter, and he tells her that Belmonte has come and has a boat moored round the point. At midnight each will be at his lady's window with a ladder. Before then, as soon as it is dark enough, he will come into the garden. He also gives her some sleeping pills to give to Osmin.

**aria** **No. 12 (2 min.)**—*Blonde:* She bubbles with delight. She can't wait to tell Constanza.

**No. 13 (3 min.)**—*Pedrillo:* He sees more clearly than Blonde the **aria** dangers. In fact, he is nervous. "Frisch zum Kampfe" (fresh to battle), he encourages himself.

Osmin enters and Pedrillo proceeds to get him drunk.

**No. 14 (3 min.)**—*Osmin and Pedrillo:* "Vivat Bacchus," they sing. **duet** But Osmin fears that Allah may see him—until after the first sip. Thereafter he joins Pedrillo in praising all women: "die Blonden, die Braunen" (the blond ones, the dark ones).

Pedrillo packs the drunken Osmin off. Belmonte sneaks into the garden and meets Constanza.

**No. 15 (5 min.)**—*Belmonte:* He rejoices in being reunited with his **aria** beloved Constanza. (Sometimes this aria is omitted here and sung at the beginning of Act III where it fits just as well—possibly better.)

**No. 16 (9 min.)**—*Constanza, Blonde, Pedrillo and Belmonte:* The lovers rejoice. Then Belmonte sighs, and Pedrillo keeps repeating "doch Herr Osmin" (but Herr Osmin). The ladies beg to know what **quartet** troubles them. The men admit they fear the ladies succumbed to Selim and Osmin. Blonde hits Pedrillo. Constanza is deeply hurt. The men apologize and, after some hesitation, the ladies forgive them. The act ends with a fugue started by Constanza in which all hope love will flame forever.

### Vocabulary, Act II

| | | |
|---|---|---|
| Oh Englander | oh Eng.lahn.der | Oh Englishmen |
| Traurigkeit | trau.rig.keight | sadness |
| bittern Schmerz | bit.tern shmairts | bitter grief |
| der Tod | der toht | the death |
| frisch zum Kampfe | frish zum kahmf | fresh to battle |
| vivat Bacchus | vee.vaht Bak.kus | long live Bacchus |
| die Blonden, die | dee blond.en dee | the blond ones, the |
| Braunen | brow.nen | dark ones |
| doch Herr Osmin | doch hair Osmin | but Herr Osmin |

## ACT III (25 min.)

The square before Pasha Selim's palace; on one side, the palace; on the other, Osmin's quarters; to the back, the sea. A few minutes before midnight.

Pedrillo and a sailor enter with a ladder which they lean up to Constanza's window in the palace. Then they place another ladder to Blonde's window in Osmin's house. Belmonte enters and Pedrillo tells him to sing. (At this point there is a long, florid aria for Belmonte, No. 17, which is invariably cut. Sometimes No. 15 is placed here.) Pedrillo now sings a serenade, which is the signal.

**aria**  No. 18 (2 min.)—*Pedrillo:* He sings of a captive maiden freed by her lover.

After what seems to the men an unreasonably long time, Constanza opens her window, and she and Belmonte flee to the ship. Pedrillo climbs to Blonde's window as Osmin comes out the door below. A mute has heard the singing and woken Osmin. Osmin is confused by the mute and sits on the bottom rung of the ladder, trapping Pedrillo and Blonde on it. Osmin discovers them, sends after the other lovers and bags all four.

No. 19 (3 min.)—*Osmin:* He jigs with excitement. Now there will be a mass hanging. He sees the ropes around their necks: "schnueren
**aria**  zu" (throttling you). He gets so excited he even hiccups a

little coloratura and then sinks to a low D, which he holds for eight measures.

(The score here calls for a change of scene to Selim's chambers. But most productions require Selim to come to the square.) The Pasha appears. Constanza begs him to spare Belmonte. Belmonte offers to pay any ransom for himself and Constanza. His father is Commandant of Oran. Selim is overjoyed. The Commandant is his greatest enemy. Selim assures them of death preceded by dreadful tortures. Osmin beams and he and Selim leave.

No. 20 (7 min.)—*Belmonte and Constanza:* They philosophically view death as a release. "Was ist der Tod" (what is death)? she
**duet**    asks. First each blames himself for the other's death and offers to die for the other. But in the end, they decide, it is better to die together: "O welche seligkeit" (O what bliss).

The Pasha reappears and announces that he will free them to prove that it is a greater pleasure to repay evil with good than in kind. Osmin is furious.

No. 21 (5 min.)—*Constanza, Blonde, Pedrillo, Belmonte:* The opera ends with a "vaudeville," which here means that each character in turn
**quartet**    sings a verse and all join in the chorus. Each thanks the Pasha, and in chorus they praise his goodness. Osmin, however, breaks in. He insists they should all be hung, strangled, ripped and torn. With tears of rage, he waddles off, and the opera closes with a final chorus of the vaudeville.

### Vocabulary, Act III

| | | |
|---|---|---|
| schnueren zu | shnoo.wren tsoo | (rope) throttling you |
| was ist der Tod | vas ist der toht | what is death |
| O welche seligkeit | o vel.ker see.lig.kite | O what bliss |

# LE NOZZE DI FIGARO
## (The Marriage of Figaro)

Opera buffa in four acts. First performed at Vienna on May 1, 1786. Music by W. A. Mozart. Libretto by L. da Ponte, after Beaumarchais' comedy, *La Folle Journée, ou Le Mariage de Figaro,* first produced in 1785.

### PRINCIPAL CHARACTERS

| | | |
|---|---|---|
| Figaro, valet to Count Almaviva | baritone | FIG.ah.row |
| Susanna, maid to Countess Almaviva | soprano | sue.SAN.nah |
| Doctor Bartolo, former guardian of the Countess | bass | BAHR.toe.low |
| Marcellina, Doctor Bartolo's housekeeper | soprano | mar.chell.EEN.ah |
| Cherubino, page to the Countess | soprano | care.oo.BEE.no |
| Count Almaviva | baritone | al.mah.VEE.vah |
| Don Basilio, the Count's musician | tenor | bah.SEAL.yo |
| Countess Almaviva (Rosina) | soprano | |
| Antonio, a gardener and Susanna's uncle | bass | |
| Don Curzio, a lawyer | tenor | |
| Barbarina, Antonio's daughter | soprano | |

The action covers one day and evening in the eighteenth century at the Count's chateau of Aguas Frescas, near Seville.

*Figaro* was Mozart's first opera with Da Ponte, who created the libretto from the play by Beaumarchais. The play had been banned both in Paris and Vienna as subversive because it ridiculed the upper class and its privileges. Even in the opera a good deal of this comes through.

The opera turns on the renunciation by the Count of the "droit du Seigneur." This feudal custom allowed the lord of the manor to claim the maidenhead of his serf on her wedding night. The Count has voluntarily renounced his rights but, as the opera begins, he sorely regrets doing so and hopes to persuade Susanna voluntarily to observe the custom. Susanna and Figaro win out by trickery. In Paris, of course, the lower class won out by revolution.

It may seem incongruous to compare Da Ponte's libretto to Jane Austen's "Pride and Prejudice." Yet each work is a comic master-piece and there is a startling similarity of construction. In "Pride and Prejudice" Darcy proposes to Elizabeth twice: the first time is exactly halfway through the story, and he makes it perfectly plain to Elizabeth how lucky she is. It takes the rest of the novel to humble him sufficiently to propose again, this time without condescending. So, in Da Ponte's libretto in the Finale to Act II when Susanna, not Cherubino, emerges from the Countess' bedroom, the Count begs his wife's pardon. But it is only form. He still suspects her and still schemes for Susanna. But in the Finale to Act IV, when he begs pardon of the Countess, he has been humbled. He has learnt something. The music plainly says so.

All of which may suggest that art is depth rather than breadth of experience. The prim little Protestant who never left her father's parsonage knew as well how to do as the brilliant Italian Jew turned renegade Catholic priest. Da Ponte was also a friend of Casanova and Austrian Emperor Joseph II; he was bankrupt in London, a greengrocer in New York and a professor of Italian at Columbia University.

## OVERTURE (4 min.)

It is probably Mozart's greatest overture and goes very fast.

## ACT I (38 min.)

A half-furnished room in the chateau. There is a large armchair. Figaro is measuring the floor to see if the bed will fit; Susanna is trying on a hat. It is morning.

No. 1 (3 min.)—*Susanna and Figaro:* Figaro counts the inches (in one **duet** melody): "Cinque, dieci, venti . . ." (five, ten, twenty). Susanna models the hat (to a contrasting melody) and asks for admiration: "guarda" (look). Finally, Figaro gives up and admires it (to her melody): She was so clever to make it; it is just right for their wedding.

> Vaguely Susanna asks what he is measuring. To see if the bed promised by the Count will fit, he explains. Susanna puts the hat aside: the bed cannot go in this room, she states firmly. Figaro is dumfounded.

No. 2 (3 min.)—*Susanna and Figaro:* It is so convenient, he protests. If the Countess rings, "din, din," you are close by. If the Count rings, **duet** "don, don," I am close by. Susanna parodies him: if some morning the Count sends you on an errand, "din, din," and I am in bed, and he's so close, "don, don." Figaro stops her: "Susanna pian, pian . . ." (softly). She promises to tell him more if he won't be jealous.

> The Count, "il Signor Conte," Susanna explains, is looking for love at home but not from the Countess. She reminds Figaro of the "droit du Seigneur." But the Count has abolished it, Figaro insists. He wants to buy it back with the dowry, the bed, the room, Susanna explains. The Countess rings, and Susanna goes leaving Figaro to think on it.

No. 3 (2 min.)—*Figaro:* "Se vuol ballare, signor Contino . . ." (if **aria** you wish to dance that style . . .), then I'll call the tune,

Figaro muses. "Saprò, saprò" (I will know how), he insists. "Ma piano, piano . . ." (but for the moment, softly), he decides.

Figaro goes out. Marcellina and Bartolo enter. She confides that Figaro once borrowed money from her and agreed, if he failed to repay, to marry her. She plans to hold him to the contract. Bartolo agrees to assist her because several years before Figaro helped the Count to carry off the Countess from under Bartolo's nose. (Rossini's *Barber of Seville.*)

**aria**    No. 4 (3 min.)—*Bartolo: "La vendetta"* (vengeance). He gloats at the thought of getting even with Figaro.

Bartolo exits quickly. Susanna returns and finds Marcellina.

No. 5 (2 min.)—*Susanna and Marcellina:* The two ladies exchange **duet**    sharp pleasantries over who shall go out the door first. Susanna triumphs on "age before beauty" and Marcellina flounces out leaving Susanna behind, laughing.

Cherubino comes through the window. He's the victim of a disaster, he sighs. The Count found him under the table in Barbarina's room, and if the Countess, his godmother, can't get him pardoned, he's to be sent away. He sees Susanna has a ribbon, and he grabs it. It belongs to the Countess, whom he adores. He offers to give Susanna a song he's composed. He tells her to sing it to the Countess, Barbarina, Marcellina, or any woman.

No. 6 (3 min.)—*Cherubino:* What is it, he wonders, excitedly, pleasure or pain, that runs up and down me when I see a woman? Why does **aria**    my heart beat faster: "palpitar" (to palpitate). And when there is no one else to hear me, he confesses, I talk of love with myself: "con me" (with myself).

The Count calls through the door. Cherubino, terrified to be caught again in a lady's room, hides behind the chair. Entering, the Count tells Susanna he loves her, and she could make him happy. Basilio, the music teacher, enters. The Count hides behind the chair as Cherubino scoots round the front and into it. Susanna covers him with a dress. Basilio, who carries messages for the Count, leers that Susanna could make the Count happy. She protests. Basilio then gossips about how everyone says that Cherubino loves the Countess . . .

No. 7 (3 min.)—*Count, Basilio and Susanna:* The Count, infuriated, bursts out that Cherubino is to be dismissed at once. Basilio insists he didn't mean a thing. Susanna attempts to faint but revives quickly as the men maneuver her toward the chair where Cherubino is con-

**trio**     cealed. Susanna begs the Count to forgive the page, a boy. The Count describes how he discovered Cherubino in Barbarina's room. He lifts the dress, as he did the tablecloth in the girl's room, and once again uncovers Cherubino. Basilio squeals with delight. The Count remarks that it is clear why Susanna was defending Cherubino. She throws up her hands in despair.

    The Count tries to use the situation to pressure Susanna into accepting his proposal. Susanna, however, resolves to rely on the truth. Figaro knows there is nothing between her and Cherubino.

**chorus**     No. 8 (1 min.)—*Peasants:* Figaro leads in a chorus that politely thanks the Count for abolishing the "droit du Seigneur."

    Figaro makes a little speech of thanks and asks the Count to place a white veil on Susanna's head as a symbol of her virtue's being intact. He hopes by such a public display to force the Count to quit his efforts. The Count evades it, however, by promising to do it later.

No. 8a (1 min.)—*Peasants:* They haven't understood the byplay and
**chorus**     are just as pleased with later as now. Figaro and Susanna, however, are dashed.

    Figaro dismisses the peasants, and Susanna explains to him that Cherubino has been dismissed. The Count relents to the extent that the page can have a commission in the Count's regiment, provided he join it at once. The Count and Basilio exit, leaving Cherubino with Figaro and Susanna.

No. 9 (4 min.)—*Figaro:* He describes the new life for Cherubino: no
**aria**     more silks and satins and chasing the girls. No, sir! The army. Death and glory—if you live. Bugles—"alla gloria militar." "Non più andrai . . ." (no more will you go . . . [after the girls]).

### Vocabulary, Act I

| | | |
|---|---|---|
| cinque, dieci, venti | chink.way, dee.chee, ven.tee | five, ten, twenty |
| guarda | gwahr.dah | look |
| pian(o) | p'yon | softly |
| il Signor conte | eel seen.yor kone.tay | the Count |
| il padrone | eel pah.drone.nay | the Count |
| saprò | sah.PRO | I will know how |
| la vendetta | lah ven.DEBT.tah | vengeance |
| palpitar | pal.pea.tar | to palpitate |
| con me | kone may | with myself |
| non più andrai | known p'you an.dry | no more will you go . . . |

## ACT II (46 min.)

Later the same morning in the Countess' boudoir. Susanna has just told the Countess of the Count's advances and is leaving the room to get a dress.

**aria**     No. 10 (4 min.)—*Countess:* Sadly she asks the God of Love to restore the Count to her or let her die. (The first line is "Porgi Amor.")

> She asks Susanna what the Count has said. With a maid, Susanna observes, the Count doesn't offer compliments but money. And he must still love the Countess, she adds, or he wouldn't be so jealous. Figaro enters. He treats the Count's advances rather lightly, which irritates Susanna. He has a plan. He has sent the Count an anonymous letter warning that the Countess plans to meet a lover in the garden tonight. The Count, he explains, will be so raging and distracted that Susanna and he can get safely married. The Countess can simply stay in her room.
>
> Susanna is doubtful. Figaro suggests another note to the Count: this time ostensibly from Susanna and suggesting an assignation in the garden. Cherubino can go dressed as Susanna, and the Countess can "discover" the Count. The ladies agree, and Figaro leaves to send Cherubino to them.
>
> The Countess regrets that Cherubino heard the Count propose to Susanna. She asks about Cherubino's song, and when he enters, they have him sing it.

**aria**     No. 11 (3 min.)—*Cherubino:* The song is a question: Is this love, this thing in my heart? Tell me, you who know: "Voi che sapete . . ." (you who know).

> Susanna measures him for a dress for the assignation. While she gets one from the closet, Cherubino shows the Countess his commission papers. She comments that the Count's secretary forgot the seal. Susanna locks the door for the fitting of the dress.

**aria**     No. 12 (3 min.)—*Susanna:* While she dresses Cherubino, she twits him on his good looks and instructs him how to behave like a girl.

> The ladies discover the Countess' ribbon binding a scratch on Cherubino's arm. The Countess suggests a band-aid instead, and Susanna goes to get one. Cherubino insists that a ribbon that has

touched some particular person may be more healing. The Countess laughs. The Count, trying to enter, demands the door be unlocked. The Countess hides Cherubino in an inner room and locks him in. The Count has received Figaro's anonymous letter. He demands an explanation from the Countess. In the inner room Cherubino knocks over a chair. The Count accuses the Countess of having her lover inside. She insists it is only Susanna.

No. 13 (3 min.)—*Count, Countess and Susanna:* The Count demands Susanna come out. The Countess urges her to stay inside. Susanna
**trio**    comes back with the band-aid and hides behind a screen. The Count and Countess warn each other to have a care: "giudizio" (be careful). Susanna despairs that there will be a real scandal.

    The Count then locks every other door in the room and insists the Countess accompany him while he gets a crowbar to pry open the door. The Countess, who has not seen Susanna, is in despair.

No. 14 (1 min.)—*Susanna and Cherubino:* Susanna calls to him to come out, and apparently he can unlock the door from his side. The
**duet**    window is the only way out of the room. For the Countess, Cherubino insists, he will risk it. Susanna urges him against it, but he jumps. She sees him off and then locks herself in the room.

    The Count and Countess return. Faced with the crowbar, she admits that Cherubino is in the room. Remembering Basilio's gossip, the Count is furious.

No. 15, *Finale* (21 min.)—(The music flows unbroken to the end of the act. Changes in situation are indicated by A, B, etc. Musicians think this finale to be one of the greatest ever written. It is not very long, but notice how much action Mozart and Da Ponte develop—without any sense of hurry—and the enormous variety obtained by different combinations of voices, starting with a duet and increasing to a septet.)

    A: The Count demands Cherubino come out. The Countess pleads with the Count not to hurt him. She explains that she was dressing
**duet**    him. At the mention of clothing, the Count demands the key —"chiave"—and threatens to disown his wife who has, he claims, stained the family honor. She insists she is guiltless. He swears he'll be revenged on Cherubino. He takes the key from her and unlocks the door.

    B: It is Susanna. She quips that "Cherubino" is ready to die. Both Count and Countess are confused. The Count can't find anyone else

in the inner room. Susanna whispers to the Countess that Cherubino
**trio**    is safely out. Then they turn on the Count. He pleads that he
loves the Countess, that the circumstances were deceiving. The Countess scorns him while allowing Susanna to urge her to forgive him.
The Count offers the anonymous letter as a cause for his conduct. The
ladies explain (a real mistake in strategy!) that Figaro invented it.
The Count begs "guardatemi" (forgive me), and the Countess graciously does.

C: Figaro enters to say that everything is ready for the wedding.
But the Count stops him. He shows Figaro the anonymous letter and
**quartet**    asks if he recognize it. Figaro denies it: "nol conosco"
(I don't know it), while the Countess and Susanna try to signal him
that they've already admitted the truth. Figaro tries to turn the subject back to the wedding, and he and the ladies beg the Count not to
spoil the festivities.

D: Antonio, the gardener, enters rather drunk, although it is still
morning. He complains that every day people throw rubbish out of
**quintet**    the windows and spoil his flowers. But today was beyond
bearing: they threw out a man. "In giardino?" (into the garden), asks
the Count, looking at the Countess' balcony. He tromped on the
carnations, Antonio wails. Susanna whispers to Figaro that it was
Cherubino. Figaro laughs and tells the Count the gardener is drunk.
The Count, however, refuses to disbelieve the story, so Figaro says it
was he. He heard the Count coming, he explains, was afraid because
of the letter and jumped—twisted his ankle, in fact. Antonio says he
thinks it was the page, Cherubino, but whoever it was, he dropped all
his papers.

Everyone reaches, but the Count gets them. He asks Figaro to
identify them and dismisses the gardener. The Countess recognizes
**quartet**    Cherubino's commission. She tells Susanna, who whispers
to Figaro, who identifies it to the Count. The Count then asks why
Figaro had it. Again the Countess to Susanna to Figaro: it lacked the
Count's seal. Balked again, the Count rips the papers in disgust. He
still suspects, while the others rejoice at the close escape.

E: Marcellina, Basilio and Bartolo enter. Marcellina demands that
**septet**    Figaro honor his contract: to pay up or marry her. Figaro
hasn't the money. The Countess and Susanna despair. The Count calls
for silence: "silenzio." Bartolo says he represents Marcellina. The act

ends with the wedding obviously delayed, and each person commenting thereon either sadly, angrily or gleefully.

### Vocabulary, Act II

| | | |
|---|---|---|
| voi che sapete | voi kay sah.PAY.teh | you who know |
| giudizio | jew.dee.tsio | take care |
| chiave | key.AH.veh | the key |
| guardatemi | gwour.dah.tay.me | forgive me |
| nol conosco | knoll con.oh.skow | I don't know it |
| in giardino | een jar.DEEN.oh | into the garden |
| silenzio | see.LEN.tsio | silence |

## ACT III (39 min.)

The same day a few hours later in a large hall of the chateau. The Count, muttering to himself, tries to sort out the intrigue. The Countess pushes Susanna in to make an assignation with him for the garden that evening. The Countess plans to go herself in Susanna's place and makes Susanna promise not to tell anyone —not even Figaro. The Count warns Susanna that the dowry he promised, which would settle Marcellina's claims, will be paid only for services rendered.

No. 16 (3 min.)—*Count and Susanna:* He suggests they meet. She **duet** agrees: "si." He fears she'll back out. She denies it: "no." He is excited—"gioja." He keeps reasking her, and she begins to get mixed up on "si" and "no."

Figaro steps in looking for Susanna. As they go off, the Count overhears her tell Figaro that they are all set now. At once the Count suspects a trick.

No. 17 (5 min.)—*Count:* As he imagines them plotting, he grows furious. He is the Count; Figaro, a servant. Who should have Susanna's **aria** charms? Figaro is presumptuous. He will have Susanna out of lust, out of vengeance—because he is the Count. (This is the Count's great moment of self-revelation, and although it is a beautiful aria, a good bass will make it horrifying, a moment when all the Count's worst characteristics combine in an evil bloom.)

Figaro, Marcellina and Bartolo enter with Don Curzio, a lawyer. The law is plain: Figaro must marry Marcellina. Figaro insists he can't marry without the consent of his parents, from whom he was stolen as a baby. Marcellina gasps. She identifies a birth-mark on Figaro's arm and announces that he is her son. Bartolo is his father.

No. 18 (5 min.)—*Count, Bartolo, Figaro, the lawyer, Marcellina and Susanna:* Bartolo and Marcellina continually embrace Figaro, sighing, **sextet** "figlio amato" (beloved son). Susanna arrives and believes that Figaro has agreed to marry Marcellina. She smacks him. There are explanations: "sua madre, suo padre" (his mother, his father), and everyone but the Count is happy.

No. 19 (6 min.)—*The Countess:* She enters alone. (This is her great aria.) She worries about the night in the garden. She and Susanna will each go disguised as the other. She now must pose as her maid to meet **aria** her lord. Softly she starts: "Dove sono . . . i bei momenti . . ." (where are they . . . the beautiful moments of love). Sadly she recalls the bygone days (two verses). Then, more excitedly, she wonders if her "constanza" (constancy) will ever win his love again. She goes off.

The Count enters and hears Antonio insist that Cherubino has not left for the regiment but is in his house being dressed as a girl. Antonio leads the Count off to show him. The Countess and Susanna enter. The Countess asks Susanna if the Count agreed to meet her. Then to clinch the assignation she dictates a love note for Susanna to send to the Count.

**duet** No. 20 (2 min.)—*Countess and Susanna:* She asks the Count to walk by the sweet-smelling pine trees. They agree that the Count will understand the rest: "il capirà" (he will understand).

They seal it with a pin. Barbarina and the other girls (among them Cherubino) enter.

**chorus** No. 21 (1 min.)—*Peasant and servant girls:* They give the Countess their flowers.

Cherubino tries to look inconspicuous, but the Countess recognizes him and is beginning to twit him when the Count and Antonio arrive and defrock him. Barbarina cries that the Count, when he kisses her, is always promising her anything she wants, and now she wants Cherubino. In the confusion the wedding march begins. All go out except the Count and Countess, who sit on a dais in the hall to receive the two couples. (Bartolo and Marcellina, Figaro and Susanna.)

No. 22, *Finale* (6 min.)—Two girls thank the Count for renouncing

**chorus and ballet**     his rights to their favors. The household dances a fandango. Susanna slips the Count the note, and he pricks himself on the pin. The girls continue to praise the Count for letting them keep their virtue.

Vocabulary, Act III

| | | |
|---|---|---|
| si . . . no | see . . . no | yes . . . no |
| gioja | je.OY.ah | joy |
| figlio amato | feel.yo ah.mah.toe | beloved son |
| sua madre | sue.ah mah.dray | his mother |
| suo padre | sue.oh pah.dray | his father |
| dove sono | doe.veh so.no | where are they |
| i bei momenti | ee bay.ee moe.men.tee | the beautiful moments |
| constanza | con.stan.tsa | constancy |
| il capirà | eel cah.pee.rah | he will understand |

## ACT IV (35 min.; with usual cuts, 23)

That evening in the garden of the chateau. Arbors to the right and left. Barbarina with a lantern is searching the ground.

**aria**     No. 23 (1 min.)—*Barbarina:* "L'ho perduta," she sighs. (I've lost it.)

Figaro and Marcellina enter. Barbarina explains that she has lost a pin that the Count told her to deliver to Susanna with a message about the sweet-smelling pines. Figaro at once suspects the worst and complains bitterly to Marcellina.

(The next two arias are almost always cut. This makes Marcellina go off, and Figaro starts immediately on his denunciaton of women at No. 26. If the arias are not cut, Figaro goes off and Marcellina stays.)

**aria (usually cut)**     No. 24 (3 min.)—*Marcellina:* She decides to warn Susanna that Figaro knows of the assignation and is planning to hide in the arbor, for, after all, women have to stick together.

Marcellina goes off. Barbarina comes on with some food for Cherubino. She looks for him in the arbor to the left. Figaro leads in Basilio and Bartolo, tells them that Susanna is about to bestow her favors on the Count. He wants them to catch her in the act and jump out of the arbor when he whistles. Bartolo is sympathetic, but Basilio thinks Figaro is silly to take on.

**aria (usually cut)**     No. 25 (4 min.)—*Basilio:* He expresses his philosophy: better not to kick against the pricks.

The two men hide in the arbor to the left. Figaro returns.

No. 26 (5 min.)—*Figaro:* He soliloquizes: only fools put any trust in
**aria** women. He urges all men: "Aprite un po quegl' occhi" (open
your eyes a little) and see what women do. (In the orchestra the horns,
symbol of cuckoldry, blow a call.)

He hides by coming down to the front of the stage. Susanna and
the Countess enter, each in the other's dress or cloak. Marcellina
whispers that Figaro is listening. The Countess and Marcellina
wander down an alley of the garden, and Susanna, knowing
Figaro is listening, sings an outrageously sensual song to the
lover she awaits. (The libretto does not make it clear whether
Susanna sings this with her disguise on or off. The implication
seems to be that she has laid the Countess' cloak aside, and most
producers stage the scene this way.)

**aria** No. 27 (4 min.)—*Susanna:* She murmurs of the perfume of
the pine needles, the soft night air.

Susanna goes off down an alley. Figaro is disgusted. Susanna
or, if sung in disguise, the Countess, joyfully deceives her husband.
At this moment Cherubino enters, spies the Countess and thinks
she is Susanna.

No. 28, *Finale* (15 min.)—A: Cherubino extravagantly pursues the
false Susanna. The Countess is terrified that the Count will arrive and
discover her in disguise with Cherubino. The Count does come and
tries to box Cherubino's ear for bothering "Susanna." But in the dark
and confusion, he hits Figaro. Cherubino and Figaro disappear into
the arbor.

B: The Count then rhapsodizes his love for "Susanna" and gives
the Countess a ring. Figaro and the real Susanna comment from the
side. The false Susanna then goes down an alley while the Count, going
out the other side, promises to join her in a minute.

C: Susanna comes out and Figaro, to be revenged on the Count,
urges the "Countess" to come with him and catch the Count "in
flagranti delicto." Susanna, however, for an instant forgets to change
her voice, and Figaro recognizes her. So now he pretends to make love
to the "Countess." Susanna, irritated, smacks him angrily until he
cries for peace: "pace, pace, mio dolce tesoro . . ." (peace, peace, my
sweet treasure). He reveals he knew her all along. They laugh and
make love even more ardently to catch the Count's attention. He
returns and is outraged at the "Countess!" He calls in everyone to see
her disgrace.

D: The "Countess" begs forgiveness: "perdono." Instead, the Count renounces her. All plead for her. Six times he repeats "no." Then the real Countess steps out and suggests that she forgive the offender. The Count realizes the true situation and, kneeling before her, asks her pardon: "Contessa, perdono" (Countess, forgive me). (The music shows that this is not a perfunctory "excuse me." The Count has suddenly seen himself as he really is.) Softly the Countess replies that she is more gentle than he and to his plea will say "si." The others observe that it is better to forget and forgive. The opera ends as all agree to go in and enjoy the wedding feast.

### Vocabulary, Act IV

| l'ho perduta | low pair.dew.tah | I have lost it |
| aprite un po quegl' occhi | ah.preet oon po quell yock.key | open a little those eyes |
| pace, pace, mio dolce tesoro | pah.chay pah.chay me.oh dole.chay tez.oar.row | peace, peace, my sweet treasure |
| perdono | pair.doe.no | forgive, pardon |

# DON GIOVANNI

Dramma giocoso in two acts. First performed at Prague on October 29, 1787. Music by W. A. Mozart. Libretto by L. da Ponte, fashioned in part after the libretto by G. Bertati for an opera, *Don Giovanni*, by G. Gazzaniga, which was first produced on February 5, 1787 in Venice.

### PRINCIPAL CHARACTERS

| Leporello, servant to Don Giovanni | bass | lep.or.ell.oh |
| Donna Anna, betrothed to Don Ottavio | soprano | |
| Don Giovanni, a young nobleman | baritone | |
| The Commendatore, father of Donna Anna | bass | com.men.dah.TOR.ay |
| Don Ottavio, friend of Don Giovanni | tenor | oh.TAHV.ee.o |
| Donna Elvira, a lady of Burgos, deserted by Don Giovanni | soprano | ell.VEE.rah |
| Zerlina, a peasant girl, betrothed to Masetto | soprano | zair.LEE.nah |
| Masetto, a peasant | bass | mah.ZET.toe |

The action takes place in and around Seville in the middle of the seventeenth century.

*Don Giovanni* is supposed to be—at least most everybody says it is —the greatest opera ever written. (Beethoven, however, preferred *Die Zauberfloete*.) But for the "greatest" opera, an extraordinary argument rages over how it should end.

Mozart wrote the opera for Prague in 1787. He ended it with a sextet in which all the characters moralize on Don Giovanni's bad end. In the course of it, Donna Elvira announces she'll retire to a convent; Donna Anna promises to marry Ottavio; Zerlina takes Masetto home for dinner; and Leporello starts for Seville to find a new master. The matter-of-fact plans mixed with the stylized moralizing stress the eighteenth-century, comic side of the opera.

However, at the Viennese première in 1788, Mozart cut the sextet and ended with Don Giovanni's descent into Hell. Throughout the romantic nineteenth century, serious burghers trudged home after a performance overwhelmed by Mozart's tremendous statement of the tragedy of Everyman.

Now in the twentieth century the trend is back to the original, Prague ending. But scattered through the audience, as the sextet comes on, is a horrified hard core with its eyes shut and its fingers in its ears.

Mozart himself left confused clues, for when he cut the sextet for Vienna, he also added a scene of broad burlesque in which Zerlina attacks Leporello with a razor and threatens to give him a "dry" shave. This is never given today, as Mozart clearly inserted it only to replace an aria which the Viennese tenor couldn't sing. But it may indicate Mozart's point of view. He himself entitled the opera a "dramma giocoso."

The original Don Giovanni in the Prague company, and for whom the part was written, was twenty-two years old, a bit of casting no modern producer has been able to equal. Alas! For occasionally some fearful sagging thighs step out in tights.

Musically the opera is a series of twenty-six numbers connected by recitative. Nos. 14 and 26 are the finales and are, of course, extended, but the others are extremely short, which in a good production gives the opera tremendous pace.

## OVERTURE (7 min.)

An ominous, slow section associated with the statue is followed by one swift and vigorous, a characterization of Don Giovanni.

## ACT I (78 min.)

---

## SCENE 1 (13 min.)

A garden in the palace of the Commendatore. Night. Leporello is watching.

No. 1 (5 min.)—*Leporello, Donna Anna, Don Giovanni and the*
**aria** *Commendatore:* Leporello complains of the lot of a servant. "Non voglio più servir, no, no, no . . ." (I do not wish anymore to serve . . . no, no, no). Don Giovanni has the fun while he watches.

Don Giovanni, trying to escape unrecognized after an attempted
**trio** rape, cannot shake off Donna Anna. She screams for help. Leporello complains that there'll be real trouble now. She drops Don Giovanni's arm and runs for help.

The Commendatore appears and challenges Don Giovanni, who refuses to fight such an old man. The Commendatore insists and is
**trio** killed. In a short trio (eighteen bars) the old man dies, Don Giovanni wishes peace to his soul, and Leporello wishes he were clear of the whole situation. (Musicians admire this tiny trio as a miracle of mood.)

Don Giovanni and Leporello escape before Donna Anna returns

with servants, lights and Don Ottavio.

No. 2 (6 min.)—*Donna Anna and Don Ottavio:* "Padre mio" (my
**duet**     father), Donna Anna sobs. When she realizes he's dead, she
faints. Don Ottavio has the body removed and then tries to console
her. But she can only moan for her father. Then rage revives her, and
she makes Don Ottavio swear to avenge him. "Lo giuro," he agrees
(I swear it).

## SCENE 2 (12 min.)

A street in Seville, one morning some time later. Leporello has
something to say, but Don Giovanni will let him talk only if he
doesn't mention the Commendatore. Leporello agrees and then
tries to warn Don Giovanni about his way of life. The lecture is
cut short by Don Giovanni's scenting a woman. Unknown to
him, it is Donna Elvira. They hide.

No. 3 (4 min.)—*Donna Elvira:* She laments that a man, a barbarian
(Don Giovanni), promised to marry her, stole her maidenhead and
**aria**     then left. Now she wants to find him and marry him or be
revenged. "Poverina" (poor lady), Don Giovanni observes to Leporello. He comes out to console her and is horrified to discover it is
Donna Elvira.

Recriminations fly back and forth. Leporello observes that it is
like a novel. Don Giovanni contrives to get her attention fixed
on Leporello and to slip away. Leporello assures her she is well
rid of Don Giovanni and as evidence sings a catalogue of his
master's conquests.

No. 4 (6 min.)—*Leporello:* The refrain is, "Ma in Ispagna . . .
mille e tre" (but in Spain . . . one thousand and three). (For purposes of the opera, Don Giovanni's conquests total 2,065—640 in
Italy, 231 in Germany, 100 in France, 91 in Turkey and 1,003 in
**aria**     Spain. His three attempts in the opera all fail.) Leporello
describes the ladies: thin, fat, old, young or tiny—"la piccina." Virgins
particularly excite him. "Voi sapete" (you know), Leporello insists
as he goes off. (The aria is generally called "madamina," its opening
word.)

Donna Elvira can only swear revenge.

## SCENE 3 (28 min.)

In the country near Don Giovanni's château later that morning.
**duet and chorus**      No. 5 (1 min.)—*Zerlina, Masetto and peasants:*
The peasants make a fuss over Zerlina and Masetto, who are to be
married today.

Don Giovanni and Leporello enter congratulating themselves on
escaping Donna Elvira. Don Giovanni's eye lights on Zerlina.
He invites all the peasants to his château for a feast and gets
Leporello to lure Masetto away. Only Masetto won't go without
Zerlina. Finally Don Giovanni, as a nobleman, orders him off.
No. 6 (1 min.)—*Masetto:* "Ho capito" (I understand), he con-
**aria**      cedes. "Vengo, vengo" (I'm coming), he calls to Leporello.
But he doesn't like it and says so in asides to Zerlina.

Don Giovanni at once sets out to charm Zerlina. He promises to
marry her and make her a lady.
No. 7 (3 min.)—*Don Giovanni and Zerlina:* "Vieni" (come), he insists. "Là ci darem la mano . . ." (you'll put your hand in mine) and
**duet**      we'll be married. Zerlina is uncertain: "Vorrei e non vorrei"
(I would and I wouldn't). Finally, she agrees: "Andiam" (let's go).

But Donna Elvira arrives and takes in the situation at a glance.
Don Giovanni protests and then tells Zerlina that Donna Elvira
loves him and is hysterically jealous.
**aria**      No. 8 (1 min.)—*Donna Elvira:* "Fuggi" (flee), she warns
Zerlina, who doesn't know whom to believe.

Donna Elvira leads her off. Donna Anna and Don Ottavio enter.
She requests Don Giovanni to help her. But before she can explain
how, Donna Elvira returns and sees Don Giovanni apparently
charming yet another victim.
No. 9 (4 min.)—*Donna Elvira, Donna Anna, Don Ottavio and Don*
**quartet**      *Giovanni:* She warns Donna Anna against him. Don
Giovanni insists that Donna Elvira is a well-known mental case. Donna
Anna and Don Ottavio are confused.

Donna Elvira goes off, and Don Giovanni hastily excuses himself from the others to be sure that Donna Elvira gets home safely.
No. 10 (6 min.)—*Donna Anna:* She launches into a dramatic, declamatory recitative. It is accompanied by the full orchestra. She rec-
**aria**      ognizes Don Giovanni's voice. He is the man. Shuddering,
she describes how he crept into her room, how she wrestled with him,

how he kept his face masked. But she is sure of the voice. She soars into an aria, calling on Don Ottavio to avenge her: "vendetta" (vengeance). (This is Donna Anna's great moment. The aria is a tour de force and, if delivered with the proper vehemence, exhausts the soprano. There is evidence that Mozart originally intended to have the opera in four acts with the first ending here.)

Don Ottavio is puzzled. He cannot believe a nobleman could behave as described. He resolves to discover the truth and either clear his friend, Don Giovanni, or avenge Donna Anna.

No. 11 (4 min.)—*Don Ottavio:* He promises to find peace of mind for **aria** Donna Anna. He will share her burden. (This was composed for the Viennese première to replace No. 22, which the tenor could not sing. Now tenors insist on singing both.)

Don Ottavio goes off, and Leporello and Don Giovanni return. Leporello reports that he has made all the arrangements for the feast, soothed Masetto and locked Donna Elvira out of the château.

**aria** No. 12 (1 min.)—*Don Giovanni:* He is pleased. He orders Leporello to keep the liquor flowing and promises by morning to have twelve new entries for the catalogue. (The aria is called by its first line, "Fin ch'han dal vino," or more popularly "The Champagne aria.")

## SCENE 4 (16 min.)

A garden with Don Giovanni's château in the background. Zerlina is trying to persuade Masetto that nothing happened. He is huffy.

**aria** No. 13 (4 min.)—*Zerlina:* "Batti, batti . . ." (beat me), she sings, but afterwards we can be friends again. "Pace, pace . . ." (peace).

Masetto is won over. Unfortunately, however, Zerlina starts at the sound of Don Giovanni's voice off stage, and all his suspicions revive.

No. 14 (19 min.)—*Finale:* (Here begins the first finale which runs unbroken by recitative and through a change of scene to the end of the act. It divides roughly into five parts which are indicated A, B, etc.)

A: (5 min.)—Masetto hides in an arbor in order to spy on Zerlina and Don Giovanni. This irritates Zerlina. But as Don Giovanni comes on instructing his servants, she decides to hide too. But Don Giovanni discovers her at once. She hesitates, and Don Giovanni leads her insistently to the arbor where Masetto is hiding. On discovering him, Don Giovanni scolds him for leaving his bride alone and takes them both in to the party.

**trio** B: (5 min.)—Donna Anna, Donna Elvira and Don Ottavio creep in, all masked, to spy on Don Giovanni. From a window Leporello sees them and, on Don Giovanni's instructions, invites them in to the party. They sing a trio asking Heaven's help and blessing: "protega . . ." (protect).

### SCENE 5 (9 min.)

The ballroom of the château opening at the back into two other rooms. In each there is an orchestra.

**chorus** C: (2 min.)—Don Giovanni is the charming host; Zerlina is nervous and Masetto sullen. Don Giovanni signals Leporello to help get Masetto away. The three masks enter. There are introductions, and all praise the gay life: "Viva la libertà" (long live liberty).

**ballet** D: (3 min.)—The orchestra in the front room (i.e. the pit) strikes up a minuet. (Theoretically, only the nobles dance to this.) Leporello tries to get Masetto away. The second orchestra strikes up a country dance (the peasants, Don Giovanni and Zerlina dance to this). The third orchestra begins a waltz and Leporello forces Masetto to dance with him to this. As everything goes on at once, Don Giovanni pulls Zerlina off.

**chorus** E: (4 min.)—Off stage Zerlina screams for help. Everyone talks about breaking the door down when Don Giovanni comes out holding Leporello by the ear. But Don Ottavio will have none of that. He unmasks and accuses Don Giovanni of all his crimes. All join in the indictment. "Trema" (tremble), they insist. A huge thunderstorm crashes down. Don Giovanni starts to duel with Don Ottavio, but in the confusion they are separated and Don Ottavio attends Donna Anna.

### Vocabulary, Act I

| | | |
|---|---|---|
| non voglio più servir | known voe.l'yo p'you sair.veer | I do not wish anymore to serve |
| padre mio | pah.dray me.oh | my father |
| lo giuro | low jure.oh | I swear it |
| poverina | poe.vair.ee.nah | poor lady |

Vocabulary, Act I (*continued*)

| | | |
|---|---|---|
| ma in Ispagna | ma een ee.spah.n'yah | but in Spain |
| mille e tre | meal eh tray | one thousand and three |
| la piccina | lah pee.chee.nah | the tiny lady |
| voi sapete | voy sah.pay.tay | you know |
| ho capito | ho cap.ee.toe | I understand |
| vengo, vengo | veng.go | I'm coming |
| vieni | v'yay.knee | come |
| là ci darem la mano | lah chee dah.rem lah mah.no | you'll put your hand in mine |
| vorrei e non vorrei | vor.eh eh known vor.eh | I would and I wouldn't |
| andiam | an.d'yahm | let's go |
| fuggi | food.jee | flee |
| vendetta | ven.debt.tah | vengeance |
| batti, batti | bah.tee | beat me |
| protega | pro.tay'juh | protect |
| viva la libertà | vee.vah lah lee.bear.tah | long live liberty |
| trema | tray.mah | tremble |

# ACT II (79 min.)

## SCENE 1 (21 min.)

A street in Seville before the house in which Donna Elvira is staying. There is a balcony. It is night.

No. 15 (1 min.)—*Leporello and Don Giovanni:* Leporello is tired of **duet** Don Giovanni's woman-chasing. He threatens to quit. He will not stay: "no." He will go: "si."

Don Giovanni gives him money, and Leporello changes his plans. But he still mutters. Don Giovanni ignores him and explains that he is now after Donna Elvira's maid. He forces Leporello to exchange cloaks with him. Donna Elvira steps out on the balcony.

No. 16 (5 min.)—*Donna Elvira, Don Giovanni and Leporello:* **trio** She wonders why she still thinks of Don Giovanni. To get her out of the way so he can pursue the maid, Don Giovanni calls to her from a concealed position while Leporello (in Don Giovanni's cloak) waves to her to come down. After much hesitation, she agrees.

Don Giovanni is pleased. Now Leporello can lead Donna Elvira down a few streets and lose her before she discovers the deception.

Leporello calls him heartless but does it—and rather enjoys it. **aria** No. 17 (1 min.)—*Don Giovanni:* He serenades the maid.

(The accompaniment, scored for a mandolin, is often faked on a violin.)

The maid appears on the balcony, but the arrival of Masetto and his friends scares her back in. Masetto is looking for Don Giovanni in order to kill him. Don Giovanni (in Leporello's cloak) pretends he is Leporello and directs them down the street where Leporello led Donna Elvira.

No. 18 (3 min.)—*Don Giovanni:* He sends some down one street, **aria** others down another. He describes exactly his own cloak, which Leporello is wearing, and warns them that the intended victim is armed. Keeping Masetto by the hand, he leads him down a third street.

Don Giovanni circles Masetto around the block and then asks him what weapons he has. Masetto hands over his pistol and sword for inspection and is promptly hit on the head, kicked and left moaning in the street. Zerlina, with a lantern, finds him.

**aria** No. 19 (3 min.)—*Zerlina:* She has a cure for his sore head. She keeps it in her heart. She takes Masetto out.


## SCENE 2 (21 min.)

A few moments later in a courtyard of Donna Anna's palace. It is very dark.

Leporello has been unable to lose Donna Elvira who, being terrified of the dark, keeps ahold of him.

No. 20 (8 min.)—*Donna Elvira, Donna Anna, Zerlina, Leporello, Don Ottavio and Masetto:* Donna Elvira complains of the dark. Leporello feels for the archway out. Just as he locates it, it is filled by servants preceding Donna Anna and Don Ottavio, who briefly lament the Commendatore's death. Donna Elvira, too, now wants to get away before being discovered. Leporello finds another arch but is caught **sextet** by Zerlina and Masetto, who are entering. All think he is Don Giovanni and prepare to beat him. Donna Elvira, revealing herself, passionately begs them to have pity: "pietà, pietà" (have pity). This surprises everyone, but they decide to go ahead with the beating anyway. Leporello at once identifies himself, at which all exclaim at length, and Donna Anna (who as a lady wouldn't stay to see a servant beaten) sails out.

The rest, however, argue briefly over who will strike the first blow.

(This may have been where Mozart originally intended to end Act III of a four-act version, in order to start the next act in the cemetery.)

**aria**     No. 21 (2 min.)—*Leporello:* He sobs for mercy, "Pietà." He admits everything, knows nothing, inches closer to the door and darts out.

Don Ottavio invites them to wait in Donna Anna's house while he gets the police to arrest Don Giovanni, who, he is now convinced, killed the Commendatore. (The police seems a rather craven solution, but according to the times the correct one, because the death of the Commendatore was not a matter of honor but of murder.)

**aria**     No. 22 (4 min.)—*Don Ottavio:* He asks them to tell Donna Anna that love and duty call him away from her side. He asks them to console her: "cercate" (enquire [after her]).

Donna Elvira stays alone. The others go off with Don Ottavio. No. 23 (6 min.)—*Donna Elvira:* She expresses her confusion. Don Giovanni has betrayed her: "mi tradi quell' alma ingrata . . ." (betrayed me that ungrateful soul); and yet: "provo ancor per lui pietà"

**aria**     (I feel still for him pity). (The aria has an almost unique flow to it. It is Donna Elvira's great moment. Mozart composed it for the Donna Elvira at the Viennese première who asked for something that would get applause. Now no Elvira will omit it.)

## SCENE 3 (7 min.)

A few moments later in a churchyard enclosed by a wall, with a statue of the Commendatore. Moonlight. Don Giovanni leaps over the wall.

Here follows an unusually long recitative. Leporello first complains of his narrow escape from a beating. Don Giovanni counters with a description of a girl he just left, who kissed him because she thought he was Leporello. Leporello is indignant. "Suppose it was my wife?" he asks. "Even funnier," Don Giovanni laughs. At this point the Statue speaks: Your laughter ends at dawn. The two men can't discover anyone hiding, so Don Giovanni makes Leporello read the inscription on the statue: "Here I wait for vengeance on the blasphemer who killed me." The superstitious Leporello is terrified. Don Giovanni insists, however, that he ask the statue to dinner.

No. 24 (3 min.)—*Leporello and Don Giovanni:* With teeth chattering, Leporello begins: "O statua gentilissima . . ." (oh most noble
**duet**     statue . . .). He breaks down. Don Giovanni threatens
him with his sword. Leporello invites it to dinner. The statue nods.
"Guardate" (look), Leporello gasps. Don Giovanni asks the statue
to speak. "Si," it says. Don Giovanni is intrigued, Leporello terrified.

## SCENE 4 (8 min.)

A room in Donna Anna's palace.

Don Ottavio reports that he has been to the police and that soon
the Commendatore's death will be avenged. He suggests to Donna
Anna that now she can marry him. She refuses. It is too soon. He calls
her "crudel" (cruel). She is hurt.

No. 25 (6 min.)—*Donna Anna:* "Non mi dir . . ." (don't call me
**aria**     . . . cruel), she asks. Then, as the aria gets increasingly
florid, she prays Heaven to ease her anguish.

     Quite carried away, she goes out. Don Ottavio observes he only
wants to lighten her burden.

## SCENE 5 (16 min.)

A hall in Don Giovanni's château. The table is set for supper. Don
Giovanni is entertaining some girls. (For some reason there is a little
fuss about the girls. Some scholars feel that Don Giovanni was not the
type to mix eating with lechery—so, in some productions, no girls.)
A small orchestra is on stage as alternate entertainment.

No. 26, *Finale* (22 min.)—A: The meal is served. Leporello steals
some for himself. Don Giovanni remarks on the wine. When the
orchestra plays a selection from Mozart's *Le Nozze di Figaro,* he orders
Leporello to sing or whistle. Leporello, who had just sneered at the
music as "a poor tune" and stuffed his mouth with pheasant, has to
do some heavy swallowing.

     B (2 min.)—Suddenly Donna Elvira bursts in. She insists she
has come to save Don Giovanni if he'll only reform. He mocks her.
Leporello comments that his master has no heart. Scorned, Elvira turns
to go but falls back from the door screaming. Without any explanation,
she rushes out the opposite side.

     C (9 min.)—Leporello investigates, screams and slams the door.

It is the statue. Leporello imitates the heavy thud of its feet. He refuses to let it in. Don Giovanni goes to the door. Leporello hides under the table.

Don Giovanni directs Leporello to set another place at the table. The statue, however, slowly explains that being dead it cannot eat mortal food. Instead it invites Don Giovanni to dine with it. "Rispondimi," it insists (answer me). Don Giovanni hesitates. Leporello urges him to decline. But Don Giovanni accepts and grasps the statue's offered hand. It is deathly cold. The statue commands him to repent: "Pentiti." He refuses: "No, no, no. . . ." "Your time has come," the statue states, sinking through the floor. Flames crackle up the walls.

An invisible chorus calls Don Giovanni to Hell. He twists, burns with fire and *slowly* disappears. (In the original production Mozart had to give the Commendatore time to change his costume in order to reappear as Masetto. The singer doubled the parts.)

### SCENE 6 (6 min.)

The burnt-out hall, later.

D (6 min.)—*Donna Anna, Donna Elvira, Zerlina, Don Ottavio, Masetto and Leporello:* All come in calling for Don Giovanni. Leporello from under the table explains that it is useless. Coming out, he **sextet** describes what happened. They exclaim. Donna Anna promises to marry Don Ottavio. The others make their plans, and all moralize to the audience about Don Giovanni.

#### Vocabulary, Act II

| | | |
|---|---|---|
| no | no | no |
| si | see | yes |
| pietà | p'yay.tah | have pity |
| cercate | chair.kah.tay | enquire (after her) |
| mi tradi quell' alma ingrata | me trah.dee quell' ahl.mah een.grah.tah | he betrayed me that ungrateful soul |
| provo ancor per lui pietà | provo an.core pear louis p'yay.tah | I feel still for him pity |
| o statua gentilissima | oh stah.too.ah gent.eel.ees.ee.mah | oh most noble statue |
| guardate | gwahr.dah.teh | look |
| crudel | crew.dell | cruel |
| non mi dir | known me dear | don't call me (cruel) |
| rispondimi | ree.spon.dee.me | answer me |
| pentiti | PEN.tee.tee | repent |

# COSÌ FAN TUTTE

## (Thus do all women)

Opera buffa in two acts. First performed in Vienna on January 26, 1790. Music by W. A. Mozart. Libretto by L. da Ponte.

### PRINCIPAL CHARACTERS

| | | |
|---|---|---|
| Ferrando, betrothed to Dorabella | tenor | |
| Guglielmo, betrothed to Fiordiligi | baritone | goo.lee.ell.moe |
| Dòn Alfonso, an old bachelor | baritone | |
| Fiordiligi ⎫ sisters living in Naples | soprano | f'yore.dee.LEE.chee |
| Dorabella ⎭ | | |
| Despina, the ladies' maid | soprano | |

The action takes place in and around Naples in 1789.

Mozart composed the opera on commission from Emperor Joseph II of Austria. There is a story that the Emperor requested him to set a current court scandal to music. Two army officers, to test their fiancées' fidelity, had departed, returned in disguise and been disappointed. Be that as it may, the plot as far as opera is concerned was original with Da Ponte.

The opera shows its court parentage. Of Mozart's well-known operas, this is the most artificial, stylized and musically sophisticated. Everything balances and contrasts: the two sisters, the two lovers; the maid, the mistress; the old man and the boys. In his orchestration Mozart continued this. He underlined every platitude with parody, every sham with truth. In its artificiality it is extremely comic and charming and often so beautiful that tears choke off laughter.

It is a long opera: given uncut and with only one intermission, it runs about four hours. Every production, however, prunes severely. Generally Nos. 7, 24, 27 and 28 are omitted entirely and others are shorn of repeats, whole sections or connecting recitative. But even so, it is not for the exhausted man of business taken against his will or for those unfortunates who find Mozart "tinkly" and "small-voiced."

The opera takes place in Naples, and to suggest its sun, sea air and the ladies' sighs, Mozart continually scored for woodwinds, bassoons, clarinets, oboes and flutes, rather than strings. The liquid quality of those instruments pervades the whole opera, giving it a unity and feeling all of its own.

## OVERTURE (4 min.)

It is shorter than most and, after a brief "andante," rushes along "presto" (which with Mozart means prestissimo). Twice, from Don Alfonso's aria (No. 30), it quotes the moral and title of the opera in broad, loud chords.

## ACT I (100 min.)

### SCENE 1 (8 min.)

A café in Naples.

No. 1 (2 min.)—*Ferrando, Guglielmo and Don Alfonso:* Don Alfonso has just announced that women, including Dorabella and Fiordiligi, **trio** cannot be faithful. Ferrando extols Dorabella's constancy; Guglielmo, Fiordiligi's. Don Alfonso, the old bachelor, argues from experience. Irately, the lovers accuse him of slander and demand satisfaction.

Calmly, Don Alfonso states that his only satisfaction these days is eating. But are these fiancées, he asks, women or goddesses? The lovers reply ecstatically: "Son donne, ma son tali . . ." (they are women, but such women).

No. 2 (2 min.)—*Ferrando, Guglielmo and Don Alfonso:* Constancy **trio** in woman is a myth: "fenice" (a phoenix), Don Alfonso states. Ferrando insists, "la fenice è Dorabella" (the myth is Dorabella); Guglielmo repeats it of Fiordiligi.

Even if they love you today, what of tomorrow? Don Alfonso queries. Kisses and sighs mean nothing. The lovers are shocked. Don Alfonso offers to bet a hundred sovereigns he can prove his point within twenty-four hours. The lovers agree and consider how to spend their winnings.

**trio** No. 3 (2 min.)—*Ferrando, Guglielmo and Don Alfonso:* Ferrando plans a serenade and Guglielmo a dinner. Don Alfonso asks to be included.

### SCENE 2 (31 min.)

The ladies' garden by the shore. Each has a locket with her lover's picture.

No. 4 (4 min.)—*Fiordiligi and Dorabella:* "Ah guarda, sorella,
**duet**    guarda" (look, sister), Fiordiligi sighs. What a noble face!
Dorabella sighs over Ferrando's likeness. Together the sisters promise
revenge to Love ("Amore") if ever they waver in constancy.

    Having sighed all the correct sentiments, they wonder a little
impatiently where their lovers are. Don Alfonso hurries in.
**aria**    No. 5 (1 min.)—*Don Alfonso:* He can't wait to break the
bad news and builds it up by pitying them extensively first, "pietà."

    It is not prison or death—but worse, the army. The ladies are
overcome: grim separation. The lovers enter in traveling clothes.
No. 6 (5 min.)—*Guglielmo, Ferrando, Don Alfonso, Fiordiligi and*
**quintet**    *Dorabella:* The men declare they are speechless at the turn
of events. The ladies request a last favor: death by a sword through
the heart. Who could want to love amidst so much sorrow?

    Fiordiligi insists she will kill herself. Dorabella promises to die
of grief without weapons. The lovers urge them to trust in God;
Don Alfonso suggests a good cry.
**duet (usually cut)**    No. 7 (3 min.)—*Ferrando and Guglielmo:* We
need your love, they assure the ladies, so live, and we will soon be
united again.

    Offstage a drum rolls. A military band accompanies a troop of
soldiers onstage. A barge moors at the landing at the foot of the
garden.
**chorus**    No. 8 (2 min.)—*Soldiers and Neapolitans:* They enthuse:
"Bella vita militar" (beautiful military life).

    The ladies protest they cannot bear it and embrace the men for
the last time.
No. 9 (4 min.)—*Fiordiligi, Dorabella, Guglielmo, Ferrando and Don*
**quintet**    *Alfonso:* "Di scrivermi . . ." (write to me) Fiordiligi
weeps. "Addio" (farewell). Don Alfonso struggles not to laugh.

    The barge pulls out with the lovers aboard. The Neapolitans
cheer, sing and exit, and Dorabella turns as if stunned: "Dove
son" (where are they)? Don Alfonso comforts the ladies.
**trio**    No. 10 (5 min.)—*Fiordiligi, Dorabella and Don Alfonso:*
They beg the breezes to blow lightly, the stars to shimmer nightly, and
all the elements to be kind to the dear departed.

    Overcome with emotion the ladies withdraw. Don Alfonso laughs
and is confident of success.
**arietta**    No. 10a (1 min.)—*Don Alfonso:* He calls a fool any man
that trusts a woman.

## SCENE 3 (41 min.)

A room in the sisters' villa; several chairs, a table, and Despina, the maid, preparing chocolate for the ladies.

Despina complains of being a maid: All the good things are for others. She sips the chocolate. The ladies enter. Fiordiligi requests a dagger; Dorabella, poison.

**aria**　　No. 11 (4 min.)—*Dorabella:* She warns Fiordiligi and Despina to flee, "fuggi," before she does something desperate. She appeals to her agony to consume her all together.

At the end she collapses in a chair. Fiordiligi does likewise out of sympathy. When Despina finally worms out of them the cause of the despair, she suggests a new romance. Fiordiligi is outraged. Despina suggests the men won't sit and groan.

No. 12 (3 min.)—*Despina:* Do unto them, she preaches, as they do
**aria**　　unto you. Women should love as it suits them, as it pleases them: "per vanità" (for amusement).

The ladies flounce out followed by an uncomprehending Despina. Don Alfonso steals in. He muses that he'd better get Despina on his side, and when she returns, he bribes her help. He explains that he has two friends who have developed a passion for the ladies and that Despina could assist in breaking down the ladies' natural reluctance to be kind to strangers. He calls in Ferrando and Guglielmo dressed as Albanians.

No. 13 (6 min.)—*Entire Cast:* Don Alfonso introduces them to Despina, who shakes her head over their mustaches and clothes. Then
**sextet**　　he retires behind a door to let Despina introduce them to the ladies. The ladies enter, furious at Despina for letting men in the house; then they turn on the men, who beg for mercy, enslaved as they are by beauty. Don Alfonso chortles from behind the door, confident that the ladies' fierce façade conceals a fickle heart.

Don Alfonso enters and pretends to recognize the Albanians as old friends. The men gush with love for the ladies. Dorabella is confused, but Fiordiligi soars into a dramatic aria (a parody) with wide leaps and runs.

**aria**　　No. 14 (6 min.)—*Fiordiligi:* She orders them out and suggests that as they go they notice how she and Dorabella are true to their men at "the front." Their love is built "come scoglio" (like a rock).

The ladies start to go, but the men stop them. They are confident they will win the bet.

**aria**    No. 15 (3 min.)—*Guglielmo:* He points out that he and his friend are both young, good-looking and rich.

The ladies sniff and leave, followed by Despina.

**trio**    No. 16 (1 min.)—*Don Alfonso, Ferrando and Guglielmo:* The lovers laugh confidently and josh Don Alfonso, who reminds them that the day is not yet over.

He has another plan. Guglielmo asks when they will eat and Ferrando replies.

**aria**    No. 17 (5 min.)—*Ferrando:* He apostrophizes the ladies. "Un aura amorosa" (a tender breath) from them will be food for their hearts.

The two go off. Don Alfonso consults Despina, who reports that the ladies are lamenting in the garden. They plot another scheme. (Ferrando's aria here raises a staging problem typical of this opera. It is an answer to Guglielmo, who should stay onstage and listen, although, being more physical about eating, he may remain unconvinced. If he responds to Ferrando's philosophy, his facial expressions or actions will distract the audience's attention; if he doesn't respond, then he sits or stands a lump. If he goes off at the beginning, the usual solution, then the aria has less point and the opera seems more than ever a string of concert arias connected by a series of unmotivated exits and entrances. What to do?)

### SCENE 4 (20 min.)

The garden of the villa. Two grassy mats on either side.
No. 18—*Finale:* The ladies sigh over the separation. Suddenly the Albanians rush in and dramatically swallow poison. Don Alfonso tries to prevent them. Sweetly the ladies comment "il tragico spettacolo" (a tragic spectacle). The men, however, insist on babbling about rejected love. The ladies sing of their speechlessness and call Despina for help. She enters, calls them heartless and suggests they could at least hold the heads of the dying men while she and Don Alfonso get the doctor.

The ladies nervously stand off. The men groan. Slowly the ladies come closer. Dorabella even feels a pulse.

Despina re-enters disguised as a doctor. She rips off some Latin, gives orders, pulls out a magnet (a spoof on mesmerism which was current in Vienna in 1789) and drags it up and down the men. They begin to quake and squirm. Despina demands help in holding their heads. The ladies no longer refuse.

The men slowly come to and extravagantly compliment their nurses, who got very nervous. Worse, the men ask for a kiss: "Dammi un bacio" (give me a kiss). The ladies are outraged and tell the men to leave at once. The men are impressed but for the first time begin to wonder if the ladies do not protest too much.

### Vocabulary, Act I

| | | |
|---|---|---|
| son donne, ma son tali | son dun.nay ma son tah.lee | they are women, but such women |
| la fenice | lah fen.EE.chay | the phoenix (a myth) |
| guarda, sorella, guarda | gwahr.dah so.RELL.ah | look, sister, look |
| Amore | ah.MORE.eh | Love (Cupid) |
| pietà | p'yay.tah | (I) have pity (for them) |
| bella vita militar | bell.ah VEE.tah mil.ee.tar | beautiful military life |
| di scrivermi | dee scree.vair.me | write me |
| addio | ah.DEE.oh | farewell |
| dove son | doe.veh son | where are they |
| fuggi | food.jee | flee |
| per vanità | pear van.ee.TAH | for amusement |
| come scoglio | ko.may skol.yo | like a rock |
| un aura amorosa | oon oar.ah (ah)more.oh.sah | a tender breath |
| il tragico spettacolo | eel trah.gee.coe speh.tah.coe.low | a tragic spectacle |
| dammi un bacio | dah.me oon bah.choe | give me a kiss |

## ACT II (104 min. without cuts)

### SCENE 1 (12 min.)

A room in the sisters' villa.

Despina scolds the ladies for being false to womanhood. The Albanians are rich, handsome, well-bred (Despina's order of attributes) and ready to die for love. When Dorabella appeals piously to Heaven, Despina reminds her that they are on earth —thank God. She persuades them that the request of the kiss was the effect of the poison. Fiordiligi worries about gossip, but Despina promises to tell all Naples that the "Albanians" came to see her.

No. 19 (3 min.)—*Despina:* She instructs them in the ways of co-
**aria** quetry. Dorabella is won over. It will be an amusement. Their engagements to the lovers will remain unbroken, as their hearts will not be engaged. Cautiously she informs Fiordiligi which Albanian she prefers.

No. 20 (3 min.)—*Dorabella and Fiordiligi:* Dorabella will take the
**duet** "brunettino" (the dark one); Fiordiligi, the "biondino" (the blonde one). In choosing, each selects the other's fiancé.

Don Alfonso enters to say that they must not miss an extraordinary party that is going on in the garden.

### SCENE 2 (42 min.)

The garden of the villa by the seashore. A barge draws up laden with flowers, a band of musicians (Mozart never missed an opportunity to show how they could be employed) and a multitude of servants in elaborate costumes.

**duet and chorus** No. 21 (3 min.)—*Ferrando, Guglielmo and Servants:* The two men softly beseech the breeze to carry a message of love to their adored. The servants repeat the plea.

During the chorus the two men rise, garlanded with flowers. Despina and Don Alfonso lead them to the astounded ladies, who are speechless. They finally manage to stammer: "What's the point?" The men, victims of their own staging, are so overcome with emotion that they forget their lines. In despair, Despina and Don Alfonso act out the part for the ladies and the men.

No. 22 (3 min.)—*Don Alfonso, Ferrando, Guglielmo and Despina:*
**quartet** Don Alfonso sues for pardon for what happened earlier. "Rispondete" (answer), he urges the embarrassed ladies. Despina answers for them and forgives the past.

Don Alfonso and Despina go off; the couples talk briefly of the weather. Then Fiordiligi and Ferrando stroll away. Guglielmo besieges Dorabella. He has a locket in the shape of a heart. He threatens suicide again if she won't wear it, and she gives in.

No. 23 (4 min.)—*Guglielmo and Dorabella:* He gives her his heart.
**duet** She can't give hers as it is already given. Not so, he argues,

for he can hear it beating "batte, batte." He insists she must wear the locket and, in placing it on her neck, he removes the locket she is wearing (with the picture of Ferrando). Then they sigh "oh cambio felice" (oh happy exchange).

They stroll off, and Fiordiligi and Ferrando come on. She resists his pleas.

**aria (usually cut)**   No. 24 (4 min.)—*Ferrando:* Someday she will melt and return his affection. Meanwhile her coldness condemns him to death.

Ferrando runs off. Fiordiligi fears she has hurt him. Even more she fears the emotions he has stirred in her heart.

No. 25 (8 min.)—*Fiordiligi:* She prays the departed Guglielmo to forgive her for the momentary lapse from constancy. She asks God to **aria**    keep it hidden. Guglielmo deserves better than she can give. (This is generally cited as *the* great aria from the opera. It is very difficult to sing, especially the slow beginning, where unless the singer can provide the necessary phrasing and continuity, the aria collapses into a mass of separate and unrelated notes.)

Fiordiligi goes off, and Ferrando and Guglielmo enter. Ferrando is delighted to report Fiordiligi's refusal. Guglielmo is terribly pleased and indulges in some smug asides. In a rough and ready way he tries to be kind about Dorabella. Ferrando, however, is inconsolable. Guglielmo knows of no way to help, so he accuses women of generally being unworthy of love.

No. 26 (3 min.)—*Guglielmo:* I have defended you "mille volte" **aria**    (a thousand times). But you fail so often, "tanti" (so much), that lovers have cause to complain: "un gran perchè" (a great why).

Ferrando is left alone.

No. 27 (3 min.)—*Ferrando:* He'd like to blot Dorabella out of his **aria (usually cut)**   heart. "Tradito" (betrayed). But he loves her still —"le voci d'amor" (the voices of love).

Don Alfonso and Guglielmo join him. Guglielmo wants to collect his share of the winnings at once, but Don Alfonso reminds him that the day is not yet over. Guglielmo remarks that Fiordiligi knows she has an unusually fine fiancé and won't give in.

### SCENE 3 (27 min.)

A room in the villa.

Dorabella confides to Despina that she capitulated and enjoyed doing so. Fiordiligi enters. She confesses she loves her Albanian, but she will not give in.

**aria (usually cut)**     No. 28 (3 min.)—*Dorabella:* She advises Fiordiligi to submit to love, which otherwise will worm its way into her heart and leave her no peace.

Dorabella and Despina leave Fiordiligi thinking of their advice, but she won't give in. She calls Despina back and orders her to unpack some old uniforms of Ferrando and Guglielmo (left over from charades?). Then she and Dorabella will journey to the front in disguise and marry their lovers. During this recitative and the following aria Don Alfonso and Guglielmo eavesdrop behind a door. Ferrando suddenly bursts in on her.

No. 29 (10 min.)—*Ferrando and Fiordiligi:* He presses hard. Her go-

**duet**     ing will kill him; better she do it now (he offers his sword). Weakly she protests, "sorgi, sorgi" (go). Softly he advises her to be ruled by her heart. She trembles and begins to weaken: "giusto ciel" (dear heaven). He has won. They embrace and quietly sing of their happiness.

Guglielmo is furious. He wants action, revenge. Ferrando and Fiordiligi go off, and when Ferrando returns, he ironically quotes some of Guglielmo's consolations. Don Alfonso suggests that the best revenge would be to marry the girls.

**aria**     No. 30 (2 min.)—*Don Alfonso:* After all, he philosophizes, women can't help it; "così fan tutte" (thus do all women). He makes his pupils repeat the lesson: "Così fan tutte."

Despina announces to them that the ladies will be ready to marry and leave Naples by evening.


### SCENE 4 (23 min.)


A large hall in the villa. An orchestra to the back. To the front a table set for four with silver candelabra. Servants in stylish livery, and Despina.

No. 31—*Finale* (23 min.): Despina directs the servants on the final preparations, and they repeat her instructions as they do them. Don Alfonso inspects and compliments Despina. The ladies and their lovers enter. The orchestra and servants sing a complimentary wedding march, and the couples thank them in return.

At the wedding table the lovers exchange compliments and propose toasts: "tocca e bevi" (toast and drink). Fiordiligi begins a slow fughetta. She suggests they drown all memories in the cup. Dorabella and Ferrando take up the tune in turn, but Guglielmo can only growl that he wished the cup held poison.

Don Alfonso announces the notary, and Despina enters in disguise. She starts to read the contract. It is very boring, and the parties agree to sign first and read it later.

The moment the ladies sign, offstage Neapolitans cheer some returning troops: "bella vita militar." Don Alfonso runs to the window. "Misericordia" (great heavens)! He reports that Ferrando and Guglielmo are coming up the street. The ladies tremble with mixed emotions. They hide the Albanians in a side room, have the table cleared and try to compose themselves.

Ferrando and Guglielmo enter in their soldier's uniforms. They gabble of their pleasure to be home. The ladies can utter only an occasional monosyllable. Suddenly the men discover Despina. She claims she was simply trying on a costume for a masquerade. The ladies grasp at the straw but sink again when the marriage contract is found. When accused, all they can do is blame Despina and Don Alfonso.

Don Alfonso agrees and, to the horror of the ladies, conducts the men to the room where the "Albanians" are hiding.

The men come back, the deception is revealed, and the couples pair off (Mozart never reveals the alignment, but presumably pre-Albanian feeling determines), and the opera ends with a moral: happy the man who can take life as it is.

### Vocabulary, Act II

| | | |
|---|---|---|
| brunettino | brew.net.tee.no | the dark one, brunette |
| biondino | be.yon.dee.no | the blonde one |
| rispondete | ree.spon.deh.tay | answer |
| batte, batte | bah.tay | beating |
| oh cambio felice | oh kahm.b'yo fay.lee.chay | oh happy exchange |
| mille volte | mill.eh vol.tay | a thousand times |
| tanti | tahn.tee | so much |
| un gran perchè | oon gran pear.kay | a great "why" |
| tradito | trah.dee.toe | betrayed |
| le voci d'amore | lah voh.chee d'ah.more | the voices of love |
| sorgi, sorgi | sore.jee | go |
| giusto ciel | jewst.oh chell | dear heaven |
| così fan tutte | ko.see fan toot.tay | thus do all women |
| tocca e bevi | toh.kah eh bay.vee | toast and drink |
| misericordia | me.zay.re.KOR.d'ya | great heavens |

# DIE ZAUBERFLOETE

## (The Magic Flute)

Opera in two acts. First performed at Vienna on September 30, 1791. Music by W. A. Mozart. Libretto by E. Schikaneder and K. L. Giesecke.

### PRINCIPAL CHARACTERS

| | | |
|---|---|---|
| Tamino, an Egyptian Prince | tenor | tah.MEAN.oh |
| Three Ladies, attendants of the Queen of Night | two sopranos and mezzo-soprano | |
| Papageno, a birdcatcher | baritone | pap.ah.GAY.noh |
| The Queen of Night | soprano | |
| Monostatos, a Moor in the service of Sarastro | tenor | mon.OH.stat.toas(t) |
| Pamina, daughter of the Queen of Night | soprano | pa.MEAN.ah |
| Three Genii | two sopranos and mezzo-soprano | |
| The Orator | bass | |
| Sarastro, High Priest of Isis and Osiris | bass | sah.RAH.stro |
| Two Priests | tenor and bass | |
| Papagena | soprano | |
| Two Men in Armor | tenor and bass | |

The action takes place in ancient Egypt near a temple of Isis and Osiris.

Mozart and Schikaneder, the first producer and the more important of the two librettists, designed the opera as a spectacular fairy tale for the public rather than the aristocracy of Vienna; thus, they wrote in German rather than Italian, used spoken dialogue instead of recitative, and made the comedy burlesque rather than wit. After an uncertain start, the opera became a tremendous success, although Mozart died before he could benefit by it.

The story is so simple that all sorts of symbolism and allegory can be found in it, and scholars squabble endlessly about just how much and what Mozart intended. It is certain that he was a Freemason and that he adapted some of the ritual (and especially the rhythms) from the Masonic rites. It is less certain that he intended the opera to represent the triumph of Freemasonry with its liberal ideas (in 1790) over Catholic reaction. Under this interpretation the Queen of Night represents the Empress Maria Theresa; Monostatos, the Roman Catholic Church or at least the Jesuits; and Tamino and Pamina, the Austrian people.

None of this is important today to enjoy the opera. Tamino and Pamina can be Everyman and Everywoman. The Queen of Night is prejudice, violence and hate; Sarastro, reason, inner peace and love. Tamino and Pamina achieve the greatest development of themselves by successfully passing through fire and water, human suffering and sorrow, to join Sarastro. Papageno is human nature at its simplest, innocent but undeveloped. Those who like the opera can and have multiplied the levels of meaning to staggering heights.

The opera provides its producer with continuous opportunity for spectacular and contrasting scenery and lighting: the Queen of Night, sinister blue, versus Sarastro, warming yellow; the fire, the water; the animals; and so on. In many ways the opera would do well in the movies. The Queen of Night, for example, is never directed to "exit" but always to "disappear." Any producer who shirks these opportunities deadens the opera beyond the quickening power of even Mozart's music, for it is long, and the spoken dialogue, designed for simple people, is painfully pedestrian. Every joke is spelt out twice. Here translation and understanding is a hindrance unless the translator has ruthlessly condensed on the ground that the audience has changed.

Musically the opera consists of twenty-one numbers of which two are finales. They vary in length from one to seven minutes. The finales, of course, run longer. The connecting dialogue varies from a sentence to several pages. One of the opera's most enchanting qualities is its mixture of popular song, fancy coloratura, slow marches and glockenspiel. The wonder of Mozart is that he could make each so perfectly expressive of the moment.

## OVERTURE (7 min.)

It is greatly admired and turns up frequently at concerts. Some scholars believe that the series of three, pounding chords that appears in the overture and later in the temple scene represents the knocking at a Masonic lodge door at the beginning of an initiation, e.g. Tamino's.

## ACT I (60 min.)

### SCENE 1 (28 min.)

A rocky gorge with trees and hills on either side.

No. 1 (7 min.)—*Tamino and the Three Ladies:* He rushes on pursued by a huge serpent. His arrows are gone. There is no help. He swoons. But Three Ladies with spears appear and kill the serpent. Then they **trio** discover Tamino. Reluctantly they admit to each other that he is extremely good-looking. A polite argument develops over who will stay and who will report to the Queen of Night. The argument increases until all three leave to make the report together.

Tamino revives, hears a man coming and hides.

**aria** No. 2 (2 min.)—*Papageno:* He describes himself as a birdcatcher and announces he'd like to catch a girl. If she were nice to him, he'd give her sugar and they'd be man and wife.

Tamino questions Papageno about the country and its king, but Papageno knows only that the Queen of Night is his mistress. He claims, however, to have throttled the serpent with his bare hands. At that lie the Three Ladies reappear and put a padlock on his mouth for telling lies. They give Tamino a picture of the Queen's daughter, and he (it being a fairy story) at once falls in love with her.

**aria** No. 3 (4 min.)—*Tamino:* He sings a love song, wishing Pamina were his.

The Three Ladies explain that Pamina is the prisoner of Sarastro, the High Priest of the temple of Isis and Osiris. Tamino swears to free her. To thunder and lightning the Queen of Night appears.

No. 4 (5 min.)—*The Queen of Night:* Pathetically she describes how **aria** Pamina was taken from her. Then fiercely she urges Tamino to rescue her daughter. (The coloratura and extremely high range—it rises to a high F—make this a tour de force. It should be delivered with tremendous vehemence.)

She disappears and the sun reappears. Tamino gazes at the portrait he has been given.

No. 5 (6 min.)—*Tamino, Papageno and the Three Ladies:* Because

of the padlock, Papageno can only hum. The ladies unlock his lips,
and in a quintet all comment on what a terrible thing it is to lie and
**quintet**    what a good cure padlocks are. Then the Three Ladies
give Tamino a magic flute from the Queen of Night to protect him in
his search for Pamina. They tell Papageno that he must accompany
Tamino and give him some magic bells. Papageno is pleased with the
bells but nervous about the quest. The Three Ladies also promise that
Three Genii will help them find their way. Tamino and Papageno start
on their search, and the five part: "Auf Wiedersehn" (till we meet
again).

### SCENE 2 (6 min.)

A room in a building connected to the temple of Isis and Osiris.
No. 6 (2 min.)—*Monostatos, Pamina and Papageno:* Monostatos
**duet**    drags on Pamina. She refuses to give him of her charms. He
has her chained and prepares to force her. She swoons. Papageno
enters. When he and Monostatos catch sight of each other, both
**duet**    panic, "Das ist der Teufel" (that's the devil), and both rush
off.

    Pamina revives, and Papageno creeps back. He explains about
the rescue party and how Tamino fell in love with her from a
portrait. He complains that no one ever falls in love with him.
**duet**    No. 7 (3 min.)—*Pamina and Papageno:* She assures him
that Nature has someone for him. The law of God is love: "Mann und
Weib" (man and woman).

    They run out.

### SCENE 3 (26 min.)

A grove with three temples. To the back the Temple of Wisdom; to
one side a Temple of Reason, to the other a Temple of Nature.
No. 8—*Finale* (26 min.): (The music flows unbroken to the end of
the act. Changes in situation are indicated by A, B, etc.)
**trio**    A: The Three Genii lead in Tamino and leave him before the
temples.

    B: Tamino soliloquizes on the meaning of life and the temples un-
til the thought of Pamina spurs him to action. He tries to enter each
temple, starting with those on the side, but each time is warned off by

voices: "Zurueck" (stand back). From the center temple a priest, the Orator, steps out.

C: He asks Tamino what he seeks. Tamino describes Sarastro as cruel and unjust. The Orator suggests that Tamino has been prejudiced by a highly emotional woman. He refuses to say whether Pamina is still alive, but the mysterious voices assure Tamino that she is.

D: Happily Tamino sits and plays his flute. Wild animals come and **aria** listen. He sings of the power of music, of how it calls his soul to lofty purposes. He wonders about Pamina, hears Papageno's pipes in the distance and rushes round the temple to find him.

**duet and chorus** E: Papageno and Pamina hurry round the opposite corner. Papageno tries again on his pipes to signal Tamino but instead brings on Monostatos and his slaves. Papageno remembers his bells, which mesmerize the slaves, and they dance grotesquely off.

F: Offstage trumpets flourish and voices announce Sarastro. Papageno and Pamina are trapped. In despair he asks her what they should say. "Die Wahrheit" (the truth), Pamina insists. (For persons sentimental about the truth, this is one of the high points of opera.)

G: Sarastro enters (the directions call for him to be in a chariot drawn by lions). Pamina confesses that she tried to escape. She pleads love of her mother as her excuse. Sarastro forbids her to talk of her mother and suggests she'd do better to love a man. At that moment Monostatos drags in Tamino. Sarastro, however, sternly rebukes Monostatos for the attempted rape and dismisses him in disgrace. Meanwhile, Tamino and Pamina gaze rapturously at each other. The act ends as the priests veil Tamino and Papageno to start the probation for admission to the good life. The chorus praises reason and the pursuit of wisdom. Sarastro leads Pamina into the temple.

### Vocabulary, Act I

| | | |
|---|---|---|
| auf Wiedersehn | owf vee.der.zane | till we meet again |
| das ist der Teufel | das ist der Toy.fell | that is the devil |
| Mann und Weib | mahn oont v'eye'b | man and woman |
| zurueck | zoo.rook | stand back |
| die Wahrheit | dee vahr.hite | the truth |

(For a discussion of Mozart's use of the flute and bells, see page 61 in Chap. VI, "Sounds of the Orchestra.")

## ACT II (79 min.)

---

### SCENE 1 (6 min.)

A grove of palms near the temples.

**march**     No. 9 (3 min.)—*Sarastro and the Priests:* They file in to a slow march.

Sarastro announces that Tamino and Papageno will be initiated into the mysteries and ways of wisdom and that he kidnaped Pamina to save her from her mother and unite her with Tamino.

**aria and chorus**     No. 10 (3 min.)—*Sarastro and the Priests:* He prays to Isis and Osiris to lead Tamino safely through the trials. (In this aria the bass must sing a low F, a thing few can do.)

### SCENE 2 (7 min.)

A porch of the temple.

Tamino and Papageno are alone. Two Priests enter with lanterns. Tamino is eager to begin the trials. Papageno is not, and only the promise of a loving wife (Papagena) leads him to agree to continue. Both men swear not to speak to Pamina, Papagena or any other woman until released from the vow. (It is not clear from the libretto just what the vow of silence was supposed to mean. Clearly, the definition is operatic not Trappist, for Tamino sings in a trio and a quintet before he is officially released. And in the beginning, he talks to Papageno, although later he gets stuffy about it.)

**duet**     No. 11 (1 min.)—*The Two Priests:* They warn the men against women, who will lead them astray.

The Two Priests go out, and at once the Three Ladies appear. No. 12 (3 min.)—*The Three Ladies:* They urge the men to flee.

**quintet**     Papageno is so inclined, but Tamino stands firm. The ladies then slander the priests and assure Papageno and Tamino that they will go to Hell if they join the priests. The men refuse to talk to the Ladies, who finally give up in despair.

The Two Priests congratulate them on passing the first test and lead them off to the next.

## SCENE 3 (13 min.)

A garden.

Pamina is asleep. Monostatos steals in, and the sight of her excites his lust.

**aria**     No. 13 (3 min.)—*Monostatos:* He swears he'll steal a kiss at least.

Just as he leans over her, the Queen of Night appears and wards him away: "Zurueck." She gives Pamina a dagger and orders her to kill Sarastro. Pamina protests.

**aria**     No. 14 (3 min.)—*The Queen of Night:* In a towering rage (four high F's) she insists that Pamina kill Sarastro or be cut off forever. Then on an instant she disappears.

Monostatos again approaches Pamina. This time Sarastro appears. Disappointed in the girl, Monostatos mutters that he'll try his luck with the mother, the Queen of Night. He goes off in search of her. Pamina begs Sarastro to spare her mother.

**aria**     No. 15 (5 min.)—*Sarastro:* He assures her that revenge is unknown in the temple. Love is supreme. "In diesen heil'gen Hallen" (in these holy halls). (It was of Sarastro's music that G. B. Shaw once wrote, "the only music yet written that would not sound out of place in the mouth of God.")

## SCENE 4 (9 min.)

A hall in the temple.

The Two Priests lead in Tamino and Papageno. Once again they enjoin the two men to be silent. Papageno at once starts chattering. Tamino tells him to be quiet, so Papageno sullenly starts talking to an ugly, old woman. She terrifies him, however, by claiming she's married to him. He asks her name, but a clap of thunder blots out her answer, and she hobbles off.

**trio**     No. 16 (2 min.)—*The Three Genii:* They deliver again the magic flute and bells and spread a table of food in front of Papageno. They urge Tamino to be brave and Papageno to talk less: "Still" (hush).

Papageno falls on the food, while Tamino plays his flute. Pamina runs in. Neither will speak to her; Papageno, because of the food in his mouth, and Tamino, because of his vow.

**aria**      No. 17 (5 min.)—*Pamina:* She laments that Tamino won't speak to her. Therefore, he must not love her. Only death can soothe her pain. Sadly she goes off.

Tamino leads the chattering Papageno off to the next test.

## SCENE 5 (7 min.)

A vault in the temple.

**chorus**      No. 18 (4 min.)—*The Priests:* They enter solemnly, singing of Tamino's progress.

Sarastro compliments Tamino and has Pamina brought in. He tells her that Tamino will take his last farewell of her.

No. 19 (2 min.)—*Pamina, Tamino and Sarastro:* She fears the worst:
**trio**      he does not love her. Tamino says he must obey the priests. Sarastro reminds him that the time has come to go.

## SCENE 6 (6 min.)

Another hall in the temple.

Papageno runs in searching for Tamino. Everywhere he turns, voices warn him to "stand back." A priests enters and informs him that he has failed the test; he will never be one of the initiated. Papageno is immensely relieved and asks for a cup of wine. Then he wonders what else he could possibly want to make him happy.

**aria**      No. 20 (4 min.)—*Papageno:* He plays the bells and sings that all he needs is a loving wife, and then he'd not envy a king. "Ein Madchen oder Weibchen . . ." (a maiden or a little woman).

The old woman hobbles in. She promises to love him if he'll take her. Papageno philosophizes that an old wife is better than none and agrees. Instantly she is transformed into a lovely girl. Papageno is entranced. But a priest calls her away and prevents him from following.

## SCENE 7 (6 min.)

A garden with the Three Genii.

No. 21—*Finale* (31 min.): The Three Genii comment that reason can make men like gods. Pamina rushes in. She has the dagger and wails that to die is better than to live without love. The Three Genii suggest that she is foolish to act so hastily. Tamino loves her. She denies it, but they assure that there were secret reasons why he couldn't speak to her. Then they inform her that they are to take her to Tamino. Excitedly, Pamina urges them to lead on.

### SCENE 8 (12 min.)

Two men in armor stand on either side of a large doorway.

The Two Priests lead in Tamino. The two men in armor explain that now he must pass through fire and water to purge himself of the fear of death. Outside, Pamina calls. The men absolve Tamino from his vow of silence, and Pamina enters. The men explain that if she, too, will pass the tests, then she can be admitted along with Tamino. She volunteers. She will help Tamino find the way. The music of the **the tests** flute will protect them. Together they enter the door and pass first through fire and then through water. At the end, Sarastro and the priests welcome them into the temple.

### SCENE 9 (7 min.)

A garden.

Papageno calls for Papagena. He has lost her and blames his eternal talking. He has a rope and plans to hang himself, for without her life is nothing. Slowly he counts to three, but she doesn't answer to stop him. The Three Genii enter and remind him of his magic bells. He plays them, and Papagena appears. Together they sing a patter song about life together, their home and children.

### SCENE 10 (6 min.)

Before the Temple.

Monostatos steals in, beckoning the Queen of Night and the Three Ladies to follow him. They plot their revenge, and the Queen of Night promises Pamina to Monostatos. But suddenly there is a clap of thunder, and Sarastro appears above them. With a shriek they all vanish.

Sarastro and the priests then officially welcome Tamino and Pamina into the band of the initiated, and all praise the power of love and wisdom.

Vocabulary, Act II

| | | |
|---|---|---|
| zurueck | zoo.rook | stand back |
| in diesen heil'gen Hallen | in dee.zen hile.gen hah.len | in these holy halls |
| still | Shtill | hush |
| ein Madchen oder Weibchen | eye'n mait.chen oh.der v'eye'b.chen | a maiden or a little woman |

# FIDELIO

An opera in two acts. First performed (three performances) in a three-act version at Vienna on November 20, 1805. Music by L. v. Beethoven. Libretto by J. Sonnleithner after P. Gaveaux's opera, *Leonore, or l'Amour Conjugal,* first produced on February 19, 1798, at Paris. *Fidelio* was revised—the libretto was reduced to two acts by S. von Breuning—and produced (two performances) at Vienna on March 29, 1806. It was revised again—the libretto was put in its present form by G. F. Treitschke—and produced at Vienna on May 23, 1814.

### PRINCIPAL CHARACTERS

| | | |
|---|---|---|
| Jacquino, the porter at the prison | tenor | |
| Marcellina, Rocco's daughter | soprano | |
| Rocco, the jailer | bass | |
| Leonora, wife of Florestan, disguised as a young man and known as Fidelio | soprano | lay.on.or.ah |
| Pizarro, governor of the prison | bass | peets.AHR.roh |
| Florestan | tenor | FLOR.es.tahn |
| Don Fernando, a Minister of State | bass | |

The action takes place in a state prison near Seville in the eighteenth century.

*Fidelio* is the only opera Beethoven wrote. Some consider it one of the greatest operas ever composed; others argue that it is poorly put together; and if it were not for the fascination that it is Beethoven's only opera, it would seldom be heard. Even these, however, grant it one stunning tenor aria, a fine chorus and quartet, and an excess of good overtures.

The disagreement, whether over the libretto or the music, can be distilled to a complaint about the opera's style which is said to be inconsistent. One minute Beethoven is sublime and the next teetering close to the ridiculous; the first act is an eighteenth-century opera with set numbers and the lyrics and music cast mostly in the form of repeating verses; the second act, or at least its first scene, is a nineteenth-century music drama proceeding on melodic recitative without word repetition, except for several incongruous lapses. The best operas, so the argument goes, have a unity of style that gives them a cumulative power that *Fidelio* does not achieve.

**BEETHOVEN**

Much of the trouble lies in Beethoven's difficulties with the libretto. It is an example of a type that once was popular—the Rescue Opera—in which a wife survives a series of trials and terrors to free her husband. In *Fidelio* the husband, Florestan, is unjustly and secretly imprisoned. His wife, Leonora, finds him by working at the prison. Disguised as a young man, Fidelio, and under dramatic circumstances, she saves his life. The full title of the opera is *Fidelio or Conjugal Love,* and on to this story of conjugal love Beethoven grafted his feelings about freedom and tyranny. These, all agree, are nobly expressed and inspiring; but his feelings on conjugal love, of which he had no personal experience, strike some as merely clichés. He does not succeed in making the relationship between Leonora and Florestan anything unique and fully expressed, such as Wagner did for Tristan and Isolde, Verdi for Otello and Desdemona, and Mozart for Rosina and the Count.

This failure, the argument runs, allows the opera to begin on a comic subplot of mistaken identity which peters out and explains why in the final scene, with its pleasant chorus of "lucky fellow to have such a wife," the protagonists have so little identity that they almost merge into the front line of the chorus. It also explains why the glories of the opera strike many as unconnected.

Those who consider the opera one of the greatest inevitably stress those parts dealing with freedom and tyranny. When the prisoners creep out of their dark cells towards the light of the sun, mumbling and fearful, Beethoven emphatically states that men must not do this to each other. A positive social program—how many houses for the workers or pensions for the aged—may be arguable, but not this; not imprisonment in the dark, in terror. So too in Florestan's aria in the dungeon the music perfectly expresses the near hysteria and agony of a man cut off from light and life. Persons who feel strongly about freedom or who have suffered for it find *Fidelio* extremely moving and a testament of faith that might is not right.

But whether the emotion is in the music or is brought to the opera house by some and not others, or whether the music plumbs unsuspected depths in those that hear it, is a question that probably will always divide any audience.

### OVERTURE (6 min.)

The overture now generally played was the fourth Beethoven wrote in an effort to work out a proper balance between it and the opera. (For a discussion of his problem, see page 5 in Chap. I, "The Overture, the Prelude and Three Chords.")

### ACT I (60 min.)

The courtyard of a prison; to the back is the main entrance with a gate and porter's lodge; to the left, barred doors leading to the cells with the jailer's house to the front; and to the right, trees and a gate to a garden. Marcellina is ironing linen outside her door with a charcoal stove to heat the iron; Jacquino is near the porter's lodge and opens the gate for persons arriving with parcels, etc. (The score does not indicate any change of locale during Act I, but producers sometimes divide it into two scenes, setting the first inside the jailer's house. The scene then changes during the march, No. 6.)

**duet** No. 1 (4 min.)—*Jacquino and Marcellina:* He hopes she has time to talk with him, but she warns him she is busy. He stammers "ich, ich habe" (I, I have) been thinking. He proposes they be engaged and the banns be published. She remarks airily that he seems to have already set the day. There is a knock and, as he goes to the door, she comments that she loves "Fidelio."

He returns, "wo, war ich" (where was I), and continues. She refuses him, "nein." He suggests she may change her mind, which she denies when again knocking at the door interrupts him.

He returns ready to start again but this time Rocco calls, and Marcellina insists he go to her father. As she watches him go, she admits she feels sorry for him, but it only makes her realize how much more she loves Fidelio.

**aria** No. 2 (3 min.)—*Marcellina:* She thinks of Fidelio and looks forward with hope "die Hoffnung," to marrying him. (The aria is in two verses.)

Rocco enters, asking for Fidelio. There is a knocking and Jacquino opens the gate. Leonora (Fidelio) enters, exhausted with carrying some heavy chains from the town. She gives the bill to Rocco, who promises her a reward, meaning Marcellina, for doing such a good job.

**quartet** No. 3 (5 min.)—*Marcellina, Leonora, Rocco and Jacquino:* Each sings his thoughts: Marcellina imagines Fidelio loves her—"mir ist so wunderbar" (it is wonderful to me); Leonora grieves that with this new complication her hope is turning to fear; Rocco is pleased at his daughter's choice; and Jacquino wonders how Fidelio can be preferred to him. (The quartet is in the form of a canon (*See* Glossary). The introductory eight bars are the first great music of the opera; they have a quality that makes everything before seem trifling.)

Rocco gives his blessing to Marcellina's choice. She is thrilled and Leonora is secretly appalled. Then he gives them some fatherly advice.

**aria** No. 4 (2 min.)—*Rocco:* Love is all very well, but it is gold, "das Gold," that fills the stomach.

Leonora suggests to Rocco that she help him with the prisoners. There are so many, and he barely can tend to them at all. Rocco agrees that he needs help, but Pizzaro is strict. Anyway, Fidelio could not help him with the prisoner who has been in the deepest dungeon for "zwei Jahre" (two years). "Zwei Jahre," Leonora exclaims, then catches herself. It is the period Florestan has been missing. Marcellina adds that no one knows the prisoner's name. Rocco observes mysteriously that he will not be a bother much longer, and when Marcellina suggests that the sight of the prisoner would be too much for Fidelio to bear, Leonora insists: "ich habe Mut und Staerke" (I have courage and strength).

No. 5 (6 min.)—*Rocco, Leonora and Marcellina:* Rocco compliments Fidelio on his courage. Leonora insists she has courage for anything, and Marcellina promises love will soothe a heart that may be too tender for jailer's work. Rocco promises to ask the Governor if Fidelio may help him in the dungeons, for it is true that he has not felt well **trio** lately. Marcellina insists her father is in fine health, and Leonora promises herself to go through with the masquerade no matter how hard. (The trio is often criticized for going on too long and reducing the drama with trivial words and music to a music-hall level. At its close there sometimes comes the change of scene, in which case Pizarro reads his letter after the march which then covers the change of scene.)

Marcellina and Leonora go off as Pizarro comes in with the change of guard which he posts. He then reads in his dispatches handed him by Rocco an anonymous note warning him that Don Fernando suspects him of tyrannizing the prisoners and plans a surprise inspection. Pizarro hesitates and then concludes he must get rid of Florestan, Fernando's friend.

**march** No. 6 (2 min.)—*The Change of Guard:* An instrumental march as the guard does some military business.

No. 7 (3 min.)—*Pizarro and Guard:* His moment of vengeance has come. Now he will kill Florestan who scorned him. "Oh Wonne" (oh **aria** bliss). "Triumph," he cries; the victory is his. The guards observe that he seems very angry. (This aria, long and difficult, is a showpiece for a bass. To make an effect it must be sung with great vehemence.)

Pizarro orders the captain of the guard to take a trumpeter with him to the tower and to give notice as soon as they sight Don Fernando's carriage. Then he calls Rocco over.

No. 8 (5 min.)—*Pizarro and Rocco:* Pizarro gives Rocco a purse, suggesting that there will be more to follow if he keeps his mouth shut and does a good job. Rocco asks what Pizarro has in mind, and the answer is "Morden" (murder). A prisoner, a threat to the state, must

**duet**  be liquidated. Rocco can only gasp, "O Herr." Finally he insists he will not do it. Pizarro at once states that then he will do it himself, but Rocco must dig the grave. There is an old cistern in the cell; all he need do is reopen it. "Und dann, und dann" (and then)? Rocco asks. Pizarro shows him a dagger: "Ein Stoss" (one blow). He exults that then he will be safe as Rocco comments that maybe the prisoner will find death a release. They go off.

No. 9 (7 min.)—*Leonora:* (She has overhead Pizarro's plan and, alone on the stage, launches into a recitative and aria which many **aria**  consider one of the glories of the opera. A minority complains that towards the end Beethoven wrote a poor vocal line in that it makes an instrument of the voice—like a horn or a violin—rather than stressing its unique qualities. The solo instrument throughout is the French horn.) "Abscheulicher" (abominable man, i.e. murderer), she cries. Has he no pity? Yet through his anger and hate she can still see in the world love and grace. She appeals to hope, "Komm Hoffnung," not to let its last star go out in despair. Let it guide her to Florestan whom she must find, for her wifely love compels her. He waits for her to release him. She will not flinch or fail; her love will support her.

> Marcellina runs in followed by Jacquino. She insists she will not hear more of love. Rocco and Leonora enter, and he tells Jacquino that Marcellina will marry Fidelio. Leonora changes the subject by asking if the prisoners mayn't be let out in the garden. Marcellina urges Rocco, and he finally consents. They open the cells, and Leonora examines every face, hoping to discover Florestan.

No. 10 (16 min.)—*Finale:* The prisoners slowly emerge into the light. "O welche Lust" (oh what a joy) to feel the sun and air. Only here **chorus**  ("nur hier") is life ("ist Leben"). One prisoner trusts in God, hoping that they may yet go free. "O Freiheit" (freedom), they murmur, wondering if it can still be theirs. Another warns them to speak softly, "sprecht leise," and never mention that word, for they are always watched. The chorus repeats and fades away as the prisoners stumble into the garden.

Rocco tells Leonora that Pizarro has approved of Fidelio's marrying Marcellina and has also allowed Rocco to take him as a helper to the darkest dungeon where they will have work to do. Leonora asks if they will release the prisoner, and Rocco at first says "nein" but then talks of digging a grave. She asks anxiously if the man is already dead, "so ist er tot?" Again Rocco denies it, and then admits that Pizarro, "der Gouverneur," plans to murder him. They must dig the grave, "das Grab." He urges her to get ready; they must start at once. She insists she will face anything and begs Heaven to help her.

Marcellina runs in to warn Rocco that Pizarro is in a rage that the prisoners have been let into the garden. Pizarro appears, and Rocco protests that it is the King's birthday, which is always celebrated by letting the prisoners out. But Pizarro orders them returned to their cells, and they go, bidding the sun good-by, "Leb' wohl." The finale builds with each character singing his views on the events of the day as the prisoners, returning to their cells, grow fewer and fewer. As the curtain falls, Rocco and Leonora start down to the dungeon.

### Vocabulary, Act I

| | | |
|---|---|---|
| ich, ich habe | ik,* ik hah.buh | I, I have (been thinking) |
| wo war ich? | voh vahr ik * | where was I? |
| nein | nine | no |
| die Hoffnung | dee hoff.noong | the hope |
| mir ist so wunderbar | meer ist so voon.der.bahr | to me it is so wonderful |
| zwei Jahre | tsvhy yahr.ah | two years |
| ich habe Mut und Staerke | ik hah.buh mooht unt shtair.kuh | I have courage and strength |
| O Wonne | oh von.uh | oh bliss |
| Triumph | tree.oompf | triumph |
| morden | mor.den | to murder |
| o Herr | o hairr | oh sir |
| und dann | unt dahnn | and then |
| ein Stoss | ine shtohs | a blow |
| Abscheulicher | ahp.shoy.lik.er | abominable man (foul murderer) |
| komm Hoffnung | kom hoff.noong | come, hope |
| o welche Lust | o velk.kuh loost | oh what a joy |
| nur hier ist Leben | noor heer ist lay.ben | only here is life |
| o Freiheit | oh fry.hite | oh freedom |
| sprecht leise | shprekt ly.zuh | speak softly |
| so ist er tot | so ist air toht | so is he dead |
| der Gouverneur | der goo.vair.noor | the Governor |
| das Grab | dah grahb | the grave |
| Leb' wohl | layb.vohl | farewell |

* Ik or ish, depending on the North or South German accent of the singer.

## ACT II (45 min.)

---

## SCENE 1 (34 min.)

A dungeon. To the back is a wall with large, irregular, barred openings, behind which steps lead up to a door in the wall; to the front at one side is a low entrance to a dark cell; on the other side is a mass of ruins and stones. The whole scene presents a ruin. Florestan is sitting on a stone; he is chained to the wall by a long chain fastened round his body.

**aria**    No. 11 (9 min.)—*Florestan:* His aria falls into three parts:

A: He cries out against the darkness and the silence, "Gott! Welch' Dunkel hier" (God! how dark it is here) and "stille" (silent), but adds that it must be God's will, "ist Gottes Wille," and he will not complain.

B: He grieves that his life has been cut short in its springtime, "in des Lebens Fruehlingstagen," and that speaking words of truth, "Wahrheit," has led him to jail. His only consolation is that he has done his duty.

C: He imagines he sees Leonora, an angel, "ein Engel," come from Heaven to lead him there to freedom, "zur Freiheit."

At the close he sinks exhausted so that his face is not visible either to the audience or to those on stage. Rocco and Leonora come down the steps; he carries a lantern and bottle of wine, she a pickax and a spade.

No. 12 (6 min.)—*Rocco and Leonora:* She remarks on the cold and tries to look at the prisoner. Rocco starts digging around the closed **duet** well and calls to her to help him. She feigns work while all the time trying to see the prisoner's face. Rocco lifts a stone off the well and asks for her help, "komm hilf," warning her to be careful, "hab acht." They roll the stone aside and continue working. Leonora aside swears to save the prisoner, whoever he is; Rocco hurries, for Pizarro will soon come down.

Leonora exclaims that the prisoner is awake. Rocco goes over to him, and Florestan turns his face so that Leonora recognizes him. "Gott! Er ist's," she exclaims, nearly fainting. Florestan asks Rocco who runs the prison, and Rocco for the first time reveals it is Pizarro. Florestan begs Rocco to send word to his wife, Leonora, in Seville. Rocco insists it is impossible, but offers Florestan some wine.

No. 13 (5 min.)—*Florestan, Rocco and Leonora:* Florestan thanks
**trio**    him, "O Dank!" Rocco insists it is nothing and then, aside,
regrets that his duty requires him to have any part in murder. Leonora,
aside, resolves to face death to save Florestan who murmurs that perhaps he yet may find liberty.

Leonora, with Rocco's permission, offers Florestan a crust of bread.
She and Rocco grieve for the unhappy man, "armer Mann," as
Florestan thanks her for her kindness.

> Rocco takes Leonora aside and insists he must give the signal.
> Florestan, near hysteria, cries out that he will never see Leonora
> again. Pizarro arrives. He orders Rocco to unchain Florestan
> from the rock but to leave his fetters on. He mutters in an aside
> that he will also have to do away with Rocco; the well will con-
> ceal all the evidence. Rocco sends Fidelio (Leonora) away, but
> she hides in the shadow.

No. 14 (5 min.)—*Pizarro, Florestan, Leonora and Rocco:* Pizarro
reveals himself to Florestan, promising him death. Florestan calmly
**quartet**    replies that then Pizarro is a murderer, "Ein Moerder."
As Pizarro steps forward to stab him, Leonora rushes between them,
insisting that Pizarro must kill her first. Pizarro orders, and Rocco
urges, her to stand back. She refuses, insisting "toet' erst sein Weib"
(kill first his wife). All exclaim "sein Weib." Pizarro, promising to
kill them both, advances, but Leonora produces a pistol and swears:
take another step "und du bist tot" (and you are dead). At that moment a trumpet call from the tower announces that Don Fernando has
been sighted. For a moment all are stunned; then the call sounds again,
this time nearer.

> Jacquino calls down the steps that "Der Herr Minister" has come,
> and Rocco thanks God while ordering that men with torches be
> quick to light Pizarro's way up to greet Don Fernando.

Rocco and Leonora rejoice with Florestan that he will be free again at
last, while Pizarro rages at being balked at his revenge.

> The men with torches escort Pizarro up the steps, and Rocco fol-
> lows with Jacquino.

No. 15 (3 min.)—*Leonora and Florestan:* They rejoice "O namen,
**duet**    namenlose Freude" (oh inexpressible joy)! They give thanks
to God and breathlessly repeat each other's names—Leonora, Florestan. Then again they thank God for such joy.

(At this point, between the scenes, some producers insert the

"Leonora Overture #3" discussed on page 5. Critics, professional and amateur, choose their sides and marshal arguments. Those against the practice point out that the overture repeats much of the material of the scene it follows; even worse, it spoils the feeling of resolution which the C Major of the final scene can produce when *not* preceded by music in the same key; it destroys the dramatic balance of the act; and, being heavily orchestrated and noisy, throws off the careful balance of instrumentation throughout the opera. These critics argue that if it must be played, then it should be placed at the end of the opera.

· Others, perhaps more mystical, agree with Marcia Davenport who states: "Heard in its true setting it literally overwhelms. We have just lived through the climax of the opera. . . . Then Beethoven the dramatist fuses with the universal Beethoven the symphonist to such tremendous effect that *Fidelio* moves beyond and above the theatrical, the visible, into the eternal realm of the spirit."

But W. H. Auden thinks opera is singing and the orchestral "Leonore 3," however fine in the concert hall, in an opera is merely "twelve minutes of acute boredom.")

### SCENE 2 (Outside the prison, 11 min.)

No. 16, *Finale:* The people and prisoners, gathered to greet Don Fernando, hail, "Heil," the happy day. Don Fernando enters and sings a short speech about the king's mercy, and Rocco presents Florestan as one needing it. Don Fernando who had thought Florestan dead is astonished, and Rocco explains how Leonora saved her husband. **chorus** Pizarro is led away, Leonora removes Florestan's fetters, and all exclaim that Florestan was blessed in his wife, while Leonora insists that only love could have supported her until Florestan was saved.

### Vocabulary, Act II

| | | |
|---|---|---|
| Gott, welch' Dunkel hier | got velk doong.kel here | God, how dark here |
| stille | shtill.uh | silence |
| ist Gottes Wille | ist got.es vill.uh | (it) is God's will |
| in des Lebens Fruehlingstagen | een dess lay.bens froo.ling.stah.gen | in the spring day of life |
| Wahrheit | vahr.hite | truth |

Vocabulary, Act II (*continued*)

| | | |
|---|---|---|
| ein Engel | eye'n eng.el | an angel |
| zur Freiheit | tsoor fry.hite | to freedom |
| komm hilf | komm hilf | come help |
| hab acht | hahb ahkt | have care |
| Gott, er ist's | got air ists | God, it is he |
| o Dank | oh dahnk | oh thanks |
| armer Mann | ahrm.er mahnn | unhappy man |
| ein Moerder | eye'n merd.er | a murderer |
| toet' erst sein Weib | tert airst sine vibe | kill first his wife |
| und du bist tot | oont doo bist toht | and you are dead |
| o namen, namenlose Freude | oh nah.men . . . loh. suh froy.duh | oh inexpressible joy |
| heil | hile | hail |

# IL BARBIERE DI SIVIGLIA

## (The Barber of Seville)

Opera buffa in two acts. First performed at Rome on February 20, 1816. Music by G. Rossini. Libretto by C. Sterbini after Beaumarchais' comedy, *Le Barbier de Séville,* first produced in 1775.

### PRINCIPAL CHARACTERS

| | | |
|---|---|---|
| Count Almaviva, a Grandee of Spain | tenor | alma.VEE.vah |
| Figaro, a Jack-of-all-trades and presently a barber | baritone | FIG.ar.oh |
| Dr. Bartolo, a physician and Rosina's guardian | bass | BAR.toe.low |
| Rosina | mezzo-soprano | roh.SEEN.ah |
| Don Basilio, a music teacher | bass | bah.SEAL.yo |
| Berta, a maid | mezzo-soprano | |

The action takes place outside and in Dr. Bartolo's house in Seville in the seventeenth century.

*Il Barbiere di Siviglia* is the only universally popular comic opera, comedy far more than tragedy often being a matter of local taste. Its only close competitor, *Le Nozze di Figaro,* has always had areas, the largest being Italy, in which it has failed to establish itself. The reason may be, as the Italians aver, that *Figaro* has melancholic overtones: the incidents of the intrigue are comic, but the audience no more than the Countess can laugh at the Count's behavior.

There are no such overtones in *Il Barbiere*. It is pure fun. Even sober-sided, moralistic Beethoven liked it. The story is simplicity itself. The Count, a tenor, outside the house, must get inside long enough to plan the soprano's escape. The enemy is Dr. Bartolo, a bass, who keeps the soprano locked in. The barber, the baritone, is the brains behind the tenor's schemes. The love interest of the tenor and the soprano is purely perfunctory; the opera is a romp.

ROSSINI

Rossini is supposed to have written the opera in thirteen days, and it has a unique scrambled spontaneity to it. The overture, the storm scene, a tenor aria, a chorus, and numerous phrases were snatched from five earlier operas and pressed into service. Don Basilio, the music teacher to whom words perhaps did not come easily, joins an Act I ensemble merely singing the notes of the scale: do, re, mi, etc. And in some of the ensembles the singers all converge on the same word and sing it over and over again.

But it is all comic because, throughout the opera, Rossini is laughing at the medium itself. In Act I Scene 1 the hired musicians, although ordered to be quiet, work up a sufficient racket to wake the dead but not one light sleeper in Seville. And the cause of the racket? The musicians were *over*paid—only in opera! In Act II when the soprano and tenor should be escaping down a ladder, they remain rooted for yet another verse while Figaro mocks them as silly operatic characters and tries desperately to get them to move. Earlier Dr. Bartolo characterizes opera as ". . . un lungo, malinconico, noioso, poetico strambòtto. Barbaro gusto! secolo corrotto!" (A long melancholy, noisy, poetical nothing. Barbarous taste, corrupted era.)

Three traditions, all bad, cling to *Il Barbiere*. The first is that Rosina is a role for coloratura sopranos. It isn't. Rossini wrote it for Signora Giorgi-Righetti, whose voice has been described as a mezzo-soprano or even a contralto. Plainly, he imagined a voice with body to it, large enough to balance the four men. Coloraturas can't begin to do this, and to sing the role at all, they have to transpose all the low notes up. Audiences need not admire this. Happily, another tradition, substituting "Home Sweet Home" or something equally inappropriate, for Rosina's aria in the Lesson Scene, seems to be dying. There remains, however, the series of small cuts, made perhaps to save the audience some recitative but which destroys the continuity of the plot. The cuts would be less serious if the librettos published by opera houses and record companies indicated them. As it is, most of the published librettos give no explanation, for example, of why Rosina in Act II greets the Count, entering by the balcony to free her, with a torrent of angry words.

The opera was originally composed in two acts with the first having two scenes. In most productions Act I Scene 2 is treated as a separate act, making three in all.

## OVERTURE (7 min.)

According to legend, Rossini wrote an overture based on Spanish themes that was lost after the first performance. The one presently and universally played was originally composed for *Aureliano in Palmira*, a tragedy; it was used again for *Elisabetta, Regina d'Inghilterra*, an historical drama; but only here reached its final resting place in a comedy.

## ACT I (101 min.)

### SCENE 1 (50 min.)

A square in Seville. To the left is Dr. Bartolo's house with a balcony. Dawn.

*Musicians:* The Count's servant, Fiorello, leads in a band of street **chorus** players, instructing them to be very quiet: "piano, pianissimo" (softly, very softly).

*The Count:* He enters and sings a serenade: "Ecco ridente in cielo"

**aria**     (lo, dawn rising . . . and you asleep)? It is directed to a young lady he saw one day in the Prado in Madrid and whom he has traced to this balcony in Seville. The serenade is unsuccessful; the girl does not appear.

**chorus**     *The Musicians:* The Count, discouraged, dismisses them and pays them so well that they excessively noise their thanks.

*Figaro:* He wanders in singing the most famous aria in all opera in
**aria**     which he describes how much he enjoys being a barber, hearing and amplifying all the gossip, arranging assignations for society, and making himself indispensable to anyone rich enough to have a problem. (It is called "Largo al Factotum" from its first line.)

*The Count and Figaro:* The Count recognizes Figaro who was once in his service. He explains that he is in Seville in disguise to court a young lady, but that he is unable to discover anything about her. Figaro informs him that he is in luck. The girl, Rosina, is the ward of Dr. Bartolo, and he, Figaro, has access to the house as barber, apothecary, surgeon and general factotum. Just then the door to the balcony opens and Figaro pushes the Count out of sight underneath.

*Rosina and Dr. Bartolo:* She appears, intending to drop a note to the serenader, but Dr. Bartolo follows her out on the balcony and demands
**usually cut**     to know what she is holding. She lies that it is only the text for an aria of the new opera, *The Useless Precaution,* and drops it over the railing. With apologies, she sends Dr. Bartolo down to pick it up, but the Count gets it first. When Dr. Bartolo appears below, Rosina pretends it blew away. He suspects she has tricked him and orders her inside.

*The Count and Figaro:* The letter states that his "assiduous attendance has piqued her curiosity." She inquires his name, condition and intentions. Figaro warns him that Dr. Bartolo intends to marry her him-
**usually cut**     self in order to enjoy her inheritance. They hide again as Dr. Bartolo comes out. (The two short scenes, together taking only three minutes, are almost invariably cut, probably only because it is cheaper to paint a backdrop than build a balcony to support a soprano and a bass.)

*Dr. Bartolo:* He orders the porter to admit no one except his friend, Don Basilio, whom he's going even now to seek in order to arrange for the wedding as soon as possible.

*The Count and Figaro:* At Figaro's suggestion the Count starts another serenade in which he explains his name is Lindoro, he is a stu-

**aria**     dent, and he intends marriage. Rosina appears on the balcony and urges him to continue. He is expanding on his love when she suddenly retires. Figaro surmises that someone has entered her room.

The Count, all excited, insists Figaro help him. Figaro agrees if **duet**     liberally subsidized. They sing in a duet that money makes Figaro's brain boil like a volcano, "un vulcano."

Figaro's first idea is that the Count be a soldier, "un soldato," billeted in the house. To this he adds the further idea that Dr. Bartolo's suspicions will be lulled if the soldier is tipsy, "ubbriaco." They agree on the plan and start to separate as the Count thinks to ask Figaro where his shop is.

**aria**     In a fast patter aria of complicated directions, Figaro explains it is "Numero quindici a mano manco" (number fifteen, to the left).

**duet**     They close with a duet; the Count is excited at his prospects with Rosina, Figaro at separating the Count from some of his money.

The score ends the scene with three lines of recitative (invariably cut) by Fiorello, who complains of serving such a master, always in love and up at all hours.

### Vocabulary, Act I Scene 1

| | | |
|---|---|---|
| piano, pianissimo | p'yah.no | softly, very softly |
| ecco ridente in cielo | eck.oh ree.dent.day een CHAY.low | lo! rising in the sky |
| mio nome | me.oh no.may | my name |
| io son Lindoro | yo sohn leen.door.oh | I am Lindoro |
| un vulcano | oon vul.KAHN.oh | a volcano |
| un soldato | oon sole.DAH.toe | a soldier |
| ubbriaco | oo.bree.AH.coe | tipsy, part-way drunk |
| numero quindici | new.may.roe kwin.dee.chee | number fifteen |
| a mano manco | a mah.no mahn.koe | on the left hand |

## ACT I SCENE 2 (51 min.)

Inside the house the next morning.

*Rosina:* She sings of her love for Lindoro, the student, whose voice has so excited her—"una voce poco fa" (a voice a little while ago) **aria**     —and then of how she must outwit her guardian. She allows that she is a nice, sweet girl until crossed in something she wants; then she can be a viper.

Figaro enters and says he has something to tell her, but he hides as Dr. Bartolo enters.

*Dr. Bartolo:* He curses Figaro, who has mixed up the medicines for the maid and porter. Berta, who should have had the sleeping pills, got the sneezing powder; and the porter now can barely stay awake. Rosina says she likes Figaro, who at least is always in a good humor, and she

**usually cut** flounces out. Dr. Bartolo then interrogates the two servants as to whether Figaro has been talking to Rosina, but they can only sneeze and yawn. (For some reason the interrogation—it lasts only a minute—is usually cut, and the audience never understands why the maid sneezes or the porter drags himself around.)

*Don Basilio:* He arrives with news: Count Almaviva, who tried to make Rosina's acquaintance in Madrid, has followed her to Seville. He suggests that Dr. Bartolo head him off by spreading a slander, "La

**aria** Calunnia." In a long aria he describes how easy it is to get a slander started—just a whisper, the merest nothing, feeds on itself and grows until it is louder than the fiercest storm, loud enough to drive the Count from Seville. Dr. Bartolo is not convinced; he thinks it would be quicker and safer to marry Rosina at once, and the two leave to make arrangements.

*Figaro and Rosina:* They resume their plotting. Figaro spells out the name of Lindoro's love: R-O-S-I-N-A. This starts a duet of, "it's me,"

**duet** "it's you." Figaro suggests she write a letter. Rosina at first protests and then produces one already written. She sings of love, and he observes as he leaves with the letter that women are strange, "donne; donne . . ."

*Rosina and Dr. Bartolo:* He wants to know what Figaro was doing in the house. Did he bring an answer to the letter dropped from the balcony? It is a shot in the dark and nearly succeeds. He accuses her of having an inky finger; he insists a sheet of paper is missing and the quill has been sharpened. But she has an answer for everything: she used the ink for a burn on her finger, the paper to wrap up some lollipops for a little girl, and the quill to draw a flower on her needle-

**aria** point. Dr. Bartolo fumes into a long aria: "A un dottor delle mia sorte . . ." (No point lying to a doctor like me. I'll find out and to keep you safe from scandal, I'll lock you in). He drives her out of the room. (In Italy particularly, another, easier aria is sometimes substituted for Dr. Bartolo: "Manca un foglio," by Romani.)

There is a knocking at the door. The porter being asleep, the sleepless maid has to come from the kitchen to open it.

*The Count and Dr. Bartolo:* The Count enters disguised as a soldier. Dr. Bartolo is disgusted, "Che brutta faccia! E ubbriaco" (such an ugly face, and tipsy)! The Count gets the Doctor's name continually wrong: Barbaro, Barnabo. He offers to embrace the Doctor as a colleague, for he is the veterinary of the regiment. Then he explains that he is billeted in the house. Bartolo is dumbfounded but produces an order exempting him from billeting.

*Finale:* The household gathers. The Count whispers to Rosina that he is Lindoro and tries to pass a letter to her by dropping it on the floor. She covers it with her handkerchief, but Dr. Bartolo at once suspects. The Count picks it up and hands it to Rosina, who explains it is only a laundry list and is able to offer one as proof from her pocket.

Rosina pretends to cry, and Dr. Bartolo offers to comfort her. The Count accuses him of mistreating her and calls him an "ugly baboon." The Doctor screams back at him, and Figaro enters. He warns them that they can be heard out in the square and that half the city has gathered. Suddenly the town guard knocks at the door. Everyone is horrified at the scandal of it, "Quest avventura" (this adventure . . . how will it end).

The guard has come to stop the riot, and everyone raises his voice further to explain and accuse the other. The Sergeant starts to arrest the Count, "in arresto," who prevents it by revealing privately to the Sergeant that he is a noble. The Sergeant then salutes him. This stuns Dr. Bartolo, who freezes with horror and indignation.

All observe Dr. Bartolo: "Fredda ed immobile come una statua" (he's cold and motionless like a statue). They remark that it quite takes their breath away. Figaro keeps repeating "Guarda Don Bartolo" (look at Bartolo . . . without a word to say). At the close of that ensemble a new finale begins in which everyone sings that the noise and pitter-patter is enough to drive a body mad.

Vocabulary, Scene 2

| una voce poco fa | oon.ah voh.chay po.ko fah | a voice a little while ago |
|---|---|---|
| la calunnia | lah kah.loon.ya | a slander |
| donne, donne | dun.nay dun.nay | women |
| a un dottor | a oon dot.tore | to a doctor |
| delle mia sorte | del.lay me.ah sore.tay | of my accomplishments |
| quest' avventura | quest ah.ven.TURE.ah | this adventure |

| | | |
|---|---|---|
| in arresto | een ah.rest.toe | in arrest |
| fredda ed immobile | fray.dah (e)dim.MOE.bee.lay | cold and motionless |
| come una statua | ko.may oon.ah sta.too.ah | like a statue |
| guarda | gwahr.dah | look at |

## ACT II (54 min.)

Inside the house that afternoon and evening.

*Dr. Bartolo:* He worries that he can't figure out who the soldier was. He has discovered that such a man is unknown in the regiment, and he suspects the man of working for Count Almaviva.

*Dr. Bartolo and the Count:* The Count enters masquerading as a music teacher. In an endless, oily refrain he calls down blessings on the house and all in it: "Pace, gioia; gioia, pace" (peace and joy). Dr. Bartolo at first thanks him, "mille grazie," and then admonishes, "ho capito" (I understand), and finally bursts out, "basta, basta" (enough). The Count lies that Don Basilio is sick and has sent him as a substitute. To stop Dr. Bartolo from canceling the music lesson, he shows him Rosina's letter to Lindoro, the one Figaro delivered. He claims he found it at the inn where he and Almaviva are staying. He suggests they tell Rosina he received it from a lady who had it from Almaviva. Dr. Bartolo thinks it a grand slander.

**the lesson scene**     *Rosina:* The music lesson begins. Rosina selects an aria from *The Useless Precaution* and injects frequent asides to the Count whom she still knows only as Lindoro, the student. (It is here that a soprano sometimes inserts an aria that she fancies she sings particularly well.)

*Dr. Bartolo:* He admires her voice, but grieves over the modern music. He starts an old-fashioned aria to demonstrate how good music sounds. Coyly he substitutes "Rosina" for the name in the aria.

*Figaro and Dr. Bartolo:* Figaro arrives to shave Dr. Bartolo, who wants to put it off, but Figaro insists he is too busy to come another day. In getting the towels and basin, he breaks some of the crockery and in the confusion slips the key to the balcony off the household key ring. Just as the shave begins, to everyone's consternation Don Basilio arrives.

*Don Basilio, Dr. Bartolo, Figaro, the Count and Rosina:* The Count reminds Dr. Bartolo that Don Basilio doesn't know of their plan about

the letter. He urges the Doctor to get rid of the fevered Don Basilio
before he blurts something out. They all comment on how sick he
looks, and Figaro diagnoses the disease as "scarlattina" (scarlet

**quintet** fever). The Count slips Don Basilio a purse, and in a
quintet all wish him, "Buona sera, mio signore" (goodnight, sir). But
Dr. Bartolo is uncertain about it.

The shave continues. As the Count whispers to Rosina to be ready
at midnight, Dr. Bartolo hears them and, in a tantrum of suspicions,
drives them all out before the Count can explain to Rosina who he is
and why he gave Dr. Bartolo the letter. Convinced he is being tricked,
Dr. Bartolo sends the porter after Don Basilio and undertakes to watch
the door himself.

**aria** *Berta:* She complains of the tumult in the house and of being
old and a spinster. (Dramatically this aria serves no function and
musically is a bit of a bore. If something must be cut, this should be
it.)

*Dr. Bartolo and Don Basilio:* Don Basilio denies knowing the substitute music teacher and surmises from the purse he received that it
was the Count. Dr. Bartolo decides to marry Rosina at once and urges

**usually cut** Don Basilio to fetch the notary. But Don Basilio
demures that it is raining and, anyway, Figaro has engaged the notary
for his niece's wedding that night. This puts Dr. Bartolo in a frenzy for
he knows Figaro has no niece. He gives Don Basilio the key to the
door and sends him off to find a notary, any notary.

*Dr. Bartolo and Rosina:* He now plays his last card, which is to show
Rosina her letter to Lindoro that the Count, disguised as the music

**sometimes cut** teacher, gave him. He suggests, and Rosina believes, that Lindoro is merely procuring for the Count. She is furious,
reveals the plot to elope, swears a "vendetta" on Lindoro, and agrees
to marry Dr. Bartolo. He goes out to summon the guard in order to
arrest Figaro and Lindoro as thieves when they appear on the balcony.

**storm scene** At this point the rain boils up into a short storm scene
for the orchestra. The stage remains bare.

*The Count, Rosina, Figaro:* The men get in by a ladder to the balcony.
Rosina hurls accusations at Lindoro who solves her problems by re-

**trio** vealing that he is both Almaviva and Lindoro. Then as
Figaro tries to hurry them, they sing a love duet at such length that
Dr. Bartolo arrives outside with the police and removes the ladder.

*Finale:* Don Basilio enters with the notary and, being influenced by the Count's bribe and pistol, orders the notary to marry the couple with himself and Figaro as witnesses. Whereupon Dr. Bartolo and the police enter. There are recriminations and explanations and the confusion and the opera end. (Immediately following the Count's revelation of his true identity to Dr. Bartolo, he has a long aria in which he tells the old man to stop fussing. It is almost always cut.)

### Vocabulary, Act II

| | | |
|---|---|---|
| pace, gioia | pah.chay je.oy.ah | peace, joy |
| mille grazie | mil.lay grah.tsee.eh | a thousand thanks |
| ho capito | hoe kah.pea.toe | I understand |
| basta | bah.stah | enough |
| scarlattina | scar.lah.TEEN.ah | scarlet fever |
| buona sera | bwon.ah say.rah | good night |
| mio signore | me.oh seen.yor.eh | my dear sir |

## L'ELISIR D'AMORE

### (The Elixir of Love)

Opera in two acts. First performed at Milan on May 12, 1832. Music by G. Donizetti. Libretto by F. Romani after the libretto by A. E. Scribe for D. F. Auber's opera *Le Philtre*.

### PRINCIPAL CHARACTERS

| | | |
|---|---|---|
| Giannetta, a peasant | soprano | |
| Nemorino, a peasant who loves Adina | tenor | ne.mo.REE.no |
| Adina, who owns her own farm | soprano | ah.DEE.nah |
| Belcore, a sergeant | baritone | |
| Dr. Dulcamara, a quack doctor | bass | |

The action takes place in and near an Italian village in the early nineteenth century.

No opera can match the simple, naive charm of *L'Elisir d'Amore*. Its story is so outrageously unsophisticated that it is impossible to describe to someone who hasn't heard the music without feeling a sort of embarrassment for opera in general that such a thing should survive. But it has, and largely because Romani had the good sense to keep it short and because Donizetti wrote delightfully artless music that perfectly reflects the sunlit, outdoors feeling of the work. Not many operas in the last two hundred years set a scene on a farm or in a small village with a single inn called "The Partridge."

The danger for the opera always is that the conductor, the tenor or the audience will take it too seriously, causing its spontaneity and fun to dry up. The opera is light entertainment and nothing more. The businessman may take time off to count his profit or loss, the hostess to seat her table, or anyone to snooze. The music, however, has some real glories such as the finale to Act I, Dr. Dulcamara's patter song, the tiny satirical soldier's march, and the Romance, which was a favorite of Caruso.

The story, such as it is, turns on Nemorino's misunderstanding of how Tristan caused Isolde to love him. Nemorino, standing to one side as Adina tells it, either does not hear or does not grasp that Isolde as well as Tristan drank the potion; so Nemorino goes off, drinks his elixir in the heat of the noonday sun and expects Adina to fall suddenly in love with him. This was composed thirty-three years before Wagner's *Tristan und Isolde,* and the audience must not think of it in terms of the later opera.

In all, Donizetti wrote sixty-five operas, of which only four are comedies. Yet all four are still given, and two of them, *L'Elisir d'Amore* and *Don Pasquale,* together with *Lucia di Lammermoor,* are at present his most successful. One reason may be that at least for modern taste melodic waltzes and marches seem more suitable for comedy. Verdi could use them for tragedy because his melodies have an urgency or thrust to them; Donizetti's lilt. He wrote them very fast; he is supposed to have written *L'Elisir d'Amore* in two weeks.

Most modern productions of the opera make one large cut, indicated below, and many little excisions. These last usually are of codas (*See* Glossary) or repeats which, since the music is well known and the audience pays more attention than in 1832, seem redundant.

## ACT I (63 min.)

### PRELUDE (3 min.)

It is mock heroic, alternating a few resounding chords with a shy, twittering descant for the flute, which traditionally is supposed to have a rustic quality to its sound. After a slow section, the orchestra introduces the opening chorus, and the curtain rises without any break.

## SCENE 1 (26 min.)

The yard of Adina's farm near the village. In the field some women are washing clothes in a brook. Harvesters, led by Giannetta, are resting in the shade of a large tree. Adina sits a little apart, reading; from a distance Nemorino gazes at her fondly. (Many productions set this scene in the locale of the next, the village square, transforming the harvesters into something more urban, such as farmers shopping in town, and, thus, avoiding the cost of a set.)

*Giannetta, the Harvesters and Nemorino:* Giannetta and her friends rejoice that the shade saves them from the heat of the sun while observ-
**chorus, aria and chorus**    ing that there is no escape from the heat of love. Nemorino sighs over Adina, "quanto è bella, quanto è cara" (how beautiful she is, how sweet). He admires her learning and reading but wonders who will ever be able to instruct him how to teach her to love him. He, Giannetta, and the harvesters then contrast their vocal lines in a duet with chorus.

*Adina et al:* She bursts out laughing and has to explain to the others that she is reading the story of Tristan, "è la storia di Tristano." They insist she read it to them, "leggi," and she begins. The cruel Isolde, "crudele Isotta," repulsed Tristan until a wise magician gave him a potion which, as soon as she had sipped, caused her to love him
**solo with chorus**    madly. Adina tells the story in two verses, exclaiming with a laugh at the end of each that she wished she had such a perfect elixir, "elisir di si perfetta." Her friends agree.

**march**    *Belcore:* He enters at the head of a platoon of soldiers and, after a short exhibition of military precision, puts the troops at ease while he presents a bouquet to Adina. Comparing himself to Paris with
**aria**    an apple, he suggests that she love and marry him. He is modest, "è modesto," she comments to the women, who admire his extravagance. It is enough that he insists that he is gallant and a sergeant, "son galante e son sargente," and, besides, there is no time to lose; the uncertainties of war may carry him away. Nemorino gasps at Belcore's boldness, but wishes he had some of it himself. Adina laughs that the soldier usually gets his reward after the battle, not
**chorus**    before it. The harvesters comment that Adina is quite able to handle herself and Belcore too.

It ends with Belcore asking matter-of-factly if he can rest his troops on her land. She agrees, offering him a bottle of wine, and he leads the troops off as the harvesters return to work.

*Adina and Nemorino:* Alone with her he asks for a word, "una parola," but she will have none of him and suggests that his time would be better spent at the bedside of his sick uncle in the city lest he be disinherited. Nemorino swears he will sooner die of love than starvation.

**duet**      Adina warns him to give up his love, for she is capricious and loves a new person each day. Why "perchè"? he asks. A silly question, she snorts; ask the breeze why it blows first this way and then that. But he likens himself to a brook, drawn to the sea by an irresistible power. She repeats that he must learn to have a new love every day, while he exclaims he cannot drive the old one from his heart, "dal cor."

### SCENE 2 (34 min.)

The village square. Outside the Partridge Inn. A cornet sounds, and the villagers gather to see what's going on.

**chorus**      *Villagers:* They all exclaim that a most important person must be arriving, at least a baron or a marquis, and Dr. Dulcamara enters, standing in his carriage with his hands full of papers and bottles. His servant follows, playing the cornet, and the villagers crowd around.

*Dr. Dulcamara:* He begins his sales talk at once: "Udite, udite o rustici; attenti, non fiatate" (listen, listen, you country folk; pay atten-

**aria**      tion, don't even breathe). He is the great Dulcamara, the one who empties hospitals; he has a cure for everything—toothache, declining vigor, wrinkles, asthma, scrofula, rickets, bugs—and all for only twenty scudi. Finally he offers, because he was born in the area,

**chorus**      to sell it for a scudi less. Come forward, "avanti," and buy, he urges. The crowd presses round his carriage and then gradually disperses, leaving him alone with Nemorino. (Dulcamara's sales talk is one of the great patter arias of Italian opera. It should be delivered with great speed and aplomb. If the singer looks even once at the prompter or conductor, the effect is half destroyed.)

*Dr. Dulcamara and Nemorino:* Nemorino cautiously asks the Doctor if he has Queen Isolde's potion. Dulcamara is at first confused and then, as he realizes that Nemorino wants something to make himself attractive to women, announces that he is the original distiller of it. Nemorino

is thrilled, inquires the cost and reveals that the most he has is a florin,
**duet**    which turns out to be just enough. "Obbligato" (much
obliged), "son felice, son contento" (I am happy, I am content), he
sings. Dulcamara mutters that he has never seen such an idiot. But
Nemorino has another question, "dottore, un momentino": the directions for taking it.

Dulcamara explains each step as Nemorino comments, "ben"
(good): take the bottle, shake it gently, uncork it, put it to your mouth
and then sip it. Soon after, in about twenty-four hours, the magic
effect will take hold. And the taste? Nemorino asks. "Eccelente," the
Doctor assures him, while commenting in an aside that it is a Bordeaux
wine.

Nemorino turns to go, when Dulcamara calls him back and swears
him to secrecy, "silenzio"; selling love is tricky business with the police.
Nemorino promises, and Dulcamara assures him that by the morning
all the girls will love him. Nemorino adds that he cares only for one.
Dulcamara observes as he enters the Inn that, in any event, by morning he will have left the village.

*Nemorino:* He hails the elixir, regretting only that he must wait a day
before reaping its benefits. He drinks at once, feels flushed and is
sure Adina even now is beginning to love him. He sits on a bench before the Inn, bites into a sandwich and, taking constant sips from the
bottle, soon begins to sing: la, la, la, la.

*Adina and Nemorino:* She is startled to see him so happy and suspects
a trick. He starts toward her and then sits again, relying on the elixir
**duet**    to make her love him. Each sings in an aside: she that he is
feigning indifference and he that "la barbara" (the cruel girl) will love
him tomorrow, "domani."

Finally Adina addresses him directly and remarks that he seems to
have taken her advice and given up sighing after love. He assures her
that in another day he will be completely cured, and they repeat their
earlier asides.

*Belcore, Adina and Nemorino:* Belcore enters muttering that in love or
war a siege is a bore; in either he prefers hand-to-hand fighting. Adina
suggests that the fortress is about to surrender and, with a glance at
**trio**    Nemorino, suggests marriage in six days. Belcore is ecstatic,
"oh gioja! son contento"; but Nemorino laughs. Belcore is angry and
Adina puzzled, as Nemorino continues to laugh and, with a knowing
look, keeps referring to the morrow.

*Giannetta, Villagers, Adina et al:* A drum rolls and Giannetta runs in, followed by the soldiers, all calling for Belcore. A courier has come with new orders. Belcore reads: they must leave in the morning, "doman mattina." The soldiers complain, and Belcore sighs to Adina, "Carina . . . domani" (sweetest, tomorrow). Nemorino chuckles, "si, si, domani."

Adina promptly offers to marry Belcore that very day, "quest' oggi"
**trio**     (today). Nemorino is horrified. He begs her to wait at least a day. Belcore, calling him a clown and a baboon, tells him to be off. Adina urges one and all to pity him for he is a simple type, and Nemorino can only gasp how unhappy he is and call vaguely for
**chorus**     Dulcamara to come to his aid. The chorus comments that Nemorino is over his depth in trying to compete with the sergeant.

Adina invites them all to a wedding feast on the farm and, taking Belcore's hand, goes out, leaving Nemorino in the center of the laughing villagers.

### Vocabulary, Act I
### Scene 1

| | | |
|---|---|---|
| quanto è bella | kwan.toe'ay bell.ah | how beautiful she is |
| quanto è cara | kwan.toe'ay kah.rah | how sweet she is |
| è la storia di Tristano | ay lah stor.yah di tris. tah.no | it is the story of Tristan |
| leggi | led.jee | read |
| elisir di si perfetta | ay.lee.ZEER dee see pair.fet.tah | an elixir so perfect |
| è modesto | ay mo.DESS.toe | he is modest |
| son galente e son sargente | son gah.LAHN.tay ay son sar.JEN.tay | I am gallant and I am a sergeant |
| una parola | oona pah.RO.lah | a word |
| perchè | pair.KAY | why |
| dal cor | dahl kor | from the heart |

### Scene 2

| | | |
|---|---|---|
| udite, udite o rustici | oo.DEE.tay...roos.tee. chee | listen...oh you country folk |
| attenti, non fiatate | aht.ten.tee non f'yah. TAH.tay | pay attention, don't breathe |
| avanti | ah.VAHN.tee | come forward |
| obbligato | ob.blee.GAH.toe | (I am) much obliged |
| son felice, son contento | son fay.LEE.chay; son kon.TEN.toe | I am happy, content |
| dottore | doh.TOR.ay | doctor |

| | | |
|---|---|---|
| un momentino | oon moh.men.TEE.noh | a little moment |
| ben | bayn | good |
| eccelente | ay.tchell.en.tay | excellent |
| silenzio | see.len.tsee.oh | silence |
| la barbara | lah BAHR.bah.rah | the cruel girl |
| domani | do.MAH.nee | tomorrow |
| oh gioja, son contento | oh je.OY.ah son kon.TEN.toe | oh joy, I am content |
| doman mattina | do.MAHN mah.TEE.nah | tomorrow morning |
| carina...domani | ka.REE.nah... do.MAH.nee | dearest tomorrow |
| quest' oggi | quest' od.jee | this day |

## ACT II (60 min., but with usual cut, 55)

---

### SCENE 1 (17 min.)

A few hours later in a room of Adina's farmhouse. Adina, Belcore, Dulcamara and Giannetta are sitting at the wedding table. Others are standing around talking and drinking. The regimental band is playing. All celebrate the marriage, although Adina has not yet signed the contract.

**chorus** *Villagers et al:* They urge each other to sing, "cantiamo," and toast the bride. In an aside Adina wishes Nemorino would come. Dulcamara suggests that he and Adina sing a new song, very popular elsewhere, about a pretty gondolier girl and Senator Threetooth. (The song is entitled a Barcarolle, but it is not in the usual triple-time [*See* Glossary] rhythm.)

*Dulcamara and Adina:* Dulcamara, as the Senator, puts his case bluntly: he is rich, "io son ricco," and she is pretty, "e tu sei bella"; he **duet with chorus** has money, she has charm. She replies with fluttering lids that she is a simple girl who wants only to marry a man of her own station. The villagers applaud and are shushed by Dulcamara. Love, he continues, is a flighty thing, blown away; gold is heavy and remains. She demurs: to make a Senator happy is too much of an honor. All congratulate Dulcamara on a fine song.

*Villagers et al:* The notary arrives to witness the contract. Adina looks for Nemorino, and then all go into another room to watch Belcore and Adina sign the contract. Dulcamara remains behind, observing that the best part of any wedding is the banquet table.

*Nemorino and Dulcamara:* Nemorino is brokenhearted. He tells the Doctor, who thinks he is mad, that he must be loved right away; tomorrow is too late. Dulcamara suggests that another bottle will work more than twice as fast, and Nemorino agrees, except that he has no more money. That, observes Dulcamara, is too bad. He will be at the Inn for another quarter of an hour if Nemorino can raise the money. He goes out, leaving Nemorino in despair, "Oh! me infelice!"

*Nemorino and Belcore:* Belcore comes in alone muttering against women: Adina swears she loves him but refuses to sign the contract until evening and will give no reason. He discovers that Nemorino is in despair for lack of money and suggests that Nemorino enlist and get
**duet** the bonus, "venti scudi" (twenty scudi), for signing up. At once Belcore launches into a description of life in the army—girls, see the world, on-the-job training, etc.—while Nemorino argues with himself that it is the only way he can raise the money for another bottle. Belcore urges, "venti scudi," hard cash, now; and Nemorino makes his cross.

Belcore shakes his hand and promises that he will soon be a
**duet** corporal. Nemorino sighs that Belcore cannot know the love that has made him enlist. Nemorino rushes off to find Dulcamara.

## SCENE 2 (38 min.)

A rustic courtyard, open at the back.

**chorus** *The Village Girls:* They bubble with excitement. Rumor has it that Nemorino's uncle has died and left him a fortune. Now he is one of the richest men in the village, a good catch for any girl. As no one has been able to find Nemorino, he doesn't know yet. They watch him curiously as he comes in.

*Nemorino and the Girls:* He has drunk, as he murmurs, bottles of the elixir and is hopeful that its magic will soon work. The girls, deciding he still doesn't know of his good fortune, begin to make much of him, and he is convinced it is the elixir.

Adina and Dulcamara, entering from opposite sides, each stop in amazement at the sight of Nemorino surrounded by girls.

(The cut most often made is of the following scene down to the scene between Adina and Dulcamara. There seems to be no good reason for it, as it robs the opera of one of its natural climaxes and,

if the singers are also good actors, of an extremely comic scene.)
Nemorino sees Dulcamara and calls out that the elixir really works.
Dulcamara is astounded. He asks the girls if Nemorino really pleases
them, and they protest that they find him desperately attractive. Adina,
**quartet and chorus**        to one side and unnoticed, is astounded, confused and a little jealous. Giannetta invites Nemorino to dance in the
shade with her, and all the girls push forward. First this one, then that,
Nemorino orders. "Misericordia," swears Dulcamara as the girls trip
into line. At that moment Adina calls, "Nemorino." "Ma tutte, tutte"
(but *every* girl)! Dulcamara gasps. Adina asks if it is true, as Belcore
says, that Nemorino has enlisted, and she tries to tell him that he has
made a mistake. But the girls are more than ever fascinated by him,
and Nemorino is sure that her interest is a sign of love. He goes out
with the girls, leaving an astounded Adina and Dulcamara.

*Adina and Dulcamara:* He insists that the credit for the change in
Nemorino's appeal is all his, and he explains about his elixir and how
Nemorino enlisted in order to buy more. Adina is impressed by the
extent of Nemorino's love and begins to sigh. Dulcamara, thinking
**duet**      perhaps he has another customer, extols his prescription.
But Adina, while conceding that it may be a most powerful potion,
says it is not for her: she will rely on her own charms and pretty face.
Dulcamara, observing in an aside that she knows more about love than
he, calls her a "bricconcella" (little flirt), while she sings that
Nemorino will not escape her. They go out together.

*Nemorino:* He sings that Adina loves him. (In the score it is entitled
"Romanza" and is the most famous aria in the opera. The solo instru-
**aria**      ment introducing it is a bassoon.) He is sure he saw a tear in
Adina's eye, "una furtiva lagrima" (a furtive tear), and he knows now
she loves him, "m'ama, si m'ama" (she loves me). All he wants of life
now is to die of love, "si può morir" (If I can die). He sees Adina
coming and resolves to continue his indifference until she admits she
loves him.

*Adina and Nemorino:* She presents him with his enlistment papers,
which she has bought back from Belcore. "Prendi" (take them), she
urges, saying that he should stay in the village where he is loved. Then
as Nemorino expects to hear that *she* loves him, she turns to go,
"addio." In despair he gives her back the papers. He would rather die
a soldier's death, "voglio morir soldato," than remain unloved. At that

she admits she loves him, "t'amo, si t'amo." He exclaims "oh, gioja," and in increasingly lengthy runs she swears to love him always, "eterno amor."

*Finale:* Belcore comes in at the head of his troops followed by Dulcamara and the villagers. Adina brushes Belcore's objections aside and announces she will marry Nemorino. Belcore muses that there are other girls, Dulcamara tries to sell a few more bottles, and the curtain falls as Dulcamara drives off in his carriage.

### Vocabulary, Act II
### Scene 1

| | | |
|---|---|---|
| cantiamo | kan.t'yah.moe | let us sing |
| io son ricco | yo son reek.ko | I am rich |
| e tu sei bella | ay too say bell.ah | and you are pretty |
| oh, me infelice! | oh may in.fay.LEE. chay | oh unhappy me |
| venti scudi | ven.tee skoo.dee | twenty scudi |

### Scene 2

| | | |
|---|---|---|
| misericordia | me.zay.re.KOR.d'yah | great heavens |
| ma tutte, tutte | mah toot.tay | but all girls |
| bricconcella | brik.kon.chell.ah | little flirt |
| una furtiva lagrima | oona foor.tee.vah lah.gree.mah | a furtive tear she loves me |
| m'ama, si m'ama | m'AH.mah | if I can die |
| si può morir | see pwoh mor.eer | take (the enlistment |
| prendi | pren.dee | papers) |
| addio | ah.DEE.oh | farewell |
| voglio morir soldato | vo.l'yo mor.eer sol.DAH.toe | I wish to die a soldier |
| t'amo, si t'amo | t'AH.moh | I love you |
| eterno amor | ay.tair.no ah.mor | eternal love |

# LUCIA DI LAMMERMOOR

Opera in three acts. First performed at Naples on September 26, 1835. Music by G. Donizetti. Libretto by S. Cammarano after the novel by Sir Walter Scott.

### PRINCIPAL CHARACTERS

| | |
|---|---|
| Normanno, captain of Enrico's retainers | tenor |
| Enrico, Lucia's brother | baritone |

Raimondo (sometimes called Bidebent), Lucia's tutor     bass

Lucia     soprano     loo.CHEE.ah
Alisa, her companion     mezzo-soprano
Edgardo, last of the Ravenswoods     tenor
Arturo, Lucia's bridegroom     tenor

The action takes place in the Scottish Lowlands outside of Edinburgh about 1705.

Sir Walter Scott's *The Bride of Lammermoor,* based on a true story, appeared in 1819. The spirit of romance was then sweeping Europe, and within twenty years four operas were made of the novel. Of these, only Donizetti's survives and that only because of its music, not its libretto, which is a fearful mishmash of Italian innocence and ignorance in the face of Scottish history and customs.

But even Scott's novel doesn't do well by the story. He has Ravenswood (Edgardo) die, for example, by accidentally riding into a bog of quicksand, a wholly irrelevant ending. Scott's achievement was a fine portrayal of the rise of the middle class in Scotland. Ravenswood is one of the land-poor aristocracy being forced to sell out. Ashton is an Edinburgh lawyer, rising politically and buying in. Ravenswood, if he had survived, would have become a Jacobite and wanted Scotland independent with Edinburgh its capital. Ashton already has agents at the court in London and in the future will be a Whig. The time of the novel is Queen Anne's Reign (1702–14) during which by the Act of Union (1707) England and Scotland joined.

None of this is in the opera. Donizetti presents simply a sentimental, old-fashioned romance set in the time of "The Troubles." The Ashtons live in Ravenswood Castle, which Enrico tricked out of the Ravenswood family by legal chicanery. Edgardo, the last of the Ravenswoods, lives in dilapidated Wolfscrag Castle nearby, the last of the family possessions. Edgardo's party is out of favor, and a marriage to him by Lucia would be fatal to her family's fortunes. Enrico therefore forces her to marry Arturo Bucklaw, whose political star is rising.

Donizetti turned out operas like detective stories. At one point he wrote ten in four years. He is supposed to have written Edgardo's final aria in thirty minutes while fighting off a headache. *Lucia* is a singers' opera and there are many traditions of cutting measures here and adding there. Sopranos use their own cadenzas and ornaments in the various coloratura arias. This probably is legitimate where the composer "improvises" the opera in a very short time. The result is an opera of perfunctory choruses, vigorous tunes, and two scenes for a soprano that are frankly and charmingly exhibitions.

## ACT I (37 min.)

### SCENE 1 (13 min.)

Near Ravenswood Castle. Enrico's retainers are hunting. There is a short prelude (2 min.).

**chorus** *Retainers and Normanno:* They decide they must tell Enrico a thing they have discovered.

*Enrico, Normanno and Raimondo:* Enrico complains that the family fortunes are sinking: Lucia must marry. Raimondo urges Enrico to give her time to mourn her mother. Normanno scoffs at that: Lucia already loves a man, a man who saved her life by shooting a bull. Enrico guesses "Edgardo?" Normanno assents.

**trio** *Enrico, Normanno and Raimondo:* Enrico curses Edgardo and threatens the absent Lucia. Raimondo asks Heaven to watch over Lucia. Normanno insists that he had, for honor, to speak up.

**chorus** *Retainers:* They murmur they know more. Edgardo that very day has just seen Lucia. He passed them on his return to Wolfscrag Castle.

**duet and chorus** *Enrico, Raimondo and Retainers:* Enrico swears that Edgardo's blood must flow—"sangue" (blood). Raimondo laments that the times are bad. The chorus supports Enrico.

### SCENE 2 (24 min.)

By a fountain near Ravenswood Castle. A harp solo (3 min.) introduces the scene.

*Lucia and Alisa:* Lucia has asked Edgardo to meet her by the haunted fountain. While they wait, she tells Alisa how one day she saw the
**aria** ghost. It tried to speak to her but she couldn't hear it. Then it disappeared under the water. The legend is that a Ravenswood killed his love, who had betrayed him, and that her spirit lives in the fountain. (The aria is in two verses, the second being greatly ornamented. Sopranos sometimes make up their own ornaments.)

Alisa is horrified and convinced that it is an ill omen. She urges Lucia to give up Edgardo.

**aria**    Lucia brightly tells her that Edgardo is everything to her; just his presence is ecstasy. (Again the aria is in two verses, the second being ornamented.)

*Edgardo and Lucia:* He tells her he must leave that night for France. He suggests that before then he speak to Enrico and ask formally for her hand. She is terrified and urges him against it. He bursts out against Enrico. She tries to calm him. "M'odi e trema," he tells her (hear me **duet**    and tremble). He starts: "Sulla tomba . . ." (on the tombs) he swore revenge against Enrico and only gave it up for her. "Ceda, céda," she urges (give it up).

Edgardo asks if she'll swear to be true to him. She agrees and they exchange gold rings and softly pledge their true love before Heaven.

Then at the thought of parting, they grow more excited until Lucia starts an extended duet, "Verrano a te" (will carry to you). Each promises that the breezes will carry the sighs of love to the other.

Vocabulary, ACT I

| | | |
|---|---|---|
| sangue | sahng.gway | blood |
| m'odi e trema | m'oh.dee eh tray.mah | hear me and tremble |
| sulla tomba | sool.lah tum.bah | on the tombs |
| cedi, cedi | CHE.dee, CHE.dee | give it up |
| verano a te | vair.rah.no ah tay | will carry to you |

## ACT II (31 min.)

———

## SCENE 1 (16 min.)

Enrico's study in Ravenswood Castle.

*Enrico and Normanno:* Enrico tells Normanno that the wedding guests are coming and that he hasn't yet told Lucia that the wedding is to be today. Normanno encourages him and gives him a forged letter in which Edgardo announces his engagement to another lady.

*Enrico and Lucia:* He asks her why she is so silent. She replies that he **aria**    shouldn't force her to marry. To what is musically the second verse, he suggests that her sense of love and duty to her family should impel her to such a marriage. She insists he knows she has promised her hand to Edgardo. Enrico begins to get angry. "Nol potevi," he repeats (you cannot). He gives her the forged letter: "Leggi" (read it).

Overcome, Lucia sinks in the chair. Pathetically she sobs her one hope in life has been shattered. Eagerly Enrico urges her to forget **duet** Edgardo: "un perfido amore" (a faithless lover). They join as she wishes she were dead, and he insists that time will help her.

Offstage trumpets announce the arrival of the wedding guests. Lucia is startled. Enrico insists that she go through with it. Angrily, he threatens her with vengeance if she doesn't: "Se tradirmi" (if to betray me). Lucia tearfully begs the Heavens for mercy. The marriage bed, she laments, will be her tomb. Enrico leaves her to welcome the guests.

(Here there is a scene between Lucia and Raimondo which is usually cut. In it he urges her more kindly, but as insistently as Enrico, to give up Edgardo. He tells her that he suspects Edgardo's letters to her and hers to him have been withheld by Enrico. But he also says that he arranged to have one of hers smuggled out to France. But still Edgardo is silent. He persuades Lucia she owes it to her brother to marry.)

## SCENE 2 (15 min.)

The Great Hall of Ravenswood Castle.

**chorus** *Guests and Arturo:* The guests hail the wedding. Arturo in an arietta formally expresses his happiness, and the guests wish him the good things of life.

*Enrico and Arturo:* Arturo asks: "Dov'è Lucia" (where is Lucia)? Enrico assures him she is coming and warns him that she still weeps a bit for her dead mother.

*Lucia, Enrico, Arturo, Raimondo, Alisa and, later, Edgardo:* Enrico introduces her to Arturo: "Ecco il tuo sposo" (here is your husband). They move over to the table where the marriage contract waits to be signed. This sets for them all the rights of dower and curtsy. Lucia hesitates. Enrico insists, "Scrivi" (inscribe it). The instant she does, Edgardo enters, and the famous sextet begins.

Edgardo first muses why he doesn't kill Enrico on the spot, then de- **sextet** cides that it is because he still loves Lucia. Enrico wonders what Edgardo plans and then, on seeing Lucia's haggard looks, fears the day may bring even worse events. Arturo has the same fears. Raimondo, Alisa and Lucia beg Heaven to help her.

Enrico and Arturo threaten to drive Edgardo out, but Raimondo urges peace, "pace."

Enrico asks what Edgardo wants. He replies he wants Lucia, his pledged love. Raimondo then shows him the contract. He forces her to admit it is her own writing: "Rispondi" (answer). "Si" (yes), she groans.

He throws her ring at her feet and roughly pulls his off her finger. "Maledetto" (curse you), he curses her. Lucia is overcome. Enrico and the guests tell him to get out; they'll be revenged later. Edgardo throws down his sword; he is ready to die now. There is nothing to live for. Finally in despair, he leaves.

### Vocabulary, Act II

| | | |
|---|---|---|
| nol potevi | knoll po.teh.vee | you cannot |
| leggi | LEH.gee | read it |
| un perfido amore | oon pear.fee.do ah.more | a faithless lover |
| se tradirmi | say trah.deer.me | if to betray me |
| dov'è Lucia | doe.v'eh loo.CHEE.ah | where is Lucia |
| ecco il tuo sposo | ek.koe eel two.oh sposo | here is your husband |
| scrivi | SCREE.vee | inscribe it |
| rispondi | ree.spon.dee | answer |
| si | see | yes |
| maledetto | mal.le.DEBT.toh | curse you |

## ACT III (with usual cuts, 35 min.)

### SCENE 1 (6 min.)

(There follows here a scene, generally cut, in which Enrico bursts in on Edgardo at Wolfscrag Castle. He tells Edgardo that the marriage ceremony has been performed and challenges him to duel to avenge the dishonor brought on the family. In an angry duet they agree to meet early the next morning. Musically, the scene is not a great addition to the opera; dramatically, it gives Edgardo more depth as a character by revealing him in his dilapidated castle and contrasting it with the good repair of his enemy's.)

### SCENE 2 (20 min.)

A hall in Ravenswood Castle. The wedding guests in groups. There is dancing.
*Raimondo:* He stops the dancing and describes the horrifying scene

upstairs: Lucia has gone mad and stabbed Arturo. The chorus begs Heaven to forgive her.

**the mad scene**     *Lucia:* She comes (in almost every production downstairs). She imagines she's talking to Edgardo. They will meet by the fountain, "presso la fonte." Suddenly, terrified, she sees the ghost, "il fantasma." It comes between them.

She imagines their wedding. The guests are there. The candles are lighted. The chorus pities her. She sees the future bright without a cloud.

(Here all sopranos put in some straight vocalizing. Tradition calls for a cadenza with flute accompaniment. This is very exacting for a soprano because a flute once tuned cannot go flat but sopranos can, and the florid passages are exceedingly tiring. The cadenza traditionally ends on a high E flat. Few sopranos sound like anything at all that high, so there is always a burst of applause if she makes it—even though this is in the middle of the Mad Scene. If she's seriously tiring, she may skip it, for tradition requires another at the end of the scene. But the audience, although entitled to a buzz of excitement, must still applaud.

(At this point six pages of the score, mostly remarks by Enrico, are cut so that the soprano won't have to share the stage with anyone.)

**aria**     Lucia then starts on an aria: "Spargi d'amaro pianto" (shed bitter tears . . . on my grave). It will only be Heaven when Edgardo joins her. (The aria is in two verses, the second, of course, being ornamented.)

At the end she falls fainting on the high E flat, which allows her to trail the note off if she hasn't really got it. And the curtain falls, cutting a brief scene in which Raimondo accuses Normanno of causing all the trouble.

## SCENE 3 (15 min.)

The tombs of the Ravenswoods in a cemetery midway between Ravenswood and Wolfscrag Castles. Night.

*Edgardo:* He is alone and does not yet know of Lucia's death. He
**aria**     imagines her enjoying the wedding feast: "ingrata donna" (ungrateful woman). He begins a mournful aria foreseeing his death in the duel. He warns Lucia not to stray near his tomb, but to forget him and let him rest in peace.

A group of Ravenswood retainers appears and tells him that Lucia has gone mad and is calling for him. A bell rings. Raimondo enters and prevents him from going to Lucia. The bell tolled her death. He is too late.

Edgardo sings: God will join us in heaven. Without you, life is nothing—"bell' alma innamorata" (beautiful, beloved soul). He draws
**aria** his dagger. They try to disarm him, but he stabs himself. He dies singing, "bell' alma innamorata . . ."

#### Vocabulary, Act III

| | | |
|---|---|---|
| presso la fonte | press.oh lah fon.tay | near the fountain |
| il fantasma | eel fan.tahs.mah | the ghost |
| spargi d'amaro pianto | spar.gee d'ah.mah.roe p'yan.toe | shed bitter tears |
| ingrata donna | in.grah.tah don.nah | ungrateful woman |
| bell' alma innamorata | bell' al.mah (i) nam.or.ah.tah | beautiful, beloved soul |

# DON PASQUALE

Opera buffa in three acts. First performed in Paris on January 3, 1843. Music by G. Donizetti. Libretto by Donizetti and G. Ruffini after A. Anelli's libretto for an opera on the same subject, *Ser Marcantonio*, by S. Pavesi, first produced on September 26, 1810 at Milan.

### PRINCIPAL CHARACTERS

| | | |
|---|---|---|
| Don Pasquale, a bachelor nearing 70 | bass | |
| Dr. Malatesta, his doctor | baritone | mal.ah.TEST.ah |
| Ernesto, his nephew | tenor | |
| Norina, a young widow | soprano | |

The action takes place in the early nineteenth century in Rome.

Donizetti composed two comic operas which are still given with some regularity outside of Italy, *Don Pasquale,* his last great success, and *L'Elisir d'Amore* (1832), one of his first. Both are minor masterworks with some of the vivacity and verve typical of Rossini combined with a melodic sentiment that was Donizetti's unique gift. No other composer has ever been able to underline his scenes with such simple, graceful and charming melodies. It is impossible to leave the theater without humming snatches.

Of the two operas *Don Pasquale* is generally considered the greater, although *L'Elisir* may have the more famous arias. But in *Don Pasquale* the melodic invention is more consistent and the libretto tighter. The opera uses the ancient story, beloved in Italy, of the old goat who forgets that love is for the young or, worse, marries to disinherit his relatives; but Donizetti's unpretentious music gives each of the stock figures a real character. In the third act when Norina slaps the foolish old man, the opera has some depth, whereas *L'Elisir,* however delightful, is never more than fluff.

In the history of opera *Don Pasquale* closes an era. It is the last of the comic operas in the style Rossini spread over Europe. In the year of its première, 1843, Wagner's *Der Fliegende Hollaender* also was first produced. The two are so different it is incredible they should touch at all. It is typical of the different approach to opera that each represents that Wagner should have worked on his for more than three years while Donizetti, legend says, spent only eleven days.

One difficulty of the opera is that it seems to excite the worst vulgarities in many of the artists who sing it. Using the fact that it is a comedy as an excuse, many turn it into a fast, slapstick number. Ernest Newman, arguing against such excesses, pointed out that it was presented in 1843 in what was then contemporary dress. Donizetti meant these to be real people, not caricatures. He wrote the characters with the necessary depth; they only need to be plumbed.

Before the opera begins, Don Pasquale, the old bachelor, has urged his nephew Ernesto to marry a suitably rich young lady. Ernesto, penniless and in love with a poor but attractive widow, has refused, and the disagreement between the two men has festered until the elder has decided to marry himself in order to discipline his nephew. He has consulted the family doctor who, as a friend to both uncle and nephew, has tried to dissuade him. But failing, the Doctor has decided it best to humor the old man and, in order to keep control of the situation, has agreed to find a suitable bride. In the first scene Don Pasquale is waiting for the Doctor to return and report on his search.

## OVERTURE (6 min.)

It is made up of melodies from the opera, mainly Ernesto's serenade from Act III and Norina's aria from Act I Scene 2, strung together without much reason except contrast and charm. It appears frequently on concert programs.

# ACT I (31 min.)

---

## SCENE 1 (A room in Don Pasquale's house—16 min.)

*Don Pasquale:* He awaits Dr. Malatesta, chortling over his plan to discipline his nephew. In the slang of the time he repeats that he will be a "Don Somaro" (Don Donkey) if he doesn't show the young man a thing or two.

*Don Pasquale and Dr. Malatesta:* Dr. Malatesta reports he has found
**aria**    just the girl for Don Pasquale. He describes her virtues in an aria, "Bella siccome un angelo" (beautiful like an angel). Don Pasquale is beside himself; "il nome" (the family name)? Malatesta explains "È mia sorella" (she is my sister). Don Pasquale is elated, "O gioja" (joy), and wants to meet her at once. That evening, "stasera," is too late. He begs Malatesta to arrange it sooner for pity's sake, "per carità dottore," and pushes him out the door.

**aria**    *Don Pasquale:* He can feel the years fall off him; he is twenty again. Already he can see a sweet wife, lovely children and himself in the center. Ernesto will learn the results of stubbornness.

*Don Pasquale and Ernesto:* Don Pasquale rehearses with his nephew the core of their disagreement. Two months earlier he'd offered the young man a wife, suitable and rich. "È vero" (it is true), Ernesto admits. He'd offered him a comfortable income; "è vero." He'd threatened to disinherit him if he refused to marry; "è vero." Now he offers the same lady again; "non posso" (I cannot), Ernesto insists, for he loves Norina. Then out of the house, Don Pasquale orders, for he announces triumphantly that he himself will marry: "Io prendo moglie" (I am taking a wife).

Ernesto at first cannot believe it and then, to the old man's fury,
**aria**    laughs. But it is true, and Ernesto sighs in a short aria over his hopes for himself and Norina. Now he must leave Rome and her, for he cannot ask her to share his life. Meanwhile, Don Pasquale observes that Ernesto seems to be taking it hard, as well he'd better.

After a short pause Ernesto suggests that perhaps Don Pasquale should consult Dr. Malatesta. His uncle announces that he already has done so and that the girl in question is Dr. Malatesta's sister, "sua sorella." This to Ernesto is the treachery of a friend, and he despairs altogether. Don Pasquale, watching him, exults that Ernesto is getting what he deserves.

SCENE 2 (A room in Norina's house—15 min.)

*Norina:* She has a novel and reads aloud a passage in which a maiden
**aria**     decimates a knight with a languishing glance. Closing the
book with a laugh, she allows as how she knows just as much about
the tricks to catch men's hearts. She characterizes herself as gay, witty,
a little vain, but goodhearted.

Her maid delivers a letter from Ernesto, and Norina sighs as she
reads it.

*Dr. Malatesta and Norina:* He bursts in, bringing good news, he announces. But she is dejected and shows him the letter which he reads
aloud. Ernesto tells her all is over; the scoundrel Malatesta has arranged a marriage for his uncle and, as he is too poor to marry her, he
plans to leave Rome at once.

Malatesta quickly explains his plan to Norina: she will impersonate
his young sister in the convent and, as Don Pasquale has never seen
either, she need only act the part to fool him. His cousin will be the
notary. After the marriage she must contrive to drive the old man mad
till he comes to his senses and they can persuade him to accept Ernesto's
**duet**     choice. Norina agrees at once and suggests that, since con-
vent-bred, she act downcast. "No, no," the Doctor advises. In tears?
Also "no." The trick he suggests is "la semplicetta" (the simple type)
with head on one side and pursed lips. She practices and he approves,
"brava." In a duet they prophesy how it will go with Don Pasquale.

Vocabulary, Act I

| | | |
|---|---|---|
| Don Somaro | don so.MAH.roh | Don Donkey |
| bella siccome un angelo | bell.ah see.KO.may oon ahn.jay.lo | like a beautiful angel |
| il nome | eel NO.may | the family name |
| è mia sorella | eh me.ah so.RELL.ah | she is my sister |
| o gioja | oh je.OY.ah | oh joy |
| stasera | stah.SAIR.ah | this evening |
| per carità dottore | pair kah.ree.TAH doh.TOR.ay | for charity's sake, doctor |
| è vero | eh VAIR.oh | it is true |
| non posso | non poss.so | I cannot |
| io prendo mogli | yo pren.doe MOE.l'yay | I am taking a wife |
| sua sorella | sue.ah so.RELL.ah | his sister |
| la semplicetta | lah sem.plee.che.tah | the simple type |
| brava | BRAH.vah | good |

## ACT II (33 min.)

A room in Don Pasquale's house. There is a short prelude (2 min.) with a horn solo that continues into the following recitative and aria. *Ernesto:* He is very dejected. To be betrayed by his friend Malatesta **aria** is bad, but worse is to be able no longer even to hope for Norina. He will go far away and be true to her forever, and if later she finds another love and marries, he will be happy for her. He sees his uncle coming and leaves.

*Dòn Pasquale:* He tells a servant that after Dr. Malatesta and his sister enter, no one else is to be admitted. Then, admiring himself, he remarks that for one nearly seventy he is a fine figure of a man, although he does not plan to advertise his age to his wife.

*Don Pasquale, Dr. Malatesta and Norina:* The Doctor enters with his "sister from the convent," who is heavily veiled and nearly fainting **aria** from the sudden exposure to the world. Don Pasquale greatly admires her "semplicità" and announces he will marry her if her beauty corresponds. She demonstrates her convent upbringing by trying to flee when she discovers, even through the thick veils, that besides her brother there is another man in the room, "un uomo."

Don Pasquale requests the veil be lifted, but Dr. Malatesta suggests that for the moment he merely talk to the shy girl. So Don Pasquale starts, "andiam, coraggio" (let's go, courage), but at once breaks down in confusion. Norina, replying to his questions, assures him that she likes to be alone, has never even heard of a theater, and likes nothing better than a little embroidery or supervising the kitchen. Don Pasquale is enchanted; he pleads for the veil, "velo," to be removed. When it is, he is smitten: "Misericordia." A bombshell, "una bomba," has exploded in his heart; he is dead with love, "son morto." The Doctor now urges them both to have courage, "coraggio," and sends for the notary, his cousin Charles in disguise. "Ecco il notaro."

Malatesta dictates the marriage agreement, stressing the "etcetera," and Don Pasquale, quite carried away, adds that his wife will be complete mistress of the house. They both sign, but the document lacks the signature of a second witness.

At that moment Ernesto bursts in, furious at being barred from the room. He does not know of the deception and sees Norina marry- **quartet** ing his uncle. Naturally he assumes her affections changed with the news that he was disinherited. Malatesta only just succeeds in persuading Ernesto to have faith, go along with them, and sign as the second witness.

The contract signed, Don Pasquale approaches to embrace his bride, "carina" (dearest). Gently she reminds him he should ask permission first. Gallantly he does, and she refuses, "No." Ernesto bursts out laughing, and Don Pasquale orders him out of the house. But Norina, calling Don Pasquale's manners boorish, asks Ernesto to remain, "restate." Don Pasquale appeals to Malatesta, who pretends to be equally surprised and confused. Norina explains that as her husband is heavy and gross, she will need Ernesto as a squire when she goes out. Don Pasquale forbids it. But she replies that it is no longer what he allows but what she wishes that matters, "voglio" (I wish).

**quartet**    When Don Pasquale remonstrates, she threatens to slap him. Incredulously, he wonders whether he is awake or dreaming. The others, watching him, crush their pity and proceed.

Norina rings the bell for the servants and is horrified to discover there are only three, "tre in tutto." She at once doubles their salaries; gives orders for hiring two dozen more; orders two carriages, a light and a heavy, with ten horses of English stock; and remarks that the furniture will have to go in the morning.

Don Pasquale in a concentrated rage inquires if she has finished. "No," and she orders dinner at 4 P.M. for fifty. Who pays? he asks. "Voi" (you), she simpers, and then calls him a peasant, "un villano."

**aria**    Overcome with rage, suffocating with anger, Don Pasquale explodes into a swift "buffo" aria on how he is betrayed. Norina explains the plan to Ernesto, who admits for a moment he doubted her; and the Doctor, while urging the lovers not to betray the scheme, urges the old man to lie down for a bit.

## Vocabulary, Act II

| | | |
|---|---|---|
| semplicità | sem.plee.che.TAH | simplicity |
| un uomo | oon woh.moe | a man |
| andiam, coraggio | an.d'yahm ko.RAHD.jo | let's go, courage |
| velo | vay.low | the veil |
| misericordia | me.zair.ee.KOR.d'yah | good God! |
| una bomba | oona bohm.bah | a bombshell |
| son morto | sohn more.toe | I am dead |
| ecco il notaro | ek.koe eel no.TAHR.oh | here is the notary |
| etcetera | et.chet.air.ah | etc. |

| carina | kah.REE.nah | dearest |
| restate | reh.STAH.tay | remain |
| voglio | vole.yo | I wish |
| tre in tutto | tray een toot.toe | three in all |
| voi | voy | you |
| un villano | oon vill.LAH.no | a peasant |

## ACT III (37 min.)

### SCENE 1 (26 min.)

The same room in Don Pasquale's house but now, on the first day of the marriage, transformed by articles of feminine apparel scattered about—hats, shawls, laces and dresses. Don Pasquale is at the desk staring at the bills. A hairdresser comes out of Norina's apartment; a maid calls directions to the servants; etc.

*The Servants and Don Pasquale:* They call back and forth, "presto, presto" (hurry), until he thinks he will go mad. He cannot believe that she really intends to dishonor him by going out alone on the first day of marriage, and he resolves once again to speak to her.

*Don Pasquale and Norina:* He begins politely: "Signorina . . . dove va" (where are you going)? She replies, "al teatro" (to the theater). He suggests that her husband, "il marito," might forbid such an expedition. She retorts that her husband may speak, but no one will listen. In a rage he orders her back to her room. With a mocking air, she suggests he go to bed and sleep, "dorma." He blocks the door, epithets fly, and she slaps him.

**duet**     He is crushed: "È finita, Don Pasquale" (it is finished). There is no more need to rack his brains; the only thing left is to hang or drown himself. It was a hard lesson; Norina is moved but tries not to show it. Finally she announces gaily that she is off. He hopes that she will never return. She urges him to go to bed and calls him "grandpa," while he insists on "divorzio" (divorce). As she goes out, she drops a note where he will see it.

He picks it up and reads directions in an unknown hand for an assignation in the garden that night; the lover will announce himself by a serenade. Immediately Don Pasquale sends a servant off for Dr. Malatesta, and then goes out himself.

**chorus**     *The Servants:* The new ones gather to discuss the household. They rehearse the domestic strife, beginning with the scene after dinner, and conclude that, although there is considerable work involved, they will do well: it is a big house and the owners spend on a large scale. They can't figure out the nephew's role. "Zitti" (sh), they advise each other as the door opens.

*Dr. Malatesta and Ernesto:* The Doctor tells Ernesto to sing a serenade and to be sure to be able to escape undetected. Ernesto goes off, and the Doctor grieves at having to cause his old friend so much pain.

*Dr. Malatesta and Don Pasquale:* Don Pasquale describes himself as a walking dead man, "un morto." He describes the scene, how he tried to prevent her going to the theater, and how she cuffed him. He shows the letter to Malatesta, and the two sit down to work out a plan. Don Pasquale suggests that with the servants they surround his wife and her lover and then march them off to the Mayor's office. But Malatesta objects that the wife is his sister and the disgrace would be too public. He suggests that the wife, merely threatened with exposure, may promise to break off the affair. But this is not enough for Don Pasquale, who insists that his wife must leave the house; nothing less will do. The Doctor agrees, provided that they hide first in the bushes and hear (thus allowing a gorgeous duet) if there really is something going on. If there is, he promises to arrange to get her out of the house provided he is given a "carte blanche" on how to do it. Don Pasquale agrees and begins to chortle over his revenge as the Doctor watches him with amusement.

## SCENE 2 (11 min.)

The garden of the house, which is to the left. A small summerhouse is on the right.

*Ernesto and some Hired Musicians:* He sings the serenade with a soft
**serenade**    chorus from outside the garden gate. It is a typical Italian serenade, "come è gentil" (how soft . . . the night air of April, but cruel Nina stays within, etc.). As he ends, Norina slips out of the summerhouse and unlocks the gate.

*Ernesto and Norina:* Like the serenade their duet is typical in all ex-
**duet**    cept its beauty: "Tornami a dir che m'ami" (turn to me to say that you love me). At its end they spy Don Pasquale and Dr. Malatesta creeping through the shrubs towards the gate to cut off the lover's retreat. Ernesto, wrapping a black cloak around himself, disappears into the house.

*Don Pasquale, Dr. Malatesta and Norina:* Don Pasquale jumps out waving a lantern and demanding the lover's name. Norina denies that anyone was there; she merely was taking the air. He orders her out of the house, and she again refuses to go. Dr. Malatesta then comes forward and tells "his sister" that she must prepare for a blow. Ernesto is going to marry her enemy, Norina, who will come to live in the house with them. She will not stay under the same roof with that woman, the real Norina cries, although she cagily announces that she will not be put off by a trick. The Doctor calls Ernesto from the house 'and urges Don Pasquale to repeat that he will bless his nephew's marriage to Norina and settle an income on them. This Don Pasquale does. All is revealed. The lovers beg his pardon, while the Doctor explains it was all for Don Pasquale's own good. The opera ends with a quartet moralizing that the old should not marry, for they gain only noise and strife.

### Vocabulary, Act III

| | | |
|---|---|---|
| presto | press.toe | hurry |
| dove va | doe.vay vah | where do you go |
| al teatro | al tay.AH.troe | to the theater |
| il marito | eel mah.REE.toe | the husband |
| dorma | door.mah | sleep |
| è finita, Don Pasquale | eh fin.EE.tah | it is finished |
| divorzio | dee.VORTS.yo | divorce |
| zitti | tsee.tee | sh! |
| un morto | oon MORE.toe | a dead man |
| come è gentil | ko.may jen.TEE'l | how it is soft |
| tornami a dir che m'ami | torn.ah.myah deer kay mah.me | turn to me to say that you love me |

# DER FLIEGENDE HOLLAENDER

## (The Flying Dutchman)

Romantic opera in three acts. First performed at Dresden on January 2, 1843. Music and libretto by R. Wagner.

### PRINCIPAL CHARACTERS

| | |
|---|---|
| Daland, a Norwegian sea-captain | bass |
| The Helmsman in Daland's crew | tenor |
| The Dutchman, Vanderdecken | baritone |
| Mary, Senta's nurse | mezzo-soprano |
| Senta, Daland's daughter | soprano |
| Erik, a hunter | tenor |

The action takes place on the Norwegian coast sometime during the eighteenth century.

The opera is the shortest and for most operagoers the most readily enjoyable of Wagner's operas. It tells its legendary story without philosophic pretensions, and the motives or themes, so confusing for the casual operagoer in *The Ring*, are only two of obvious importance and easily grasped. Finally, the sea music is extraordinarily exciting and evocative, so that even nautical types, while reserving their right to criticize the ship's rigging, confess a sneaking affection for the opera. The title, *Der Fliegende Hollaender*, refers to both the skipper and his ship.

WAGNER

It is impossible to identify one verson of the legend as primal. Evidently at the beginning of the nineteenth century, several were current. Ernest Newman in *The Wagner Operas* outlines four.

One involved almost no supernatural elements. A Dutchman outward-bound swore to round the Cape of Good Hope if it took forever, and in his case it seemed to be going to. He would hail passing ships, forcing them to share his bad weather, and give them letters to deliver in Holland. But the addressees, including the man's wife, had all long since died. The story's point was the man's affection, after all the years, for his wife.

Another version, a novel called *The Phantom Ship* by Captain Marryat, involved a Dutchman who swore to round the Cape if it took till Judgment Day. He swore by a piece of the Holy Cross owned by his wife, and the celestial powers took offense. As his only release was to view the relic, his wife sent their son out to sea with it. When the unfortunate, dutiful young man finally met up with his father, the ship supporting them both immediately sank beneath the waves.

Still another version, recounted by Heine in his *Memoirs of Herr von Schnabelwopski,* had the Dutchman in the usual navigational difficulties swear by all the devils, at which the infernal powers took offense. Release this time could be had only through the love of a woman faithful unto death, whom he finally found in Katharina, daughter of a Scottish skipper.

In these three versions the Dutchman's name was Vanderdecken, and he was clearly from the North Sea area. Just why operatic tradition should have him dress in a Spanish costume is uncertain. The score states only that he has a pale face, dark beard, and wears a black cloak. Perhaps the Spanish influence comes from the fourth version, which has a Mediterranean background.

Here an Algerian captain killed a dervish who was foolish enough to reprove him for his piratical ways. In revenge the dervish swore that neither the captain nor his crew should live or die until their heads were buried in the earth. At once the crew massacred each other, and thereafter they were dead by day and live by night, unable ever to make port and signifying death to any other ship that sighted them. In this story the decks were red with blood, the captain nailed to the mast, and all the details extremely gory and colorful. This may be the source of Wagner's blood-red sails and black masts.

Wagner intended the opera to be given in one unbroken act, and it sometimes is. Only a few opening and closing bars need be cut for the acts to join directly with short orchestral interludes. He also revised the orchestration and closing bars of the overture and Act III. The orchestration he merely made less noisy, and this second version is invariably used. The original overture and close of Act III ended with the Dutchman's theme booming out fortissimo. In the revision Wagner closed in both places with Senta's music, redeeming the Dutchman from his curse. Most persons feel this to be the more satisfactory of the two, but both versions are still given. The difference in time is only a minute.

## OVERTURE (11 min.)

Amid a raging gale the Dutchman's theme sounds, a simple horn call on the horns and bassoons that is repeated almost at once by the trombones and tuba. Then after the music calms, there are three soft beats on the kettledrum followed by Senta's theme on the woodwinds and horns, peaceful and redeeming. Wagner expands and contrasts these, adding other sea music from the opera, and ends either with the Dutchman or Senta, depending on the version being performed.

## ACT I (32 min.)

A cove in the Norwegian coast surrounded by steep, rocky cliffs. Daland's ship has dropped anchor, and the crew is furling the sails. Daland has come ashore to reconnoiter.

**chorus**     *Sailors:* They have a short chorus in which the French horns carry their calls off in a windy echo.

*Daland:* He recognizes the cove; the storm has driven them seven miles off course. It is tantalizing after a long voyage to be blown past his house, "mein Haus," and child, "Senta, mein Kind." Who trusts the wind trusts Satan's mercy, "Satans Erbarmen." He tells the helmsman, "Steuermann," to stand watch while he goes below to sleep.

*Helmsman:* He sings to his girl friend, "mein Maedel," and of the **aria**     Southwind, "Suedwind," that will take him to her. But exhausted by the storm, he soon falls asleep.

*The Dutchman:* His ship pulls in and drops anchor beside Daland's. While the ghostly crew silently furls the sails, he comes ashore. He then has a long monologue introduced by a few bars of recitative and thereafter divided into three parts. In the recitative he explains that another seven years have passed and he can again set foot on land; the **monologue**     sea can have a rest from him but never he from his search. In the first part of the aria he describes how he has tried to kill himself in reckless sailing and begging the pirate to strike, but he never can find a grave or death: "Nirgends ein Grab! Niemals der Tod!" He closes with "Dies der Verdammnis Schreckgebot" (this is the fate for the accursed). In the second part he asks the kind angel, "Engel," who won him the chance every seven years at redemption if that chance was to be no more than a mockery. This part is intense but quiet. Lastly, he despairs. The only hope, "Hoffnung," is for the Day of Judgment to come. In the destruction of all he too will pass into peace.

From within the ship comes a sigh from the ghostly crew.

*Daland and the Dutchman:* Daland coming on deck finds the helmsman asleep, wakes him and together they call over to the ghost ship. There is no answer. Then Daland sees the Dutchman ashore and joins him. When asked, the Dutchman explains vaguely that he has been sailing many years and has no home. (This is the dullest part of the act, as it repeats the monologue; but, because the Dutchman now speaks only half-truths, it is all at a much lower level of intensity.) The Dutchman offers Daland a chest of precious stones in return for a night's shelter. Daland marvels at the value of the chest, and the Dutchman offers him the entire cargo. What good is treasure, he laments, when he has no wife or child? He inquires directly: "Hast du eine Tochter" (have you a daughter)? And when Daland admits he does, the Dutchman breaks out "Sie sei mein Weib" (let her be my wife).

The two men sing a duet in which Daland begins to realize that he may be able to make something out of his daughter, and the Dutchman offers him all his treasure, "meine Schaetze dahin" (my treasure
**duet**     within). Then, as the music gets rather bouncy, Daland thanks the storm for driving him ashore, and the Dutchman gives way again to hope, "Hoffnung."
*Sailors:* The helmsman calls that the wind has shifted to the south, "Suedwind," and the two captains part, the Dutchman agreeing to
**chorus**     follow Daland up the coast. The sailors up-anchor and away with a shanty.

### Vocabulary, Act I

| | | |
|---|---|---|
| mein Haus | mine house | my house |
| Senta, mein Kind | mine kint | my child |
| Satans Erbarmen | sah.tahns air.barm.en | Satan's mercy |
| Steuermann | SHTOY.er.mahn | helmsman |
| mein Maedel | mine MAY.dell | my maiden |
| Suedwind | sood.veend | southwind |
| nirgends ein Grab | nearg.ens eye'n grahb | nowhere a grave |
| niemals der Tod | nee.mahls dair toht | never death |
| dies der Verdammnis Schreckgebot | deece dair fair.DAHM. nis schreck.ge.boat | this is the fate for the accursed |
| Engel | ENG.ell | angel |
| Hoffnung | hoff.noong | hope |
| Hast du eine Tochter | hast do eye.nuh tawk.ter | have you a daughter |
| Sie sei mein Weib | zee z'eye mine v'eye.b | let her be my wife |
| meine Schaetze dahin | mine shahts dah.hin | my treasure within |

## ACT II (62 min.)

A large room in Daland's house; on the wall at the back is a portrait of the Dutchman, pale with a dark beard and in a black suit. Mary and the village girls are spinning; Senta gazes at the portrait. *Village Girls:* They sing of their lovers out at sea who would be home **spinning song** if only the wind went as fast as the spinning wheel. The second verse is more calculating: the better they spin, the more gold their lovers will give them.

Mary nags at Senta to spin with them, but the girls remark that Senta has no need; her lover is a hunter who brings home game not gold. Mary continues to pester Senta, who bursts out with, "Der arme Mann" (the wretched man). The girls all giggle that Senta is in love with the Dutchman, "sie ist verliebt," and prophesy trouble with Erik. Senta warns them not to laugh, but they spin and sing louder so as not to hear her. Finally Senta suggests that Mary sing the ballad of the Dutchman and, when Mary refuses, she begins it herself.

*Senta:* The ballad falls into three verses with a refrain after each and a coda at the end:

*Verse 1:* She describes the ship with blood-red sails and black masts, its sleepless captain, and the wind whistling endlessly.

*Refrain:* He will be released only if he can find a girl who will love **the ballad** him even unto death. (This is the music associated with Senta and redemption throughout the opera.)

*Verse 2:* She recounts his oath while rounding the cape, how Satan heard it and condemned him to sail on forever.

*Refrain:* But an angel showed him how he could be freed. The girls, much moved, joined Senta on the refrain.

*Verse 3:* Every seven years he can look for a wife who will be true, but never yet has found one.

*Refrain:* Senta remains silent while the girls softly wonder where such a wife may be found.

*Coda:* In a burst of ecstasy Senta insists it is she. May the angel guide him to her.

**chorus** Mary, the girls and Erik, who has just entered, are terrified: Senta has gone mad. Erik distracts them by announcing that Daland's ship is in, and Mary and the girls go off in an excited chorus. *Erik and Senta:* He detains her and asks if she will tell her father that she loves him. Daland, Erik feels, is interested only in money and will not look with favor on a poor hunter. Senta, still in a daze, says she must go to the ship. Erik insists his heart will break with anguish, "dieses Herz im Jammer bricht," if she doesn't give up her infatuation with the portrait of the Dutchman. He accuses her of singing the song again, "und die Ballade." She defends herself by claiming to be only a child, "ich bin ein Kind," not knowing what she sings. But she draws Erik to the portrait and asks if he can imagine the pain and grief the Dutchman must feel and how the thought of it stabs her heart.

Erik, horrified, warns her (to eleven pounding chords) that Satan has snared her. He tells her of his vision. He saw Daland and a stranger (the orchestra gives the Dutchman's theme) walking up from the village. As Senta urges him on, Erik slowly describes the pale face, dark **Erik's vision** beard and black clothes of the Dutchman. Then he points to the portrait. Eagerly Senta asks if she appeared in the vision. Erik saw her come out, greet her father, kiss the stranger and then put to sea with him. Senta, in the wildest excitement, cries that her fate is the Dutchman's; she will wait for him. Erik rushes out in despair while Senta, gazing at the portrait, asks that Heaven will soon lead the Dutchman to some true woman. At that moment Daland and the Dutchman enter.

*Senta, the Dutchman and Daland:* Senta gasps, and for the balance of the act, in one of Wagner's long looks, the two stare at each **aria** other. Daland, at first nonplused by their intensity, introduces them in a bluff, jocular aria, telling what he knows of the Dutchman and praising her as a good girl. He tries to interest her in the jewelry the Dutchman has offered for lodging and states that she can have more if she will marry him: "ist morgen er dein Mann" (tomorrow he is your husband). Then he leaves them alone.

*Senta and the Dutchman:* The orchestra sounds first his theme on the horns and then hers on the softer woodwinds, suggesting his redemption. Their duet divides roughly into four moods:

A: Each soliloquizes about the other. The Dutchman marvels that the girl of his longing should now be before him. He wonders if he can feel love and decides it is rather a desire for salvation. He hopes that through such an angel as this girl he can find peace: "Engel mir zu Teil" (angel to me a share [of peace]). She wonders if she is awake or dreaming. The Dutchman so tortured is now before her, and she can release him. (This is the longest of the four parts.)

B: He addresses her directly, asking if she will abide by her father's choice. Without hesitation she agrees, and he rejoices, "du bist ein Engel" (you are an angel).

C: To the familiar sea music he asks if she understands what her fate will be if she joins hims; can she be true? In a line of pure German romanticism, often parodied, she insists: "Wohl kenn' ich Weibes heil'ge Pflichten" (well do I know woman's holy duties). She will be "true to death": "Die Treue bis zum Tod."

D: The last section is climactic: he exults at the end of Satan's hold over him, and she marvels at the strange power she feels within herself, while asking Heaven to help her be true.

*Daland, Senta and the Dutchman:* Daland enters to urge them to come
**trio**    to the party celebrating the ship's safe return. He asks Senta if she will have the Dutchman, and she replies: "Hier meine Hand! Und ohne Reu' " (here is my hand, and without regret). Daland is pleased; the Dutchman rejoices; and Senta promises again to be true to death.

Vocabulary, Act II

| | | |
|---|---|---|
| Der arme Mann | dair ahr.muh mahn | the wretched man |
| sie ist verliebt | zee ist fair.leebt | she is in love |
| dieses Herz | dee.ses hairts | this heart |
| im Jammer bricht | im yahm.err brickt | in anguish bursts |
| und die Ballade | oont dee bah.LAH.duh | and the ballad |
| ich bin eine Kind | ish * been eye'n kint | I am a child |
| ist morgen er dein Mann | ist more.gen air dine mahn | tomorrow he is your man |
| Engel mir zu Teil | eng.ell meer zoo tile | an angel to me peace |
| dubist ein Engel | do bist eye'n eng.ell | you are an angel |
| wohl kenn' ich Weibes heil'ge Pflichten | vole ken ish * vhy.bes hile.ge flick.ten | well know I woman's holy duties |
| hier meine Hand | here mine hahnt | here is my hand |
| und ohne Reu' | oont own.nuh roy | and without regret |

* Ish or ik depending on South or North German accent of singer.

## ACT III (28 min.)

A bay with rocky shore. To the back, the ships of Daland and the Dutchman; to the front, Daland's house. It is a clear night. Daland's crew is celebrating and the ship is lighted. The Dutchman's is dark and gloomy.

*Sailors and the Girls:* The sailors sing a chorus during which the girls
**chorus**    arrive with food and drink for the celebration. They call
to the Dutchman's crew to come and join them, but neither they nor
the sailors can raise an answer. The sailors begin to joke that it must
be The Flying Dutchman and the crew all dead. Hailing the ship again
they ask if there is any mail to be delivered to persons long since dead.
Still there is no reply, and the girls, now thoroughly scared, withdraw.
The sailors, after another round of drinks, try again to rouse the
Dutchman's crew.

This time the sea around the strange vessel begins to froth. A bluish
flame flares on board, and the ghostly crew sings of its captain's curse
and cynically inquires if he has found a true wife. The Norwegians
are terrified and ask, "ist es Spuk" (is it a ghost)? They try to en-
courage themselves by singing louder, but the Dutchman's crew sings
even louder and, as the Norwegians, crossing themselves, hurry below
decks, ends with a burst of laughter.

*Erik and Senta:* Senta runs out of the house followed by Erik. He asks
her how she could go back on her word to him and how she could give
her hand to a man she has only just met. She has no answer except
**aria**    "ich muss" (I must); she is obeying a higher duty. He reminds her in an aria that she has no higher duty than her vow to be
true to him.

*The Dutchman, Senta and Erik:* The Dutchman overhears Erik's account of Senta's vow and assumes she has already deserted him. In
despair he cries out, "Verloren" (abandoned). Senta tries to stop him,
but he signals his crew to up-sail and calls farewell, "leb'wohl," to her.
**trio**    In a trio she urges him to stay, for she is true; he states he will
not hold her to her promise, which he sees now was only a jest; Erik
urges Senta to turn to him and break the spell that Satan has cast over
her.

The Dutchman tells her the fate she has escaped. If she had sworn
before God and deserted him, she would be damned forever. But as
she only swore to him, he will release her from her vow. She cries that
she knew her fate; she recognized him. He refuses to believe that she
could and, pointing to the red sails, announces that he is the "fliegende
Hollaender." His ship pulls out. Senta breaks away from Erik and the
others who have gathered around her and rushes to the edge of the
cliff. Calling out that she is true even unto death, she throws herself
off. At once his ship sinks in a whirlpool and, if the revised ending is

being used, her form and his, in an embrace, soar Heavenward from the sea. (This is impossible to stage well and awaits the day when opera houses will discover how to integrate movies with the stage action, for this is a true, cinematic, glorious, technicolor finish.)

### Vocabulary, Act III

| | | |
|---|---|---|
| ist es Spuk | ist es shpook | it is a ghost |
| ich muss | ish moose | I must |
| verloren | fair.LORE.en | abandoned |
| leb'wohl | layb.vohl | farewell |
| fliegende Hollaender | flee.gen.duh holl.an.der | flying Dutchman |

# TANNHAEUSER

Opera in three acts. First performed at Dresden on October 19, 1845; a revised version was given at Paris on March 13, 1861. Music and libretto by R. Wagner.

### PRINCIPAL CHARACTERS

| | | |
|---|---|---|
| Venus | soprano | |
| Tannhaeuser, known at the Wartburg as Heinrich | tenor | tan.hoy.zer |
| A shepherd | soprano | |
| The Landgrave of Thuringia | bass | |
| Wolfram von Eschenbach, a knight | baritone | |
| Elisabeth, the Landgrave's niece | soprano | eh.LEE.zah.bet |

The action takes place early in the thirteenth century in Thuringia. Venusberg is inside a mountain called Hoerselberg, which looks across a valley to another mountain on which is the Landgrave's castle, the Wartburg.

The full title of the opera is *Tannhaeuser and the Contest of Song at the Wartburg,* an unwieldy title but honestly representing the two legends Wagner combined in his opera. The first, a mixture of several stories, is based on an historical Tannhaeuser (c. 1200–70) who came from Salzburg. He was an impoverished knight more interested in poetry than business, and several poems survive which, according to Ernest Newman, give the impression of one who lived high and handsome. The poet acknowledged he had a reputation for "fair women, good wine, dainty meats, and baths twice a week." (Pepys records that Mrs. Pepys took one bath in nine years.) At the end of his life Tannhaeuser was bankrupt, but during it he had been on a Crusade in 1228 and had traveled in Italy and Sicily.

Newman conjectures that Tannhaeuser became associated with Venus only sometime later as the middle class displaced the aristocracy. The middle class with its different, stuffier standards used the poet, known for his sensuality and poverty, as an example of one who left virtue for Venus. And by the fifteenth and sixteenth centuries, when the Tannhaeuser legends took final shape, they all associate him with Venus and send him on a pilgrimage to Rome where the Pope refuses absolution. There are several endings, however, depending on the temperament of the later poets. Some send the Pope, Urban IV (1261–64) to Hell for refusing absolution, and other have the miracle of the staff take place and Tannhaeuser redeemed.

The second legend, *The Contest of Song at the Wartburg,* is also based on historical figures. There was a Landgrave, Hermann, famous as a patron of the arts, who ruled Thuringia from 1190 to 1217. He collected at his court a number of famous poets, among whom were Wolfram von Eschenbach, an historical figure, and Heinrich von Ofterdingen, possibly an historical figure. Wolfram and Heinrich compete for an attractive widow, Matilda. Heinrich employs the aid of a magician, Klingsor, and for a while is victorious, turning Matilda into "an uncanny something" (words failed the poet) "that was neither woman nor man." Eventually Wolfram triumphs, restores Matilda to her former recognizable state and forces Heinrich to flee. In all of this there is nothing about Venus, Tannhaeuser or the Pope, and it is not hard to see how Wagner merged the two legends.

It is usual to speak of two versions of the opera, the Dresden and the Paris. The terminology is unfortunately inexact, and it would be better to speak of an earlier and later version, including in each a number of changes that Wagner made in years immediately following the premières in each city. The advantage of the earlier version is a consistent musical style and the overture in the form in which most persons expect it. The advantage of the later version is a shortened overture with a musically more exciting Venusberg scene and some cuts made in the song contest in Act II. For the record: after the first few performances in Dresden, Wagner changed the end of Act III to bring Elisabeth's bier on stage and cut the orchestral introduction to Act III almost in half; at the Paris première the earlier overture in its entirety was played and followed by the new Venusberg music; after Paris, Wagner dovetailed the overture and new Venusberg music together. In concerts this last often appears, with the call of the sirens omitted, as the "Tannhaeuser Overture and Venusberg Music." The earlier uncut version of the overture is called "The Tannhaeuser Overture." And, if the new Venusberg music is played alone, it is called simply "The Venusberg Music." The earlier version is recounted below with the later changes indicated.

## OVERTURE (15 min.)

It opens with the Pilgrims' Chorus, first as if from a distance, then closer and finally passing away. It is followed by the Venusberg music, a swirl of rising sound which culminates in Tannhaeuser's song to Venus, a foursquare melody. Again the Venusberg music swirls around, ending another stanza of Tannhaeuser's song a semitone higher. (At this point the later version goes directly into the expanded Venusberg scene.) Then gradually the tension eases as the Pilgrims' Chorus returns and dominates the Venusberg music, suggesting the triumph of piety over Venus and the flesh.

## ACT I (44 min.; the later version, 62 min.)
----
### SCENE 1 (The Venusberg—5 min.)

Inside the mountain. A wide cave bends back to the right and ends in a lake in which Naiads are bathing. To the front Venus, on a couch, with Tannhaeuser kneeling beside her. On either side are nymphs and sirens resting and dancing. A rosy light fills the cave.

*Sirens and Nymphs:* They do a wild, orgiastic dance. From the end of the cave a group of sirens call: come to this land where love ends **ballet** longing. The dance grows even wilder, then lessens and finally stops as a mist gradually sinks to the floor of the cave, concealing all but Venus and Tannhaeuser. From far in the distance the sirens repeat their call: come to this land. (The later version, which follows the overture without a break, is expanded into a more complicated ballet with three Graces and a cloud picture of the Rape of Europa; the music is infinitely more exciting.)

## SCENE 2 (19 min.)

*Tannhaeuser and Venus:* He starts, as if waking from a dream, and she asks his thoughts. He dreamt that he heard the sound of bells and asks how long he's been away from the earth's surface. She wonders that he can already be tired of love and calling him "mein Saenger" (my **song** singer) urges him to sing of love, "die Liebe." He does in three verses, each starting off in praise of Venus and love but ending with a plea to be released: "O Koenigin! Goettin las mich zieh'n" (O Queen! Goddess, let me fly). Between each, Venus tries to persuade him to remain, first by reason, then by anger and seduction (solo violin accompaniment), and after the last verse in a fury she orders him to go. She warns him that he will be scorned by the world and will suffer torments remembering her. He insists repentance will heal his heart. She insists Heaven holds no deliverance, "Heil," for him. "Mein Heil," he exclaims, is in the Virgin Mary. With a cry, Venus vanishes and the scene instantly changes around Tannhaeuser.

## SCENE 3 (9 min.)

He is standing in a valley. Behind, on a hill to the right, is the Wartburg; to the left is Hoerselberg. To the front is a small shrine to the Virgin. It is daytime, and sheep bells can be heard. A shepherd on a rock watches his herd while playing his pipe.
*The Shepherd:* His pipe is played by an English horn. He sings about the coming of May. (Both he and the Pilgrims who interrupt him sing a cappella [*See* Glossary], and the contrast of sound with the lush orchestration of the Venusberg scene is striking and deliberate.)
*The Pilgrims:* They cross the stage slowly, singing of God's mercy and their search for grace. The Shepherd wishes them Godspeed to Rome, and Tannhaeuser sinks to his knees murmuring of the greatness of God's mercy. In his prayer he repeats the Pilgrims' music as he swears never to cease searching for divine pardon. The last of the Pilgrims slowly disappears as a horn call in the distance warns of a hunting party's approach.

## SCENE 4 (11 min.)

*The Landgrave, Wolfram, Tannhaeuser et al:* To a fanfare on twelve French horns the Landgrave and his knights appear. They are astonished to find what they think is a lone pilgrim, but they quickly recognize him and greet him as Heinrich. At first the knights are uncertain whether to greet him as a friend or foe. Wolfram, however, at once hails him as a friend and the others soon do likewise. When the Landgrave asks where he has been, Tannhaeuser answers vaguely and insists that he must depart. They all protest he must never leave again, "O bleib" (oh stay). A septet develops in which Tannhaeuser insists he must go while the others urge him to stay. Finally Wolfram exclaims, "Bleib bei Elisabeth" (stay near Elisabeth). Tannhaeuser repeats the name ecstatically. Wolfram then asks the Landgrave's permission to tell Tannhaeuser of the prize he won.

**aria** *Wolfram:* He describes how Tannhaeuser's song won the heart of Elisabeth and, when he disappeared, she lost all joy and interest. He urges Tannhaeuser to stay for her.

*The Landgrave, Wolfram, Tanhaeuser et al:* They all urge him and Tannhaeuser joins them, singing of his joy in spring and Elisabeth. The entire hunting party gathers and starts off to the castle.

### Vocabulary, Act I

| | | |
|---|---|---|
| mein Saenger | mine SENG.er | my singer |
| die Liebe | dee LEEB.eh | love |
| O Koenigin | o KERN.ig.in | O Queen |
| Goettin | GERT.in | goddess |
| lass mich zieh'n | lahss mik tseen | let me fly |
| Heil | hile | deliverance |
| o bleib | o bly'b | oh stay |
| bleib bei Elisabeth | bly'b by el.EE.sah.beth | stay near Elisabeth |

## ACT II (74 min. but with usual cut, closer to 65)

There is a short prelude (2 min.) and then the curtain reveals the Hall of Minstrels in the Wartburg with the valley, seen through an open wall at the back.

### SCENE 1 (4 min.)

**aria**    *Elisabeth:* She enters alone. (Her aria, greeting the Hall of Song, is always an emotional moment for singers and others sentimental about song.) She sings, "Dich, theure Halle" (you, dear hall), where first she heard Tannhaeuser's song and to which he has at last returned. "Sei mir gegruesst" (I salute you).

### SCENE 2 (13 min.)

*Elisabeth, Tannhaeuser and Wolfram:* She is startled by the men and tries to leave, but Tannhaeuser prevents her by kneeling at her feet. She gives thanks for his safe return and asks where he has been. He replies vaguely and exclaims that only a miracle led him back—"Ein **aria**    Wunder war's." Ecstatically Elisabeth praises the miracle, "Ich preise dieses Wunder." Then she describes, naively and sweetly, the effect of his song on her and how, when he disappeared, no other singer could touch her heart. She asks him, "Heinrich," what has happened to me? (Wagner imagined her a young girl, not a middle-aged soprano.) "Den Gott der Liebe" (the God of Love), Tannhaeuser exclaims, has touched his harp and, through his song, spoken to her. **duet**    Together they praise, "gepriesen," the power of love. (Mendelssohn particularly liked this duet.) At the back of the hall, Wolfram despairs that Elisabeth will never love him. Tannhaeuser leaves with Wolfram.

### SCENE 3 (5 min.)

*Elisabeth and the Landgrave:* He is pleased that she will attend the song contest and asks what starts her interest up again. But she is con-**arietta**    fused and cannot speak, "Sprechen kann ich nicht." He remarks that she may keep her secret and goes on to say that all the knights will attend the contest since she will give the prize. A trumpet fanfare announces the contest, and the guests begin to gather.

### SCENE 4 (The Tournament of Song—52 min.)

**march**    *The Knights and Ladies:* They enter to a march, which they later sing, hailing the Landgrave and the Hall of Song. (The whole gathering with chorus lasts 7 min.) Then the Minnesinger (*See*

Glossary) enter and are seated by the Pages.

*The Landgrave:* He makes a speech of welcome, reminding them that the art of song is as highly prized as that of war. He refers to Tannhaeuser's return, the cause of which is a mystery, and he declares the theme of the contest to be Love. (This speech [7 min.] is not very exciting, nor are the first songs in the contest.) The assembly hails the Landgrave again, and the Pages collect the names of the Minnesinger in a cup and announce the first contestant: "Wolfram von Eschenbach, beginne."

*The Contest:* It departs from the usual pattern almost at once. They sing in this order:

| | |
|---|---|
| *1. Wolfram:* | He imagines Elisabeth as a fountain of pure, healing love. He prays never to contaminate it with impure thoughts. The crowd applauds. |
| *2. Tannhaeuser:* | He knows the same fountain, but he would not approach it without desire, the flame of truest love. Only Elisabeth starts to applaud. |
| *3. Walter:* | He undertakes to instruct Tannhaeuser about the fountain, which soothes and ennobles only those with pure thoughts. The crowd applauds. (Two and three, omitted in the later version, are often cut.) |
| *4. Tannhaeuser:* | He advises Walter to adore the stars, distant and perfect; human love is pure and best enjoyed when consummated. Consternation in the crowd. |
| *5. Biterolf:* | Angrily he challenges Tannhaeuser. They are friends no more. To defend noble womanhood, virtuous love is worth a blow. The crowd applauds. |
| *6. Tannhaeuser:* | He suggests Biterolf has never experienced love or he wouldn't talk such twaddle. The knights draw their swords, but the Landgrave calls for peace. |
| *7. Wolfram:* | He begs Heaven to inspire him so that he may do justice to noble love which, fanned by an angel's wing, has an immortal fire. |
| *8. Tannhaeuser:* | (To his Venusberg music.) He calls on the Goddess of Love to inspire him. He advises the knights to search out Venus before they sing of love. At this all the ladies except Elisabeth quit the Hall. |

The knights draw their swords and move towards Tannhaeuser who stands as if in a trance to one side. Elisabeth, coming between them, orders the knights back. Death cannot hurt as much as the wound Tannhaeuser has dealt her: "Was ist die Wunde" (what is the wound)? The knights are amazed at her, but she insists he must be given a chance to save himself. But again the knights close in on him, saying that he is cursed by Heaven.

**aria** *Elisabeth:* She shames them: one against so many. Then in an aria she asks if mercy is not Heaven's law. Who are they to decide that Heaven has abandoned any man? "Ich fleh' fuer ihn" (I beg for him), she implores. Don't deny him a chance at pardon.

Tannhaeuser, now crushed with remorse, sobs! "Weh! weh!" (woe . . . lost forever).

*Finale:* The knights sing of Elisabeth as an angel sent to disclose Heaven's will. Tannhaeuser begs Heaven's pardon for his profanity: "Erbarm dich mein" (have pity on me). (The score allows the chorus either to sing or not during Tannhaeuser's lines. Wagner designed it, however, as a large ensemble.)

The Landgrave banishes Tannhaeuser from the kingdom and suggests that only by joining the Pilgrims and going to Rome can he win pardon. A group is forming even now in the valley.

The knights urge him to go, promising that if he returns unshriven, they will kill him: "dies Schwert" (this sword . . . will find you). Elisabeth begs Heaven to pardon him; Tannhaeuser hopes through her to be pardoned. From the valley comes the sound of the pilgrims' voices, and Tannhaeuser rushes out calling, "nach Rom" (to Rome), which they all repeat.

### Vocabulary, Act II

| | | |
|---|---|---|
| dich, theure Halle | dik toy.er hahll | you, dear hall |
| sei mir gegruesst | sigh meer ge.groost | I salute you |
| ein Wunder War's | eye'n voon.der varce | it was a miracle |
| ich preise dieses Wunder | ik* prize deezes voon.der | I praise the miracle |
| den Gott der Liebe | den got der leeb.eh | the God of Love |
| gepriesen | ge.preeze.en | be praised |
| was ist die Wunde | vast ist dee voon.deh | what is the wound |
| ich fleh' fuer ihn | ik* flay feer een | I beg for him |
| weh, weh | vay | woe |
| Erbarm dich mein | air.bahrm dik mine | have pity on me |
| dies Schwert | deez shvairt | this sword |
| nach Rom | nahk rohm | to Rome |

* Ik or ish depending on the North or South German accent of the singer.

## ACT III (54 min.)

There is a long (8 min.) introduction suggesting Tannhaeuser's pilgrimage to Rome, starting with a phrase on the horns from the Pilgrims' chorus in Act I, which is at once contrasted with the woodwinds, sounding part of Elisabeth's plea for Tannhaeuser in Act II. The climax sounded twice on the brass is a new melody associated with Rome. It ends quietly with Elisabeth's plea.

## SCENE 1 (18 min.)

As in the first act, the valley below the Wartburg. Elisabeth is kneeling at the Virgin's shrine. Wolfram enters.

*Wolfram:* He stops on seeing Elisabeth. He muses that she is always at the shrine, waiting for the Pilgrims, wondering if Tannhaeuser will come back repentant and absolved. "Dies ist ihr Fragen, dies ihr Flehen" (this is her question, this her prayer), he comments. He hopes that she will never know the anguish he feels each time he sees her.

**chorus** The Pilgrims: Their song comes first from a distance; then they cross the stage and go out. Elisabeth and Wolfram stand where they can see them. Tannhaeuser is not among them. Softly Elisabeth says, "Er kehret nicht zurueck!" (he does not return).

**prayer** *Elisabeth:* She prays to the Virgin. She asks to be released from life, "O! nimm von dieser Erde mich," and to enter Heaven as a maid. If she has sinned in loving Tannhaeuser, then she will abjure it and live a maid, always serving the Virgin. Finally she begs the Virgin to pardon Tannhaeuser. Then, gently refusing Wolfram's company, she starts for the Wartburg alone. (She goes to a solo passage for woodwinds, flutes, clarinets, oboe and bassoons. A bass clarinet introduces the melody.)

## SCENE 2 (5 min.)

*Wolfram:* Night falls, and he notices how the evening star brightens
**evening star** the twilight. Taking his harp he asks it to greet Elisabeth's soul, to carry her out of sadness into joy: "O du mein holder Abendstern" (oh you, my lovely evening star). He falls silent (and the cello echoes his thought).

## SCENE 3 (23 min.)

*Tannhaeuser and Wolfram:* Tannhaeuser stumbles in, ragged and exhausted. Wolfram's at first mistakes him and then worries that Tannhaeuser has returned unrepentant and unabsolved. The knights will kill him. Tannhaeuser replies that he is looking for Venusberg. Wolfram is horrified and asks if he went to Rome. Furiously, Tannhaeuser tells him not to speak of Rome. But Wolfram sympathetically urges him to tell what happened, and Tannhaeuser says with surprise, "Bist du denn nicht mein Feind" (are you then not my foe)? As Wolfram goes to sit beside him, Tannhaeuser warns him away: "zurueck von mir" (back from me); the very spot he sits is accursed.

Tannhaeuser then begins his Rome narrative, which musicians think **Rome narrative** the finest part of the score. It divides roughly as follows:

*To Rome:* (To a predominantly string sound.) He started contrite and penitent, thinking of the angel, "ein Engel," who had pleaded for him. After a pause he describes himself carrying others' burdens, going without water, taking the hard road, thinking always of the angel who awaited his return. (This section ends with a buzz on the violins.)

*At Rome:* (To high, silvery tones.) At last at Rome the bells pealed, a choir sang, the pilgrims rejoiced. (The section ends with another buzz.)

*The Audience:* (Still to the buzz.) They came before the Pope, who that day pardoned thousands, "tausenden," (to horns). Then (to strings) Tannhaeuser drew near, confessed his sin to the Pope who replied as Tannhaeuser now intones: You who have dwelt in Venusberg will be forever accursed, "verdammt!" As this staff in my hand, "in meiner Hand," will never put forth a leaf, so you will never find salvation. At which Tannhaeuser swooned (described in a whisper).

*At Rome:* (To high, silvery tones.) When he recovered, he was alone and forsaken, and in the distance he could hear prayers and singing.

*The Return:* (To Venusberg music.) There was nothing left but to find Venusberg. In a frenzy he calls to Venus: he will surrender to her. Only she can stop the pangs of yearning.

*Tannhaeuser and Wolfram:* Wildly Tannhaeuser calls to Venus as Wolfram tries to stop him, "Halt' ein." A rosy mist fills the valley as

Venus appears. She calls to Tannhaeuser, "O komm," but Wolfram holds him back. Desperately Wolfram reminds him of "Elisabeth." At her name Tannhaeuser stops, while from the valley comes the sound of a funeral procession. With a cry, Venus and the rosy mist vanish. The knights enter with Elisabeth on a bier, and Wolfram leads Tannhaeuser to it. He kneels beside it: "Heilige Elisabeth, bitte fuer mich" (saintly Elisabeth, pray for me). He dies, and all invert their torches as the dawn lights the valley. A group of pilgrims enter, exclaiming over a staff that miraculously put forth leaves, and all join in a final chorale.

### Vocabulary, Act III

| | | |
|---|---|---|
| dies ist ihr Fragen | deez ist eer FRAH.gen | this is her question |
| dies ihr Flehen | deez eer FLAY.en | this her prayer |
| er kehret nicht zurueck | air kayr.et nikt tsoo.ruk | he will not return |
| o! nimm von dieser Erde mich | o nim fon deez.er air.de mik | free me from this earth |
| o du mein holder Abendstern | o doo mine holt.er AH.bent.shtairn | oh you, my lovely evening star |
| zurueck von mir | tsoo.ruk fon meer | stand off from me |
| ein Engel | eye'n ENG.el | an angel |
| tausenden | TOWZ.ent.en | thousand |
| verdammt | fair.DAHMT | be accursed |
| in meiner Hand | in mine.er hahnt | in my hand |
| Halt' ein | hahlt eye'n | stay |
| O Komm | o kom | come |
| Heilige Elisabeth | hile.ik | saintly Elisabeth |
| Bitte fuer mich | bit.eh feer mik | pray for me |

# LOHENGRIN

Romantic opera in three acts. First performed at Weimar on August 28, 1850. Music and libretto by R. Wagner.

### PRINCIPAL CHARACTERS

| | | |
|---|---|---|
| The King's Herald | baritone or bass | |
| Henry I, King of Saxony | bass | |
| Friedrich von Telramund, a Count of Brabant | baritone | FREED.rik |
| Elsa von Brabant | soprano | AIL.sah |
| Lohengrin | tenor | LO'en.grin |
| Ortrud, Friedrich's wife | soprano | |

The action takes place in Antwerp about 933 A.D.

The political background of the opera is historically accurate. Henry I, known as "the Fowler," was king of Saxony from 919 to 936. At that time Saxony was the most important of the German states, and Henry was considered their leader, although he was not formally acknowledged as such. His great contribution was stopping the advance of the Hungarians from the East. In 924 he made a nine-year truce with them, during which time he fortified his towns, created a cavalry and retrained his army. The opera begins as the truce is about to end and Henry is making sure of his ally, Brabant.

˙The opera has always been the most popular of Wagner's, which is curious, inasmuch as the story has, even for opera, a peculiarly unhappy ending. Lovers dying together is common, e.g. *Aida* and *Tristan und Isolde;* but lovers separating because of something more powerful than their love, the Grail and Elsa's distrust, is most unusual (*La Traviata* is another example). From the first the ending bothered sentimentalists. For a day or two even Wagner considered changing it, but on second thought he stood firm; clearly, given Lohengrin's character, it must end as it does.

One theory of the opera's popularity, generally propounded by men, is that it strikes some deep chord in the female psyche. Most ladies, argue the theoreticians, find their husbands or lovers somehow disappointing—merely human—and long always for a knight in shining armour. Each easily identifies herself with Elsa until the unfortunate question is asked, at which moment the lady smugly assures herself that, of course, *she* never would have doubted. Men, according to the theory, tend to find the character of Lohengrin faintly ridiculous and sympathize with Friedrich that the magic is unfair. It is curious, but seems to be true, that men and women in recounting the story consistently emphasize a different side of it; the women stress the mystical and the men the practical.

## PRELUDE (10 min.)

In it Wagner depicts a vision of the Grail gradually emerging clearer and closer until its glory seems about to envelop the beholder; then the vision slowly fades.

## ACT I (53 min.) SCENE 1 (11 min.)

A meadow on the Scheldt near Antwerp. King Henry sits under a large oak flanked by his Saxon knights. Opposite him are the knights of Brabant led by Friedrich, who is accompanied by Ortrud.

*The Herald:* He advances from the King's party and calls the meeting to order. They are gathered to consider the problem of mutual defense.

*King Henry:* He has come to warn them of the danger to "die deutsches Land" from the Hungarians in the East. Nine years earlier he made a truce with them and used the time to fortify the towns. Now the truce is ended, and the Hungarians are preparing to attack. "Nun ist es Zeit" (now is the time), he insists, to defend the German land and state, "das deutsche Reich." His Saxon knights clash their arms as a sign of support; the Brabantians listen.

The King adds that he had come to enlist the Brabantian knights in the cause but found them feuding and the Duchy in disorder. He calls on Friedrich to state the reason.

*Friedrich:* He assures King Henry that he will speak the truth, "die Wahrheit." He recounts how the late Duke of Brabant died leaving two children in his care, Elsa and Gottfried, the latter being the heir to the Duchy. One day Elsa went into the forest with her brother but came back alone. He searched for the boy but never found him, and when he questioned Elsa, she stammered so it seemed a confession of guilt. He was horrified and canceled his prospective marriage to her, although her father had blessed it. Instead he married Ortrud. He presents her to King Henry.

Solemnly Friedrich lays a charge, "Klage," against "Elsa von Brabant": the murder of her brother, "des Brudermordes." Then he claims the dukedom in his own right and that of Ortrud, whose ancestors once had ruled Brabant. On the charge, "die Klage," he suggests, let the King, "Koenig," give judgment. All the knights are astounded. King Henry exclaims that it is such a fearful "Klage" that he can scarcely believe it. But Friedrich insists that Elsa, a dreamer, has some secret lover whom she preferred to him and with whom she probably intends to consort openly when she controls Brabant.

King Henry stops him and proclaims a court to find the truth. The knights indicate the solemnity of the proceeding by drawing their swords; the Saxons strike theirs into the ground while the Brabantians lay theirs down flat. King Henry orders the Herald to summon Elsa.

## SCENE 2 (18 min.)

Elsa enters as the knights murmur at her beauty and the gravity of the charge.

*King Henry:* He asks if she is "Elsa von Brabant." She nods. She agrees, also by nodding, that she accepts Henry as her sovereign and that she knows the charge against her. Even when he asks if she can disprove it or will confess to it, she merely shakes her head and sighs, "mein armer Bruder" (my unfortunate brother). The knights wonder, and the King urges her to speak.

*Elsa:* In a dreamy voice she explains that she used to pray for Heaven **Elsa's dream** to aid her and her brother. Then one day Heaven answered her as she fell asleep. King Henry urges her to defend herself before the court. But she continues with her dream. She saw a knight, calm and splendid, leaning on his sword. He had a gold horn, "ein golden Horn," at his side. He will be her champion, "er soll mein Streiter sein."

*King Henry and Friedrich:* The knights are impressed, and King Henry warns Friedrich to be careful in his accusations. Friedrich, however, insists her vision is proof of a secret love. But he offers to fight to back his word, "hier mein Schwert" (here is my sword). He asks who will fight for Elsa, and all the Brabantian knights decline. King Henry accepts Friedrich's suggestion of a trial by battle. He drives his sword into the ground and solemnly asks Friedrich if he will fight for life and for death, "auf Leben und auf Tod," leaving to Heaven to pass on the truth of the charge, "Klage." "Ja," Friedrich agrees. King Henry then repeats the question to Elsa, who also agrees, "Ja." The King then orders her to choose a champion, "Streiter."

*Elsa:* The knight she dreamed of will be her champion, and she will give him all her lands, title and love. On the King's orders the trumpeters sound a flourish; the Herald calls for the knight, but no knight appears. Elsa asks for another flourish, for her knight lives far away and may not have heard the first. This time, after the trumpets and the Herald, Elsa prays, and the knights nearest the river see Lohengrin approaching in a skiff drawn by a swan. All the knights and ladies call it a miracle, "ein Wunder," and greet the unknown knight as a hero. Ortrud at the sight of the swan shivers.

## SCENE 3 (24 min.)

*Lohengrin:* He stands in the skiff gazing calmly before him. He wears a
**farewell to the swan**     silver coat of mail and shining helmet; he
stands leaning on his sword with a golden horn at his side. He steps
ashore and softly bids the swan good-by: "Nun sei bedankt, mein lieber
Schwan" (now be thanked, my beloved swan), "leb'wohl" (farewell).

The knights and ladies exclaim "wie ist er schoen" (how handsome he is). Lohengrin greets the King and then turns to Elsa.

*Lohengrin and Elsa:* He asks if she will have him as her champion. She
hails him as "mein Held, mein Retter" (my hero, my savior). He asks
whether if he fights for her, she will have him as her husband. She
agrees. Then he puts the condition: she must never ask his country,
rank and name, "noch wie mein Nam' und Art!" She swears, but he
repeats it. Calling him "mein Engel" (my angel), she swears to cherish
his command, and he sighs, "Elsa, Ich liebe dich" (I love you). The
knights and ladies murmur their approval.

*Lohengrin et al:* He announces he is ready to fight; Friedrich's charge
was false. All the knights urge Friedrich not to fight, for clearly
Lohengrin has some special power, but Friedrich insists that as he has
not lied, God will help him. The king then announces the contest,
knights measure off the area of combat, the Herald announces the
rules of the fight, and the King leads everyone in a prayer asking the
Deity to support the right and fell the wrong. They fight; Lohengrin
wins; he spares Friedrich's life; and all rejoice at the outcome.

### Vocabulary, Act I

| | | |
|---|---|---|
| die deutsches Land | dee doyt.shes lahnnt | the German land |
| nun ist es zeit | noon ist es tsite | now is the time |
| das deutsche Reich | dahs doyt.she rike | the German realm |
| die Wahrheit | dee VAHR.hite | the truth |
| Klage | KLAH.geh | charge, accusation |
| Elsa von Brabant | AIL.sah fon brah.BAHNT | Elsa of Brabant |
| des Brudermordes | des BROOD.er.mort.es | of her brother's murder |
| Koenig | KER.nik | king |
| mein armer Bruder | mine AHRM.er BROOD.er | my unfortunate brother |
| ein golden Horn | eye'n GOLL.den horn | a golden horn |
| er soll mein Streiter sein | air zol mine shtreye.ter zine | he shall be my champion |

| | | |
|---|---|---|
| hier mein Schwert | here mine shvairt | here my sword |
| auf Leben und auf Tod | owf LAY.ben oont owf toht | for life and for death |
| ein Wunder | eye'n VOON.der | a miracle |
| nun sei bedankt mein lieber Schwan | noon sy be.DAHNKT mine LEEB.er shvahn | now be thanked, my beloved swan |
| leb'wohl | layb.vohl | farewell |
| wie ist er schoen | vee ist air shern | how fair he is |
| mein Held, mein Retter | mine helt . . . RET.ter | my hero, my savior |
| noch wie mein Nam' und Art | nok vee mine nahm oont ahrt | not now my name and rank |
| mein Engel | mine ENG.el | my angel |
| ich liebe dich | ik* leeb.eh dik* | I love you |

* Ik or ish depending on the North or South German accent of the singer.

## ACT II (81 min.; but with cuts, closer to 72)

There is a short (1 min.) prelude, sombre and brooding; musicians think it particularly expressive. It is night at the castle at Antwerp; to the back, the knights' wing; to the left, the ladies' wing; and to the right, the church. Ortrud and Friedrich sit in the dark on the church steps watching the lights in the knights' wing.

### SCENE 1 (20 min.)

*Friedrich:* He tells Ortrud to come; they must leave the castle before **aria** dawn. She murmurs that she cannot go until she has revenge. Friedrich looks at her. He wonders why he cannot leave her. She led him on to shame and disgrace. Death would have saved his honor, "mein Ehr'." He throws himself beside her as trumpets sound in the hall of the knights' wing.

*Ortrud and Friedrich:* She asks why he blames her. Because she lied to him, he insists; she let him stake his life and honor on a falsehood. "Wer log" (who lied)? she asks. "Du," Friedrich replies. The judgment in the duel was clear. "Gott" (God), she laughs scornfully: she can show him how to change God's judgment. Friedrich shudders, "du wilde Seherin" (you wild seer). Then in a dialogue she works him into a fury. If Lohengrin's name and rank are known, he will be powerless. Only Elsa can learn them, and she must be either induced or forced to ask. Failing that, they must wound Lohengrin, for his preserving spells will fail when his blood is spilt. Friedrich rages at losing his honor in an unfair fight, wonders if he can regain it, and threatens Ortrud if she is **duet** lying. She tells him to sit beside her and learn about revenge. They sing "der Rache werk" (the vengeance work); while others slumber, they are at work. (This "vendetta" duet could come from any Italian opera, even a bad one.)

## SCENE 2 (19 min.)

**aria** *Elsa:* As Ortrud and Friedrich murmur against her from below, she sings to the night breezes, which had comforted her in sorrow, now to cool the ardor of one in love, "in Liebe."
*Ortrud and Elsa:* Ortrud tells Friedrich to save himself for Lohengrin; she will handle Elsa. She calls up to her, asking if Elsa having robbed her of all but life now intends to disown her. Elsa is astonished and denies that she is the cause of Ortrud's misfortune. Ortrud says Friedrich is overcome with remorse and yet will be banished. Nothing is left for them except to leave in order not to spoil Elsa's happiness. Elsa, beginning to feel guilty at her happiness, promises to come down at once.
**aria** *Ortrud:* She calls on her Gods, Wotan and Freia, to help her work her revenge, "meine Rache."
*Elsa and Ortrud:* Elsa comes out: "Ortrud, wo bist du" (where are you)? Ortrud kneels at her feet, and Elsa is aghast at her bedraggled appearance. She promises to ask Lohengrin to pardon Friedrich. She urges Ortud to dress and accompany her to the church, where she will meet Lohengrin and "vor Gott sein Eh' gemahl zu sein" (before God his bride to be). Ortrud grovels her thanks and adds that she has only one thing to give in return: a warning. Elsa does not understand, and Ortrud suggests that as Lohengrin came mysteriously, he may just as suddenly and mysteriously leave.

Elsa, secretly fearful for a moment, turns away. Then she tells Ortrud of a faith and love that has no fear. It is a good fortune without **duet** blemish: "es giebt ein Glueck, das ohne Reu'!" Proudly she repeats it as Ortrud murmurs she will use this very pride to destroy her faith. Elsa leads Ortrud in, and Friedrich remarks, "So zieht das Unheil in dies Haus" (so moves evil into the house).

## SCENE 3 (11 min.)

(During this scene day breaks, rather abruptly; but the fault is only partly Wagner's. Most productions have cuts in the choruses, which are difficult, and also cut the scene with the four knights.)

*Knights:* Two wardens blow reveille on a nearby turret and are an-
**chorus** swered by others off stage. The knights gather singing that the day promises very much, "gar viel," either of good or evil.

*The Herald:* Four trumpeters announce him. He recites that King Henry has banished Friedrich: "In Bann und Acht ist Friedrich Telramund." Whoever aids or protects him will also be banished. The knights and soldiers all curse Friedrich or anyone who aids him. The Herald continues: the stranger who defended Elsa has been entitled the Protector of Brabant: "Schuetzer von Brabant." The knights hail him, "Heil." The Herald concludes that the Protector invites all to the wedding and that on the next day they will leave to join King Henry's army. The knights exclaim with excitement. They will win because Lohengrin has been sent from God, "von Gott."

*Four Knights:* They complain, one to another, of the Protector's military policy and wonder who would dare to question it. Friedrich reveals himself, suggesting he be their leader. They urge him to conceal himself, as pages announce the coming of Elsa.

## SCENE 4 (11 min.)

*Knights and Ladies:* Elsa enters, preceded and followed by the ladies of
**chorus** the court; to the rear and shunned by the others is Ortrud. The knights, joined later by the ladies, greet Elsa. As she starts up the steps to the church, Ortrud rushes to the front and confronts her.

*Ortrud:* "Zurueck, Elsa" (stand back). She declares that she should lead and Elsa follow. All exclaim as Ortrud repeats it more fiercely. Elsa in confusion wonders about the night when Ortrud was wailing at her door. Ortrud recites Friedrich's past honor, which all could see and know, but Elsa does not know even the name of her knight. The knights and ladies murmur against Ortrud as she asks Elsa for Lohengrin's name.

*Elsa:* She recites Lohengrin's virtue, proved in the fight, and the crowd murmurs for her.

*Ortrud:* Ortrud concludes that if Elsa does not dare ask the question of Lohengrin, it is because she fears the answer.

## SCENE 5 (20 min.)

*Elsa and Lohengrin:* Trumpeters announce the King and Lohengrin. Elsa, clinging to Lohengrin, explains how she took in Ortrud out of kindness only to be repaid by being taunted for her trust in him. Lohengrin orders Ortrud away: "steh ab von ihr" (stay off from her). He asks Elsa if Ortrud has succeeded in raising doubts and, when Elsa denies this, urges her to come to the church.

*Friedrich and Lohengrin:* Friedrich bars the door. The knights surge forward to kill him. Furiously Friedrich insists that he has been unjustly dishonored. Lohengrin should have revealed his name. Friedrich demands to know it. Lohengrin refuses, and Friedrich urges King Henry to command him to reveal it. Lohengrin states that he would refuse even the King; only Elsa can ask the question. He turns to her and with dismay sees her struggling with doubts.

*Finale:* Ortrud, Friedrich, Lohengrin and Elsa all exclaim in glee or fear on the doubts now obviously troubling Elsa. The King and knights all state Lohengrin's deeds are recommendation enough. The knights each shake Lohengrin's hand as a sign of homage.

Friedrich leaves the church door to whisper to Elsa that he can convince her of his charge; only a drop of Lohengrin's blood need be spilled, and then she will know. He will be close by that night if she calls. Elsa insists she never will.

Lohengrin sees Friedrich and Ortrud by Elsa and orders them away. He asks Elsa if she wants to put the question. With an effort she insists that love will conquer all doubt: "meine Liebe steh'n" (my love stands).

The procession reorganizes itself, and they all enter the church.

### Vocabulary, Act II

| | | |
|---|---|---|
| mein Ehr' | mine air | my honor |
| wer log | vair log | who lied |
| du | doo | you |
| Gott | got | God |
| du wilde Seherin | do vilt.eh SAY.her.in | you wild seer |
| der Rache werk | der RAH.keh vairk | the revenge work |
| in Liebe | in LEEB.eh | in love |

| | | |
|---|---|---|
| meine Rache | mine RAH.keh | my revenge |
| Ortrud, wo bist du | voh bist doo | where are you |
| vor Gott sein | for got sine ay'ge.mahl | before God his bride |
|   Eh'gemahl zu sein |   tsoo sine |   to be |
| es giebt ein Glueck | es geebt eye'n gloock | it casts a fortune |
|   das ohne Reu' |   dahs oh.ne ray |   without blemish |
| so ziehet das Unheil | so tsee.et dahs oon.hile | so enters evil |
|   in dies Haus |   in dees hows |   in that house |
| gar viel | gahr feel | very much |
| in Bann und Acht | in bahn oont ahkt ist | under ban and exile is |
|   ist . . . | | |
| Schuetzer von Brabant | shoo.tser fon . . . | Protector of Brabant |
| heil | hile | hail |
| von Gott | fon got | from God |
| zurueck, Elsa | tsoo. rook AIL.sah | stand back, Elsa |
| stah ab von ihr | stay ahp fon eer | stay off from her |

## ACT III (64 min.; but with usual cuts, closer to 55)

### PRELUDE (3 min.)

It depicts the excitement of the marriage and its celebration, and occasionally it turns up on concert programs for which a few closing bars are added. It leads directly into the bridal march.

### SCENE 1 (5 min.)

The bridal chamber; to the right, a window.
*Ladies and Knights:* The ladies lead in Elsa; the King and knights, Lohengrin. When the two trains meet, Elsa and Lohengrin embrace and eight ladies circle round them twice. King Henry congratulates the **bridal chorus** couple, blesses them, and the two trains retire. Throughout, they sing the bridal chorus. (Wagner, wherever he is, must get a laugh out of middle-class Christian America, which has taken his march to the bridal bed, with its constant reference to the joys of the body, as a suitable accompaniment for a march to the bridal altar, with its connotations of the bonds of the spirit; and the reference to the faithless Elsa is, of course, wildly inappropriate.)

## SCENE 2 (23 min.)

(This scene, the most lyric in the opera, is a test of the dramatic tenor's ability to sing without bellowing.)

*Lohengrin and Elsa:* At last they are alone, for the first time. "Elsa, mein Weib" (my wife). She replies: "Fuehl' ich zu dir so suess mein **duet** Herz entbrennen" (I feel for you so sweet my heart enflames). They rhapsodize that love is a gift from God. He states that love led him to her, and she describes how she first saw him in a vision. But then she starts: "Ist dies nur Liebe" (is this then love)? How is it shown? He sighs, "Elsa." How sweet, she continues, to hear my name on your lips: whisper yours to me.

Lohengrin embraces her and points to the garden out the window. The smell of flowers, he remarks, comes mysteriously on the breeze and can be enjoyed without question. So he first loved her when she was accused before all of murder. But she wishes she could do something to prove her love for him: she could keep his secret even to death. She presses more urgently, and he begs her to be silent. He steps back from her: "Hoechstes Vertrau'n" (highest trust) has he shown her in believing her free from guilt. If her faith in him wavers, their love is lost.

Then, fondly again, he moves to embrace her, "an meine Brust" (on my breast). Even if the King should offer him his crown, he would refuse, for "muss ich in deiner Lieb erseh'n" (must I in your love shine forth).

But Elsa is not convinced. She accuses him of trying to confuse her. She fears one day he will go without warning, as he came. She overrides all his protestations. How can she bind him to her? Almost in a trance she sees the swan coming for him, "der Schwan." He cannot compel her to trust him. She insists: "Dem Namen sag' mir an" (the name tell me then). Lohengrin sobs, "weh" (woe).

At that moment Friedrich and the four knights burst in, but Lohengrin kills Friedrich with one blow. He orders the knights to take the corpse before King Henry. Then he pulls a bell and directs the ladies who respond to lead Elsa to the King, where he will answer all her questions.

The curtain falls, although the music continues unbroken into the next scene.

SCENE 3 (33 min.; but with cuts, closer to 27)

In the meadow by the Scheldt. It is early morning.
*King Henry and the Knights:* The knights gather to march against the Hungarians. Four Counts and then the King enter, each on horseback and with a full retinue. (Wagner intended this to be a tremendous spectacle. Opera houses that cannot stage it frequently cut some of the martial music.) The troops hail the King, and he addresses them. He thanks the knights of Brabant for joining him against the Hungarians: "Fuer deutsches Land das deutsche Schwert" (for German land the German sword). The men repeat it.

The four knights carry in Friedrich's corpse: Elsa follows, and then Lohengrin, with the chorus commenting on each. King Henry greets Lohengrin, stating that the troops wait only for him to lead them.
*Lohengrin:* He replies that for reasons he will explain he must forego the campaign—"darf ich nicht" (I may not). All are aghast. He uncovers Friedrich's corpse and, after explaining why he killed him, asks to be judged. They acquit him. Then he adds that he must part from Elsa, who insisted on asking "mein Nam und Art!" He will now tell them who he is and whence he comes.

He begins. "In fernem Land" (in distant land) in a castle, "eine Burg," called "Monsalvat" there is the Grail, "der Gral." The knight serving it can champion right against wrong with its strength so long as his name and country are unknown. But once known, he loses its power and must return to Monsalvat. He states proudly, "mein Vater Parzival" (my father is Parsifal) and "ich bin Lohengrin genannt" (I am named Lohengrin).

Everyone exclaims, and Elsa faints.
*Lohengrin, Elsa, King Henry and the Knights:* (This section, down to the entry of the swan, is frequently cut.) Lohengrin turns to Elsa, grieving that he must say farewell. She is filled with remorse and begs him to stay, "bleibe hier." But he must go, "ich muss." Elsa continues her plea. King Henry begs him to stay to fight the Hungarians, but Lohengrin explains that the rules of the Grail forbid it. He prophesies victory, however. Suddenly some knights sight the swan, "der Schwan."
*Lohengrin:* He greets it, "mein lieber Schwan," regretting that if Elsa had been true for only a year, it could have resumed its human form. He hands Elsa his horn, "dies Horn," his sword, "dies Schwert," and his ring, "den Ring," to give Gottfried if he returns. Then he bids Elsa

farewell, "Leb'wohl." All grieve.

*Ortrud:* She urges him to be gone. She enchanted Gottfried into the swan; now he will never return. On her the Gods of vengeance have smiled.

*Lohengrin:* He prays silently until the white dove, symbolic of the Grail, hovers over the skiff. Lohengrin rises, takes the gold band off the swan's neck and, as the swan sinks, lifts Gottfried ashore. Then stepping into the skiff pulled now by the dove, Lohengrin departs. Ortrud collapses; Elsa dies in Gottfried's arms; and all exclaim, "weh" (woe)!

## Vocabulary, Act III

| | | |
|---|---|---|
| Elsa, mein Weib | AIL.sah, mine vibe | Elsa, my wife |
| fuehl' ich zu dir so suesse mein Herz entbrennen | fuel ik tsoo deer so soo.se mine hairts ent.bren.en | I feel for you so sweet my heart enflames |
| ist dies nur Liebe | ist dees noor LEEB.eh | is this then love |
| hoechstes Vertrau'n | herk.stes fair.trown | highest truth |
| an meine Brust | ahn MINE.eh broost | on my breast |
| muss ich in deiner Lieb erseh'n | moos ik in diner leeb er.sayn | must I in your love shine forth |
| der Schwan | der shvahn | the swan |
| dem Namen sag' mir an | dem nah.men sahg meer an | the name tell me then |
| weh | vay | woe |
| fuer deutsches Land das deutsches Schwert | fur doyt.shes lahnnt dahs doyt.shes shvairt | for German land the German sword |
| darf ich nikt | dahrf ik nikt | I may not |
| mein Nam und Art | mine nahm oont ahrt | my name and rank |
| in fernem Land | in fair.nem lahnnt | in distant land |
| eine Burg | eye.neh boork | a castle |
| der Gral | der grahl | the Grail |
| mein Vater Parzival | mine FAH.ter Par.see.vahl | my father Parsifal |
| ich bin Lohengrin genannt | ik bin . . . ge.nahnt | I am named Lohengrin |
| bleibe hier | blibe here | stay here |
| ich muss | ik moos | I must (go) |
| mein lieber Schwan | mine leeb.er shvahn | my beloved swan |
| dies Horn | dees horn | this horn |
| dies Schwert | dees shvairt | this sword |
| den ring | den ring | this ring |
| leb'wohl | layb.vohl | farewell |

# TRISTAN UND ISOLDE

Opera in three acts. First performed at Munich on June 10, 1865. Music and libretto by R. Wagner.

### PRINCIPAL CHARACTERS

| | | |
|---|---|---|
| A sailor's voice | tenor | |
| Isolde | soprano | is.OLD.uh |
| Brangaene, her lady in waiting | soprano | bran.GAIN.uh |
| Kurvenal, Tristan's friend and retainer | baritone | KOOR.ven.ahl |
| Tristan | tenor | TRIS.tahn |
| Melot, a knight | baritone | |
| Marke, King of Cornwall | bass | |
| A shepherd | tenor | |

The action takes place in legendary times on a ship nearing Cornwall, Cornwall, and in Brittany.

The legend on which Wagner based his opera was the most popular of medieval Europe and existed in many versions. But all except the most debased stressed the tragic beauty of an overpowering love that could not be satisfied except in death. So great was the love that the medieval audience excused it from the usual standards of behavior, and the poets indicated divine absolution of the lovers with vines or trees growing out of their graves and interlocking where all could see.

In every culture there are heroes with attributes so great that they are considered touched in some way by the divine and not responsible for the effects of their actions. In ancient Greece there were Achilles and Helen. Achilles did not always behave well at Troy, but there was a splendor about him that Homer granted neither Odysseus nor Hector, the noblest of the merely human. Likewise, Helen's beauty was merely a tragic fact. There is a delightful account in the *Iliad* of Helen on the walls of Troy identifying the Greek warriors for Priam. He treats her with the greatest courtesy and without the slightest suggestion of personal responsibility for the slaughter going on below them.

Wagner recreated the Tristan legend for his opera, greatly emphasizing the mystical quality of the love and enriching it with an oriental negativism, equating love with death. The legend, as Wagner used it and before the curtain rises, is as follows:

Morold, a knight of Ireland, came to Cornwall to collect its tribute which Marke, the King, had withheld. Tristan, Marke's nephew, killed Morold in a battle but was himself wounded, and the wound would not heal. Soon the odor from it was so terrible that he had himself set adrift in a small boat. In time he came to Ireland where, calling himself Tantris (anagram of Tristan), he was cured by Isolde, the Princess who had been engaged to Morold. From Morold's body she had taken a tiny piece of Tristan's sword, and one day she discovered it perfectly fit a notch in the sword of Tantris. She hurried to kill him and had the sword raised when he looked up at her. After a moment she let it drop unused. Thereafter she kept secret his true identity and allowed him to depart as Tantris.

Back in Cornwall Tristan, to prove to jealous nobles that he had no designs on the throne, recommended that Marke marry and suggested Isolde as the finest Princess in the world. Marke then sent Tristan to fetch her, authorizing him to make peace between Cornwall and Ireland. This was done, and the opera begins as Tristan is returning with Isolde.

Over the years *Tristan* has become one of Wagner's most popular operas and possibly now is given more often than any other. Many persons consider it the most musical and therefore the greatest opera ever written. Others consider it unhealthy in its negative attitude, equating love with death, and the work of a man suffering a mental breakdown. These argue that those who admire the work have never examined the imagery of the libretto. The admirers retort that the libretto is at best elliptical and obscure and that the detractors have never listened to the music, which explains all.

The libretto is difficult, perhaps even obscure. Most mystical works are. And Wagner did not bother with irrelevancies. In spite of all the monologues reviewing the past, no character mentions whether Isolde by Act II had married Marke, whether the meeting was her first with Tristan, why she couldn't heal Tristan in Cornwall as well as in Brittany, or how much time elapsed between any of the acts. The literal-minded will continue to complain of this while lovers expostulate that there is no time—there is only being together or apart.

## PRELUDE (11 min.)

It is unnecessary to recognize themes in the Prelude. Wagner wrote it before he wrote the opera and stated that it was neither dramatic nor pictorial. It merely and perfectly captures the mood and urgency of a love that can never be released or satisfied except in death. It is one of the few preludes or overtures during which most opera houses refuse to seat the latecomers.

## ACT I (76 min.)

Isolde's quarters on the ship taking her to Cornwall. A marquee has been set up for her on deck, and she is screened from the crew by heavy curtains hung to the back and sides; a companionway leads to the cabin below.

## SCENE 1 (7 min.)

Isolde is on a couch with her head buried in the cushions. Brangaene, holding back a curtain, gazes over the ship's rail.
*Sailor's Voice:* He sings of the ship headed east while his thoughts swing west after his Irish girl.
*Isolde:* She starts up, offended at what she thinks is a slight on her, who could not remain in Ireland. She asks where they are. About to land in Cornwall, says Brangaene. Never. Not today or tomorrow, Isolde bursts out. Brangaene, startled, drops the curtain as Isolde furiously calls on the winds to sink the ship.
*Brangaene:* She begs Isolde to confide in her, to reveal her secret pain. Why did she leave her father and mother, "der Vater und Mutter," and Ireland without a word; why is she fasting and sleepless? Isolde merely tells her to raise the curtain.

## SCENE 2 (10 min.)

With the curtain raised, the length of the ship aft can be seen. Sailors are lolling about; behind them are knights and squires; standing apart is Tristan, his arms folded, gazing thoughtfully out to sea; at his feet lounges Kurvenal.

*Sailor's Voice:* He repeats a verse of his song.

*Isolde:* She stares at Tristan. "Mir verloren" (I, abandoned!), she muses. Indicating Tristan, she asks Brangaene what she thinks of such a hero. Brangaene thinks him a noble knight, but Isolde calls him a coward, afraid throughout the voyage to face her. Brangaene offers to ask Tristan to join her now, and Isolde tells her to order him as her vassal. She is a Princess and the affianced bride of a King.

*Tristan, Brangaene and Kurvenal.* Three times Brangaene asks Tristan to go to Isolde, but he always replies evasively: the voyage is almost over, he'll come to lead her to King Marke, and he cannot leave the helm of the ship. She asks why he mocks her, adding that Isolde commands him to come. At that Kurvenal leaps up and answers for Tristan. Loudly he repeats the story of Ireland's shame—how Tristan defeated Morold and now is bringing Isolde to Marke. Tristan orders him below, but the sailors repeat the story as Brangaene retreats and drops the curtain behind her.

## SCENE 3 (21 min.)

*Isolde and Brangaene:* Brangaene reports, but halfway through Isolde stops her: she heard Kurvenal and the sailors. But she could if she **Isolde's narrative** wished repay them in kind with a different story. She starts her narrative, which is in three parts, each ending with a comment by Brangaene.

1: She recalls how Tristan came first to Ireland in disguise, a man with a wound that would not heal; how she nursed him to health, "Isolde's Kunst . . . und Balsamsaft" (Isolde's skill and balsam juice); how she discovered that he had killed her fiancé, Morold; how she raised a sword to kill him and, when their eyes met, could not (music from the prelude).

Brangaene is astonished that she never recognized the Tristan who later came to claim Isolde for Marke as the sick man, Tantris, Isolde healed. "O Wunder."

2: But hear how he swore to be ever grateful and true to her. She helped him go, still in disguise. But then he returned to take her not for himself but for his Uncle Marke, to make her marry a man who once paid her tribute. She should have struck with the sword; instead now she is the vassal, "dem Vasallen."

Brangaene insists that peace, "Da Friede," was sworn between the two countries.

3: Isolde sweeps on: "O blinde Augen" (blinded eyes) that could not see. Her silence saved Tristan, and how did he repay it! He returned to Cornwall and told the King and court of a nice Princess for the King who could be had for the asking and whom Tristan would be glad to fetch. Curse him. Curse him. Vengeance, "Rache." Death, "Tod."

(Sometimes a cut is made to join Isolde's second verse directly to her curses in the third, omitting Brangaene's second comment and Isolde's image of how Tristan spoke of her in Cornwall. This is a serious cut, indicating that either the musical director responsible has no taste or that the soprano lacks ability. It leaves the narrative without any climax. In the measures cut are two B's, Isolde's highest notes throughout the entire act. Other possible cuts are far less damaging.)

Brangaene, who does not yet understand that Isolde loves Tristan, is horrified. "O suesse! Traut" (Sweet. Beloved). She embraces Isolde and argues that she sees Tristan's actions just backwards. What greater honor could he offer than to make her his Queen? (Notice that even before the love potion Isolde is deeply in love with Tristan and struggling with the problem of reality, her view of it and the world's.)

But Isolde has not heard. Staring vacantly in front of her, she murmurs on low notes: unbeloved, yet always near him, how can I endure it?

Unbeloved? Brangaene repeats, thinking Isolde means Marke. Confidentially she reminds Isolde of her mother's magic potions: "Kennst du der Mutter Kunste nicht" (know you not of your mother's skill)? Isolde orders her to get the box. Brangaene comments "Fuer Weh und Wunden Balsam hier" (for woe and wounds balsam is here). She indicates a bottle, the love potion, calling it the greatest. "Du irrst," Isolde says, "ich kenn ihn besser" (you err, I know a better). She points to the death potion.

*Sailors:* They call to let go the sail, get ready the anchor. They are almost to Cornwall.

## SCENE 4 (11 min.)

*Kurvenal and Isolde:* He enters without ceremony, telling the ladies to prepare to land. Isolde with dignity replies that she will not go ashore until Tristan comes to beg pardon for an offense. Kurvenal is impressed and, although grumbling, leaves with the message.

*Isolde and Brangaene:* Isolde hurries to Brangaene, gasps a farewell and orders her to prepare the death potion. Brangaene, beginning to understand, is terrified. Ironically, Isolde quotes: "Kennst du der Mutter Kunste nicht; fuer weh und Wunden gab sie Balsam." For the greatest pain there is the death potion, "Todestrank." Kurvenal announces Tristan, and Brangaene retires. (The end of this scene and the first twelve minutes of the next until the first sailors' chorus are the least exciting moments of the act, and if a snooze is unavoidable, this is the place for it.)

## SCENE 5 (29 min.)

*Tristan and Isolde:* They begin what is essentially no more than a medieval wrangle, although it exposes the conflict between the lovers' world and reality. Honor, Tristan explains, kept him from her during the voyage. Honor, she says, should have brought him to her. Custom, he insists, requires that he not be intimate with his future Queen. Custom, she retorts, requires the bloodguilt of Morold's death be absolved between them. So it was in public, he claims; but not in private, she insists, and rehearses her healing and sparing of him although she knew that he had killed Morold. She wants vengeance for Morold, "Rache fuer Morold."

Tristan offers her his sword. She remarks (often cut) that Marke will hardly be pleased with his bride if she slays his favorite knight. Put up your sword and we'll drink an atonement.

Sailors' voices break in on them. They are at Cornwall. She asks if he will drink with her. Again sailors' voices break in.

Isolde offers the cup to Tristan while making a sardonic speech (often cut) of what he might say to Marke when he delivers her to the King. The sailors call again. Tristan takes the cup, believing it contains death, and drinks. She snatches it from him and finishes what is left.

They gaze at each other. Believing they are about to die, they abandon themselves to truth and acknowledge that they love. The sailors hail King Marke coming out to meet them. Brangaene, who could not face death, laments her foolish fraud. Isolde and Tristan wonder how his supposed honor and her supposed shame could have so misled them. Brangaene, rushing to separate them as the curtains are raised, whispers that she substituted the love potion. Isolde, terrified, sobs "must I live then?" Hardly aware of what surrounds them, she and Tristan turn to face the coming of Marke and the world.

### Vocabulary, Act I

| | | |
|---|---|---|
| der Vater und Mutter | dar fah.ter oont moot.ter | the father and mother |
| mir verloren | mere fair.LORE.en | I, abandoned |
| Isolde's Kunst | koonst | Isolde's skill |
| und Balsamsaft | oont bal.sahm.sahft | and balsam juice |
| O Wunder | voon.der | oh wonder |
| dem Vasallen | dem fah.sahl.len | the vassal |
| da Friede | dah freed.eh | when peace |
| O blinde Augen | blint.uh ow.gen | blinded eyes |
| Rache | rah.kuh | revenge |
| Tod | toe.ht | death |
| O suesse | sue.suh | sweet |
| Traute | trow.tuh | beloved |
| Kennst du der Mutter Kunste nicht | kenst doo dare moot.ter koonst.uh nikt | know you not your mother's skill |
| Fuer Weh und Wunden Balsam hier | feer vay oont voon.duh bal.sahm here | for woe and wounds balsam is here |
| du irrst | doo eerst | you err |
| ich* kenn ihn besser | ik kenn een BESS.er | I know a better |
| Todestrank | toe.tes.trank | death drink |
| Rache fuer Morold | rah.kuh feer Morold | revenge for Morold |

\* Ish or ik depending on the North or South German accent of the singer.

## ACT II (93 min.; but with cuts, probably 70)

A garden with tall trees from which steps lead up one side to Isolde's chamber in the castle. A torch burns by the door. It is a clear summer night.

There is a prelude (3 min.) expressing Isolde's excitement at the coming meeting with Tristan. As the curtain rises, Brangaene is listening to the horns of Marke's hunting party. Isolde comes from her chamber.

### SCENE 1 (14 min.)

*Isolde and Brangaene:* Isolde asks if Brangaene can still hear the horns; she herself cannot. They are still near, Brangaene insists. Isolde listens but claims to hear nothing. She can hear the water in the well but not horns, and she scolds Brangaene for deliberately delaying the tryst. Brangaene pleads with her to take care. She warns that from the first day on the ship one of the knights has plotted against Tristan: "von Melot seid gewarnt" (of Melot be warned). Isolde mocks Brangaene's fears: Melot is Tristan's best friend. He arranged the hunt so that the lovers could meet. Give the signal, she insists, "das Zeichen." She welcomes darkness; put out the torch.

Brangaene delays, lamenting that she ever substituted the love potion. But Isolde scornfully assures her that it was none of her doing. Love did it; love, more powerful than death. And now wherever love leads she will follow. The potion robbed you of reason, Brangaene warns; be guided by mine: leave the torch lit. But Isolde, crying that love wants darkness, throws the torch to the ground, where it slowly burns out, and orders Brangaene to the tower to watch for the hunting party.

The orchestra builds a climax as Tristan approaches.

### SCENE 2 (49 min.)

(Generally cuts in the act are made in this scene, which is physically but not psychologically static. From Tristan's entrance to Kurvenal's at the beginning of the next scene, nothing "happens" on stage. Musically the scene is an almost steady curve down from the wild excitement of the first moments of physical meeting with broken, breathless phrases to the broad, mystical intensity of the final section of the duet, from which the human quality of the lovers is almost purged. **love duet** The long duet divides roughly into six sections, including Brangaene's warning. These are indicated with the stage directions which are generally faithfully observed.)

*Tristan and Isolde*—1: He rushes in and they embrace, gasping out, "Tristan, Isolde, mein, mein und dein. Ewig (always)." (It is here that Isolde has her two famous high C's, the highest notes she sings in the opera. They pass very quickly and seldom sound like more than a shriek because Wagner did not prepare for them with a gradual ascent. On the first the soprano's voice must leap more than an octave while traveling at high speed, about as easy as remaining upright on a jump from a moving car.)

2: The first gush of personal encounter over, the lovers at only a slightly slower pace praise the night, which has brought them together, and decry the day, which caused such miseries. Tristan complains, "Das Licht" (the light, i.e. the torch as a symbol of day). The sun went down and still there was the torch. (The continuation of this section [about 13 min.] is cut almost everywhere but Bayreuth, so that the audience loses both the philosophical and musical preamble to the later sections of the duet.) They outbid each other as to who has suffered most from day. Day, the pursuit of honor as the world conceives it, led Tristan to suggest Isolde as a bride for Marke. Day, a feeling of shame in terms of the world, led Isolde to hate Tristan whom she loved. The death potion let night conquer day within Tristan so that he could admit his love. But the death potion was really love. They hail the potion which opened their eyes to true reality. But day had its revenge, they confess, for when it is day, there is only yearning and endless longing for the night.

3: Tristan leads Isolde to a flowery bank, kneels before her and lays his head on her arm. After a short orchestral introduction, he begins, "O sink' hernieder, Nacht der Liebe" (Oh sink upon us, night of love). Extinguish day; free them from the world. "Herz an Herz dir, Mund an Mund" (heart on heart, mouth on mouth).

**Brangaene's warning**     4: As they lie beside each other, Brangaene sings from the tower where she is watching. "Habet Acht" (have a care). Night is ending.

5: The lovers murmur. Tristan does not want to wake to day. Day is death to love, but love can live in death. (There is usually a short cut here [6 or 7 min.] of the philosophical conversation.) Tristan and Isolde: "Dein und mein." They are bound by a word, "und," but can a word die? They can die but the binding power of the word cannot. (Wagner is deliberately using the rather meaningless words of the meeting in the first section to carry now his deepest meaning, thus binding the sections together.) Then Tristan begins the most familiar part of the duet: "So stuerben wir" (so let us die), "ewig einig" (always one), "ohne End" (without end), and she joins him.

From the tower Brangaene briefly warns, "Habet Acht."

6: Tristan smiles: Shall I waken? Then more seriously he adds: must the day waken Tristan? Leave the day for death, Isolde cries. Let us flee into everlasting night. She rises, Tristan following her, and they embrace (frequently they cross the stage first) beginning the final section of the duet. This is built on the music of section five with a more exciting accompaniment beneath.

It ends on a shriek from Brangaene in the tower as Kurvenal rushes in crying to Tristan to protect himself.

## SCENE 3 (27 min.)

*Tristan, Isolde, Melot and Marke:* The hunters with Marke, led by Melot, enter. They stare at the lovers. "Der oede Tag zum letzten Mal" (the dreary day for the last time), Tristan observes. Melot eagerly **Marke's address** directs Marke's eye to the lovers, and the King begins a monologue in a broken voice. (Marke's address [15 min.] is the least interesting part of the act.) A bass clarinet accompanies him. Marke observes that his own honor is not increased by Tristan's dishonor. Tristan exclaims, "Ghosts of day, morning dreams, disappear." Marke then recites all the world's counts against Tristan—favor, affection, pride and trust, all blasted by betrayal. He ends with a question: why must he who has not earned the Hell endure it without hope of Heaven when his best friend and wife betray him?

Tristan sadly and honestly replies, "O Koenig, das kann ich dir nicht sagen" (oh King, that can I not tell you); what you ask never will be answered. He turns to Isolde and asks if she will follow, "folgen," where he soon will go (death). She replies that she has already followed him to one strange land; she will again to another. Tristan kisses her on the forehead.

Melot draws his sword, urging the King to avenge his honor. Tristan observes that Melot, once a friend, has himself behaved with questionable honor. Dropping his sword, he allows Melot to wound him.

### Vocabulary, Act II

| | | |
|---|---|---|
| von Melot seid gewarnt | fon . . . side ge.vahr.nt | of Melot be warned |
| das Zeichen | dahs tseye.ken | the signal |
| mein und dein | mine oont dine | mine and thine |
| ewig | ay.vig | always |
| das Licht | dahs likt | the light |
| o sink' hernieder | o sink hair.nee.der | oh sink down low |
| Nacht der Liebe | nahkt dare leeb.uh | night of love |
| Herz an Herz dir | hairts an hairts dear | heart on heart |
| Mund an Mund | moont an moont | mouth on mouth |

| | | |
|---|---|---|
| habet Acht | ha.bet ahkt | have a care |
| so stuerben wir | so shtur.ben veer | so let us die |
| ewig einig | ay.vig eye.nig | always one |
| ohne End' | oh.nuh end | without end |
| der oede Tag | dare er.duh tahg | the dreary day |
| zum letzten Mal | tsoom lets.ten mahl | for the last time |
| O Koenig | o ker.nig | oh King |
| dass kann ich dir nicht | dahs kahn ik dear nikt | that can I not tell you |
| sagen | sah.gen | |
| folgen | fol.gen | follow |

## ACT III (86 min.; but with cuts, probably 60)

The garden of Tristan's castle in Brittany where Kurvenal has brought him in an effort to heal the wound received from Melot. The garden is on a rocky cliff overlooking the sea. To one side are turrets; on the other, a low breastwork with a castle gate to the back. "The scene," in Wagner's words, "gives an impression of absentee landlordism with the buildings in poor repair and grounds unkempt."

There is a prelude (4 min.) expressing the desolation of the place and the spiritual loneliness of Tristan. As the curtain rises, he is on a couch under a lime tree. Tending him is Kurvenal. From the distance comes the sound of a shepherd's pipe.

## SCENE 1 (54 min.)

*The Shepherd and Kurvenal:* The shepherd plays a sad tune (3 min.; on an English horn) and then, appearing over the wall, asks if Tristan is awake. Kurvenal shakes his head and remarks it is better he sleep until Isolde comes. Is there no sign of a ship, "Schiff?" The shepherd promises to pipe a merry tune, "lustig," if one appears and goes off repeating the sad tune.

*Tristan and Kurvenal:* Tristan wakes and wonders where he is, "wo bin ich?" Kurvenal excitedly explains he is in Brittany, in his own house, which he left to go to Cornwall. Tristan barely remembers, and Kurvenal (to hearty, foursquare music) reminds him of his fame and deeds in Cornwall and how he came in a ship to Brittany. But now at home, Kurvenal rejoices, Tristan will recover.

*Tristan:* He begins a monologue (11 min.), which divides into three sections (the middle one is sometimes cut). First he says he has been in the land of night and peace but not quite dead, for Isolde, still alive and in the day, pulled him back. In the middle section he dreads the longing that day will bring. Already the door back to day, almost shut, is opening and light streams in. Lastly he curses the day, "Verfluchter Tag." When will Isolde put out the torch so that his longings can cease? (This is what he must have felt waiting for her to put out the torch at the beginning of Act II, but now it has added meaning.) Exhausted, he sinks back; the light, "das Licht," when will it die?

*Kurvenal and Tristan:* Kurvenal assures him Isolde is on her way while Tristan murmurs that the light still shines. Kurvenal explains he sent a ship to fetch her. He knew that Isolde, who had cured the wound from Morold, could cure this one from Melot.

*Tristan:* "Isolde kommt" (Isolde comes), he bursts out. He tries to embrace Kurvenal, his most faithful friend, who has stood by him always, even when he betrayed Marke. There is nothing Kurvenal would not suffer for him, but he cannot know the pangs of yearning and longing. If he could only imagine them, he would be on the tower watching for the ship. Tristan imagines the ship; he almost see it, the flag at the mast; now it has crossed the bar. "Das Schiff! Das Schiff!" Furiously, he asks Kurvenal if he doesn't see the ship.

*Kurvenal:* The shepherd plays the sad tune, and Kurvenal answers that there is no ship yet.

*Tristan:* He has another monologue (11 min.), roughly in three sections (the last two are sometimes cut). The shepherd's sad tune has awakened memories in Tristan. First he recalls it sounded when his father died, "des Vaters Tod," and when he was told that his mother had died at his birth. "Die alte Weise" (the old tune) brought sorrow to them also. For what fate, "Zu welchem Los," was he born? "Mich sehnen und sterben" (for me yearning and death). In the next section he decides that "sehnen" keeps him alive to see Isolde. He thinks how he first met her, how she spared his life, how they drank the potion. "Der Trank" (the potion), he cries, is keeping him alive by having uncovered his longing. In the last section he philosophizes on the potion. He is fated for night, but everywhere the sun shines. There is no cure for his wound, love, because it burns like the sun, pressing back night. He curses the potion, "verflucht," and the man who brewed and drank it, himself. Tristan falls senseless.

*Kurvenal:* He cries out in terror, cursing love which has laid Tristan so low. He listens for a breath. There is one. No. "Er lebt" (he lives).

*Tristan:* He begins the last monologue (6 min.), which is a vision of

Isolde coming in the ship, "das Schiff." (The music starts very quietly.) He imagines the ship with her floating to shore on waves of flowers. She brings peace and release. "Ah, Isolde. Wie schoen bist du" (how fair you are). Can't Kurvenal see her? Why isn't he watching on the tower for "das Schiff"? Suddenly the shepherd's pipe sounds a merry tune.

*Kurvenal and Tristan:* Kurvenal cries, "Freude" (joy). He runs to the wall. Tristan makes him describe every inch of the ship's approach. Then it is out of sight. Perhaps lost on the reef. No. Saved. Isolde waves. Tristan orders him to go and help her. Kurvenal tells him to stay on his couch.

## SCENE 2 (11 min.)

*Tristan:* He tosses on the couch in the wildest excitement. Now he blesses the day; his blood runs faster. He must get up to join the others. (Beneath Tristan's voice the orchestra repeats a theme used in the last two sections of the duet in Act II, but now Wagner rhythmically disjoints it. Something has snapped in Tristan.) He raises himself. Once bloody and wounded, he'd gone to meet Morold; now bloody and wounded, he'll meet Isolde. He tears his bandage off the wound, laughing at the blood which gushes out. (On some theory of sparing the ladies, this stage action is often omitted or a gesture substituted, but Wagner would have scorned such bowdlerizing.) She who can cure me comes, Tristan cries.

From outside, Isolde calls his name. I hear the light, he chokes, the torchlight. It's gone out. I go to her, to her, "zu ihr." (Wagner is deliberately mixing the senses, "hearing light"; the music recalls Tristan's running to meet Isolde in Act II.)

Isolde catches Tristan as he sinks. He murmurs her name and dies.

*Isolde:* It is I, she cries. Come once again when I call. I've come to die with you. Live an hour with me, only an hour. I'll heal the wound; then we'll extinguish the light of life together. But his heart is still, "still das Herz." She is cheated of dying with him. Just once more, speak, she begs. She sinks senseless on his body.

## SCENE 3 (17 min.)

*Kurvenal et al:* He has been watching. Now the shepherd warns him of another ship. A helmsman confirms the news. (Why Wagner created a role of one line at this point is a mystery.) Brangaene calls. Kurvenal, in a frenzy, fights off Marke and his men and joyfully kills Melot. Brangaene runs to Isolde while Kurvenal, fatally wounded, crawls to Tristan's feet and dies.

Marke sadly observes that no one lives to hear the good news. But Brangaene has revived Isolde. Eagerly she tells Isolde that she has told Marke of the potion; he will free Isolde to be with Tristan. Marke confirms it but sadly observes that his coming has only increased the dead. Isolde, already in a world of her own, does not hear them.

**love-death—Liebestod**     *Isolde* (7 min.): Fixing her eyes on Tristan, she remarks how he smiles, "mild und leise" (mild and gentle). His eyes open and he rises, radiant in starlight. He speaks. Can they, too, hear it? Tristan's glorious melody surrounds and engulfs her, foretelling peace and release. Trumpet blasts sound clear and nearer; are they waves of perfume? Shall she breathe them, drink them, and finally in the depths of the world go down to the highest bliss?

She sinks to Tristan's body, and Marke blesses the dead.

### Vocabulary, Act III

| | | |
|---|---|---|
| Schiff | shif | ship |
| lustig | loost.ik | merry |
| wo bin ich | voh been ik | where am I |
| verfluchter Tag | fair.flook.ter tahg | accursed day |
| das Licht | dahs likt | the light |
| Isolde kommt | komt | Isolde comes |
| des Vaters Tod | dess fah.ters toht | of the father's death |
| die alte Weise | dee ahl.tuh veye.zuh | the old tune |
| zu welchem Los | tsoo vel.kem lohs | for what fate |
| mich sehnen und | mik sayn.en oont | for me yearning and |
| sterben | shtir.ben | death |
| der Trank | dair trahnk | the potion |
| er lebt | air leap't | he lives |
| wie schoen bist du | vee shern bist doo | how fair you are |
| Freude | froy.duh | joy |
| zu ihr | tsoo ear | to her |
| still das Herz | shtill dahs hairts | still the heart |
| mild und leise | milld oont lye.zuh | mild and gentle |

# DIE MEISTERSINGER VON NUERNBERG

## (The Mastersingers of Nuernberg)

Opera in three acts. First performed at Munich on June 21, 1868. Music and libretto by R. Wagner.

### PRINCIPAL CHARACTERS

| | | |
|---|---|---|
| Walther von Stolzing, a young knight from Franconia | tenor | VAHL.ter |
| Eva, Pogner's daughter | soprano | AY.vah |
| Magdalene, Eva's companion | soprano | |
| David, apprentice to Hans Sachs | tenor | DAH.veed |
| Veit Pogner, a goldsmith | bass | POY.nyer |
| Sixtus Beckmesser, the town clerk | bass | BECK.mess.er |
| Hans Sachs, a cobbler | bass | hahns sahks |
| Fritz Kothner, a baker | bass | |

The action takes place in and near Nuernberg about 1560.

The opera is Wagner's only comedy and one of the greatest in opera. But its comedy lies in its philosophic view of humanity rather than in any actual laughter, of which there is little compared to Rossini or Mozart. Anyone seeing it for the first time would do well to anticipate a genial romance rather than a comedy.

It is, however, the most accessible of Wagner's later operas, and it steadily and quietly made its way into the repertory, perhaps because it survived translations and cuts better than the others. Outside of Bayreuth it is invariably cut, as with intermissions it runs more than five hours.

The picture the opera gives of Nuernberg is historically accurate. Wagner studied chorales, folk songs and histories of the time, and all the Meistersinger (the word is both singular and plural) were real persons. Sachs, of course, was a well-known poet, and the chorale in Act III is set to one of his poems. At the time of the opera, the historical Sachs (1494–1576) would have been sixty-six and, as portrayed, a widower, which he remained only briefly.

Wagner does not specify Sachs' age in the opera, and some artists play him as though he were only forty or so. This pleases those who like to view the opera as a beau geste by Sachs as regards Eva in favor of Walther. These good people lay great stress on Sachs' remarks about Tristan and Isolde, and for them it is one of the great moments of the opera. Another is when Eva bursts into tears on Sachs' shoulder and he hands her to Walther. Others find this sentimental and argue that Sachs from the first says he is too old for Eva and if he didn't truly believe it, he would be ludicrous, even as Beckmesser is. In fact, the historical Sachs' second wife was forty years younger than he. Singers with make-up and acting play it first one way, then another, and the argument continues pleasantly in the intermissions.

The opera begins on the afternoon before a holiday honoring St. John the Baptist. Walther had come from Franconia on business and had spent the previous night at Pogner's house, where he met and fell in love with Pogner's daughter Eva.

## PRELUDE  (9 min.)

Although Wagner wrote the prelude before the opera, it admirably prepares the listener for the drama that follows without revealing its details. It falls roughly in four parts: first, the Meistersinger, four-square, honorable men, marching along in traditional forms; second, Walther swirling around in a glorious but unformed Prize Song; then, the Meistersinger again, but this time seen from their disapproving, pedantic and picayune side; and lastly, youth and tradition combining in a triumphant rush of sound in the finale. The listener need not fuss with this, for the strength and interplay of the thematic material succeed quite independently. In the opera the prelude merges directly into the first scene; concert performances add some closing bars.

## ACT I  (75 min.; but with usual cuts, nearer 65)

The nave of St. Catherine's church in an oblique view with only a few pews visible. To the front is the open space before the choir which is later closed off from the nave by a black curtain.

## SCENE 1  (11 min.)

*Congregation:* It sings a chorale to end the afternoon service. Walther, **chorale** leaning against a pillar, signals Eva in the last pew to remain. She returns his glances, although her nurse Magdalene nudges reprovingly.

*Walther, Eva and Magdalene:* He begs Eva for a word, "ein Wort, ein einzig Wort." Although Eva sends Magdalene back first for her kerchief and then for her pin, and then Magdalene has to fetch her prayerbook, which she left while searching for the pin, Walther only just gets his question put: is Eva a promised bride, "Braut?" Eva, just as confused, repeats the question to Magdalene, who is eager to leave before they are seen. But Walther insists, "Nein, erst dies Wort." Then because she sees David, who loves her, enter in the back, Magdalene delays.

Eva and Magdalene between them explain that Eva is promised but to a man as yet unknown—the winner of a singing contest for Meistersinger to be held the next day. "Dem Meistersinger?" Walther asks, astonished, but Eva promises to have only him. She sighs to Magdalene that he looks just like David. Magdalene thinks Eva means her David, or at least Saint David, but Eva means David who slew Goliath.

Magdalene's David announces that the Meistersinger will soon gather there to hold trials for their pupils, and Magdalene suggests that Walther try to qualify for the contest. She tells David to help him. Walther promises to meet Eva that evening and bursts out, "Neu ist mein Herz" (new is my heart). Eva joins him while Magdalene urges her to leave.

## SCENE 2 (16 min.)

*Apprentices:* They gather to erect a stage for the examination and make sly remarks at David, who prefers supervising to work.
*David and Walther:* David has been appraising Walther and suddenly calls out, "Fanget an" (now begin). Walther is astonished, and David explains, "so ruft der Merker" (so calls the Marker). "Wer ist der Merker" (who is the Marker)? Walther asks, revealing he knows nothing about the Meistersinger. David asks if he has ever qualified as a poet, a singer, a school friend or even a scholar. But Walther knows none of the categories, and David sighs "O Lene, Magdalene." David, **David's instruction** enjoying his knowledge, starts to instruct Walther in mastersinging. He does so in seven parts, each with a comment by Walther.

1: He explains he has worked twelve months with Sachs learning the cobbler's craft and also all about words and syllables. Walther observes David ought at least be able to make a good pair of shoes.

2: He briefly describes the stanza used by the Meistersinger in terms of the cobbler's craft. "Hilf Gott!" Walther exclaims: more of singing and less of cobbling.

3: He lists the phrases and tones the Meistersinger use for special colors, flowers, fruits and trees. Walther cries, "Hilf Himmel."

4: He describes the arts of singing, breathing, pronunciation and coloratura. He warns Walther to heed the lesson, for before he can be a Meistersinger, he must be a singer and a poet.

The apprentices call to David to help them as Walther asks what may be a poet if all this is only a singer.

5: David explains: a poet makes up his own words and rhymes but uses another's tune.

The apprentices accuse David of endless chattering as Walther asks who is a Meister.

6: David defines a Meister as one who can create both the words and music.

Walther bursts out that with God's help he will create a mastersong, and David scolds the apprentices for setting up the stage for a singing school rather than an examination. They joke at what a good teacher David has become.

(David's instruction is lengthy, and a usual cut is from the middle of Part 3 to Part 5 or 6. The cut and the following twenty-five minutes are the least exciting in the act and are the moments, if such there must be, to nod.)

7: David advises the apprentices to save some laughter for Walther, who will try to create a mastersong that afternoon. Turning back to Walther he points out the slate, "Die Tafel," on which the marker, the examiner, chalks the mistakes; only seven, "sieben," are allowed. He wishes Walther success.


### SCENE 3 (48 min.)

*Pogner and Beckmesser:* They are the first of the Meistersinger to arrive. Pogner is telling Beckmesser of his plan for the contest and Beckmesser points out that if Eva can refuse the winner on personal grounds, the winner may win nothing. Pogner remarks that if Beckmesser is uncertain of Eva's affection, he shouldn't compete.

*Pogner, Walther and the Meistersinger:* Walther greets Pogner and states that he wants to be a Meistersinger. Pogner is complimented and agrees to introduce him to the others. Beckmesser is at once suspicious.

Kothner calls the roll, and all are present except one who is ill. Then **Pogner's address** Pogner addresses them. He recites that the morrow is a holy day with a festival in the meadow outside of town and prizes for competitions. He knows that throughout most of Germany the burghers such as he are said to be interested only in gold, and to show his interest in art he offers with all his goods "Eva mein einzig Kind" (Eva, my only child).

He ignores the murmurs of approval to add that, of course, Eva must agree. Beckmesser grumbles that there is no point then to singing, but Pogner explains that she must choose a Meistersinger or no one.

Sachs suggests that instead of the Meistersinger, the people, "das Volk," decide the contest, since they are more likely to pick a man acceptable to Eva. But none approve of the people, a wild lot. Sachs, however, adds that it might be good to forget the rules once in the year. But opinion runs against him.

Pogner then introduces Walther, and all the Meistersinger except Beckmesser are pleased he wants to join them. They ask Walther to describe his experience and teacher.

**aria** Walther in an aria, "Am stillen Herd" (by quiet hearth) sings in three stanzas that in the winter he studied from a book, in the summer his school was the woods, and now he will try to offer them a mastersong. The Meistersinger interrupt each verse with gloomy comments, but they agree to let him try. Walther rejects a biblical subject in favor of love.

Beckmesser goes to the Marker's box. He explains to Walther that he will chalk up faults on the slate; seven, "sieben," disqualify the singer. He then enters the box and draws the curtain.

Kothner explains the group's aesthetic theories. (This aria with its coloratura for a bass is occasionally cut, probably not so much to save **aria** time as the expense of hiring a good bass to do one aria.) Each stanza, "Bar," must consist of two "Stollen," sung to the same melody, and an "Abgesang," sung to a different melody. (This is explained more fully at the end of the synopsis.)

Walther is unnerved when told he has to sing sitting—"Hier in den Stuhl?" (here in the chair)—but it is the custom. Kothner calls "Der Saenger sitzt" and from behind the curtain Beckmesser orders "Fanget an."

Walther repeats the "Fanget an," using it as a motive for his song:
**aria**  so cried the spring throughout the land as winter hid away.
There is a constant sound of chalk on a slate. Walther begins the
second stanza "Doch fanget an" (his heart too heard the cry). But
before he is barely started, Beckmesser emerges with his slate filled.

All but Sachs agree that Walther has failed. Sachs would let him
finish. Beckmesser attacks Sachs for a fool who'd let the rabble set the
rules, to which Sachs replies that Beckmesser is one candidate for Eva's
hand and should not mark another. Beckmesser furiously suggests that
Sachs get on with his cobbling, as he is behind on the shoes which
Beckmesser ordered.

While the rest rehearse Walther's faults, Sachs urges him to finish
if only to irritate the Marker. Pogner, starting to suspect why Walther
attempted to become a Meistersinger, begins to regret the contest for
Eva's hand. The apprentices, sensing a fiasco (*See* Glossary), begin to
sing and laugh. In the hubbub Beckmesser takes a count and all but
the musing Pogner and Sachs vote to fail Walther. Walther contemptuously runs from the church, and the Meistersinger slowly follow him;
Sachs, however, remains behind for a moment, musing on the song.

### Vocabulary, Act I

| | | |
|---|---|---|
| Die Meistersinger | dee MY.ster.sing.er | the Mastersingers |
| ein einzig Wort | eye'n eye'n.tsik vort | a single word |
| Braut | browt | bride |
| nein, erst dieses Wort | nine airst deez.es vort | no, first this word |
| neu ist mein Hertz | noy ist mine hairts | new is my heart |
| fanget an | fahn.get AHN | begin then |
| so ruft der Merker | so rooft der MAIR.ker | so calls the Marker |
| wer ist der Merker | vair ist | who is the Marker |
| Hilf Gott, Himmel | hilf got him.el | help, God, Heaven |
| die Tafel | dee tahf.el | the slate |
| sieben | SEE.ben | seven |
| Eva, mein einzig Kind | mine eye'n.tsik kint | Eva, my only child |
| das Volk | dahs follk | the folk |
| am stillen Herd | ahm shtill.en hairt | by quiet hearth |
| Bar | bahr | stanza |
| Stollen | SHTOE.len | interior divisions of stanzas |
| Abgesang | AHB.ge.sang | |
| hier in den Stuhl | here in den shtool | here in the chair |
| der Saenger sitzt | der SENG.er sits | the singer sits |

ACT II (61 min.; but with usual cuts, nearer 50)

Evening the same day. A street runs across the front of the stage, intersected at the center by a narrow alley winding toward the back. To the right is Pogner's house, rather grand with a lime tree before it. To the left is Sach's house and shop with an elder tree. It is a summer twilight and, during the first scene, night gradually falls. There is a short prelude and, as the curtain rises, David and the apprentices are shutting the windows on the alley.

## SCENE 1 (4 min.)

*Apprentices, David and Magdalene:* The apprentices sing of "Johannistag," St. John's day, which they will celebrate in the morning. From the steps of Pogner's house Magdalene signals across the alley to David, who pretends not to see her. The apprentices advise him to be less stuffy, for she has a basket of food. She wants to know how Walther fared at the trial, and David reports that he failed. Magdalene, discouraged, pulls the basket out of David's reach and retires as the apprentices laugh at his cold reception. When they begin to joke that his Lene is a little old for him, he loses his temper. He is threatening to cuff them when Sachs arrives, dismisses the apprentices and takes David in to close his shop.

## SCENE 2 (6 min.)

*Pogner and Eva:* They come down the alley after a stroll, Pogner wondering if his offer of Eva's hand was wise, and she thinking of Walther. He asks for her thoughts, "Und du mein Kind" (and you my child), but she replies evasively that children should speak only when spoken to. Tenderly he remarks, "wie klug, wie gut" (how sensible, how good). He sits under the lime and she joins him, nervous and anxious, as he inquires her feelings about the morning "wenn Nuernberg" will gather in the meadow to sing for her hand. "Lieb Vater," she asks, "muss es ein Meister sein" (dear father, must he be a meistersinger)? Pogner assures her he must. Magdalene calls them into dinner and, as Eva is plainly surprised that Walther has not been invited, Pogner for the first time realizes her interest in Walther. Magdalene and Eva linger behind, and Magdalene reports that Walther failed.

Eva decides to ask Sachs what happened. But after supper, Magdalene advises, adding that she has a message. From Walther? No, Beckmesser. But Eva cares so little, she doesn't wait to hear.

## SCENE 3 (7 min.)

*Sachs and David:* Sachs has David place a cobbler's bench under the elder and then sends him off to bed. The scent of the elder, "der Flieder so mild, so stark und voll" (the elder so sweet, so sturdy and full) sets his mind on poetry. But he reminds himself that work, "Arbeit," must come before poetry, "Poetrei." And he cannot forget Walther's song. It was old yet new, a song of the birds, a command from spring, "Lenzes Gebot," as if Walther himself was a bird, "dem Vogel," taught by Nature.

## SCENE 4 (10 min.)

*Eva, Sachs and Magdalene:* He starts work again as she comes across the alley to greet him, "Gut'n Abend, Meister." He asks if she has come about her new shoes, "die neuen Schuh," and she confesses that she hasn't yet tried them. He remarks that she will wear them in the morning as a bride, "Braut," and she, hoping to hear about Walther, asks if he knows who the groom will be. But Sachs answers evasively, and she grows impatient. He remarks that he is working on shoes for Beckmesser, who hopes to win her; there aren't many bachelors free to compete. Softly she asks, "Koennt's einem Wittwer nicht gelingen" (could not a widower succeed)? But Sachs discounts himself as too old, although the thought had crossed his mind. She still cannot get Sachs to talk of Walther, and in her irritation she tell Sachs he is fuddled. Drily he admits it; an event at the examination has filled his mind. He describes it, and Eva learns that Walther failed.

Magdalene calls, but Eva ignores her. Was it a hopeless failure? It was, Sachs observes; not one was for him. Eva proudly asserts that Walther will prove his worth in spite of the Meistersinger and Hans Sachs and abruptly leaves to join Magdalene. Sachs, who has learned more than Eva, watches her go, remarking to himself that now he will have to help her get what she wants. He withdraws into his shop from whence, unobserved, he can watch the alley.

Magdalene tells Eva that Beckmesser plans to serenade her that night. Eva who expects Walther any minute is unimpressed. She suggests that Magdalene stand at the window in her place, and Magdalene, thinking that David might see her being serenaded by someone else, agrees. Pogner calls and Magdalene is pulling Eva indoors when Walther comes.

## SCENE 5 (8 min.)

*Eva and Walther:* Eva rushes to him, declaring that in spite of the examination he is a poet, a hero, her only friend. He despairs of winning her, but she promises to be his. He reminds her, "Ein Meistersinger muss es sein. Doch diese Meister" (but all these Masters)! he bursts out bitterly. He suggests they elope, swearing that he cannot endure any more of the Meistersinger (often partly cut).

The Nightwatchman's horn sounds, and Walther reaches for his sword. Eva soothes him, telling him to hide under the lime tree as the watchman passes, while she goes into the house for a minute.

The Nightwatchman announces, "die Glock hat zehn geschlagen" (the bell has struck ten) and blows his horn loudly (Wagner scored it deliberately off key).

Sachs from his shop murmurs that no good will come from an elopement and that he must prevent it. Eva comes out in Magdalene's cloak, and she and Walther are about to start up the alley when Sachs shines a light directly across it. "O weh! Der Schuster" (oh woe! the cobbler), Eva gasps. They retire to the lime and are discussing what to do when Beckmesser comes up the alley, tuning his lute for the serenade. When Walther realizes it is "der Merker," he is for strong measures, but Eva fears it will wake her father. So they remain hidden to wait out the serenade.

## SCENE 6 (21 min.)

*Sachs and Beckmesser:* Beckmesser tunes the lute and prepares to sing, when *thwack!* Sachs starts cobbling. He has moved his bench to the door of the shop and is flooding the street with light. He starts a loud, **cobbling song** hearty song about the kind God who sent an angel to make shoes for Adam and Eve, who were stubbing their toes on the rough ground outside the gate of Eden. Beckmesser is frantic and pleads with Sachs to forget about the shoes even though they are for him. (Sachs' song is in three verses; frequently the second is cut. Each starts, "Jerum, Jerum," a hey-nonny-nonny.)

At the end of the song Magdalene appears at the window in Eva's dress. Beckmesser first begs and then threatens Sachs to be quiet. Sachs soberly insists that Beckmesser will complain if the shoes aren't ready in the morning. The only solution is for the cobbling and the serenade to proceed together—Beckmesser singing and Sachs "marking" with his hammer. In desperation Beckmesser agrees. (This is a long section and often as much as eight minutes is cut, although in bits and pieces.)

Sachs calls "Fanget an," and Beckmesser starts. (The serenade is in three verses with the second often cut.) Sachs finishes the shoes before Beckmesser does the serenade, and the noise wakens the neighborhood. David sees Beckmesser serenading Magdalene and rushes out to assault him. All the neighbors and apprentices join in the free-for-all.

## SCENE 7 (5 min.)

The tumult grows until the entire town is in the alley, pushing and pulling at each other. Sachs puts his bench in the shop and watches Eva and Walther who are increasingly afraid they will be discovered. As they start down the alley, hoping to get by in the confusion, the Nightwatchman blows his horn. Everyone starts to scatter. Pogner seeing a girl whom he believes to be Magdalene calls to her to come in. Sachs separates Walther and Eva, pushing her towards Pogner and dragging Walther into his shop. The alley quickly clears and, when the Nightwatchman arrives, it is empty: "die Glock hat elfe geschlagen" (. . . struck eleven). He blows the horn off key, and the full moon uncovers, shining brightly down the alley.

### Vocabulary, Act II

| | | |
|---|---|---|
| Johannistag | yoh.HAHN.is.tahg | St. John's Day |
| und du mein Kind | oont doo mine kint | and you my child |
| wie klug, wie gut | vee klook vee goot | how sensible, how good |
| wenn Nuernberg | ven nerrn.berg | when Nuernberg |
| lieb Vater | leep faht.er | dear father |
| muss es ein Meister sein | moos es eye'n . . . sine | must he be a Master |
| der Flieder | der FLEED.er | the elder tree |
| so mild, so stark und voll | so milld . . . shtark oont foll | so sweet, sturdy and full |
| Arbeit | AHR.bite | work |
| Poeterei | poe.et.er.RYE | poetry |

| | | |
|---|---|---|
| Lenzes Gebot | lents ge.BOHT | spring's command |
| dem Vogel | dem fohg.el | the bird |
| gut'n Abend, Meister | goot'n AH.bent | good evening |
| die neuen Schuh | dee noy.en shoo | the new shoes |
| Braut | browt | bride |
| koennt's einem Wittwer | kernts eye.nem vit.ver | can a widower not |
| nicht gelingen | nikt ge.LING.en | succeed |
| doch diese Meister | dok deez.eh | but all these Masters |
| die Glock | dee glock | the bell |
| hat zehn geschlagen | haht tsain ge.SHLAH.gen | has struck ten |
| o weh, der Schuster | o vay der SHOO.ster | oh woe, the cobbler |
| der Merker | der MAIRK.er | the Marker |

## ACT III (128 min.; but with cuts, closer to 90)

### PRELUDE (8 min.)

It pictures Sachs grieving over the folly of humanity but with resignation rather than sarcasm or bitterness. It opens with a phrase for cellos later taken up by violas and violins. Then the brass sound part of the chorale with which the townspeople later greet Sachs. Isolated phrases of the cobbling song rise high in the violins; the brass return with more of the chorale; and the prelude closes with the first phrase again on the strings. Wagner described it as "a massive expression of the perturbation of a profoundly-stirred soul."

### SCENE 1 (16 min.)

Sachs' shop. To the back a door leads to the street; on the left a window looks out on the alley; and to the right a door leads to his house. Sachs is in a chair by the window reading a large book as David enters from the street with a basket of food decorated with ribbons and flowers.

*David:* He fears a reprimand for his part in the riot and sneaking in begins to prattle an explanation: an apprentice can't always behave, Magdalene had rebuked him before the other apprentices, and when he saw her at the window being serenaded, he just naturally attacked the man. Sachs, lost in his thoughts, does not hear, and David thinks he must be very angry. In a fright he begs, "Ach Meister! Sprecht doch nur ein Wort" (speak only a word).

*Sachs and David:* Sachs, still musing, closes his book and for the first time sees David with the basket beribboned and flowered. Softly he inquires what the decorations are for. David reminds him that it is a holiday in honor of St. John the Baptist. Sachs asks him to sing his song in honor of St. John, and David begins, but to the tune of Beckmesser's serenade, and has to stop and start again. "Am Jordan Sanct Johannes stand . . ." (St. John stands on the Jordan . . .).

The song describes a Nuernberg mother who took her child to the Jordan to be baptized. The boy was named Johannes but when he returned to the Pegnitz, Nuernberg's river, he was called Hans. Excitedly David bursts out that it is Sachs' name day too. He offers Sachs his basket of food, urging him to compete for Eva and observing that the town thinks Beckmesser will not compete if Sachs does. Sachs sends David off to dress for the competition and is left alone musing.

**monologue** *Sachs:* The monologue divides roughly into three parts, the universal folly, the folly of Nuernberg, and what Sachs can do about it.

1: "Wahn! Wahn! Ueberall Wahn" (folly, everywhere folly)! In vain has he searched in books for the explanation of it, a reason for the struggles and rages of men against each other. They get nothing from it; yet strife is constant, never long subdued.

2: Last night in Nuernberg to prevent a folly of youth, an elopement, a cobbler unwittingly let loose a maddened population in the streets, kicking and clawing at each other. "Gott weiss, wie das gaschah" (God knows how that happened). After a pause Sachs decides it must have been a goblin, "ein Kobold," or a glowworm looking for his mate. Perhaps it was the elder tree, "der Flieder war's," on "Johannisnacht" (St. John's eve). "Nun aber kam Johannistag" (but now comes St. John's Day).

3: He wonders how he can turn the folly to some purpose.

### SCENE 2 (20 min.)

*Sachs and Walther:* Walther appears from Sachs' house and, after they greet each other, Walther remarks that he had a beautiful dream. Sachs suggests that he use it to win the prize, Eva. Walther sees no hope in singing, but Sachs urges him to try again: the Meistersinger may be mistaken, but they are not dishonorable (often cut). He goes on to explain that art is more than mere youthful passion; every man is a poet in his youth. Walther softly breaks in "ich lieb ein Weib" (I love a woman). Then use your art to win her, Sachs urges. He promises to take down Walther's words, leaving him free to think only of the dream (often cut).

Walther begins "Morgenlich" (in the morning) and stops at the end of a long phrase. "Das war ein Stollen," Sachs comments (that was a **the dream, verses 1 and 2**      Stollen). He tells Walther to make another just like it. "Warum ganz gleich?" (why just alike) Walther asks. To make it plain that instead of being single you wish to be married, Sachs answers. Walther then sings another Stollen, and Sachs tells him to add an aftersong, "Abgesang." He explains this to Walther as the child of the two Stollen, alike yet different. Sachs is moved by Walther's "Abgesang" but warns him that his melody is very free.

Walther sings a second verse of two Stollen and an Abgesang without interruption. It begins "Abendlich" (in the evening).

Sachs urges him to do a third but, as Walther is growing impatient, does not press him. Instead Sachs leads Walther into the house to dress for the contest.

## SCENE 3 (15 min.)

*Beckmesser:* He enters and has three minutes of mime during which he acts out his frustration, the humiliation of the night before, his hopes for Eva, his fears of Walther, and his despair at being unable to compose a good song. Finally he sees Sachs' draft of Walther's dream and at once suspects that Sachs intends to compete for Eva and deliberately **aria**      spoiled the serenade the previous night. When at that moment Sachs enters, Beckmesser in a rage recites all his complaints against Sachs, beginning with the ill-fitting shoes. He ends by accusing him of planning to woo Eva. Sachs denies it, and Beckmesser produces the draft. Sachs offers it to him, and Beckmesser is overjoyed. He explains (often cut) that he is too upset to compose his own. He proposes the song be a gift of peace between them. But, still suspecting, he makes Sachs promise never to claim the poem as his own. Sachs warns him, however, that it will be hard to sing and will need careful study. Beckmesser protests his admiration for Sachs and blames Walther for misleading him (often cut). He departs, promising to buy all of Sachs' poems and to support him for "Merker." Sachs is left musing on the malice of the man.

## SCENE 4 (22 min.)

*Sachs, Eva, and Walther:* Eva enters, and Sachs compliments her on her dress. She complains, however, of her shoe which pinches, and he, knowing she wants news of Walther, pretends to be unable to find the trouble until Walther enters. Then he takes the shoe off to one side and grumbles at the cobbler's lot (often cut) as the lovers gaze at each **the dream, verse 3** other. He adds that lately he heard a song that lacked a third verse. Walther sings it as Sachs comments to Eva after the Stollen: "das ist ein Meisterlied" and "that is the kind of singing there is in my house." During the Abgesang he fits the shoe and asks if it still pinches.

Eva bursts into tears on Sachs' shoulder, but he withdraws leaving Walther to support her. To cover his emotion he chatters about the trials of being a cobbler: everyone complains about the shoes, wants help with his wooing, yet calls the cobbler dull and foolish (often cut). Eva stops him with a cry, "O Sachs. Mein Freund" (my friend). He has been everything to her. What good there is in her he nurtured through her childhood. If love had not robbed her of choice, she would give him the prize. He replies, "Mein Kind, von Tristan und Isolde" (my child, of Tristan and Isolde I know), and would not play the role of Marke.

He calls in David and Magdalene and announces that a mastersong has been created in the shop and must be named. He and Eva are godparents but two witnesses are needed. As an apprentice cannot be a witness, he makes David a journeyman with a light blow on the ear. He names the song "The Morning Dream" and asks the godmother to speak an appropriate word for it.

**quintet** Eva begins the quintet. She sings of her coming happiness of which the song contains the secret; Walther, that love inspired the song and will win him his heart's desire; Sachs, that he must conceal his personal pain and rejoice that love will triumph through the poet's prize. David and Magdalene rejoice at the change in his status that will let them now get married.

At its close they all leave for the meadow.

## SCENE 5 (47 min.)

The scene shifts to a meadow by the Pegnitz with Nuernberg in the distance. There is no break in the music, which builds (3 min.) a festive atmosphere with many horn and trumpet calls. To the right is a platform for the Meistersinger, surrounded with the banners of the various Guilds already arrived. The burghers and journeymen watch the Guilds arrive while the apprentices act as marshals and heralds. *The Guilds:* First come the shoemakers. Then the tailors, who recite a story of a tailor who once raised a siege of Nuernberg by sewing himself in a goatskin and being taken by the enemy for a devil. They bleat in his honor. Then come the bakers. Only the Meistersinger are left to come.

*The Apprentices:* They start a dance and urge David to join them. At first, conscious of his new status, he refuses, but he soon gives in, although he hesitates when they twit him that Magdalene is watching. *The Meistersinger et al:* The Meistersinger come in a procession. Pogner leads Eva to the seat of honor. When each is at his place, the marshals call, "Silentium" (silence). As Sachs, who has been chosen the speaker for the day, comes forward, the entire assembly honors him with a chorale (the words were written by the historical Hans Sachs to greet Luther and the Reformation).

*Sachs:* Much moved, he thanks them. Then (often cut) he explains that Pogner has offered Eva and a dowry as a prize to the winner of a song contest held before all the folk. (It is most unfortunate that this speech is often cut and, worse, not printed in most librettos. In it Sachs deliberately blurs the rules of the contest by constantly mentioning the folk so that the folk will feel they have some say in the contest and the Meistersinger will hesitate to decide against popular opinion.) Pogner recognizes the probable effect of Sachs' speech and thanks him. (To persons unaware of what has been cut, he seems overeffusive.) Sachs remarks to Pogner that it was a bold move, but they will not fail. He turns to Beckmesser (often cut) and asks if he has the song by heart. Beckmesser complains that the song is impossible and Sachs has deliberately tricked him. He begs Sachs to use his favor with the crowd to help him.

*Beckmesser:* Kothner calls to him as the eldest contestant to begin. Beckmesser comes forward and complains that the singer's stand is rickety. The crowd murmurs that Eva will surely refuse him. Kothner calls "fanget an," and Beckmesser nervously twangs his lute. He gets the song all wrong: "my beauty steaming, faster dreaming," instead of "the air with beauties teeming, past all dreaming," etc. The crowd begins to laugh, softly at first and then outright. Beckmesser furiously leaves the stand and shouts curses at Sachs, saying it was Sachs' song and foisted on him. He runs off into the crowd.

*Sachs and the Crowd:* He explains that he did not write the song. He insists (often cut) that it is a good song and needs only its author to sing it. The crowd murmurs its disbelief. To clear his name, Sachs asks permission to call as a witness the song's author, who will sing it. (Thus he gives Walther, who doesn't qualify to sing in the contest, a chance to be heard.) The Meistersinger, who now recognize what is going on, exclaim, "Ah Sachs, you're very sly; today though we'll pass it by."

*Walther:* He sings the Prize Song as the crowd murmurs its ap-
**Prize Song**    proval. (It is not exactly like the morning dream, but each verse starts with the former's music and then varies it. The verses begin "Morgenlich," "Abendlich" and "Huldreichster Tag," which explains the poet's vision of Paradise and Parnassus set forth in the first two verses. Some productions and librettos cut the second verse.)

The crowd urges Eva to proclaim Walther the winner, Pogner thanks Sachs, and all the Meistersinger urge Pogner to make Walther a Meistersinger by giving him the symbolic chain with medallion. Eva places the wreath on Walther's head, but when Pogner advances, Walther refuses the chain. All are disconcerted and look to Sachs.

*Sachs:* He takes Walther's hand and tells him not to scorn the Meistersinger but to honor their art, which has won him Eva. He expounds on how the Guild has kept German art holy and pure from foreign thoughts and ways. (The speech has occasionally offended non-Germans, who feel that such chauvinism is out of place in art. Newman reports that Wagner was for cutting it, but his wife Cosima, a German by adoption, insisted that he keep it. Wagner's theatrical instinct was sound. The speech to most non-Germans is long, so obviously untrue it is silly and, worst of all, a bore.)

In the final chorus Eva takes the wreath from Walther's head and places it on Sachs', and Sachs, taking the chain from Pogner, hangs it round Walther's neck. The Meistersinger and the people meanwhile hail Sachs as their leader.

## Vocabulary, Act III

| | | |
|---|---|---|
| Ach Meister | ahk MY.ster | alas, Master |
| Sprecht doch nur ein Wort | shprek dok noor eye'n vort | speak only a word |
| am Jordan Sanct Johannes stand | an . . . shtahnnt | on the Jordan St. John stands |
| Wahn! Wahn! ueberall Wahn! | vahn . . . oo.ber.ahl | folly, everywhere |
| Gott weiss, wie das geschah | got vice vee dahs ge.shah | God knows how that happened |
| ein Kobold | eye'n KOH.bohlt | a goblin |
| der Flieder war's | der FLEED.er var's | it was the elder tree |
| Johannisnacht | yo.HAHN.is.nahkt | St. John's eve |
| ich lieb ein Weib | ish* leep eye'n vibe | I love a woman |
| Morgenlich | MOR.gen.lik | in the morning |
| das war ein stollen | das var eye'n SHTOE.len | that was a stollen |
| warum ganz gleich | vah.room gahnts glike | why just alike |
| Abgesang | AHB.ge.sang | aftersong |
| Abendlich | AH.bent.lik | in the evening |
| Merker | MAIRK.er | Marker |
| das ist ein Meisterlied | dahs ist eye'n my.ster.leed | that is a mastersong |
| O Sachs, Mein Freund | mine froynt | my friend |
| mein Kind, von Tristan und Isolde | mine kint fon . . . | my child, of Tristan and Isolde I know |
| Silentium | see.lent.ee.uhm | silence |
| fanget an | fahn.get AHN | begin |
| Huldreichster Tag | hoolt.rike.ster tahg | hallowed day |

* Ish or ik depending on the South or North German accent of the singer.

Since the opera is about song, the form of song plays an unusually large part in it. The Meistersinger imagined a song as follows: the entire song would consist of three stanzas or "Bar." A stanza is a number of verses grouped so as to compose a pattern that is repeated in the song. An individual stanza was composed of three rhetorical units, each being several verses long. The first two, called Stollen, were musically and in rhyme identical. The last, almost twice as long and called an Abgesang, was different but related. The aesthetic theory was that the singer stated his melody, repeated it so that the audience grasped it, and then varied it.

A number of the arias fit the form. The first and easiest to follow is Walther's aria in Act I explaining his background, "Am stillen Herd."

His actual test song also follows the form but on such a vast scale that it appears to be formless. Beckmesser's serenade is perfect in form. Walther's first two stanzas of the dream that he sings to Sachs are almost perfect. The actual Prize Song is freer. Some say the entire opera is cast in the form: the first two acts are Stollen, identical in that both, for example, end with a riot leaving a single man on stage; the third act, as the Abgesang, reconciles the traditionalists and the proponents of free form.

The text of the song was to consist of a vision or conceit presented in the first Stollen and then repeated in a different guise in the second; the two were then to be combined and explained in the third—as morning, evening and the significance of the day; or, in the Prize Song, a vision of Eve in Paradise, of the muse of poetry on Parnassus and of both merging to become Eva.

# DER RING DES NIBELUNGEN
## (The Ring of the Nibelung)

*The Ring* complete, or any of the individual operas, with the possible exception of *Die Walkuere,* is not for the casual operagoer. All the operas are long; even *Das Rheingold,* short by comparison, compensates for that by playing to the end without intermission. All the operas have dull stretches lasting sometimes more than half an hour. To make these rough places plain requires considerable work: reading at least two books in addition to the libretto and spending several hours at the piano or victrola. If the operagoer does not care to put in that time or has not done so, he would do better to stay home, even if offered free seats.

The work would be well rewarded, however, for *The Ring* is possibly the most awesome, imposing masterwork of the nineteenth century in any form. Because of it Wagner has been compared to Aeschylus and Michaelangelo. The comparisons are too complimentary. *The Ring* at its close produces no new concept of justice or guilt such as the *Oresteia* nor does it have the artistic unity of the Sistine ceiling. But its defects are as interesting as its glories, and to be completely ignorant of *The Ring* is to be poorly educated, ignorant of what a great man thought on an important subject and as poor as those who have never considered Plato's Cave.

No short synopsis can do justice to *The Ring*. Most synopses simply move the characters on-and-offstage without any attempt to discuss what the opera is all about. And either it *is* about something or else, as many say, it is a windy bore, ineptly put together and best approached through orchestral excerpts in the concert hall from which the words and thoughts have been removed. In the outline below the story is told briefly; Wagner's allegory of the evolution of man towards a better world is suggested in this preamble and the parentheses thereafter. *Die Walkuere,* the most popular of the four operas and the only one presented independently with any frequency, is also given an independent synopsis (*See* p. 380) in which it is treated as a story without philosophic pretensions, the way most operagoers undoubtedly see and hear it.

*The Ring* technically consists of three operas and a prelude, *Das Rheingold;* everyone except pedants, however, calls it a tetralogy. After *Das Rheingold* the operas in order are *Die Walkuere, Siegfried* and *Goetterdaemmerung.*

Wagner conceived of the universe at the time his drama begins as containing the usual stars, rocks, rivers, primitive man of no account, and three other orders of humanity—dwarfs, giants and gods. The gods were neither omnipotent nor even omniscient; they were merely the most attractive of the three orders, all of which were struggling to make themselves comfortable and powerful in a hostile world.

When Wagner through his chief god, Wotan, conceives of a higher, better order than dwarfs, giants or even gods, it is man as the hero. The idea of man in any form being a higher development than the gods is a conception that could only be taken seriously at certain times in history, as for example the nineteenth century, the Renaissance or in Athens in the fifth century B.C. The Middle Ages could not have grasped the concept and the twentieth century, remembering its gas chambers and race riots, doubts it. This is one reason for the decline in popularity of *The Ring;* its basic concept is at the moment incomprehensible or at least out of fashion.

In the universe of *The Ring* the three orders are dramatizations of kinds of men or of three strains within an individual man, and Wagner uses the story to talk about man as he existed in nineteenth-century Europe. The giants are lazy, nonintellectuals who want money merely to make themselves comfortable—a ranch-type house with a TV set and money in the bank (Wagner talking). The dwarfs are more complicated: they want power and, looking at the giants, they realize that money is the way to get it. Deep in the earth Alberich, the head dwarf, mines gold, forcing hundreds of other dwarfs to work for him. Bernard Shaw saw Alberich as a typical capitalist. The gods are the intellectuals, the only ones troubled by ideas of what is fair or just and who, in order to carry out the ideas, devise institutions and laws to settle disputes and to bring an order into the jungle of life.

The principal characters by opera are:

| | Das Rheingold | Die Walkuere | Siegfried | Goetter-daemmerung |
|---|---|---|---|---|
| THE GODS | Wotan Fricka Loge | Wotan Fricka Bruennhilde | The Wanderer (Wotan) Bruennhilde | |
| NATURE OR FERTILITY SYMBOL | Erda | | Erda | |
| RHINEMAIDENS | Rhinemaidens | | | Rhinemaidens |
| THE GIANTS | Fafner Fasolt | | The Dragon (Fafner) | |
| THE DWARFS | Alberich Mime | | Alberich Mime | Alberich |
| THE HEROES | | Siegmund Sieglinde | Siegfried | Bruennhilde Siegfried |
| COMMON FOLK | | Hunding | | Gunther Gutrune Hagen |

Wotan is the chief god, Fricka his wife. Erda is sometimes called a goddess, but she neither dwells on Wahlhall (Valhalla) with the others nor shares their interest or fate; and, throughout, she has a special role. The Rhinemaidens are sui generis, perhaps distant cousins of the gods.

The Walkuere (Valkyries) are nine daughters of Wotan and Erda; Bruennhilde is one. She starts life as a god but ends it as a human or hero, although which is one of the arguable points in *The Ring*.

Alberich and Mime are brothers and members of the Nibelung family; hence the tetralogy's title refers to Alberich, who made the ring.

Of the heroes, Siegmund and Sieglinde are twin brother and sister, children of Wotan by some nameless lady of no account. Siegfried is the son of the twins and Wotan's grandson.

Of the common folk, Hagen is Alberich's son by the mother of Gunther and Gutrune. Hunding is married to Sieglinde. He is the only character in all four operas whose actions at least on stage are always decent and honorable. Wagner treats him like dirt.

Some of the confusion about *The Ring* can be cleared up by examining the order in which the librettos and the music were written. The librettos were written backwards; the music forwards but with a long gap in the middle during which Wagner wrote *Tristan und Isolde* and *Die Meistersinger*. The dates necessarily are approximate, as he kept making small changes.

| Librettos | Music |
| --- | --- |
| *Goetterdaemmerung* (first called *Siegfried's Death*) 1845 | *Das Rheingold* 1853–54 |
| *Siegfried* (first called *Young Siegfried*) 1851 | *Die Walkuere* 1854–56 |
| *Die Walkuere* 1852 | *Siegfried*, Acts I and II, 1856–57 |
| *Das Rheingold* 1853 | (*Tristan und Isolde*, 1857–59) |
| The entire poem was printed privately in 1853 and publicly with a few changes in 1863. | (*Die Meistersinger*, 1861–67) |
| | *Siegfried*, Act III, 1869 |
| | *Goetterdaemmerung*, 1869–74 |

A glance at the list of principal characters shows that *Goetterdaemmerung* is peopled almost entirely with common folk and heroes; there are no gods and no giants. This was the libretto with which Wagner started and, if taken as a single opera, the bulk of it is not very different from Wagner's *Der Fliegende Hollaender*. There is an attractive man under a curse, Siegfried, who is redeemed after death by a great love of a woman, Bruennhilde. This is the stuff of romantic opera, and Bernard Shaw used to irritate Wagnerites by stating that *Goetterdaemmerung* wasn't a music drama at all but an old-fashioned opera.

As Wagner worked his poem backward from *Goetterdaemmerung*, he began to see all sorts of philosophic and allegoric meanings in the action. These he refined and polished, so that for persons interested in the allegory, the discussion of the evolution of man and the problem of evil, *Das Rheingold* is the best of the librettos. It sets the problem clearly and with a wealth of consistent detail. But most persons find the music which was written first less interesting and exciting than that of *Goetterdaemmerung*. The opera with the best balance is generally conceded to be *Die Walkuere*.

Why did Wagner stop at the end of Act II of *Siegfried* and turn to *Tristan und Isolde?* The best answer seems to be twofold: first, he was excited by the idea and music of *Tristan* which flooded his mind; and second, after four librettos and two and two-thirds operas, as his biographer Ernest Newman conjectures, he was just plain tired of *The Ring.* Shaw, who loved the allegory more than the old-fashioned opera, grieved that Wagner, when he came years later to write the music for *Goetterdaemmerung,* had lost his interest in the allegory and did not prune and revise the libretto to reflect the allegory as he had developed it in the earlier operas, i.e. the later librettos. Many persons disagree with Shaw and feel that Bruennhilde's immolation is the only conceivable ending: out of the ashes of her great love will rise a world freed of evil, for only love can conquer evil. Newman concedes that the ending is intellectually disappointing but argues that it is musically satisfying; in trying to continue the allegory with the character of *Goetterdaemmerung,* Wagner may have faced an artistic problem that was insoluble without rewriting the four operas. Within the range of these views each operagoer must take up his own position.

## DAS RHEINGOLD

### (141 min.) (The Rhinegold)

### SCENE 1 (The bottom of the Rhine—23 min.)

Three Rhinemaidens sport around a rock which cradles a lump of gold, the Rhinegold. A dwarf, Alberich, approaches with propositions of love, and they first tease and then deny him. Suddenly the sun strikes through the water and lights up the gold. Alberich asks what it is, and they explain that it is a magic lump which, if made into a ring, would give the possessor power over all the world. But only a man who has forsworn love can forge the ring and that man, they laugh, is clearly not Alberich. Thwarted in love, however, he seizes the gold, renounces love forever and runs off to forge the ring. (Deprivation of affection leads to juvenile delinquency and violence or, on a more philosophic level, a denial of love is the fundamental cause of evil.)

### SCENE 2 (An open space on a mountain—45 min.)

The gods are asleep. As the sun rises, Fricka wakes her husband, Wotan, and points to Wahlhall which the giants have built for the gods. It is a grand castle, and in return for it the gods have agreed rather vaguely to give the giants Freia, the goddess of youth and love. The giants—two of them—lumber on stage to collect their pay, and Wotan who does not want to lose Freia casts around for some acceptable substitute. But the giants insist on their contract. Loge, the god of fire, suggests that perhaps the giants would take gold instead of Freia. They agree, provided that the gold is enough to conceal Freia completely from their sight; in the meantime, however, they take Freia as a hostage. Wotan and Loge leave to find Alberich who, having forged the ring, has forced all the dwarfs to mine gold for him.

(Wotan has one eye; the other he gave up to marry Fricka. He represents man at his freest and noblest; she represents law and institutions. Man gives up something when he agrees to live in society and abide by law. When the gods want to abrogate the contract they have with the giants, they begin to talk, which is standard intellectual procedure—free trade, but special preference to certain nations, or the Bill of Rights for all citizens except, or the United Nations for all nations but. In the end they persuade the giants to settle for gold, which the gods can procure only by a crime—theft. In Wagner's cosmos the gods, the highest order, are not yet willing to renounce the passion of "me first" to keep evil out of the world.)

### SCENE 3 (Alberich's mine—23 min.)

Alberich has tyrannized the other dwarfs and forced his brother Mime to make him a magic helmet, which allows the wearer to become invisible. Wotan and Loge arrive and Alberich taunts them that soon he will be rich enough to subvert the world. To show off his power, he puts on the helmet and turns himself first into a serpent, then into a toad. Wotan steps on the toad; Loge rips the helmet off; and the two gods lead the dwarf back to the mountain.

### SCENE 4 (The open space on the mountain—40 min.)

Wotan makes Alberich pile gold in front of Freia and, as the last bar is put on, the giants claim they can still see Freia. So Loge throws on the magic helmet but still, through a tiny chink, they can see her hair. They suggest Wotan put on Alberich's ring, but he refuses. Then Erda (variously called by critics the goddess of wisdom, the first mother, or Earth) appears and warns Wotan that he must give up the ring, so he adds it to the pile, but with poor grace. The giants release Freia and fight between themselves over the gold until Fafner kills Fasolt. Fafner then goes off with the gold, turns himself into a dragon, and sits on it. The gods cross a rainbow to their new castle as the sound of the Rhinemaidens wailing over their stolen gold reminds Wotan that the castle is built on a crime.

(*Das Rheingold* sets the problem of the drama. The three orders— dwarf, giant and god—are set in conflict by a denial of love which lets evil into the world. The drama then evolves from the efforts of the most intelligent, Wotan, to rid the world of evil which constantly burgeons. First there was Alberich's theft of the gold, then Wotan's theft of the ring, and finally the murder of one giant by another. All the orders are equally involved. Each man, then, *is* his brother's keeper and equally responsible, whether rich or poor, upper or lower class, for poverty, disease, backward nations, evil, etc. Fafner is typical of most men, who will trade youth and love for money for which they have no use except to guard fiercely like a dragon.)

Between *Das Rheingold* and the next opera, *Die Walkuere*, Wotan broods on the problem of evil. To protect the gods against assault by the giant who has the ring or by Alberich, if he should regain it, Wotan has sired by Erda nine daughters, the Walkuere, of which Bruennhilde is his favorite. They collect fallen warriors and take them to Wahlhall, where they feast and form a defensive army for Wotan. To rid the world of evil, Wotan plans to raise a new order of humanity—a hero who will be free of all taint inherent in being either a dwarf, a giant or a god. This hero will kill the giant and return the ring to the Rhinemaidens, thereby breaking the ring's power for evil and also preventing Alberich from regaining it. Wotan explains this in his long narrative to Bruennhilde in the second act of *Die Walkuere*. In order to produce the hero, Wotan lived on earth for a while with a human wife by whom he had two children, Sieglinde and Siegmund. At an early age the girl was carried off and married to one of the common folk, Hunding. The boy, Siegmund, was trained by Wotan to be a superb physical specimen—a hero. Then Wotan disappeared leaving Siegmund, he hoped, to retrieve the ring and to rid the world of evil. At this point *Die Walkuere* begins.

## DIE WALKUERE

### (The Walkuere)

### ACT I (Hunding's hut—61 min.)

Siegmund bursts into the hut to escape from a storm. He explains to Sieglinde that he has been in a fight and lost his sword. The two, who do not recognize each other as brother and sister, fall in love. Hunding enters, recognizes Siegmund as the man who has been harassing Hunding's kin and challenges him to fight in the morning. Meanwhile, under the laws of hospitality, Siegmund is welcome in the hut. After Hunding goes to bed, Sieglinde shows Siegmund a sword left by Wotan stuck in a tree. He pulls it out, she recognizes him as her brother and savior, and they run away together.

### ACT II (On a rocky height—87 min.)

Wotan is pleased, for Siegmund evidently is developing into the fearless man or hero who will be able to kill the giant and return the ring to the Rhinemaidens. He tells his daughter Bruennhilde to let Siegmund defeat Hunding. But at that moment Fricka appears. Hunding has called to her for justice, and the gods must support their laws without exception. She recites all the laws Siegmund has broken and demands he be punished. Wotan is forced to give in even though it means abandoning his plan to rid the world of evil. As Fricka points out to him, it was his plan, conceived and aided by him, and therefore tainted. (Fricka, symbolizing law and institutions, understands nothing of Wotan's grander plan. She sees only that Hunding has correctly filed his complaint, has a cause of action, and must receive justice according to precedent and the gods' own ordinance.)

Wotan, in a long monologue, explains to Bruennhilde his plan which Fricka has just blasted with her logic and orders Bruennhilde now to protect Hunding. (This is one of the moments persons interested only in the fairy tale of *The Ring* find extremely dull; for those interested in the allegory, it is one of the most crucial and moving moments in the four operas.) Bruennhilde grasps Wotan's plan; if not completely, at least emotionally she understands its importance to him, and later, in the fight between Siegmund and Hunding, she disobeys Wotan and protects Siegmund. Wotan arrives, furious at her disobedience, lets Hunding kill Siegmund, and starts off in pursuit of Bruennhilde, who has fled with Sieglinde.

(The conflict between Fricka and Wotan is the eternal one of the ends and means or, viewed differently, of the state or individual having to work through laws or institutions devised by a previous generation and which no longer fit the pattern of daily experience. Thus General Billy Mitchell is the revered and honored prophet of the air age in the United States, yet the Army court-martialed him for expressing his views.)

## ACT III (A rocky height—72 min.)

**the ride of the Walkuere**     The Walkuere gather; Bruennhilde comes last with Sieglinde and tells her that she will bear Siegmund's child, Siegfried. She urges Sieglinde to flee into the forest and hide from Wotan while she stays to face him. Wotan's anger terrifies the other Walkuere, who leave. Bruennhilde explains her disobedience as an act of love. She knew that Wotan in his heart loved Siegmund and wished to save him. Wotan brushes that aside. He cannot save the world by any plan; the best he can do is to enforce the laws in effect. He sen-
**fire music**     tences Bruennhilde to sleep on a rock until a man awakens her. He agrees to surround her with fire that only a hero will dare to pierce.

(The farewell between father and daughter is extremely moving because Wagner made it so very human. Some argue the allegory loses throughout by Wagner's humanizing the gods too much, and that if he was going to write an opera, he should have done so and cut out the monologues.

(Bruennhilde's plea of love is that of every radical and is rejected by every state and institution because it fears that an exception will undermine its authority. General Mitchell *had* to be court-martialed. All visionaries are feared, prophets dishonored, and poets declared insane. In banishing Bruennhilde, Wotan recognizes that he is banishing part, perhaps the best, of himself. It is the part of intuitive love; henceforward, he will be a shell or institution, the church and the state, without any quickening spirit. Bruennhilde, however, being the part of Wotan that is love, will be saved for Siegfried, who was conceived in love; they, representing the new man, the hero, may be able to redeem the world. In this last act Wotan, the god, realizes that for the hero to come, the gods must pass away, a mere phase in the evolution to a higher order. When he next appears, Wagner calls him "The Wanderer," not "Wotan," and gives him a passive and resigned personality.)

————

By the beginning of the next opera, *Siegfried*, the hero is born and is a strapping young man. (Wagner intended him to represent the culmination of man in his natural state, uncorrupted by society or its institutions. Siegfried is the descendant and heir of Rousseau's Noble Savage, the French Revolution, and the hopes and beliefs of radicals in Europe that the common man, given the chance, would be able to fashion a better society. This was revolutionary doctrine at the time, and Wagner intended it as such. But it is a different concept from that of the founding fathers of the American revolution, who viewed man as a thoroughly imperfect creature needing in his government the most carefully contrived checks and balances. This latter was more of an eighteenth-century view of man. Wagner's view was much more Marxian and of the nineteenth century. For him man was perfectible, and the state need only wither away. Dramatically it is curious that Siegfried, as Wagner drew him, is not an attractive character.)

Siegfried lives with Mime, a dwarf and brother of Alberich. Sieglinde fled into the forest and was taken in by Mime, who raised Siegfried after Sieglinde died in childbirth. Mime remembers Alberich's power with the ring and covets it for himself; he also knows that only Siegfried can kill the giant, Fafner, who has turned himself into a dragon and sits on the gold. Mime hopes to be able to use Siegfried to retrieve the ring for him just as Wotan had hoped to use Siegmund. The difference is that Wotan, the intellectual, wanted to redeem the world from evil; Mime wants merely to be powerful and rich. Each, representing the old order or establishment, hoped to subvert the new political force to strengthen his position; in the end each is destroyed by it.

## SIEGFRIED

### ACT I (A cave in the forest—76 min.)

Siegfried despises Mime and enjoys terrifying him. He makes Mime promise to forge him a sword, but the dwarf cannot make one that Siegfried cannot break. He knows that the only sword that will withstand the boy's blows will be one made from the pieces of Siegmund's sword, but he cannot forge them himself nor can he imagine who will be able to. At that point Wotan, the Wanderer, enters and tells Mime that Siegfried will forge the sword. (Wotan's position now is one of disinterested observer. He recognizes that Siegfried, as a higher form of evolution, will do away with them all.) Siegfried returns, forges the sword, splits the anvil with it, and rushes off to seek adventure, specifically to kill Fafner, the dragon. (Fafner, through his love of money, has gone backwards in evolution.) Siegfried has no interest in the gold; he hopes the dragon will teach him fear, the only thing Mime has that Siegfried can't understand.

## ACT II (In the forest—68 min.)

Outside the dragon's cave lurks Alberich, hoping somehow to retrieve the ring. The Wanderer appears and warns both Alberich and the dragon that Siegfried is coming. Siegfried arrives and to the dragon's great surprise slays him easily. Mime and Alberich, who have been watching, quarrel furiously over the gold which they have not yet got and hide when Siegfried comes out of the cave. He licks some of the dragon's blood off his fingers and thereby is able to understand the birds. One warns him that Mime will try to poison him, and when Mime appears with a cup, Siegfried cuts off his head. Then advised by the bird, he sets out to find Bruennhilde, a wife for himself and another adventure.

It is here that Wagner stopped in 1857 and did not resume until 1869.

## ACT III

### SCENE 1 (At the foot of Bruennhilde's rock—30 min.)

Wotan consults Erda about how to avert the doom of the gods' world and learns that there is no way. The new order can come only on the passing of the old. Wotan exclaims that he doesn't care anymore, and Erda disappears.

Siegfried comes on and tells Wotan to get out of the road. He is so rude that Wotan has a surge of the old passion and threatens him. Siegfried smashes the old man's spear, the symbol of his authority. Wotan slowly collects the pieces and passes out of *The Ring*. The new order is at hand. (Those who like the allegory feel that with this scene it ends and that Wagner in what remains rises or descends, depending on the point of view, into the purely operatic.)

### SCENE 2 (Bruennhilde's rock—42 min.)

Siegfried passes through the fire and awakens Bruennhilde with a kiss, and they soar off into a typical love duet in which she is at first hesitant and then joins him. (Parsimonious producers sometimes allow

Siegfried's kiss to extinguish the fire as well as awaken Bruennhilde. This is wrong; the fire burns continuously around the rock. Siegfried must pass through it again in *Goetterdaemmerung*.)

---

The time of the action of *Goetterdaemmerung* is soon after *Siegfried*. But the cast of characters and scenery are so different that it seems like a different world. Much of the action takes place in the hall of the Gibichungs, a bewildering step forward in domestic architecture from Hunding's hut built around a tree trunk. Equally astounding is the transformation of Bruennhilde and Siegfried. He is no longer the young, noble savage but a sophisticated knight of the world; she is a typical proud princess raging with jealously and plotting murder. Clearly the concept of man as a higher order of evolution has been discarded or, as the librettos were written backwards, not yet conceived. The Gibichungs, in whose hall much of the action takes place, consist of Gunther, King of the area; Gutrune, his sister; and Hagen, his half brother. Gunther and Hagen shared the same mother, but Hagen's father was Alberich, the dwarf, and his loyalty is all to his father, not his brother. The mother is dead.

## GOETTERDAEMMERUNG

### (The Twilight of the Gods)

### PROLOGUE (At Bruennhilde's Rock—40 min.)

Three Norns, Norse fates, sit outside a cave in which Bruennhilde and Siegfried are asleep. The Norns spin and predict the doom of the gods after reciting everything that has led up to the present moment. The strand of destiny parts and the Norns sink into the earth to join Erda. (Already the old order passes and, as Siegfried will control his **dawn or daybreak** own destiny, the fates no longer have a function and pass away.) After dawn comes (orchestral interlude), Bruennhilde and Siegfried come out of the cave. As proof of her love, she gives him her horse; he gives her the ring he took from Fafner. They embrace and he starts down the Rhine Valley in search of adventure.
**Siegfried's Rhine journey** The prologue connects without break to Act I by a seven-minute orchestral interlude, known as Siegfried's Rhine journey. The concert hall version, not following an impassioned

duet, starts with a drum roll and adds an additional four minutes of music at the beginning. This consists almost entirely of themes associated with Siegfried and Bruennhilde and in the opera is the orchestral interlude accompanying dawn. Thus the concert version is correctly entitled "Dawn and Siegfried's Rhine Journey."

## ACT I (74 min.)

### SCENE 1 (The hall of the Gibichungs—41 min.)

Hagen suggests a bride would enhance Gunther's fame in the Rhine Valley; specifically he suggests Gunther marry Bruennhilde. He describes her lying encircled by fire; only a hero named Siegfried can win her. But Hagen has a plan, which he offers to Gunther and Gutrune. They will drug Siegfried so that he forgets his past. When Siegfried arrives, Gutrune offers him the drink and he takes it, forgetting Bruennhilde and beginning to love Gutrune. Then Gunther describes Bruennhilde circled by fire, which he confesses he cannot penetrate although he wishes her for a bride, and Siegfried offers to win her for Gunther. Then Hagen tells Siegfried of the helmet's magic power to transform the wearer into anything he wishes, and Siegfried, who was unaware of the helmet's power, proposes to pierce the fire disguised as Gunther.

### SCENE 2 (Bruennhilde's rock—33 min.)

From Wahlhall comes one of Bruennhilde's sisters, Waltraute. She begs Bruennhilde to give the ring back to the Rhinemaidens and thus save Wotan and the other gods from perishing. (This is inconsistent with Wotan's remarks earlier to Erda and with the pattern of the allegory, which is that the gods are beyond saving, and Wotan knows this.) Bruennhilde refuses to help the gods. (Her rejection of Wotan is in a manner so out of hand and brutal that she clearly is a different person from the Bruennhilde of *Die Walkuere*.) Waltraute departs in despair.

Siegfried comes through the fire, announces he is Gunther and tears the ring from her finger. He drives her into the cave and prepares to spend the night with his sword between them as a symbol for Gunther that he has not dishonored the bride.

ACT II (On the shore in front of the Gibichung's hall—65 min.)

Alberich appears to his son, Hagen, in a dream and urges him to gain the ring from Siegfried. He urges Hagen to hate and lust for power, and Hagen promises. Alberich disappears; soon dawn comes and with it Siegfried. He has left Gunther to bring Bruennhilde down the river and has journeyed ahead to see Gutrune. Hagen assembles the vassals to announce Gunther's marriage, and they greet their king as he steps ashore with Bruennhilde. (This is the only chorus in *The Ring*.)

When Bruennhilde sees Siegfried who, still under the influence of the drug, does not recognize her, she almost faints with despair and confusion. Then she notices the ring on his finger and begins to realize that he must have come through the fire disguised as Gunther. She is convinced of it when the real Gunther reveals by his confusion that he knows nothing about the ring.

Bruennhilde insists that she is Siegfried's wife and that the marriage has already been consummated. Siegfried denies it. Bruennhilde then accuses him of betraying Gunther by forcing her love during the night just passed. (This is either a lie, or Siegfried lied to Gunther. In any event the allegory about the heroes has dwindled into all too human deceit.) Siegfried swears on a spear that Bruennhilde lies, and she swears that he lies. He laughs and, saying that he cannot stay around to bicker with a woman, goes off with Gutrune. Bruennhilde, Hagen and Gunther plot "Siegfried's Tod" (Siegfried's death). (This was the original title of the opera, and the phrase is whispered twice in the crucial scene of the opera. At this point the characters call on Wotan, a distant and impersonal god. The gods as characters are retired.) Bruennhilde reveals that Siegfried can be killed only by a wound in the back, and they plan to kill him on a hunting party.

## ACT III (85 min.)

### SCENE 1 (A wooded place on the Rhine—53 min.)

The men are out hunting, but Siegfried has become separated from the main party. The Rhinemaidens call to him to return the ring, but he refuses. They warn him of death, and he replies that he is unafraid. They disappear.

The hunting party comes up and stops for a rest. Siegfried talks of his early life with Mime, and Hagen gives him a drink that restores his memory. To the horror of the vassals and Gunther, Siegfried describes how he first went through the flames to waken Bruennhilde and marry her. As Siegfried turns to watch two ravens, Hagen spears him in the back. Siegfried sings a farewell to Bruennhilde, dies, and is borne on a shield by the hunters back to the hall of the Gibichungs.

**Siegfried's funeral march**    There is no break between this scene and the next as an orchestral interlude known as Siegfried's Funeral March (7 min.) covers the change. The concert-hall version of it runs almost twice as long and includes, without the voice, the music of Siegfried's farewell to Bruennhilde as he is dying.

SCENE 2 (The hall of the Gibichungs—32 min.)

Gunther lies to Gutrune that Siegfried was killed by a boar, but she accuses Gunther of murdering him. Gunther blames Hagen and, in a fight, is killed. Hagen turns to the corpse to pull the ring from Siegfried's hand, but the corpse's fist clenches and rises against him.

Bruennhilde enters. She orders Siegfried laid on a pyre, lights it, sings of her love for him and, mounting her horse, Grane, rides into the flames. The hall collapses; the Rhine overflows, allowing the Rhinemaidens to retrieve the ring. Hagen drowns. In the background Wahlhall, home of the gods, burns; in the orchestra the "great theme of Redemption by love" soars out.

(Musically the scene is a success; intellectually it seems contrived and irrelevant. Shaw was very scornful of the panacea of sexual love, which he felt was dragged in by Wagner as a sure-fire ending for the middle-class audience. And it is true that the great lovers of history have all headed for a bungalow by a lake and let the world go hang without fussing much about the problems of evil and evolution. Sexual love is an essentially selfish emotion.)

# DIE WALKUERE

Music drama in three acts. First performed at Munich on June 26, 1869. Music and libretto by R. Wagner.

### PRINCIPAL CHARACTERS

| | | |
|---|---|---|
| Siegmund | tenor | |
| Sieglinde | soprano | |
| Hunding, Sieglinde's husband | bass | |
| Wotan | baritone or bass | VOE.tahn |
| Bruennhilde | soprano | BROON.hild |
| Fricka | mezzo-soprano | |

The action takes place in mythological times in the north country.

*Die Walkuere* has always been the most popular of the four operas in *The Ring,* and at present the discrepancy in the number of performances between it and the others is increasing. If the trend continues, it may soon become the only one produced on a repertory basis.

There are a number of explanations for its popularity, not all musical. It is easier to cast than either *Siegfried* or *Goetterdaemmerung:* the tenor part, for example, is considerably shorter and not so difficult, and the role of Bruennhilde has a lower tessitura (*See* Glossary) than the one in *Siegfried.* Of the four operas *Die Walkuere* has the least complicated plot and the emotions of the characters are simple and easily grasped; there is not the amnesia of *Goetterdaemmerung* or the musically difficult business of fear of *Siegfried.* Also, it portrays its characters, particularly Siegmund, exhibiting their most attractive qualities; the young Siegfried, on the other hand, is hard to love. Musically it is clearly stronger than *Das Rheingold* and relies far less than the succeeding two operas on musical reference to what has gone before; unless the musical references in *Goetterdaemmerung* are understood, the opera inevitably seems windy.

Persons going to a performance of *Die Walkuere* as an independent opera, not part of a *Ring* cycle, need not fuss with the larger implications. Of course the opera is richer if they do, but they need not. It is sufficient to know that there are gods and heroes; that through the heroes the gods, who are not omnipotent, hope to banish evil from the world by returning a stolen ring to the Rhinemaidens; that the gods abetted the original theft and, so, are themselves morally flawed; and that the heroes, to succeed, must do so independently, uncontaminated by help from the gods. As the opera begins, the hero is about to act independently and embroil the gods in a dilemma that requires Wotan, the chief god, to sacrifice both his daughter whom he loves and the hero whom he also loves. Such, says Wagner, is the effect of evil in the world.

For those who find this view of life too pessimistic to be faced, the opera can be enjoyed on a lower level of purely human emotions— love, fear, death, and farewell. The music is magnificent.

## ACT I (61 min.)

There is a short (3 min.) prelude depicting a storm in the forest and culminating in a tremendous roll of thunder on the drums followed by lightning. (Music invariably reverses the order of nature and has thunder precede lightning, probably because, as thunder is easily imitated and lightning is not, the latter is recognizable only by association with something that has gone before.)

## SCENE 1 (12 min.)

As the storm ends, Siegmund bursts into a wooden hut built round the trunk of a huge ash tree.

*Siegmund and Sieglinde:* He enters, exclaims "hier muss ich rasten" (here must I rest) and sinks exhausted on the hearth. Sieglinde, thinking it is Hunding, comes out and is attracted by the stranger. Raising his head, Siegmund gasps "ein quell! ein quell" (a drink). While he drinks, they gaze at each other (cello solo) and he asks with interest who she is. "Diess Hause und diess Weib sind Hundings eigen," she replies (this house and this woman are Hunding's own). "Waffenlos bin ich" (weaponless am I) and wounded, Siegmund states, wondering whether Hunding will welcome him. Sieglinde offers to tend his wounds, but he makes light of them, and instead she gives him a drink of mead. He offers it to her first, and then the two gaze at each other. (Throughout the scene there are tiny orchestral interludes, much admired by musicians, in which love develops.)

Siegmund breaks off, remarking that misfortune, "misswende," pursues him and he must leave. "So bleibe hier" (then stay here), she insists, where misfortune already is. I call myself "Wehwalt" (woeful) he states, adding that he will wait for Hunding. Again they gaze at each other, and then Hunding's music sounds—massive, foursquare music on the deep brass.

## SCENE 2 (18 min.)

*Sieglinde, Hunding and Siegmund:* Sieglinde explains that she found Siegmund lying exhausted on the hearth and has given him some mead. Hunding observes to Siegmund: "Heilig ist mein Herd: heilig sei dir mein Haus" (sacred is my hearth: sacred be my house to you). Then taking off his armor he tells her to serve dinner. He notices a resemblance between his wife and the stranger and decides in an aside that he does not like the man. But still he asks Siegmund politely how and whence he came. Siegmund confesses that the storm confused him, and he doesn't know where he is. Hunding identifies himself and his kinsmen and asks for Siegmund's name in return. Siegmund remains for a minute lost in thought, and Hunding, seconded by Sieglinde, repeats the request.

Siegmund begins his narrative. (It divides in three parts, each closing with a comment by Hunding and Sieglinde. It runs about twelve minutes and is the least interesting part of the act.)

1: His name is not "Friedmund" (peaceful) but "Wehwalt" (woeful). His father's name was Wolfe; his mother was killed and his sister disappeared when he was very young. Thereafter, he and his father lived and hunted in the forest. Hunding comments that he has heard of them; Sieglinde urges Siegmund to continue.

2: One day their traditional enemies (the orchestra sounds Hunding's music) fell on them, and they were separated. He never found any trace of his father except a wolf skin, "den Vater fand ich nicht." He left the forest and tried to ally with other people, but always some argument or feud drove him out. Hunding comments that the Norns (the Fates) have been unkind; Sieglinde asks about the most recent fight.

3: He heard "ein trauriges Kind" (a sad child). Some brothers, "Brueder," were forcing their sister to be a bride, "Braut." He killed all the brothers, but then, as "Wund und waffenlos stand ich" (wounded and weaponless stood I), others of her kinsmen killed the girl. He escaped. But his name is not "Friedmund" (peaceful).

Hunding announces that it was his kinsmen Siegmund killed. He states that according to the rules of hospitality Siegmund is welcome for the night; but tomorrow, "morgen," they will fight. He orders Sieglinde to prepare a nightcap and watches her go about it. She tries with her eyes to indicate to Siegmund a sword sunk in the ash tree. Hunding gestures her into the bedroom and, remarking that a man should be armed "mit waffen," follows her.

## SCENE 3 (28 min.)

(Throughout this scene and the end of the last, the sword theme, a typical trumpet call, sounds on various instruments.)

*Siegmund:* His father had promised him a sword, "ein Schwert," in his hour of greatest need. Now he is "waffenlos" in an enemy's house. He has seen a woman, "Weib," who excites him. He calls to his father by a name he did not reveal, "Waelse, Waelse. Wo ist dein Schwert" (Waelse, where is your sword)? The fire flares, and the sword handle gleams, but the sparkle reminds him of Sieglinde's eye, and he does not see the sword. Instead he sings of her.

*Siegmund and Sieglinde:* She returns, explaining that she has drugged Hunding and has come to show him a weapon, "eine Waffe." She recounts how at her wedding an uninvited guest drove the sword into the tree saying it was for the man who could pull it out. None could, and she, married to Hunding against her will, realized that the man who could would deliver her from Hunding. Ecstatically she declares Siegmund to be the man. They embrace.

Siegmund promises to deliver her and rejoices that she is everything he has sought.

Suddenly the outside doors fly open. It is a spring night with full moon. Startled, Sieglinde asks who went out; Siegmund replies that spring, "der Lenz," came in.

**aria**    He sings to her of spring and love as brother and sister. Spring came to love to free her, and so they are one.

"Du bist der Lenz" (you are the spring), she exclaims, thawing a heart congealed by a loveless marriage.

They begin an extended love duet. (At the time he composed it, Wagner believed that as in real life persons did not speak at the same time, so on stage they should not sing at the same time. Consequently, the voices never overlap. Later Wagner discarded the theory.) Sieglinde begins to recognize Siegmund's face and the sound of his voice, but she cannot place them. "Du bist das Bild" (you are the image) he had in his heart, Siegmund insists. "O still" (hush), she stops him, trying to remember. "Wehwalt" are you called, and "Friedmund," she muses, and was "Wolfe den Vater?" That was what his enemies called him, Siegmund acknowledges, but his real name was "Waelse." She is astounded and recognizes him now as her brother. She cries that the sword was for him and names him "Siegmund." He starts up, repeating it, grasps the sword handle and exclaims that now he needs it. He names the sword "Nothung" (needed) and pulls it out. With this sword he will free her to follow spring and love. But if you are Siegmund, I am Sieglinde, she cries: he has won the sword and sister together. "Braut und Schwester" (bride and sister) she can be to him; the children of Waelse forever. They rush out into the forest.

## Vocabulary, Act I

| | | |
|---|---|---|
| hier muss ich rasten | here moos ik* RAHST.en | here must I rest |
| ein quell | eye'n kvel | a drink |
| diess Haus und diess Weib sind Hundings eigen | deez hows oont deez vibe sint eye'gen | this house and woman are Hunding's |
| waffenlos bin ich | vahff.en.losh been ik* | weaponless am I |
| Misswende | miss.vend.eh | misfortune |
| so bleibe hier | so bly.beh here | then stay here |
| Wehwalt | vay.vahlt | woeful |
| heilig ist mein Herd | hile.ik* ist mine hairt | sacred is my hearth |
| heilig sei dir mein Haus | hile.ik* sigh deer mine hows | sacred be my house to you |
| Friedmund | freed.munt | peaceful |
| den Vater fand ich nicht | den fah.ter fahnt ik* nikt | the father found I not |
| ein trauriges Kind | eye'n trow.rig.es kint | a sad child |
| Brueder | brood.er | brothers |
| Braut | browt | bride |
| wund und waffenlos stand ich | voont oont vahff.en.lohs shtahnnt ik* | wounded and weaponless stand I |
| morgen | MOR.gen | tomorrow |
| ein Schwert | eye'n shvairt | a sword |
| Waelse | vale.seh | the family name |
| wo ist dein Schwert | vo ist dine shvairt | where is your sword |
| der Lenz | der lents | the spring |
| du bist das Bild | doo bist das bilt | you are the image |
| o still | oh shtill | oh hush |
| nothung | NO.toong | needed |
| Braut und Schwester | browt unt shvest.er | bride and sister |

* Ik or ish depending on the North or South German accent of the singer.

ACT II (87 min.; but with usual cuts, closer to 76)

There is a short (2 min.) prelude depicting the flight of the lovers and introducing Wotan and Bruennhilde. The scene is a wild, rocky gorge.

### SCENE 1 (19 min.)

*Wotan and Bruennhilde:* Wotan calls to her to let Hunding die in the
**the war cry**     fight but not to bring him to Walhall, "nach Walhall." She gives her battle cry, hojo-to-ho, warns him that Fricka is approaching, and withdraws. ˙
*Wotan and Fricka:* He fears a scene but prepares to stand up to her: "Doch stand muss ich hier halten." She has heard Hunding's cry for vengeance and has sworn to punish the lovers. Wotan expresses surprise; they have only followed spring, "der Lenz." But they have broken the marriage oath, "heiligen Eid," she insists. He characterizes an oath that binds in a loveless marriage as "unheilig." Worse than the broken oath, she observes, is the incest, "Schwester und Bruder." Wotan makes light of it. They love each other, and she should bless the bond.

At this point Fricka begins her dialogue with Wotan. It falls in four parts:

1: She accuses him of breaking his own laws to benefit his children. She wails over his past infidelity, bad enough, but this is the worst.

2: He responds "Nichts lerntest du" (you have learnt nothing). The gods must raise a hero who, free of their help and laws, will save them from the curse of the ring. She accuses him of trying to fuddle her with talk. Siegmund is not the hero. He was born of Wotan, raised by him and lastly armed by him with "das Schwert" (the sword). Her logic defeats him.

3: He asks, "was verlangst du" (what do you demand)? She retorts "Lass' von dem Waelsung" (abandon the child of Waelse). He must also order "die Walkuere" not to shield Siegmund, for otherwise Bruennhilde will do what she knows Wotan secretly wishes. Wotan breaks out that he cannot fell Siegmund, who found his sword. Then destroy its magic, she replies. Bruennhilde approaches.

4: Fricka demands from Wotan an oath on it, "von Wotan den

Eid." In despair he gives it, "Nimm den Eid." Fricka leaves, telling
Bruennhilde to hear her new orders.

### SCENE 2 (28 min.)

*Bruennhilde and Wotan:* She tries to console him as he observes that he
is bound by his own fetters. "Goetternoth" (the despair of the gods),
he cries. "Vater," she begs, what is the trouble? If he tells her, he remarks, he will lose some of the power of his will. She denies it, for
she is merely an instrument of his will. Wotan then begins his narrative;
it falls in four parts. (Most operagoers find it dull. It lasts, uncut, about
twenty-one minutes; with cuts, closer to twelve minutes.)

1: He recounts how he cheated Alberich of the ring and used it to
pay the giants who built Walhall, how Erda prophesied doom for the
gods, and how he fathered the Walkuere so that they might bring
heroes to Walhall to protect the gods.

Bruennhilde remarks that the Walkuere were doing that and so there
is nothing to fear.

2: But, he continues, there is another threat. If Alberich can obtain
the ring (the usual cut is from here to just before "das Ende" in 3), he
will be able by its power to subvert the heroes. Therefore, Wotan must
get the ring first. Fafner, a giant, has it by agreement with Wotan, who
must honor the agreement. He had hoped to raise a hero who, free of
Wotan's will, would kill Fafner and return the ring to the Rhinemaidens.

That is Siegmund, Bruennhilde interjects.

3: Wotan repeats Fricka's arguments. The moral curse of the
stolen ring has followed him, Wotan despairs. He cannot fashion anything but a slave. So you let Siegmund die? Bruennhilde gasps. There
is nothing to do but wait for "das Ende" (the end of the gods). Erda
prophesied (a usual cut is from here to just before Wotan's bequest
at the end of 3) that if Alberich, who forswore love to steal the ring,
begot a child, the gods would soon fall. And now rumor states that
Alberich with gold has bought a woman's love and fathered a child.
Furiously Wotan bequeaths the world to the child of hate.

Confused and alarmed, Bruennhilde asks what she should do.

4: Wotan orders her to fight for Fricka; there is nothing else to do.
Bruennhilde protests: "Zurueck das Wort" (take back the word);
"Du liebst Siegmund" (you love Siegmund). But he orders her to aid

Hunding. She refuses, and Wotan thunders at her. As he leaves, he orders, "Siegmund falle" (strike down Siegmund)! "Dies sei der Walkuere Werk" (this be the Walkuere's task). He strides out.

Bruennhilde goes slowly off, musing on his anger and grieving over Siegmund. "Weh, mein Waelsung" (woe, my child of Waelse).

## SCENE 3 (12 min.)

*Sieglinde and Siegmund:* He calls to her to stop running. But "weiter! weiter!" (further), she insists. "Nicht weiter," he says, catching and trying to calm her. She is her brother's bride, "Braut"; "Siegmund is der Gesell" (Siegmund is your mate).

She rests for a moment and then wants to push on. She wails that her life with Hunding has made her impure, dishonored. She should leave Siegmund. Again he soothes her, promising that Hunding's death will wipe out any dishonor; therefore, let them stay for him.

Sieglinde starts again; she hears Hunding's horns. The clan has gathered; she can hear the hounds baying. For a moment she stares blankly. "Wo bist du, Siegmund?" (where are you); then she collapses, sobbing, on his chest. But again she hears the horn, "das ist Hundings Horn!" She imagines the dogs attacking. "Siegmund, wo bist du?" she cries in terror. A sword is no defense. The hounds will tear his flesh, drag him by the feet. She sees him falling. "Bruder, mein Bruder! Siegmund!—ha———." She faints. "Schwester! Geliebte!" (sister, beloved), he calls. He sits, holding her head in his lap.

## SCENE 4 (19 min.)

*Siegmund and Bruennhilde:* She watches him as he gazes at Sieglinde; then she calls to him. "Wer bist du, sag" (who are you, say), he asks. She replies that she is death's image and who sees her must die. Siegmund gazes steadily at her and then asks where she takes the dead. "Nach Walhall" (to Walhall), she states. "In Walhall's saal" (in Walhall's hall), he asks, whom will he find? The heroes; and Wotan's daughter, "Wotan's Tochter," will fill his cup. Then he asks if "Bruder" and "Schwester" will go together, and she replies that Siegmund will not find Sieglinde there.

Siegmund looks at Sieglinde, kisses her gently and turns to Bruennhilde: "so gruesse mir Walhall, gruesse mir Wotan, gruesse mir Waelse" (then greet for me Walhall, etc.). Then he states firmly that he will not go.

Bruennhilde replies that he has no choice: he has seen death. Hunding will strike the blow. Siegmund shows her his "Schwert"; it will win. She denies it and tells him that the magic has been taken from it. Siegmund grieves for Sieglinde. Shame, he cries, on Wotan who bestowed the sword only to break it. If he must die, he will stay on earth. (The foregoing paragraph is often cut.)

Bruennhilde is impressed and questions his judgment. Bitterly he tells her to be gone if she stays only to mock him. She offers to care for Sieglinde, but he warns her away; better he and Sieglinde die together, "zwei Leben" (two lives). He draws the sword.

Bruennhilde, much moved, stops him. She will help him: he will kill Hunding. She runs out leaving Siegmund gazing at Sieglinde.

## SCENE 5 (9 min.)

*Siegmund, Sieglinde, Hunding, Bruennhilde and Wotan:* Siegmund muses over Sieglinde who now seems so happy in her dreaming. He hears Hunding's horn and, slipping from under Sieglinde, goes to the backstage to prepare for the fight.

Sieglinde in her dream imagines that she is a child again and is being carried off; her mother, "mutter," is dead and her father and brother away. She wakes in terror as Hunding and Siegmund call to each other. They meet and fight, Bruennhilde urging Siegmund on. But Wotan appears, breaks Siegmund's sword, and Hunding spears him. Bruennhilde rushes off with Sieglinde as Wotan with a gesture kills Hunding. Then in a fury Wotan starts after Bruennhilde.

### Vocabulary, Act II

| | | |
|---|---|---|
| nach Walhall | nahk vahl.hahl | to Walhall |
| doch stand muss ich hier halten | dok shtand moos ik here hahlt.en | but I must stand from here |
| der Lenz | der lents | the spring |
| heiligin Eid | hile.iken eye't | sacred oath |
| unheilig | oon.hile.ik | unholy |
| Schwester und Bruder | shvest.er unt brood.er | sister and brother |
| nichts lerntest du | nikts lairn.test doo | you have learned nothing |
| das Schwert | dahs schvairt | the sword |
| was verlangst du | vas fair.lahngst doo | what do you wish |

| | | |
|---|---|---|
| lass' von dem Waelsung | lahs fon dem VALE.soong | abandon the child of Waelse |
| die Walkuere | dee VAL.koo.ree | the Walkuere |
| von Wotan den Eid | fon voh.tahn den eye't | from Wotan the oath |
| nimm den Eid | nim den eye't | take the oath |
| Goetternoth | gert.er.note | God's despair |
| Vater | fah.ter | father |
| zurueck das Wort | tsoo.rook dahs vort | take back the word |
| du liebst Siegmund | doo leepst . . . | you love Siegmund |
| Siegmund falle | . . . fahl | Siegmund strike down |
| dies sei der Walkuere werk | deez sigh der . . . vairk | this be the Walkuere's work |
| weh, mein Waelsung | vay mine VALE.soong | woe, my child of Waelse |
| | | |
| weiter, weiter | vy.ter | further |
| nicht weiter | nikt vy.ter | no further |
| Braut | browt | bride |
| Siegmund is der Gesell | . . . ist der ge.ZEL | Siegmund is the mate |
| wo bist du, Siegmund | voh bist doo . . . | where are you, Siegmund |
| | | |
| das ist Hundings Horn | dahs ist . . . horn | that is Hunding's horn |
| geliebte | ge.leep.te | beloved |
| wer bist du, sag | vair bist doo, sahg | who are you, say |
| im Walhall's saal | im . . . sahl | in Walhall's hall |
| Wotan's Tochter | . . . TOHK.ter | Wotan's daughter |
| so gruesse mir Walhall | so groos.eh meer . . . | so greet for me Walhall |
| | | |
| zwei Leben | tsvy LAY.ben | two lives |
| mutter | moot.er | mother |

## ACT III (72 min.; but with usual cuts, closer to 60)

---

### SCENE 1 (17 min.)

**the ride of the Walkuere**     The Walkuere are gathering on a rocky precipice. To the right is a pine wood, to the left a cave. There is a short (1 min.) prelude depicting the Walkuere galloping to the rock. As the curtain opens, four of the nine have arrived and wait for the others.

*The Walkuere:* They whoop back and forth to each other, greet the late-comers, laugh at their horses kicking in the pine woods, and wonder why Bruennhilde is so slow. They sight her with a woman instead of a hero across her saddle, and some go offstage to the pine woods to help her.

*The Walkuere, Bruennhilde and Sieglinde:* Bruennhilde rushes in, breathless, supporting Sieglinde. She asks her sisters to hide them from Wotan who is pursuing her. Two of the Walkuere report that a storm cloud is approaching. Quickly Bruennhilde explains how she disobeyed Wotan. She appeals for a horse to save Sieglinde who asks only to be killed. Bruennhilde tells her she is pregnant and must live for Sieg-mund's child. Sieglinde's mood immediately changes, and she calls eagerly to be saved. (Wagner usually is accused of *over*preparing his developments. This is a rare instance where he simply tried to skid by on a cliché.)

The Walkuere confess they dare not hide Sieglinde, and Bruennhilde urges her to fly alone, directing her to Fafner's country where Wotan does not like to go. She gives Sieglinde the pieces of Siegmund's sword and names the unborn child "Siegfried." Sieglinde thanks her, rejoices ecstatically in her child and rushes out alone. From the distance Wotan's voice calls to Bruennhilde to stay.

## SCENE 2 (15 min.)

*Wotan, Bruennhilde and the Walkuere:* He strides in; "wo ist Bruenn-hilde" (where is Bruennhilde)? The Walkuere conceal her behind them. He sees them and orders them to stand aside. They murmur nervously, and he sarcastically compliments them on their courage. He recites her crime: "keine wie sie . . ." (no one but she) knew his mind and saw to his soul. Now she has broken faith; let her stand forth. Slowly she comes out: "hier bin ich Vater" (here I am, father), punish me.

Wotan states that he cannot punish her; she has already sentenced herself. He recounts what she had been to him; ". . . wars't du mir" (were to me) a handmaiden, a shield, a caster of destinies, a goad to heroes. He states each category broadly, following it with an angry phrase stating her betrayal in each. She is none any more.

Bruennhilde is astounded; it is a denial of existence. Wotan explains that "nicht" (not) again will she ride from "Walhall," etc., for "gebro-chen ist unser Bund" (broken is our bond). The Walkuere gasp. For here, Wotan continues, on the mountain, "auf den Berg," he will put her to sleep, "Schlaf," till some man shall capture the maid, "der Mann dann fange die Maid." The Walkuere are horrified. Wotan warns them to cast Bruennhilde out or share her fate. He orders them off, and they go.

### SCENE 3 (40 min.; but with cuts, closer to 28)

*Wotan and Bruennhilde:* She remains at his feet. Then slowly she asks, "war es so schmaehlich" (was it so shameful), "war es so niedrig" (so disgraceful), "war es ehrlos" (so dishonorable)? She asks him to explain her guilt. A dialogue begins (parts of which are often cut) in which she claims she did what she knew he wanted, and he points out she disobeyed him. She describes Siegmund's remarks and his effect on her. When she saw how he loved Sieglinde and knew their bond for the bond between Wotan and herself, she defied his order which she knew was imposed on him. He chides her for giving way to emotion and not understanding the higher logic of life. She murmurs (a usual cut is from here through the talk of the Waelsung) that she was not fit to serve him: she merely loved what he loved. She asks if asleep she can be won by any man; she insinuates that the best will be Siegfried, but Wotan forbids her to talk of the Waelsung.

He tells her that he must impose the punishment and put her to sleep, "Schlaf." She pleads that he grant one thing: "dies Eine musst" (this one thing must you grant): that he surround her with terrors to repel all but a hero. Wotan says it is too much to grant. In despair, as she grasps his knees, she begs "Dies Eine musst," or let her die. At least he can circle the rock with fire.

**Wotan's farewell**    He is moved and agrees. Raising her up, he says farewell, "Leb'wohl." She was his greatest love. He will encircle her with fire, so that only a hero, a man freer even than the gods, can win her. They gaze at each other. He remarks on the beauty of her eyes, which he will see no more. He kisses her lids: "so kuesst er die Gottheit von dir" (so kisses he the godhead from you).

He places her on a mossbank under a fir tree and covers her with her shield. Then he summons Loge, the god of fire, "Loge, hier," and casts a spell over the mountain where Bruennhilde will wait for the hero, Siegfried.

### Vocabulary, Act III

| | | |
|---|---|---|
| wo ist Bruennhilde? | voh ist BROON.hild | where is Bruennhilde |
| keine wie sie | ky.neh vee see | no one but she |
| hier bin ich, Vater | here been ik FAH.ter | here I am, Father |

Vocabulary, Act III (*continued*)

| | | |
|---|---|---|
| wars't du mir | varst doo meer | were to me |
| nicht | nikt | not |
| gebrochen ist unser Bund | ge.bro.ken ist OON.ser boont | broken is our bond |
| auf den Berg | owf den bairk | on the mountain |
| Schlaf | shlahf | sleep |
| der Mann dann fange die Maid | der mahn dahnn fahn.ge dee mite | the man then captures the maid |
| war es so schmaelich | vahr es so shmay.lik | was it so shameful |
| . . . so niedrig | need.rik | . . . disgraceful |
| . . . so ehrlos | air.lohs | . . . dishonorable |
| dies Eine musst | dees eye.neh moost | this one thing must you (grant) |
| | | |
| leb'wohl | layb.vohl | farewell |
| so kuesst er die Gottheit von dir | so kest er dee goht.hite fon deer | so kisses he the godhead from you |
| Loge hier | low.geh here | Loge, here |

# PARSIFAL

A Stage-Consecrating Festival Play in three acts. First performed at Bayreuth on July 26, 1882. Music and libretto by R. Wagner.

## PRINCIPAL CHARACTERS

| | |
|---|---|
| Gurnemanz, a knight of the Grail | bass |
| Kundry | soprano |
| Amfortas, King of the Knights of the Grail and sick with a wound that will not heal | baritone |
| Parsifal | tenor |
| Titurel, father of Amfortas | bass |
| Klingsor | bass |

Wagner described the scene of the action "in the territory and the castle of the Knights of the Grail, Monsalvat. The scenery is in the style of the northern mountain ranges of Gothic Spain. Klingsor's magic castle is on the southern slope of this range, facing Arabic Spain."

Few operas are so pleasing as *Parsifal* to those who like it and none so irritating to those who don't. Undoubtedly because of the religious nature of its subject, men feel strongly about it and are apt to express themselves with unexpected violence either for or against it. Those who like it talk of its otherworldliness, its reverence; those who don't are apt to base their attack on what are primarily either literary, religious or musical grounds.

The literary attack aims at the libretto which Wagner, as always, wrote himself. He based it in part on a medieval romance, popular about 1100 A.D., which, as Jessie L. Weston has demonstrated in *Ritual to Romance* (1920), was essentially a pagan story or ritual common in one form or another to people everywhere. It is a vegetation or fertility rite. The king or ruler has lost his vitality either through sickness, old age or a wound. His illness affects the fertility of his land and people; the women bear no children and the land becomes a waste (T. S. Eliot's *The Waste Land*). The task of the hero is to restore the vitality of the king and the prosperity of the land. After a number of trials and adventures, he succeeds. Pagans acted out this drama or, in fact, killed the old king to make way for the new.

In the ritual were two symbols, a spear and a cup, always associated together. They were symbols of the male and female reproductive energies. They were so before Christianity appeared and still are today among primitive people. But in Christian art and tradition, at least before Wagner, they are not associated symbols.

The medieval poets, looking at their material, found a hero, a sick king, a spear and cup, and a number of adventures. They did not know why the king was sick or the significance of the spear and the cup, but being Christian poets they attempted to tell the adventures in Christian terms. The result was a romance filled with inexplicable symbols, curious incidents and contradictory versions which for the last thousand years has intrigued and irritated scholars, critics and its audience.

The literary theorists say that Wagner attempted on this pagan base to build a Christian superstructure of his own design; but, unfortunately, like the medieval poets, he was not aware of the meaning of his material. Thus when Parsifal in Act III brings back the spear to the Grail's domain, it is consistent to have spring fill the meadow with flowers and the waste land grow green; but when Parsifal sticks the spear in the ground, kneels, and worships it, nothing could be more wildly inappropriate to Wagner's Christian context of ascetic knights in a monastic order who hear heavenly voices.

Wagner, of course, had a right to use the symbols in any way he wished, but literary operagoers who dig deep to determine the meaning of *Parsifal* soon come to Weston's book and are apt thereafter to find the libretto increasingly unsatisfactory.

Those who object to the opera on religious grounds are apt to argue that the Christian religion and ritual are important to them and that they do not enjoy seeing it used to bolster a story of knights, a magic garden with flower girls, and a magician. Thus the stage picture of Kundry washing Parsifal's feet, drying them with her hair, and then anointing them with oil inevitably reminds the Christian audience of Christ and the sinning woman who washed His feet, etc. (Luke 7:37). Ernest Newman, the great Wagnerian critic, wrote on this: "The spectator should guard against the too common error of identifying Parsifal vaguely with Christ. Any suggestion of that sort angered Wagner. 'The idea of making Christ a tenor!' he said: 'phew!' " But many persons on this point find Newman simple and Wagner disingenuous. The error, as Newman himself suggests, is common, and the picture most deliberately staged. The religious objectors would have preferred an opera on Christ rather than having their emotions manipulated in this fashion. After all, they say, there is the Oberammergau Passion Play in which the artists face up squarely to the drama of Christ rather than merely pilfering it for its images and connotations.

Another primarily religious objection is that Wagner did not understand Christianity. What Parsifal brings to the knights is a Nirvana, an escape from pain and suffering into a blissful nonexistence in which all the senses and the soul are soothed. This seems to be the effect on much of the audience, at any rate, and unquestionably it is what Wagner intended. But it has little to do with exciting the audience to do its duty, love its neighbor, or even worship only one God.

Lastly, and by far the least violent, are those who find it musically dull. First there is its length, and the pace throughout is deliberate and slow. Rhythmically, they say, it is monotonous: the knights, for example, gather in the first Grail scene to a heavy skip rhythm that continues throughout most of the scene. Melodically, Wagner used the themes stated in the prelude over and over again, often with little variation. Finally, some of the orchestration is unimaginative, such as the simple swoosh up the harp as Klingsor hurls the spear at Parsifal.

But those who like the opera—and they are a considerable number —are not bothered by these flaws, if such they be. The opera has almost no lyrical passages, and yet it draws and holds an attentive audience, most of whom consider it a religious rather than a musical experience. For these Wagner has superbly caught the essence of reverence and worship, binding the knights and the audience into a common attitude unspoilt by the egotism of priest or minister or the divisive words of dogma. They find Wagner in the prelude and Good Friday music at the height of his orchestral powers, the scene between Kundry and Parsifal as dramatic as any he wrote, and the opera as a whole with its two sacred acts and one profane ideally paced.

At Bayreuth, according to Newman, the custom is to applaud after the second and third acts; in New York the audience applauds only after the second act.

### PRELUDE (13 min.)

It is made up of themes from the opera that are used to create a religious atmosphere without indicating the drama. Wagner once described it as based on three themes of "Love," "Faith" and "Hope?" The question mark was Wagner's. Nietzsche, although he later wrote famous harsh words of the opera, thought no painter had "ever depicted so sorrowful a look of love as Wagner does in the final accents of his prelude." The curtain rises directly. (The concert version of the prelude is identical except for the addition of several closing bars.)

### ACT I (100 min.)

### SCENE 1 (62 min.; but with usual cut, 55)

In the country of the Knights of the Grail. A deep forest, shady not gloomy, with a glade in the center. To the left a road rises to the castle; to the right at the back the ground slopes away to a lake. It is daybreak. Gurnemanz, old but vigorous, and two squires, young men, are lying asleep under a tree. Reville sounds from the castle.

*Gurnemanz and the Squires:* He calls to them to get up, and they all begin the day with a silent morning prayer. Then he directs them to prepare for Amfortas' bath, "Bad," in the lake, for the knights acting as heralds have already come.

*Gurnemanz and the Knights:* He asks, "wie geht's Amfortas heut" (how is Amfortas today)? Gawain had brought a new salve. But the knights report that the pain of the wound seemed just as bad and that Amfortas was eager for the bath, "das Bad." Gurnemanz nods sadly: there is only one man, "nur der Eine," who can help Amfortas. But when asked who he is, Gurnemanz evades the question by talking of "das Bad."

At that moment they all hear Kundry galloping up on her horse, and they exclaim at her speed.

*Kundry and Gurnemanz:* She runs in, almost staggering. (Wagner imagined her with black hair; red-brown complexion; dark eyes sometimes flashing, sometimes fixed and staring; and in a tattered dress with a snakeskin girdle trailing long ends.) "Hier," she gasps. "Balsam" brought from Arabia. She sinks to the ground to rest: "ich bin muede" (I am weary).

At that moment the knights arrive with Amfortas on a litter, and Gurnemanz turns from Kundry. "O Weh'" (woe)! he grieves, sorrowing that their leader should be a slave to sickness.

*Amfortas:* He asks to be put down and confesses he had a tortured night. He asks for Gawain only to learn that knight has already left to search for another salve. Amfortas fears Gawain may be trapped by Klingsor. The only cure, as Amfortas repeats, will be through one "durch Mitleid wissend" (who finds understanding through compassion). Gurnemanz agrees. He will be, Amfortas continues, "der reine Thor" (the innocent boy). (The translation of these words is most important and very unsatisfactory. Most librettos translate "Thor" or "Tor" as "fool" or "simpleton" and "reine" as "pure," "chaste," "guileless" or "blameless." Yet Wagner did not expect the audience to spend five hours giving serious attention to the world being saved by a virginal moron. The word "Thor" can also connote inexperience rather than stupidity; and "reine" can mean innocence in the sense of "untested" rather than of "deliberate continence." Wagner never gives Parsifal's age or a stage direction about the passage of time, but a good argument can be made that in Act I Parsifal is about twelve, in Act II fifteen, and in Act III twenty. If the ages are accepted, the concepts of "untested" or "inexperienced" are reasonable; a free translation, then, is "the innocent and inexperienced boy." Certainly the usual "blameless" or "guileless fool" is enough to prevent any audience from identifying itself with the hero, which is a bad beginning for the drama. Most satisfactory of all, of course, is to let a good performance of the role give the words their meaning.)

Amfortas muses that perhaps this savior will be death, "den Tod ihn nennen" (death to name him). Gurnemanz gives him Kundry's balsam, and he promises to try it. She refuses his thanks, "Nicht Dank," with poor grace, and the knights carry him off to the lake.

*Gurnemanz and the Squires:* The squires scold Kundry for her rudeness, but Gurnemanz stops them. She has never done them harm, and often she has done the knights good. The squires complain that she hates them, is spiteful, and is a heathen, "Eine Heidin ist's." Gurnemanz concedes that she may have sinned and be atoning for it by service. One squire suggests that her guilt may be the cause of their present distress, and Gurnemanz does not deny that evil sometimes befalls the knights when she is away. Calling to her he asks where she was when Amfortas lost the spear, "als unser Herr den Speer verlor?"

Kundry will not reply and, when asked again, she denies that she ever helped the knights. The squires suggest that if she is so helpful she be sent to recover the missing spear.

(This remark starts Gurnemanz on his narrative, in which he explains to the squires that Titurel is Amfortas' father and that Titurel founded the Order of the Grail. He also identifies Amfortas and Klingsor and describes how Amfortas got his wound. The narrative runs on for sixteen minutes and is the dullest part of the opera. Sometimes the middle section, seven minutes, is cut; but even so this is the spot to snooze.)

*Gurnemanz:* Gloomily he remarks that recovering the spear is beyond them all. With a great cry he despairs that he saw the holiest spear, "heiliger Speer," wielded by the unholiest hand, "unheiligster Hand."

**the narrative**  He recalls how Amfortas went out, armed with the spear, to overthrow Klingsor and how, near the walls of the castle, "Schloss," he was bewitched by a beautiful woman, "schoenes Weib." As he lay in her arms, Klingsor stole the spear, "der Speer," and wounded Amfortas. Gurnemanz helped Amfortas escape, but there was a wound, "eine Wunde," in Amfortas' side. Turning to the squires, he explains: this is the wound, "die Wunde ist's," that will not heal.

At this point two squires come up from the lake. Gurnemanz asks, "wie geht's dem Koenig" (how is the king)? They reply that the bath and the balsam have eased the pain. But Gurnemanz repeats "die wunde ist's" that will never heal. The squires ask him to continue about Klingsor.

Gurnemanz remarks that Titurel knew Klingsor well. Once when the pagans pressed the Christian knights hard, Christ appeared in a vision to Titurel and gave him the Grail and the spear. The Grail was the cup used both at the Last Passover Feast and to catch Christ's blood from the wound He received on the cross from a soldier's spear.

(The following paragraph is the usual cut.) To guard the relics Titurel built the castle and enrolled knights, pure in heart, to do God's work. Klingsor sought to join and was rejected. He then sought to seize the Grail by force and was defeated. He studied magic and, on the other side of the mountain in a desert, made a lovely garden filled with beautiful women, whom he uses to lure knights to sin. When Titurel grew old, Amfortas started off to destroy Klingsor and the garden. Instead he lost the spear, and Klingsor expects soon to win the Grail. The squires exclaim that the first job is to get the spear back.

Amfortas, Gurnemanz continues, prayed to the Grail, "dem Grale," and in a vision heard that he would be healed by one "durch Mitleid wissend, der reine Thor" (who finds understanding through compassion, the innocent boy). The squires repeat the prophecy.

*Gurnemanz, Parsifal and the Squires:* There is a commotion by the lake; someone has shot a swan, "den Schwan." It flies feebly overhead and then sinks midscene and expires as a knight draws an arrow from its breast. (It is usually carried on, taxidermied, with the arrow falling out because of its own weight.) The knights push Parsifal forward, and he confesses to Gurnemanz that he killed it. The squires and knights urge that he be punished.

Gurnemanz asks how the swan had ever hurt Parsifal. It probably was looking for its mate and now is dead because of a childish whim. He makes Parsifal look at the drooping wings, the sad eyes. (The scene is ludicrous if, as most tenors portray him, Parsifal is forty or older.) Parsifal breaks his bow and throws aside his arrows.

Gurnemanz asks if Parsifal understands what he has done, but Parsifal does not. Gurnemanz asks the boy's name, his father, from whence he comes, and to all Parsifal responds, "das weiss ich nicht" (that know I not). Gurnemanz exclaims that he is as dull as Kundry and sends the knights and squires back to the lake.

*Gurnemanz, Parsifal and Kundry:* Gurnemanz questions Parsifal again, and the boy admits he has a mother, "ich hab eine Mutter," named "Herzeleide." Gurnemanz wonders that Parsifal has only a bow, for he looks nobly born. When Parsifal remains silent, Kundry explains that his father was killed in battle and that his mother raised him ignorant of the world and its ways.

Parsifal exclaims that one day some knights passed and he followed but was unable to overtake them. Kundry continues that he fought off enemies—beast and man. The wicked, she calls them. But he naively asks who then are the good?

Gurnemanz replies that his mother is good and must grieve for her lost son. Kundry laughs that his mother is dead, "seine mutter ist todt." Parsifal protests, but Kundry claims to have seen her die. Parsifal springs at Kundry, and Gurnemanz pulls him off her while lecturing him on his violence. Parsifal sits down feebly, and Kundry gets him water, which Gurnemanz praises as an act in the spirit of the Grail. But Kundry mutters that she never does good. She wants only to sleep, "schlafen," to achieve eternal repose. Hell is not to sleep, "nicht schlafen." She shambles off, muttering "schlafen."

To the back the knights return with Amfortas to the castle. Gurnemanz determines to take Parsifal to the Grail or Communion feast. But when Parsifal asks what it is and what it means, Gurnemanz replies that this is revealed only to those called to its service. They start walking and the Transformation Scene begins.

(In the Transformation Scene [5 min.] Gurnemanz and Parsifal appear to walk, and behind them the scenery changes from the forest to rocky cliffs and finally into the castle itself until they reach a large hall with a high, vaulted dome and clerestory windows. From the heights above the dome, chimes sound. A Transformation Scene is one of the theater's oldest effects, but the audience is entitled to ask Wagner just what he thought he gained by this one. It is a producer's nightmare and generally disappointing.)

SCENE 2 (In the hall of the castle—38 min.)

The knights gather in a processional celebrating the Communion
**processional**     feast. (In a pattern that he uses and reverses throughout the scene, Wagner has first the knights, tenors and basses; then sounding from halfway up the dome the younger men, tenors and altos; and lastly from the top of the dome boys' voices, sopranos and altos. Producers sometimes cheat on this by not having the voices come from different heights and, worse, by using female sopranos and altos, whose voices sound far less ethereal than do those of boys.)

Amfortas is carried in and placed on a raised couch behind an oblong, stone altar on which stands the Grail, covered. When all are in place, there is a pause; then Titurel's voice comes from behind "as though out of a tomb." He asks Amfortas to reveal the Grail to start the service. Amfortas begs to be excused for he has sinned, but Titurel insists that only by service can Amfortas atone. "Nein," Amfortas breaks out. In a long speech he hopes that none of them will ever know his anguish in being the only sinner and yet having to perform the holy office. When the Grail is revealed and Heaven's light falls on it, he feels the Savior's grace pour into his body, mixing the Holy Blood with his own. But his own, lustful and evil, boils in a rage and pours out through the wound, "die Wunde," renewing again his lust and sense of guilt which no repentance can still. "Erbarmen" (have mercy), he cries to Christ. "Erbarmen." Heal his wound and let him die now, pure.

From the top of the dome, voices call, "Durch Mitleid wissend, der reine Thor," and urge him to wait for the appointed healer. The knights demand he reveal the Grail. With an effort Amfortas begins the service and the lights in the hall dim. At the mystical moment, as Amfortas consecrates the blood and wine, a dazzling ray of light falls on the Grail, which glows with an ever-softer, richer purple. From the back, Titurel hails the greeting from Christ.

The squires recover the Grail and distribute the consecrated bread and wine to the knights. Gurnemanz signals to Parsifal to partake of the service, but he stands apart as though in a trance. The service concludes. Amfortas sinks back, and the squires attend to his wound which **recessional** has broken out afresh. He is carried out, followed by the knights in a recessional.

*Gurnemanz and Parsifal:* Gurnemanz asks Parsifal if he understood the service. Parsifal remains silent and slightly shakes his head. Disappointed and irritated, Gurnemanz calls him only a fool, "nur ein Thor," and orders him to get on his way.

From the top of the dome an alto solo repeats the prophecy and other high voices intone, "Blessed are the Faithful."

### Vocabulary, Act I

| | | |
|---|---|---|
| das Bad | dahs baht | the bath |
| wie geht's Amfortas heut | vee gaits . . . hoyt | how is Amfortas today |
| nur der Eine | noor der eye.nuh | only the one |
| hier . . . Balsam | here . . . bahl.sahm | here . . . balsam |
| ich bin muede | ik* bin mer.duh | I am weary |
| o Weh | oh vay | oh woe |
| durch Mitleid wissend | doohrk mit.lite viss.ent | through compassion, understanding |

| | | |
|---|---|---|
| der reine Thor | der rine.uh tohr | the innocent boy (the pure fool) |
| den Tod ihn nennen | den toht een nen.en | death him to name |
| nicht Dank | nikt dahngk | no thanks |
| eine Heidin ist's | eye.nuh hide.in ists | a heathen she is |
| als unser Herr den Speer verlor | ahls oon.ser hairr den shpair fair.lor | as our master the spear lost |
| heiliger Speer | hile.ik.er shpair | holy spear |
| unheiligster Hand | oon.hile.ik.ster hahnnt | unholy hand |
| Schloss | shloss | castle |
| schoenes Weib | shern.es vibe | beautiful woman |
| der Speer | der shpair | the spear |
| eine Wunde | eye.nuh voon.duh | a wound |
| die Wunde ist's | dee voon.duh ists | the wound it is |
| wie geht's dem Koenig | vee gaits dem ker.nik | how is the King |
| dem Grale | dem grahl | the Grail |
| den Schwan | den shvahn | the swan |
| das weiss ich nicht | dahs vise ik* nikt | that I know not |
| ich hab eine Mutter | ik hahb eye.nuh moot.ter | I have a mother |
| seine Mutter ist todt | zine.nuh moot.ter ist toht | thy mother is dead |
| schlafen | shlah.fen | to sleep |
| nein | nine | no |
| erbarmen | air.bahr.men | have mercy |

* Ik or ish depending on North or South German accent of the singer.

## ACT II (67 min.)

### SCENE 1 (17 min.; with usual cut, 14)

After a short (2 min.) prelude the curtain reveals the inside of a tower in Klingsor's magic castle. Stone steps lead up to the battlements, down to a rampart and on into darkness at stage level. There are "magical instruments and necromantic appliances." Klingsor sits before a metal mirror.

*Klingsor:* In his mirror he sees Parsifal approaching and prepares to call up Kundry. He descends a few steps and ignites some incense which fills the background with a blue smoke. Then he reseats himself before his magical instruments. "Herauf" (up here), he calls. "Dein Meister ruft dich" (your master calls you). He repeats it insistently, calling her by her various names throughout time, such as Herodias (wife of the Herod who executed John the Baptist and was ruling at the time of Christ's death) and Gundryggia (one of the Valkyrie serving the Norse God Odin). In the blue smoke Kundry appears as though asleep. As she wakes, she gives a terrible cry. Klingsor laughs: she is in his power. He inquires sarcastically if she has been serving the knights. She mutters brokenly, "Schlaf" (sleep), ever deeper sleep and then death, "Tod." He mocks her, and she moans, "Sehnen, Sehnen" (longing).

Klingsor reminds her that the knights can give her nothing, whereas he can conquer their strongest and wound him with his own spear. He warns her that the most dangerous knight of all is coming—one protected by his innocence. She murmurs that she will not, "ich will nicht," harm him.

(The usual cut [3 min.] is the following paragraph.) He reminds her that he is her master, for he alone can resist her charms. She taunts him, "bist du keusch" (are you chaste)? Klingsor turns on her furiously and then relapses into grieving that all his efforts to be worthy of the Grail (including, by implication, self-castration) have resulted only in having Kundry mock him. Yet soon he will destroy the knights and himself guard the Grail. (For a brief period Wagner considered having a castrato sing Klingsor.) Klingsor in turn taunts Kundry by asking if she found Amfortas to her taste. She grieves that even he succumbed to her.

With a cry she sighs that all men are weak and that she will never find peace. He urges her to see if Parsifal can resist her. She refuses to try; "ich will nicht" (I will not). Klingsor climbs the tower steps and gazes into the darkness: Parsifal is coming. "O Wehe! Wehe" (woe)! Kundry moans. "Muss ich? Muss" (must I)? Klingsor laughs that Parsifal is handsome, and Kundry sobs again. Klingsor blows a horn, summoning his knights of evil to bar the way to Parsifal. He describes how Parsifal cuts his way through them. With a shriek Kundry vanishes; the blue light disappears; and Klingsor greets the still distant Parsifal: every hero carries home a wound. He calls to Kundry to be ready and hails Parsifal as his slave.

(The tower with Klingsor sinks into the darkness, and in its place rises a magic garden with tropical flora. It rises in terraces to the extreme background bounded by the castle wall and the side wings of the castle, which is in the Arabian style. Parsifal appears on the wall and gazes in astonishment at the garden. From all sides rush in the flower maidens, forming a confused, colorful throng and appearing to be just waking from sleep.)

SCENE 2 (In the garden—50 min.; with the usual cut, 47)

(The maidens in their filmy veils have some of the opera's most lyric music and yet are almost invariably visually disappointing. It is well to remember that the scene is intended not so much as a seduction scene as a psychological moment in Parsifal's development.)

*The Flower Maidens and Parsifal:* They call back and forth, at first ignoring Parsifal and then accusing him of killing their lovers. Grad-

**chorus** ually they insinuate that he must love them, and naively he agrees. In ones and twos they disappear only to return actually dressed as flowers. Their advances grow more ardent, and a quarrel breaks out over whom he shall kiss first. Half angry, Parsifal turns away, when Kundry's voice calls to him to remain, "Parsifal." At the strange sound of a name his mother, "die Mutter," had called him but which he had forgotten, he stays, and Kundry gradually appears. When she calls again, the maidens, terrified, retreat. Still in the distance she orders them away, and they withdraw, leaving Kundry, a beautiful woman, lying on a couch and dressed in veils "in the Arabian style."

*Parsifal and Kundry:* He asks how she can name him who has no name. She starts with a play on his name, "Fal-par-si," Arabian for "foolish pure one," and "Par-si-fal," the pure fool. Kundry explains that his father, who died in Arabia, named him.

He asks if she, like the maidens, lives in the gardens. She explains that her home is far away and that she waited only to see him. (She then sings the most lyrical passage in the opera, a description of Parsifal's childhood and mother.)

She saw him as a babe, the one joy of his widowed mother, who sang

**aria** him to sleep even as she wept for her dead husband. To save him from her husband's death, his mother raised him ignorant of arms and men. One day he wandered off and did not return. His mother searched, hoped and finally died of a broken heart.

Parsifal sinks at Kundry's feet: "Wehe! Wehe" (woe). "Mutter" (mother)! How could he have been so thoughtless? Kundry explains that he must know grief in order to know the healing power of love. But Parsifal can think only of his mother, "die Mutter," and wonder who else he has injured.

Kundry bends over him. From guilt comes knowledge, and he must learn of love: his father's for his mother, and his mother's for him. Kundry brings, as his mother's blessing, his first kiss, "ersten Kuss!"

With a tremendous cry, pressing his hand as if in pain to his heart, Parsifal calls, "Amfortas! Die Wunde, die Wunde." It burns in him now. "Klage! Klage" (moaning). "Hier, hier" (here). But no, it is not the spear wound: "Nein! Nein! Nicht die Wunde ist es!" It is his own heart, the terrible longings of lust. Kundry stares at him, amazed. Parsifal appears to fall into a trance as he remembers the ritual he saw.

His gaze, he continues quietly, is on the Grail. In every pure heart it brings divine joy, but it does not soothe his own. But over the Grail's sanctuary he could hear the Savior crying to be saved from the hands of the guilty. He heard it in his soul and now he has come to this garden. Falling to his knees, he begs the Redeemer, "Erloeser," to let him atone for his failure to understand.

Kundry tries to persuade Parsifal to look at her, but he remains kneeling, gazing blankly before him. Thus it was, he continues, when Amfortas fell: those lips, that encircling arm, the same voice and finally that kiss, "dieser Kuss." He leaps up and thrusts Kundry aside.

Kundry pleads that she too is a sinner. She laughed at the Savior carrying His cross: "ich sah ihn, ihn, und lachte" (I saw Him, Him, and laughed). She describes (3 min. and often cut) how she wanders seeking redemption but how whenever she sees the Savior's face she laughs again. But love can redeem her: let Parsifal love her.

Parsifal rejects her. They would better be damned forever if, forgetting his mission which he now understands, he spent an hour with her. He must also save the knights who, although they cannot help themselves, know that the source of salvation is in Grail. The blind world seeks salvation through the soul's destruction.

Kundry replies that if he learned this from one kiss, then he should have another and be a God, redeeming the world through love. He offers her redemption; she pleads for love. But when he asks to be shown the way to Amfortas, "zu Amfortas," she breaks out in a fury; Amfortas is not worth saving—a man who fell by his own spear. Parsifal asks who dared to wield it. He who will use it on Parsifal, she cries. Then she begs for pity, "Mitleid." Let him spend one hour with her.

Parsifal thrusts her aside. She shrieks for help, cursing any road that leads him from her and promising Klingsor as a guide. Klingsor appears on the rampart with the spear, which he hurls at Parsifal; "it remains floating over his head." Parsifal grasps it, makes a sign of the cross, and calls to an end the existence of the castle and its illusion.

"As in an earthquake the castle falls, the garden withers to a desert, and the Flower Maidens lie like shriveled flowers on the ground." Parsifal turns to Kundry: she knows where they will meet again.

Vocabulary, Act II

SCENE 1

| herauf | hair.OWF | up here |
|---|---|---|
| dein Meister ruft dich | dine MY.ster rooft dik | your master calls you |
| Schlaf | shlahf | sleep |
| Tod | toht | death |
| Sehnen | SAY.nen | longing |
| ich will nicht | ik vill nikt | I will not |
| bist du keusch | bist doo koysh | are you chaste |
| oh Wehe, Wehe | oh vay.uh vay.uh | oh woe |
| muss ich | moos ik | must I |

SCENE 2

| die Mutter | dee moot.ter | the mother |
|---|---|---|
| ersten Kuss | airst.ten koos | first kiss |
| Amfortas, die Wunde, die Wunde | ahm.FOR.tahs dee voon.duh | Amfortas, the wound |
| Klage | klah.guh | moaning |
| hier | here | here |
| nein, nicht die Wunde ist es | nine, nikt dee voon.duh ist es | no, it is not the wound |
| Erloeser | air.ler.ser | Redeemer |
| dieser Kuss | dee.zer koos | this kiss |
| ich sah ihn, ihn und lachte | ik sah een een oont lahk.tuh | I saw Him, Him, and laughed |
| zu Amfortas | tsoo ahm.FOR.tahs | to Amfortas |
| Mitleid | mit.lite | compassion |

## ACT III (75 min.)

---

## PRELUDE (6 min.)

It suggests Parsifal growing, as time passes, in experience of the world and searching always for the Castle of the Grail where he knows Amfortas waits for him. But no one can find the castle unless the Grail itself leads him to it. The prelude leads without break into the act which begins shortly before Parsifal re-enters the domain of the Grail.

## SCENE 1 (52 min.; with cuts, 49)

It is Good Friday and early spring. Meadows rise to the back; to the right the forest stretches off to rocky ground. By the edge of the wood is a spring. To the left is a hermit's hut against a mass of rock. Gurnemanz appears, grown very old. It is early morning.

*Gurnemanz and Kundry:* He steps from his hut and listens; a groan comes from a thicket; he discovers Kundry almost frozen. He recognizes her, although he has not seen her in a long time. He urges her to get up, to awake, for it is spring. At last she seems to wake, neatens her hair and dress, and moves off "as though a maid in service."

Gurnemanz remarks "ist diess der Dank" (is this the thanks) for stirring life back into her. She mutters "dienen, dienen" (to serve). She looks around her, sees the hut and enters it. Gurnemanz wonders at her strange behavior. She reappears with a pitcher and starts for the spring. She points out to Gurnemanz a knight approaching.

Parsifal enters in black armor with the visor lowered; he carries the spear. He sits on a grassy mound.

*Gurnemanz:* He gazes in astonishment at the strange knight. Then he greets him and offers to direct him on his way. Parsifal nods but does not speak. Gurnemanz rather more sharply reminds the visored knight that on Good Friday, "Charfreitag," morn he should not bear arms, "Waffen." Parsifal slowly rises, lays aside his helmet and sword and, sticking the spear in the ground, kneels before it in prayer.

Gurnemanz watches with surprise and emotion. He beckons to Kundry: it is the boy, now a man, who killed the swan, whom he drove from the chapel, and who now has returned with the lost spear, "der Speer." He praises the day, "O Heiligster Tag" (oh holiest day), that he should see it. Kundry turns her face away.

*Gurnemanz, Parsifal and Kundry:* Parsifal recognizes Gurnemanz and greets him. Parsifal wonders aloud if he has finally reached his goal, and when Gurnemanz asks what that is, Parsifal replies that it is to find Amfortas and relieve his suffering. He describes how he wandered as though cursed, never able to find the right road, fighting battles, but always preserving the Grail's holy spear, "des Grales heil'gen Speer." "O Wunder," Gurnemanz exclaims. Gurnemanz assures Parsifal that if a curse kept him from the road, it must be broken, for he is now in the Grail's domain. (The balance of the paragraph is sometimes cut.) Gurnemanz describes how poorly the knights have fared. Amfortas, hoping death would ease his pain, refused to uncover the Grail and to perform his office. The knights, refused their spiritual sustenance, declined in their power to do good.

Gurnemanz concludes that he himself retired to be a hermit and that Titurel has died. Parsifal bursts out·that the death is his fault because he could not find the way back sooner. He reels, and Gurnemanz lowers him to the bank. Kundry fetches a basin of water, but Gurnemanz waves that aside and asks for water from the holy spring: perhaps that day Parsifal will do holy work and assume a holy office; he should be purified. Kundry takes off the greaves of his armor, Gurnemanz the breastplate. Parsifal asks when they will lead him to Amfortas, and Gurnemanz replies immediately, for the service for Titurel awaits only them. Gurnemanz bathes Parsifal's head while Kundry washes his feet, annoints them with an oil and dries them with her hair. Parsifal then hands the vial of oil to Gurnemanz so that his head as well as his feet may be anointed, for that day, he explains, he will be appointed King of the Knights. Gurnemanz pours the oil over Parsifal's head and blesses him, hailing him as King "als Koenig."

As his first act, after taking some water from the spring, Parsifal baptizes Kundry while telling her to trust in the Redeemer. She sinks to the ground, weeping.

Turning to gaze at the meadow, Parsifal exclaims that it has never **Good Friday music** seemed more beautiful. Gurnemanz adds, "das ist Charfreitag's-Zauber, Herr" (that is Good Friday's spell, Lord). For Good Friday, Parsifal observes, the flowers should weep. Gurnemanz explains that flowers can see only the joy of Heaven, not Christ upon the cross. And men today, in memory of their Lord, will walk with soft steps and spare the flowers which, too, rejoice in their deliverance. Parsifal looks down and sees that Kundry is crying. He urges her to look at the flowers and kisses her gently on the forehead. (The immense difference in language sounds is demonstrated in the German, English and French titles for the concert versions of the Good Friday music; the German is "Charfreitagszauber," the English "The Good Friday spell" and the French "Enchantement du Vendredi Saint.")

In the distance the castle bells toll. Gurnemanz remarks that it is noon, "Mittag." The time has come to go to the castle.

There is a Transformation Scene as in Act I to the castle hall for the ritual of the Grail or Communion feast.

## SCENE 2 (23 min.)

*The Knights:* They gather in two processions, one bearing Amfortas to his position behind the Covered Grail, the other bearing Titurel's **processional** coffin, which is placed before the Grail. They sing of the Grail so long denied them, of how Amfortas failed to perform his office and to reveal the Grail, and of how as a result Titurel died in sorrow. They urge Amfortas to perform his office.

*Amfortas and the Knights:* He grieves. "Wehe, Wehe" (woe). They should grieve for him. He'd prefer it if they would kill him. They open the coffin and he gazes down on his father, "mein Vater." He intended only death for himself, yet he gave it to another. He pleads with his father to beg Heaven for his release. He wants only death, "Tod."

The knights press forward, insisting that he reveal the Grail. Never, he cries. Death is finally near. He tears off the bandages; here is the wound. He urges them to plunge their swords deep, up to the hilt, into his blood. The knights shrink back.

*Parsifal et al:* He steps forward with the spear: "Nur eine Waffe taugt" (only one weapon serves). He touches it to Amfortas' side. Amfortas totters with emotion. Parsifal intones that Amfortas is absolved. He gazes at the spear which he holds aloft. In a miracle Holy Blood appears on its tip, flowing, as Parsifal says, to join that in the Grail, which he orders uncovered. The service proceeds accompanied by voices from the dome; a white dove hovers over Parsifal's head; Kundry expires; and all kneel to Parsifal, who holds the Grail in blessing over their heads.

### Vocabulary, Act III

| | | |
|---|---|---|
| ist diess der Dank | ist dees der dahnk | is this the thanks |
| dienen | dee.nen | to serve |
| Waffen | vahf.fen | weapons |
| Charfreitag | kahr.FRY.tahk | Good Friday |
| der Speer | der shpair | the spear |
| o helligster Tag | oh hile.ik.ster tahg | oh holy day |
| des Grales heil'gen Speer | des grahl.es hile.gen shpair | the Grail's holy spear |

| | | |
|---|---|---|
| o Wunder | oh voon.der | oh wonder |
| als Koenig | ahls kern.ik | as King |
| das ist Charfreitag's-<br>   Zauber, Herr | dahs ist<br>   kahr.FRY.tahk's-<br>   tsow.ber hairr | that is Good Friday's<br>   spell, Lord |
| Mittag | mit.tahg | midday |
| Wehe, Wehe | vay vay | woe, woe |
| mein Vater | mine faht.er | my father |
| Tod | toht | death |
| nur eine Waffe taugt | noor eye.nuh vahf.fuh<br>   towgt | only one weapon<br>   serves (the purpose) |

# NABUCCO

(Full title is *Nabucodonosor,* i.e. Nebuchadnezzar)

Opera in four acts. First performed at Milan on March 9, 1842. Music by G. Verdi. Libretto by T. Solera.

### PRINCIPAL CHARACTERS

| | | |
|---|---|---|
| Zaccaria, High Priest and Prophet<br>   of the Hebrews | bass | |
| Ismaele, nephew of the King of the Hebrews | tenor | |
| Fenena, daughter of Nabucco and loved<br>   by Ismaele | soprano | fay.NAY.nah |
| Abigaille, purported daughter of Nabucco | soprano | ah.bee.gah.EEL.ay |
| Nabucco, King of Babylon | baritone | nah.BOO.coe |
| The High Priest of Bel, the God of Babylon | bass | |
| Abdallo, an old soldier faithful to Nabucco | tenor | |

The action takes place in Jerusalem and Babylon about 586 B.C. *Nabucco* was Verdi's third opera, first great success, and the earliest of his operas to survive in the repertory. Those who like Italian opera and Verdi in particular find it good fun. Others complain that it is naive and bombastic. Undoubtedly it is, and those who enjoy it probably do so by mixing their admiration with amusement—admiring the frequent sparks of a young and inexperienced genius and grinning at the anachronisms and artificialities of Italian romantic opera.

In 1842 Italian opera stressed the intensity of the moment rather than the dramatic seriousness of the whole. No one cared if the opera pulled and pushed the characters around like puppets so long as when they came face to face they were passionate or pleading, mad or in

VERDI

love, and behaved generally like Italians. No one expected Verdi to know anything about Jerusalem or the Temple, and the audience happily recognized the opening chorus of Virgins, Levites and Hebrews as the Vestal Virgins, Senators and Populace of the Roman Forum. For the Hebrews in captivity the audience understood Italy dismembered and occupied by Austria. Certainly no one cared that the librettist was unable to distinguish between the Babylonians and the Assyrians; the Guelphs and the Ghibellines were equally confusing.

What mattered was that it should be an Italian opera for the Italians. It must have a "preghiera," or prayer, which was always particularly intense if sung by a soprano costumed as a virgin. *Nabucco,* having a religious subject, happily allowed *every* character sooner or later to drop to his knees. There also must be a mad scene and several marches, in to dinner or a wedding if there were no soldiers. But if there were soldiers, then there had to be a horse, and someone, preferably the rider, had to have a plume. And each act had to be individually entitled. Solera, the librettist, offered a bonus of such opportunities in *Nabucco,* and it was thought at the time to be an excellent libretto.

The opera survives today, however, not because the clichés are historically amusing but because every now and again Verdi made them real, infusing into the stock situations a vigor and violence that was new in Italian opera and that, because of its simple honesty seems still to find an audience. Particularly admired today are the music of

Abigaille and Zaccaria and most of the choruses. Of the principal characters, Ismaele fares least well.

The Italians have always had a particular fondness for *Nabucco,* and they selected it to reopen La Scala in 1946 after repairing the damage of World War II. Again the chorus of the captive Hebrews had a political connotation. For those determined to have the opera about the historical Nebuchadnezzar: he lived c. 605–562 B.C. and appears in the Bible in II Kings 24-25, Jeremiah and Daniel. In the last, his madness takes the form of eating grass, which might have been sensational on the stage except that it obviously interfered with singing.

### OVERTURE  (8 min.)

It is made up of music from the opera and is mainly interesting as a demonstration of how a melody can be more or less effective when played rather than sung. The rather bouncy chorus of the Levites in Act II Scene 2, seems to do better in the overture, but the famous chorus of the captive Hebrews certainly does not.

### ACT I  (Jerusalem—32 min.)

#### (Inside Solomon's Temple)

*Hebrews, Levites and Virgins:* All the Hebrews not actually fighting have gathered in the Temple to pray to Jehovah to scatter the Babylo-
**chorus**    nian armies and strike down Nabucco. The prayer passes between the groups, varying from a soft plea by the Virgins alone to a full forte shout by everyone, in which they all attempt to shame Jehovah into working for them.

*Zaccaria et al:* He urges them not to lose heart: Jehovah has given
**solo with chorus**    them a hostage. He exhibits Fenena, Nabucco's daughter. They must restrain their fear, "freno al timor," and have faith in Him, "in Lui," who never fails to save his people in their hour of need, "estremo."

Ismaele enters with a small band of soldiers and reports that Na-
**solo with chorus**    bucco is winning. Zaccaria hands Fenena to Ismaele and then leads everyone in a vigorous prayer asking Jehovah to blast the false God of Bel and kindle within the Hebrews a fire to

consume the Assyrians. At its end all go out except Ismaele and Fenena.

*Ismaele, Fenena and Abigaille:* Ismaele reminds Fenena of how in Babylon, where he had gone as Judah's envoy, she had saved his life. Now he will save hers. She protests that he will violate his sacred duty. But he insists he loves her and is about to lead her out through a secret door—"vieni" (come)—when Abigaille enters, sword in hand, followed by a troop of Babylonian soldiers disguised as Hebrews.

**trio**  She greets the lovers scornfully, threatening Fenena with death for loving a Hebrew. Then moving close to Ismaele, Abigaille confesses to him that she has loved him, "io t'amava"; her love is a fury, "una furia è questo amore." If only he could love her, "Ah se m'ami," she could save him and all the Hebrews. He rejects her suggestion; he can give her his life but not his heart. Fenena, to one side, begs the God of Judah to protect Ismaele.

*Finale:* Hebrew women run in terrified by the sight of Nabucco on his horse; Levites wail that the battle is lost; and the Hebrew soldiers enter, throwing aside their arms. Abigaille comes forward crying, "viva Nabucco," as her soldiers throw off their disguise. More Babylonian soldiers pour in (to a march associated with them throughout the opera), and suddenly Nabucco appears at the entrance on his horse.

**chorus**  Zaccaria opposes him, promising to kill Fenena before he will let Nabucco profane the Temple. Nabucco dismounts, observing to himself that he must disguise his wrath for the moment but that later it can break out in a sea of blood, "in mar di sangue." In a chorus Fenena begs him to spare the Hebrews, Abigaille observes that perhaps Fenena will be killed, and Zaccaria and all the Hebrews beg Jehovah to save them.

**chorus**  Nabucco orders the Hebrews to bow before him. He has conquered them in battle and even their God, Jehovah, fears him. Zaccaria raises his knife over Fenena. As he is about to stab her, Ismaele stops him and frees Fenena, who collapses in her father's arms. Savagely Nabucco promises that nothing will restrain him now. In the final chorus Nabucco orders his soldiers to burn and pillage. Abigaille rejoices that the cursed Hebrews will be destroyed and that her hate, if not her love, will be fulfilled. Fenena and Ismaele grieve that his love has brought him dishonor and beg the Hebrews to have pity on him. Zaccaria and the Hebrews curse Ismaele for betraying them.

Vocabulary, Act I

| | | |
|---|---|---|
| freno al timor | fray.no ahl tee.mor | restrain your fear |
| in Lui | in loo.ee | (have faith) in Him |
| estremo | es.TRAY.moe | extreme (hour of need) |
| vieni | v'YAY.nee | come |
| io t'amava | yo t'ah.MAH.vah | I have loved you |
| una furia è questo amore | oona foo.r'yah ay quest' ah.MOR.ay | a fury is this love |
| ah se m'ami | ah say m'ah.me | ah, if you loved me |
| in mar di sangue | in mahr dee sahn.gway | in a sea of blood |

## ACT II (The Blasphemer—33 min.)

Nabucco took all the leading Hebrews back to Babylon with him. Then he left Fenena, the younger of his two daughters, as his Regent, while he went off to fight more battles.

SCENE 1 (An apartment in the Babylonian palace—13 min.)

*Abigaille:* She enters holding a paper and rejoicing that at last she discovered where Nabucco had hidden it. It is evidence that she is not his daughter but the child of slaves. No one but she and Nabucco know it. With dramatic declamation, she swears to humble them all—Fenena, Nabucco, even the kingdom—in her furious hatred.

**aria**      She remembers how her heart once warmed to love: she wept for another, hoped for another. But who will return her even a single day of that lost illusion? "Chi del perduto incanto" (who of the lost spell) "mi torna un giorno sol" (returns to me a single day)?

*Abigaille, Babylonian High Priest and Others:* The High Priest complains that Fenena is freeing the Hebrews. He suggests that Abigaille assume the throne; he and the other priests have spread the rumor that Nabucco has died in battle.

**aria**      Abigaille agrees. She will be a ruthless ruler and Fenena, a royal princess, will have to beg mercy of a humble slave, "l'umil schiava." The priests and the vengeance of Bel will support her. (The aria is a typical cabaletta [*See* Glossary] and the second verse, an exact repetition of the first, is often cut.)

## SCENE 2 (20 min.)

Another room in the palace. To the right a door leads to a gallery; to the left another leads to Fenena's apartment. It is evening, and the room is lit with lamps. Zaccaria enters accompanied by a Levite carrying the Tables of the Hebrew Law.

*Zaccaria:* He explains to the Levite that they are God's chosen instru-
**"preghiera"**       ment, for they will convert an infidel, Fenena. He prays, beginning "Tu sul labbro" (you from the lips) "de' veggenti" (of the prophets) did thunder. Now speak through my lips to all of Babylon so that in every temple, "ogni tempio," sacred hymns, "e di canti," will resound to Thee and over the broken idols Thy law shall rise.

He and the Levite enter Fenena's apartment.

*Ismaele and the Levites:* The Levites gather, wondering why they have
**solo with chorus**       been called to meet. Ismaele tries to speak to them, but they refuse to have anything to do with him. He has been ostracized by Zaccaria for releasing Fenena. He begs to be forgiven, "pietà" (have pity), as they reject him as one cursed by God, "maledetto dal Signor."

*Finale:* Zaccaria enters with Fenena and announces her conversion. The sound of a riot breaks in on them, and an old Babylonian, Abdallo, hurries in urging Fenena to flee, "fuggi." Nabucco is dead and Abigaille has seized the throne.

Abigaille enters followed by the priests. She walks directly to Fenena and demands the crown. Fenena starts to protest; and then pushing his way through the crowd with a small band of soldiers, comes Nabucco. He puts the crown on his own head and turns to Abigaille: "dal capo mio la prendi" (take it from *my* head!). The crowd draws back in terror.

Nabucco starts an aria in which Abigaille, Ismaele and Fenena enter
**chorus**       in turn, as in a round, and which the whole chorus joins. They sing that the moment of a fatal rage is nearing which will bring a day of death and mourning—"il terror" (the terror).

Nabucco in a frenzy of excitement rejects the Babylonian God for it taught his people to be traitors. He rejects the Hebrew God for he conquered it in battle. From now on there will be one God, the King, "il vostro Re." Zaccaria is outraged, and when Nabucco orders everyone to kneel and worship him, the Hebrews, including Fenena, refuse. Nabucco starts to force her to her knees, insisting he is God. At that moment a bolt of lightning knocks the crown from his head and leaves him plainly mad. Everyone exclaims.

**Mad Scene**     Nabucco stutters in a daze. Who takes his scepter? What specter pursues him? Who pulls his hair, casts him down, "chi m'atterra"? Who will help him? His daughter, "oh, mia figlia"? The sky, red with blood, has fallen on him. Why do his eyes fill with tears: "ah, perchè . . . una lagrima"? He feels weak. (It is a rare bass who goes mad in opera—although Boris is another; sopranos, however, hover continually on the brink of insanity.)

Zaccaria thunders that Heaven has punished the blasphemer. Abigaille picks up the crown, remarking that Babylon, however, will not lose its splendor.

## Vocabulary, Act II

| | | |
|---|---|---|
| chi del perduto incanto | key del pair.doo.toe in.kahn.toe | who of the lost spell |
| mi torna un giorno sol | me tor.nah oon je.OR.no sol | will return me a single day |
| l'umil schiava | l'oo.meel skee.AH.vah | a humble slave |
| tu sul labbro | too sool LAH.broe | you on the lips |
| de' veggenti | day ved.jen.tee | of the prophets |
| ogni tempio | own.ye tem.p'yo | every temple |
| e di canti | ay dee kahn.tee | and of songs |
| pietà | p'yay.tah | have pity |
| maledetto dal Signor | mahl.eh.det.toe dahl seen.yore | the cursed of the Lord |
| fuggi | food.jee | flee |
| dal capo mio la prendi | dahl kahpo me.ɔh lah pren.dee | from my head take it |
| il terror | eel tair.or | the terror |
| il vostro Re | eel voh.stroh ray | your king |
| chi m'atterra | key m'ah.tair.rah | who knocks me down |
| oh mia figlia | oh me.ah feel.ya | oh, my daughter |
| ah, perchè . . . una lagrima | ah pair.kay . . . oona LAH.gree.mah | ah, why . . . a tear |

## ACT III (The Prophecy—26 min.)

---

## SCENE 1 (16 min.)

The hanging gardens of Babylon. Abigaille is on the throne; at her feet are the nobles and people of Babylon. Near the altar, with its gold statue of Bel, are the priests.

**chorus** *The People and Priests:* They sing that Babylon now has a queen and the power of Bel rules over the land. The previous king had ruined the country with his foreign wars; now there is peace.

*The High Priest, Abigaille, Nabucco and Abdallo:* The priest asks Abigaille to hear the prayers of her people: the Hebrews must die. He carefully reminds her that Fenena betrayed Babylon and also should die. He hands Abigaille the sentence of death to approve, and she is pretending not to understand when Nabucco, shabbily dressed and still mad, wanders in. The soldiers led by Abdallo make way for him.

Abigaille orders Nabucco to be led back to his room, and Abdallo with kindness tries, but Nabucco orders him away, "lasciami." They are waiting for him, he raves; "perchè, perchè" (why) must he be helped? It is true he is weak, but they must never know; he will find his place himself. He advances towards the throne and is outraged to see it occupied by a woman. Abigaille asks everyone to leave them.

*Abigaille and Nabucco:* In amazement he asks her who she is. She replies that she came to protect his throne. He scoffs "o frode" (fraud); he never asked her. She explains that he was ill and that the people **duet** cried for vengeance on the Hebrews. She shows him the death sentence. "Soscrivi" (sign it), she insists. When he hesitates, she sarcastically urges the Hebrews to rise up, for Nabucco is no more. Death, death to them, "a morte," he cries, and puts his seal on the sentence. Abigaille rejoices.

But Nabucco remembers Fenena, "è sangue mio" (she is my blood). You cannot save her, Abigaille insists as she hands the sentence to a guard; besides, she insinuates, he has another daughter, "un altra figlia." Kneel down, "prostrati," oh slave, "schiava," he thunders at her. Fool, she retorts: I, a slave, "io schiava"? Learn the truth, he cries, searching in his clothes for the evidence of her slave birth. Triumphantly she pulls it from her bosom and tears it to pieces before his eyes.

Nabucco grieves at his shame. He is only a wretched old man, a shadow of the king, "l'ombra tu sei del re." Abigaille exults that a throne is worth the loss of a father.

A trumpet sounds. When she reveals that it heralds death for the Hebrews, he tries to call the guards, only to learn from her that he is now a prisoner, "prigionier."

He begs her to have mercy on an old man, "perdona." She can keep the throne, but let him have Fenena. He is an old man, begging. She tells him to go away. He raised her only for dishonor and slavery; now she is queen.

### SCENE 2 (10 min.)

On the banks of the Euphrates, where the Hebrews are being worked as slaves.

*The Hebrews:* They sing "Va, pensiero" (fly, my thought) on golden wings back to the hills of Jerusalem, the ruined towers of Zion. "Oh mia patria sì bella e perduta" (oh, my fatherland, so beautiful and **chorus** lost). (This chorus and particularly the last quoted line was immensely moving to Italians in 1842 when Austrian armies still occupied much of Italy. The chorus became a national song. When Verdi died almost seventy years later, his will directed: "My funeral shall be very modest, at dawn or at the time of the Ave Maria in the evening, without singing or music." The clause was a terrible blow to Italians who expected to honor their hero, but the directions were observed scrupulously. Luckily a second clause in the will directed that he be buried in the Casa di Reposo, the old musicians' home that he had founded, and such a burial required special authorization. There was a delay and a second internment. For this, distinguished persons gathered from all over Europe, and a crowd, it is said, of more than two hundred thousand Milanese lined the streets. As the cortège passed, the people mysteriously began to sing, and what they sang was "Va, pensiero. . . .")

*Zaccaria et al:* He asks them who weeps, who cries like a cowardly **solo with chorus** woman? Through him Jehovah speaks. Someday their bondage will end and the Lion of Judah will arise. Someday Babylon will be a stubble field with dust stirred by the wind. The Hebrews exclaim at the fire of the old man and promise themselves that Judah will arise.

Vocabulary, Act III

| lasciami | LAH.shah.me | leave me |
| perchè | pair.kay | why (must I be helped) |
| o frode | o fro.day | oh fraud |
| soscrivi | so.skree.vee | sign (it) |
| a morte | ah MOR.tay | to death |
| è sangue mio | ay sahn.gway me.oh | (she) is of my blood |
| un' altra figlia | oon' ahl.trah FEEL.yah | another daughter |
| prostrati, o schiava | pro.strah.tee o skee.AH.vah | kneel, o slave |
| lo schiava | yo skee.AH.vah | I, a slave |
| l'ombra tu sei del re | l'om.brah too say.ee del ray | the shadow you are of the king |
| prigionier | pree.joan.yair | prisoner |
| perdona | pair.doh.nah | have mercy |
| va, pensiero | vah pen.see.ay.roh | go, thought |
| oh mia patria sì bella e perduta | oh me.ah pah.tree.ah see bel.lah ay pair.doo.tah | oh, my country so beautiful and lost |

## ACT IV (The Idol Broken—23 min.)

### SCENE 1 (12 min.)

An apartment in the palace as in Act II. Nabucco sits gazing in a stupor.

*Nabucco:* He behaves as if waking. This is his body, and yet wasn't he just now fleeing through the woods like a hunted animal? He decides that it was all a terrible dream, "terribil sogno." Outside trumpets sound, and he reaches for his sword, but he has none. The crowd shouts for Fenena as a funeral march begins. Nabucco, going to the gallery, sees her being led, bound and weeping, between files of soldiers. He rushes to the door and discovers he is a prisoner, "ah prigioniero io **"preghiera"** sono." Returning to the gallery, he kneels and calls on the God of the Hebrews. If Jehovah will save him from so great a father's sorrow, "tanto affano," he will build him a temple and worship him forever, "adoranti ognor saprò." He rises to try the door, and it is opened by Abdallo.

*Nabucco, Abdallo and soldiers:* Abdallo urges him not to expose his disordered mind to the jeers of the crowd, and the soldiers say that they **solo with chorus** have come to defend him. But Nabucco insisting his mind is now clear asks for a sword, "il brando," to save Fenena. The soldiers swear to follow him, promising that the traitors will fall like locusts to the ground. Nabucco swears that they will again see the flashing of his crown in the sun, "di mia corona, corona al sol."

## SCENE 2 (11 min.)

The hanging garden as in Act III. The High Priest of Bel is beneath the peristyle of the temple next to an expiatory altar (with drains to catch the blood). On either side is a headsman with an ax. Fenena and **march** the Hebrews arrive to a funeral march. As Fenena arrives midstage, she stops and kneels before Zaccaria.
*Zaccaria and Fenena:* He urges her quietly to go on. She will find her fatherland in Heaven.
**"preghiera"** She sees Heaven open before her and Jehovah promising her joy: she bids the earth and stars farewell, "addio." Her soul flees, "fugge l'alma," and flys to Heaven, "e vola al ciel."
*Finale:* Outside there is a cry of "Viva Nabucco," and he runs in followed by Abdallo and the soldiers. He orders the men to tumble the statue of Bel, but it falls by itself and shatters. The crowd takes it as a sign from Heaven. Nabucco calls on the Hebrews to build a new **chorus** Temple, for only Jehovah is great and strong. All praise "immenso Jehovah."

Abigaille enters having taken poison. She humbles herself to Fenena, calls on the Hebrew God to comfort her in affliction, and dies, begging him not to curse her, "non maledire a me." She dies, and Zaccaria promises Nabucco that as the servant of Jehovah he will be the king of kings.

### Vocabulary, Act IV

| | | |
|---|---|---|
| terribil sogno | ter.ee.bil so.n'yo | terrible dream |
| ah prigioniero io sono | ah pree.joan.yair.oh yo so.no | ah, I am a prisoner |
| tanto affano | tan.toe ah.fah.no | so great sorrow |
| adorarti ognor saprò | ad.dor.rahr.tee own.yore sah.proh | I shall worship Thee forever |
| il brando | eel brahn.doe | a sword |
| di mia corona | dee me.ah kor.OWN.ah | of my crown |
| corona al sol | kor.OWN.ah ahl sole | crown in the sun |
| addio | ah.DEE.oh | farewell |
| fugge l'alma | food.jay l'ahl.mah | the soul flees |

Vocabulary, Act IV (*continued*)

| | | |
|---|---|---|
| e vola al ciel | ay vo.lah ahl chell | and flys to the sky |
| immenso Jehovah | ee.men.so | mighty |
| non maledire a me | known mahl.lay.deer' | don't curse me |
| | ah may | |

# MACBETH

Melodrama in four acts. First performed at Florence on March 14, 1847; revised version given at Paris on April 21, 1865. Music by G. Verdi. Libretto by F. M. Piave, after Shakespeare's play, first printed in 1623.

### PRINCIPAL CHARACTERS

| | | |
|---|---|---|
| Macbeth, Thane of Glamis and one of Duncan's generals | baritone | mac.BEH.toe |
| Banquo, another general | bass | |
| Lady Macbeth | soprano | |
| Macduff, Thane of Fife | tenor | |
| Duncan, King of Scotland | (silent part) | |
| Fleance, son of Banquo | (silent part) | |

The action takes place in and near Glamis Castle, Scotland, in 1040 A.D.

Of all his early operas Verdi loved *Macbeth* the best. Shakespeare was his favorite poet, and with the opera Verdi felt he was attempting something new. The opera has neither hero, heroine, nor romantic role for a tenor, only the inexorable effect on the two criminals of their crime. And in them is the opera's power, for however much the witches may seem like a group of girl scouts haunting on Halloween, Macbeth and Lady Macbeth are real persons, suffering, triumphant, terrified and finally broken.

It is not important to know the details of the revision; most critics agree that Verdi improved the opera. However, because the new production was for Paris, Verdi had to include a ballet. He inserted this in Act III before the apparitions and had Hecate appear from the underworld; most productions omit it. He also changed or added Lady Macbeth's aria at the beginning of Act II, the duet between her and Macbeth that ends Act III, the exiles' chorus in Act IV, the fugue for the battle, and the final hymn of victory.

In a letter to Salvatore Cammarano, a librettist with influence at the

San Carlo in Naples, Verdi wrote about a production of the opera:

"I know you are rehearsing 'Macbeth,' and since it is an opera which interests me more than all my others, you will permit me to say a few words about it. They gave the role of Lady Macbeth to Tadolini . . . Tadolini's appearance is good and beautiful, and I would like Lady Macbeth twisted and ugly. Tadolini sings to perfection, and I don't wish Lady Macbeth really to sing at all. Tadolini has a marvelous, brilliant, clear, powerful voice, and for Lady Macbeth I should like a raw, choked, hollow voice. Tadolini's voice has something angelic, Lady Macbeth's voice should have something devilish. Pass on these reflections to the management . . .

"Tell them that the most important numbers of the opera are the duet between Lady Macbeth and her husband and the Sleep Walking scene. If these two numbers are lost, then the opera falls flat. And these two numbers absolutely must not be sung:
> "They must be acted and declaimed
> With very hollow voice,
> Veiled: otherwise it will
> make no effect.
> The orchestra 'con sordini' (with mutes)."

There is no record of whether or not Verdi saw Tadolini's performance or was pleased with the reports of it. Probably he would have been disappointed; the sopranos of the time were trained in a different tradition. The Lady Macbeth of the 1847 première complained in her memoirs that Verdi demanded more than 150 rehearsals of the first-act duet and insisted on a dress rehearsal, a thing unheard of. Clearly he tried to create something quite different from the usual soprano role.

## PRELUDE (3 min.)

Its music reappears in the Sleepwalking Scene.

## ACT I (43 min.)

### SCENE 1 (13 min.)

A wood near a battlefield. It is the end of the day. Amidst thunder and lightning three groups of witches gather.

**chorus** *The Witches:* They greet each other and discuss their business. A drum roll interrupts them. "Vien, Macbetto," they call (come, Macbeth).

Macbeth and Banquo enter, fresh from battle with the rebellious Thane of Cawdor. Macbeth accosts the witches who hail him "Salve, O Macbetto" (hail . . .), first as Thane of Glamis, which he is, then as Thane of Cawdor and lastly as King of Scotland.

Banquo asks them to prophesy for him: he will be lesser yet greater than Macbeth; not so happy, yet much happier; not king himself, but the father of kings. Then the witches vanish.

Soldiers enter and salute Macbeth as Thane of Cawdor, newly created at the King's command. Macbeth is startled.

*Macbeth and Banquo:* Macbeth comments in an aside that he will **duet and chorus** never raise "la man rapace" (the hand rapacious) to seize the throne. Banquo, also aside, wonders at the prophecy and its effect on Macbeth. The soldiers wonder why Macbeth seems so worried. They all go off.

**chorus** *The Witches:* They reappear for a chorus in which they prophesy that Macbeth will come to them again.

## SCENE 2 (30 min.)

The courtyard of Glamis Castle. It is night.

*Lady Macbeth:* She reads a letter from Macbeth in which he describes the prophecy, Cawdor and King, and how it is already half fulfilled. **aria** The letter excites her. She fears (first part of the aria) Macbeth's vacillating, honest spirit. She urges him to come, "vieni," so that she can stir his ambition. He must be King. "Che tardi" (what holds you back)? she argues. A messenger from Macbeth announces that Duncan will spend the night in the castle. "Qui" (here), "qui, la notte" (here, tonight), she gasps. Then (second part of the aria) she calls on the spirits of Hell to "unsex me here" and strengthen her for murder that night.

*Macbeth and Lady Macbeth:* She greets him as "Cawdor" and inquires when the King will depart. Tomorrow, Macbeth replies. He must not, she insists. "Intendo" (I understand), Macbeth agrees. Then they prepare to welcome Duncan, who marches in with Banquo, Malcom **march** and Macduff.

*Macbeth:* Alone in the courtyard, he sees a dagger before him. Is it a sign from the witches or the imaginings of a fevered brain? The dagger leads him up to Duncan's chamber and he follows it.

*Macbeth and Lady Macbeth:* She enters looking for him. He appears from Duncan's chamber, dagger in hand and distraught. "Tutto è **duet** finito" (all is finished), he gasps. He heard voices in the room—some praying, some saying Macbeth had murdered sleep— and he couldn't even add "amen" for Duncan's soul. She warns such thoughts are folly, "follie." He must go back and smear the grooms with blood so that they will be accused. Macbeth refuses. She takes the dagger and goes off. He notices the blood on his hands. A knocking at the gate startles him. Lady Macbeth insists that a little water will clean their hands. She pulls Macbeth off as the knocking grows louder, and he wishes the deed had never been done.

**aria** *Banquo:* He and Macduff enter, and Macduff goes off to wake the King. Banquo remarks on the strangeness of the night, so full of signs and sounds.

*Finale:* Macduff discovers the murder—"orrore" (horror)—and rouses **chorus** the castle. All are horrified. (It is important to remember that in the Middle Ages the murder of a King was more than merely a crime against a person: it was an assault on the entire moral and political structure of society. Critics greatly admire the "a cappella" writing and Verdi's use of it in this chorus.)

### Vocabulary, Act I

| | | |
|---|---|---|
| vien, Macbetto | v'YAYN Mac.BEH.toe | come, Macbeth |
| salve, O Macbetto | sahl.vay oh . . . | hail, oh . . . |
| la man rapace | lah mahn rah.pah.chay | the hand rapacious |
| vieni | v'YAY.nee | come |
| che tardi | kay tar.dee | what holds you back |
| qui | kwee | here |
| qui, la notte | kwee lah NOT.tay | here, tonight |
| intendo | een.TEN.doe | I understand |
| tutto è finito | toot.toe eh fee.NEE.toe | all is finished |
| follie | foh.LEE.eh | folly |
| orrore | or.roar.ray | horror |

## ACT II (27 min.)

### SCENE 1 (6 min.)

A room in Glamis Castle.

*Macbeth and Lady Macbeth:* He is pensive; she, restless. She cannot understand why he is always sunk in thought. The deed is done; Macbeth is King; and Malcolm fled to England, considered by all to be his father's murderer. Macbeth worries about Banquo and his son, Fleance, whom the witches prophesied would be King. He and Lady Macbeth agree, and he leaves to arrange the murder of Banquo and Fleance.

*Lady Macbeth:* The day wanes; night once again must come to hide the
**aria** bloody hand. More blood, "nuovo delitto" (new crime). But it is necessary, "è necessario," she resolves. The throne, the crown, the thrill of power soothe the soul.

### SCENE 2 (7 min.)

A park. In the distance Glamis Castle.
**chorus** *The Murderers:* They gather (to a chorus that almost parodies itself). "Trema, Banquo" (tremble, Banquo).
*Banquo:* He enters with Fleance on his way to the banquet at the
**aria** castle. The night reminds him of Duncan's murder, and he fears for himself and Fleance. The murderers strike him down, but Fleance escapes.

### SCENE 3 (14 min.)

The Great Hall in Glamis Castle. A banquet is spread.
*Finale—Macbeth, Lady Macbeth, Macduff and Lords and Ladies:*
The banquet begins normally enough as the Lords hail Macbeth as King and Lady Macbeth as Queen. In return they welcome their guests and Lady Macbeth sings a "brindisi," a toast.

One of the hired assassins signals Macbeth from the side and reports that Banquo was killed but Fleance escaped. Macbeth turns back to his guests and remarks that Banquo is delayed but, to complete the circle of brave warriors, he will sit in Banquo's seat.

As he goes to sit down, Banquo's ghost appears (to Macbeth alone) with bleeding wounds. Macbeth swears to the ghost that he did not cause its death: "never shake your gory locks at me." The astounded Lords think Macbeth is sick and prepare to leave. Lady Macbeth urges them to stay and whispers to Macbeth to pull himself together. Macbeth insists to her that Banquo was there. But he regains his composure, and she starts the "brindisi" again.

Again the ghost appears. This time Macbeth collapses in terror. He begs it to be gone, "fuggi . . . fantasma tremendo" (flee . . . awful phantasm). It disappears and Macbeth broods on what it wants: "sangue a me . . ." (blood from me . . .). He resolves to visit the witches, "alle streghe" (to the witches). Lady Macbeth insists the dead cannot return. Macduff decides to flee to England and the Lords fear for the country whose King has such dark secrets.

Vocabulary, Act II

| | | |
|---|---|---|
| nuovo delitto | n'woe.voe deh.lit.toe | new crime |
| è necessario | eh neh.chess.SAHR.yo | it is necessary |
| trema, Banquo | TRAY.mah . . . | tremble, Banquo |
| fuggi . . . fantasma tremendo | food.jee . . . fan.tahs.mah tree.men.doe | fly . . . awful phantasm |
| sangue a me | sahng.gway ah may | blood from me |
| alle streghe | ah.leh stray.geh | to the witches |

## ACT III (18 min., without ballet)

A dark cavern. Witches surround a cauldron.

**chorus**     *The Witches:* Double, double, toil and trouble; fire, burn; and cauldron, bubble. Eye of newt, and toe of frog, wool of bat and tongue of dog.

(Here comes the Hecate ballet, which is usually cut.)

*Macbeth and the Apparitions:* He enters the cave and demands the witches reveal his fate. They offer to speak themselves or to let him hear from those whose ministers they are. He chooses the apparitions.

On a clap of thunder the first, a head covered with a helmet, rises from the ground. "Dimmi, o spirto" (speak to me), Macbeth insists impetuously. "Taci" (be silent), the witches admonish. The apparition warns him to beware of Macduff.

The second apparition, a bloody child, assures him that no man born of woman can harm him. Happily, Macbeth hopes to spare Macduff but then on second thought decides to kill him.

The third apparition, a child with a crown on its head and a tree in its hand, assures him that no harm can befall him till Birnam wood shall come to Dunsinane. Macbeth rejoices, for never even by magic has an entire wood been moved.

Macbeth turns to the witches. He demands to know if Banquo's sons will sit on the throne. The witches warn him not to ask. But he insists "Io voglio" (I wish it) and threatens them with his sword. The cauldron sinks into the ground, and the witches crouch and watch.

Eight Kings pass over the stage. The last is Banquo, who holds a looking glass and points at his descendants. "Fuggi, regal fantasima . . ." (flee royal phantasm), Macbeth cries to the first. But they keep coming: "un terzo, un quarto, un quinto . . ." In despair Macbeth sobs "O mio terror" (oh my terror). He tries to attack them with his sword. Then drawing back, he asks if the apparitions will live. They will live, the witches assure him. Macbeth swoons.

(Here there is another short ballet and chorus for witches. It too is usually cut.)

*Macbeth and Lady Macbeth:* She enters and he repeats the riddles of
**duet**     the apparitions. Together they vow death and destruction on Banquo's issue and Macduff: "vendetta" (vengeance).

Vocabulary, Act III

| | | |
|---|---|---|
| dimmi, o spirto | dee.me oh spear.toe | speak to me, oh spirit |
| taci | tah.chee | be silent |
| lo voglio | low voh.l'yo | I wish it |
| fuggi, regal fantasima | food.jee ray.gal fan.tahs'ee.mah | flee, royal phantasm |
| un terzo | oon tair.tso | a third |
| un quarto | . . . kwahr.toe | a fourth |
| un qunito | . . . kwin.toe | a fifth |
| o mio terror | oh me.oh ter.oar | oh my terror |
| vendetta | ven.DEBT.tah | vengeance |

## ACT IV (27 min.)

Some months later. Macbeth has tried to force the country to accept him but has won, at best, only sullen obedience. Malcolm, Duncan's son, is in England raising an army. Many of the Thanes, including Macduff, have secretly joined him. Macbeth's murderers, seeking Macduff and not finding him, have slaughtered Lady Macduff and his children.

## SCENE 1 (12 min.)

The ravaged countryside near the English border. Scottish refugees from burned-out farms and villages clog the road.

**chorus**    *Scottish Refugees:* They lament the fate of Scotland, "la patria oppressa" (oppressed country), where each day fathers die, orphans wail, and the deathknell never stops tolling.

**aria**    *Macduff:* He laments for his children and his wife who, when they needed him most, called for him in vain. (This is the only tenor solo in the opera.) "Ah, la paterna mano" (ah, the paternal hand). *Malcolm and Macduff:* Malcolm enters with troops. Macduff and his

**chorus**    few followers join him. The refugees urge them on. Malcolm directs the troops to cut branches from the trees in Birnam wood to carry before them so that Macbeth may be confused as to their number.

## SCENE 2 (12 min.)

A room in Glamis Castle. It is night.

*Lady Macbeth:* Her lady in waiting brings in a doctor to observe her.

**aria**    Lady Macbeth appears, sleepwalking. She murmurs "una macchia" (a spot). She tries to wipe Duncan's blood off her hands. Then she thinks of Macduff's wife and children and, finally, of Banquo. Then it is again the night of Duncan's murder. Macbeth is with her. They hear the knocking and she urges him to come to bed so that no one will suspect them. "Andiam, Macbetto" (let us go, Macbeth).

## SCENE 3 (13 min.)

A hall in Glamis Castle. Macbeth is alone.

*Macbeth:* He blusters that the rebellious Thanes and Malcolm will fix

**aria**    him even more firmly on the throne. But then he regrets that honor, respect and love will never be his, even in old age; he will have only curses, "ahi lasso" (alas).

The lady in waiting runs in. She announces that Lady Macbeth, "la regina" (the Queen), is dead. Macbeth despairingly comments that life is a tale told by an idiot, full of sound and fury, signifying nothing. *The Battle:* Macbeth's soldiers announce that Birnam wood seems to

**fugue**    be marching against them. It is Malcolm's army fulfilling the third prophecy. Macduff will fulfill the other two in himself and his birth. His mother died before he was born, and he was ripped from her womb.

Macduff enters and, after a fight, fatally wounds Macbeth. (In the

Paris version Macbeth here goes off fighting with Macduff and is not
**arietta**    seen again. In the original version Macbeth had a final aria,
and this is often kept. In it Macbeth curses the witches and the crown
which set him at war with heaven and earth.)
**chorus**    *People and Soldiers, Macduff and Malcolm:* They all praise
God and hope for better times for Scotland in a "Hymn of Victory."
"Vittoria" (victory).

Vocabulary, Act IV

| la patria oppressa | lah pah.tree.ah oh press.ah | oppressed country |
|---|---|---|
| la paterna mano | lah pah.tair.nah mah.no | the paternal hand |
| una macchia | oona mahk.y'ah | a spot |
| andiam, Macbetto | an.d'yahm | let us go, Macbeth |
| ahi lasso | aye.lah.so | alas |
| la regina | lah ray.JEE.nah | the Queen |
| vittoria | vee.TOR.ee.ah | victory |

(Some producers present the opera in three acts, generally cutting
the final "vendetta" duet in Act III and in the battle in Act IV, presumably because it is difficult to stage, Birnam wood's approaching
Dunsinane. The third act, as so presented, has four scenes. The cuts
are serious. They make the last act a long one (always a mistake),
leave the famous prophecies unfulfilled, and conceal Lady Macbeth's
disintegration from cool assurance at the banquet in Act II through
near hysteria in the duet in Act III to haunted sleepwalking in Act IV.)

# RIGOLETTO

Opera in three acts. First performed at Venice on March 11, 1851.
Music by G. Verdi. Libretto by F. M. Piave after a play by Hugo,
*Le Roi s'amuse.*

### PRINCIPAL CHARACTERS

| The Duke of Mantua | tenor | |
|---|---|---|
| Rigoletto, his jester and a hunchback | baritone | |
| Sparafucile, a professional cutthroat | bass | spa.rah.foo.CHEEL |
| Gilda, Rigoletto's daughter | soprano | SHJEEL.da |
| Maddalena, Sparafucile's sister | contralto | |

The action takes place at Mantua in the sixteenth century.

*Rigoletto* is undoubtedly one of Verdi's best operas. No aria or scene need be cut or shifted; there are no "versions"; it is all one piece, theatrically and musically, perhaps because in a burst of inspiration Verdi rattled it off in forty days.

At the time Verdi himself knew how good it was. During the rehearsals for the premiere in Venice in 1851, he withheld the music for "La Donna e Mobile" (woman is fickle) until two days before the performance in order to prevent the cast from humming it around town. And on opening night it stopped the show.

In a different way it stopped the show again a few years ago when the tenor, collecting breath for one of the high notes, gulped down his false mustache.

The opera is based on Victor Hugo's play, *Le Roi s'amuse.* Hugo, however, instead of being complimented, was outraged and in an effort to stop the Paris production of the opera, sued the theater manager. But he lost and in later years more graciously admitted that the fourth-act quartet and second-act scene with Sparafucile even improved on his play.

The plot is simple. Count Monterone curses the Duke for debauching his daughter (who has died, apparently of shame). Rigoletto, the Duke's hunchbacked jester, taunts the old man, who furiously curses the jester for jeering at a father's agony. This is the first act. The next three show the curse working itself out: the Duke debauches Rigoletto's daughter, the jester's scheme for revenge is frustrated, and the daughter dies. Verdi's original title for the opera was *La Maledizione,* but for some mysterious reason the censors objected to it.

The opera as written is in three acts; the first has two scenes. Most productions separate the two scenes by an intermission and present four acts.

## ACT I (16 min.)

The opera begins with a short (3 min.), ominous prelude, related to Monterone and his curse. This is interrupted by tinkly dance music, and the rising curtain reveals the Duke of Mantua's court dancing and gossiping in the main hall of the palace.

*The Duke and Borsa:* The Duke remarks impatiently to the courtier that his intrigue with the unidentified girl in town should progress.

For three months now he has secretly met her, disguised as a student. (The girl is Rigoletto's daughter, Gilda, unknown at court.) Then noticing the Countess Ceprano, the Duke praises her figure. Borsa suggests he is unfaithful to his student love.

**aria**     The Duke sings, "Questa o quella" (this girl or that), each a flower to be plucked and discarded. The aria has two verses.

*The Duke and Countess Ceprano:* He extravagantly praises her. Although embarrassed, she accompanies him to another room. Count Ceprano is agitated and follows them. Rigoletto suggests to the courtiers that they amuse themselves by watching Ceprano squirm as the Duke besieges his wife, and some of the courtiers go out with him.

*Marullo:* He enters and excitedly tells his friends that Rigoletto keeps a mistress; he has discovered her (actually it is Gilda). The courtiers are surprised.

*The Duke and Rigoletto:* The Duke wonders how he can get rid of Ceprano for a night. Rigoletto suggests arrest or execution. Ceprano **quintet**     is furious. To his friends he swears revenge: "vendetta" (vengeance). The Duke warns Rigoletto against the courtiers, but Rigoletto is sure they wouldn't dare harm the Duke's jester. The Duke, Rigoletto, Ceprano and the courtiers work the contrasting ideas into a quintet with chorus.

*Monterone, Rigoletto et al:* The old man forces his way into the hall and demands to see the Duke. Rigoletto sprawls on the throne and imitates the Duke giving an audience. He complains that he has graciously forgiven Monterone for treason and shouldn't have to listen to these old tales of dishonoring the man's daughter. The Duke and courtiers laugh. Monterone vows God will avenge him. The Duke, irritated, orders the guards to arrest him. Monterone then curses the Duke and Rigoletto: "sii Maledetto." He calls the Duke vile to loose a jackal jester on him, and he curses Rigoletto for mocking a father's agony.

The Duke and the courtiers urge the old spoilsport to be gone. Rigoletto, however, with his secret daughter, is terrified: "orrore" (horror).

### Vocabulary, Act I

| quest(a) o quella | quest(a) oh quail.ah | this girl or that |
|---|---|---|
| vendetta | ven.DEBT.tah | vengeance |
| sii maledetto | see mal.eh.DEBT.toe | curse you |
| orrore | or.roar.ray | horror |

## ACT II (35 min.)

The act divides roughly into four parts: Rigoletto and Sparafucile (7 min.), Rigoletto and Gilda (11 min.), Gilda and the Duke (12 min.) and the abduction of Gilda (5 min.). The almost unbroken succession of duets is unique to the opera and an example of Verdi's ability to vary the mood and pace of music even within one form.

Night. A deserted street in Mantua. On one side behind a wall is Rigoletto's simple house and garden; on the other, Count Ceprano's palazzo looms over the street.

*Rigoletto and Sparafucile:* Rigoletto still worries about the curse. Sparafucile accosts him and offers to put his sword at Rigoletto's **duet** service. He explains that his sister acts as a decoy and that the killing is actually done at his hut on the bank of the river Mincio. It costs twice as much to kill a noble as a commoner. Rigoletto sends him off after asking where he can find him again.

Left alone, Rigoletto muses, "Pari siamo" (alike we are): he stabs at night and I, with my tongue, by day. Then he rails at his deformity and the debasement of being a jester. Most of all he hates the courtiers whom he must try to please. His mood changes as he remembers Gilda and enters his garden.

*Rigoletto and Gilda:* They embrace—"mio padre," "figlia" (my father, daughter)—and exclaim how much each means to the other. She tries to comfort him and asks if there is something in their family that haunts them (evidently Rigoletto has told her nothing about his job or the court; in fact, he has only just moved her from the country **arietta** to the town). She asks who her mother was. In an arietta Rigoletto laments that his wife died. "Moria, moria" (she died). This **duet** leads to a duet in which Gilda urges him to forget, and he sighs that she alone is left to comfort him.

The duet continues as Gilda asks him about "patria" and "famiglia" (country, family), and he insists she is all of them to him.

Suddenly he fears that in the three months she's been in town she may have attracted someone's attention. Gilda lies that she's seen no one. Rigoletto then warns the nurse to guard "questo fiore" (this **duet** flower). In between the two verses Rigoletto rushes into the street to make sure no one is there. Behind his back the Duke slips in, seen only by the nurse, whom he bribes. The Duke discovers for the first time that it is Rigoletto's daughter. After a reprise of "questo fiore," Rigoletto leaves.

*The Duke and Gilda:* She starts to tell the nurse how badly she feels for lying. The Duke, disguised as a student, interrupts and passionately **aria** announces that he loves her. She shyly holds him off. Then in a two-verse aria he tries to overcome all her objections. Outside in the street Ceprano and Borsa make a noise that alarms the nurse. The Duke swears under his breath that if it is Rigoletto, he will kill him. **duet** Gilda now, however, has the nurse on her side, and the Duke goes. He and Gilda sing an "addio" (good-by) duet. (The Duke is a bravura role, and although it is not in the score, tenors sometimes end the last "addio" on a high D flat—or they try to.)

Gilda, left alone, rhapsodizes on the "student's" name—Gualtier **aria** Maldè. The aria starts "caro nome . . ." (dear name . . . carved on my heart). She repeats it lovingly, while outside the house the courtiers gather to abduct the girl whom they suppose is Rigoletto's mistress.

*The Abduction:* Rigoletto comes on them and is terrified for Gilda. But by hiding Ceprano and showing Rigoletto the key to Ceprano's house (with the Count's crest), which they claim to have stolen, the courtiers persuade him that they plan to abduct the Countess Ceprano for the Duke. Rigoletto then agrees to hold the ladder.

Claiming they are all masked, they put a mask on Rigoletto that **chorus** effectively blinds him. There is a chorus—"zitti" (sh!)— during which they get in the house and away with Gilda before Rigoletto realizes he has been duped.

### Vocabulary, Act II

| | | |
|---|---|---|
| pari siamo | par.eee see.ah.moe | equal we are |
| mio padre | me.oh pah.dray | my father |
| figlia | feel.yah | daughter |
| moria | more.ee.ah | she died |
| patria | pah.tree.ah | country |
| famiglia | fah.meal.yah | family |
| questo fiore | quest.oh fee.yor.eh | good-by |
| addio | ah.DEE.oh | farewell |
| Gualtier Maldè | Gwal.tee.air Mahl.day | Walter Malde |
| caro nome | kah.roe no.may | dear name |
| zitti | zee.tee | sh |

## ACT III (31 min.)

Later the same night in a room of the Duke's palace; to the back is a hall and on the left a large portrait of the Duke.

**arietta**     *The Duke:* He is agitated. When he stole back to see Gilda, the house was broken open and deserted. In an arietta he wonders where she is, whether she is weeping and wishes he could rescue her.

**chorus**     *The Duke and the Courtiers:* They describe excitedly how they fooled Rigoletto into assisting them to abduct his own "mistress." The Duke realizes the courtiers have mistaken Gilda for Rigoletto's mistress and is delighted to hear that they have brought her to his **aria**     rooms. He sings a quick two-verse aria of excited anticipation at the joys of love. (Sometimes this aria or a verse of it is cut.) *Rigoletto:* He enters, greets the courtiers absently and looks for evidence of Gilda, hoping he can find her without revealing that she is his daughter. (This is one of the great scenes in opera for baritones, separating the artists from the mere singers. It can take all the singing and acting ability a baritone can give it and in its context, when well done, it is heartbreaking.)

A page enters and asks for the Duke. The courtiers say that he is asleep. Not so, replies the page, because he just passed him in the hall. He's out hunting, the courtiers suggest. It is too late, the page insists. The courtiers hurry the page out.

Rigoletto, however, realizes that the Duke is at that moment dishonoring Gilda. With a terrible cry he announces she is his daughter— "mia figlia." He tries to push past the courtiers to the Duke's room, but they throw him back.

He swears at them: "cortigiani" (courtiers). He accuses them of selling his daughter. He threatens them, calls them "assassini" (assassins). Again they throw him back from the door.

Now in despair, he begs Marullo to be kind to him, to tell him that Gilda is not really behind the door: "non è vero" (it isn't true). "Tu taci" (you are silent), he sobs.

Then he pleads with the courtiers, beginning, "Miei signori . . ." (my lords). He continues, "Perdono, pietà" (forgive, have pity). She was dearer to him than anything in the world—"tutto, tutto al mondo" (all, all in the world). The courtiers are unmoved.

*Gilda and Rigoletto:* She rushes out of the Duke's room, obviously ravaged. Rigoletto refuses to believe the worst, but Gilda admits it. Rigoletto then imperiously orders the courtiers to leave them alone.

Gilda brokenly explains how every morning at church the "student" first watched her, then whispered to her and promised love.

Rigoletto muses on how perversely Heaven has answered his prayers for Gilda.

**duet**    They join in a duet, Rigoletto trying to comfort her—"piangi, fanciulla" (weep, little girl)—and Gilda sobbing that he is the best of fathers.

*Monterone:* At the back, guards lead Monterone to prison. Monterone shakes his fist at the portrait of the Duke and wails that his curse has been in vain.

*Rigoletto and Gilda:* Rigoletto promises the vanishing Monterone that
**duet**    an avenger is at hand. Turning to the portrait of the Duke, he swears to kill him: "si, vendetta" (yes, vengeance). Gilda is horrified and urges her father to forgive the Duke and not to draw Heaven's wrath on himself: "perdonate" (forgive him).

### Vocabulary, Act III

| | | |
|---|---|---|
| mia figlia | me.ah feel.yah | my daughter |
| cortigiani | core.tee.JAH.nee | courtiers |
| assassini | ah.sah.SEE.knee | assassins |
| non è vero | non eh vair.oh | it isn't true |
| tu taci | two TAH.chee | you are silent |
| miei signori | m'yea seen.yor.ee | my lords |
| perdono, pietà | pear.doe.no p'yay.tah | forgive, have pity |
| piangi fanciulla | p'yahn.jee fan.chule.ah | weep, little girl |
| si, vendetta | see ven.debt.tah | yes, vengeance |
| perdonate | pair.doe.nah.teh | forgive him |

## ACT IV (28 min.)

Night. By the river Mincio; in the background, Mantua; and on the left, Sparafucile's hut. Rigoletto and Gilda are outside; Sparafucile, inside.

*Rigoletto and Gilda:* She confesses she still loves the Duke because, in spite of what's happened, he really loves her. Rigoletto promises to reveal how well the Duke loves her. They peek in the house.

*The Duke:* He is in disguise for an assignation with Maddalena,

**aria**    Sparafucile's sister. While waiting, he sings, "La donna è mobile" (woman is fickle). (Tenors traditionally demonstrate their taste and ability by inserting a cadenza of their own invention to end the aria.) At the end when Maddalena enters, Sparafucile steps out to ask Rigoletto when he wants the Duke killed. Rigoletto suggests later in the evening.

**quartet**    *The Duke, Rigoletto, Maddalena and Gilda:* The Duke gaily tells Maddalena that he's loved her always. Maddalena laughs but, outside, Gilda is stunned. Rigoletto keeps asking her what she thinks now. The Duke courts Maddalena in extravagant terms: "bella figlia dell'amore . . ." (beautiful daughter of love). Maddalena accuses him of flattery. Gilda sobs that these are the words he sighed to her. Rigoletto urges her to forget the Duke and promises to avenge her.

At the end Rigoletto tells Gilda she must quickly return to Mantua, disguise herself as a boy and flee to Verona, where he will join her. Then Rigoletto gives Sparafucile the down payment on the Duke's murder and says he'll return for the body at midnight.

*The Duke, Sparafucile and Maddalena:* A storm threatens. The Duke, with an eye on Maddalena, suggests he spend the night. Sparafucile agrees, but Maddalena, charmed by the Duke, urges him to leave. Sparafucile, however, takes the Duke upstairs.

*Sparafucile, Maddalena and Gilda:* Gilda returns, in her disguise, to see the Duke again. She overhears Maddalena and Sparafucile argue about whether to kill him. Sparafucile insists he has made a bargain and will stick by it. Finally he agrees to spare the Duke if some victim **trio**    can be found before midnight. Maddalena despairs that no one will be out on such a stormy night. Gilda begs Heaven's pity and her father's forgiveness, for she will save the Duke. She knocks; they pull her inside and the storm beats itself out.

*Rigoletto:* He returns. Midnight strikes (usually six strokes in Italian operas). Sparafucile brings out a body in a sack. Rigoletto pays him off and, left alone, exults over the corpse.

Suddenly he hears the Duke's voice—"La donna è mobile."

He rips the sack and discovers Gilda: "mia figlia" (my daughter). With her last breaths she explains that she loved the Duke and asks **duet**    for her father's forgiveness. Rigoletto can only sob "non morire" (don't die), and "No, lasciarmi non dei" (no, don't leave me).

Gilda promises that she and her mother in Heaven will pray for him. Then as she dies, he remembers the curse: "ah, la maledizione."

Vocabulary, Act IV

| | | |
|---|---|---|
| la donna è mobile | lah dun(a) ay mow.bih. lay | woman is fickle |
| bella figlia dell'amore | bell.ah feel.ya dell' ah.more.ray | beautiful daughter of love |
| mia figlia | me.ah feel.ya | my daughter |
| non morire | known more.rear | don't die |
| no, lasciarmi non dei | no lash.are.me known day | no, don't leave me |
| ah, la maledizione | ah lah mal.eh.dee.tsee. own.nay | ah, the curse |

# IL TROVATORE

## (The Troubadour)

Opera in four acts. First performed at Rome on January 19, 1853. Music by G. Verdi. Libretto by S. Cammarano and L. E. Bardare after the play by A. G. Gutierrez, first produced in 1836.

### PRINCIPAL CHARACTERS

| | | |
|---|---|---|
| Ferrando, captain serving under the Count di Luna | bass | |
| Leonora, a lady in waiting to the Queen | soprano | lay.on.OR.ah |
| Count di Luna, one of the Queen's generals | baritone | |
| Manrico, captain serving under the Prince of Biscay in revolt against the Queen | tenor | man.REE.coe |
| Azucena, a gypsy who has raised Manrico | mezzo-soprano | ah.tsoo.CHAIN.ah |

The action takes place in Aragon and Biscay during the fifteenth century.

This is one of the most popular of Verdi's operas, although the libretto is constantly cited as the most confusing and silliest in opera. Possibly it is; but the charge is made sooner or later against every libretto, and to a large extent it is a matter of fashion. The opera is based on a Spanish play produced in 1836 at the height of the Romantic Age. Byron died twelve years earlier fighting for Greek independence. Berlioz in 1831, carrying a chambermaid's dress in his bag as a disguise, set out from Rome for Paris to murder his faithless fiancée and her mother. That same year Victor Hugo published his *Nôtre Dame de Paris*. It was an era of extravagant passions, and in Spain, where gypsies were a familiar part of the landscape, the story may not have seemed improbable.

The music, however, has never ·gone out of fashion. The arias are short, melodic and extremely vigorous. A good performance of the opera seems to race to its conclusion leaving the audience breathless and cheering with excitement. The orchestration is simple, mostly a tum-ti-tum on the strings, which places the burden of carrying the opera squarely on the singers. The characters have little depth to them, and none develops, so that no amount of acting ability can compensate for vocal inadequacy. More than many operas, *Il Trovatore* requires great singing.

## ACT I (26 min.)

### SCENE 1 (10 min.)

The duty room of the guards' barracks in the Aliaferia Palace in Aragon. It is the fifteenth century.

*Ferrando and the soldiers:* Stay awake, "all' erta," he warns the men. The Count is restless and watching Leonora's window. The soldiers grumble that the Count is jealous of the unknown troubadour. They beg Ferrando to keep them awake with a story—the one about Garcia, the Count's younger brother.

The Count's father, Ferrando starts, had two sons, and one day the **aria** nurse of the younger awoke to see—(the story is told in a song of two verses with Ferrando always hesitating at the most dramatic moment and the soldiers urging him on)—an old gypsy woman bending over the boy. She said she was merely casting his horoscope, but the nurse and everyone else said it was a spell. Sure enough, the child sickened. So they burned the old woman at the stake. Her daughter, for revenge, stole the boy. And, though no one saw her do it, the next day they found the blackened and burnt bones of a boy at the foot of the stake.

The soldiers are deliciously thrilled and ask what happened to the daughter. No one ever found her, Ferrando replies, but the Count is still searching for her and his brother, whom he believes alive. Ferrando is certain he could recognize the witch even now, twenty years later.

He warns them not to joke about the gypsy's being a witch and flying around at midnight. One man who struck her died horribly: "mori" (he died), he repeats. The soldiers are terrified, and when the clock unexpectedly strikes midnight (six strokes), they excitedly curse the witch.

### SCENE 2 (16 min.)

A few minutes later in the gardens of the palace; on the right, a staircase. Dark clouds drift over the moon.

*Leonora and Inez:* Inez warns Leonora that she must soon go in. The Queen has asked for her. But Leonora lingers, hoping the troubadour will come. She describes how she saw him first at a tourney and how they—he from Biscay and she from Aragon—were separated by the **aria** civil war. But one night "tacea la notte . . ." (still was the night . . .), his voice came up to her. (In a broad, rising line she describes how deeply it thrilled her.)

Inez, however, foresees trouble in loving a traitor and urges Leonora to forget him. Leonora is indignant. Now in agitated gasps—almost hiccups—she insists that he alone can win her. Inez remains pessimistic. They go in to the Queen.

*Di Luna and Manrico:* The Count steals into the garden. From the lights in the windows he decides that the Queen has gone to bed but that Leonora is up. The thought of her overcomes him, and he is about to break into her chamber when Manrico, from a distance, be- **aria** gins his serenade. "Io fremo," the Count rages (I tremble).

*Leonora, Di Luna and Manrico:* She too has heard the serenade and rushes out. In the darkness she assumes that the Count, the only man she sees, is the troubadour. Manrico arrives in time to see her start towards the Count. "Infida" (unfaithful woman), he calls scornfully. She persuades him it was the darkness; she loves him alone. "Io t'amo" (I love you). This enrages the Count, who demands the troubadour **trio** reveal himself. It is Manrico, the rebel. The two men berate each other and prepare to duel while Leonora tries to stop them. But honor is engaged and, swearing to kill each other, they go off leaving Leonora to swoon.

Vocabulary, Act I

| all' erta | al air.tah | stay awake |
| mori | mor.EE | he died |
| tacea la notte | tah.chay la NOT.tay | still was the night |
| io fremo | yo FRAY.moe | I tremble |
| infida | in.FEE.dah | unfaithful woman |
| io t'amo | yo T'AH.moe | I love you |

## ACT II (33 min.)

### SCENE 1 (17 min.)

In the mountains of Biscay to the north where the revolt is centered. Manrico won the duel with the Count and was about to "thrust home" on his opponent when some mysterious urging stayed him. He spared the Count and, in return, later in a battle was severely wounded by the Count and left for dead. Azucena found him, took him to the mountains and nursed him back to health.

**Anvil Chorus**     *Gypsies:* They sing of gypsy life, girls and drink as some of the men work at their anvils.

*Azucena:* She has been gazing into the fire, and the flicker of the flames has unsettled her memories. She describes in horrible detail a victim being led out to the stake, prodded by the soldiers, kicked by the **aria**     crowd, bound and burnt. The aria is in two verses, each beginning, "Stride la vampa" (crackles the flames). At the close she turns to Manrico and sobs, "Mi vendica, mi vendica" (avenge me).

The chorus goes out.

*Azucena and Manrico:* Her remark confuses him and he questions her. She reveals that it was her mother who was burnt and who called out to her as she watched helplessly with her little boy in the crowd: "mi **aria**     vendica." Then she describes how she stole the baby boy, the present Count's brother, and in the night went back to the stake, relit the fire and, as the flames rose, heard again and again her mother's voice: "mi vendica." Blackness clouded her mind and eyes and, when it cleared, she realized that the stolen baby was by her side and that the burnt one was her own child—"il figlio mio" (my son). The memory of it haunts her.

Manrico then asks, "Non son tuo figlio" (I am not your son)?

His question reminds Azucena of her plot for vengeance: to use

Manrico to kill the Count. Instantly she tries to cover anything she may have revealed. She insists her story was just an hallucination. She reminds him that she fed him, cared for him, loved him. She asks how he could have spared the Count: "Strana pietà, strana pietà" (strange pity).

**duet**     Manrico describes how at the very last moment something seemed to stop him. Azucena then makes him swear to strike at the next opportunity. Manrico agrees: "Si, lo giuro" (yes, I swear it).

*Messenger:* The Prince of Biscay, the rebel leader, asks Manrico to lead the defense of the fortress of Castellor. As a goad he reports that Leonora, believing Manrico to be dead, is that very evening entering a convent near Castellor.

**duet**     *Manrico and Azucena:* He at once prepares to go. She tries to stop him. Leonora for her is a side issue. She insists that his wounds aren't healed and that if he goes, he doesn't love his mother. But Manrico states plainly that Leonora is the most important person in his life, and he goes, with Azucena trying vainly to stop him.

## SCENE 2 (16 min.)

That evening in the cloisters of the Convent near Castellor.

**aria**     *Di Luna:* The Count enters with Ferrando and a few followers. He sings of Leonora and his love for her—"ah, l'amor, l'amor" (the aches of love)—and how only she can calm "la tempesta del mio cor" (the tempest in my heart). (The aria is called "Il balen" from its first words.)

A bell rings to signify that Leonora will soon be coming. He places **aria and chorus**     his men. Passionately he bursts out that not even God will snatch Leonora from him, ". . . rapirt(i) a me" (snatch from me). He repeats it throughout the chorus: "no, no . . . rapirt(i) a me."

**chorus**     *Nuns:* Offstage in the chapel the nuns sing of consolation for the daughters of Eve. Slowly they proceed onstage with Leonora. She stops to comfort her companion, Inez, and insists she will find peace in the convent.

*Di Luna, Manrico and Leonora:* The Count furiously interrupts, "No giammai" (no, never). Manrico arrives with a company of soldiers. Leonora can't believe he is really alive: "Sei tu . . ." (it's you), she gasps. The Count, who also thought Manrico dead, is furious, and he and Manrico exchange threats.

The act ends with a quintet in which Leonora is overcome at what
**quintet and chorus**      she can scarcely believe. Inez thanks God for
helping Leonora. Manrico and the Count continue to growl at each
other, and Ferrando advises the Count not to fight against such odds.
The Nuns and soldiers exclaim appropriately.

### Vocabulary, Act II

| | | |
|---|---|---|
| stride la vampa | stree.day lah vah.mpah | crackles the flames |
| mi vendica | me ven.dee.kah | avenge me |
| il figlio mio | eel feel.yo me.oh | my son |
| non son tuo figlio | known son two.oh feel.yo | I am not your son |
| strana pietà | strah.nah p'yay.tah | strange pity |
| si lo giuro | see lo JUR.oh | yes, I swear it |
| ah l'amor | ah lah.more | ah (the pangs of love) |
| la tempesta del mio cor | lah tem.pes.tah del me.oh cor | the tempest in my heart |
| rapirti a me | rah.peer.t'ya may | snatch from me |
| no, giammai | no jam.EYE | no, never |
| sei tu | say two | it's you |

## ACT III  (22 min.)

### SCENE 1  (12 min.)

Count di Luna's camp outside the walls of Castellor.
**chorus**      *Soldiers:* They sing of how they're just resting now but in a
little while in battle will be regular demons.
*Di Luna:* He steps out of his tent and gazes at the walls of Castellor:
Leonora is there. Ferrando drags in a spy for questioning. It is
Azucena, who is trying to join Manrico inside the city.
*Di Luna, Ferrando and Azucena:* She does not know the Count except
**aria**      by name and does not recognize him. She admits she is a
gypsy from Biscay. She claims her only joy in life was a son who
deserted her and whom she now seeks. She begs to be released.

But the Count questions her about the stolen baby and the fire. Her
nervousness convinces Ferrando that she is the witch, and he identifies
her to the Count. In despair she wails for Manrico to save her. The
Count is delighted to learn that his rival's mother is in his power.

The scene ends as Azucena, realizing for the first time that her in-

**trio**     terrogator is the hated Count, spits out her defiance of him; the Count gloats how he can torture Manrico by torturing his mother; and Ferrando warns her that the fire at the stake is just a warm-up for the scorching she'll undergo in Hell.

## SCENE 2 (10 min.)

Inside the fortress in a room near the chapel.

*Leonora and Manrico:* The constant fighting has broken her nerve. She
**aria**     fears for Manrico. He consoles her by insisting that her love will make him stronger, but that if on the morrow his fate is to die, then death for him will be only going to Heaven before her. There they will be together.

The organ sounds for the wedding in the chapel, and they pledge their love.

A messenger runs in, announces that Azucena has been captured and that the Count is about to burn her. Black smoke and orange fire-light fill the sky.

**aria**     Leonora can't understand. The gypsy is, he reveals, his mother. Rushing to center stage he begins, "Di quella pira . . ." (from that pyre). The smoke, the heat, he feels already. The Count had better quench the flames or his blood will douse them. She was his mother before he loved her, he tells Leonora, as he prepares to go. He must save Azucena. Troops gather. Bugles blow. The battle is joined and Leonora left. (In this aria tenors traditionally insert a high C. The story is that one of the first Manricos was so carried away by the music's excitement and the beauty of his own singing that he inserted the note by accident, and Verdi allowed it to stay. Presuming on this most tenors now also attempt to finish the act on a high C.)

Vocabulary, Act III

di quella pira          dee quail.ah pee.rah          from that pyre

## ACT IV (41 min.)

---

## SCENE 1 (23 min.)

A courtyard in the Aliaferia Palace. To the back is the Prisoners' Tower. The sortie was successful and Azucena was saved. But later

Castellor fell and Manrico was captured. The Count has imprisoned him and Azucena in the tower. Leonora has disappeared and the Count has not yet found her. It is night.

*Leonora:* She enters heavily veiled and wearing a ring that conceals poison. Only the prison wall separates her from Manrico, but she can **aria** get no closer. She appeals to the sighing wind to carry her love to Manrico, to comfort him, but not to betray "le pene del mio cor" (the pain in my heart).

**miserere** Offstage the monks begin the "Miserere" as the death bell tolls for Manrico. Leonora is aghast. Suddenly from the tower Manrico's voice soars. He begs death to hurry and bids Leonora farewell: "Addio, Leonora." She is overcome.

Again she hears his voice. This time he begs her, "Non ti scordar di me" (don't you forget me). "Di te scordar-mi" (forget you)! she repeats.

**aria** She loves him forever. She will either save him or die with him. (This aria is sometimes cut.) A door opens and Leonora hides.

*Di Luna and Leonora:* The Count comes out. He orders an attendant to execute Manrico at dawn and to burn Azucena. He wonders where Leonora might be.

**duet** She reveals that she has come to beg life for Manrico. The Count refuses.

She kneels to him. He can kill her, "ma salva il Trovator" (but save the troubadour). The Count replies that the more she loves Manrico the more he hates him. He turns to go.

Finally she offers to marry him in return for a few minutes with Manrico and for his freedom. The Count agrees and each swears to it: "Lo giuro" (I swear it).

The Count calls the guard and countermands the order for the execution. Leonora secretly sips the poison from the ring.

The scene closes with Leonora ecstatically singing that Manrico is saved, while the Count exults that she is his.

### SCENE 2 (18 min.)

Minutes later in a cell in the Prisoners' Tower. Azucena lies on a cot; Manrico sits beside her.

*Manrico and Azucena:* She complains that she can't sleep. She thinks she is going to die before they burn her, but then she imagines they're coming to get her. He soothes her: "Alcuno . . ." (there's no one). "Il rogo" she sobs (the stake). The memory of her mother's death overcomes her. She sinks exhausted in his arms.

**duet** Then more quietly she agrees to lie down. She asks him to wake her if she dreams of the stake. He calms her "Ripos(a), o madre" (sleep, mother). With longing she remembers Biscay: "Ai nostri monti . . ." (to our mountains we'll return). Sleep, he soothes.

**duet** *Leonora and Manrico:* She urges him to flee at once, but he refuses to leave without her. Suddenly he guesses that she has bargained his freedom for her love. Furiously he turns on her: "Ha, quest' infame . . ." (ha, this faithless woman). She insists she has not betrayed him. Desperately, as she feels the poison begin to work, she urges him to go: "Fuggi, o sei perduto" (flee, or you are lost).

**trio** From her bed, half awake, half asleep, Azucena dreams of the mountains. Manrico continues to berate Leonora till finally she falls at his feet, gasping out the truth. She tries to push him out, but he stays with her.

**trio** Slowly she begins the final trio: she'd rather die Manrico's than live another's. The Count enters, sees them and promises himself revenge. As Leonora dies, the Count orders the guards to take Manrico out and execute him. Manrico calls farewell to Azucena, who advises the horrified Count that he has executed his brother. She has avenged her mother.

## Vocabulary, Act IV

| | | |
|---|---|---|
| le pene del mio cor | lay pay.neh del me.oh cor | the pain in my heart |
| addio | ah.dee.oh | farewell |
| non ti scordar di me | known tee scor.DAR dee may | don't forget me |
| di te scordarmi | dee.tay scor.DAR.me | forget you |
| ma salva il trovator | ma salv(a) eel trow.vah.tor | but save the troubadour |
| lo giuro | lo JUR.oh | I swear it |
| alcuno | al.COON.no | there is no one |
| il rogo | eel row.go | the stake |
| ripos(a) o madre | ree.pose.ah o mah.dray | sleep, mother |
| ai nostri monti | eye nos.tree MON.tee | to our mountains |
| ha quest' infame | ha quest' een.FAH.may | this faithless woman |
| fuggi | FOOD.jee | flee |
| o sei perduto | oh say pair.DEW.toe | or you are lost |

# LA TRAVIATA

Opera in three acts. First performed at Venice on March 6, 1853. Music by G. Verdi. Libretto by F. M. Piave after the play and novel by A. Dumas *fils, La Dame aux Camélias.*

### PRINCIPAL CHARACTERS

| | | |
|---|---|---|
| Violetta Valery | soprano | vee.oh.LET.ah |
| Flora Bervoix, her friend | mezzo-soprano | |
| Alfredo Germont | tenor | al.FRAY.doe |
| Annina, Violetta's maid | soprano | |
| Giorgio Germont, his father | baritone | |
| Dr. Grenvil, Violetta's doctor | bass | |

The action takes place in and near Paris in 1846 and 1847.

*La Traviata* is probably the world's most popular opera. This may be partly because it requires a smaller cast and orchestra than *Aida, La Bohème* or *Carmen,* and consequently is far more often performed than these in the smaller houses, and partly because the singers find the music lies well for their voices. But most persons would say it was because Verdi cared about Violetta. Somewhere inside his gruff exterior, he wept for her, and his feeling comes out in the music, brushing aside the operatic conventions, pulling up the audience and making even poor performances of the last act moving. *La Traviata* is one of the great operatic love stories; it is more human than *Tristan und Isolde,* which has a slight symbolic remoteness, and less contrived than *Madama Butterfly.*

The humanity of *La Traviata* comes to it naturally, for Violetta was an historical figure, Marie Duplessis, born January 15, 1824, and died February 3, 1847, of what was then called consumption and today tuberculosis. She seems to have been an extraordinary person, a mixture of sensuality and disinterestedness, simple yet loving luxury, gay and yet with a strain of sadness. She is said to have had great tact and breeding. Certainly her lovers, among whom were the Duc de Gramant, Liszt and Alexandre Dumas *fils* had nothing but good to say of her.

In 1846 she married the young Vicomte de Perregaux in London. Just why they married is unclear; they do not seem to have lived together. Before him, her accredited lover was an exceedingly rich man, Comte de Stackelberg, who was almost eighty. Dumas states that "the Count, notwithstanding his great age, sought in her not, like Oedipus, an Antigone, but, like David, a Bathsheba." These two, the grand old man and the young husband, followed her coffin to a temporary grave. Four days later she was reburied in the Montmartre Cemetery. Her stone records her true name, Alphonsine Plessis.

The opera was written in three acts, each being a day in Violetta's life. The two scenes of Act II, however, are frequently referred to as separate acts, making a total of four.

"Traviata" is the past participle feminine of the verb "traviare," meaning "to go astray." The title, therefore, means literally "the woman having gone astray." The title and story have inspired some remarkable prose as, for example, these last two sentences of one synopsis: "The fragile flower, broken on its stem, can never more raise its beauteous head. One gleam of happiness, the purest and the brightest that she has known, arising from her lover's assurance of his truth, and his desire to restore her reputation, gilds the closing moments of her life, as with a gentle sigh her soul parts tranquilly from its fragile tenement of clay."

## PRELUDE (4 min.)

It opens with a passage for violins, which appears again in the prelude to Act III when Violetta is dying. It then states and repeats with a more elaborate accompaniment Violetta's farewell to Alfredo in Act II. It leads directly with deliberate contrast into the gaiety of Violetta's party.

## ACT I (24 min.)

Violetta's drawing room; doors at the back to another room; at one side, a fireplace with a mirror; in the center of the room, a table set for dinner. Violetta from a sofa greets some guests, among whom are the Marquis, with Flora on his arm, and the Baron. It is a summer evening in August.

*The Party:* During the small talk, Gaston enters with Alfredo, whom he introduces to Violetta. They sit at the table, Violetta between Alfredo and Gaston, and Flora opposite her between the Baron and the Marquis. Gaston tells Violetta that Alfredo called for news of her each day while she was sick. She twits the Baron that he was not so faithful. He defends himself by saying that he has known her only a year, to which she replies that she has only met Alfredo that evening. The Baron confides to Flora that he doesn't like Alfredo. They all call on Alfredo for a song.

**brindisi**  He sings a verse and then she; all join in the refrain. It is a typical drinking song about youth, wine and love: "libiamo" (let us drink). At its end Violetta's orchestra (off stage) strikes up in the room to the back; but as they go to dance, Violetta staggers, almost fainting. She urges the others to leave her for a minute, and they do; all but Alfredo.

*Violetta and Alfredo:* He begs her to take better care of herself. Her gay life will kill her. She replies that it is no matter; she will hardly be **aria**  missed. He insists he will miss her; he has loved her for a year. He sings "un di felice" (one happy day) when at the sight of her he first knew love, "di quell' amor" (of that love), that brought mysteriously, "misterioso," sorrow and gladness, "croce e delizia," to his heart, "al cor."

Violetta is touched, but suggests he should find another: she is capa-**duet**  ble only of friendship. He sings of love, but she insists he will find it easy to forget her. Finally she forbids him to talk of love, so he turns to go. Stopping him, she gives him a flower to bring back when it fades. He is ecstatic: "Io son felice" (I am happy). They say farewell, "addio."

**chorus**  *The Party:* The guests bid their hostess good night.

*Violetta:* She now has her great "scena" consisting of one long aria in **aria**  four parts and a reprise. The aria covers many emotions and is one of the great tests of a soprano's ability to act with her voice, for there is no action of any sort. She begins:

1: "È strano! è strano! in core . . ." (it's strange . . . in my heart his words are engraved). She wonders if a real love would be a misfortune for her. (This part is very short.)

2: "Ah, fors'è lui" (ah, perhaps he is the one). She wonders if from such a love sorrow and gladness, "croce e delizia," would come into her heart, awakening it to life. (A second verse of this is usually cut.)

3: She dismisses the thought: "follie, follie . . . gioir" (folly . . . joy)! Love, she decides, is not for her, only joy. (This part is short.)

4: "Sempre libera" (always free), she sings, convinced, until suddenly she hears Alfredo under her balcony singing of love. To herself she insists "follie . . . sempre libera." (Some sopranos, claiming tradition, interpolate a high E flat as the last note. But it is not in the score, and most musicians deplore it.)

### Vocabulary, Act I

| | | |
|---|---|---|
| libiamo | lee.BYAH.moe | let us drink |
| un di felice | oon dee fay.LEE.chay | one happy day |
| di quell' amor | dee quail ah.MOR | ah, that love |
| misterioso | me.stair.ee.O.zo | mysterious |
| croce e delizia | kro.chay day.LEE. tsee.ah | torment and delight |
| al cor | ahl kor | to the heart |
| io son felice | yo son fay.LEE.chay | I am happy |
| addio | ah.DEE.oh | farewell |
| è strano | ay STRAH.no | it is strange |
| ah, forse'è lui | ah, for.say LOO.ee | ah, perhaps it is he |
| follie | fol.LEE.ay | folly |
| gioir | je.OY.ear | joy |
| sempre libera | sem.pray LEE.be.rah | always free |

## ACT II

### SCENE 1 (32 min. with usual cuts)

January of the following year. A room on the ground floor of a house outside Paris. In the center at the back are a fire and mantelpiece with clock and mirror. There are chairs, tables and a desk. Alfredo enters in hunting clothes and puts away his gun.

**aria**  *Alfredo:* He sings of how happy he is and reveals that the liaison is now three months old.

*Alfredo and Annina:* She comes from Paris where, she confesses to Alfredo, Violetta has been selling her possessions to pay for the country house. He is horrified and plans to raise the money himself. He then has an aria (almost always cut) in which he expresses his remorse, "o mio rimorso," in not realizing the cost sooner. He leaves for Paris.

*Violetta:* She asks after Alfredo from Annina and is surprised to hear he has gone to Paris. The butler delivers a letter; it is an invitation from Flora for a party. With a laugh Violetta throws it aside; that life is past. The butler announces a visitor, and Germont *père* enters.

*Violetta and Germont:* He starts out stuffily accusing her of living off his son's inheritance. She flares up and, as evidence of the true situation, shows him the receipts for sale of her property. Germont is impressed and more politely states that he has come to ask a concession.

**aria** He explains that his daughter's fiancée threatens to break the engagement if Alfredo continues the liaison. He describes his daughter as "pura siccome un angelo" (pure as an angel).

**aria** Violetta offers to part temporarily, but he insists it must be forever. "Ah, no! giammai" (ah, no, never), she cries. In an outburst she exclaims, "Non sapete" (you do not know) what it would mean: she'd prefer to die, "morir preferirò."

**aria** Germont tries to soothe her: "È grave il sacrifizio" (the sacrifice is great) but she will meet someone else. She cuts him off. He then starts his big appeal: someday when her beauty is gone, "un di quando le veneri," she will have to face old age alone. No permanent happiness can come from a liaison unblessed by God or man. "È vero"

**duet** (it is true), she sighs. God has given her this chance, he continues, to be the saving angel of his two children. She is overcome at the demands of a cruel world.

**duet** Weeping, she says, "Dite alla giovine, si bella e pura" (tell the young girl, so beautiful and pure) of what I've done for her. Germont tries to comfort her with "piangi, piangi, o misera" (weep, unhappy woman).

She cannot think how to part from Alfredo. Germont suggests that she simply leave; she replies that Alfredo would follow. He tells her to say she does not love him; he wouldn't believe it, she answers. Then she realizes the only way and, without telling Germont, warns him to stay in the garden to comfort Alfredo when he learns. "O generosa" (oh generous woman), Germont exclaims.

**duet** Violetta bursts out, "morrò" (I shall die), but Germont urges her to live, insisting that somehow her sacrifice will be rewarded. They part; he goes to the garden; "addio."

*Violetta and Alfredo:* She writes a note to Flora, accepting her invitation to a party that evening. Annina gasps when she sees the address. Then Violetta tries to write to Alfredo, but he arrives before she can finish.

Alfredo asks what she is writing, but she refuses to tell him. He explains that he must wait to see his father, whom he knows will love Violetta. Close to tears, she asks him to say he loves her, "tu m'ami."

"Oh, quanto" (how much!) he replies and asks why she is crying. She insists it is nothing; she is calm again. (But the music pounds along underneath.) She promises to wait in the garden while he sees his father and to come when he calls. Desperately she clings to him: "Amami, Alfredo" (love me). "Addio."

*Alfredo and Germont:* The butler announces that Madame and Annina have left for Paris and, immediately after, a gardener delivers a note to Alfredo. In it Violetta says that they are parted forever. With a cry Alfredo turns and sees his father, "Padre mio." Alfredo sinks to the couch in despair.

**aria**    Germont tries to comfort him by reminding him of the joys of home in Provence, "di Provenza il mar, il suol" (of Provence, the sea, the sun). In a second verse he urges Alfredo to come home.

(In the theater the aria is usually followed by long applause, which stops the action. Then Alfredo has a few remarks, discovers Flora's invitation, gives a great cry and rushes off: curtain. It seems like a clumsy, flat way to end the act; Verdi must have expected and hoped for the applause. Actually Germont has another aria, universally cut because it expresses the same thought as "Di Provenz " but to duller music. As it ends, precluding any applause, Verdi had Alfredo discover the invitation, give his cry and rush off.)

Alfredo leaves for Paris and the party that night, followed by his father.

### Vocabulary, Act II Scene 1

| | | |
|---|---|---|
| pura siccome un angelo | POO.rah sik.KO.may oon AHN.jay.lo | pure like an angel |
| ah, no! giammai | jam.MAH.ee | never |
| non sapete | non sah.PAY.teh | you do not know |
| morir preferirò | mo.REER pray.fay.ree.roh | I would prefer to die |
| è grave il sacrifizio | ay grahv eel sac.ree.fee.tsio | the sacrifice is heavy |
| un di quando le veneri | oon dee kwan.doe lay vay.nay.ree | one day when the beauties (have gone) |
| è vero | ay VAIR.oh | it is true |
| dite alla giovine si bella e pura | DEE.tah lah je'oh.vee.nay see bell.ah eh poo.rah | tell the young girl so beautiful and pure |
| piangi, piangi, o misera | p'YAHN.jee . . . me.zer.ah | weep, unhappy woman |

| o generosa | jen.nay.RO.sah | generous woman |
| morrò | mo.ROH | I will die |
| addio | ah.DEE.oh | good-by |
| tu m'ami | two m'ah.me | you love me |
| oh quanto | kwan.toe | how much |
| amami, Alfredo | ah.mah.m'ahl.FRAY.do | love me Alfredo |
| padre mio | pah.dray MEE.oh | my father |
| di Provenza il mar | dee pro.VEN.ts'eel mahr | of Provence the sea |
| il suol | eel soo.ol | the sun |
| | | (have you forgotten) |

## ACT II

### SCENE 2 (20 min.)

That night at Flora's party. To the right of the room is a gaming table; to the left, a table with flowers and refreshments. Seated on sofas Flora, her Marquis, Dr. Grenvil and other guests are conversing while they await more friends, who are coming masked.

*Flora and the Marquis:* She remarks that she expects Violetta and Alfredo. The Marquis, however, thinks it more likely Violetta will come with the Baron, for she is rumored to have broken with Alfredo.

*The Gypsies:* (Verdi's concept was that these would be some of Flora's feminine guests in costume and thus the palm reading would be amusingly personal. Most productions treat them as though they were entertainers hired by Flora.) The gypsies strike a few poses and one reads in the Marquis' hand that he has a roving eye. Flora pretends to

**chorus** be very hurt. The disguised ladies give a refined version of a gypsy chorus, consisting mostly of banging tambourines, and the Marquis presses Flora's hand.

*The Matadors:* Some gentlemen guests rush in dressed as matadors and picadors, being careful to announce in their opening words exactly what they are supposed to be in case their costumes were not suf-

**chorus** ficiently evocative. They sing of a young matador who won his lady by killing five bulls in a single afternoon. The gypsies strike their tambourines for a final chorus, everyone unmasks and the party continues. (Inevitably the bigger the opera house, the more likely this bit of home entertainment is to become a full ballet, even spectacle, curiously at odds with the rest of opera, which is intimate rather than grand.)

*The Party:* Alfredo arrives alone, and a few eyebrows go up in surprise. But the guests include him at once at the card table. Violetta then arrives with the Baron who, on seeing Alfredo, forbids Violetta to talk to him. Violetta is terrified the Baron will pick a fight with Alfredo and, in an aside, begs Heaven to have pity on her: "Pietà, gran Dio, di me!"

Alfredo wins constantly, makes ironic remarks in a loud voice and irritates the Baron. Violetta appeals again to Heaven. Alfredo gambles against the Baron and wins; he wins again on doubled stakes; and the Baron quits as dinner is announced. For a third time as she leaves for dinner, Violetta begs Heaven to help her. Alfredo and the Baron go in together exchanging social unpleasantries.

*Violetta and Alfredo:* She returns followed by Alfredo. She begs him to leave before there is trouble. He asks why she should care; does she fear for the Baron? She swears not. He will go, he says, if she goes with him. "Ah no, giammai" (never), she replies. She has sworn an oath. To whom? he insists. To the Baron, she lies (actually, of course, to Germont). Alfredo finally forces her to say she loves the Baron: "Dunque l'ami" (then you love him)? "Ebben . . . l'amo" (well then . . . I love him).

*Finale:* Alfredo calls everyone in. He at once begins his denunciation of Violetta with "questa donna conoscete" (you know this woman)? Violetta gasps, "Ah, taci" (ah, keep silent).

Alfredo then starts on pounding notes: "Ogni suo aver . . ." (all her wealth) she squandered on me. To pay her back, he throws the money he has won in her face. At that moment, in time to see it but too late to stop it, his father arrives. (Some original critic complained that there was no reason for Germont to turn up at Flora's party, and it is usual to reiterate his complaint. But why should Germont be denied the natural feelings of a father who knows he has created the situation in which his son is about to act violently and under a misapprehension? Naturally, he followed Alfredo to Paris to try to reason with him. He knew his son planned to go to Flora's party, so he followed him there. His only fault, if it be one, was that, being stuffy, he took the time to dress and so arrived too late.)

Violetta swoons, and all are aghast at Alfredo's action. They order him to leave at once. His father, angry and disappointed, asks, "dove mio figlio" (where is my son)? It is shameful to insult a woman. Alfredo pays no attention to any of them but, in an aside, struggles with his mixed feelings of love, jealousy and resentment. The guests continue their criticism of him; the Baron pontificates about honor and duels; and Germont sadly observes that he alone knows how much Violetta has sacrificed.

The final chorus begins with Violetta breaking down completely. She starts it off as a solo with "Alfredo, Alfredo, di questo core . . ." (of this heart) you cannot understánd all the love. She hopes that God will spare him remorse, for even when she is dead she will love him. The guests insist that time will mend her heart; Alfredo continues his remorse; Germont his lament; and the Baron his talk of duels. Germont leads his son out, followed by the Baron.

### Vocabulary, Act II Scene 2

| | | |
|---|---|---|
| pietà, Gran Dio, di me | p'yay.TAH gran DEE. oh dee may | have pity, Gran Dio, on me |
| ah, no giammai | jam.MAH.ee | ah no, never |
| dunque l'ami | doon.kway l'ah.me | then you love him |
| ebben . . . l'amo | ay.bayn l'ah.moe | well then . . . I love him |
| questa donna conoscete | ques.tah.DUN.nah ko.no.shay.teh | this woman you know |
| ah, taci | ah TAH.chee | ah, keep silent |
| ogni suo aver | own.ye sw'ah.vair | all her wealth |
| dove mio figlio | DOE.veh me.oh FEEL. yo | where is my son |
| Alfredo, di questo core | . . . dee quest.oh ko. ray | Alfredo, of this heart |

## ACT III (28 min.)

Some weeks later. Violetta's bedroom. She is dying of consumption. A bed with curtains half drawn at the back; a window closed by shutters; a table with a night light burning; a sofa; and in the grate a fire. It is seven o'clock in the morning on a day in February.

## PRELUDE (4 min.)

It is a tradition in most opera houses to play it with the curtain up and Violetta in bed. Most musicians consider this the best purely symphonic music that Verdi composed. It is what the Metropolitan played to honor both Toscanini on the day he died and Leonard

Warren, the great Verdi baritone, who died on stage during a performance of *La Forza del Destino*.

*Violetta, the Doctor and Annina:* He tells Violetta she is improving, but to Annina he admits she has only a few hours to live. Annina reports that they have little money left, but Violetta is more interested in the mail and sends Annina out to see if it has come.

*Violetta:* She pulls a letter from her bosom. It is from Germont, who writes that the duel took place, the Baron was wounded, and Alfredo was forced to leave the country. He adds that he has revealed her sacrifice to Alfredo, who is returning to implore her pardon, and that he too will come to see her. "È tardi" (it is late), she gasps.

**aria**    She sings "Addio del passato . . ." (farewell to life and the past). Now "tutto finì" (all is finished). (A second verse is usually cut.)

**offstage chorus**    Outside, some late partygoers sing on their way home.

*Violetta and Alfredo:* Annina announces Alfredo, and there is an impassioned duet of "nothing can part us."

**duet**    Then he starts a more formal duet: "Parigi, o cara, noi lasceremo" (Paris, dearest, we shall leave) and live together. She repeats it happily. Away from the world, she'll regain her health.

She rises, suggesting they go to church to thank God for his safe return, and for the first time Alfredo realizes how sick she is. She tries to put on her coat but hasn't the strength: "Gran Dio! non posso" (I cannot). Annina runs for the doctor.

Violetta in despair sings, "Ah! Gran Dio! morir si giovine . . ."
**duet**    (to die so young). (Marie Duplessis was twenty-three years, twenty days old.) Alfredo tries to calm her, "calmati."

*Violetta, Alfredo, Germont, Annina and the Doctor:* Violetta says she is going to die, and Germont and Alfredo exclaim with remorse and despair.

Violetta then begins the final trio by turning to Alfredo: "Prendi,
**trio**    quest' è l'immagine . . ." (take this picture) in remembrance. Alfredo interrupts, "No, non morrai" (no, don't die). Germont asks her forgiveness for breaking her heart, "perdonami."

There is a break, and then Violetta begins again: "Se una pudica vergine . . . sposa ti sia" (if you meet a nice young girl . . . let her be your wife). Give her this picture and tell her that one in Heaven
**quintet**    prays for her and thee. The others quietly grieve and

despair. Then, reviving, Violetta starts up: "È strano . . . in me rinasce" (it's strange . . . in me is reborn) a new strength and vigor. She feels life returning. She will live. "Oh gioja." And she dies.

Alfredo gasps "Violetta?" The Doctor pronounces her dead, and the curtain falls on their grief. (The last remarks after her death are sometimes cut.)

### Vocabulary, Act III

| | | |
|---|---|---|
| è tardi | ay tar.dee | it is late |
| addio del passato | ah.DEE.oh del pah.sah.toe | good-by to the past |
| tutto fini | TOOT.toe fe.nee | all is finished |
| Parigi, o cara, noi lasceremo | pah.ree.jee o kah.rah noy lah.shay.ray.moe | Paris, oh dearest, we shall leave |
| Gran Dio, non posso | gran DEE.oh non poss. so | Gran Dio, I cannot |
| ah, Gran Dio, morir si giovine | . . . mo.reer see je'oh.vee.nay | . . . to die so young |
| calmati | kahl.mah.tee | be calm |
| prendi, quest' è l'immagine | pren.dee quest'ay l'im.MAH.je.nay | take, this is the picture (of me) |
| no, non morrai | no, non mor.rye | no, don't die |
| perdonami | pair.do.NAH.me | forgive me |
| se una pudica vergine . . . sposa ti sia | say oona poo.dee.ka VAIR.je.nay . . . spo.za tee see.ah | if (you meet) a nice young girl, let her be your wife |
| è strano . . . in me rinasce | ay STRAH.no . . . in may ree.nah.shay | it is strange . . . in me is reborn |
| oh gioja | oh je.OY.ah | oh joy |

# SIMON BOCCANEGRA

Melodrama in a prologue and three acts. First performed at Venice on March 12, 1857. Revised version first performed at Milan on March 24, 1881. Music by G. Verdi. Libretto by F. M. Piave, founded on a play by A. G. Gutierrez. Libretto revised by A. Boito.

### PRINCIPAL CHARACTERS

| | | |
|---|---|---|
| Paolo, a leader of the plebian party | bass | |
| Pietro, his lieutenant | baritone | |
| Simone Boccanegra, a sea captain later elected Doge | baritone | see.MOH.nay |

| | | |
|---|---|---|
| Fiesco, a Genoese nobleman, leader of the patrician party, father of Maria whom Simone loves, and calling himself in disguise "Andrea" | bass | |
| Amelia Grimaldi, a foundling later revealed to be Simone's lost daughter | soprano | ah.MAY.l'ya |
| Gabriele Adorno, a patrician in love with Amelia | tenor | |
| Maria, daughter of Fiesco and unwed mother of Amelia by Simone. | mute (appears only as a corpse in the Prologue) | |

The action takes place in and near Genoa in the fourteenth century.

Verdi more than any other composer favored baritones with great roles, and one of the greatest is Simone Boccanegra. The opera's plot may creak at times, but it does give the singer in the title role a chance to portray a rounded, mature man in an extraordinary number of situations and some of which, such as those involving municipal politics, seem very modern.

The opera has always been criticized for being gloomy and confused. The first charge rests almost entirely on the Prologue which is set at night and presents some conspiratorial political maneuverings, the grief of two men following an offstage death, and a dialogue of quiet anger and hate. Actually it is not so much gloomy as subdued. Perhaps it was a theatrical mistake not to open with something more arresting, such as the gaiety of *Rigoletto* and *La Traviata* or the storm of *Otello*. Certainly it does not catch the audience up with the same speed, although the music has its rewards in subtlety and beauty. The actual deaths in the opera are far fewer than in *Il Trovatore*, *Tosca* or *Tristan und Isolde*. In fact, outside of the comedies, few operas have less of death and torture. The gloom comes mainly because Verdi succeeds in making the audience care for Simone, and so it hates to watch him die.

The charge of confusion is more apt. There are a number of revelations, secrets and hidden identities with loose ends that trip the plausibility of the plot. But these tend to dwindle if the politics of the plot are clearly grasped. The division between the plebians and the patricians dominates every scene and relationship; even the love interest does not cut across it directly. The opera's unique distinction and success lie in its portrayal of the politics of Genoa and of Simone's efforts to be a statesman; the love interest is quite secondary.

There are a number of other small confusions about the opera. The revised version is always given. The most famous scene, the one in the Council Chamber, was Boito's creation, and the music was wholly new. Much of the rest of the music was reorchestrated and some was rewritten. Verdi did this between *Aida* and *Otello,* so that musically the opera is much later than the date of its première suggests.

Another confusion is the century of the action. For some reason many librettos and synopses give it as the fifteenth. Clearly it is the fourteenth, for in the Council Chamber scene Simone reads a letter from Petrarch, who lived from 1304 to 1374. But more than that, in 1339 the Genoese elected their first Doge, the historical Simone Boccanegra (?–1363). Boccanegra, a member of a minor noble family, from the first led the plebian party. The people, exhausted by the feuds between the nobles, first offered him the position of abbot, a sort of magistrate. Boccanegra refused, and the people made him Doge by acclamation. He served from 1339 to 1344 and then resigned, retiring to Pisa. After twelve years of anarchy the city called him back and he served as Doge from 1356 to 1363. He died after a banquet in honor of the King of Cyprus, and it was generally believed he was poisoned. He was succeeded by Gabriele Adorno who represented the new merchant aristocracy. The feuds between the old noble families were part of the general Guelph-Ghibelline war that divided most of Italy. In Genoa the Doria and Spinola families were Ghibellines and the Grimaldi and Fieschi families Guelphs.

The historical Simone Boccanegra seems to have been similar to the operatic character. A contemporary historian recorded with astonishment that he spared the life of a Grimaldi who was a personal enemy and under him Genoa had a successful foreign policy and a period of peace.

One last confusion: tradition in English-speaking countries has generally translated the opera's title, like *Macbeth* for *Macbetto,* but of course onstage Simon is called Simone.


## PROLOGUE (29 min.)

A piazza in Genoa; to the back the church of San Lorenzo, on the right the Fieschi palazza with a large balcony. In the buttress of the balcony is an icon of the Virgin with a tiny lantern before it; on the left are other houses. Streets lead in and out of the piazza. It is night. The curtain rises almost at once.

*Paolo and Pietro:* They discuss the possible candidates for Doge. Pietro favors a certain Lorenzino, but Paolo suggests the man who defeated the Barbary pirates, Boccanegra. If they can elect him, they will have "oro" (gold), "possanza" (power) and "onore" (honor) for themselves. Pietro sees the possibilities, agrees and goes off to organize the campaign.

*Paolo and Simone:* Paolo, alone, curses the hated patricians, "patrizi," and asks Simone when he enters if he would like to be elected Doge. Simone laughs until Paolo reminds him that Maria is held a prisoner in the Fieschi palazzo, but that even they could not refuse a Doge. The election is certain, Paolo insists, and all he wants is a share in the danger and power. "Sia" (so be it), Simone agrees. He goes off and Paolo hides as Pietro leads in a mob.

*Pietro, Paolo and the Mob:* Pietro announces that the candidate Lorenzino has sold out to the Fieschi. The mob is aghast: then who? Pietro suggests a hero, a commoner. "Simone Boccanegra," cries **aria** Paolo, advancing from the shadows. He points to the Fieschi palace and orates on the beautiful Maria kept prisoner by her proud, patrician father. The chorus murmurs for Maria. When a light appears at a window, Paolo urges the people to exorcize it and the house of evil. The mob goes off with Paolo and Pietro, promising to vote for Simone.

*Fiesco:* He comes out of the palace where Maria has just died, "sepolcro dell' angiolo mio" (tomb of my angel). He curses, "oh maledetto," her seducer. Gazing at the icon, he accuses the Virgin of permitting his daughter to be ravished and then begs pardon for the **solo with chorus** blasphemy, "ah, mi perdona." He sings of his grief, begging his daughter in Heaven to pray for him: "Prega, Maria, per me." Inside the palazzo the servants sigh, "e morta" (she is dead) and "miserere." (This is one of the great bass arias of Italian opera. The orchestral close of it is much admired.)

*Simone and Fiesco:* Simone enters. His name is in every mouth. Perhaps soon he can marry Maria. When he sees Fiesco, he kneels before him, "padre mio, pietà t'imploro" (my father, have pity I beg you). Fiesco repels him, "tardi è omai" (it is too late). Simone begs, "non sii crudel" (don't be cruel). For Maria's sake he tried to better himself. **duet** Coldly Fiesco admires Simone's bravery but promises to hate him until his death. For peace between them Simone offers his sword: let Fiesco kill him now. But the proud man refuses to be a murderer.

Instead, "ascolta" (listen), he proposes. If Simone will give him the child, the grandchild Fiesco has never seen, then there will be peace between them. But Simone cannot, "nol poss'io." The child and its nurse lived alone, and the child disappeared when its nurse unexpectedly died, "morta." He has never been able to trace it. Fiesco turns from him: without the child there can be no peace.

Desperately Simone cries, "m'odi" (hear me), but Fiesco walks away, "addio." From a distance he watches to see Simone suffer when he discovers Maria is dead.

*Simone, Fiesco, Paolo and the Mob:* Seeing the palazzo door ajar, Simone pushes in. When he discovers her corpse, he sobs out "Maria" and Fiesco takes cold comfort in the cry. Simone staggers out: it is a dream, "è sogno." At that moment Paolo and the mob appear (to a tune as banal as most political songs), calling for him as Doge. But Simone can only gasp, "una tomba" (a tomb)! Paolo insists "un trono" (a throne). The mob cheers Simone, the people's choice.

### Vocabulary, Prologue

| | | |
|---|---|---|
| oro, possanza, onore | OR.o poss.AHN.tsah on.OR.ay | gold, power, honor |
| patrizi | pah.TREE.tsee | patricians |
| sia | see.ah | so be it |
| sepolero dell'angiolo mio | say.POLL.kro dell ahn.je'OL.oh me.oh | tomb of my angel |
| oh maledetto | oh mal.eh.DEBT.toe | curses |
| ah, mi perdona | ah me pair.DOH.nah | oh, forgive me |
| prega, Maria, per me | pray.gah . . . pair may | pray, Maria, for me |
| e morta | ay mon.tah | she is dead |
| padre mio, pietà, t'imploro | pah.dray me.oh p'yay.TAH t'im. PLOR.oh | my father, have pity, I implore you |
| tardi è omai | TAR.d'yo.MY | it is too late |
| non sii crudel | non see kroo.dell | don't be cruel |
| ascolta | ah.SCOLE.tah | listen |
| nol poss'io | nol poss yo | I cannot |
| morta | MOR.tah | dead |
| m'odi | M'OH.dee | hear me |
| addio | ah.DEE.oh | farewell |
| è sogno | ay so.n'yo | it is a dream |
| una tomba | oona TOM.bah | a tomb |
| un trono | oon TRO.no | a throne |
| miserere | mee.zayr.RAY.ray | miserere (have mercy) |

## ACT I (56 min.)

Twenty-five years later. The plebian party, led by Boccanegra, has proscribed many of the patricians including Fiesco and the men of the Grimaldi family. But Fiesco, whom Simone believes dead, has returned to Genoa in disguise under the name "Andrea" and, to preserve the Grimaldi estates from confiscation, has brought with him a girl he claims is Amelia Grimaldi. In fact the true Amelia is dead, and Fiesco has substituted a foundling who is, of course, his lost grand-daughter, Maria. No one, including herself, however, knows her true identity.

### SCENE 1 (35 min.)

The garden of the Villa Grimaldi outside Genoa; to the left the villa, to the back the sea. It is early morning.

**aria**  *Amelia:* She sings of the beautiful day. It stirs faint memories of the night her nurse died and she was left a foundling. Then she thinks of her love, Gabriele Adorno, a patrician whose father Simone had executed.

**duet**  *Amelia and Gabriele:* He sings to her from off stage, and they meet with a lovers' duet in which she accuses him of being delayed because of more political plotting with Andrea (Fiesco); he urges her not to think about politics. The refrain for both is "ripara i tuoi pensieri" (shelter your thoughts) in the port of love, "al porto dell' amor."

A servant announces Pietro who asks if the Doge, who has been hunting, would be welcome at the villa. Amelia agrees to receive him. Gabriele is astounded the Doge should come, but Amelia explains he hopes to persuade her to marry Paolo. She urges Gabriele to find

**duet**  Andrea and to arrange for their marriage at once. They sing "sempre vivrai con me" (always you shall live with me), and Amelia goes in to prepare for the Doge as Andrea comes out.

*Gabriele and Andrea (Fiesco):* Gabriele announces his intentions but Andrea stops him: there is a mystery about Amelia which he should hear before deciding. He explains that she is not "la figlia dei Grimaldi" (the daughter of the Grimaldi) and consequently the Grimaldi fortune will not go with her. She is a foundling whom Andrea substituted

when the true Grimaldi died to prevent the Doge from confiscating
**duet**    the Grimaldi property. Gabriele insists he loves Amelia, not
the fortune, and Andrea gives the marriage and Gabriele his blessing:
"Vieni a me, ti benedico" (come to me, I bless you). Trumpets announce the Doge, and the two men leave in order not to be seen.

*Amelia and Simone:* Simone enters telling Paolo and the others to be
ready to leave in an hour. He comes quickly to the point: he will pardon her exiled brothers. He shows her the pardon already written. Then
he asks if she has ever thought of marriage. Amelia, who understands
exactly what is afoot, replies that she loves a man dearly but is bothered
by another, who lusts after the Grimaldi gold, "l'or de' Grimaldi
brama." "Paolo," Simone exclaims. You named him, she says. (At
this moment, when the two clearly are beginning to like each other,
comes one of the serious flaws in the libretto. Amelia announces that
she is not a Grimaldi. Considering that she has been raised by Fiesco
and knows the possible political and financial consequences of such a
revelation, it is inconceivable. The best that can be said for it is that
she hopes by it to end Paolo's suit. Perhaps she relies on the difficulty
of proving that she is *not* a Grimaldi to continue to preserve the
Grimaldi estates. But it is best swallowed whole.)

Amelia makes her announcement: "Non sono una Grimaldi."
**duet**    Simone is astounded, and she explains about her childhood.
She was raised in Pisa by an old woman who before dying gave her a
picture of her mother. Simone fears only that if it is a dream he must
wake. He questions her: did anyone ever visit them? She replies, "a
sailor." Was the nurse called "Giovanna"? She was. He draws a locket
from his neck, and they compare the pictures. "Maria," he cries. "Il
**duet**    nome mio," she exclaims. "Mia figlia!" "Padre!" Each rejoices in finding at last what he and she wanted most. Finally she
leaves him to talk with Paolo. (Again it is inconceivable that "Andrea"
never would have seen the picture in her locket; but no matter. Well-
made plays are easier to write than great operas.)

*Simone, Paolo and Pietro:* Paolo asks how his suit was received.
Simone tells him to give up all hope. Paolo gasps, "Doge, nol posso"
(I cannot). "Il voglio" (I wish it), Simone replies and goes out. Paolo
is furious: this to him who made the sailor a Doge. He tells Pietro to
abduct the girl from the beach at night and to take her to Lorenzino's
house in Genoa. (This short scene is sometimes cut.)

## SCENE 2 (21 min.)

The Council Chamber of the Doge's Palace. On one side sit twelve Councilors of the plebian party, on the other twelve of the patrician party. Seated apart are four Maritime Councilors and the Constables. Paolo and Pietro sit on the plebian side.

*The Business of State:* Simone reviews the terms of a trade treaty with Tartary, and all the Councilors agree to it: "Si." Then, quoting a letter from Petrarch in his support, he asks for a vote for peace with Venice. The Councilors all cry, "Guerra a Venezia" (war on Venice). Simone pleads that both cities have the same fatherland, but the Councilors insist, "È nostra patria Genova" (our country is Genoa).

*The Riot:* The sound of it from the streets interrupts the Council. At first no one can make out its cause; then Simone sees Gabriele and Andrea (Fiesco) fighting a mob. He asks for a herald and orders the doors sealed so that none of the leaders can get out. From the square come cries of "Morte ai patrizi" (death to the patricians) and "viva il popolo" (up the people). The patrician Councilors start to draw their swords, and the riot is threatening to spill into the Council Chamber.

When the mob outside shouts, "Morte al Doge" (death to the Doge), Simone angrily orders the herald to open the palace doors and announce that the Doge has heard the mob's cry and awaits them in the Chamber. Simone reports from the window: the herald's trumpet . . . the herald speaks . . . "tutto e silenzio." Inside the Chamber they wait. Suddenly the mob outside cries, "Eviva il Doge," and in a second the people burst into the Chamber, pushing Gabriele and Andrea before them.

*Simone and Gabriele:* They confront each other. Simone asks why Gabriele has a sword in hand. Because he has killed Lorenzino, Gabriele replies, who kidnaped Amelia Grimaldi. The mob calls him a liar, but Simone suspects the truth. Gabriele adds that Lorenzino, in dying, claimed that someone powerful had ordered him to do it. Gabriele accuses Simone and attacks him, but he is seized and disarmed as Amelia enters.

*Amelia:* She begs both Gabriele and Simone to stop, and Simone orders the guards to release Gabriele. She explains that she was seized on the beach and taken to Lorenzino's house. There she so confused and terrified the man with threats of the Doge's vengeance that he finally let her go. But she knows who put him up to it. She gazes at Paolo. Simone understands, but the patrician Councilors accuse the plebians, who retort in kind, and the riot threatens to start up again. *Simone et al:* Furiously he cries, "Fratricidi" (fratricides). "Plebe!" **aria**    "Patrizi!" "Popolo!" With all the sea to sail and goods to be traded, all they can do is hate by inheritance and kill each other. "E vo gridando: pace! E vo gridando: amor!" (I cry to you: peace . . . love).

The Councilors and the mob are moved and murmur their admira- **chorus**    tion. Gabriele rejoices in Amelia's safety; she urges peace and love to Andrea (Fiesco) who rages at seeing Genoa ruled by a common sailor. Paolo and Pietro fear they are discovered.

At the end of the chorus Gabriele offers his sword for the Doge, who refuses it but insists that Gabriele remain in custody until the abduction plot is cleared up.
*Simone and Paolo:* Simone turns to Paolo. He points out that Paolo has the people's trust and can help him find the one in power who organized the abduction. Simone thinks he knows who it is, and he asks Paolo after him to curse the unknown man: "Sia maledetto! e tu ripeti il giuro" (let him be accursed! and you repeat the oath). To avoid confessing, Paolo does, but as all repeat it, he staggers from the Council, terrified.

### Vocabulary, Act I Scene 1

| | | |
|---|---|---|
| ripara i tuoi pensieri | ree.pah.r' ee twoy pen.s'air.ee | shelter your thoughts |
| al porto dell'amor | ahl por.toh dell'ah.MOR | to the port of love |
| sempre vivrai con me | sem.pray vee.vry kon may | always you will live with me |
| la figlia dei Grimaldi | lah feel.ya day.ee gree.MAHL.dee | the daughter of the Grimaldi |
| vieni a me, ti benedico | v'YAY.nee' ah me tee bay.nay.dee.ko | come to me, I bless you |
| l'or de' Grimaldi brama | l'or day . . . brah.mah | the gold of the Grimaldi covets |
| non sono una Grimaldi | non so.no oona . . . | I am not a Grimaldi |
| il nome mio | eel NO.may me.oh | my name |
| mia figlia | me.ah FEEL.ya | my daughter |
| padre | PAH.dray | father |
| Doge, nol posso | do.jeh nol poss.so | Doge, I cannot |
| il voglio | eel vol.y'oh | I wish it |

## Scene 2

| | | |
|---|---|---|
| guerra a Venezia | gwair.r'ah ve.NEH.tsia | war on Venice |
| è nostra patria Genova | ay nos.tra pat.ria JEH.no.va | our country is Genoa |
| morte ai patrizi | mor.t' eye pah.TREE.tsee | death to the patricians |
| viva il popolo | vee.vah il po.po.lo | up the plebians |
| morte al Doge | mor.t' ahl do.jeh | death to the Doge |
| tutto è silenzio | toot.to' ay see.len.tsio | all is silent |
| fratricidi | frah.tree.CHEE.de | fratricides |
| plebe | play.bay | plebians |
| patrizi | pah.TREE.tsee | patricians |
| popolo | PO.po.lo | the people |
| e vo gridando: pace | ay vo gree.DAHN.do PAH.chay | I cry to you: peace |
| e vo gridando: amor | ay vo gree.DAHN.do ah.MOR | I cry to you: love |
| sia maledetto | s'ya mah.le.DET.toe | be accursed |
| e tu ripeti il giuro | ay too ree.peh.tee eel jur.oh | and you repeat the oath |

## ACT II (24 min.)

A room in the Doge's palace; doors at either side; and at the back a balcony overlooking the city. On a table there is a carafe and goblet. Night is falling.

*Paolo and Pietro:* Paolo sends Pietro to bring up the two prisoners, **aria** Gabriele and Andrea (Fiesco). Alone Paolo rants at the Doge whom he put on the throne. Already the Doge's curse has isolated him politically; he is rejected by the Council and scorned by the people. There remain only flight and revenge. He pours a poison into the carafe. If he cannot persuade the prisoners to murder the Doge, perhaps the poison will do it.

*Paolo and Andrea:* Paolo hints that he knows Andrea is Fiesco and that the Doge has ordered Andrea's death. Paolo offers to save Andrea at a price: the murder of Simone as he sleeps. "Osi a Fiesco . . ." (you dare to a Fiesco) suggest such a crime? Andrea replies. "Tu rifiuti" (you refuse)? Paolo asks. "Si" (yes); and Andrea is led back to prison.

*Paolo and Gabriele:* Gabriele, too, scorns Paolo until the latter suggests that the Doge loves Amelia and has designs on her. Paolo quickly goes out, leaving Gabriele to think about it.

*Gabriele:* He curses the Doge who killed his father and now robs him of his bride. A furious jealousy boils in his blood. If the Doge had a
**aria**    thousand lives, he could not kill him often enough. But anger at the Doge he decides is delirium, "delirio," when he should be thinking of Amelia. He weeps, "io piango," and begs Heaven to have pity, "pietà, pietà, gran Dio," and to restore Amelia unsullied.

*Gabriele and Amelia:* He at once accuses her of betraying him. She confesses the Doge loves her and she him, but only with a pure love.
**duet**    She will explain it later, she says. (Just why Amelia is coy about her relationship to the Doge is not clear, and nothing seems to be gained by saving the revelation for the Doge to make several pages later.) Gabriele pleads with her to explain, and she asks him to have faith.

A trumpet announces the Doge, and Amelia hides Gabriele on the balcony.

*Simone and Amelia:* He remarks she has been weeping. She confesses that she loves and he asks the man's name. She replies that it is Gabriele Adorno. "Il mio nemico" (my enemy), Simone cries. She pleads for Gabriele and Simone refuses, "nol posso" (I cannot). She swears then she will die with Gabriele. Simone is impressed, softens and agrees to pardon him.

Then Simone, going to the couch, says he will rest for a bit. She, fearing Gabriele on the balcony, tries to stay, but Simone insists that she need not and finally asks to be left alone. He muses on the quirks of life, takes a drink from the poisoned carafe and lies down on a couch, sighing, "oh, Amelia . . . ami un nemico" (Amelia loves an enemy).

*Gabriele, Amelia and Simone:* Gabriele comes in from the balcony prepared to avenge his father's death by murdering Simone. Amelia, who feared this and waited outside the door, comes back in and stops him. Simone awakes and sarcastically urges Gabriele to kill him. Gabriele accuses him of murdering his father. Simone retorts that Gabriele has robbed him of his daughter, "la mia figlia." Gabriele stammers, "suo padre sei tu" (her father is you)!

Gabriele begins a trio begging Amelia to forgive his doubt of her, "perdon." Then to Simone he admits that he is an assassin, "un assassin
**trio**    son io," and offers his life, "dammi la morte." Simone wonders whether he should spare an enemy and decides that his tomb should be the altar of friendship between Italians. Amelia begs her mother in

Heaven to move Simone's heart to pardon Gabriele who sinned only because of love.

Outside there is the sound of a mob gathering around the palace. It is a patrician uprising. Simone sends Gabriele out to disperse the mob with a message of peace and pardon from the Doge. He calls after Gabriele that he may marry Amelia.

### Vocabulary, Act II

| | | |
|---|---|---|
| osi a Fiesco | os'yah fyay.sko | you dare to a Fiesco |
| tu rifiuti | two ree.f'yoo.tee | you refuse |
| deliro | day.lee.ro | delirium |
| io piango | yo p'YAHN.jo | I weep |
| pietà, pietà, gran Dio | p'yay.tah . . . gran dee.oh | have pity, Gran Dio |
| il mio nemico | eel me.oh nay.me.ko | my enemy |
| nol posso | nol poss.so | I cannot |
| oh Amelia . . . ami un nemico | . . . ah.me oon nay.me.ko | you love an enemy |
| la nia figlia | lah mee.ah FEEL.yah | my daughter |
| suo padre sei tu | soo.oh pah.dray say.ee two | her father is you |
| perdon | pair.don | forgive |
| un assassin son io | oon ah.sahs.seen son ee.oh | an assassin am I |
| dammi la morte | dah.me la MOR.tay | give me death |

## ACT III (27 min.)

Inside the Doge's palace; to the back, a balcony through which Genoa can be seen lighted for a celebration; behind Genoa, the sea. Later that night. The act begins with the music of the riot that ended the last act. In the distance crowds hail the Doge.

*Andrea (Fiesco) and Paolo:* The guards release Andrea and return his sword. On being told of the defeat of the patricians in the revolt, he grieves, "o triste libertà" (oh sad freedom). Paolo is brought in under guard. He explains to Andrea that he joined the revolt, was captured and was condemned to death by Simone. But he adds that if he must die, so, too, must Simone, who has drunk the poisoned water. Andrea is horrified. From the chapel in the palace comes the sound of a wedding chorus. Paolo regrets that Gabriele, not he, is marrying Amelia. He confesses that he ordered Amelia abducted as the guards

lead him off. Andrea muses that poison was not the revenge he had hoped to have of Simone. He hides in a shadow as a herald appears.
*The Herald:* From the balcony he calls to the people to end the celebration in honor of those who died.
*Simone:* He enters alone. Already he feels dizzy from the poison.
**aria**　　He goes to the gallery and gazes at the sea, "il mare," free and clean, where he first won his glory untrammeled by the city. He wishes he could have died then, in the sea; "ah, perchè, perchè" (ah, why not)?
*Simone and Andrea (Fiesco):* Andrea comes out of the shadows remarking that it would have been better if Simone had died. Simone threatens to call the guards, but then waits to hear what Andrea has to say. (This begins the second long duet between Simone and Fiesco, tying the prologue and the finale together. It is longer and more intense than the first and falls into three parts.)
**aria**　　1: Andrea warns him that his days of glory are over. He will join the spirits, "le larve," of his many victims in the tomb, "la tomba."

Simone wonders at the voice, and Andrea reveals himself as Fiesco, returned from the dead.
**duet**　　2: Fiesco says he appears like a phantom, "come un fantasima," to avenge an ancient wrong. Simone insists Fiesco comes to make peace between them, reminding him of the condition set twenty-five years earlier. In a rising phrase "in Amelia Grimaldi," he reveals, is the long lost child, Fiesco's granddaughter. "Perchè" (why), Fiesco gasps, did Heaven conceal it so long?

He turns abruptly from Simone, who remarks, "tu piangi" (you weep)!

3: I weep, "piango," Fiesco explains, because through Simone he hears the voice of Heaven reproving his hate, even in Simone's pity, "nella tua pietà." Simone begs him "vien" (come). Fiesco's pardon will be balm to his soul.

In broken phrases Fiesco explains that Paolo has poisoned the water. Simone urges him to be quiet as the wedding guests enter with Amelia and Gabriele.
*Finale:* Simone reveals Fiesco's identity to Amelia and she rejoices that the feud is ended. Then he announces that he is dying, blesses the lovers and asks the Councilors to elect Gabriele the new Doge. Amelia sobs, "non, non morrai" (no, don't die); Gabriele exclaims at how soon the hour of happiness has ended; Fiesco grieves that the human

heart is a fountain of tears; and the Councilors and ladies agree.

Fiesco goes to the balcony and calls to the people that Gabriele Adorno is the new Doge. They cry: "No, Boccanegra!" Fiesco explains, "È morto" (he is dead). "Pray for him." All kneeling murmur "Pace per lui."

### Vocabulary, Act III

| | | |
|---|---|---|
| o triste libertà | o triss.tay lee.bair.TAH | oh sad freedom |
| il mare | eel mahr.ray | the sea |
| ah, perchè, perchè | ah pair.kay | ah, why (did I not die) |
| la larve | lay lahr.vay | the shades (of the dead) |
| la tomba | lah tom.bah | the tomb |
| come un fantasima | ko.may oon fahn.tah.see.mah | like a phantom |
| in Amelia Grimaldi | een ah.may.l'ya gree.mahl.dee | in Amelia Grimaldi |
| tu piangi | two p'YAHN.jee | you weep |
| piango | p'YAHN.joe | I weep |
| nella tua pietà | nell.ah two.ah p'yay.tah | in your pity |
| vien | v'YAY'n | come |
| no, non morrai | no non mor.rye | no, don't die |
| è morto | ay mor.toe | he is dead |
| pace per lui | pah.chay pair lwee | peace for him |

# UN BALLO IN MASCHERA

## (A Masked Ball)

Opera in three acts. First performed at Rome on February 17, 1859. Music by G. Verdi. Libretto by A. Somma after a libretto by A. E. Scribe for D. F. Auber's opera *Gustave III*, first produced in 1883 at Paris.

### PRINCIPAL CHARACTERS

| | | |
|---|---|---|
| Oscar, the King's page (sometimes called Edgar) | soprano | |
| Riccardo, the King | tenor | |
| Renato, his minister | baritone | |
| Ulrica, a sorceress | contralto | |
| Amelia, Renato's wife | soprano | ah.MAIL.ya |
| Sam } conspirators | bass | |
| Tom } | bass | |

The action takes place in Sweden in 1792.

The opera is regrettably and unduly famous for its libretto troubles with the censors. The silly business has obscured its real virtues: well contrasted scenes, consistently brilliant melodies and some of the finest quarters and quintets Verdi wrote. It is also extremely well-knit. It runs, for example, almost thirty-five minutes less than *Aida*.

The libretto was based on a play by Scribe, which in turn was based on the assassination of Gustaf III of Sweden. The King was murdered at a masked ball in the Stockholm Opera House in 1792. The murderers were a former Captain of the Royal Guards, Count Anckarstroem and Counts Horn and Ribbing. They represented, or were the tools of, a reactionary, aristocratic clique that disliked the King's liberal leanings. The ball was a natural place to find the King, as he was a patron of the arts. On this particular night he received a note from a disaffected conspirator warning him of the plot, but as such notes apparently were common, he ignored it. He died two weeks later. Of the conspirators, Anckarstroem was executed and the others exiled.

Scribe's play, entitled *Gustaf III*, kept the Swedish and royal setting. Verdi first offered the opera with that setting to San Carlo in Naples for the 1859 season. But Orsini had just thrown his bomb at Napoleon III of France, and King Ferdinand of Naples was not going to have any king killed on stage. The censors required so many changes that Verdi withdrew the opera and offered it to the Rome house. Perhaps he thought Rome, being a Papal State, would view regicide with more equanimity. But again there was a long hassle, and finally a ludicrous compromise was reached: the action would be transferred from the Swedish Court to Colonial Boston. The King would be a Royal Governor and Counts Horn and Ribbing would be just plain "Sam" and "Tom." And for some reason that totally escapes the twentieth-century mind, "Amelia" was thought to be less subversive than "Adelia."

The opera, based on the morality and politics of a small European Court, was given for a number of years in this incongruous setting. Later the locale was shifted to Naples, and more recently back to Sweden. But some of the Boston names have stuck. The program lists "Sam" and "Tom" and uses "Riccardo" instead of "Gustaf."

But after the curtain goes up, none of it is important. There is the King, there are the courtiers, the page and the conspirators. The Italians, who have never been to Colonial Boston and wouldn't believe it if they had, go merrily on enjoying the Boston locale with Gobelin tapestries hanging on split-log palace walls and uninhibited Puritans partying every night.

## OVERTURE (5 min.)

It is built around two contrasting themes: one, lyrical and associated throughout the opera with the King's love for Amelia; the other, gruff and jagged, for the conspirators. As Verdi's overtures go, this one is admired for being neither too short nor too long and doing its job of introducing the opera simply and aptly.

## ACT I (42 min.)

### SCENE 1 (15 min.)

A reception hall in the palace. The courtiers and the people await the King (Riccardo). Among them are the conspirators, Sam and Tom, and their adherents.

**chorus**    *Courtiers and Conspirators:* The courtiers croon that the King can rely on the hearts of his loving people. The conspirators growl that he has had military reverses, lost lives and that they're out to get him.

*Oscar, Riccardo and Courtiers:* Oscar announces the King, who enters, grants a few petitions and goes over the list of invitations to the royal **aria**    masked ball. He finds the name of Amelia, the wife of his minister, Renato, and muses on how much he loves her: "La rivedrà" (I shall see her) and "la sua parola udrà" (I shall hear her words). The chorus murmurs how hard he seems to be working for their benefit. The conspirators mumble that there are too many people: it's not the time. Then they all go out.

*The King and Renato:* The minister informs the King that he has discovered everything. The King, horrified, thinks Renato is referring to his love for Amelia: "Gran Dio," he gasps (Great God). But Renato has uncovered a conspiracy against the King. The King is so relieved **aria**    he won't even hear the conspirators' names. Renato then pleads with the King to take care: "Te perduto, ov'è la patria" (with you lost, where is the country)?

*Oscar, the Chief Justice and the King:* Oscar shows in the Chief Justice who requests an order banishing Ulrica, a sorceress. The judge explains that she attracts the riffraff of the kingdom and is undoubtedly **aria** the center of a conspiracy. The King turns to Oscar who, in a brilliant aria, pooh-poohs the judge's fears, says Ulrica is a grand fortuneteller with a great sense of theater, undoubtedly is in league with the Devil, and is a big addition to the kingdom.

*Courtiers, the King, Renato et al:* The King invites everyone to join him in disguise that afternoon on a visit to Ulrica. Renato protests that **chorus** it is too dangerous. Oscar is delighted. The conspirators see a possible opportunity for regicide. They all agree to meet at three at Ulrica's den: "Alle tre" (at three).

### Vocabulary, Act I Scene 1

| la rivedrà | lah ree.vay.drah | I shall see her |
| la sua parola udra | lah ree.vary.drah oo.drah | I shall hear her words |
| Gran Dio | gran(d) dee.oh | Great God |
| te perduto | tay pair.DEW.toe | with you lost |
| ov'è la patria | of eh lah pah.tree.ah | where's the country |
| alle tre | al.lay tray | at three |

## SCENE 2 (27 min.)

At Ulrica's den. There are a large caldron, skulls, bones and other tools of the trade scattered about. Ulrica, in a trance, has started her invocation. A crowd watches her, fascinated.

**aria** *Ulrica:* She calls to the Devil. Everything has happened correctly: the owl has hooted, the salamander has spat, the corpse has croaked. In the middle of it the King arrives in disguise. Looking around, he wonders aloud where the rest of the court is. The crowd, its eyes glued on Ulrica, tells him to stand back, which he does with a laugh.

Suddenly Ulrica ecstatically bursts out: "È Lui, è Lui" (it's he). She grows more excited. "Nulla, più Nulla" (nothing) is hidden from my sight, she cries. The crowd, popeyed, murmurs its appreciation. "Silenzio" (silence), she warns them.

**arietta** *Silvano and Ulrica:* Silvano, a sailor, steps forward. He sings of his life in the navy and asks for his future. Ulrica takes his hand. Promotion and money, she forecasts. The King has recognized Silvano. He hastily writes a commission and slips it and a purse into

Silvano's pocket. The sailor pulls them out. Sensation in the crowd. Ulrica doesn't reveal her thoughts.

At that moment there is a knock at the side door. A footman enters and asks for a private audience for his lady, who is in the coach outside. Ulrica dismisses the crowd on the ground that she must talk to the devil alone to straighten their fortunes out. Everyone goes out except the King, who has recognized the footman as one of Amelia's and who hides.

*Amelia and Ulrica:* Ulrica asks what has upset her. Amelia replies that it is a secret love that she must tear out of her heart. The King is thrilled to hear that she, in turn, secretly loves him, but he is distressed **aria** at her anguish. Ulrica knows a cure. She reveals that it is a special herb that grows in moonlight at the foot of the gibbet. Amelia, **trio** terrified, then starts a trio in which she prays for strength to go and get it. Ulrica tells her not to be afraid, and the King (still in hiding) swears that he will follow her there to protect her.

Outside, the crowd, joined now by the court in disguise, grows restive. They call to Ulrica. Hurriedly Amelia goes out.

*Ulrica, the King, the Crowd et al:* The crowd insists she tell more fortunes, and the King steps forward. He imitates Silvano and sings a song of a sailor's life (only his is in two verses and flashier than the simple sailor's). Ulrica examines his hand and announces that it's the hand of a noble. Then she abruptly refuses to continue. Everyone, including the King, insists. Reluctantly she forecasts death by a friend's hand. Courtiers and conspirators are equally aghast.

**quintet** The King then starts what becomes a quintet. He shrugs "E Scherzo" (it's a joke). Ulrica warns him not to mistake her. Sam and Tom fear she will reveal their plot and their names. Oscar cares for the King and is horrified at the suggestion of assassination.

Still laughing, the King asks, "By whose hand?" "By the next to grasp yours," she replies. The King then offers his hand around, but no one will take it. Except at that moment Renato arrives, late. He grasps the King's hand. Oscar and the courtiers sigh with relief. "He's my best friend," the King tells Ulrica. "Riccardo," Renato says on recognizing him. The King throws off his disguise and, giving Ulrica a purse, orders her to leave the country. She tries again to warn him, but he cuts her off.

Silvano then leads the courtiers and people in the local national **chorus** anthem. The conspirators vow they'll get the King next time; Ulrica asks them enigmatically what they're laughing about; Renato tries to warn the King of hidden dangers; and Oscar compliments the King on the love of his people. The King asks why he should fear when his subjects are so loyal. Then all join for the last verse of the Anthem.

### Vocabulary, Act I Scene 2

| | | |
|---|---|---|
| è Lui, è Lui | eh loo.we | it's he, it's he |
| nulla, più nulla | NOOL.ah p'you NOOL.ah | nothing, no nothing (is hidden from my sight) |
| silenzio | see.len.tsio | silence |
| è scherzo | eh scair.tso | it's a joke |

## ACT II (28 min.)

Outside the city gates. On one side, the gibbet on which the criminals are hung. It is close to midnight and there is a moon.

*Amelia:* She enters alone. The place, the night, the errand terrify **aria**    her. As her courage begins to fail, she urges her heart to be stony, to betray itself by picking the herb or to stop beating and let her die. A bell tolls midnight (usually six strokes in Italian opera). Suddenly she sees a figure, a vision. It moves. She's overcome with terror. Passionately she prays to Heaven to guard her. The vision materializes into the King.

*Amelia and the King:* In great agitation she begs him to leave at once **extended duet**    and preserve her honor. He insists no one cares more for her honor than he who loves her. She reminds him she belongs to his best friend. He doesn't deny it but starts an arietta, reciting how many sleepless nights he passed to earn this moment with her.

Again she begs him to go: "Mi lascia, mi lascia" (leave me). She urges him, but he insists, "Un sol detto" (one sole word). The music quiets and slows as she gives in: "Ebben, si, t'amo" (well then, I love you). Ecstatically he repeats, "M'ami, Amelia" (you love me).

Then he begins a duet in which first he and then she sings a verse; then, in a third, they join. He's ready to die for love, but she sees no good in it. Renato arrives.

*Renato, the King and Amelia:* Breathlessly he tells the King that the conspirators have set an ambush. He overheard them discussing that the King was at the gibbet with a lady. He insists the King leave at once. Amelia, keeping her face veiled, joins him. The King refuses to leave Amelia, but she threatens to throw off the veil if he doesn't go. Greatly troubled, the King makes Renato swear to take the veiled lady to the city gate without looking at or speaking to her and to leave **trio** her there. Renato swears: "Lo giuro" (I swear it). Then a trio develops: Renato and Amelia urge the King to hurry—"Va" (go) —while he laments that love makes him leave just when he ought to stay to protect Amelia.

*Renato, Amelia, Sam, Tom and the Conspirators:* The conspirators stop Renato and Amelia. Balked of the King, they insist on unveiling the lady. Renato prepares to fight against them all. In despair Amelia unveils. The conspirators burst out laughing: "Sua moglie" (it's his **quartet** wife). Renato is shattered: "Amelia," he repeats. The conspirators nudge each other. What a lover, what a husband. Midnight at the gibbet. What a story to spread around the town. Renato can get out only little broken phrases. Amelia wails that no one will believe the truth or her tears.

Renato suddenly interrupts the quartet to ask the conspirators to meet at his house in the morning. Surprised, they agree and go out still snickering. Renato roughly pulls Amelia after him back to the city.

### Vocabulary, Act II

| | | |
|---|---|---|
| mi lascia | me lah.shah | leave me |
| un sol detto | oon sole debt.toe | one sole word |
| ebben, si, t'amo | eh.ben see t'ah.moe | well then, I love you |
| m'ami | M'AH.me | you love me |
| lo giuro | lo JUR.oh | I swear it |
| va | vah | go |
| sua moglie | sue.ah MOE.l'yay | his wife |
| Amelia | ah.MAIL.ya | Amelia |

## ACT III (44 min.)

----

## SCENE 1 (23 min.)

Early next morning in the library in Renato's house. A large portrait of the King dominates the room.

*Renato and Amelia:* He tells her that her tears cleanse nothing. Blood is needed, and he will kill her. She swears that she did not dishonor him. "Hai finito," he commands (have done). It will take blood,

**aria**    "sangue." Brokenly, she makes one request: to see her son, "mio figlio." The aria is in two verses each beginning "morrò" (I shall die). It closes with a little, sobbing coda on the words "che mai più" (who never more—will see her son).

*Renato:* He is moved and gruffly orders her to the nursery. He decides not to kill her. She is too tender. Instead, another's blood must cleanse his name. He gazes at the portrait of the King: "Il sangue tuo" (it's **aria**    your blood). Then he sings the great baritone aria of the opera, "Eri tu" (it was you) who soiled that soul, the delight of my life. "Traditor" (betrayer) of your best friend. Then the aria softens as he remembers Amelia: "O dolcezze perdute" (oh bliss that I have lost); Amelia truly loved me. "E finita" (it's over). "O speranze d'amor, d'amor" (oh hopes of love).

*Renato, Sam and Tom:* They greet him suspiciously. He asks to join **trio**    the conspiracy. To prove himself to them, he burns some papers incriminating them. Finally he offers his son as a hostage. They agree, and in a trio they swear vengeance on the King: "La vendetta sarà, sarà" (revenge will be).

Renato insists he strike the blow and, as an argument starts, he gets a vase to draw lots—"la sorte." Amelia enters to say that Oscar has come with a message from the King, and they make her draw the lots. Sam reads the name: "Renato." "Il mio nome" (my name), Renato **quartet**    exults. Amelia, guessing what is going on, is horrified. In a quartet the conspirators resolutely close ranks, while Amelia wails her fears for the King.

*Oscar, Amelia, Renato, Sam and Tom:* Oscar announces that the King has invited them all to a masked ball that night. Amelia quickly refuses, but Renato corrects her: they will go. The scene ends with a quintet led by Oscar: he excitedly chatters of the glitter and blaze of the ball, the conspirators chortle over the "dance of death" and Amelia nearly faints with despair while wondering how she can get a message to the King.

### Vocabulary, Act III Scene 1

| | | |
|---|---|---|
| hai finito | hi fee.NEE.toe | have done |
| sangue | SAHNG.gway | blood |
| mio figlio | me.oh FEEL.yo | my son |
| morrò | more.oh | I shall die |
| che mai più | kay my p'you | who never more (will see her son) |

Vocabulary, Act III Scene 1 (*continued*)

| il sangue tuo | eel SAHNG.gway two.oh | it's your blood |
| eri tu | eh.rhee two | it was you |
| traditor | trah.dee.tor | betrayer |
| O dolcezze perdute | oh doll.che.tsay pair.doo.tay | oh bliss that I have lost |
| è finita | eh fin.NEE.tah | it's over |
| O speranze d'amor | oh spair.antsay d'ah.more | oh hopes of love |
| la vendetta sarà, sarà | lah ven.debt.tah sah.rah sah.rah | revenge will be |
| la sorte | lah sor.tay | lots, chances |
| il mio nome | eel me.oh NO.may | my name |

## SCENE 2 (21 min.)

The King's palace in the evening. The ball is about to begin. Actually the scene is in two parts, the first being a private closet of the King, which dissolves, without a break in the music, into the ballroom (which stage designers often represent as in the Stockholm opera house).

**aria**  *The King:* He worries about Amelia and wonders what happened. He decides that honor requires him not to see her again. He signs an appointment of Renato as Ambassador to Finland. Amelia will go with him.

He hears music from the ballroom and wonders if Amelia is there. Resolutely he determines not to go. Oscar enters with a message from an unknown woman. It warns the King against the ball. Oscar looks at him expectantly. The King decides to go to prevent anyone from calling him "coward." Excited now, he sings ardently of seeing Amelia again. *The Ball:* Courtiers dance by. The chorus wishes the night would last forever. Sam, Tom and Renato are frustrated: they cannot find the King. Oscar identifies Renato who, annoyed, pulls off Oscar's mask.

**aria**  Renato asks him to identify the King. Oscar deliberately irritates him by singing an "ask-me-no-questions-I'll-tell-you-no-lies" song. The refrain is an arch "tra-la-la-la." Dancers separate them. Renato new frantically tries to persuade Oscar that it's a matter of state. Finally Oscar reveals that the King is in a black cape with a pink bow. Again the dancers sweep by, this time leaving the King and Amelia to the front.

(The orchestra here starts a little mazurka tune that wanders hesitantly through the rest of the scene. Somehow it greatly increases the tension.)

In a whisper she begs him to leave the ball. At first he doesn't recognize her. Then when she urgently raises her voice, he calls her an angel. Passionately she admits that she loves him, but she insists that he must go: "Fuggi" (flee). He only tells her how much he loves her. Then he tells her that he is sending Renato as Ambassador to Finland in the morning, that he will never see her again, and that his heart is broken. She can only sob "Riccardo."

(Underneath the mazurka Verdi has introduced a tiny screw-turn figure on the cellos. It repeats quietly but insistently for twenty-nine measures. It can't go on forever. On the thirtieth and thirty-second measures, as the King sings "addio," it misses. On the thirty-third it starts again. Then Renato strikes. A good conductor can make it thrilling.)

Guards grab Renato. The Courtiers want to execute him instantly. The King forbids it and pardons him. With his dying breath he promises Renato that Amelia is pure. He admits he loved her but pulls out the ambassadorial appointment as evidence of his honorable intentions. Renato is overcome. The courtiers, led by Amelia, pray for a merciful God to spare him. The King bids them all farewell, "Addio per sempre miei figli" (farewell for ever my children), and dies.

### Vocabulary, Act III Scene 2

| | | |
|---|---|---|
| fuggi | FOOD.jee | flee |
| addio | ah.DEE.oh | farewell |
| per sempre miei figli | pair sem.pray m'yay feel.ye | for ever my children |

# LA FORZA DEL DESTINO
### (The Force of Destiny)

Opera in four acts. First performed at St. Petersburg on November 10, 1862. Revised version first performed at Milan on February 20, 1869. Music by G. Verdi. Libretto by F. M. Piave, after a play *Don Alvaro,* by the Duke of Rivas. Libretto revised by A. Ghislanzoni.

PRINCIPAL CHARACTERS

| | | |
|---|---|---|
| Marquis of Calatrava | bass | |
| Leonora, his daughter | soprano | lay.on.OR.ah |
| Don Alvaro | tenor | al.VAR.oh |
| Don Carlo | baritone | |
| Preziosilla, a camp follower | mezzo-soprano | |
| Melitone, a monk | bass | mel.ee.TOE.nay |
| Padre Guardiano, head of the monastery | bass | |

The action takes place in the middle of the eighteenth century: Act I is in Seville; Act II in an inn and a monastery near Hornachuelos, Spain; Act III near Velletri, Italy; and Act IV at the monastery.

The opera, with great blobs of passion, gloom, love and hate, tells the history of a Spanish blood feud. The play on which it is based has a better balance between light and dark by reason of the excellent scenes of Spanish village life. Some of these were lost in compressing the play into the opera.

The feud which is wholly one-sided exists between the Calatrava family and a noble Spaniard, Don Alvaro. The family is led, until destiny strikes in the first act, by the Marquis; thereafter by his son, Don Carlo. A flaw in the libretto is that Don Carlo's first appearance, in the second act, is in disguise.

Don Alvaro, the hero, is the only child of a renegade Spanish nobleman who, out in Peru, married the last Inca Princess and attempted to revive the Inca nation. But the revolt failed and Alvaro was born in prison. Shortly thereafter his parents were executed. The high Spanish types, the Calatrava family, continually sneer at Alvaro for being a mulatto and the child of a slave.

The skeleton of the plot, which in the opera is visible only in bits and pieces, is that Alvaro in eloping with Leonora accidently kills her father, the Marquis of Calatrava. In the ensuing confusion, off stage, Alvaro is wounded, and he and Leonora are separated. Don Carlo at once sets out to kill both of them—Alvaro for killing his father and Leonora for disgracing the family name. He pursues her first.

They meet when both are in disguise. He suspects that it is she, but she eludes him after overhearing him say that Alvaro has returned to America. In despair, with no home to which to return, she flees to a monastery where she persuades the Father Superior to let her live out her life as a hermit.

Don Carlo, meanwhile, joins the Spanish Army in Italy. There, still in disguise, he meets Don Alvaro, also in disguise, who believes Leonora is dead. Alvaro saves Don Carlo's life, and the two men swear eternal friendship. But as soon as Don Carlo suspects who Alvaro may be, he rifles his friend's belongings for evidence and finds a picture of Leonora. Then he provokes Alvaro to a duel, but they are separated.

Alvaro returns to Spain determined to give up the sword and become a monk. He joins the same monastery in which Leonora is a hermit. Don Carlo pursues him there. Once again he provokes Alvaro to a duel. The fight takes them near the hermit's grotto. Alvaro fatally wounds Don Carlo. He begs the hermit to emerge and hear the dying man's confession. Finally Leonora appears. The lovers recognize each other and are horrified at the circumstances.

Leonora runs to comfort Don Carlo who, recognizing her, stabs her. The Father Superior comes in and she dies, contented to find peace but leaving Alvaro desolate. (In Verdi's first version and in the play, Alvaro jumped off the precipice by the grotto.)

This skeleton gives no idea of the extraordinary beauty and excitement of almost all the music. But it does suggest why, when the opera was first revived, Verdi tinkered with it and why at every subsequent revival the producer has cut a scene here, switched an aria there, and tried to make the story comprehensible, if not believable.

But no amount of snipping and splicing can make the story believable to a twentieth-century audience that does not contribute, as Francis Toye suggests; "an effort of constructive imagination." He points out that "in an age when the principle of the blood-feud was accepted, facts, not intentions, were what mattered, and the facts remained undeniable." Alvaro killed the Marquis; Leonora put love before blood. At the height of the Romantic Age—the play came out in 1835—audiences reveled in blood and thunder.

## OVERTURE (8 min.)

It is exciting and built entirely of melodies from the opera. It opens with six hammer blows of destiny, flows at once into an agitated melody associated with Leonora fleeing from her brother and contrasts that with her appeal to the Virgin in Act II. (The Metropolitan has played the overture after the first scene.)

## ACT I (18 min.)

Seville. The entrance hall of the Calatrava palace.

*Marquis and Leonora:* He bids her good night, "buona notte," and is puzzled by her sadness. He reminds her that her recent visit to the country has made her forget Alvaro and that she must trust her father to make a suitable match.

*Leonora:* As soon as the Marquis has left, she and her maid start pack-
**aria**     ing. The maid urges her to be ready for Alvaro when he comes, but Leonora is listless and dreads the thought of leaving Spain. She sings a farewell to her country: "Ti lascio, ahimè . . . Addio" (I leave you, alas . . . farewell).

*Leonora and Alvaro:* Finally he arrives, excited and eager. But she is hesitant. To a broader melody he tries to give her confidence—he loves her and God will bless them—but she stops the maid from packing.
**arioso**     Excitedly he urges her to hurry. Again to another broad melody (this time with his agitation showing through it) he describes the waiting priest and how they will be married. But she suggests they leave tomorrow: she must see her father again. Alvaro is hurt and
**duet**     angry: if she doesn't love him, he absolves her of her prom-ise. Leonora gives in. They sing together of their future happiness. "Andiam, andiam" (let's go). But now it is too late. The noise has woken the Marquis.

*Marquis and Alvaro:* The Marquis thrusts Leonora aside calling her "degraded." Alvaro insists her virtue is unsullied and offers his life as proof. He bares his chest for the Marquis' sword. But the Marquis re-fuses to touch his sword to a baseborn mulatto. He orders his servants to arrest Alvaro and then hang him. Alvaro pulls his pistol, insisting he will surrender only to the Marquis. He offers his chest again and then throws the pistol at the Marquis' feet. It explodes, and the Marquis falls fatally wounded (said to be the only accidental death in opera). Leonora rushes to her father, but he dies cursing her: "Ti maledico" (I curse you). In the confusion Alvaro leads Leonora out with him.

### Vocabulary, Act I

| | | |
|---|---|---|
| buona notte | bwahn.ah NOT.tay | good night |
| ti lascio | tee LAH.show | I leave you |
| ahimè | aye.MAY | alas |
| addio | ah.DEE.oh | farewell |
| andiam | an.d'yahm | let's go |
| ti maledico | tee mal.eh.DEE.coe | I curse you |

## ACT II (51 min.)

## SCENE 1 (17 min.)

The village of Hornachuelos, several weeks later. In the large kitchen of an inn the innkeeper and his wife are preparing the supper for some peasants, muleteers, students and the Alcalde (the village mayor). (This is one of the scenes that producers cut or parts of which they push and pull into other scenes: dramatically it is the least interesting and the most confusing, and musically it is below par for the opera except for the Pilgrims' chorus and the baritone aria.)

**ballet and chorus**    *Peasants and Muleteers:* While they wait, they dance.

*Student (Don Carlo) and Trabucco:* The Alcalde asks the student to say "grace." Thereafter, as plates are passed, the student in an aside reveals that he is Don Carlo and is relentlessly pursuing his sister. He tries to question Trabucco (who is fasting) about a boy traveling with him and who has not come down to supper. (It is Leonora.) But Trabucco won't talk.

*Preziosilla:* She is a camp follower and she announces that Spain has declared war on Germany (the War of the Austrian Succession, 1740–48, known in the United States as the French and Indian War).

**aria**    The fighting is in Italy, and everyone is going. She sings a martial song, the refrain of which is "è bella la guerra, eviva" (war is glorious).

**chorus**    *Pilgrims:* They pass outside the inn singing a processional, and everyone at the inn joins them. Leonora (in disguise) peeks in from another room, sees her brother (in disguise) and joins the chorus, in which all ask for God's mercy.

*Don Carlo and Trabucco:* He again questions the muleteer, who still refuses to talk and leaves to sleep with his mules, "who ask fewer questions."

**aria**    *Don Carlo:* Then at the Alcalde's suggestion Don Carlo describes himself, claiming to be a student at Salamanca University. His best friend, he says, is Don Carlo of Calatrava, a fine fellow. He joined Don Carlo in pursuing his sister, Leonora, and her ravisher, Don Alvaro. But Alvaro had gone to America and it was rumored that the sister had died. (Leonora overhears all this and believes till the last

scene that Alvaro, thinking her dead, had returned to America.)
**chorus** *Preziosilla, Peasants et al:* There is a final chorus to which all leave. "Buona notte; andiam."

Vocabulary, Act II Scene 1

| | | |
|---|---|---|
| è bella la guerra | eh bell.ah lah gwair.rah | war is glorious |
| eviva | eh.VEE.vah | hurrah |
| buona notte | bwahn.ah NOT.tay | good night |
| andiam | an.d'yahm | let's go |

SCENE 2 (34 min.)

Night, several weeks later, at the monastery of the "Madonna degli Angeli" high on a mountain near Hornachuelos. The large chapel doors are closed. Light shines through the rose window. The monks are at service. The moon lights a stone cross set in a courtyard.
*Leonora:* She stumbles in, exhausted with the climb. Despairingly she repeats her brother's lie which she overheard in the tavern: Alvaro has **aria** returned to America, deserted her. She kneels and passionately prays: "Madre, madre pietosa Vergine . . ." (Mother, merciful Virgin). "Deh! non m'abbandonar . . ." (don't abandon me). "Pietà, pietà di me, Signore" (have pity on me, Lord). The monks chant at service in the chapel as she repeats it.
*Leonora and Melitone:* She rings the bell, and Melitone answers. He is a Chaucerian monk—lazy, curious, fond of the good life, intensely human and rarely elevated by his religion. Now he grumbles at Leonora for coming so late. She insists on seeing the Father Superior. As Melitone goes off, she prays again: "Vergin, m'assisti" (Virgin, help me).
*Padre Guardiano and Leonora:* Guardiano enters. Dramatically she describes her situation and then reveals who she is. Calmly he tells her **aria** to stand by the cross and let Heaven guide what she has to say. The cross seems to calm her. Already, she says, the sound of her father's curse grows fainter. She desires, she explains, to serve God by living in disguise in the Hermit's Grotto and seeing no one— **extended duet** ever. Guardiano warns her against it: she is too young, she is upset. "Guai" (woe), he mutters. But she is determined. Ecstatically she insists that Heaven has told her this is the place—at this cross. Guardiano is impressed and praises God: "Thy Will be

done." At the close of the duet he calls to Melitone to gather all the monks in the chapel.

**duet**     Then he tells Leonora to dress in monk's clothes. She praises God for his help and comfort. Guardiano joins her.

*The Monks, Guardiano and Leonora:* The monks assemble. Guardiano **chorus**     tells them that a penitent soul will live in the Grotto. No one is to go there. The monks curse anyone who breaks the rule— "maledizione." Then Guardiano explains to Leonora that he and he alone will bring her food. He gives her a bell to ring in case of great danger or death. The monks softly praise the Virgin as Leonora goes off to the Grotto.

### Vocabulary, Act II Scene 2

| | | |
|---|---|---|
| Madre, madre pietosa vergine | MAH.dray . . . p'yay. toe.zah vair.jin.nay | Mother . . . merciful Virgin |
| deh! non m'abbandonar | day known m'ah. BAHN.doe.nar | don't abandon me |
| pietà, pietà di me, Signore | p'yay.tah . . . dee may Seen.YOR.eh | have pity on me, Lord |
| Vergin m'assisti | Vair.jin mah.sis.tee | Virgin, help me |
| guai | gw'eye | woe |
| maledizione | mah.leh.deets.ee. OWN.nay | be accursed |

## ACT III (46 min.)

### SCENE 1 (25 min.)

Near Velletri, Italy, where the Spanish are fighting the Germans. To the right, in a tavern, the voices of men gambling. It is night.

**aria**     *Alvaro:* He advances out of the gloom, thoughtful and melancholy. He recalls his parents, Peru, Seville and Leonora. Nothing has turned out for the best. He was wounded on the night of the elopement and believes that Leonora was killed. He begs Leonora in Heaven to give him peace.

*Alvaro and Don Carlo:* The gamblers fight. Alvaro rushes in and returns with Don Carlo, who thanks Alvaro for rescuing him. Both men are in disguise and under false names, but Alvaro has made his the most famous in the army. Don Carlo is proud to be indebted to **duet**     him. They swear eternal friendship, "amici" (friends). A skirmish starts at the edge of the town and they rush off together.

(The score here has a change of scene to an officer's quarters where a surgeon is watching the skirmish and preparing to take in the wounded. Some producers omit the change as unnecessary.)

*Alvaro and Don Carlo:* Alvaro is brought in on a stretcher. The surgeon is gloomy about his chances. Don Carlo promises him as a reward for his bravery the order of Calatrava. Alvaro is shocked by the name and murmurs a refusal. Then he turns to Don Carlo and begins, "Solenne in quest' ora . . ." (in this solemn hour). He gives Don Carlo a key to his strongbox and makes him promise to burn unread a packet of letters. Don Carlo assures him, "Lo giuro" (I swear it). Alvaro then (to a broader phrase) says he can now die happy. Don Carlo urges him to have faith in Heaven, and they sing farewell to each other: "Addio."

*Don Carlo:* The surgeon takes Alvaro off to operate, and Don Carlo is left alone. He wonders why Alvaro started at the sound of "Calatrava." Is the man he knows as "Federico" in fact the mulatto? He opens the **aria**  box. In an aria beginning "urna fatale . . ." (fateful letters), he remembers his oath to burn them unread; but his oath concerned only the letters. He rummages until he finds a portrait of Leonora. **aria**  At that moment the surgeon announces Alvaro will live. With a burst of joy Don Carlo exults that now Alvaro will die by his sword.

### Vocabulary, Act III Scene 1

| | | |
|---|---|---|
| amici | ah.ME.chee | friends |
| solenn(e) in quest'ora | sole.en(e) een quest'or.ah | in this solemn hour |
| lo giuro | lo JUR.oh | I swear it |
| addio | ah.DEE.oh | farewell |
| urna fatale | oor.nah fa.TAL.lay | fateful letters |

## SCENE 2 (21 min.)

Here again the score calls for a change of scene (to a military camp near Velletri) that is frequently disregarded. Sometimes producers let the curtain fall to indicate a passage of several weeks. The score also has here a duet between Don Carlo and Alvaro. Most producers place it at the end of the act, which is where Verdi had it originally.

**chorus**  *Soldiers, Townspeople and Preziosilla:* She leads them in a martial chorus.

**aria**    *Trabucco:* The peddler sells his "bargains" in a sort of Verdian "Poor Little Buttercup."

**chorus**    *Beggars, Recruits and Preziosilla:* The Beggars complain of the war and ask for bread; the Recruits complain of being drafted; and Preziosilla scorns them both. (This chorus is frequently cut.)

**ballet and chorus**    Everyone joins in a tarantella, the refrain of which is that life is short and death is long. In the middle of it Melitone, the monk, arrives to give a sermon.

**aria**    *Melitone:* The sermon is a series of puns, such as "the crowd prefers bottles to battles." He scolds them until they get bored and drive him off.

**rataplan**    *Preziosilla and Soldiers:* She leads them in a "rataplan" (*See* Glossary). At the end, all go off.

*Alvaro and Don Carlo:* A few soldiers pass by. Then Alvaro and Don Carlo come forward. Don Carlo asks if Alvaro is well enough to defend himself. Alvaro doesn't understand. Don Carlo explains that he **extended duet**    saw the portrait. Alvaro refuses to fight: The Marquis' death was an accident and Leonora herself, he believes, died soon after. She lives, Don Carlo insists, but only until I can find her. Alvaro hears only that she lives: "E vive." Eagerly he suggests they search for her together. But Don Carlo contemptuously calls such a plan "stolto" (madness). He rehearses all the stains on the family honor until Alvaro, in a rage, pulls his sword.

The camp patrol separates them and arrests Don Carlo. Alvaro looks at his sword and throws it away, swearing to give it up forever. He will seek peace in a monastery.

### Vocabulary, Act III Scene 2

| | | |
|---|---|---|
| e vive | eh VEE.veh | and she lives |
| stolto | stole.toe | madness |

## ACT IV (37 min.)

---

### SCENE 1 (22 min.)

In a courtyard of the monastery.

**chorus**    *Old Men and Women and Melitone:* They beg for food— "la carità" (charity). Melitone staggers out with a big cauldron of soup. The old women nearly knock him down, and he begins to get irritated. One woman insists that she should get double portions because God gave her six children. Melitone suggests that if she spent the night in prayer, God wouldn't be so overly generous. The altercation is interrupted by the old men asking for more of the "scrapings." Melitone explodes: scrapings—the charity of the Lord? They are all lazy gluttons. They retort that Father Raphael (Alvaro) is much kinder to them. Melitone's feelings are hurt and he calls them "bricconi" (scoundrels). Guardiano tries to soothe him. The old people, however, keep right on calling Raphael "un angelo" (angel) and "un santo" (a saint). Furiously Melitone drives them all out.

*Melitone and Guardiano:* Guardiano mildly rebukes Melitone's impatience and tells him to ignore the crowd's preference for Father **duet** Raphael. Melitone asks why Raphael is so solitary and strange, always muttering to himself, and Guardiano replies that it is the effect of constant fasting and praying. Melitone observes that either alone would be enough to drive a man mad. A bell rings and Guardiano leaves as Melitone admits Don Carlo, who immediately asks for Father Raphael. Melitone, muttering, goes off to find him.

*Don Carlo and Alvaro:* Alvaro at first doesn't recognize him. Don **extended duet** Carlo eagerly offers Alvaro a sword. Alvaro (to a calm phrase) declines, as a monk, to fight and urges Don Carlo, "Lasciatemi" (leave me). Don Carlo calls him a coward. Alvaro quietly replies by asking Don Carlo to forgive him for any wrong, as he is trying now to atone for his sins: "O fratell' pietà, pietà" (oh brother, have pity, forgive).

Don Carlo recites Leonora's dishonor. Alvaro denies it and, to a lyrical phrase, insists that he still loves her: "L'am'(o) ancor." Alvaro then kneels to Don Carlo. A sign of the slaveborn, Don Carlo quips. Alvaro leaps up and demands a sword, "un brando." Then he stops. Don Carlo strikes him. Grabbing a sword, Alvaro leads him off to fight.

### Vocabulary, Act IV Scene 1

| | | |
|---|---|---|
| la carità | lah kah.ree.tah | charity |
| bricconi | bree.KO.nee | scoundrels |
| un angelo | oon AHN.jay.lo | an angel |
| un santo | oon sahn.toe | a saint |
| lasciatemi | lah.SHAH.tay.me | leave me |

| o fratell' pietà | oh frah.TELL p'yay.tah | oh brother, have pity, forgive |
| l'am(o) ancor | la.ah m'an.core (as sung) | I love her still |
| un brando | oon.BRAN.doe | a sword |

## SCENE 2 (15 min.)

The Hermit's Grotto: "a valley of inaccessible rocks crossed by a brook."

**aria** *Leonora:* She comes to the mouth of the cave. She prays for peace for her heart, which is still troubled by love for Alvaro. "Pace, mio Dio" (peace, O Lord). As she picks up the bread left for her by Guardiano, she hears Alvaro and Don Carlo fighting and rushes into the cave.

*Alvaro, Leonora and Guardiano:* Alvaro fatally wounds Don Carlo. He begs the hermit (unknown to him) to hear the dying Don Carlo's confession. In a panic Leonora rings the bell for Guardiano. But Alvaro urges the hermit to hurry. Leonora comes out. They have only a second for recognition. She rushes to Don Carlo who, also recognizing her, stabs her. Guardiano arrives in time to support her for the **trio** final trio. It begins with Alvaro cursing Heaven. Guardiano and Leonora reprove him. "Piangi," she says, and "prega" (weep, pray). "Prostrati," Guardiano insists (humble yourself). With difficulty, but for her, Alvaro forces himself down to his knees.

The feeling of the trio at once changes. Leonora is certain now that they will meet in Heaven where their love will be blessed. Guardiano rejoices at the translation of suffering into grace. But Alvaro remains human and earth-bound. At the end he can only sob, "Deh'non lasciarmi" (don't leave me). "Morta" (dead), he cries. "Salit(a) a Dio" (gone to God), Guardiano reminds him.

### Vocabulary, Act IV Scene 2

| pace, mio Dio | pah.chay me.oh dee.oh | peace, O Lord |
| piangi | p'YAHN.jee | weep |
| prega | pray.gah | pray |
| prostrati | PROH.strah.tee | humble yourself |
| deh, non lasciarmi | day known lah.SHAHR.me | don't leave me |
| morta | MORE.tah | dead |
| salit(a) a Dio | sah.leet ah DEE.oh | gone to God |

# DON CARLO

Opera in five acts. First performed at Paris on March 11, 1867. Music by G. Verdi. Libretto by C. Du Locle and F. J. Méry, adapted from Schiller's play, *Don Carlos*. Revised version by Verdi and A. Ghislanzoni, reducing it to four acts, first performed at Milan on January 10, 1884.

### PRINCIPAL CHARACTERS

| | | |
|---|---|---|
| A monk | bass | |
| Don Carlo, son of King Philip by his first wife | tenor | |
| Rodrigo, Marquis di Posa, an idealist and liberal | baritone | |
| Eboli, a Spanish Princess | mezzo-soprano | |
| Elisabetta, Queen of Spain and Philip's third wife | soprano | |
| Philip II of Spain | bass | fee.LEE.poe |
| The Grand Inquisitor | bass | |

The action takes place in and near Madrid about 1560 A.D.

One side of Verdi that many persons find attractive, both in the man and his operas, is his wide sense of reality. As a man he knew and cared not only about the theater but also about politics, agriculture, old folks' homes and hospitals. In his operas the lovers generally are not isolated from life, as those of Puccini and Wagner are apt to be; even in *La Traviata* there is talk of bills and relatives. In most of his later operas Verdi attempted to create a whole society as did Mozart in *Le Nozze di Figaro* and Wagner in *Die Meistersinger*. In two operas in particular, *Simon Boccanegra* and *Don Carlo*, Verdi tried to put politics and statesmanship on the stage, and any operagoer searching for a musical romance a la Puccini will probably find both unsatisfactory.

*Don Carlo* shows the Spanish court in the early years of the reign of Philip II, and the fictional love story is told against a background that is historically fair and is used to build the characters into real persons. The most important in the opera is King Philip (1527–98), who became king in 1556. He inherited on his father's abdication the larger share of an immense empire; on the other side of the world the Philippines are named after Philip. Administering such an empire had exhausted Charles V, and he retired to a monastery, where in 1558 he died, only fifty-eight years old.

Philip's efforts to administer his empire transformed him into an original bureaucrat. He worked extremely hard, read and signed everything himself so that the administration lagged months behind events, and tried hard to be just and fair. To his surprise many found him rigid and inhuman. It is typical of Philip's orderly mind that under him the Spanish court developed a protocol that most foreigners found ludicrous and stifling. There are hints of this in the opera: the Queen may walk alone only in the cloister of the convent and she may receive only those persons of whom Philip approves. Verdi presents her as a woman used to the greater freedom of the French court and slowly suffocating under the Spanish restrictions.

The historical Elisabetta, Elisabeth of Valois (1545–68), was Philip's third of four wives and was eighteen years younger than he. The others, in order, were Maria of Portugal, Mary I of England and Anne of Austria. Elisabeth died in 1568, having borne Philip two daughters but no heir. He seems to have been kind to her and fond of her gaiety and extravagance. There is no evidence of an affair between her and Don Carlo, Philip's son by his first wife. Don Carlo (1545–68) was physically deformed and apparently mentally unbalanced. His father imprisoned him as he was about to flee to the Netherlands, and he died in prison. Protestant and Catholic historians have always wrangled over whether Philip murdered his son.

Eboli is also an historical person (1540–92) and she was important in court intrigue. She is reported to have been extremely beautiful, although she lost an eye as a young girl. Sopranos sometimes wear a black patch to indicate this. Eboli probably never had an affair with Philip, although it is arguable; she was the mistress of Antonio Perez, who was for a number of years Philip's most trusted adviser. In 1579 Philip and Perez had a sensational falling out in which each publicly accused the other of murdering the secretary of Don John of Austria. Eventually on Philip's instigation the Inquisition accused Perez of heresy, and he fled to France. Eboli shared his disgrace and after 1579 lived either in prison or enforced retirement. Gossip at the time suggested that the murdered secretary was merely a blind and that Philip and Perez were really fighting over Eboli.

Rodrigo, the Marquis of Posa, was an invention of Schiller, but the model existed in Philip's greatest opponent, William the Silent (1533–84). William, who eventually led the Dutch out of the Spanish Empire, had been the favorite courtier of Charles V and one of Philip's ablest diplomats at the time of the opera. He constantly advised Philip against a policy of repression in the Netherlands and finally, when Philip began a policy of systematic terror through the Duke of Alva's soldiers and the Inquisition, William took up active opposition. And it soon became evident that Philip, for all his soldiers and priests, could not force the Netherlanders led by William to resign their political privileges under various municipal charters or to accept the Roman Catholic religion as the only one permissible. Philip then published his famous "Ban" in which he declared William to be out-side the law, all his property free for the taking, and offered 25,000 gold crowns and a patent of nobility to anyone kind enough to kill William. In reply William published his "Apologia" in which he started with arguments *ad hominem,* accusing Philip of murdering not only Don Carlo but also Elizabeth. Then he went on to suggest what really shot eyebrows up and started tongues wagging: that a prince by bad government could forfeit his right to rule. Thereafter Catholic sharpshooters took aim. One succeeded only in shooting away most of William's jaw; another got him on the stairs of his house in Delft. The Dutch have preserved the bullet holes in the plaster wall under a sheet of glass and polished the stairs so that they shine.

Verdi, of course, was not an historian and did not attempt to debate the issues. He wanted only to present human beings in the tangle of life—thinking, feeling, struggling to do what each conceives to be his duty—each able to control only a small part of his destiny; in fact, say some operagoers, he wished to show life as opposed to romance.

The opera exists in versions. The first was written for Paris with a French text, five acts and a ballet. Since the original run this version has never been performed. Verdi revised the opera, cutting out the first act and ballet, making other small changes and rewriting the text in Italian. This, the second version, is the one most often given and the one described below. A third version restores the first act and attempts to save time by cuts elsewhere. It is debatable whether this version had Verdi's approval, although it was published in his life-time.

The first act, cut from the second version, is set in the forest of Fontainbleau where Elisabetta has been riding. She loses her way, and a stranger offers to protect her while her page goes for help. He introduces himself as a member of the Spanish Ambassador's suite. She asks him about Don Carlo, whom she is to marry as a condition of peace between France and Spain. He, of course, is Don Carlo, and he has been axious to see her for himself. He is charmed by her, reveals himself, and they sing of their happiness. The page returns leading a large crowd that salutes her as Queen of Spain. Philip has decided to marry her himself. Duty to her country forces her to agree, and she and Carlo lament their lost happiness.

## ACT I (63 min.)

### SCENE 1 (19 min.)

The cloister of the convent of San Giusto. To the right, a lighted chapel through the gilded gates of which is the tomb of Charles V. The cloister is ringed by high cypress trees. It is dawn. In the chapel a monk leads several others in prayer.

*Monks:* They pray for Charles' soul, asking the all-powerful God to **solo with chorus**      forgive the Emperor whose greatest sin was pride. Only God is mighty, only He is great. Don Carlo, entering, uncovers and listens. The prayer ends, and the monks disperse. One, however, remains at prayer in the shadow of the tomb.

*Don Carlo:* He thinks of Elisabetta, whom he loves. "Io l'ho perduta" **aria**      (I have lost her), he grieves. He recalls how he courted Elisabetta "nella foresta di Fontainbleau" (in the forest of Fontainbleau), how they loved each other and how their happiness was cut short when Philip sent word that he and not his son would marry Elisabetta. (In the five-act version this scene in the forest forms the first act.) "Ahimè" (alas), Carlo sobs, "io l'ho perduta."

The last monk rises and departs, murmuring that peace can be found only in Heaven. Don Carlo imagines that the voice is his grandfather's, Charles V, who is rumored to be still alive. He gasps "O terror!"

*Rodrigo and Don Carlo:* Rodrigo starts to talk of the troubles in Flanders and then stops to ask why Don Carlo is pale and weeping. Carlo confesses that he is in love, "amo," and with "Elisabetta." "Tua madre" (your mother)! Rodrigo exclaims. It is sad for me, "tristo me," Carlo remarks, when even you abandon me. Rodrigo insists he will help Carlo and urges him to petition the King to be sent to Flanders.

**duet**      A bell announces the King and Queen on their way to prayer. Quickly Rodrigo and Don Carlo swear eternal friendship under God, who gives them a love of liberty, "di libertà."

Philip and the Queen pass through, the King kneeling for a moment before his father's tomb. Elisabetta and Carlo each tremble with emotion at the sight of the other. Monks in the King's train intone their prayer, as Carlo sobs again, "Io l'ho perduta."

Then with desperation and enthusiasm Carlo joins Rodrigo: "Vivremo insiem e morremo insiem" (we will live together and die together) and all for "libertà." (Francis Toye, a Verdi scholar, considered this friendship tune one of the most banal Verdi ever wrote. Lord Harewood, another operatic scholar, finds it "a noble expression of feeling." Much depends on the style with which the singers take it.)

### SCENE 2 (44 min.)

A sunny spot at the entrance of the San Giusto cloister; a fountain, grassy banks, clumps of orange, pine and lentil trees. In the distance at the back are the blue mountains of the Estremadura. At the back to the right are the gates of the convent. In the garden, awaiting the Queen, who is alone in the cloister, is her court, led by the Princess Eboli and the Countess of Aremberg. A page plays a mandolin.

**chorus**      *The Ladies:* They sing of the pleasures of the garden, the sound of the fountain, the shade from the sun, the flowers.

*Eboli:* She enters, remarking (for the benefit of the audience) that the convent's cloister is one of the few places where the Queen may walk **The Song of the Veil**      alone. Eboli proposes a song to pass the time. (It is in two verses and is called the "Canzone del Velo," "The Song of the Veil." The second verse is sometimes cut even though it reveals what was behind the veil.) Mohammed, King of the Moors, crept into the garden and whispered love to the veiled beauty, promising to make her Queen and swearing that there was no Queen. The lady consented, and when she removed her veil, "Allah!" exclaimed Mohammed, "it is the Queen!" The page and ladies sing the chorus which advises that veils favor love.

*Elisabetta, Eboli and Rodrigo:* Elisabetta enters, and a page announces Rodrigo. He ostentatiously delivers to her a letter from her mother in **trio**      Paris and underneath it slips her a note from Don Carlo. Then he deliberately walks Eboli away from the Queen, and a trio develops of Eboli's questions, his answers and Elisabetta's asides.

Eboli asks about the festivities, fashions and beauties at the French court, and Rodrigo insists that the best dressed and most beautiful lady is in Spain by his side. Elisabetta after hesitating reads Carlo's note, which urges her to trust Rodrigo.

Elisabetta announces that in return for bringing the letter from her mother, Rodrigo may ask a favor. He refuses anything for himself, but asks an audience with the Queen for Don Carlo. Elisabetta fears that to see Don Carlo will only cause them both pain. Eboli, not knowing Carlo loves the Queen, wonders if he loves her, for often at court he seems strangely moved by emotion. Elisabetta agrees, Don Carlo is shown in and Rodrigo leads Eboli and the others aside.

*Don Carlo and Elisabetta:* He kneels before her. As the interview proceeds, the ladies in waiting, slightly embarrassed by a situation which they don't understand, drift away until the two are left alone. Carlo announces that he seeks the Queen's help to persuade the King to send him to Flanders. Upset, she gasps, "mio figlio" (my son). He exclaims against the name and, as she starts away, begs her to have pity on him, "pietà." She promises to help him and again moves to close the interview.

He accuses her of indifference, and she replies that he should understand her silence, "silenzio"; she is trying to do her duty.

Sadly he recalls their love in the forests of Fontainbleau: "Perduto ben" (lost altogether), "mio sol tesor" (my only treasure). She replies softly, it is farewell, "O Carlo addio"; if on earth they could be joined, she would think it Heaven.

Excitedly Carlo insists that he will die of love at her feet, and he swoons in an epileptic fit (only most tenors are too inhibited as actors to attempt it). She believes he is dying. In his fit he imagines they are in Heaven and that she speaks of love. "O mio tesor, sei tu" (my treasure, you are), he insists. The fit passing, he regrets he did not die, for he loves her, "Io t'amo."

He tries to embrace her, and she draws quickly away, asking if he intends to kill the father to lead the mother to the altar. Horrified at the picture, Carlo cries, "Ah! maledetto io son" (I am accursed), and rushes off.

Elisabetta kneels and thanks God, "Signor," for saving them from themselves.

*Philip and Elisabetta:* The page announces the King, and the court hastily reassembles. He asks why the Queen is alone, "perchè sola è la Regina," in spite of his orders and he dismisses her lady in waiting,

**aria**    the Countess of Aremberg, who came with her from France. The Countess bursts into tears, and the Queen consoles her; they can still be friends though separated. She gives the Countess a ring in remembrance and urges her not to speak in France of her friend's grief and tears (this second verse is sometimes cut). The ladies comment on her noble spirit, but Philip in an aside insists she feigns it.

The Queen departs, followed by her court, leaving Rodrigo and Philip.

*Philip and Rodrigo:* Philip orders Rodrigo to remain and asks why he has not requested some preferment for his service to the state. Rodrigo replies that he wants nothing for himself, "nulla per me," but for others, "ma per altri." Philip urges him to speak.

Rodrigo describes the plight of the people in Flanders—the homeless children, the grieving mothers, the rivers red with blood. (The "Spanish Fury," which fell on Antwerp, was still to come in 1576. It profoundly shocked all of Europe, including many Spaniards. Philip, of course, argued that his internal policies were no affair of the family of nations. Others argued that his policies were so extreme that they affected world peace, world trade, etc.) Rodrigo thanks God, "Ah! sia benedetto Iddio," that he has been allowed to tell the King the agony of Flanders.

Philip replies calmly that by bloodshed he brings peace to the world and combats the heretics. When Rodrigo protests, Philip asks him to consider Spain where the people are peaceful, prosperous and Catholic. That same peace Philip will give to Flanders.

Rodrigo bursts out "Orrenda, orrenda pace" (horrible peace), "la pace dei sepolcri" (the peace of sepulchers)! He begs the King not to be remembered in history as another Nero. In the Empire the priests are executioners, the soldiers bandits, and the people curse the King, "maledir, si maledir." He urges the King to bring happiness to the world: "Date la libertà" (give liberty).

Philip is impressed but refuses to hear more. In fact he will not remember what he has heard. He warns Rodrigo, however, to beware of the Grand Inquisitor, "ti guarda dal Grande Inquisitor!"

Then, putting affairs of state aside, Philip asks Rodrigo to stay at court. With difficulty he explains that he suspects the Queen is unfaithful with Don Carlo. Rodrigo protests. With an outburst of grief, Philip complains that Don Carlo has robbed him of peace, and he asks Rodrigo to find the truth, giving him permission to see the Queen at all times. Rodrigo exclaims at the honor, and the act ends with Philip repeating his warning: "Ti guarda dal Grande Inquisitor."

## Vocabulary, Act I Scene 1

| | | |
|---|---|---|
| io l'ho perduta | yo l'oh pair.doo.tah | I have lost her |
| nella foresta di | nell.ah fo.RESS.tah dee | in the forests of Fon- |
| Fontainbleau | fon.tay.neh.blow | tainbleau |
| ahimè | eye.may | alas |
| o terror | oh ter.ROR | oh terror |
| amo | ah.moe | I love |
| tua madre | two.oh mah.dray | your mother |
| tristo me | triss.toe may | unhappy me |
| Dio . . . di libertà | dee.oh . . . dee lee.bair.TAH | God (gives us a love) of liberty |
| vivremo insiem | vee.vray.moe in.see.aim | we will live together |
| e morremo insiem | e mor.ray moe . . . | and we shall die together |

### Scene 2

| | | |
|---|---|---|
| mio figlio | mee.oh feel.yo | my son |
| pietà | p'YAH.tah | have pity |
| silenzio | see.len.tsio | silence |
| perduto ben | pair.doo.toe bayn | lost altogether |
| mio sol tesor | m'yoh sohl tay.zor | my only treasure |
| O Carlo, addio | . . . ah.DEE.oh | farewell |
| o mio tesor, sei tu | oh mee.oh tay.zor say two | oh my treasure, you are |
| io t'amo | yo t'ah.moe | I love you |
| ah! maledetto io son | ah mal.eh.debt.toe yo son | ah, I am accursed |
| Signor | seen.yore | Lord |
| perchè sola è la Regina | pair.kay so.lah ay lah red.JEE.nah | why is the Queen alone |
| nulla per me | nool.lah pair may | nothing for me |
| ma per altri | mah pair ahl.tree | but for others |
| ah! sia benedetto Iddio | ah see.ah ben.eh.debt.toe ee.DEE.oh | ah, blessed be God |
| orrenda, orrenda pace | or.ren.dah . . . pah.chay | horrible peace |
| la pace dei sepolcri | lah pah.chay day say.poll.kree | the peace of the sepulchers |
| maledir, si maledir | mah.lay.deer see . . . | curse, yes curse |
| date la libertà | dah.tay lah lee.bair.TAH | give liberty |
| ti guarda dal Grande Inquisitor | tee gwahr.dah dahl grand een.kwee.see.tor | beware of the Grand Inquisitor |

## ACT II (39 min.)

### SCENE 1 (14 min.)

The Queen's gardens in Madrid. A grove; to the back, under an arch of laurel, a fountain and a statue. The night is clear. There is a short prelude (2 min.).

*Don Carlo:* He enters reading a letter: at midnight in the Queen's gardens near the fountain. It is unsigned. He is certain it is from Elisabetta, "mio ben, mio tesor" (my best, my treasure). Eboli enters, veiled.

**duet**  *Don Carlo and Eboli:* Taking her to be the Queen, he pours out his love: "Sei tu, sei tu, bell' adorata" (it is you, beautiful adored one). Eboli rejoices as he continues, "Io t'amo" (I love you). As she unveils, he gasps in an aside "Ciel, non è la Regina" (Heavens, it is not the Queen). (Small point: this neat turn on the words and situation in "The Song of the Veil" explains why that song, rather than some other, was composed to introduce Eboli.)

Eboli, uncertain why he has drawn back, assures him of her love, "Io v'amo." She can help him politically, too; she knows of a plot against him. She heard the King whispering with Rodrigo about him. Don Carlo is surprised and attempts to use it to disentangle himself. He should not have come, he exclaims; happiness for him is impossible. But now Eboli senses the truth. "Voi la Regina amate" (you love the Queen), she accuses. Rodrigo enters and hears her.

**trio**  *Rodrigo, Eboli and Don Carlo:* A trio develops in which Rodrigo threatens Eboli to keep silent, she swears to destroy them both by speaking out and Don Carlo grieves at the trouble he has brought on the innocent Queen. Rodrigo draws his dagger, but Don Carlo forbids him to use it. Eboli threatens Carlo the more, "trema," and the trio continues until she leaves in a rage.

*Rodrigo and Don Carlo:* Rodrigo points out that Don Carlo must at once dispose of any incriminating papers in his chambers and suggests that Don Carlo give them to him. Don Carlo hesitates, and Rodrigo asks if he is no longer trusted. Carlo assures him that he is, and the act closes with the orchestra sounding the friendship theme.

### SCENE 2 (25 min.)

A large square in front of the Cathedral of Our Lady of Atocha. To the right, the cathedral with steps leading up to it; to the left, the palace; to the back, more steps leading down to a square in which is the pyre for the heretics and the top of which can just be seen. Large buildings and distant hills form the horizon. Bells ring, and guards hold back a large crowd.

(The scene is almost entirely spectacle built up on successive choruses. Only at the very end is the plot picked up and advanced. In the corresponding scene in his next opera, *Aida,* Verdi integrated the plot and spectacle much more closely; for example, he uses the spectacle to introduce Amonasro, an important character. The two scenes are an interesting study in their similarities and differences. Both are effective, but the later one is extraordinarily developed and refined.)

The crowd praises Philip, falling silent when the monks in a processional lead the heretics across the stage and into the lower square to be burned. (The heretics were always made to walk barefoot, to carry long green candles, and to wear "sanbenitos," a short smock with red crosses on the front and back.) From the palace the court emerges also in a procession, including delegates from all the provinces of the Empire, the Grandees of Spain, Rodrigo, the Queen surrounded by her ladies, and a Royal Herald. The Herald faces the closed doors of the Church and asks the Church to reveal the King for the court to behold. The doors open and Philip, under a canopy and surrounded by monks, walks to the top of the steps. The nobles bow and the people kneel. Philip repeats his coronation oath: to pursue God's enemies with fire and sword. He starts down the steps to lead the court into the square to watch the heretics burn when suddenly Don Carlo leads in six deputies from Flanders. The deputies kneel before Philip and ask him to reverse his policy in Flanders. Philip calls them unfaithful to God and their King and orders them removed from his presence under guard. The court and people beg for mercy for the deputies; the monks urge Philip to treat them like rebels.

(The scene thus far is an interesting demonstration of the variety a composer can achieve within one rhythm, the march, by changing his types of melody and orchestration. The crowd, as befits a mixture of men, women and children, alternates a roar with a series of short notes hit one after another like shouts. The melody ranges over almost two octaves. The monks leading the heretics have a melody of broken phrases that stays mournfully within a single octave. The court arrives to a melody more elegant than the crowd's with long-held notes followed by graceful turns and with a range of well over an octave. The herald makes his request and the court repeats it a cappella, which makes it appear more solemn and serious after all the brassy sounds than if merely a different accompanying instrument were used. The Flemish deputies, men of the world, present their plea to a suave, rhythmical melody suggesting that the speech was prepared and polished before being delivered. As the King tries to pass on and Don Carlo addresses him, the rhythm changes briefly to triple time, the only few bars in the scene not in march time.)

At the end of the plea for the deputies Don Carlo steps forward and asks the King to give him Flanders so that he may learn to rule. The King brusquely refuses, and Don Carlo draws his sword, swearing by Heaven that he will be the Savior of Flanders. All are aghast at the affront to the King, who furiously orders the guards to disarm Carlo. When they hesitate, the King seizes a sword himself.

At that moment Rodrigo advances to Don Carlo and demands his sword: "A me il ferro." Carlo gasps "Tu" (you), "Rodrigo"; (the orchestra sounds the friendship theme on mocking woodwinds). Don Carlo surrenders his sword to Rodrigo, who gives it to the King. The King at once makes Rodrigo a Duke, takes the Queen's hand and proceeds, followed by the court, to take up his position to watch the heretics burn. As the flames light up the square, the crowd praises Philip, the monks intone about God's law and mercy, and the Flemish deputies wonder how God can allow such things to be done in his name. From Heaven a voice promises the heretics God's own peace.

## Vocabulary, Act II

| | | |
|---|---|---|
| mio ben, mio tesor | mee.oh bayn . . . tay. ZOR | my best, my treasure |
| sei tu bell adorata | say too bell ah.dor.AH. tah | you are my beautiful adored |
| io t'amo | yo t'AH.moe | I love you |
| ciel, non è la Regina | chell non ay lah ray.JEE.nah | Heavens, it is not the Queen |
| io v'amo | yo v'AH.moe | I love you |
| voi la Regina amate | voy lah ray.JEE.n'ah. MAH.tay | you love the Queen |
| trema | TRAY.mah | tremble |
| a me il ferro | ah may eel fair.roh | (give) to me the sword |
| tu, Rodrigo | too Rod.REE.go | you, Rodrigo |

## ACT III (52 min.)

---

## SCENE 1 (37 min.)

The King's study in the palace in Madrid. Philip is deep in thought. The table is littered with papers. It is early morning.

*Philip:* "Ella giammai m'amò (she never loved me), he broods about **aria** the Queen. "Amor per me non ha" (she has no love for me). He recalls her sad look when she first came from France and saw his white hair. He muses on his end as King: "Dormirò sol" (I will sleep alone) wrapped in a mantle in the tombs of the Escorial. "Se il serto regal" (if only the royal scepter) could give him the power to read men's hearts, the traitor's heart, the Queen's heart. But for the King the future is only "dormirò sol." After a pause he murmurs again "Ella giammai m'amò; amor per me non ha!"

*The Grand Inquisitor and Philip:* The Grand Inquisitor, blind and ninety years old, is led in by two Dominican friars. Philip explains Don Carlo's disobedience, amounting to treason, and asks if the **duet** Church would absolve a father who executed his son. The Inquisitor replies that God did not hesitate to sacrifice His son. Philip demurs that he cannot silence his paternal feelings. The Inquisitor replies that all must be silenced to exalt the faith. "Sta ben" (very well), Philip concedes.

The Inquisitor then complains that there is one man at court, far more dangerous than Don Carlo, who wishes to undermine the Church. Philip interjects that he has found one man at last who can be a true friend, a loyal subject. Why be a King if another man is to be equal? the Inquisitor starts. But Philip cuts him off, "Non più, frate" (no more, friar)! The Inquisitor furiously accuses Philip of harboring heretical ideas and forsaking his vows to the Church. He demands of Philip Rodrigo, "il Signor di Posa." "No, giammai" (never), Philip refuses. The Inquisitor assures Philip that only his royal position saves him from the Inquisition. Philip orders the Inquisitor to stop such talk, and then the Inquisitor asks why he was summoned. Philip insists that there must be peace between them. "La pace?" remarks the Inquisitor as he goes. "Forse" (perhaps). Thus the crown must always bow before the altar, Philip observes alone again.

*Elisabetta and Philip:* She enters calling for justice, "giustizia"; her **duet** jewel box has been stolen. He hands her the box from his table and asks her to open it. When she refuses, he breaks the lock and finds amidst the jewels "il rittratò di Carlo" (the portrait of Don Carlo). She confesses it is hers but denies she has been unfaithful to him. He knows well that she was engaged to the son before she was married to the father. He warns that if she has been untrue, he will kill her. Then as she attempts to answer, he calls her an adulteress and she faints. He calls for her lady in waiting and Eboli enters followed by Rodrigo.

*Philip, Elisabetta, Rodrigo and Eboli:* At the sight of the Queen, Eboli is aghast that perhaps she went too far in advising Philip of the portrait and intimating that the Queen was unfaithful. Rodrigo asks Philip if, **quartet** with half the world to control, he cannot control himself. A quartet develops in which each sings his thought as an aside. Philip regrets his jealousy and decides the Queen was not unfaithful. Rodrigo sees the political disagreement between Don Carlo and his father aggravated by the domestic one and resolves to die if necessary to aid Spain. Eboli gasps "La perdei" (I betrayed her), "rimorso" (remorse). Elisabetta grieves that she is alone in a strange land, "Ah! sola, straniera."

Philip hesitates for a moment and then leaves, followed by Rodrigo. *Eboli and Elisabetta:* Eboli begs for pardon, "Pietà." She confesses that she stole the casket and accused the Queen to the King, naming Don Carlo—all because she loved him and he spurned her. Elisabetta asks her to rise, but Eboli has yet another sin to confess: that of which she accused the Queen, she herself committed with the King. Quietly the Queen asks Eboli to return the crucifix she gave her. Then ordering Eboli to choose between exile and the cloister, the Queen leaves. *Eboli:* With despair she cries that she will never see her Queen again. **aria** She curses her beauty: "O don fatale" (oh fatal gift), "o don crudel" (cruel gift); "ti maledico, o mia beltà" (I curse you, my beauty). She grieves that she sacrificed her Queen, "o mia Regina," to the passions of her heart. And Carlo will be executed the next day. Only one day before she must enter the cloister is left to her to save him, "un di mi resta," and she resolves to do it.

# SCENE 2 (15 min.)

The prison, a dark subterranean room. To the back, an iron gate leading to a courtyard, in which guards come and go. A stairway leads from the room up into the building. Don Carlo is seated with his head in his hands.

*Rodrigo and Don Carlo:* Rodrigo comes to tell Carlo that he will soon be released. Rodrigo explains that he is posing as the leader of the Flemish rebellion and that all of Don Carlo's incriminating papers **aria** were found in his room. Take heart, "No, fa cor," he urges. He is happy to die for Spain, and Carlo, apparently no longer at odds with the King, can be sent to Flanders.

Two men, unseen by Don Carlo and Rodrigo, descend the prison stair. One is an inquisitor, the other a guard. The inquisitor points out Rodrigo, and the guard aims his musket. Don Carlo, meanwhile, insists that he will reveal the plan to the King rather than let Rodrigo die. The guard shoots, and Rodrigo falls in Carlo's arms.

**aria** Rodrigo gasps "O Carlo, ascolta" (listen). Elisabetta will meet him at the cloister in the morning. Then, "Io morrò" (I shall die), he sings, happy to have given Spain a savior. "Ah, di me non ti scordar" (don't forget me)! he pleads.

*Philip, the Inquisitor and The Riot:* (This scene [4 min.] is sometimes cut.) Philip enters and offers to return Don Carlo his sword, which Carlo violently refuses, calling his father Rodrigo's murderer. Outside, a riot starts with the people shouting against Don Carlo. The King orders the gates opened, and the crowd surges in. Among them is Eboli in disguise, who urges Carlo to use the confusion to escape. The crowd is getting out of hand when the Grand Inquisitor is led in, and he cows them, "Vi prostrate," into kneeling to the King, God's annointed.

### Vocabulary, Act III Scene 1

| | | |
|---|---|---|
| ella giammai m'amò | el.lah jam.eye m'ah.moe | she never loved me |
| amor per me non ha | ah.mor pair may non ha | love for me she has not |
| dormirò sol | dor.mee.row sohl | I will sleep alone |
| se il serto regal | say eel sair.toe ray.gahl | if only the royal scepter |
| sta ben | stah bayn | very well |
| non più, frate | non p'you frah.tay | no more, friar |
| il signor di Posa | eel seen.yor dee PO.zah | the Marquis of Posa |
| no, giammai | no jam.eye | no, never |
| la pace | lah pah.chay | peace |
| forse | FOR.say | perhaps |

Vocabulary, Act III Scene 1 (*continued*)

| | | |
|---|---|---|
| giustizia | joo.stee.tsiah | justice |
| il rittrato di Carlo | eel ree.TRAH.toe dee . . . | the portrait of Carlo |
| la perdei | lah pair.dye | I betrayed her |
| rimorso | ree.MOR.soh | remorse |
| ah, sola, straniera | ah so.lah strahn.yair.ah | ah, alone, a stranger |
| pietà | p'yay.tah | have pity |
| o don fatale | o don fah.tah.lay | oh fatal gift |
| o don crudel | o don croo.del | oh cruel gift |
| ti maledico | tee mal.eh.dee.ko | I curse you |
| o mia beltà | o mee.ah bell.tah | oh my beauty |
| o mia Regina | o mee.ah reh.jee.nah | oh my Queen |
| un di mi resta | oon dee mee RESS.tah | one day remains to me |

Scene 2

| | | |
|---|---|---|
| no, fa cor | no fah kor | no, take heart |
| oh Carlo, ascolta | ah.SKOL.tah | oh Carlo, listen |
| io morrò | yo mor.roh | I shall die |
| ah, di me non ti scordar | ah, dee may non tee skor.dahr | ah, don't forget me |
| vi prostrate | vee pro.STRAH.tay | prostrate yourself |

## ACT IV (22 min.)

The cloister of the convent of San Giusto. It is a moonlit night. Elisabetta enters, approaches the tomb of Charles V and kneels before it.

*Elisabetta:* (Her aria divides roughly into five parts, with the last re-
**aria**      peating the first. It expresses the Queen's personality from a number of sides, just as did "O don fatale" for Eboli.)

1: She appeals to the dead Charles: "Tu che le vanità" (you who knew the vanity) of the world and found peace in the tomb, if tears are shed in Heaven, "piangi" (weep) for my grief and bear my tears to the throne of God. "E porta il pianto mio al trono del Signor."

2: She thinks of Carlo, for whom she waits. He must go to Flanders; she promised Rodrigo. Carlo will win glory and, as for her, she will soon die.

3: After a pause, a happier tune begins, and she thinks of France, "Francia," where she had been happy, and of "Fontainbleau." Perhaps

Carlo will walk again in the gardens where they swore eternal love, an eternity that lasted a day.

4: She bids farewell, "addio," to youth, love and illusion. Her heart's one desire now is the peace of the tomb.

5: She appeals again to the dead Charles, "Tu che le vanità," to bear her tears to the throne of God.

*Elisabetta and Don Carlo:* Carlo enters; one word only, she insists. She entrusts him to Heaven, and he must forget her and live. He must think of Rodrigo. Carlo promises to create a monument for Rodrigo of happy people in Flanders or to die in the attempt, knowing that she will mourn or applaud him in her heart. (There then follows a duet, often cut, in which he exclaims that her love inspires him and she urges him to go and save the Flemish.)

He sees she is weeping, and she says they are tears for a hero. **duet**    She promises that they will meet again in a better world, "Ma lassù ci vedremo" (but up there we shall meet), "in un mondo migliore." He repeats it and they say farewell forever, "addio, per sempre."

*Philip, the Grand Inquisitor et al:* "Yes, forever," cries the King, pulling her away. He tells the Grand Inquisitor that he may have Don Carlo, and the Inquisition guards surge forward. Carlo draws his sword and backs against the gate to the tomb. A monk suddenly appears. It is the dead Charles V in royal robes. He tells Carlo that the grief of the world follows man even into the cloister, and he leads Carlo to safety inside the tomb (Carlo symbolically dies?), leaving Philip and the others astounded and terrified.

(The ending has always been criticized. In the play Philip hands Carlo over to the Grand Inquisitor, who will have him legally murdered. In the opera it is seldom clear whether the producer intends to portray Charles as actually alive, an apparition or merely being impersonated by a monk. The score states flatly that it is Charles V. But in the opening scene, where Don Carlo thinks he recognizes his grandfather's voice, the score describes the man merely as a friar.)

### Vocabulary, Act IV

| tu che le vanità | too kay lah vah.nee. TAH | you that the vanity of the world have known |
| --- | --- | --- |
| piangi | p'YAHN.jee | weep |

### Vocabulary, Act IV (*continued*)

| | | |
|---|---|---|
| e porta il pianto mio | ay por.tah eel p'yahn. toe mee.oh | and bear my tears |
| al trono del Signor | ahl tro.no del seen.yor | to the throne of God |
| Francia | FRAHN.chah | France |
| addio | ah.DEE.oh | farewell |
| ma lassù | mah lah.SOO | but up there |
| ci vedremo | chee vay.DRAY.moe | we shall meet |
| in un mondo migliore | een oon mon.doe meel. yor.ay | in a better world |
| addio, per sempre | ah.DEE.oh pair sem. pray | farewell, forever |

# AIDA

Opera in four acts. First performed at Cairo, Egypt, on December 24, 1871. Music by G. Verdi. Libretto by Verdi and A. Ghislanzoni after a précis by F. A. F. Mariette and C. du Locle.

### PRINCIPAL CHARACTERS

| | | |
|---|---|---|
| Ramphis, the High Priest | bass | |
| Radames | tenor | rah.dah.MACE |
| Amneris, the King of Egypt's daughter | mezzo-soprano | ahm.NAIR.ees |
| Aida, daughter of Amonasro and slave to Amneris | soprano | ah.EE.da |
| The King of Egypt | bass | |
| Amonasro, King of Ethiopia | baritone | am.oh.NAS.roh |

The action takes place in Memphis, Egypt, during the time of the Pharaohs.

*Aida,* like other very great operas, suffers from being given too often; the performances frequently torpedo the opera. All singers try to have it in their repertory, for it comes up often and to sing is to eat. Late or soon most are rushed in as replacements without rehearsal.

But it is an excellent opera. The libretto is beautifully constructed. Consider the implications, memories and contrast between Aida's appeal to the Gods, "Numi, pietà," in the first act and Amneris' appeal with the same words in the fourth. Or how the character of the chief priest, a small role, is developed as priest, prime minister and judge. Or consider the musical wealth and confidence that the last scene represents: there is no reprise of "Celeste Aida" but two new arias and a superb duet. Further, Verdi somehow managed by the split stage, his idea, to preserve the intimacy of Aida's death while fringing it with the trappings of grand opera.

In spite of legend the opera was not commissioned for the opening of the Suez Canal, nor even for the opening of the Italian Theatre in Cairo in 1869. The first offers, with these openings in mind, Verdi refused, and by the time a contract was signed, the première was scheduled for January, 1871. But the Franco-Prussian war trapped the scenery in Paris and delayed the première almost a year. In order, however, not to disappoint those who revel in legends: it is true that veiled ladies from the Khedive's harem attended the première in Cairo in three boxes on the first tier.

## PRELUDE (3 min.)

It has contrasting themes: the quiet is associated with Aida's love for Radames and the more dramatic with the priests.

## ACT I (34 min.)

### SCENE 1 (24 min.)

A hall in the palace at Memphis. Ramphis, the High Priest, and Radames are discussing the rumors of war.

*Ramphis and Radames:* Ramphis says his scouts will soon report whether the Ethiopians are marching up the Nile to Thebes. He adds that the Gods have already selected the general for the Egyptians. "Oh, lui felice," Radames exclaims (oh, happy he). But Ramphis doesn't reveal the name and departs to report to the King.

*Radames:* Alone, Radames hopes it will be he. Glory, power, and all **aria** for Aida. He sings, "Celeste, Aida, forma divina" (heavenly Aida, form divine). (This aria is difficult for tenors because it comes so early in the opera. The last note, a B flat, is scored to be sung very quietly, which is exceedingly difficult. Most tenors unabashedly hit it hard. Jean de Reszke, one of the greatest tenors, invariably omitted the aria on the ground that he would not compete with late-comers tramping down the aisle.)

*Amneris and Radames:* Amneris enters remarking how happy he looks.

**duet**    He hastily lies that he was thinking of war. Insinuatingly she suggests he was dreaming of love. He fears she has guessed he loves Aida. His agitation unnerves her: "Oh, guai," she gasps (woe), for the first time jealous.

*Amneris, Radames and Aida:* His glance at Aida, who enters, fires Amneris' fears. Sweetly she asks Aida why she is sad. The preparation for war, Aida replies. Something more personal, Amneris suggests.

**trio**    The three then turn aside and each expresses his secret thoughts. Amneris recites her rage at Aida: "Trema" (tremble). Aida wails that her love is doomed: "Pianto" (weeping). Radames fears that Amneris will upset all his plans: "Guai."

*The King, Ramphis et al:* They gather to hear the messenger, who reports that the Ethiopians have crossed the border led by Amonasro. "Mio padre," Aida gasps (my father). The Egyptians call for "guerra" (war). The King announces the Egyptian General: Radames. Then he leads several choruses of "Egypt forever" punctuated by cries of "guerra" and topped by Aida's lament for love and country. At the end Amneris addresses Radames: "Ritorna vincitor" (return victorious). The crowd repeats and goes out.

*Aida:* "Ritorna vincitor," Aida repeats. Then in an aria she poses the
**aria**    problem of the opera. How can she hope Radames will be victorious—over her father? In a swift rising phrase she asks the Ethiopian Gods to scatter, "struggete," the Egyptian arms. Then she remembers Radames: "E l'amor mio" (and my love)? Father, lover—it is insoluble. Desperately she appeals to the Gods to let her die: "Numi, pietà, del mio soffrir" (Gods, have pity, on my sufferings).


### SCENE 2 (10 min.)

Inside the temple at Memphis. The priests and Radames gather to consecrate his sword.

**chorus, and ballet**    *Priests:* They call on the God, "Immenso Phtha, noi t'invochiamo" (Almighty Phtha, we invoke you). The priestesses dance while a silver veil is placed on Radames.

**duet**    *Ramphis and Radames:* Each in turn directly appeals to the God for strength: "Nume" (God).

**chorus**    *Priests:* All join in the final appeal to Phtha. (Note: Sometimes the final "o" of "invochiamo" is not sung.)

Vocabulary, Act I

| | | |
|---|---|---|
| oh lui felice | oh louis feh.LEE.che | oh, happy he |
| celeste Aida | che.less.tay ah.EE.dah | heavenly Aida |
| forma divina | for.mah dee.VEE.nah | form divine |
| oh, guai | oh gweye | oh, woe |
| trema | TRAY.mah | tremble |
| pianto | p'yahn.toe | weeping |
| mio padre | me.oh PAH.dray | my father |
| guerra | gwair.rah | war |
| ritorna vincitor | ree.turn.ah vin.chee.<br>tor | return victorious |
| struggete | strew.jet.teh | scatter |
| e l'amor mio | eh l'ah.more me.oh | and my love |
| Numi, pietà | new.me p'yay.tah | Gods, have pity |
| del mio soffrir | dell.me.oh soh.frear | on my sufferings |
| immenso phtha | ee.men.so ftha | Almighty Phtha |
| noi t'invochiamo | noy t'in.vo.k'yahm.oh | we invoke you |
| Nume | new.may | God |

## ACT II (40 min.)

### SCENE 1 (14 min.)

The apartments of Amneris. The Egyptians have defeated the Ethiopians and Amneris' slaves are dressing her for the triumphal procession.

**solo, chorus and ballet** *Amneris and Slaves:* Gently they sing of love and victory while Amneris yearns for Radames: "Oh vieni, vien(i), amor mio" (Oh come, come, my love). Young Moorish slaves dance.

*Aida and Amneris:* The sight of Aida excites Amneris' fears and jealousy. Determined to discover if Aida is a rival for Radames' love, she first consoles her for her country's defeat. Then she suggests that love might ease the pain. Aida bursts out: "Amore, amore" (love), a **duet** joy and a torment, a boon and a curse, she wails. Amneris watches her closely. Then she suggests to Aida that Radames may be dead. "Misera" (miserable woman), Aida wails. Finally, to make certain, Amneris then tells Aida that Radames lives: "Vive" (he lives). Rapturously, Aida repeats it.

Amneris rages: "Trema" (tremble), she warns Aida who, remembering with difficulty that she is a slave, begs for "pietà" (pity). The trumpets announce the procession outside. Angrily, Amneris goes off, threatening to take care of Aida later. Aida, alone, prays again to her Gods for mercy.

### SCENE 2 (26 min.)

An avenue in Memphis leading out to Thebes: on the right a temple, on the left a reviewing stand for the King, and at the back a triumphal arch. Egyptians line the avenue to welcome the victorious troops.

(This scene is one of the great operatic spectacles. It is a finale that lasts twenty-six minutes—longer than most symphonies. Again and again it seems impossible that Verdi can cap the preceding climax. Yet he succeeds not only musically but dramatically. Even with all his characters trapped at a parade, he continues to unfold his plot— one cause of the scene's success.)

**chorus and ballet**     The people and priests sing "Glory to Egypt," the King takes up his position, and the parade of victorious troops begins. Thereafter comes the ballet. (It is almost always disappointing— often because the choreographer has tried too hard to be Egyptian and, with a succession of frozen stances and rigid movements, taken all the frenzy and excitement out of the dancing.)

More troops parade, more chorus sing, leading up to the entrance of Radames. The King proclaims him The Savior of Egypt and offers to grant him any boon he requests. Radames asks that the prisoners be led in first.

The Ethiopians stumble in. The last is the King, Amonasro, Aida's father, disguised as a mere officer. Aida recognizes him and gasps, "Mio padre" (my father). All hear it but think only that her father is an officer. "Tu prigionier," she sobs (you, a prisoner). He warns her: "Non mi tradir" (don't betray me).

Amonasro then proudly admits that he fought for his country. The **aria**     Ethiopian King, he lies, died at his feet. Then, launching into a broad aria, he begs mercy for the prisoners. "Ma tu, Re" (but you, **chorus**     King . . . have the power to spare us). The crowd takes up the plea, but the priests call for death.

Aida passionately pleads for her father. Radames admiringly watches her, while Amneris, watching him, flames with jealousy. The Egyptian King decides clemency is a royal virtue. Amonasro plots for **sextet and chorus**     the morrow and Ramphis, the chief priest, insists on death. The crowd scolds the priests and begs for mercy, as do also the prisoners. (Throughout, Verdi is writing an average of fifteen different vocal lines.)

In a moment of silence, Radames demands his boon: freedom for the prisoners. The priests are furious. Ramphis urges the King to go back on his word. He chides Radames for being a fool in foreign policy. Radames insists that with Amonasro dead, as he believes, the Ethiopians will be peaceful. Ramphis then urges the King at least to keep Aida's father as a hostage. The King agrees to this and frees the other prisoners. Then he publicly announces that he will give Amneris and succession to the throne to Radames.

**sextet and chorus**    The final chorus begins with the crowd and priests rejoicing in victory and praising the Gods; the prisoners rejoice in freedom. Aida wails that all hope is gone. Amneris is triumphant. Radames is horrified: to refuse Amneris would be treason, yet he loves Aida. Amonasro plots vengeance. Ramphis intones to the Gods.

### Vocabulary, Act II

| | | |
|---|---|---|
| ah vieni, vien(i) amor mio | ah v'yay.nee v'yayn ah.more me.oh | oh, come . . . my love |
| amore, amore | ah.MOR.eh | love |
| misera | ME.zer.ah | miserable woman |
| vive | VEE.veh | he lives |
| trema | TRAY.mah | tremble |
| pietà | p'yay.tah | have pity |
| mio padre | me.oh pah.dray | my father |
| tu prigionier | two pre.joan.air | you, a prisoner |
| non mi tradir | known me trah.deer | don't betray me |
| ma tu, Re | mah two ray | but you, King |

## ACT III (31 min.)

On the bank of the Nile. To one side in shrubs is a temple. Stars and a moon.

*Amneris and Priests:* They accompany her to the temple, where she will spend the night in prayer preparing for her marriage to Radames.
*Aida:* She wonders why Radames asked her to meet him here. If just to bid her farewell, then, looking at the Nile, she will seek peace in death.

**aria**    She begins a long aria: "O patria mia" (my country). She laments that she will never again see its green hills and blue sky. "Mai più" (never more).

*Aida and Amonasro:* A sound startles her. It is not Radames but Amonasro. He has a plan. He sees that she loves Radames. If she helps, **duet** they can recover their country, his throne and her love. Craftily he reminds her of the country, green and happy before the Egyptians came, and the wasteland, red with blood that it was after. As her memories stir, she joins him.

The Ethiopians are again on the march, he says. They plan an ambush. But they must know the pass into the hills that the Egyptians will use. Entice this information out of Radames, he urges. "No, no, giammai" (no, never), she refuses.

Savagely he calls her the curse of her country, a daughter of death. "Pietà" (have pity), she sobs. In the shadows he claims he sees the withered hand of her mother stretched out to curse her. Aida, terrified, sinks to the ground. The music softens, and she agrees to do it. Amonasro at once lifts her up, comforts her and, hearing Radames, hides in the bushes.

*Aida and Radames:* He is thrilled to see her again and alone. She, however, asks him what he intends to do about Amneris. Accompanied by trumpets, he describes his soldier's plan. He will again defeat the Ethiopians and with even greater glory will explain to the King and **duet** ask another boon—Aida's hand. She is unconvinced and suggests flight together, now: "Fuggir" (to flee).

Softly she urges it. But for him it means abandoning his country. "Va" (go), she repeats scornfully: Amneris waits for you. "No, **duet** giammai," he resolves. Together, passionately, they resolve to flee. They are leaving when Aida stops to ask how the Egyptian troops are going, so that they can avoid them. "By the gorges of Napata," he answers.

At once Amonasro, emerging, exults that he will station his troops there. Radames is stunned: "Tu . . . Amonasro . . . tu . . . il Re" (you . . . Amonasro . . . you . . . the dead king). On pounding notes he exclaims, "Io son disonorato" (I am dishonored) **trio** . . . forever, a traitor. Aida tries to calm him, and Amonasro remarks that it was fate. Both urge him to flee with them.

But Amneris has come out of the temple: "Traditor" (traitor), she accuses. Aida and Amonasro flee, and Radames surrenders to the priests.

Vocabulary, Act III

| | | |
|---|---|---|
| o patria mia | oh pah.tree.ah me.ah | oh my country |
| mai più | my p'you | never more |
| no, no giammai | no no jam.EYE | no, never |
| pietà | p'yay.tah | have pity |
| fuggir | food.jeer | to flee |
| va | vah | go |
| tu il Re | two eel ray | you the King |
| io son disonorato | yo sewn dis.own.nor. RAH.toe | I am dishonored |
| traditor | trah.dee.tor | traitor |

## ACT IV (30 min.)

———

## SCENE 1 (22 min.)

A hall in the palace; on the left the entrance to the courts of justice and on the right the prison. The Egyptians have again defeated the Ethiopians. This time Amonasro died; Aida disappeared. Radames knows none of this and believes that Amneris has had Aida killed.

*Amneris:* She argues to herself that Radames is not a traitor. Then as she remembers his attempted flight, she rages and wishes him dead; but she admits, "Io l'amo, io l'amo sempre" (I love him for always). She determines to see him, and the guards bring him in.

She urges him to speak in his defense, and she will beg his pardon **duet** from the King. He refuses. He disclosed the secret, but he is not a traitor. Still, there is nothing to live for.

"Morire" (you'd die)? she bursts out. You must live—for me. She offers to give up her country, her throne, her life for him. He refuses. Life is nothing without Aida.

Angrily she cuts him off. He accuses her of killing Aida. She denies it: "No, vive Aida" (no, Aida lives). She describes how Amonasro died and Aida disappeared. To a broad phrase Radames rejoices that Aida lives and hopes that she'll reach her homeland.

Again Amneris offers to save him if he will swear to give up Aida. He replies, "Nol posso" (I cannot).

Furiously she swears that nothing will save him now. He answers that death is a blessing: "È la morte" (it is death). The guards take him out.

*Amneris and Priests:* Alone she sobs: "O chi lo salva" (oh, who will save him now)? She watches the priests enter the courtroom offstage with dread. The priests call the court to order. Amneris appeals to the Gods: "Numi pietà" (Gods have pity). "O chi lo salva," she repeats as she watches Radames enter the prisoner's box.

Three times Ramphis calls Radames to the bar. Then he reads the first charge, ending "Discolpati" (defend thyself). "Egli tace," he reports (he's silent). "Traitor" (traitor), the priests judge. "Pietà, Numi, pietà," Amneris sobs at the door. (This is repeated twice more for a total of three charges.)

The priests then condemn him to death. Slowly they file out muttering "traditor." Amneris rages at them hysterically and curses them as bloodthirsty hounds of heaven. But they ignore her, and she is powerless.

## SCENE 2 (8 min.)

The scene is divided. Above is the interior of the temple; below, the death chamber. Two priests have just lowered Radames into it and are relaying the heavy stone.

*Radames:* He is thinking of Aida, when he hears a groan. It is she. She explains that she foresaw his fate and earlier crept in to die with him.

**aria**    "Morir, sì pur(a) e bella," he begins (to die, so pure and lovely).

**aria**    The lack of food and air has already affected her. She sees an angel come to take them to heaven, where at last they can be happy and free to love.

Above them the priests begin to chant.

**duet**    Softly Aida sings, "O terr(a) addi(o)" (oh earth farewell); for us, she says, "si schiud(e) il ciel" (itself the heaven opens).

Above them the despairing Amneris begs the Gods to give him peace, "pace t'imploro" (peace, I implore for you), as Aida dies in the arms of Radames.

### Vocabulary, Act IV

| | | |
|---|---|---|
| io l'amo, l'amo sempre | yo l'ah.moe . . . sem. pray | I love him for always |
| morire | more.rear.ay | to die |
| no, vive Aida | no vee.veh ah.EE.dah | no, Aida lives |
| nol posso | knoll pos.so | I cannot |

| | | |
|---|---|---|
| è la morte | eh lah more.tay | it is death |
| pietà, Numi, pietà | p'yay.tah.new.me | have pity, Gods |
| oh, chi lo salva | oh key lo sal.vah | oh, who will save him |
| discolpati | dis.kol.pah.tee | defend yourself |
| egli tace | eh.lee TAH.chay | he is silent |
| traditor | trah.dee.tor | traitor |
| morir, sì pur(a) e bella | more.rear see poor(a) eh bell.ah | to die so pure and lovely |
| o, terr(a) addi(o) | oh, tair.ah.dee | Oh earth farewell |
| si schiud(e) il ciel | see skood(e) eel chell | itself the heaven opens |
| pace t'imploro | pah.chay t'im.plor.oh | peace, I implore for you |

# OTELLO

A lyrical drama in four acts. First performed at Milan on February 5, 1887. Music by G. Verdi. Libretto by A. Boito after Shakespeare's play, first printed in 1622.

### PRINCIPAL CHARACTERS

| | | |
|---|---|---|
| Cassio, Otello's captain | tenor | CASS.ee.oh |
| Iago, Otello's ensign | baritone | ee.AH.go |
| Roderigo, a young Venetian noble | tenor | |
| Otello, a Moor, general for the Venetians | tenor | oh.TELL.oh |
| Desdemona, his wife | soprano | des.DAY.moan.ah |
| Emilia, Iago's wife | mezzo-soprano | eh.MEAL.ya |
| Bianca, beloved of Cassio | (never appears) | |

The action takes place in a seaport of Cyprus at the close of the fifteenth century.

*Otello* is usually cited as the greatest Italian opera of the nineteenth century, and it is fair to ask why and, even before that, what such a statement means. By definition the nineteenth century as so used refers to a period of style, rather than of time. Thus Rossini's early operas, such as *Il Barbiere di Siviglia* (1816), are excluded, while by the time of his last, *William Tell* (1829), the period had begun. It corresponds to the Romantic Age in all the arts—the novels of Scott and Hugo, the plays of Schiller, the revival of Shakespeare, and the operas of Bellini, Donizetti, Verdi, Weber, Wagner and Meyerbeer. All have in common a multiplicity of scenes instead of the unities of time, place and action; an emphasis on extravagant passions extravagantly expressed rather than on feelings restrained and refined by reason; and a wholly new feeling for nature—the more wild and rugged the better. Rossini wrote an *Otello* in 1816, and it has many beauties; but in its rather static, formalized passion and its alternative endings, tragic and happy, it only prophesies the coming age. The period ended before 1900 with the advent of *verismo* (*See* Glossary) opera which changed the emphasis again.

Verdi's *Otello* exhibits all the signs of a typical Romantic drama. In its scenes of storm, fire and calm night during the first act it exploits nature. It observes the unity of place but not of time or action. Based on Shakespeare, whom the Romantics resurrected, it matches passion with poetry and heads inevitably for its tragic ending.

It is better than others of its kind because it combines the moments of Romantic passion, so often isolated in the inferior operas, into one inexorable sweep. From Otello's magnificent entrance in the first act to his murder of Desdemona in the last, the opera gathers pace and connotations so that Otello's suicide at the end is not stagy but inevitable as a last flicker of his former greatness. Such pacing was built into the libretto by Boito. Ernest Newman felt that there were perhaps two points in the otherwise perfect libretto where it was unnecessarily slowed: the fire scene in Act I and Desdemona's reception of the Cypriots in Act II. The defense of the first usually offered is that without something like the fire scene, Iago's embroiling of Cassio would be too sudden after the excitement of the storm, Otello's entrance and

Iago's explanatory remarks to Roderigo; and of the second that it is the only scene before the last act in which Desdemona is seen apart from Otello and gives her needed substance as a person.

The opera is the best of the *Italian* repertory because it so plainly and perfectly makes use of all the stock in trade of Italian opera: the storm scene, victory chorus and drinking song in Act I; the friendship duet at the close of Act II; the big choral scene with trumpets, plumes and banners in Act III; and finally the Mad Scene and prayer in Act IV. Typical of Verdi's transformation of an old form is the Mad Scene. Desdemona isn't the least bit mad when she sings her Willow Song, and yet standing behind her in feeling and atmosphere are Lucia and Ophelia. In the same way with the drinking song of Act I Verdi took an old-fashioned set number and gave it new purpose.

For the Paris production Verdi wrote five dances, Ballabili (*See* Glossary), which were inserted at the start of the finale to Act III. They are performed only in Paris, although the music sometimes turns up elsewhere at concerts.

## ACT I (31 min.)

Outside Otello's castle in Cyprus; a tavern is to one side; to the back, the sea and a quay.

*Soldiers and Cypriots:* Some men (four tenors and four basses) with Cassio and Montano watch and exclaim as Otello's ship tries to make the harbor. Others (more chorus) join them, as do Iago and Roderigo.

**chorus**    The ship manages to moor safely, and a boat puts off for shore. Off stage (more chorus) sailors shout directions to each other. Suddenly all join in a single "Evviva" as Otello jumps from the boat up the quay and onstage.

*Otello:* "Esultate" (rejoice), he cries. Briefly he announces that the war is over and the Turkish fleet is sunk. (Notice how carefully Verdi has built up the chorus from the original eight voices to the full resources of the Opera House. The effect of Otello's solo voice immediately following the final "Evviva" of the chorus can be tremendous.) Otello at once enters the castle followed by Cassio, Montano and the soldiers.

**chorus**    *Soldiers and Cypriots:* They exult, "Vittoria," and, the excitement over, begin to disperse.

*Iago and Roderigo:* Iago encourages Roderigo to hope for Desdemona.

Her marriage will not last, and he, Iago, will help to destroy it because Otello passed over Iago to make Cassio his lieutenant.

*Soldiers and Cypriots:* As the storm passes, the fire outside the tavern
**fire chorus**    flares up; the people gather and comment on how it burns. (This is simply "fire music" and although the orchestration is brilliant, the evocation is essentially vocal, whereas in *Die Walkuere* it is essentially symphonic, a difference between Verdi and Wagner.)

*Iago, Roderigo and Cassio:* Cassio joins the others at the fire. Iago urges him to drink, but Cassio refuses. Then Iago toasts Desdemona, and Cassio must join him. Before drinking, however, he comments on Desdemona's loveliness and innocently suggests that Iago sing a song in her praise.

*Iago:* In an aside to Roderigo Iago insinuates that Cassio is a serious rival for Desdemona and Roderigo decides that it is in his own interest
**brindisi**    to ruin Cassio. Iago then sings a drinking song, the refrain of which is "beva con me" (drink with me). Cassio joins in and drinks too much.

*Iago, Roderigo, Cassio, Montano and Otello:* Montano enters and reminds Cassio that he has the watch. Roderigo twits Cassio for being too drunk to do his job, and Cassio retorts. They start pushing each other and draw swords. Montano tries to separate them and is wounded. Iago turns the brawl into a riot, sending Roderigo off to ring the alarm bells.

Otello comes out and demands an explanation. But Cassio is confused: Roderigo is gone, Montano wounded. Iago gives an ambiguous explanation. The brawl has awakened Desdemona, and on the sight of her coming out, Otello cashiers Cassio on the spot: "Cassio non sei più capitano" (Cassio, you are no more a captain). Then he dismisses everyone and states that he will watch at the quay.

*Otello and Desdemona:* Together and alone, they begin a love duet; she is gentle and soothing; he, at first, is still rough and agitated from the brawl, but then falls quiet as he remembers courting her in Venice.
**duet**    "She loved me for the dangers I had passed, and I loved her that she did pity them." Finally relaxed and at peace, he asks for a kiss, "un bacio . . . ancor(a) un bacio." The storm at sea has passed. For a moment they gaze at the stars and then go in. (During the duet Otello has a slight epileptic seizure. He has another at the end of Act III. Some tenors ignore this altogether.)

### Vocabulary, Act I

| | | |
|---|---|---|
| evviva | eh.vee.vah | eviva |
| esultate | eh.sul.TAH.tay | exult, rejoice |
| vittoria | vee.TOR.ya | victory |
| Desdemona | des.DAY.moan.ah | Desdemona |
| beva con me | bay.vah kone may | drink with me |
| Cassio non sei più capitano | . . . non say.ee p'you cap.ee.tah.noe | Cassio, you are no more a captain |
| un bacio | oon BAH.choe | a kiss |
| ancor(a) un bacio | ahn.kor oon BAH.choe | yet another kiss |

## ACT II (33 min.)

A hall on the ground floor of the castle looking out on a garden. *Iago and Cassio:* Iago counsels Cassio that the way to gain the favor of his love, Bianca, is to regain his captaincy, and the way to do that is through Desdemona. "Vanne" (go then), he advises Cassio, indicating Desdemona in the garden. After Cassio leaves, he repeats it cynically.

**credo** *Iago:* Alone, he describes himself and his faith: "Credo in un Dio crudel" (I believe in a cruel God . . . words are lies . . . life only food for the worms of death). Just before the end, very hushed, he states, "La Morte è il nulla" (after death, there is nothing.)

*Otello and Iago:* Cassio has joined Desdemona in the garden. Iago watches them. He pretends not to see Otello approaching and mutters aloud about them. Otello questions Iago, who answers ambiguously and finally simply repeats the questions as though to avoid answering. This infuriates Otello. Iago ostentatiously appears to soothe him by telling him to beware of jealousy; it is the green-eyed monster. Again Otello bursts out: evidence is needed before he'll doubt Desdemona.

*Cypriots:* The chorus starts in the background while Iago suggests that **chorus** evidence is to be seen if Otello will look for it. (Verdi scored the chorus to be accompanied in part by bagpipes, but most opera orchestras fake it.) At the end of the chorus, as Desdemona comes forward, Otello almost forgets Iago's innuendos.

*Otello and Desdemona:* But unfortunately she at once asks about Cassio and begs Otello to forgive him: "Gli perdona." "Non ora" (not now), Otello replies, getting angry as she repeats it. Desdemona is confused and offers to wipe his brow with her handkerchief. He throws it on the floor and orders her out.

**quartet** *Iago, Otello, Emilia and Desdemona:* Each now sings his feelings of the moment. Iago roughly forces Emilia to give him the dropped handkerchief. Emilia is suspicious at first but then is intimidated. Desdemona can't understand what's happened. Otello laments that his sure faith is gone. Finally, Otello orders them all out. *Otello and Iago:* Iago, however, lurks in the background. Otello argues with himself; but now on her lips he'll find Cassio's kisses. **aria** "Addio," he sings, to peace, content, even the glory of war. Iago comes forward; but Otello turns on him: some evidence or he'll kill him.

Iago pretends to be angry and sulks. Otello despairs. He wants evi- **aria** dence, but he won't spy on Desdemona. Iago then, in a sinuous aria—"Era la notte" (during the night)—invents that Cassio in his dreams called out for Desdemona, imagined that he kissed her, caressed her—all as though he'd done it often before. The description almost persuades Otello. Iago then adds as concrete evidence that he's seen Desdemona's handkerchief, "il fazzoletto," in Cassio's hand. **duet** This topples Otello's last doubt. "Sangue, sangue, sangue" (blood). Love is gone. Only anger and vengeance are left, he swears. Iago joins him, urging him on.

### Vocabulary, Act II

| | | |
|---|---|---|
| vanne | VAH.nay | go then |
| credo in un Dio crudel | cray.doe'nun dee.oh crew.dell | I believe in a cruel God |
| la morte è il nulla | lah more.t'eel NUL.lah | after death, nothing |
| gli perdona | lee pair.doan.ah | forgive him |
| non ora | none.OAR.ah | not now |
| addio | ah.DEE.oh | farewell |
| era la notte | err.ah lah not.tay | during the night |
| il fazzoletto | eel fats. oh. LET.oh | the handkerchief |
| sangue | SAHNG.gway | blood |

## ACT III (35 min.)

The great hall of the castle.

*Otello and Iago:* A herald announces that the Venetian ambassador's ship has entered the harbor. Iago tells Otello that Cassio is coming and urges him to watch and listen and from Cassio's own mouth and actions he will have proof of Desdemona's betrayal. But instead of Cassio, Desdemona enters, and Iago retires.

*Otello and Desdemona:* She greets him, and he takes her hand, suggesting that it needs the help of prayer. She answers that it is the hand that gave her heart to him. Then she adds she has asked Cassio to come for an audience. Otello complains of a cold and asks for a handkerchief. Desdemona gives him one, but it is not the special one he gave her. He grows furious: "Il fazzoletto." She promises to find it and tries to take refuge in matters of state: Cassio is coming. He accuses her of being a whore. She is horrified and weeps. He accuses her again and she denies it. Ironically he takes her hand and says that he made a ghastly mistake; he thought it was the hand of the whore that married him. Then he pushes her out of the hall.

**aria** *Otello:* Otello, left alone, breaks down. He laments that he could have withstood shame, disgrace, captivity, anything, if in secret moments he could have comforted himself in his heart that Desdemona loved him. But she has destroyed that inner strength. He'll make her confess her vileness and then kill her: "Confession, confession."

*Iago, Cassio and Otello:* Iago sets up the scene so that Otello can have evidence of Desdemona's alleged betrayal. He will talk with Cassio by the pillars, while Otello hides behind them on the terrace. Cassio enters and tells Iago that he was to meet Desdemona here. "Her name," Otello groans, hearing only half the remark. Iago then questions Cassio about Bianca. Cassio laughs, and Otello is infuriated. Iago keeps moving Cassio so that Otello never can hear more than snatches of the words. Then Cassio tells Iago that he has found a handkerchief in his **trio** lodgings. He pulls out Desdemona's missing handkerchief. Iago examines it carefully, holding it this way and that so that Otello can see it. Then ironically he remarks that it is a spider's web that will catch Cassio in its silken threads. Cassio admires the beauty of the needlework as Otello moans for revenge. The trumpets announce the Venetian ambassador, and Cassio leaves. Otello rushes forward to Iago: "What will I do? How will I kill him?" Iago replies that he will take care of Cassio and suggests that Otello strangle Desdemona in the bed she defiled.

**chorus** *Cypriots et al:* The ambassador, Ludovico, enters. Desdemona and Emilia come to greet him, and there is polite conversation as Otello reads the official message from Venice. Ludovico asks Desdemona about Cassio. She tells of his fall from favor but adds that he may regain Otello's favor soon. Otello overhears this and, in a rage, raises his arm to strike her. The crowd is horrified.

Cassio enters, and Otello reads the message aloud: he is recalled to Venice and Cassio is to remain in command. Iago despairs. Ludovico suggests that Otello comfort Desdemona. Otello instead throws her to the ground: "A terra! È piangi" (on your knees and weep)! Everyone is stunned.

Desdemona starts the big choral scene of the opera: "A terra, si . . ." (yes, here in the dust . . . I feel the icy breath of death . . . His pity and love are gone). Emilia, Cassio, Roderigo and Ludovico join in a quartet. Emilia protests Desdemona's innocence; Cassio is nervous at his new command in such unhappy times; Roderigo despairs that Desdemona will be leaving Cyprus; and Ludovico can't believe what he has seen. Otello remains seated; Iago and he exchange a few asides about killing Cassio. Then the whole chorus joins in pleading for Desdemona and protesting at Otello's strange behavior. Otello remains silent throughout. (This is unusual. In most operatic great choruses, *Aida* for instance, every character sings. But Otello's silence, if properly staged, provides great drama. It hangs over the stage. What is he going to say? And when?)

Suddenly he breaks in: "Fugite" (get out)! He shrieks at them again. Desdemona runs to him, but he curses her: "Ti maledico" (curses on you). Emilia leads Desdemona away. Only Iago lurks behind.

Otello, left to himself, bursts out and begins to have convulsions: "Il fazzoletto, il fazzoletto." He falls in a fit on the floor. (In both Shakespeare and the opera libretto there are references to his being an epileptic.) Meanwhile, outside, the crowd hails Otello: "Gloria al Leon di Venezia" (glory to the lion of Venice). But inside, Iago points at the prostrate Otello. "Ecco il Leone" (behold the lion).

### Vocabulary, Act III

| il fazzoletto | eel fats.oh.LET.toe | the handkerchief |
| confession | con.fess.ee.OWN | confession |
| a terra | ah tair.rah | to earth (down on your knees) |
| è piangi | eh p'YAHN.jee | and weep |
| fugite | food.jee.tay | get out |
| ti maledico | tee.mal.eh.DEE.coe | curses on you |
| ecco il Leone | ek.ko eel lay.OWN.nay | behold the lion of Venice |

## ACT IV (27 min.)

Desdemona's bedroom. There are a bed, prayer stool, table, looking glass and chairs. A burning lamp hangs in front of the icon of the Madonna over the prayer stool; a door is to the left. A lighted candle is on the table. It is night.

There is a short prelude. Emilia is assisting Desdemona to bed. *Emilia and Desdemona:* Desdemona is deeply depressed, and she asks Emilia to make the bed with the wedding-night sheets and, should she die, to use them for a shroud. Then as she goes to the looking glass, **Willow Song** she remembers a lament that her mother's maid used to sing: a girl's lover left her, and she went down to the river bank, weeping; and so pretty was her song that the birds came down to hear her sighing and the stones wept for pity; for the lover was destined for glory, but she to love and die. (The song is roughly in three parts, the first two being very alike except for an increasingly agitated accompaniment. The refrain is "Salce Salce Cantiamo" (willow, willow . . . let us sing). In the middle of the third part a gust of wind terrifies Desdemona, but she finishes the song and says good night, "buona notte," calmly to Emilia. But then as Emilia leaves, Desdemona loses her composure and breaks out in a terrified and impassioned "addio." **Ave Maria** *Desdemona:* She kneels before the icon and prays. She begins intoning on one note with the formal words, "Ave Maria piena di grazia." But as her appeal becomes more personal, she falls into melody: "Prega . . . prega per noi" (pray . . . for us; pray for her whose early hopes of bliss are dying). She closes, "Ave . . . Amen." *Otello:* Opera houses stage the next few minutes in various fashions. Verdi's directions, each separated by a few bars of music, are: "At the first note Otello is seen standing on the threshold of a secret door. He comes forward. He lays a scimitar on the table. He stands before the candle doubtful whether to blow it out or not. He looks at Desdemona. He extinguishes the candle. A gesture of fury. He goes toward the bed. He stops. He raises the bed curtains and looks for a long time on the sleeping Desdemona. He gives a kiss to Desdemona; another kiss; another kiss. She wakes."

*Otello and Desdemona:* He asks if she has prayed tonight; he does not want to kill her soul. He accuses her of loving Cassio; she gave the handkerchief to Cassio; he saw it in Cassio's hands. She denies it all and tells Otello to call Cassio and ask him. He's dead, Otello replies —"morto." On this, Desdemona breaks down completely. She begs to live the night, an hour, an instant, while she prays. "È tardi" (too late), he cries and stifles her.

*Emilia, Desdemona and Otello:* Emilia bursts in to report to Otello, the general, that Cassio has killed Roderigo. A groan from the dying Desdemona interrupts her. Emilia rushes to the bed and asks who attacked her. "No one," Desdemona replies. "I die innocent; commend me to Otello." And she dies. Otello shouts that he killed her; she was a whore. He threatens Emilia, but she calls the guard. Ludovico, Cassio and Iago come in. With everyone present, the strands of Iago's web unravel, and he flees. Otello's first quivering reaction is to strike at someone, but then he drops the sword. The great general is no more: "Otello fu" (finished). He gazes at Desdemona, calls her name. "Morta" (she is dead). He stabs himself. "I kissed thee ere I killed thee: no way but this, killing myself, to die upon a kiss." "Bacio" (kiss) . . . "un altro" (another).

### Vocabulary, Act IV

| | | |
|---|---|---|
| salce | SAHL.chay | willow |
| cantiamo | kahn.T'YAHM.oh | let us sing |
| | (The two together are a sort of "heigh-ho.") | |
| prega . . . per noi | PRAY.ga . . . pear noi(se) | pray . . . for us |
| morto | MORE.toe | he's dead |
| è tardi | eh TAR.dee | it is too late |
| fu | foo | gone, finished |
| bacio | bah.choe | kiss |
| un altro | oon al.tro | another |
| buona notte | bwahnah not.tay | good night |
| addio | ah.dee.oh | farewell |
| Ave Maria | ah.vay mah.ree.ah | Ave Maria |

# FAUST

Lyric drama in five acts. First performed in Paris on March 19, 1859. Music by C. F. Gounod. Libretto by J. Barbier and M. Carré after Goethe's tragedy.

PRINCIPAL CHARACTERS

| | | |
|---|---|---|
| Dr. Faust | tenor | |
| Méphistophélès | bass | |
| Valentin, Marguerite's brother | baritone | |
| Siebel, a boy in love with Marguerite | mezzo-soprano | see.BELL |
| Marguerite | soprano | |
| Martha, a neighbor | mezzo-soprano | |

The action takes place in a German town during the sixteenth century.

*Faust,* like *Carmen,* was composed in the opéra-comique form with spoken dialogue between the numbers, and in this form it first succeeded in France and the rest of Europe. Only ten years later, when it was produced at the Paris Opéra, did Gounod add the recitatives and ballet. During the ten years, during the rehearsal period at the Opéra, and even for a time thereafter, a bewildering number of arias and scenes were added, dropped or rewritten. The constant change, coupled

GOUNOD

with Gounod's complaisance, make it almost impossible to determine his original concept of the drama, supposing he had one. To some extent, therefore, *Faust* is a producers' opera rather than Gounod's; it is the antithesis of an opera such as *Tannhaeuser,* for each note of which Wagner was prepared to do battle. The version of *Faust* familiar all over the world today is the one finally settled on by the Paris Opéra with an aria or the ballet sometimes cut.

Gounod was probably wise to follow the many suggestions, although they led constantly away from Goethe's drama of good and evil toward a light, sentimental romance. But Gounod's gift was not for drama but lyric melody, and productions that frankly emphasize the operettalike quality of many of the scenes seem to be the most satisfying. Persons go to *Faust* to hum and tap their feet, not to consider the problem of evil. The German theaters recognize this by calling the opera *Margarethe* and stating flatly that any resemblance to Goethe is purely coincidental.

The endless changes and light music, however, have damaged the libretto. The scenes in Dr. Faust's study, the church and the prison attempt to do more than be merely charming, yet Méphistophélès is presented as a sardonic boulevardier, not a prince of evil. He is exorcised in Act II by some crossed swords, yet he dares in Act IV to play a whole scene in a church. Faust is the title role, yet from Act III, on, the opera is Marguerite's. Valentin is easily the stuffiest, most one-dimensional character in opera. Nothing is done with Siebel.

Yet none of this matters. The music has always, and rightly, been admired. Sunk into the memory of even the most casual operagoer is the soldiers' chorus, the waltzes, the serenade, the jewel song, the flower song, several trios and the love duet. For easy melody *Faust* hardly can be surpassed.

The opera is in five acts, but today except in Paris it is more often given in four or even three. Most productions give Acts I and II as scenes of a single act and cut the first scene in Act IV. The Walpurgis Night scene in Act V is also often cut. There is a confusion about what constitutes the ballet music of the opera, since there are really two *Faust* ballets. The first has a good deal of singing through it in which Méphistophélès presents, and Faust comments on, the courtesans of antiquity. Then Faust sees the vision of Marguerite and insists on leaving. During all this the corps de ballet can do considerable dancing, but what with an offstage chorus and the two principals, the scene remains essentially operatic. Imbedded in it, although cut almost everywhere except Paris, is the second *Faust* ballet, the music for which often appears on band or "pop" concert programs. It is fifteen minutes of real bowwow music straight out of the Follies. Helen of Troy appears with all her court, and they do seven dances for Faust. The music is delightful, vulgar and totally out of keeping with the story and other music. When Gounod realized what was expected of him, he demurred, believing that it would conflict with his religious principles, and he asked Saint-Saens to write it for him. Saint-Saens agreed but in such a way as to shame Gounod into writing it himself. Ironically, it has survived most of his religious music.

## OVERTURE (6 min.)

Gounod or his publisher referred to it as an introduction, and it is slight and curiously ineffective, considering the drama of good and evil that follows. The melody treated in the second half is Valentin's aria in Act II.

## ACT I (Dr. Faust's study—19 min.)

*Faust:* He complains bitterly of old age and failure; his pursuit of science has led in the end only to death, which is slow in coming. He has **aria** discovered nothing, "rien," learnt nothing. In an aria he hails his last day on earth: "Salut! O mon dernier matin." He pours poison into a glass and is about to drink when outside a chorus sounds. (Some tenors look out the window; others pretend that they hear it in their minds.)

**chorus** *The Townspeople (off stage)*: First the girls sing of love and spring. Faust raises the glass but hesitates. Then the men sing of work and God.

*Faust:* "Dieu," he cries and curses life, prayer and faith. Each thought begins, "Maudite soit" (cursed be). He ends with "À moi, Satan! À moi" (to me, Satan).

*Méphistophélès:* "Me voici" (here I am). He bows: "At your service, Dr. Faust, with a feather in my hat and a blade at my side." He first offers Faust "l'or" (gold), then "la gloire" (glory), and finally "la puissance" (power). But Faust wants "la jeunesse" (youth).

**aria**     *Faust:* He sings an aria in which most of the verses begin, "À moi . . ." (mine be the caresses, the desires, the energy of youth). (The aria poses a problem for the tenor: should he let go on it and stop pretending he is an old man or act the part and then have to share the glories of the aria in a repeat later with the bass at the close of the scene?)

*Méphistophélès and Faust:* The two negotiate that Faust will serve Méphistophélès in hell, "la Bas" (down there), and that the latter will **vision**     offer supernatural service to Faust here. To excite the hesitant Faust, Méphistophélès shows him a vision of Marguerite spinning at her wheel. Faust signs in blood. Méphistophélès gives him the poison to drink and Faust's gray hairs turn to brown and he is **duet**     young. The two then sing a duet—Faust, "À moi . . ." (mine be the caresses, etc.), and Méphistophélès, "À toi . . ." (yours be the caresses, etc.)

### Vocabulary, Act I

The sign (n) indicates that the preceding syllable is to have a nasal twang.

| | | |
|---|---|---|
| rien | ree.an(n) | nothing |
| salut! o mon dernier matin | sah.loo oh mon(n) dair.nee.ay mah(n).tan(n) | hail, oh my last |
| Dieu | dee.yuh | God |
| maudit soit | moh.dee swat | cursed be |
| à moi, Satan | ah mwa Sah.tan(n) | to me, Satan |
| me voici | muh vwah.cee | here I am |
| l'or | lor | gold |
| la gloire | lah glwahr | glory |
| la puissance | lah pwee.sawnse(n) | power |
| la jeunesse | lah shje.ness.uh | youth |
| la bas | lah bah | down there, hell |

### ACT II (The Fair, La Kermesse—26 min.)

At one of the city gates. At the left is an inn with a statue of Bacchus sitting on a keg for its symbol.

*Townspeople:* They are students, soldiers, merchants, young girls and
**chorus**  old matrons. Each group sings an appropriate sentiment—
wine, war, worry, flirting, gossip. The melody passes from group to
group. (Saint-Saens felt that conductors always took this so fast it
sounded like a "hullabaloo," not music.)

*Valentin:* He arrives, greets his friends and Siebel, and sings of his departure for war. He gazes at a medallion Marguerite has given him and
grieves that after he goes there will be no one to care for her. Their
**aria**  parents are dead. Then as the aria gets more martial he sings
of glory and the chance to win honor. Everyone assures him about
Marguerite, and one of the students, Wagner, starts a song about a rat.
Then Méphistophélès interrupts.

*Méphistophélès:* He sings (to music almost vulgarly vital, compared to
Valentin's aria) of the power and fascination of money—"le veau
**aria**  d'or" (the calf of gold). The aria has two verses; it replaced
one about a beetle. The brilliance, intensity, and possibly the truth of
it shocks the townspeople. And they are not soothed when he reads
palms and predicts death for the student and a hand that withers
flowers for Siebel. He further annoys them by sneering at the local
wine, which he ostentatiously transforms into a superior vintage. Then
he toasts Marguerite's health. This last infuriates Valentin and he attacks Méphistophélès, who breaks his sword.

**chorale**  *The Townspeople:* They now realize who he is. They cross
their swords and arms and exorcise him to a hymn tune. Méphistophélès cringes and disappears, and the townspeople wander off.

*Méphistophélès and Faust:* Faust complains that he hasn't yet seen
the girl of the vision. Méphistophélès, returning, urges patience. The
waltz that is starting up will bring her out.

**the waltz chorus**  *The Townspeople:* They gather again and sing
the famous waltz. Throughout it Siebel refuses to dance and hunts for
Marguerite. At a break in the chorus, she appears. Méphistophélès
constantly prevents Siebel from getting to her, and Faust has a chance
to speak to her.

*Faust and Marguerite:* He offers her his arm and she, somewhat coyly,
refuses. He is enraptured. She goes off alone.

**chorus**  The scene closes with the waltz.

## ACT III (48 min.)

Marguerite's garden. At the back a wall with a little door; to the left a bower; to the right a pavilion with a window facing front.

**flower song**    *Siebel:* He arrives with some flowers. During the first verse, they wither. Then he dips his fingers in holy water in a font on the wall of the pavilion and picks more flowers. These don't wither and, with a second verse, he leaves them to speak to Marguerite for him. Méphistophélès and Faust have seen the end of Siebel's scene and Méphistophélès leaves to get something more effective than flowers. *Faust:* Alone in the garden, he sings a love song to the house where

**aria**    she lives: "Salut! demeure chaste et pure" (Hail, dwelling chaste and pure), where lives an angel. (This is an extended aria and it sets the hushed quality of the love music throughout the entire act.) Méphistophélès returns with a box of jewels, which he leaves where Marguerite will see them.

**aria**    *Marguerite:* She sits at the spinning wheel and sings a two-verse song about a mythical king. She interrupts each verse to remark on how attractive Faust had been.

Then she discovers Siebel's flowers and is not much interested, but

**the jewel song**    the jewels fascinate her. She tries them on and sings a vivacious aria again in two verses in which she admires herself and wonders what Faust would think of her now.

*Martha and Méphistophélès:* A neighbor, Martha, arrives for a visit. She compliments Marguerite on the jewels, which can come only from some lord who loves her. Her own husband, Martha observes, was not so generous to her. To draw her off, Méphistophélès introduces himself and reports that he has bad news for her. Her husband is dead. Martha is moderately concerned but quite able to listen to his innuendos that he might replace the deceased. He admits that he travels, but he is old and lonely. The two wander off into the garden.

*Marguerite and Faust:* She tells him about herself: "Mon frère est soldat . . ." (my brother is a soldier . . .). But before the love scene can get started, Méphistophélès and Martha come back. Méphistophélès sees that Faust needs help and wearily decides to go off with Martha again, but he gives her the slip long enough to throw a spell over the garden.

**aria**    *Méphistophélès:* He sings an incantation to the night: "O nuit, étends sur eux ton ombre . . ." (oh night, stretch your shadows over them so they have no thought of remorse . . .).

*Marguerite and Faust:* The remainder of the act is an extended love
**aria**    duet. Faust starts with an aria: "Laisse-moi, laisse-moi con-
templer ton visage" (let me, let me look on you). Marguerite at first is
coy, and she gains time by doing "he loves me not" on a daisy: it
comes out that he loves her.

**aria and duet**    He then starts in an even more hushed manner, "O
nuit d'amour . . ." (oh night of love . . .), and finally she joins him.

But she pulls away to agitated music. She must go in. He soothes her
with another verse of "O nuit d'amour . . ." and she joins him again.
But he is not forceful and this time she leaves him, insisting she must
go in. She begs him to help her leave him: "Partez; j'ai peur" (depart,
I am afraid). She agrees he can return tomorrow, "demain," very
early. She runs in; "Adieu" (farewell).

Méphistophélès has seen the end of it and tells Faust he is a fool not
**aria**    to press his advantage. Listen to her, he suggests. Marguerite
is at her window, and she sings of how much she loves Faust. Faust
goes to her, and she lets him in. Méphistophélès laughs.

### Vocabulary, Act III

| | | |
|---|---|---|
| salut! demeure chaste et pure | sah.loo duh.murr.uh shahst ay purr.uh | hail, dwelling chaste and pure |
| mon frère est soldat | mon(n) frair ay sole.dah | my brother is a soldier |
| O nuit, étends sur eax ton ombre | o nwee ay.ten(n) surr uh ton(n) ombruh | oh night, extend over them thy shade |
| laisse-moi, laisse-moi contempler ton visage | layss.mwa . . . con(n).tem.play ton(n) vee.sah.shje | let me look at your face |
| O nuit d'amour | o nwee d'ah.moor | oh night of love |
| partez | pahr.tay | leave |
| j'ai peur | shjay purr | I am afraid |
| demain | duh.man(n) | tomorrow |
| **Adieu** | ah.d'yuh | farewell |

## ACT IV (37 min.; but with cuts, 29)

(The first scene in this act traditionally is cut in England and the
United States. The second and third scenes are sometimes reversed in
order.) Faust visited Marguerite many times and fathered her child.
Then he deserted her.

## SCENE 1 (A room in Marguerite's house—8 min.)

*Marguerite:* She is at her spinning wheel. Outside, some girls sing of a stranger who loved and left as they laugh at her misfortune. She philos-**spinning song** ophizes that the world is cruel: hers was not a wanton love. Then, as she spins, she begins an aria (generally cut when the scene is given): "Il ne revient pas" (he will not return). (Saint-Saens considered the aria one of the finest in the score and blamed its disappearance on the laziness of sopranos, who found it exhausting to sing.) Marguerite ends in tears.

*Siebel and Marguerite:* He swears to avenge her, but she protests she **aria** still loves Faust. He sings a two-verse song of condolence, and she thanks him, saying she will go to the church to pray for Faust and her child.

## SCENE 2 (In the church—9 min.)

*Méphistophélès and Marguerite:* He interrupts her prayer, and a chorus of demons calls her to hell. She is terrified. He taunts her by recalling her lost innocence: hell is for her. The choir sings that God's mercy is infinite. She tries to pray. The music builds to a climax as he insists, "À toi malheur! À toi l'enfer" (for you unhappiness and hell). Desperately she calls, "Seigneur, accueillez la prière" (Lord, hear my prayer). (The music, as she begins, shifts its key, quietens and broadens.) The choir joins her. But Méphistophélès insists, "Sois maudite" (be cursed). "À toi l'enfer." She faints.

## SCENE 3 (The street outside Marguerite's house—20 min.)

*Soldiers, Valentin and Siebel:* They march into the street, happy to put down their arms and rejoin their families. Valentin sees Siebel, who reports that Marguerite is in church. Valentin assumes she is praying **soldiers' chorus** for him and is pleased. The soldiers sing the chorus honoring the glorious dead and promising the civilians that they will hear some terrifying war stories. Valentin asks Siebel to join him in a drink, but Siebel refuses, enigmatically urging Valentin to be merciful and forgiving. Valentin rushes off, suspecting the worst of Marguerite.

*Faust and Méphistophélès:* Méphistophélès asks why they must return to see Marguerite. He will show Faust better girls at the Walpurgis

Nacht (the demons' revels on a mountain top). But Faust insists, and with a shrug Méphistophélès serenades Marguerite for Faust.

**serenade**    *Méphistophélès:* The serenade is cruelly flip. The refrain for the two verses is "Don't go to bed before you're wed." It produces not Marguerite but Valentin (who presumably understood from the mere sight of the baby the cause of Siebel's distress and the identity of Marguerite's lover).

*Valentin, Méphistophélès and Faust:* Valentin asks who will fight and Faust draws. In a trio each sings his own sentiments—anger, scorn and remorse. Valentin tears Marguerite's medallion from his neck: he will not be helped by anything of hers. Then they duel: "En garde." With the aid of Méphistophélès, Faust fatally wounds Valentin. As a crowd gathers, Méphistophélès pulls Faust away and they go out.

*Valentin:* Marguerite, returning from church, breaks through the
**aria**    crowd to her brother. In an aria he accuses her of causing his death and curses her: "Soit maudite." He dies proudly: "Je tombe en soldat" (I die a soldier). The crowd, which has been urging him to forgive even as he hopes in Heaven to be forgiven, is shocked by his bitterness. Marguerite is stunned.

Vocabulary, Act IV

| | | |
|---|---|---|
| il ne revient pas | eel nuh r.vyahn(n) pah | he will not return |
| à toi malheur | ah twa mal.err | for you, unhappiness |
| à toi l'enfer | ah twa lon(n).fair | for you, Hell |
| Seigneur, accueillez la prière | sane.yurr ah.kool.yay lah pree.air | Lord, hear the prayer |
| sois maudite | swa moh.DEE.tuh | be accursed |
| en garde | on(n) gahr.duh | on guard |
| soit maudite | swat moh.DEE.tuh | be accursed |
| je tombe en soldat | shje toh.mbuh en(n) sole.dah | I fall a soldier |

## ACT V (25 min.)

Valentin's curse and her own grief have driven Marguerite mad, and she has killed her child. She has been tried, found guilty of murder, and waits in prison for her execution.

### SCENE 1 (Walpurgis Night—25 min., if both ballets included)

Méphistophélès takes Faust to a mountaintop, where he shows him the beautiful courtesans of antiquity, among whom are Cleopatra and

Helen of Troy. (Here is the ballet that is often cut.) Faust is unimpressed and manages in the middle of the revels to see a vision of Marguerite. (Sometimes she has a red ribbon on her neck or blood to foreshadow her execution for killing the child.) Faust insists on leaving.

### SCENE 2 (The prison—15 min.)

*Faust and Méphistophélès:* Méphistophélès gives Faust the keys to Marguerite's cell, warns him that dawn is coming and that the scaffold is already raised, and goes out to watch the main entrance. Faust is overcome with remorse. He supposes Marguerite must have been mad indeed to kill her child. He calls softly to her, "Marguerite."

**aria** *Marguerite and Faust:* She sings that it is the voice of the one she loves: "Oui, c'est toi, je t'aime" (yes, it is you, I love you). Now she has no fears. He answers that he loves her and will save her.

**aria** *Marguerite:* Her mind wanders. She repeats exactly the phrases she sang when they first met (the waltz from the second act). She sees again the garden, the night. He urges her to come, "viens," but she won't leave with him. And when Méphistophélès appears to hurry them, with her mad eye she sees clearly that he is "le demon."

**trio** *Marguerite, Méphistophélès and Faust:* She kneels and begs the angels to save her soul, "Anges purs! Anges radieux" (angels pure, angels radiant)! Faust urges her to come, "viens," and Méphistophélès tries to hurry Faust away. She pleads again to the angels and, as she dies, Méphistophélès cries triumphantly "Jugée" (condemned). But a chorus of angels contradicts him, "Sauvée" (saved). And according to the stage directions, the prison walls open; the soul of Marguerite rises towards Heaven; Faust gazes after her with despair and then falls to his knees in prayer; and Méphistophélès is turned aside by the shining sword of an archangel.

### Vocabulary, Act V

| | | |
|---|---|---|
| oui, c'est toi, je t'aime | we say twa shje t'eh.muh | yes, it is you, I love you |
| viens | vyahn(n) | come |
| le demon | le dee.mon(n) | the demon |
| anges purs | ahn.je purr | angels pure |
| anges radieux | ahn.je rah.dee.yuh | angels radiant |
| jugée | shjoo.jay | condemned |
| sauvée | so.vay | saved |

# SAMSON ET DALILA

## (Samson and Delilah)

Opera in three acts. First performed at Weimar on December 2, 1877.
Music by C. Saint-Saens. Libretto by F. Lemaire.

### PRINCIPAL CHARACTERS

| | | |
|---|---|---|
| Samson | tenor | sam.sohn(n) |
| Abimelech, satrap of Gaza | bass | |
| The High Priest of Dagon, the God | baritone | |
| of the Philistines | | |
| An old Hebrew | bass | |
| Dalila, a priestess of Dagon | mezzo-soprano | dah.lee.LAH |

The action takes place in Old Testament times, c.1136 B.C., in
Gaza and the valley of Sorek outside it.

Saint-Saens wrote twelve operas, of which the most successful is
*Samson et Dalila;* some of the others are occasionally revived in France.
His first, a one-act opera called *La Princesse Jaune* (1872), started
the fad for Japanese subjects that culminated thirty-two years later in
Puccini's *Madama Butterfly.*

*Samson* was originally planned as an oratorio in the style of Handel's
*Saul* or *Israel in Egypt,* but at some time during its six years of gesta-
tion Saint-Saens decided to recast it as an opera. The first act, however,
still has an oratorio atmosphere in its solo voices, massive choirs and
little or no dialogue. The scenes succeed each other like postage stamps,
each a vignette and only loosely attached to its neighbor. The second
act is more operatic and closely woven.

The opera is based on the biblical story recounted in Judges 16. To
modern notions the biblical Samson was an impossible man, arrogant,
selfish and wholly undisciplined. For Anglo-Saxons Milton's poetry in
*Samson Agonistes* made of him, eyeless in Gaza, a moving and tragic
figure—doubly so in view of Milton's own blindness. Saint-Saen's
Samson falls somewhere between. His sense of identification with the
Israelite nation is far stronger in the opera than in the Bible, and in
modern terms consequently more heroic. But at the same time it makes
his continued dalliance with Dalila more stupid, even criminal. A
twentieth-century libretto might have attempted a real tragedy by re-

vealing a great man wrestling against, and finally wrecked by, a fatal flaw of hypersexuality. But this was impossible in the nineteenth century, and in the opera Samson is hardly more than a nice furniture mover who couldn't say no.

SAINT-SAENS

Even so the opera has survived now almost a hundred years. There are powerful scenes in each act, but generally they are the wrong ones for building a powerful drama. In Act I there is Samson's appeal and the Israelite chorus in response, "Israel! romps ta chaine"; in Act II the dialogue between Dalila and the High Priest; and in Act III Dalila's mockery of Samson. But Samson's struggle with his desire, his subsequent remorse and his prayers to his God are among the weakest moments in the score. The final scene, which ought to be cathartic, is given over largely to a delightful but sometimes ludicrous ballet.

What the opera has in abundance is charm. If the Dalila is good-looking with a voice that melts over the caressing phrases, it succeeds. Not because seduction really happens that way, but because everyone agrees that it would be nice if it only did. The opera has the courage of its clichés. It tells the old story with a smile, some gorgeous music, several ballets and a stage falling in pieces as the curtain comes down.

In the synopsis, although there is a change of scenery only in Act III, the scene divisions of the score are indicated to show how Saint-Saens constructed the acts.

## ACT I (46 min.)

A public square in Gaza; to the left, the Temple of Dagon, God of the Philistines. Dawn. The light increases steadily until by Scene 5 the sun is fully risen.

## SCENE 1 (14 min.)

**chorus**    *Israelites:* The opera begins with a chorus from behind the curtain (5 min.) in which the captive Hebrews pray to Jehovah to smile on them again. The curtain rises revealing the Israelites massed in the square. Again they call to Jehovah as the chorus culminates in a fugue (*See* Glossary) led by the basses and closing with a series of unison phrases.

*Samson:* He steps forward. "Arretez, o mes frères" (cease, my
**arioso**    brothers), he calls, suggesting that perhaps relief is at hand. In his heart a voice is raised: "C'est la voix du Seigneur" (it is the voice of God). He calls on the Israelites to break their chains and raise an altar to Jehovah.

**chorus**    *Israelites:* "Hélas" (alas), they moan, it is in vain. The only weapons left them are tears.

*Samson and Israelites:* He urges them on: Jehovah is on high—the God of the Red Sea. But they mumble that the past is dead. He insists that to doubt is blasphemy. Pray for victory, "la victoire," for "c'est le Dieu" (it is Jehovah), the God of battles and armies, who will aid them. The Israelites feel a change and are convinced. Jehovah is with Samson and they will march with him, "et marchons avec lui."

## SCENE 2 (7 min.)

*Abimelech:* He asks who dares to raise his voice. It would be more to the point to invoke the mercy of the Philistines than the power of the
**aria**    Israelite God. Then in an aria he slanders Jehovah as weak, trembling and fearful before Dagon. It is too much for Samson. He replies in kind, and the Israelites support him. Turning to them he calls,
**solo with chorus**    "Israel! romps ta chaine. O peuple lève-toi" (Israel, break your chain; people, lift yourself up); "Le Seigneur est en moi" (Jehovah is in me), he insists, and the Israelites take up his cry. Samson kills Abimelech and holds off the Philistine guards while the Israelites clear the square.

## SCENE 3 (1 min.)

*The High Priest and Guards:* He asks why they did not cut Samson down, and they confess that their blood had turned to water.

## SCENE 4 (3 min.)

*Messenger, Guards and the High Priest:* The messenger reports that an Israelite band led by Samson is ravaging the country. The guards urge
**aria**    flight: "Fuyons" (let us flee). The High Priest, however, stands firm and curses the Israelite people and, in subsequent verses, Samson, his mother and his God. Each verse begins, "Maudit soit" (cursed be). The guards continue to advocate flight as they carry off Abimelech's corpse.

## SCENE 5 (6 min.)

**bass chorus**    *Israelite Old Men and Women:* The basses of the chorus praise Jehovah. As Samson and the armed band enter, an old Hebrew continues alone, and then the chorus joins him.

## SCENE 6 (15 min.)

*Priestesses of Dagon:* The temple gates open, and Dalila comes out,
**chorus**    followed by her colleagues. For the moment she remains silent, while they sing of spring, the time of flowers, youth and love.
*Dalila, Samson and the Old Hebrew:* She addresses Samson directly: "Je viens célébrer la victoire" (I come to celebrate the victory . . . of him who reigns in my heart). She wishes to add her love to his glory and urges him to come to the valley of Soreck where she will open her
**trio**    arms to him. Samson, already beginning to totter, gasps out an appeal, "O Dieu" (O God), for strength. The old Hebrew, increasingly nervous, warns Samson to beware. Her gentle voice will sap his strength and leave him accursed.
*Priestesses:* They dance seductively (2 min.) before the Israelite war-
**ballet**    riors. (One of the tests of a good Dalila is whether the director has been able to work her into the ballet or left her like a big peg around which the dance revolves.)
*Dalila:* She begins "Printemps qui commence" (spring which begins
**aria**    . . . bringing hope to lovers). But she quickly gets more personal, describing how she waits at night for Samson, who no longer comes. But if he should, she would be as tender as before. The old Hebrew succinctly characterizes her to Samson as a poisonous snake.

Dalila and her colleagues retire as she repeats that she is waiting and will be tender when he comes.

Vocabulary, Act I

The sign (n) indicates that the preceding syllable is to have a nasal twang.

| | | |
|---|---|---|
| arretez, o mes frères | ah.reh.tay oh may frair.uh | cease, oh my brothers |
| c'est la voix du Seigneur | say lah vwa do sane.yure | it is the voice of Je-hovah |
| helas | ay.lahs | alas |
| la victoire | lah veek.twahr | victory |
| c'est le Dieu | say luh d'yuh | it is Jehovah |
| et marchons avec lui | ay marsh.on(n) ah.vek lwee | and let us march with him |
| Israel! romps ta chaine | is.rah.ell romp(n) tah shane | Israel, break your chain |
| O peuple lève-toi | oh per.pluh lev.uh twa | oh people lift yourself up |
| fuyons | f'yon(n) | let us flee |
| maudit soit | moh.dee swat | cursed be |
| je viens célébrer la vic-toire | shje v'yahn(n) sell.ay.bray . . . | I come to celebrate the victory |
| printemps qui com-mence | pran(n).tomp(n) key ko.mahn.suh | spring which begins |

## ACT II (37 min.)

The valley of Sorek; to the left, Dalila's house surrounded with "luxuriant tropical creepers." Night falls during the act.

## PRELUDE (2 min.)

It suggests a languorous, warm evening with the hint of a storm in the distance.

## SCENE 1 (4 min.)

*Dalila:* She is alone. Samson is coming, and she rejoices that her hour
**aria** of vengeance is at hand. In her aria she begs the God of Love to assist her in humbling Samson by pouring his poison through Samson's heart: "Amour viens aider ma faiblesse" (love, come to aid my weakness).

## SCENE 2 (12 min.)

*The High Priest and Dalila:* He reports that Samson has sacked the town. Slyly he adds that Samson laughed at Dalila. She retorts proudly that she will triumph and scorns his offer of a reward for capturing Samson: Dalila's vengeance is not for sale. He is impressed but uncertain. She confesses that three times already she has failed to discover Samson's secret, but for this last combat of love she has prepared. **duet** Samson will succumb to her tears. Excitedly the High Priest and she imagine Samson cowering before them. They end together in unison: "Unissons-nous tous deux. Mort, mort au chef des Hebreux" (let us be as one . . . death to the leader of the Hebrews). The High Priest leaves, and Dalila waits for Samson.

## SCENE 3 (19 min.)

*Samson and Dalila:* A storm rumbles at the end of the valley as Samson enters. He comes, although urging himself to flee, "fuyons." (Like many men, he thinks of himself on occasion in the plural.) Dalila glides swiftly up to him: "C'est toi, c'est toi, mon bien-aimé" (it's you, my well-beloved). She murmurs that life is nothing without him. Sternly he orders her to stop. He loves her but he has made his vow.

To a brass accompaniment he describes Israel's rebirth; Jehovah has set the day. For her, Dalila points out, Israel's victory means only that she is spurned and abandoned by the man to whom she gave everything. She weeps. Samson begs her to stop. "Je subis une loi suprême" (I obey a supreme law), he explains, but he insists he still loves her, "Je t'aime" (I love you). She claims to serve a higher God, Love, and she at least is constant to it. Again he swears he loves her. In the most famous aria of the opera, "Mon coeur s'ouvre à ta voix," she rejoices in his love and asks him to declare it again, to return her words of love and caresses. "Réponds a ma tendresse . . . Ah verse-moi" (reply to my endearments . . . ah turn to me). Ardently he swears that he loves her (on a high B flat). Immediately there is a crash of disapproving thunder.

She grieves that he offers only words, easily and often broken. He protests that he has come even in spite of his God. (Throughout the scene the thunder and lightning draw closer.) She asks for complete trust, to know all about him—the secret of his strength. As long as he withholds that, it is proof that he does not trust her, does not love her. He refuses to reveal it, pleading that the thunder is the voice of his God. Furiously she calls him "coward" and, retreating to her house, orders him away, "Adieu." Samson hesitates and then follows her. There is a short orchestral interlude with tremendous crashes of thunder, and then Dalila runs out (sometimes holding his shorn hair) and calling for guards. Samson sobs "Trahison" (treason, i.e. I'm betrayed).

### Vocabulary, Act II

| | | |
|---|---|---|
| amour viens aider ma faiblesse | ah.moor v'yan(n) ay.day mah fay.bless.uh | love, come to aid my weakness |
| unissons-nous tous deux | u.knee.son(n)-new too duh | let us be as one |
| mort au chef des Hebreux | more oh shef days he.bruh | death to the leader of the Hebrews |
| fuyons | f'yon(n) | let us flee, i.e. I should go |
| c'est toi mon bien-aimé | say twa mon(n) b'yan(n)-ay.may | it is you my well-beloved |
| je subis une loi supreme | shje soo.bee oon lwa soo.prem.uh | I obey a supreme law |
| je t'aime | shje t'ehm | I love you |
| mon coeur s'oeuvre à ta voix | mon(n) kerr so.vruh ah tah vwa | my heart opens at your voice |
| résponds à ma ten-dresse | ray.pon(n) ah mah ton(n).dress.uh | reply to my endear-ments |
| ah verse-moi | ah vair.suh mwa | ah turn to me |
| adieu | ah d'yuh | farewell |
| trahison | trah.hee.son(n) | treason, I am betrayed |

## ACT III (35 min.)

The Philistines have put out Samson's eyes and set him to turning the millstone. The defeated Israelites are again slaves.

## PRELUDE (2 min.)

It suggests Samson's despair and the monotonous turning of the millstone.

## SCENE 1 (8 min.)

In a mill. Samson, replacing donkeys, is pushing the stone.

*Samson:* He bewails Israel's fate and offers his life to Jehovah as a sacrifice for his people. An offstage chorus of Israelites calls to him, "Samson," and accuses him of having betrayed his people into slavery for a woman. Samson prays to Jehovah not to forget the Israelites. For himself he asks nothing. He blesses the hand that has struck him down. Soldiers come to take him up to the temple.

The score calls for a transformation scene and provides fifty-nine bars to cover it. At its most elaborate, Samson should walk in place while the scenery changes behind him; less complicated is a fade in and out; and easiest of all is closing the curtains, which most opera houses do.

## SCENE 2 (10 min.)

Inside the Temple of Dagon. There is a statue of the God and an altar. The High Priest and Dalila are present, surrounded by lesser priests and priestesses. The Philistine nation has come to mock Samson. (According to the Bible, there were three thousand watching on the roof, which must have been open to the sky.) Day is breaking.

**chorus** *The Philistines:* They softly sing of love and hail the rising sun. The music is the same as the flower chorus of Act I, scene 6.

The ballet then dances the bacchanal (7 min.). (This ballet un-doubtedly influenced Hollywood's concept of Middle Eastern lascivi-**ballet, the bacchanal** ousness. It may be doubted that in a land and culture where the women are heavily veiled and seldom allowed out-of-doors, they would be likely to indulge so suddenly in such an orgy of nakedness, bumps and grinds.)

## SCENE 3 (14 min.)

*The High Priest, Samson, Dalila et al:* The High Priest ironically hails Samson, who is led in by a boy. The Philistines urge him to join in their revels and honor Dalila. Then the High Priest and Dalila in turn mock his God and his love. Samson turns his blind eyes up to Jehovah: Samson sinned, punish him, but do not let Jehovah's name be mocked in Dagon's Temple.

The High Priest and Dalila begin the Dagon ritual. It is in the form of a canon (*See* Glossary) with chorus. At its end the High Priest urges Samson to join them in worshiping Dagon. Samson prays: "Seigneur, inspire-moi, ne m'abandonne pas" (Lord, breathe strength into me, do not abandon me). He whispers to the boy to lead him to the pillars supporting the roof. (In the traditional Paris production a moving moment is made when, placed between the pillars, Samson kisses the boy on the head and sends him out to safety.) The Philistines build a long chorus in praise of Dagon, "Gloire à Dagon." Suddenly they become aware that Samson is between the pillars. To Jehovah he calls, "Souviens-toi de ton serviteur" (remember thy servant). He asks for his strength again, if only for an instant, to avenge his lost light and Jehovah by killing the Philistines in their Temple. And with the curtain the Temple falls.

### Vocabulary, Act III

| | | |
|---|---|---|
| Seigneur, inspire-moi | sane.yure ah(n)spear.uh-mwa | Lord, breathe strength into me |
| ne m'abandonne pas | nuh m'ah.bon(n). don(n).uh pah | do not abandon me |
| souviens-toi de ton serviteur | sue.v'yahn(n).twa duh ton(n) sair.vee.teur | remember thy servant |

# CARMEN

Opera in four acts. First performed in Paris at the Opéra-Comique on March 3, 1875. Music by G. Bizet. Libretto by L. Halévy and H. Meilhac after P. Merimée's novel.

### PRINCIPAL CHARACTERS

| | | |
|---|---|---|
| Micaela | soprano | me.kah.AIL.ah |
| Don José corporal of the guard | tenor | don joe.ZAY (Sp: hoe.ZAY) |
| Zuniga, captain of the guard | bass | zoo.NEE.gah |
| Carmen | mezzo-soprano | karrrr.MEN |
| Escamillo, a toreador | baritone | es.cah.ME.yo |

The action takes place in and near Seville in 1820.

*Carmen* along with *Aida* and *Don Giovanni* is constantly cited as the perfect opera. It clearly deserves the nomination however meaningless the contest may be. But, like every opera, it has detractors as well as supporters.

Ernest Newman tersely summarized its strength: "It is the most Mozartian opera since Mozart, the one in which enchanting musical invention goes hand in hand, almost without a break, with dramatic veracity and psychological characterization." Carmen's habanera and seguidilla are her natural and inevitable response to her situation; Don José's music grows increasingly dramatic throughout the opera as he grows in experience and despair; and the entr'acts or preludes, while extremely short, are wholly successful in setting the mood and style of the succeeding act and, in addition, are beautifully orchestrated.

BIZET

The detractors, while admitting the opera's qualities, make some interesting observations. They point, for example, to *Don Giovanni* in which Mozart successfully characterized three sopranos; with Bizet there is only Carmen, for Micaela, they say, is cardboard. Likewise, where Mozart offers both Don Giovanni and Leporello, Bizet offers only Don José, for Escamillo is merely a prop to sustain Carmen's loss of interest in José. In *Aida,* say the detractors, there are four main characters and also the High Priest, who is musically more important and developed than Zuniga or any of Carmen's band of friends. The complaint is twofold: first, because the opera has only two roles, it verges on being monotonous; and second, it is really a psychological study, an intimate opera like *La Traviata* or *Madama Butterfly,* blown up into four acts of grand opera by tacking on ballet, chorus and spectacle. And of course it is true that Bizet connected the arias with spoken dialogue and that the recitatives generally in use today were all added after his death.

Whether the complaint is justified or not, it does indicate the direction in which poor performances are likely to veer. Particularly if the Carmen and Don José are not good, there is apt to be an excess of fake Spanish color and dancing as though the story took place in a night club. One outdoor performance even included a real bullfight!

The opera is of great historical importance. Many persons in 1875 hailed it as the answer to Wagner. The most articulate was Nietszche, who used it as the point of departure in his essay, "The Case against Wagner," for an all-out attack that even today leaves readers gasping. More to the point, however, was the effect of its success on a generation of Italian composers, among whom were Puccini, Mascagni and Leoncavallo. *Carmen,* with its concentration on the soprano and tenor, its earthy passion, and death in the square, was the prototype of those Italian veristic operas, of which *Cavalleria Rusticana* is the most famous.

**No. 1**  PRELUDE  (4 min.)

It is short and in an ABAC form, the first and third sections being the entry into the arena from the fourth act, the second the Toreador song, and the last an important motif, sometimes labeled "Fate" or

"Destiny," associated with Carmen. If the conductor and orchestra are good, C will tremble with incipient disaster.

## ACT I (45 min.)

A square in Seville. On the right a tobacco factory; on the left a guard house; at the back a bridge. Soldiers from a regiment of dragoons lounge by the guard house.

**No. 2**  *Soldiers, Morales and Micaela:* The soldiers with a corporal,
**chorus**  Morales (who disappears after this scene), observe the people crossing the square: "Sur la place, chacun passe, chacun vient, chacun va . . ." (on the square, each person passes, each comes, each goes). They conclude that people are queer.

Micaela enters looking for Don José. (The libretto requires her to be in a blue skirt, the costume of a girl from Navarre, to plait her hair, and to be seventeen years old.) Morales tries to joke with her. She is shy but firm. Morales explains that Don José will come, "il y sera" (he will be here), when the guard changes. Meanwhile he urges her to remain. She declines and promises to return later, "Je reviendrai" (I will return).

The soldiers go back to watching the people.

**No. 3**  *Street Boys:* (The libretto says that they are to be as tiny as
**chorus**  possible.) They poke fun at the soldiers by imitating a guard mount. Morales tells Don José that Micaela was looking for him.

> After the change of guard, Zuniga and Don José exchange a few remarks in recitative, during which Don José abruptly confesses that he loves Micaela. The spoken dialogue, which the recitative replaced, was considerably fuller. In it Don José explained that he originally came from Navarre, where he was training to enter the church but from whence he had to flee following a duel over a game of paume (hand tennis). His mother, a widow, followed him with her adopted daughter, Micaela, and the two now live just outside of Seville. He further explains to the interested Zuniga that men are not allowed into the cigarette factory during working hours because the girls, four or five hundred of them, work in dishabille. Don José starts to repair his gun, and Zuniga stares at the factory.

**No. 4**  *Cigarette Girls and Men of Seville:* The factory bell rings;
**chorus**  the men begin to gather and the girls saunter out, smoking.

The men murmur of love and ogle the girls, who sing of the joys of smoking, "la fumée" (the smoke). The men ask for Carmen.

**No. 5**      *Carmen:* She makes her entrance to her motif from the prelude but now played very fast. Earlier it had gone DAH deedeedee DAH, bump, bump; now it goes deedleedee, plink, plink. The men beg
**habanera**      to know when she will give her heart to one of them. She replies vaguely and begins, "L'amour est un oiseau rebelle . . ." (love is a wild bird . . . it does not come when called but when it pleases). She warns them that it is safe for a man to love her, but if a man doesn't love her, then she will love him, and he'd better watch out: "Prends garde a toi" (take care to yourself).

**No. 6**      *Cigarette Girls and Men of Seville:* The young men surround her, except for Don José, who continues to work on his gun. Carmen (to her motif played slowly) throws a flower in his face. Don José is nonplused. The crowd laughs and, as the factory bell rings, the square clears.

Don José picks up the flower and muses that if there really are witches, Carmen must be one. Micaela enters.

**No. 7**      *Don José and Micaela:* He asks for news of his mother:
**duet**      "Parle-moi de ma mère" (speak to me of my mother). Micaela reports that the mother is well and has sent Don José a little money, a letter and, somewhat to Micaela's embarrassment, a kiss— "un baiser de ma mère" (a kiss from my mother). Don José is deeply moved. He remembers his home and village and happier times—"O souvenirs" (oh memories).

As the duet ends, Don José muses that the kiss from his mother may have saved him from Carmen. Happily, he sends his love and a kiss via Micaela back to his mother, and they sing again of memories of home. (On the very last "souvenir" the tenor is directed to sing a high A very quietly. Very few can; some blast it out and some take the note falsetto. Either way is always worth a comment in the lobby during the following intermission.)

Micaela insists on retiring while Don José reads the letter, but she promises to come back: "je reviendrai" (I will return). The letter evidently admonishes him to settle down and marry Micaela, for aloud he protests that he loves her and will marry her. As for that Carmen—he is about to throw the flower away when a riot breaks out in the factory.

**No. 8**      *Cigarette Girls:* They pour into the square, continuing the
**chorus**      fight, some blaming Carmen and some Manuelita. With

difficulty Zuniga learns that Manuelita announced that she intended to hire an ass to ride and that Carmen made an unfriendly observation. Zuniga sends Don José into the factory to find out what happened. Don José returns with Carmen and reports that she has wounded Manuelita. The spoken dialogue explains that Carmen cut a cross on the girl's cheek.

**No. 9**   *Carmen, Zuniga and Don José:* Carmen refuses to answer any questions and attempts to flirt with Zuniga, who binds her arms and leaves her with Don José while he procures an order to put her in prison. The excitement over, the crowd clears the square. Carmen suggests to Don José that he could help her and undoubtedly will because he loves her. He denies it, but she points out he has kept her flower. Angrily he forbids her to talk. So she sings to him.

**No. 10**   *Carmen:* She describes the inn of her friend, Lillas Pastia, **seguidilla**   where she will go to dance the seguidilla and drink wine. But the real fun will begin when her lover comes. Not a captain or a lieutenant—just a corporal—good enough for a gypsy like her.

She promises to meet him here, and he loosens the ropes.

**No. 11**   *Finale:* Zuniga returns with the order for prison, the crowd reassembles and, as Don José leads Carmen to the bridge, she pushes him aside and loses herself in the laughing crowd.

### Vocabulary, Act I

The sign (n) indicates that the preceding syllable is to have a nasal twang.

| | | |
|---|---|---|
| sur la place, chacun passe . . . | Soor lah plah.suh, shack.uhn(n) pah.suh | on the square, everyone passes |
| . . . chacun vient, chacun va | shack.uhn(n) v'yen . . . vah | each comes, each goes |
| il y sera | eel ee sir.ah | he here will be |
| je reviendrai | shje reh.v'yahn(n).dray | I will return |
| la fumee | lah fume.ay.uh | the smoke |
| l'amour est . . . | l'ah.moor ate | love is |
| . . . un oiseau rebelle | uhn(n) wah.zoh re.bell.uh | a wild bird |
| prends garde a toi | pren guard ah twa | take guard to yourself |
| parle-moi de ma mère | par.leh.mwa duh ma mare.uh | speak to me of my mother |
| un baiser de ma mère | uhn bay.zay duh ma mare.uh | a kiss from my mother |
| o souvenirs | oh sue.ven.ear | oh memory |
| je reviendrai | shje reh.v'yahn(n).dray | I will return |

## ACT II (35 min.)

Lillas Pastia's inn two months later. For his part in Carmen's escape, Don José was court-martialed, demoted and sentenced to serve two months in prison. Carmen smuggled him a file which, to her surprise, he did not use, for he felt that escape would have been desertion and dishonorable.

## PRELUDE (2 min.)

The tune is the same as that which Don José will sing offstage as he approaches the inn later in the act.

**No. 12 song** *Carmen, Frasquita and Mercedes:* Carmen sings a song describing gypsies dancing and singing. The song is in three verses and grows faster and wilder with each. The others sing the chorus.

    Frasquita announces that Pastia wants to close, and the soldiers, led by Zuniga, reluctantly agree to go. Carmen complains to Zuniga that the army must have killed Don José, and he replies that on the contrary it has just released him from prison.

**No. 13 chorus** *Men of Seville:* Offstage they sing a chorus of hurrahs. Zuniga reports that it is the famous toreador, Escamillo.

**No. 14 Toreador song** *Escamillo and others:* He launches directly into his song in which he describes a bullfight. The chorus is "Toréador, en garde" (toreador, get ready) . . . "l'amour t'attend" (love awaits you). The score directs the chorus to be sung "fatuously," which suggests that Bizet may have intended to portray Escamillo as a rather smug oaf.

    Escamillo suggests to Carmen that perhaps he could love her, but she dismisses both him and Zuniga, who follows Escamillo and the crowd out. The smugglers (the men) then ask the three women to join them on a job.

**No. 15 quintet** *Dancaire, Remendado, Mercedes, Frasquita and Carmen:* The quintet is rightly one of the opera's famous numbers, and if well done, it can make a unique impression of vocal sound. It falls roughly into four parts. First, the men insist gaily and gallantly that it is always better to have the women in on the job. Naturally, the three women agree. Second, they all agree to depart at once, except Carmen who finally admits that she is in love: "Je suis amoureuse."

Third, the men try to joke her out of it, but she replies to their tune that tonight love comes before duty. Fourth, they return to their original plea: that to succeed they must have the women on their side.

Carmen explains how Don José went to prison for her. The men, however, doubt whether he will turn up.

**No. 16**
**song**
*Don José:* He sings an unaccompanied song in two verses as he comes up the road to the inn. The men, between the verses, comment that he is a fine figure of a man and that maybe he will join them.

When Don José enters, Carmen asks if he regrets his time in prison, and he swears he does not. She asks if he loves her, and he swears he does. As a reward she offers to dance for him.

**No. 17**
*Carmen and Don José:* She starts her dance, but soon Don José hears the bugle sounding retreat, "la retraite," and announces that he will have to return to the barracks. She is furious and, imitating the bugle treats him like a little boy and orders him to be off. Sadly he insists that he never, "jamais," has loved any woman as he loves her. She refuses to listen because it might make him late. He demands she listen.

**Flower Song**
From his coat he draws the flower she threw at him in the square. He tells her how in prison it reminded him that no matter how much he might curse her, he lived only to see her again. (The aria is exceptional in having almost no repeats, even of phrases. It also requires the tenor in the next to last phrase to climb the scale to a high B flat very quietly. Few can do it.) As the aria ends, Don José insists, "Carmen, je t'aime" (I love you).

She denies it: "Non, tu ne m'aimes pas" (you don't love me). If he did, he would follow her to the mountains, and they'd live a life of freedom. He begs her not to tempt him. Finally, desperately, he breaks away from her. He will not desert his flag: that is shame and dishonor. She curtly dismisses him, and he prepares to go. "Adieu pour jamais" (farewell forever).

**No. 18**
*Finale:* But before Don José gets out, he hears Zuniga calling to Carmen. The captain, finding the door locked, breaks it down. When he sees Don José, he observes to Carmen that she exhibits poor taste in preferring an enlisted man to an officer. He orders Don José to get out. Instead, Don José draws his sword. Carmen prevents a fight by calling in the gypsies, who disarm Zuniga. Then addressing Zuniga ironically as "bel officier" (handsome officer), she

suggests that he take a walk. The smugglers adopt her ironic tone and hustle Zuniga out.

Carmen then asks Don José to join the smugglers. With a sigh, he observes that he no longer has any choice. She remarks that his reply, **chorus** while not polite, is satisfactory. Led by Carmen, all promise him a life of freedom, "la liberté." At the end, carried away with excitement, Don José joins them.

### Vocabulary, Act II

| | | |
|---|---|---|
| toréador, en garde | tor.ay.ah.door ehn(n) ga.a.a.r.duh | toreador, get ready |
| l'amour t'attend | l'ah.moor t'ah.tend(n) | love awaits you |
| je suis amoureuse | shje sweez ah.more.erse | I am in love |
| la retraite | lah reh.tray.tuh | retreat |
| jamais | shjam.ay | never |
| je t'aime | shje t'eh.muh | I love you |
| non, tu ne m'aimes pas | no(n), too ne m'ehm pah | you don't love me |
| adieu pour jamais | ah.d'yuh poor shjam.ay | farewell forever |
| bel officier | bell oh.fees.eeay | grand officer |
| la liberté | lah lee.bear.tay | freedom |

## ACT III (35 min.)

The smugglers, Don José and Carmen with them, have been to the coast, collected the contraband, and are now back in the mountains around Seville. They hope to get the goods into the city through a breach in the wall where, generally, only one revenue officer is posted.

## PRELUDE (3 min.)

A flute plays a simple, pastoral tune with harp accompaniment; later a clarinet and then violins weave around the melody.

**No. 19** *Smugglers and Gypsies:* As they gather at the meeting **chorus** place for the attempt to get into Seville, they advise each other to be alert: "Écoute . . . prends garde" (listen . . . take care). **sextet** The leaders announce that smuggling is a good life but a hard one, requiring courage and a certain "sans souci" (without care) approach.

All join in a final chorus of "prends garde" sung quietly. (This is the sort of number that Gilbert and Sullivan satirized in *The Pirates of Penzance.*)

Dancaire tells them all to wait while he reconnoiters the wall. Don José muses that his mother lives close by. Carmen, evidently continuing a quarrel, suggests that he return home, for he clearly never will make a smuggler. He warns her not to talk of parting, and she asks whether he intends to kill her. He doesn't reply, and she shrugs, "Le destin est le maître" (destiny is master).

**No. 20**    *Mercedes, Frasquita and Carmen:* The women tell their **duet**    fortunes by cards. Frasquita sees a lover who loves her madly and in time becomes a great chief. Mercedes finds a rich man who loads her with jewels and houses and quickly dies, leaving her his sole heir. "Amour," rejoices one; "fortune," the other.

**aria "The Card Scene"**    Carmen, who has been watching, cuts her pack. She turns up only diamonds, spades and death. So be it, she remarks, first her, then him. Then—as the score directs "with simplicity and very evenly"—she observes that the cards do not lie. Again it is "la mort, toujours la mort" (death, always death).

**trio**    The three join. Frasquita chants "amour"; Mercedes chortles "fortune"; and Carmen intones "la mort."

Dancaire returns with the news that there are three revenue officers at the wall instead of the usual one. The women promptly offer their talents, which are accepted. This infuriates Don José, who is ordered by Dancaire to stay behind and guard the goods for the second trip. He is authorized to shoot on sight.

**No. 21**    *Smugglers, Frasquita, Mercedes and Carmen:* The women **trio with chorus**    assure the men that the revenue officers will be no problem. The men agree that the officers will undoubtedly be gallants who will enjoy responding to feminine advances. All go off carrying bales and trunks. Don José follows them out to take up his sentinel's post.

**No. 22**    *Micaela:* She wanders in looking for Don José (in the text **aria**    she has a hired guide). Her aria is in ABA form. (*See* Chapter II, "Melody, Aria and Recitative, p. 14.) First she asks the Lord's protection: ". . . protègerez Seigneur"; then she resolves to meet Carmen and rescue Don José; lastly she returns to the Lord for help: "Protègez-moi."

Her aria done, she spies Don José on a crag and calls to him. But he raises his gun and shoots at another figure. Micaela hides and

Escamillo appears with his finger through a hole in his hat.

**No. 23** *Escamillo and Don José:* Escamillo identifies himself and explains that he has come to look up a gypsy girl who, rumor has it, has tired of a soldier. Don José asks her name and it is "Carmen." He reminds Escamillo that he must pay for Carmen and with blood. For the first time Escamillo realizes that he is talking to the soldier. They agree to fight. Escamillo's knife breaks and Don José is about to kill him when Carmen re-enters and prevents him.

**No. 24** Finale: Escamillo gaily offers to fight again soon, but Dancaire, who is eager to get on with the business of smuggling, dismisses him. As he leaves, Escamillo pointedly invites all who love him to the bullfight. The smugglers prepare to leave with the remainder of the bales when Remendado discovers Micaela. She begs José to go to his mother. When Carmen also urges him, he refuses: only death will separate him from Carmen. All urge him to go, but more resolutely he refuses. Finally, Micaela tells him, "Ta mère se meurt" (your mother is dying). At that he agrees to go, but "nous nous reverons" (we shall meet again), he says bitterly to Carmen. From the mountainside comes the sound of Escamillo singing the refrain of his Toreador song—"l'amour t'attend."

## Vocabulary, Act III

| | | |
|---|---|---|
| écoute . . . prends garde | eh.coot.uh prend guard | listen . . . take care |
| sans souci | sahn(n) soo.see | without care |
| de destin est le maître | le des.tahn(n) ay le maytre | destiny is master |
| amour | ah.moor | love |
| fortune | for.tune.uh | fortune |
| la mort, toujours la mort | la mor, two.shour la mor | death, always death |
| protègerez, Seigneur | pro.tay.shjer.ay sayn.yure | will protect, Lord |
| protègez-moi | pro.tay.shje-mwa | protect me |
| ta mère se meurt | tah mair suh mer | your mother is dying |
| nous nous reverons | new new reh.vair.ons(n) | we shall meet again |
| l'amour t'attend | lah.moor t'ah.tend(n) | love awaits you |

## ACT IV (17 min.)

A square in Seville outside the arena. Some time has passed since Don José left to see his mother. He was seen in her village, but when soldiers arrived to arrest him for desertion, he had gone. Carmen now thinks only of Escamillo.

## PRELUDE (2 min.)

With the possible exception of the habanera, this is the best known music from the opera. For many it is the epitome of Spanish bullfight excitement.

**No. 25**    **chorus**    *People and Peddlers of Seville:* They call to each other and advertise their wares. (Sometimes a ballet is inserted here. If so, the music is generally taken from Bizet's *L'Arlésienne*. The ballet may run anywhere from two to six minutes.)

**No. 26**    *People of Seville, Escamillo and Carmen:* The procession into the arena begins, and the people cheer their favorites. Lastly comes **duet**    Escamillo with Carmen brilliantly dressed. Quietly he tells her, "Si tu m'aimes" (if you love me), she will be proud of him. She responds "Je t'aime" (I love you). Escamillo enters the arena followed by the Alcalde (the mayor).

Frasquita and Mercedes warn Carmen that Don José is in the crowd. They urge her to "prends garde" (take care), but Carmen announces calmly that she will wait for Don José. The crowd goes in, leaving only Carmen and Don José outside.

**No. 27**    *Carmen and Don José:* She tells him that she has been warned he will kill her. But she was never one to run. He wants only to forget the past and go away together. Calmly she tells him that between them "tout est fini" (all is finished). He begs her to let him save her, "laisse-moi te sauver," and—a profound psychological touch—by saving her to save himself, "et me sauver avec toi" (and me to save with you). But she is firm.

Twice he asks her, first anxiously and then with despair, "Tu ne m'aimes donc plus" (you love me no more)? Cooly she replies, "Non, je ne t'aime plus" (no, I love you no more). He bursts out: he will do anything for her, even join the smugglers, but she must not forsake him. She was born free, she insists, and she will die free.

From the arena comes the sound of the crowd applauding Escamillo. Carmen starts to go in. He blocks her way. "Laisse-moi" (leave me), she insists. Don José demands her to say that she does not love Escamillo. "Je l'aime" (I love him), she insists.

The crowds cheer again. Don José threatens her. Angrily she turns to him, throws a ring he gave her in his face and starts for the arena. As the crowd cheers, he kills her.

### Vocabulary, Act IV

| | | |
|---|---|---|
| si tu m'aimes | see two m'em.uh | if you love me |
| je t'aime | shje t'em.uh | I love you |
| prends garde | pren guard | take care |
| tout est fini | toot ay fee.nee | all is finished |
| laisse-moi te sauver | lay.suh mwa teh sew.vay | let me save you |
| et me sauver avec toi | ay muh sew.vay ah.vek twa | and save myself with you |
| tu ne m'aimes donc plus | two nuh m'em.uh donk(n) ploo | you love me no more |
| non, je ne t'aime plus | naw shje nuh t'em.uh ploo | no, I love you no more |
| laisse-moi | lay.suh mwa | leave me |
| je l'aime | shje l'em | I love him |

# BORIS GODUNOV

Opera in prologue and four acts. First performed in St. Petersburg on February 8, 1874. Music and libretto by M. Mussorgsky, after a drama by Pushkin and a history by N. M. Karamzin.

### PRINCIPAL CHARACTERS

| | |
|---|---|
| Boris Godunov | bass or baritone |
| Pimen, an old monk | bass |
| Grigori, later "the false Dimitri" | tenor |
| Vaarlam, a drunken monk | bass |
| Prince Shuiski, Boris' minister | tenor |
| Marina, a Polish Princess | mezzo-soprano |
| Rangoni, a Jesuit priest | bass or baritone |
| The Idiot | tenor |

The action takes place in Russia and Poland from 1598 to 1605. For nearly 1100 years two families, the descendants being real or pretended, ruled Russia—the Ruriks (862–1598) and the Romanovs (1613–1917). The change-over was difficult; there was a period of intrigue, assassination, pillage and famine. For the first part of it Boris Godunov was the dominant figure, and the eight years of anarchy after his death in 1605 came to be known as the "Time of Trouble."

The opera, based on a drama by Pushkin, begins a month after the death of the last Rurik Tsar, Feodor I (1584–98). He was rather simple-minded, passionately interested in the church and, in his father's opinion, should have been a bell ringer. His father was Ivan "the Terrible." Ivan's chief minister was Boris Godunov. Feodor married Boris' sister and, when he became Tsar, continued Boris as chief minister. Feodor died childless and the Tsarina, as custom then demanded, retired to a convent.

The throne was vacant; there were no Rurik heirs. It fell to Boris. His position was nearly unassailable. He had been chief minister for two Tsars and the state administration was in his control. His sister was the old Tsarina; his son and heir a nephew of the old Tsar. It was a connection, however tenuous, with the Rurik dynasty, and it might have succeeded.

But after five years a challenger arose, calling Boris a usurper. This man, generally called "the false Dimitri," claimed to be a son of Ivan, a half brother of Feodor I and a Rurik by blood. Ivan, just before he died, had married a sixteen year old Princess and by her had a child, Dimitri. This child died during Feodor's reign. Boris, as chief minister, sent out a committee headed by Prince Shuiski to investigate the death. The committee reported that the child had died accidentally by falling on his dagger.

Gossip at the time, Pushkin in his play and Mussorgsky in his opera assume that Boris ordered Dimitri killed. History clears him of the charge. Indeed, he would have had to be an unusually patient man to have waited seven more years for Feodor to die. But for purposes of the opera, Boris had Dimitri murdered, and Shuiski knows it.

Boris, "the Mad Tsar," ruled from 1598 to 1605. His son, Feodor II, succeeded him, but for only a few months. "The false Dimitri" then reigned, but again for only a few months. He had married a Polish Princess, Marina, and Poles swarmed over Moscow. The Russians, naturally, weren't going to stand for that. Dimitri was succeeded by Prince Shuiski who, as Basil IV, ruled from 1606 to 1610. There then followed three years of anarchy until the election of a compromise candidate to the throne in the person of Michael Romanov. Actually, however, his uncle, a Romanov and a priest, was the power behind his throne. During the period 1610–13 a second "false Dimitri" claimed the throne. Marina married him, too, claiming that he was her first husband returned.

**MUSSORGSKY**

The opera, by latest count, exists in nine versions or revisions: three by Mussorgsky, two by Rimsky-Korsakov and the others by various publishing and opera houses. The squabble is technical. It is important to know only that Mussorgsky had trouble getting the opera produced, put in Marina later as a sop to convention, and ended with the revolution in the Kromy forest. The opera was only moderately successful. Rimsky-Korsakov reorchestrated the entire score to make it more brilliant and put the death of Boris at the end. (His version also leaves out the St. Basil scene, as did two of Mussorgsky's.) This version Chaliapin sang. The trend today, however, is to deplore Rimsky-Korsakov and up Mussorgsky.

The account of the opera that follows includes all possible scenes. Most opera houses, however, will either omit the St. Basil's scene or condense the two Polish scenes.

The opera is a series of spectacles of Russia life and history held together by the figure of Boris and his sense of guilt as developed in the four monologues. Of a total of ten scenes, Boris appears in only five and never in a scene with "the false Dimitri." The scenes can be cut and combined and some can even be shifted without confusing the story.

One difficulty of the opera is its length: with all scenes, uncut, and with intermissions it runs well over four hours. It is an epic, and every scene is crammed with local color: the nurses' song is interesting as an example of what nurses sang in Moscow in 1604, but it delays the Tsar's monologue. The opera, however, is tremendously exciting whenever Boris or the crowd dominates the scene; and, curiously enough, no matter which scene ends the opera, it builds to a superb climax.

## PROLOGUE (25 min.)

### SCENE 1 (The Monastery—14 min.)

The courtyard of the Novodevichi Monastery in February, 1598. Feodor I has been dead a month, and the Boyars (the Nobles) have divided into pro- and anti-Godunov factions. Boris has passed the month in the monastery, searching his soul and steadily refusing the crown offered to him by the Patriarch and the pro-Godunov faction. The latter have filled the courtyard with peasants whose jobs it is to cry constantly for Boris.

The peasants are bored and, as they complain, hoarse. Police guards threaten to whip them unless they cry louder. The peasants offer to give a big chorus of cries in exchange for a breathing spell, and the guards agree.

The chorus is so loud that the secretary of the Duma (Council of Nobles) comes out to tell them that once again, in spite of all pleas, Boris has refused the throne.

Some pilgrims enter singing that they have come from the Don and Vladimir, at the direction of the Archangel, to greet the Tsar. The peasants are awed and respectful. "God's people," they say.

### SCENE 2 (The Coronation—11 min.)

The Square in the Kremlin. To the back is the Red staircase leading up to the Tsar's chambers. On either side are the porches of the Cathedrals of the Archangel and the Assumption. Boris has accepted the crown and the Coronation is just over. He comes out of the Cathedral of the Assumption and crosses the square to pay homage to the preceding Tsars buried in the Cathedral of the Archangel. On his way, he dramatically stops and offers a public prayer.

**monologue**      This is the first monologue (3 min.) and it is a typical officeholder's public prayer for guidance by the Deity. But only to Prince Shuiski in 1598 or to an audience at Mussorgsky's opera years later are the opening lines especially significant. These are, "My soul is sorely anguished. Strange involuntary fears and forebodings clutch my heart."

## ACT I (40 min.)

### SCENE 1 (Pimen's cell—19 min.)

Five years later—1603. A cell in the Monastery of Chudovo. Pimen, an old monk, is writing. Grigori (later to be "the false Dimitri") is asleep.

To himself Pimen rejoices in his role of chronicler of the times, the bearer of truth to succeeding generations.

Offstage monks sing a prayer and Grigori wakes. Silently he watches Pimen scratching away and envies him his tranquillity. He asks for a blessing.

He complains of a dream he has had three times: falling from a high tower into a Moscow square (this refers to a version of how he died during Prince Shuiski's coup).

Pimen puts it down to young blood and confesses to wild dreams himself. But Grigori enviously reminds him that he had been a soldier and a courtier. Pimen replies that even Tsars seek out the religious life in the end. He cites Ivan and Feodor. Under them Russia was happy. Under Boris, the regicide, suffering stalks the country. He recounts how he was present at the murder of Dimitri and how the killers confessed and named Boris. Dimitri would have been just Grigori's age.

A bell summons the monks to morning prayer. Grigori hangs back. He calls aloud to Boris that though now no one dares recall Dimitri, still he cannot escape the judgment of God or man.

### SCENE 2 (Vaarlam's song: The siege of Kazan—21 min.)

An inn on the Lithuanian border.

**aria**  The hostess has caught a drake. She is infinitely pleased with herself and clucks a barnyard song.

**aria**  Two runaway monks and Grigori enter. One of the monks, Vaarlam, sings a rollicking song about the Siege of Kazan when Ivan the Terrible blew up 83,000 Tartars.

Vaarlam complains that Grigori never will drink, but wants only to get to Lithuania. The hostess warns Grigori that there are guards stopping everyone. But she describes a road to avoid them.

The police officers arrive. Vaarlam identifies himself as a humble monk collecting alms for charity. He complains that no one gives any more, so that he might as well drink. The officer stares at Vaarlam and says that he's the runaway monk whom they're to pick up. He hands the warrant to Grigori to read the description. Grigori sees his own name on the warrant, but instead of reading the description of himself, he describes Vaarlam. And although it doesn't say so on the warrant, the police officer insists that the monk is to be hanged. At that Vaarlam grabs the description and spells it out slowly. It fits Grigori, who has slipped out the window and started for the border.

### ACT II

(Two monologues: "I have attained the highest
power" and "The Clock Scene"—32 min.)

A room in the Tsar's chambers in the Kremlin. Xenia is weeping. Feodor is studying maps. The nurse does needlework.

**aria**  Xenia weeps inconsolably for her fiancé, who has died.

**aria**     The nurse tries to distract her with a song about a gnat. Feodor complains that it is a sad song.

**duet**     He and the nurse play "Khloyst," in which they sing and clap hands. At the end Boris enters.

He has a kind word for the nurse and Xenia, who go out, and then he examines Feodor's knowledge of Russian geography. Feodor continues to study the map while Boris delivers the second monologue (6 min.).

**monologue**     "I have attained the highest power. For five years I've ruled in peace. But I have no happiness. Not even in my family can I arrange for it or find it: Xenia's poor bridegroom carried off before the wedding. I've prayed, endlessly, to all the saints, but my soul is in torment. Outside famine, pestilence and sedition disrupt the country— and all blame me. It is a punishment for my sins. Even at night sleep is gone, and I see that little child, covered with blood, pleading for mercy. His wound gapes. I hear his scream. Oh God, my God."

Backstage there is a ruckus among the nurses. Boris angrily sends Feodor out to investigate.

A Boyar announces that Prince Shuiski requests an audience. Before he leaves, he whispers to Boris that a servant has revealed that Shuiski last night met secretly with other Boyars. (There is a scene in Pushkin at Prince Shuiski's house that shows him in communication with the dissident Boyars.)

Feodor returns and at great length describes how a parrot attacked one of the nurses. Boris compliments him on telling the story so clearly and prettily.

Prince Shuiski enters saying that he has important news. Blandly he confesses, when asked by Boris, that it is the same news he received in the secret meeting. It is that a pretender has appeared in Lithuania claiming to be Dimitri. Boris asks Feodor to leave and gives orders for closing the border. Hysterically he asks Prince Shuiski if a dead child can rise or if Shuiski is certain that it was Dimitri who was killed. Violently he threatens Shuiski with torture if he doesn't tell the truth. Quietly Shuiski answers that for five days he guarded the body and investigated the death. Softly he describes the gaping wound, the child's radiant face, the small hand clutching the toy.

Boris stops him and dismisses him. Then he sinks back into an armchair. Prince Shuiski stops in the door and watches him. The clock incessantly ticks, and Boris delivers his third monologue (3 min.).

**monologue, Clock Scene**     "I'm stifling. I feel as though all my blood were in my face. What a torment conscience is. One blot and remorse beats, beats in my ears. My head reels. There, in the corner; it's coming nearer. Don't touch me. It was the people's will. Not I. Go way, Go way. God, you have not wished my death for the crime. Have mercy on the sinful soul of Tsar Boris."

## ACT III (The Polish Act—31 min.)

### SCENE 1 (17 min.)

At the Voyevode's (Governor's) Castle in Sandomir in Poland. The Voyevode, Mnishek, was a powerful member of the Polish aristocracy. At that time Poland, after merging with Lithuania in 1569, was the largest country in Europe. The King was, however, weak and the nobles were correspondingly strong. Thus Marina can, not unrealistically, think of herself as a Polish princess of equal rank with a Tsar, since Russia was then a country of only similar size. The Crimea, for example, was still wholly under Tartar control. The scene is in Marina's rooms.

**chorus**     *Ladies in waiting:* They entertain Marina with a chorus about a beautiful lady, obviously Marina, who laughs at love and breaks the hearts of men.

*Marina:* She scolds them for singing of love and tells them in the future **aria**     to sing of Poland's history, war and battles. She dismisses them and muses on "the false Dimitri," who has gathered an army and, for love of her, is lingering at her father's palace. He can give her glory and excitement.

*Rangoni and Marina:* He complains that the Roman Catholic Church has lost ground. He urges her to be God's instrument in converting the Russians. He slyly suggests that she might become Saint Marina.

She is tempted at the thought but protests that she is too material, too social to be a saint.

**aria**     He counters that she can use all her charms on Dimitri, first giving of them and then holding back, to make him the servant of the true church. For that end, without remorse, she can sacrifice anything, even honor. Marina protests, but Rangoni, accusing her of the sin of pride, terrifies her further with a description of Hell opening beneath her. Abjectly she falls at his feet.

## SCENE 2 (24 min.)

**Near** a fountain in the castle garden. It is a moonlit night. Marina is entertaining with a ball.

**aria** *Dimitri* (formerly Grigori): Alone in the garden, awaiting Marina, he sings passionately of his love for her.

*Dimitri and Rangoni:* Rangoni assures Dimitri that Marina returns his love, and Dimitri, encouraged, swears that he'll make Marina his wife and queen and Rangoni his chief adviser.

**Polonaise** The guests dance a polonaise in which all pay homage to Marina and in which she glitters hard and cold. She joins Dimitri in the garden.

*Dimitri and Marina:* Passionately he woos her. He will throw over throne and glory for her. Sarcastically she rebuffs him. She loves the **duet** Tsar not the man. He should be marching, fighting and winning, she lashes him. Stung, he proudly tells her off. He is the Tsarevitch, she a mere Pole. He will march tomorrow, and after he has won, he will laugh at her. Now she swears she loves him, and the scene closes with a love duet. Rangoni hovers in the background.

## ACT IV (54 min.)

### SCENE 1 (Before St. Basil's Cathedral—9 min.)

Boris and the Boyars are attending a service inside the Cathedral. It is ostensibly a mass for the soul of the real Dimitri, but it gives the clergy an opportunity to curse "the false Dimitri." Outside the peasants listen and discuss the merits of "the false Dimitri." Some think he is the Tsarevich, others a pretender. A group of boys tease an idiot. The Tsar comes out of the Cathedral. A Boyar ahead of him scatters alms. The idiot asks Boris to stop the boys from teasing him and to have them killed. The Boyars start to seize him, but Boris forbids it. Instead, as he leaves, he asks the idiot to pray for him, but the idiot calls after him that he cannot pray for a child murderer.

### SCENE 2 (The Duma—26 min.)

The council room in the Kremlin. The Duma is in special session; the Boyars are discussing what punishment to mete out to "the false

Dimitri"—when they catch him.

They argue—some for hanging, some for burning and some for catching him first. Prince Shuiski arrives, apologizing for being late. He at once ominously and suggestively worries about the Tsar's health and mind. In detail he describes Boris "seeing" the child, begging it to go away. He is repeating Boris' very words as Boris enters. In a daze Boris repeats them again: "Go away, go away."

Then, composing himself, Boris sits on the throne. Prince Shuiski requests an audience for an old monk who has a secret to reveal.

**aria**     It is Pimen. In a long aria he describes a miracle. A man blind from birth has recovered his sight. In his darkness the man heard a child's voice directing him to the grave of the child, Dimitri. The blind man, led by his grandson, went and knelt by the grave. As he prayed, his tears washed away the darkness and he began to see.

It is too much for Boris, who staggers up and then falls back on the throne. He gasps for his son, Feodor, and holy vestments. (Traditionally the Tsar was supposed to die a monk. Thus a request for vestments is tantamount to a statement of imminent death.) He dismisses everyone except Feodor.

**monologue**     His last monologue (12 min.) falls roughly into three short parts—"The Farewell, Prayer and Death of Boris."

In the "farewell" he addresses Feodor. He must rule. He ascends the throne legitimately. He must be stern but just and he must trust the Boyars. He must guard the Faith and venerate the saints. He must protect his sister, Xenia.

In the "prayer" he begs God, for the tears of a sinning father, to grace his children, to protect his boy.

Slowly a bell begins to toll, announcing his death to the city. Boris calls again for the vestments so that he can leave for the monastery. Offstage a chorus begins to wail. "Oh God," Boris begs, "is there no pity, no mercy for me?" Monks and Boyars enter in a ritual procession. Pushing himself up, Boris thunders, "I am still Tsar." He collapses, begging God's forgiveness. He points to Feodor: "There is your Tsar." His last word is "forgive."

SCENE 3 (Revolution in the Kromy forest—19 min.)

On the edge of the forest. To the back are the walls of Kromy. The war has stopped all work, broken down ancient customs and given over life to the whims of the idle and the violent. Dimitri and his troops are close to Kromy.

A group of peasants and riffraff enters. They have captured a minor Boyar, whom they tie to a stump. They give him some retainers to stand by him, an old woman to love and a whip to use on honest folk. Then they pretend to worship him.

Some boys plague an idiot and steal his money.

Vaarlam and Misail, the two runaway monks, roll in and excite the crowd to scream for Dimitri and curse Boris.

Two Jesuit priests enter praying for Dimitri in Latin. At once the Orthodox monks urge the crowd to lynch the Jesuits.

Dimitri rides in. He releases the Boyar and the Jesuits and urges everyone to follow him on to Moscow. Only the idiot is left. "Weep, weep," he cries. "Darkness is coming. Woe, awful woe to Russia." But no one is left to hear him.

# EUGENE ONEGIN

Lyric scenes in three acts. First performed at Moscow on March 29, 1879. Music by P. Tchaikovsky. Libretto by Tchaikovsky and K. S. Shilovsky, after the poem by Pushkin.

### PRINCIPAL CHARACTERS

| | |
|---|---|
| Tatiana ⎱ daughters of Mme. Larina | soprano |
| Olga ⎰ | contralto |
| Madame Larina, a widow | mezzo-soprano |
| The nurse, Filapyevna | mezzo-soprano |
| Vladimir Lensky, a neighbor, aged 18 and engaged to Olga | tenor |
| Eugene Onegin, his friend, aged 19 | baritone |
| Triquet, a Frenchman | tenor |
| Prince Gremin, an old General | bass |

The action takes place in the country and nearby St. Petersburg in the 1820's.

The opera's title is misleading, although it repeats the title of Pushkin's poem on which the opera is based. But Tchaikovsky felt far more for Tatiana than he did for Onegin, and it is her story that he tells: her love for Onegin, her humiliation by him and finally, although admitting her love, her rejection of him. Musically and dramatically her letter scene in the first act is successful and the seed from which the rest of the opera grows; in fact, Tchaikovsky composed it first. But his short monologue for Onegin in Act III in which the twenty-six-year-old dandy expresses his weariness and boredom is, by comparison, a failure.

## TCHAIKOVSKY

Tchaikovsky always insisted that he was writing not an opera but lyric scenes, and these probe deeply into the mood of the character at the moment. But they do not develop the plot as in *Tosca* or the character as in *Otello*. They are, as some editions of the score call them, *tableaux,* pictures in which the sets and costumes tell much of the story, leaving the music free to expose the variations and gradations of a character's emotions. Thus in the first scene Onegin has no music of his own. The St. Petersburg clothes and manners he displays must set him apart from the simpler Lensky and the Larina household, so comfortable and middle class, and suggest that he will reject Tatiana with cold scorn. Likewise, Tchaikovsky does not show Tatiana developing from a naive country girl into a loved and admired St. Petersburg Princess; but the audience hears her husband's testimony and sees her functioning successfully in a new and brilliant environment. It rightly assumes that she has learned a discipline and sophistication that will make her rejection of Onegin inevitable and believable. In the first act the peasants dance with high jumps and kicks, the men apart from the women; in the second the gentry waltz in couples; and in St. Petersburg, society, in couples, does a polonaise but in rigid patterns with formalized gestures. In a few short ballet sequences Tchaikovsky has given a picture of Russian life that makes the real buildings of *Tosca*—the church, palazzo and castle—seem like only the most superficial evocation of Rome.

The instant and continuing success of *Onegin* surprised Tchaikovsky. He felt the style of lyric scenes, essentially static, would never appeal to audiences, and he feared the usual hard-faced prima donna, paunchy tenor and blustering baritone would destroy his shy, eager, young characters. That they have been unable to do so is evidence of the opera's melodic strength. For each character, with the possible exception of Onegin, Tchaikovsky seemed to find just the right key to unlock his innermost feelings: Prince Gremin has only one aria, but in its five minutes it reveals more of a real person, an older man surprised by love, than the entire score of *South Pacific*.

## OVERTURE (2 min.)

It is a slight introduction of music associated with Tatiana, shy, eager and uncertain.

## ACT I (67 min.)

### SCENE 1 (29 min.)

Twilight in the garden of Mme. Larina's house. To the back is a dilapidated fence and in the distance are the village and its church. Larina and the nurse are making preserves. Through the door of the house on the left Tatiana (almost always on stage called Tanya) and Olga can be heard practicing a duet.

**duet** *Tatiana and Olga:* The two girls enter still singing the duet. The refrain is pensive: "Did you ever sigh, listening to the gentle voice of the singer?" The song stirs memories in Larina and the nurse, who then start a conversation, so that the two duets merge into a quartet. *Larina and the Nurse:* Larina reminisces that when young in the city she loved a guardsman who gambled, and her parents, disapproving, quickly married her off to a country squire, the father of the girls. The **duet** nurse clucks along and comments: "Still your husband really loved you." Larina agrees: "He always trusted me." Each comment is repeated. The chorus of this duet is that "household routine is given to us by God to replace happiness."

(Because there are two duets going at once, Larina's words—even when sung in English—are almost completely lost. But they are important, as they reveal the sort of "happy" home and "good" people Tatiana has known and also the values she probably will accept as guiding her own life. Prince Gremin later will say of her that her virtue shines like a star. And yet it's just the sort of home atmosphere that, understandably, could induce Tatiana, a very young girl, to write to Onegin: "I am alone here. No one understands me.")

**chorus and dance** *Peasants:* They sing of work done and present Mme. Larina with sheaves symbolizing the harvest.

**aria** *Olga:* I am not made like Tanya, to dream and sigh. I am gay, happy and life is sweet. At the end of this aria the mother, nurse and Olga fuss over Tanya: she looks sick; she reads too much.

*Tatiana, Olga, Lensky and Onegin:* The men arrive, and in the quartet **quartet** they comment on the two girls. Lensky loves Olga, and Onegin favors Tanya, who has a more "interesting" face. Olga says that people will gossip about Onegin and Tanya. Tanya, in an aside, recognizes that Onegin will be the great love of her life.

**aria** *Lensky:* While Onegin and Tatiana walk in the garden, Lensky sings his love to Olga. The scene ends as all four go into the house, and the nurse starts the speculative gossip about Tanya and Onegin.


SCENE 2 (The Letter scene—26 min.)

Tatiana's bedroom, simply furnished with dressing table, bookshelf and desk.

*Nurse and Tatiana:* The nurse fusses about the room. Tanya muses about love, asks the nurse what it is like and then doesn't listen. She tells the nurse she is in love, but the nurse doesn't understand.

**aria**    *Tatiana:* This is her great moment of self-revelation. Her aria is extended and is itself a drama culminating in her decision to send the letter. It divides:

1: I'm in love and at last alive. Thank God. Even if it kills me. (This is a big outburst in song and orchestra. Musically, it's in two verses, both short.)

2: She starts writing to Onegin, ʹstops and then continues. She tells him that she must write to him and that she counts on his not humiliating her. (Musically this section is quiet. An oboe rises up the scale, like a pen across the page, and then various instruments, ending with a splash of harp, drop swiftly down the scale so that the oboe can start again at the next line.)

3: She loses her courage, stops and then presses on more excitedly. This section is short.

4: She writes: why did you come down here and upset me? I might have been happy married to a neighbor. (The thought of being married to someone else produces the next outburst.)

5: Another! she muses to herself. Never. I've known you always. When I saw you, a fire burnt through me. (This is a long, excited section. It is followed by a long, quiet one, starting on a sustained high note.)

6: She writes again: are you my guardian angel or some tempter? I am alone here. No one understands me. I will trust all to you. Then, after hesitating and a burst of music, she quickly signs and seals the letter. She goes to the window and looks out. Everything is at peace but she.

*Nurse and Tatiana:* Tanya asks the nurse to have her grandson deliver the letter to Onegin. The nurse who is deaf, finally understands.


SCENE 3 (Onegin rejects Tatiana—11 min.)

A part of the gardens on Mme. Larina's estate; flowering bushes, an old wooden bench.

**chorus**    *Peasant Girls:* "Come out and pick berries."

*Tatiana:* Why, why did I ever mail it? He'll just laugh. I know it. I realize it now.

**aria**    *Onegin:* "You wrote me," he begins, "and I will reply." He then describes himself with smug satisfaction as a rake and a bachelor by choice. Then, as the chorus drifts back, he condescendingly advises her to cultivate some self-control; "not everyone will be as nice as I."

**chorus**     *Peasant Girls:* "Come out and pick berries."

## ACT II (41 min.)

### SCENE 1 (The birthday party—26 min.)

A large room in Mme. Larina's house. It is Tatiana's birthday.

**waltz and chorus**     *Guests:* "What a wonderful party." Then, as Tanya and Onegin waltz by, the matrons comment on what a dreadful person he really is. The gossip irritates Onegin and in a pique he sets out to dazzle Olga and upset Lensky.

**aria**     *Triquet:* A Frenchman living at a neighbor's house sings a formal song in Tanya's honor, as it is her birthday. At the end of it the dancing starts again.

*Lensky and Onegin:* To the background of a mazurka the two men have increasingly angry words until Lensky challenges Onegin. At that moment the mother rushes up: "Not in our house. Please. Not in our house." This starts Lensky on a musical flash back.

**aria**     *Lensky:* In your house I grew up and was so happy. Now I have learned that life is ugly, a friend untrustworthy, and a girl deceiving.

*Olga, Lensky, Onegin et al:* The finale works directly out of Lensky's aria. Everyone comes in at the second or third verse and sings his own view of the situation.

### SCENE 2 (The Duel—15 min.)

Dawn. By a wooded stream near a village mill. A winter landscape.

*Lensky:* While waiting for Onegin, Lensky sings his great aria. First he

**aria**     wonders what happened to his future, which once seemed so happy. Then, as if to have expected happiness was too much, he accepts fate without questioning. He begins to think of Olga and how his love for her was the best of his short life, which leads him back to questioning the future.

*Onegin and Lensky:* Just before the duel begins, the two men sing a canon, i.e. the same tune, the same words but (as in a round) with

**canon**     Onegin always a verse behind, so that the two never get together. "Before always together and now enemies; shouldn't we laugh and shake hands? No, no."

Lensky is killed.

## ACT III (29 min.)

Seven years have passed. Tanya has married Prince Gremin, a great nobleman in St. Petersburg. It is her achievement that she has been able to make this older, cultivated and complicated man extremely happy.

### SCENE 1 (The St. Petersburg Ball—21 min.)

**polonaise**     As the scene opens, the guests are dancing a polonaise. Towards the end of it, Onegin enters.

**aria**     *Onegin:* He stands apart from the guests and sings of his boredom with travel and disgust with a life in which at twenty-six he has accomplished nothing but the death of a friend.

Tanya enters, and the guests murmur in admiration. Onegin recognizes her and she him, but they do not speak. Prince Gremin enters, and Onegin, who is his cousin, asks to be introduced to his wife, admitting that they were neighbors once in the country.

*Prince Gremin:* Before he introduces Onegin to Tanya, Gremin tells him what she has meant to him. Love came to him late. He was bitter and tired of the selfish, quarrelsome, toadying world in St. Petersburg, and then she transformed it and set "my life, my youth, yes, youth, and happiness afire."

As he closes, Gremin introduces Onegin to Tanya. They exchange a few pleasantries, and then Tanya says that she's tired, and she goes out on Gremin's arm.

*Onegin:* Left alone, he wonders what's happening to him. His music

**aria**     becomes Tanya's of the letter scene. Even if it kills him, he will pursue love. He sees her face, hears her voice everywhere.

**polonaise**     Onegin leaves while the guests continue dancing.

SCENE 2 (Tatiana rejects Onegin—8 min.)

A reception room in Prince Gremin's palace. Tanya holds a letter from Onegin in which, in an echo of her first-act letter to him, he offers her his love and urges that they flee together.

**aria** *Tatiana:* The scene starts with a short aria for Tanya: how hard it is that Onegin should return. Then, as he enters and kisses her hand, she reminds him of her letter and his response and asks why he now pursues her: is it because she is rich and famous and so her disgrace would be a feather in his cap?

*Onegin and Tatiana:* He insists he loves her and she, weakening, be-
**duet** gins to cry. The music quietens and together, answering each other, they sing of how close happiness had been to them. But then she reminds him she is married and he must leave. He refuses: the only bliss is to love and live with her. This is followed by a stormy section in which she insists he leave; and then, suddenly and very quietly, she admits she loves him. The exchange between them thereafter gets constantly more heated: he urges her to run away and she insists that Gremin is her life. Finally she rises and, walking out the door, leaves him. He curses his lot to continue wandering, alone and rejected.

# MANON

Opera in five acts. First performed in Paris at The Opéra-Comique on January 19, 1884. Music by J. Massenet. Libretto by P. Gille and H. Meilhac, after Abbé Prévost's novel, first published in 1733.

### PRINCIPAL CHARACTERS

| | | |
|---|---|---|
| Guillot de Morfontaine, a very rich nobleman | tenor | guee.oh |
| De Brétigny, a tax collector | baritone | |
| Lescaut, a guardsman and Manon's cousin | baritone | less.coe |
| Manon | soprano | mah.non (nasal) |
| Chevalier Des Grieux, a young nobleman | tenor | day gree.yuh |
| Comte Des Grieux, the Chevalier's father | bass | |

The action takes place in Amiens, Paris, and near Le Havre about 1720.

*Manon, Faust* and *Carmen* form the great triumvirate of French opera. Of the three it is the most French. It has none of Goethe's philosophic overtones, which linger around Gounod's version of *Faust*, and little of the Mediterranean passion of *Carmen*. Possibly as a result, out of France it is not as popular as its fellows.

The story is based on Abbé Prevost's *Les Aventures du Chevalier des Grieux et de Manon Lescaut*, published in 1733 and often called the first French novel. The Abbé describes the gradual moral disintegration of a young nobleman infatuated by an attractive but amoral girl who is a thief as well as a whore. Massenet's opera changes

MASSENET

the emphasis. The French have always been fascinated by the "femme fatale"—Carmen and Dalila are two more—and the opera, unlike the novel, is wholly Manon's story. Each act is tailored to show her steady decline from a giddy girl into a hardened courtesan. Des Grieux remains decent but ineffective, as he must, or the audience would soon come to care for him and hate Manon.

The opera is set in France during the Regency (1715–23) following the death of Louis XIV. It was a time of general cynicism and immorality, perhaps most clearly demonstrated by Guillot's offhand destruction of Manon out of jealous pique.

The peculiarly French quality of the opera lies in its indirection, restraint and extremely sensitive setting of the words. When Manon decides in Act II to abandon Des Grieux for De Brétigny, she does not, like her Italian sisters, make a grand scene of it; nor, as a German or English girl might, does she consider the right or wrong of it. Rather, she merely quietly and sadly sings "adieu" to the "petite table" at which night after night she sat across from Des Grieux. And the music is allowed to flow out of the rhythm and quality of the words rather than having the words fitted to it. Sometimes, on first hearing, the opera seems talky, but on rehearing it reveals subtle charms which wear as well as or, for many, better than the sentimental *Faust* or flamboyant *Carmen.*

Massenet's first name, Jules, is frequently indicated by its initial because he disliked the name and during his life refused to have it spelt out in announcements or publications.

## PRELUDE (3 min.)

It consists of music from the last three acts: first, the bustle of the Cour la Reine in Act III; then, Des Grieux's characterization of Manon as "sphinx" from Act IV; and finally the music of the guards who take Manon to Le Havre for deportation. It ends on enigmatic chords—as though Massenet, when queried "Manon," shrugged his shoulders.

## ACT I (40 min.; with cuts, usually 30)

The courtyard of an Inn at Amiens. At one side is a summerhouse in which Guillot and De Brétigny are entertaining three actresses.

*Guillot, De Brétigny, Pousette, Javotte and Rosette:* The service is
**quintet** slow, and the men call loudly to the innkeeper. Angrily they conclude he must be dead, "il est mort." The ladies add their voices: "Voyons, monsieur l'hôtelier" (come on, innkeeper). He finally appears followed by waiters.

*Innkeeper and the Guests:* He calls off the menu as the dishes are car-
**sextet** ried past into the summerhouse. The hungry guests exclaim "À table" (let's sit).

A crowd gathers in the yard to watch the coach arrive.

*Villagers, Lescaut, two Guardsmen and Travelers:* The villagers chatter about the coach. Lescaut, who has come to meet his cousin, agrees
**chorus** to join his fellow guardsmen later for a drink. The coach arrives, and as the passengers get out, the villagers laugh at their sore backs, mislaid luggage and short tempers.

*Manon and Lescaut:* She stands looking on the hubbub with astonish-
**aria** ment. Lescaut introduces himself. She explains that it is her first trip: "Je suis encor tout étourdie" (I am still all overcome . . . with the excitement). "Ah, mon cousin, excusez-moi" (my cousin, excuse me), she begs as her eyes wander back to the crowd.

**chorus**    *Villagers and Travelers:* With the coach about to depart, the travelers again dispute over seats and luggage while the villagers laugh at them. (This second chorus is often cut.) After the coach pulls out, Lescaut goes off to find Manon's luggage, and the villagers disperse.

From the summerhouse Guillot spies Manon alone and tries to make an assignation with her, but her friends interrupt and he only has time to whisper that he will hire a coach and send the postboy to her. Lescaut returns, and Guillot retires in confusion.

*Lescaut:* He recognizes the aim of Guillot's attentions and lectures
**aria**    Manon on behavior. But his friends want him for cards, and he hurries the advice: "Ne bronchez pas, soyez gentille" (don't go astray, and be a lady).

*Manon:* She promises to try, but as she waits for him, the sounds from
**arietta**    the summerhouse distract her. Sadly she reminds herself that she is on her way to a convent: "Voyons, Manon, plus de chimères" (come on, Manon, no more dreams). Her envy of the actresses, however, bursts through in a short explosion of desire for a gay life, but then she quickly reminds herself of the convent.

*Des Grieux and Manon:* He enters thinking of his father and home. Then he sees Manon; ecstatically he wonders if she is a dream. He introduces himself and is enchanted by her as she explains that she is a young girl (16), not wicked but, as her family often tells her, too fond
**arietta**    of pleasure. So they are putting her in a convent. "Et c'est là l'histoire de Manon" (and that is there the history of Manon). (These are also the last words Manon says as she dies.)

He insists it shall not be: he will take her away. She grows excited. The postboy announces that a carriage (the one ordered by Guillot) is at her service, and they plan to run off in it.

**duet**    They sing "Nous vivrons à Paris, tous les deux" (we will live in Paris, both of us together). Briefly she wonders if she is doing wrong, but he urges her to come: "Viens." Laughter from the summerhouse stops her, and she thinks how superbly Guillot's actresses were dressed. Again Des Grieux urges "Viens, partons" (come, let us go). They run out to the carriage. (Most productions end Act I here.)

*Lescaut, Guillot, Innkeeper and Villagers:* Lescaut returns to find Manon gone. He accuses Guillot of smudging the Lescaut family honor. The innkeeper reports that Manon left in Guillot's carriage. The villagers snicker, Guillot's friends laugh and Lescaut blusters and rants.

## Vocabulary, Act I

The sign (n) indicates that the preceding syllable is to have a nasal twang.

| | | |
|---|---|---|
| il est mort | eel ay mor | he is dead |
| voyons | vwhy.awhn(n) | come on now (literally, let us see) |
| monsieur l'hôtelier | muh.syuh l'oh.tell.yay | Mr. the hotelkeeper |
| à table | ah tah.ble | let's sit down |
| je suis encor tout étourdie | shje sweez en(n).kor two ay.tour.dee | I am still all overcome |
| ah, mon cousin, ex-cusez-moi | ah mon(n) koo.zan ex.scus.ay.mwa | ah, my cousin, excuse me |
| ne bronchez pas | ne bron(n).shay pah | don't go astray |
| soyez gentille | swhy.eh sjen(n).tee | be a lady |
| voyons, Manon, plus de chimères | ploo de shee.mair.eh | come on now, Manon, no more dreams |
| et c'est la l'histoire de Manon | ay say lah least.twa de Manon | and that there is the story of Manon |
| nous vivrons | new vee.vrons(n) | we will live |
| à Paris | ah Paree | in Paris |
| tous les deux | two lay duh | both together |
| viens | vee.y'ahn(n) | come |
| viens, partons | par.ton(n) | let us go |

## PRELUDE  (2 min.)

It combines the broad, noble theme associated with Des Grieux with a new, pizzicato (*See* Glossary) phrase for Manon, more vapid and empty than her arias of the previous act.

## ACT II  (23 min.)

The apartment of Des Grieux and Manon in the Rue Vivienne, Paris.

*Des Grieux and Manon:* He is at the desk and explains to her, "J'écris à mon père" (I am writing my father). She asks "Vous avez peur" (you have fear)? And he admits it: "Oui, Manon, j'ai très peur" (yes, I have great fear). She suggests they read the letter together. She starts aloud; he follows silently:

"Her name is Manon, and she was sixteen yesterday; in her are joined all beauty, grace and youth; no voice sounds so sweet, no glance **duet**   so full of charm and tenderness." Des Grieux repeats the phrase and Manon exclaims that she knew he loved her, but not so much. "Je t'adore" (I adore you), he bursts out. They continue with the letter. At the end Des Grieux explains he wants to marry her.

He is about to leave to mail the letter when he notices an expensive bouquet and asks where she got it. She lies that someone threw it in the window. Just then an uproar starts outside the door. The maid explains that two guardsmen are forcing their way in. One claims to be a cousin of Manon. The other, she whispers to Manon, is De Brétigny in disguise. As Manon knows, he sent the bouquet.

**quartet** *Lescaut, De Brétigny, Des Grieux and Manon:* Lescaut blusters at Des Grieux, who warns him to speak more softly, "plus doucement." De Brétigny also tries to calm Lescaut. The four work into a quartet in which Manon nearly expires from fear, Des Grieux attends to her, Lescaut threatens and De Brétigny holds him back.

Lescaut finally promises to put "très poliment" (very politely) his question to Des Grieux: "Répondez, oui; repondez, non; voulez-vous épouser Manon" (answer yes or no, do you wish to marry Manon)?

Des Grieux laughs and offers to show Lescaut the letter. Lescaut, in order to leave De Brétigny alone with Manon, takes the letter and Des Grieux over to the window.

De Brétigny tells Manon that Des Grieux's father intends to kidnap his son that very evening in order to end the affair. Lescaut begins to read the letter aloud. Des Grieux interjects that he truly adores Manon. De Brétigny promises Manon that, if she joins him, she will be queen of all Paris. She is confused and dismayed.

Lescaut officiously blesses Manon and Des Grieux; then he and De Brétigny leave, and Des Grieux follows to mail the letter.

*Manon:* De Brétigny's remarks trouble her. She loves Des Grieux, but to be queen of all Paris—fortune, fame! She wonders if the future will be like the past.

**aria** She gazes at the table where dinner for two is set: "Adieu nôtre petite table." It is her farewell to the past, filled with regret, but she will not save Des Grieux from his father.

**arietta, "Le Rêve de Manon"** *Des Grieux:* He returns and tells Manon of a "dream" he had while posting the letter. He saw a cottage by a brook in a wood. It was paradise, or would be if she wanted to make it so.

*Des Grieux and Manon:* There is a knock at the door. He rises to go, and she gasps "Adieu." Des Grieux is astonished: "Comment" (how so)? She clings to him without explaining. Gently he disengages himself and, promising to return, goes to the door.

There is a cry, a struggle, and Manon rushes to the window. "Mon pauvre chevalier," she sobs. (my poor chevalier).

(In some productions De Brétigny enters as his theme surges up in the orchestra just as the curtain falls.)

### Vocabulary, Act II

| | | |
|---|---|---|
| j'écris à mon père | shj'ay.cree ah mawn(n) pair.uh | I am writing to my father |
| vous avez peur | vou'sah.vay purr | you have fear |
| oui, Manon, j'ai très peur | we . . . shj'ay tray purr | yes . . . I have great fear |
| je t'adore | shje t'ah.dor | I adore you |
| plus doucement | ploo doos.eh.mawn(n) | more gently |
| tres poliment | tray pol.ee.mawn(n) | very politely |
| répondez, oui; répondez, non | ray.pawn.day we . . . nawn(n) | reply yes or no |
| voulez-vous épouser Manon | voo.lay.vous ay.poos.ay . . . | do you wish to marry Manon |
| adieu nôtre petite table | ah.d'yuh no.truh peh.tee.tuh tah.bluh | farewell our little table |
| comment | kuh.maw(n) | how's that |
| mon pauvre chevalier | mon(n) po.vruh shuh.vahl.yay | my poor chevalier |

## PRELUDE  (3 min.)

Manon now is living with De Brétigny. Des Grieux has entered the seminary at St. Sulpice. He has not seen Manon since the kidnaping.

## ACT III

### SCENE 1  (31 min.)

On the Cours-la-Reine, Paris. Booths are set up under the trees and vendors with their wares pursue the promenaders. To the right is a pavilion for dancing. (The Cours-la-Reine was a boulevard on the right bank of the Seine where society bowed and nodded, drawing the distinctions dear to it. It was laid out in 1628 by Marie de Medici

(1573–1642) who as the wife of Henry IV introduced Paris to the Florentine custom of driving out in the cool of the evening. The boulevard was lined with horse-chestnut trees imported to France from India by Cardinal Richelieu (1585–1642) and for many years were know in his honor as *cardinals.* The boulevard still exists running down the right bank from the Place de la Concorde to the Grand Palais.)

**chorus** *Vendors and Townspeople:* The vendors advertise their wares and the Parisians extol the Cours-la-Reine as a place of gaiety, food and drink.

*Pousette, Javotte and Rosette:* They flirt with some young men, remarking that Guillot must never discover them. (This is sometimes cut.)

*Lescaut:* The vendors surround him and insist that he choose a present
**aria** for his current love. Lescaut has been winning and declares that he will take everything: "A quoi bon l'économie" (to what good economy)? He interrupts his philosophizing to sing a sentimental ballad about a Rosalinda, then returns to "à quoi bon" and wanders off into the crowd pursued by the vendors.

> Guillot and his three actresses meet, much to their confusion and his indignation. De Brétigny ironically asks Guillot not to take Manon away from him. But Guillot, knowing that De Brétigny refused to hire the ballet of the Opéra to dance for Manon, determines to try, happy to be at work on an intrigue.

*Vendors:* They murmur with excitement as Manon enters. She is now the queen of the Cours.

*Manon:* She coquettishly consents to be admired and impudently de-
**arietta** scribes how she conquers everywhere she goes. The men murmur "bravo." (This aria is really a fanfare for the voice with trumpet accompaniment. It must be sung brilliantly or it is awfully flat.)

**gavotte or fabliau** She then sings a set piece celebrating youth, love and laughter. (The one originally written is a gavotte. For another soprano Massenet wrote a fabliau. The latter is perhaps more showy, the former lovelier.)

De Brétigny is entranced, but his graceful compliments bore Manon and she goes upstage to examine the booths.

> De Brétigny meets the Comte des Grieux, the chevalier's father. The Comte explains that he has come to Paris to hear his son's first sermon at St. Sulpice. He inquires if Manon was his son's

amour and remarks that he can see why De Brétigny was so solicitous for his son's moral welfare. Manon has overheard enough to realize that the Comte is Des Grieux's father. Now she asks De Brétigny to match a bracelet she has found, and he goes off.

*Manon and Comte des Grieux:* She inquires, she explains, for a friend whose love for his son was returned; but they were separated, she says. The Comte suggests poetically that it is best not to ask where the **duet**    summer has gone. But Manon persists: was he unhappy? The Comte replies firmly but not unkindly that his son healed his heart by forgetting: "On oublie" (one, i.e. he, forgets). Manon repeats it sadly, and the Comte withdraws.

Guillot returns with the Opéra ballet, and De Brétigny is staggered. Guillot sends Lescaut to buy drinks for all.

**ballet**    *Divertissement by the Ballet de l'Opéra:* The crowd cheers the ballet, which performs four dances. In the middle of the last, Manon calls for a carriage to take her to St. Sulpice. She admits to the stunned Guillot that she hasn't noticed any of the ballet.

The act ends with the vendors and strollers celebrating the Cours-la-Reine.

## SCENE 2 (22 min.)

The reception room of the St. Sulpice Seminary. The service is just over.

**chorus**    *Congregation:* The women exclaim over the new minister: "Quelle éloquence" (what eloquence). When Des Grieux enters, they devoutly lower their eyes and exit.

*Comte des Grieux and his Son:* The Comte compliments his son on the sermon but wonders kindly whether Des Grieux's decision to enter the church is for the best. An unfortunate affair, he suggests, is not the **arietta**    end of the world. He recommends instead marriage and a family. "Épouse quelque brave fille, digne de nous, digne de toi" (marry some fine girl, worthy of us, worthy of you). But Des Grieux is fixed in his decision. The Comte then promises to send him his inheritance at once.

*Des Grieux:* Alone, Des Grieux thinks of Manon, the memory of whose love will soon be erased by love of God. He urges the memory

**aria**     of her face to leave forever: "Ah! fuyez, douce image" (ah, flee, gentle image). He begs God to purify his soul. Passionately he exorcises the memory of Manon, "Fuyez, loin de moi" (flee, far from me). He leaves to attend a service.

*Manon:* The porter shows her in and goes to summon Des Grieux. In the seminary the choir intones the Magnificat. Manon prays God to forgive her, "pardonnez-moi," and to restore Des Grieux to her.

Des Grieux enters. She admits that she was to blame, "je suis coupable." She pleads with him to remember their love. He is adamant: "Ah perfide, Manon" (perfidious Manon). She weeps. Isn't this my hand, my voice, my love? Remember it. "Tout comme autrefois" (everything as before), she insists. He begins to break down. "Je t'aime" (I love you), she insists. Finally he gives in, and they leave together.

### Vocabulary, Act III Scene 1

| | | |
|---|---|---|
| à quoi bon l'économie | ah qwa bohn(n) lay.kon.no.me.uh | to what good economy |
| bravo | brah.voh | bravo, hurrah |
| on oublie | ohn(n) oo.blee.uh | one forgets |

### Scene 2

| | | |
|---|---|---|
| quelle éloquence | kell ell.oh.kahnce | what eloquence |
| épouse quelque brave fille | ay.poos.uh kell.kuh brah.vuh fee | marry some nice girl |
| digne de nous, digne de toi | deen.yuh de noo . . . twa | worthy of us . . . you |
| ah fuyez, douce image | ah fwee.yay, doos.ee.mahje | ah flee, gentle image |
| fuyez, loin de moi | . . . lwahn(n) de mwa | far from me |
| pardonnez-moi | pahr.dun.nay.mwa | forgive me |
| je suis coupable | shje swee koo.pah.bluh | I am guilty |
| ah perfide, Manon | pair.fee.duh | perfidious Manon |
| tout come autrefois | two kom oh.truh.fwa | all as before |
| je t'aime | shje t'em.uh | I love you |

## ACT IV (23 min.; with usual cuts, 18)

The "Hotel Transylvanie," a gambling house in Paris. Manon and Des Grieux are still together, although he has run through his inheritance.

*Dealers, Players, Guillot's three Actresses and Lescaut:* They set the atmosphere. The dealers call "Faîtes vos jeux, messieurs" (make your **trio** bets, gentlemen); the players call out the amounts; the ac-**arietta** tresses remark on the delights of the Transylvanie; and Lescaut sings to his secret love—the Queen of Spades. (Cuts are sometimes made here.)

*Guillot:* He insists on reciting to his friends a lampoon that he has composed on the Regent. Cautiously he leaves out all the slanderous words, relying on pantomime.

*Manon and Des Grieux:* They enter to considerable commotion. Everyone wants to see the exquisite Manon. Des Grieux is unhappy. She asks **arietta** if he does not love her. Passionately he bursts out: "Manon, sphinx étonnant" (Manon, astounding sphinx). He acknowledges that she lives for pleasure and gold, but still he loves her. Guillot admits to Lescaut that he cannot bear to see Manon prefer Des Grieux.

*Manon, Des Grieux and Lescaut:* She suggests that Des Grieux gamble. The inheritance has run out, and they need money. He is opposed, but **trio** Lescaut reminds him that Manon does not like poverty. He repeats his description of her as a sphinx while Lescaut and Manon urge him on to play. He sits down with Guillot.

*Manon, Pousette, Javotte and Rosette:* They chatter that this is life: "C'est la vie." (Sometimes the gavotte from the Cours-la-Reine scene **aria and trio** is sung here.) Manon leads the ladies in a song celebrating the sound of gold and laughter.

*Lescaut, Des Grieux and Guillot:* Lescaut has lost and stops. Des Grieux has won heavily. Guillot suggests double or nothing, and Des Grieux wins again. Manon is pleased, but Guillot accuses Des Grieux of cheating. All are shocked. Guillot leaves threatening to be heard from again and soon.

*Finale:* The gamblers assure each other that cheating is unheard of at the Hotel Transylvanie.

Suddenly there is a pounding at the door. It is the police. Hurriedly everyone hides the chips and cards, and Lescaut rushes to the roof. Guillot enters with the police and the Comte des Grieux (whose pres-**finale** ence is unexplained). Manon and Des Grieux are arrested. His father refuses to help him, saying that he will be released soon enough. Guillot gleefully orders Manon to the women's prison. Manon nearly faints with fear. She feels it is the end of her gay life. Des

Grieux is overcome at the thought of separation. The crowd urges the young lovers to be spared.

Vocabulary, Act IV

| | | |
|---|---|---|
| faîtes vos jeux, mes- sieurs | fate vo's.yuh | make your bets |
| Manon, sphinx éton- nant | sfanx eh.tone.awhn(n) | sphinx astounding (i.e. inscrutable charm) |
| c'est la vie | say lah vee | this is the life |

## ACT V (22 min.; with cuts, 14)

On the road to Le Havre. Des Grieux has been released, but Manon was sentenced to be deported to Louisiana. Guards are taking her and others from Paris to the boat and will soon pass the spot where Des Grieux and Lescaut await them.

*Des Grieux and Lescaut:* Des Grieux begs Heaven to help him. But when Lescaut enters, he admits that the men he had hired to help him have all deserted. Des Grieux, overwrought, first calls him a liar and then orders him away.

Suddenly they hear singing from down the road. It is the guards with Manon. Lescaut restrains Des Grieux from attacking immediately. He promises to work out something with the guards and persuades Des Grieux to hide behind some large bushes.

*The Guards and Lescaut:* The guards enter slowly. One remarks to the Sergeant that one of the women is sick and about to die. Lescaut bribes the captain to let him talk to his "niece," Manon. The Captain finally agrees and posts a soldier to remain with Lescaut while he and the rest march off. Lescaut leads the soldier aside with war stories.

Manon comes down the road, broken and dying. Des Grieux is over- come. He promises her that she will be free; they will live together. But she has only self-reproach. She adored him, but she was too fickle, un- grateful. She begs his pardon, "pardonnez-moi."

Then almost delirious, she foresees brighter days, but they lead her **duet**      back to the past and she recalls the inn, the little table. Des Grieux insists that they can flee and find happiness, but she knows she is dying. He points out the evening star, "C'est la première étoile" (it is the first star). "Ah! le beau diamant" (ah, a beautiful diamond), she comments. Passionately he tries to recall her to her waning life, but she insists, "Je meurs" (I am dying); "il le faut" (it is necessary, i.e. fated); her last words are those when she first met him: "C'est là l'histoire de Manon Lescaut."

### Vocabulary, Act V

| | | |
|---|---|---|
| pardonnez-moi | pahr.dun.nay.mwa | forgive me |
| c'est la première étoile | say lah prem.y'air ay.twol | it is the first star |
| ah! le beau diamant | le bow dee.ah.mawn | ah, the beautiful diamond |
| je meurs | shje murr | I am dying |
| il le faut | eel luh fow | it is necessary |
| c'est là l'histoire de Manon Lescaut | say lah least.twa | that is the story of Manon Lescaut |

# I PAGLIACCI

Opera in prologue and two acts. First performed at the Teatro dal Verme in Milan on May 21, 1892. Music and libretto by R. Leoncavallo.

### PRINCIPAL CHARACTERS

| | |
|---|---|
| Tonio, the speaker of the Prologue, deformed clown and Taddeo in the play | baritone |
| Canio, head of the traveling troupe, Pagliaccio in the play, and considerably older than Nedda | tenor |
| Nedda, Canio's wife and Colombina in the play | soprano |
| Beppe, another clown and Arlecchino in the play | tenor |
| Silvio, a villager in love with Nedda | baritone |

The action takes place in Calabria, near Montalvo, on the day of the Feast of Assumption, about 1870.

The title means "The Clowns"—plural. Hence, when sobbing to himself, Canio sings, "Ridi Pagliaccio"—singular. Often the title is given as *Pagliacci* without the article. There seems to be no right or wrong, only custom.

The story, in one form or another, is very old and constantly used for discussion of what is real. Even so, Leoncavallo was sued for plagiarism. The suit was almost immediately dropped, but Leoncavallo's defense is interesting. He stated that as a child he had attended the trial of a jealous player who had killed his wife after a performance. In fact, his father had been the judge. The player was convicted, imprisoned and later released.

The "real" world in the opera is represented by the great throbbing tunes, the "play" world by arch minuettes and gavottes. Leoncavallo's switching from one to the other and even melding them is brilliantly done. For example, in the first act the "real" Nedda repulses the "real" Tonio by sarcastically singing music from the play. And the more serious Tonio becomes in the following duet, the more Nedda refuses to treat his proposal seriously until he forces her to a "real" response.

The play itself, entitled "A Comedy," is not particularly clear, and the staging of it is often so cramped that it becomes almost impossible to follow what goes on. In it Colombina (Nedda) sits at home alone. She looks out the window for her lover, Arlecchino (Beppe). Pagliaccio (Canio), her husband, will not return till late that night. Taddeo (Tonio), her goofy servant, has not yet returned with the groceries for the tryst dinner. Arlecchino sings a serenade. Excitedly, Colombina goes to the window, makes sure it's he, and then waits a moment before signaling, in order to compose herself. Taddeo comes with the food. He is madly in love with his mistress and thinks that when he delivers the chicken would be a good time to tell her. She pays no attention but signals Arlecchino, who jumps through the window. He drives out Taddeo, who apologizes for intruding on lovers. The lovers sit down to talk of love but decide to eat first. Arlecchino gives her a vial with sleeping potion for Pagliaccio. Taddeo pops his head in to warn them that Pagliaccio is returning, very angry and looking for weapons.

Arlecchino hastily jumps out the window, telling Colombina to put the drug in Pagliaccio's coffee. Pagliaccio enters in a jealous rage. Columbina explains the table set for two by saying that it was for Taddeo. He backs up her story. At this point in the opera, the play dissolves into reality. The play should end with Colombina, the clever wife, making a fool of her noisy, jealous husband and enjoying her tryst with Arlecchino.

The opera starts with a prologue, which is unusual. It also has a short intermezzo. This latter is usually played after an intermission as the prelude to Act II.

## PROLOGUE (8 min.)

There is a short orchestral introduction (3 min.), and then Tonio puts his head round the curtain: "Si può" (may I)? (At once controversy arises on how to do it: should he be fully costumed, "in character" as the hunchback Tonio? Half costumed? Or is he just a cheeky, poised actor chatting before the curtain goes up?)

He's there, he explains, because the author, liking prologues, put him there. But not to say the actors' tears aren't real; oh no, tonight the story is true, and the audience must know that actors rage and weep like other men. "Andiam" (let's go), he calls into the wings. "Incomminciate" (begin).

## ACT I (41 min.)

On the edge of town. (Although the curtain never falls, structurally the act divides into four scenes of almost equal length: the parade through the town and the announcement of the show; Nedda's rejection of Tonio; Nedda's agreement to flee with Silvio; and Canio's discovery of the lovers and his breakdown.)

## SCENE 1 (12 min.)

**chorus**    *Townspeople:* They push each other, cheer the players and for a while refuse to let Canio speak.

**aria**    *Canio:* "Un grande spettacolo," he announces (a great performance). You'll see the ragings of the jealous Pagliaccio and the foiling of Taddeo's plot. It begins: "A ventitre ore" (at twenty-three hours—i.e. eleven P.M.).

*Townspeople:* They repeat the time and help the players get down from the cart. They invite the men to the tavern for a drink and then laugh at Canio for pushing Tonio away from Nedda. They joke that maybe Tonio would like to make love to Nedda.

**aria** *Canio:* He takes it too seriously: "Un tal gioco, credetemi" (such a joke, believe me). He warns them not to think that because he laughs in the play about Colombina's infidelity, he'd laugh in real life.

**chorus** *Townspeople:* They josh him back into a good humor. The vesper bell rings and everyone goes back to town imitating the bells. Nedda stays behind. Tonio, who is feeding the donkey, also stays.

## SCENE 2 (9 min.)

*Nedda:* She wonders why Canio was upset over the joke. Does he **aria** suspect her? Some geese fly overhead. She envies their freedom—"liberamente" (freely). Nothing hinders them, traps them; they just fly on and on: "E van" (and they fly).

*Nedda and Tonio:* He admires her song. She laughs scornfully. "Non rider, Nedda," he begs (don't laugh). Then he tells her how much he loves her, how everyone jokes about his ugliness, but still he loves **duet** her. Sarcastically she suggests that he save his speech for the play—"stasera" (this evening). He begs her not to laugh.

He gets more forceful and tries to kiss her. She hits him with a whip, and he swears revenge.

## SCENE 3 (12 min.)

*Silvio and Nedda:* He drops over a wall to the back. First he soothes her agitation over Tonio; then he urges her to stay in the village with **duet** him: "rimani" (remain) or, better, they'll flee together— "fuggi con me" (flee with me). She hesitates and he urges her. (Sometimes a small bit here is cut.) Finally he accuses her of not loving him. But she insists that she does. (Tonio, meanwhile, has been watching and gleefully goes to get Canio.)

Silvio starts again to win her over and an extended duet develops. "Tutto scordiam," he urges (let's forget everything). She repeats it and agrees to flee with him that night.

## SCENE 4 (9 min.)

*Canio, Tonio and Nedda:* Canio has heard the end of it and pursues Silvio over the wall. "Bravo," Nedda sneers at Tonio. Canio returns, having lost Silvio in the woods. He demands to know his name: "Il nome" (his name). Nedda refuses. Canio threatens her with a knife, but Beppe holds him back and persuades Nedda to go dress for the play. Tonio insinuatingly whispers to Canio that he'll continue to keep watch. Then he leaves to beat the drum for the show.

**aria**     Left alone, Canio despairs. "Recitar" (to recite . . . my part). He reminds himself: "Tu sei Pagliaccio" (you are Pagliaccio). "Vesti la giubba" (put on your costume) and "Ridi Pagliaccio" (laugh, Pagliaccio)—even though your heart is breaking.

### Vocabulary

#### Prologue

| | | |
|---|---|---|
| si può | see puo | may I |
| andiam | an.d'YAHM | let's go |
| incomminciate | een.ko.min.CHAH.tay | begin |

#### Act I

| | | |
|---|---|---|
| un grande spettacolo | oon gran.deh spet.tah.kol.oh | a great performance |
| a ventitre ore | ah ven.tee.tray oar.ay | at eleven P.M. |
| un tal giocco, credetemi | oon tal jok.oh, creh.det.eh.me | such a joke, believe me |
| liberamente | lee.bear.ah.men.tay | freely |
| e van | eh van | and they fly |
| non rider, Nedda | known ree.dare, Ned.dah | don't laugh, Nedda |
| stasera | stah.SAY.rah | this evening |
| rimani | ree.mahn.knee | remain |
| fuggi con me | food.jee con may | fly with me |
| tutto scordiam | toot.toe score.d'yahm | let's forget everything |
| il nome | eel no.may | his name |
| recitar | ray.chee.tar | to recite |
| tu sei Pagliaccio | two say Pal.yah.choe | you are Pagliaccio |
| vesti la giubba | ves.tee lah ju.bah | put on your costume |
| ridi, Pagliaccio | ree.dee Pal.yah.choe | laugh, Pagliaccio |

## ACT II (26 min.)

The scene is the same, later that evening. The intermezzo (3 min.) introduces the act. (Again, although the curtain does not fall, the act divides structurally into scenes.)

## SCENE 1 (6 min.)

*Townspeople:* They gather for the show. Tonio drums them to their places. Beppe settles arguments about seats and Nedda collects the money. When she gets to Silvio he whispers that he'll be waiting, and she warns him to be careful. (Sometimes this exchange is cut and Beppe collects the money.) The crowd demands "silenzio" (silence) and the show begins.

## SCENE 2 (17 min.)

The comedy unfolds as described before. Carefully Leoncavallo has made Taddeo's confession to Colombina reminiscent of Tonio's to Nedda, and as Canio enters, he hears Colombina's farewell to Arlecchino set to the same words and music as Nedda's farewell to Silvio that afternoon.

Canio forces himself on with the play. Taddeo confirms that the dinner was for him: Colombina cannot lie. The audience's laughter unsettles Canio, who demands the lover's name. Nedda jokes him, **aria** "Pagliaccio." Furiously he breaks out: "No, Pagliaccio non son" (I am not Pagliaccio). I am Canio. I am the fool who cared for you, gave you my name and whose love for you has become a burning passion. He collapses into a chair.

More lyrically and sadly he describes how he believed in her but she turned out to be a serpent.

She tries to continue with the play. He insists on "il nome" (his name). Defiantly she refuses to tell him. He stabs her. She calls for Silvio, who comes up from the crowd. Canio stabs him. Then, stunned, he turns to the audience: "La commedia è finita" (the comedy is finished). (In the original orchestral score Leoncavallo gave this famous last line to Tonio, the baritone, from whose lips it sounds as a ghastly, cynical comment on his night's work and balances with his prologue. Tenors always covet the line, and Caruso is said to have started the tradition of the tenor *speaking* it in a heart-broken voice. The score, however, indicates it should be sung—on eight B naturals, divided by a pause: "La commedia . . . è finita.")

Vocabulary, Act II

| | | |
|---|---|---|
| silenzio | see.len.tsio | silence |
| no, Pagliaccio non son | no Pal.yah.choe non sewn | no, I am not Pagliaccio |
| il nome | eel no.may | his name |
| la commedia è finita | lah koe.may.d'yah eh fee.knee.tah | the comedy is finished |

# MANON LESCAUT

Lyric drama in four acts. First performed at Turin on February 1, 1893. Music by G. Puccini. Libretto by R. Leoncavallo, M. Praga, D. Oliva, L. Illica, G. Giacosa and G. Ricordi, after Abbé Prevost's novel, first published in 1733.

PRINCIPAL CHARACTERS

| | | |
|---|---|---|
| Edmondo, a friend of Des Grieux | tenor | |
| Des Grieux, a student | tenor | day gree.YUH (hard g) |
| Lescaut, a Sergeant of the King's Guards | baritone | less.coe |
| Geronte di Ravoir, a rich old man | bass | jair.ON.te (soft g; nasal "on") |
| Manon Lescaut | soprano | mah.no (nasal "no") |

The action takes place in Amiens, Paris, Le Havre and Louisiana about 1720.

Manon is a young girl, eighteen, impetuous, passionate and giddy; her story is not so much tragic as pathetic. If she'd been only a little older, a little wiser, it might have ended differently.

The libretto is based on a novel by Abbé Prevost (1697–1763), published in 1731 and entitled *The Story of the Chevalier des Grieux and of Manon Lescaut*. The Abbé's story is a Rake's Progress: Des Grieux, a nice enough young aristocrat to start with, in his blind pursuit of Manon, here not much more than a middle-class harlot, sinks steadily from bad taste and poor judgment into debauchery and crime. Puccini changed the emphasis, and Manon became the pro-

PUCCINI

tagonist. The opera turns on her inability to choose, resolutely, between love and luxury.

The Abbé's story, so far, has been used by three composers: Auber wrote his *Manon Lescaut* in 1856; Massenet his *Manon* in 1884; and Puccini this opera in 1893. It is the earliest Puccini opera to survive in the repertory. Massenet's opera is given regularly in France and periodically elsewhere. It is a masterpiece of melody, charm and grace but less passionate than Puccini's.

## ACT I (35 min.)

At Amiens in a square near the Paris Gate. At one side is an inn. The square is filled with students, soldiers and citizens. Edmondo is the leader of the students.

**chorus, aria and chorus**      *Students, Edmondo and Des Grieux:* They laugh about girls and love until Des Grieux, a fellow student, appears. When he doesn't join them, they twit him on being in love. To show his independence, he sings to the girls: "Tra voi, belle, brune e bionde" (among you beautiful girls, brunettes and blondes) . . . which will win me? The students join him.

Manon, her brother Lescaut and Geronte arrive on the coach from Arras. Lescaut is taking Manon, on her parents' orders, to a convent. He is a gambler and has been eyeing Geronte as a rich victim. Geronte has been eyeing Manon as a possible mistress. So the two men have struck up an acquaintance and agree to dine together. They enter the inn with the keeper to arrange for rooms and leave Manon without. *Des Grieux and Manon:* He is struck by her and asks her name. She replies, "Manon Lescaut mi chiamo" (they call me Manon Lescaut).

He is entranced. She explains that her brother is taking her to a convent. Des Grieux insists that she join him in the square later, when it is dark. Hesitantly she agrees and goes to her room.

**aria**    Des Grieux bursts out, "Donna non vidi mai . . ." (I never saw such a lovely girl). Then he rapturously quotes, "Manon Lescaut mi chiamo." The students tease him about Manon, and he stomps off angrily.

*Students, Geronte and Lescaut:* The students flirt with the girls while Lescaut explains to Geronte that Manon will leave in the morning for the convent. Geronte goes to get the innkeeper, and Lescaut wanders over to watch some students playing cards. He soon joins them.

*Geronte and Innkeeper; Edmondo and Des Grieux:* Geronte arranges to have a carriage waiting behind the inn to take a man and girl to Paris. Edmondo overhears the plot and informs Des Grieux. They plan to substitute Des Grieux for Geronte. Lescaut continues at cards.

*Manon and Des Grieux:* She says that she shouldn't have come, but he urged her so passionately. They talk of Paris and the gay life she is **duet**    leaving. Des Grieux gets more personal and finally bursts out that he loves her: "V'amo, v'amo" (I love you). She is more restrained; there is the convent tomorrow.

Lescaut's voice rises at the card game. Quickly Des Grieux explains Geronte's plan to Manon and urges her to go off with him instead. Edmondo urges them to hurry. At first Manon refuses but then agrees, and they go off in Geronte's carriage.

*Geronte, Lescaut and Students:* The old man comes out and asks for Manon. Edmondo points to her disappearing with Des Grieux in the carriage. Geronte is first angry and then philosophical. Lescaut assures him that it is only a matter of time: Des Grieux, a student, will run out of money, and then Manon will be glad to share a palace with Geronte as her "father." The students snicker at the old man's misadventure.

### Vocabulary, Act I

| | | |
|---|---|---|
| tra voi, belle, brune e bionde | trah voy bell.eh broon(eh) eh b'yon.deh | among you beautiful girls, brunettes and blondes |
| Manon Lescaut mi chiamo | . . . me k'YAH.moe | they call me Manon Lescaut |
| donna non vidi mai | dun.ah known vee.dee my | I never saw such a lovely girl |
| v'amo | v'ah.moe | I love you |

## ACT II (38 min.)

In Paris. Manon is now in Geronte's house. She had stayed with Des Grieux in a cottage on the edge of Paris. There Lescaut found them and, as Des Grieux's money began to run out, lured her away with descriptions of Geronte's house, the clothes, the jewels. Manon's apartment is elegantly furnished, her dress exquisite. As the act opens, her hairdresser is preparing her to go out on the Boulevard with Geronte. *Manon and Lescaut:* She cannot decide where to place her beauty patches. Lescaut enters and is struck by her charm. He congratulates himself and her on her escape from the simple cottage—however full of kisses—to Geronte's town house.

Manon interrupts him to ask after Des Grieux. She admits that she **aria** misses him; she left him without a word or a kiss. In an aria beginning "In quelle trine morbide . . ." (in these soft, silk curtains) she confesses a chill now freezes her heart after the warmth of Des Grieux's kisses. The cottage seems like a vision of peace and love.

Lescaut watches her nervously. He admits that he sees Des Grieux; **duet** in fact, he is teaching him to gamble and cheat. Some day, he suggests, Des Grieux will win enough to take her back. Manon hardly hears. She remembers only the old days and wishes love could come again and bring back the past.

**madrigal** *The Levée:* First come the singers, who perform a madrigal Geronte has composed. Manon is bored by it. She gives Lescaut some money to reward the singers, but he pockets it and suggests to them that art is for art's sake. Next a dancing master enters. He is followed by Geronte, who introduces Manon to some of his **minuet** friends. Manon and the dancing master practice a minuet. All the old men admire her and congratulate Geronte. Lescaut worries, however, about her lack of interest. In an aside he decides to ar- **aria** range a visit from Des Grieux and leaves. Manon sings a verse of the minuet. Geronte is eager to show her off on the boulevard and dismisses everyone. He urges Manon to hurry with her toilette. She is left alone.

*Des Grieux and Manon:* "Tu, tu . . ." (you), she cries as he suddenly appears at the door. Then she fears that he doesn't love her anymore: "Non m'ami più" (you no longer love me). It is almost too much for him; "Taci," he cries gruffly (be silent). But she pleads with him: although she betrayed him, her love is constant. "O tentatrice,"

he sobs as he begins to falter (temptress). I'm yours, she insists. He
**duet**  gives up: "Più non posso lottar" (I can resist no more). They
soar off together about eyes, lips, love and forever.

*Geronte, Manon and Des Grieux:* Geronte arrives. He is icily polite
and reproaches Manon for bad manners in betraying him in his own
house. She laughs and thrusts a mirror before his face. Did he expect
her to love those wrinkles? Geronte stiffens. He warns Manon as he
leaves that they will meet again—and soon: "Arrivederci" (till we
meet again).

*Manon and Des Grieux:* She turns to him: "Liberi, liberi" (we're free),
she laughs thoughtlessly. He warns that they must leave at once. She
**aria**  sighs at leaving the jewels, the riches. Bitterly Des Grieux
characterizes her "sempre la stessa" (always the same)—betraying
love for luxury. He despairs of their future, but she promises she will
be true: "lo giuro" (I swear it).

*Manon, Des Grieux and Lescaut:* Lescaut rushes in to warn them that
Geronte has been to the police. Both try to hurry her, but she insists on
collecting her jewels. She delays too long. The police arrive, and before
their eyes she spills the jewels on the floor. Geronte shrugs, and the
police take her away while Lescaut restrains Des Grieux.

### Vocabulary, Act II

| | | |
|---|---|---|
| in quelle trine morbide | een quell.lay tree.nay more.bee.day | in those soft silk curtains |
| tu, tu | two two | you, you |
| non m'ami più | known mah.me p'you | you no longer love me |
| taci | TAH.chee | be silent |
| o tentatrice | oh ten.tah.TREE.chay | oh, temptress |
| piu non posso lottar | p'you known poe-so loh.tar | I can resist no more |
| arrivederci | ah.ree.veh.DAIR.chee | till we meet again |
| liberi, liberi | LEE.bear.ee | free |
| sempre la stessa | sem.pray lah steh.sah | always the same |
| lo giuro | lo JUR.oh | I swear it |

## ACT III (22 min., including the Intermezzo)

Manon is in prison at Le Havre. A court convicted her on charges
pressed by Geronte of being an abandoned woman. The sentence was
deportation to the French possession, Louisiana.

**intermezzo**   An intermezzo (5 min.) precedes the act. (It supposedly represents the trip from Paris to Le Havre, but no one need attempt to imagine the details of the journey. Puccini has an intermezzo probably because Mascagni three years earlier (1890) scored such a success with his intermezzo in *Cavalleria Rusticana* and the form became a fashion.)

At Le Havre just before dawn. To one side is the prison; to the back a wharf and a ship, which at dawn will sail with Manon to Louisiana. (This scene, always known as "The Embarkation Scene," is original with Puccini and does not appear in the Abbé's novel.)

*Lescaut and Des Grieux:* They have followed Manon to Le Havre. Des Grieux is in despair, but Lescaut has bribed a sentinel and has a plan **arietta**   for freeing Manon. In an arietta Des Grieux bewails his ill-starred fate.

*Des Grieux and Manon:* After the guard changes, Lescaut recognizes his friendly sentinel. Manon comes to the window of the prison. She and Des Grieux exchange gasps and sobs. A lamplighter strolls by singing a song. The sky begins to brighten. Des Grieux warns her to be ready for the jail break.

Suddenly a shot, followed by shouts, echoes up the street. Lescaut rushes in calling that the plan has failed. Manon pulls back from the window and then returns to urge Des Grieux to flee. Lescaut pulls him away as a crowd gathers.

*The Sergeant, Manon and Des Grieux:* The abandoned women are led out of prison and lined up. The Sergeant calls out each woman's name and she walks over to the gangplank to the admiring or sneering com-**duet and chorus**   ments of the crowd. Des Grieux manages to get close to Manon, and they sing a mournful duet of love and farewell.

Lescaut tries without success to work up the sympathies of some of the citizens to rescue Manon.

The Sergeant orders all the women aboard ship. Des Grieux holds Manon and threatens anyone who tries to touch her. The Captain of the ship appears, and Des Grieux starts to threaten him.

**aria**   *Des Grieux:* But he realizes that force will not save Manon. Then in the great tenor aria of the opera, "No . . . pazzo son" (no, I am mad), he begs the Captain to take him along as a hired hand, anything; only let him accompany Manon to Louisiana. "Pietà" (have pity). The Captain is touched and gruffly remarks that if Des Grieux wants to help populate Louisiana, he can get aboard.

Vocabulary, Act III

| no, pazzo son | no paht.tso sewn | no, mad am I |
| pietà | p'yay.tah | have pity |

## ACT IV (21 min.)

Manon and Des Grieux are wandering on a desert in Louisiana. The libretto is not specific about the reason, but the Abbé, who is also responsible for the desert in lush Louisiana, explains in his novel that the nephew of the Governor of Louisiana had cast his eye on Manon and that Des Grieux had killed him in a duel. Now Des Grieux and Manon are fleeing to the neighboring English colony. Manon, however, is dying from exhaustion. The act is often cited as Puccini's greatest dramatic blunder, for it has no action at all. Some critics, however, greatly admire the music. The act is a test for the two singers, for its effect rests wholly on the use of their voices.)

*Des Grieux and Manon:* He tries to help her. She utters a little cry, **aria** denies that it was anything, and then faints. Des Grieux pleads, "Vedi . . . rispondi a me" (look at me, answer me).

**duet** Manon revives slowly and they sing a duet. She says, "It really is you," and Des Grieux tells her how much he loves her.

Then she begs him to find some water, and he leaves reluctantly to search for a house or an oasis.

**aria** *Manon:* She knows she is dying. "Non voglio morir" (I don't want to die), she insists passionately, but adds, "Tutto è finito" (all is finished). In her fatigue she begins to have hallucinations of the past. *Manon and Des Grieux:* He rushes back to her, and they talk of their great love. She begs him to remember her. As she dies, her last words are, "Ma l'amor mio . . . non muore" (but my love . . . will never die).

Vocabulary, Act IV

| vedi | VAY.dee | look |
| rispondi a me | ree.SPON.dee ah may | answer me |
| non voglio morir | known voe.l'yo more. rear | I don't want to die |
| tutto è finito | toot.toe eh fin.EE.toe | all is finished |
| ma l'amor mio . . . | mah lah.more mio | but my love will never |
| non muore | known mwore | die |

# LA BOHÈME

Opera in four acts. First performed at Turin on February 1, 1896. Music by G. Puccini. Libretto by L. Illica and G. Giacosa, after H. Murger's novel, *Scènes de la Vie de Bohème,* first published in 1848, from which Murger and T. Barrière had made a play, *La Vie de Bohème.*

### PRINCIPAL CHARACTERS

| | | |
|---|---|---|
| Marcello, a painter | baritone | mar.CHELL.oh |
| Rodolfo, a poet | tenor | row.DOLL.foe |
| Colline, a philosopher | bass | col.LEAN |
| Schaunard, a musician | baritone | show.nar |
| Benoit, the landlord | bass | ben.wah |
| Mimi | soprano | |
| Musetta | soprano | |

The action takes place in Paris in 1830.

The opera is based on a novel by Murger (1822–61), *Scènes de la Vie de Bohème,* which first appeared in 1848 as sketches in a literary magazine. Murger then, with a collaborator, worked the sketches into a play, *La Vie de Bohème,* which had a tremendous success in Paris.

Both the sketches and the play are episodic rather than dramatic, and Puccini's librettists faced a problem in adapting them into an opera libretto. They determined, however, to reproduce the spirit of the sketches and the atmosphere of Paris rather than trying to tell the story of one particular young man and girl. In this they succeeded brilliantly.

*La Bohème* is a masterpiece and popular—in spite of a libretto that displays all the defects held by the public to be typical of opera. The characters are stock—the poet, the musician, etc.; huge chunks of action take place off stage—Rodolfo's jealous attacks on Mimi, her leaving him to live with a rich Vicomte; there is no dramatic development of character; and Mimi's death is wholly adventitious. No matter. Puccini and his librettists caught the spirit of youth, its gaiety and pathos.

But *La Bohème* is unusual in opera. It makes its effect atmospherically in scenes, like a series of impressionist paintings, not by the usual developing dramatic action. It and *La Traviata* are thus poles apart. This different approach was possibly the cause of *La Bohème's* slow success. The technique is not often used. Charpentier, however, succeeded with it in *Louise*—also about Paris.

Puccini knew firsthand of the Bohemian life. At the Milan Conservatory he had three friends, Mascagni, Buzzi-Peccia and Tirandelli. One time the four of them went to visit Ghislanzoni, the librettist of *Aida,* and Tirandelli described it as follows:

". . . Signor Ghislanzoni put us all in one big room with four beds. Mascagni was always up to some trick or other, so as soon as we were in bed and the light out, a shoe came flying through the air! Puccini, not to be outdone, threw two shoes, and Buzzi-Peccia followed suit with the candlestick, and I let fly pieces of the bedroom china until everything in the room nearly was in the air and the cry of all was 'Si salvi chi può' (save himself who can)! We were not out of our teens, you see!"

## ACT I (34 min.

Christmas Eve. A garret shared by the four Bohemians. A large skylight frames the roofs and chimneys of Paris. The furniture is simple—a few books, many packs of cards, two candlesticks.

*Rodolfo and Marcello:* Rodolfo is trying to write an article for a magazine; Marcello is painting a picture of the Red Sea (in the third

act it will hang over the tavern door). Both complain of the cold—
which makes Marcello think of his onetime love, Musetta. In desperation, Marcello suggests burning a chair. Rodolfo suggests instead his
five-act tragedy, which every theater in Paris has rejected.

*Rodolfo, Marcello and Colline:* Colline enters just as they are about
to burn the second act. He is in a bad humor because the pawnshops
are closed. "Atto secondo" (the second act), Rodolfo cries. Colline
cheers up at the sight of the fire. They joke about the love scenes burning blue and warm, the intermissions cold.

*Rodolfo, Marcello, Colline and Schaunard:* Schaunard appears with
fuel, food and money. They all pay mock homage to Louis Phillipe,
"Luigi Filippo," whose image is on the coins. Schaunard tries to tell
how he earned the money. It's a long story about an Englishman, and
no one listens; they fall on the food. But Schaunard stops them: on
Christmas Eve drink at home but eat out. As they are about to have a
toast on it, there is a knock at the door.

*The Four and Benoit:* It is the landlord, who wants the rent. Marcello
shows him the money and gives him a drink. After several more drinks,
they lure the old man into boasting of his extramarital conquests. They
all feign horror and throw the "lecher" out—with the rent still lying on
the table. All leave for the Café Momus except Rodolfo, who stays to
finish the article. Colline trips on the stairs, and there is an offstage
bump and a crash in the orchestra.

*Rodolfo and Mimi:* There is a knock. It is a woman "una donna." Her
candle has gone out and she needs a match. She coughs and half faints
from climbing the stairs. (The libretto never states where she lives. It
is incredible that she should live on the same landing or even in the
same building as the four friends and never have been seen by one of
them, and yet no one climbs to the attic of some neighboring building
to ask for a light. No matter.) Rodolfo is struck by her, revives her
with a little water on the brow, and regretfully sees her on her way.
"Buona sera" (good evening). (Till now the music has been very
quiet. It suddenly boils up as she returns.)

*Rodolfo and Mimi:* She's lost her key. She must have dropped it when
she fainted. In the draft of the door, her candle flickers out. Rodolfo's,
too, goes out. (In the libretto it is accidental, but in most productions
Rodolfo purposely blows it out.) By moonlight they search the floor
for the key. "Cerco" (I am looking). He finds it and puts it in his
pocket.

**Rodolfo's aria**     Both on the floor, he takes her hand. "Che gelida manina" (what a cold little hand). Then he describes himself: "Sono un poeta" (I am a poet). He is poor in money but rich in dreams and hopes. Then he inquires about her.

**Mimi's aria**     She starts, 'Mi chiamano Mimi" (they call me Mimi). She embroiders, makes fake flowers as a hobby and lives alone in an attic (somewhere) that looks out on the sky. (Her tone tells him that it is lonely, but the music broadens and her tone warms as she describes spring's coming to her window.) "Ma quando vien lo sgelo . . ." (but when comes the spring), then a rose she has begins to grow again. Rodolfo is entranced.

Her aria ends as Schaunard, Colline and Marcello call up the stairs **interruption**     to Rodolfo. He promises to be just a minute longer but announces that he is no longer alone and suggests they save two places. "Non son solo; siamo in due" (I am not alone; we are two).

**final duet**     Rodolfo turns back from the door and, gazing at Mimi, declares that he loves her: "O soave fanciulla . . ." (oh lovely young girl). She joins him, and they go out to the Café Momus.

(It is interesting in different productions to watch how the scene is played. The libretto is unclear as to how innocent either Mimi or Rodolfo is at this moment. For example, Rodolfo first insinuates that they should stay in the garret to keep warm; then he asks, "E al ritorno" (after the café)? And Mimi's reply is perfectly equivocal, "Curioso!" Most singers and most audiences like it played pure as the driven snow. But then, what of Musetta and Marcello?)

## Vocabulary, Act I

| | | |
|---|---|---|
| atto secondo | ah.toe say.KON.doe | second act |
| Luigi Filippo | loo.ee.gee fee.leap.oh | Louis Phillipe |
| una donna | oona dun.nah | a girl |
| buona sera | bwahn.ah SAY.rah | good evening |
| cerco | chair.koe | I am looking |
| che gelida manina | kay jell.ee.dah mah.neen.ah | what a cold little hand |
| sono un poeta | so.no oon poe.EH.tah | I am a poet |
| mi chiamano Mimi | me k'yah.mah.no mee.mee | they call me Mimi |
| ma quando vien lo sgelo | ma kwan.doe v'YAYN lo s'JAY.lo | but when comes the spring |
| non son solo | known son solo | I am not alone |
| siamo in due | see.YAH.moe een do.eh | we are two |
| o soave fanciulla | oh SO.AH.veh fahn.CHOOL.ah | oh lovely young girl |

# ACT II (18 min.)

A few minutes later outside the Café Momus. As it is Christmas Eve, the street is crowded with last-minute shoppers, promenaders and children. The shops are lit and festooned. The entire act is one long crowd scene; its only purpose for the plot is to rejoin Musetta and Marcello.

*Crowd Scene:* Amidst all the noise, Schaunard buys a horn, Colline buys a book, and Rodolfo buys Mimi a little hat. Marcello, still thinking of Musetta, stands alone, commenting cynically on the crowd. Mimi and Rodolfo look at a necklace and then join the others at the café.

**arietta**     *Rodolfo:* He introduces Mimi to the others as his Muse. They laugh.

*Parpignol:* He sells toys from a barrow and is always followed by a mob of children. Throughout his scene, the four order dinner. One boy complains loudly that his mother should buy him a little horse.

**aria**     *Mimi:* She shows them her present from Rodolfo, the little hat. All make nice comments about hats and love except Marcello.

*Musetta:* She comes in with a rich old man. Mimi observes that she is well dressed. Rodolfo comments that "angels go naked." Marcello describes her to Mimi as a bird of prey feeding on the hearts of men—which is why he has none.

Musetta, bored with the old man, sets out to cause a scene and get Marcello to take her back. She smashes some plates because they smell of onions, but Marcello remains frosty. Schaunard observes, however, that lovers adore their chains.

**Musetta's waltz**     Musetta than launches into her waltz, in which she sings of her charms. She announces that Marcello loves her still, although he will never admit it. To get rid of the old man, she pretends that her shoe pinches her foot and sends him off to the cobbler with it. She throws herself at Marcello, and he, relenting, catches her.

**military tatoo**     A band passes playing a military tattoo, and everyone goes out. The old man, returning with the shoe, finds that he's been left with the bill.

(How far to go as Musetta is a problem each soprano solves differently. After all, it is Christmas Eve; Musetta undoubtedly has had a few drinks; and she is a lady of easy virtue. The fabulous Ljuba Welitch, however, pushed it so far that one critic thrilled over seeing and hearing at this late date a new Puccini opera, *Musetta,* that rivaled *Salome.* There may be a clue in the fact that before using the waltz in the opera, Puccini used it in a ceremony to launch a battleship.)

## ACT III (24 min.)

February. Near a toll gate on the edge of Paris. Marcello and Musetta are living at the tavern while he paints some murals. His "Red Sea" hangs over the door, and he has painted a Turk and a Zouave on either side of it. Rodolfo has also left the garret and set up elsewhere with Mimi, except that he has just left her after a fight and joined Marcello at the tavern.

*Small Chorus and the Guard:* Dawn comes up slowly. It is snowing. First some street sweepers enter, then some farmers' wives with their vegetables. Occasionally voices, of which Musetta's is the loudest, sound from the tavern. Mimi comes alone, coughing and weak. She asks a woman to get Marcello out of the tavern. (This mood scene is about a quarter of the act.)

**aria**     *Mimi and Marcello:* She begs his help. In aria she tells him that Rodolfo is insanely jealous; that he screams at her to go out and find another lover.

Marcello suggests that they separate, and Mimi agrees that they must. Only that night, she says, Rodolfo left her saying "è finita" (it is **duet**     finished). Marcello promises to speak to Rodolfo for her and is urging her to go home when Rodolfo himself comes out of the tavern. Mimi hides behind a tree.

*Rodolfo, Marcello and Mimi:* Rodolfo asks Marcello to help him leave Mimi. He accuses her of being a flirt. Marcello dismisses that as untrue. "Invan, invan . . ." (in vain), Rodolfo confesses, he tries to smother **aria**     the real reason. Mimi is dying. "Ma ho paura" (but I am afraid). Mimi has "una terribil tosse" (a terrible cough), and he can do nothing for her. He has no money for medicine.

Mimi, overhearing her death sentence, is aghast, and Rodolfo discovers that she's been listening. Marcello hears Musetta laughing in the tavern and runs back in.

**aria**     *Mimi:* "Addio," she says to Rodolfo (good-by). She tells him that she must leave him and go back to her attic and flowers; she will send for her things, but he may keep as a memento the little hat he gave her. "Addio," she repeats and adds, "senza rancor" (without bad feelings).

*Mimi, Rodolfo, Musetta and Marcello:* Rodolfo and Mimi sing "addio"
**quartet** to love, dreams and quarrels. In the middle of it Marcello
and Musetta come out and have a bitter quarrel, in which she calls
him a house painter and a toad. He calls her a viper and a witch. The
sight and sound of it are too much for Mimi and Rodolfo, and they
decide to put off parting till the spring, when the flowers are out. Mimi
hopes that winter will last forever.

### Vocabulary, Act III

| | | |
|---|---|---|
| è finita | eh fee.NEE.tah | it is finished |
| invan, invan | een.vahn | in vain |
| ma ho paura | mah hoe pah.OOR.ah | but I am afraid |
| una terribil tosse | oona tay.ree.bill toss. say | a terrible cough |
| addio | ah.dee.oh | good-by |
| senza rancor | sen.tsah rahn.kor | without bad feelings |

## ACT IV

Sometime later in the spring. Rodolfo and Marcello have rejoined
Schaunard and Colline in the garret. Musetta has another rich old man,
and Mimi is living with a Viscount.

*Rodolfo and Marcello:* They are trying to work, but memories hinder
**duet** them. In a duet (really two asides) each laments his lost love:
for Rodolfo there is no life without Mimi and love, for Marcello it is
more hopeful, as Musetta will probably come back.

*Rodolfo, Marcello, Schaunard and Colline:* Schaunard and Colline
come in with food, and the four of them indulge in some extended
horseplay.

*The Four, Musetta and Mimi:* Musetta bursts in and announces that
Mimi is on the stairs and too exhausted to get up. Rodolfo brings her
in, and they try to make her comfortable on the bed (or chair).
Musetta explains to Marcello that Mimi had left the Viscount and was
found nearly dead in the street. Her one wish was to die with Rodolfo
by her.

Mimi complains that her hands are cold. Musetta goes off to get a
muff, and Marcello takes her earrings to pawn for a doctor.

*Colline:* He gazes fondly at his old coat, which he will sell to raise
**arietta** money for medicine. It had never bowed its back to the

rich and mighty and always had given shelter to poets and philosophers in its roomy pockets. "Addio," he sighs. He and Schaunard go out. (Purists complain that the arietta stops the action and distracts from Mimi and Rodolfo. At one performance the bass' voice gave out, and Caruso, with his back to the audience, sang it for him. No one noticed the difference. This was in Philadelphia.)

*Mimi and Rodolfo:* She tells him that his love was her whole life.

**aria**     Then together they remember how they first met—the candle, the key—and she confesses that she knew he'd found it.

Musetta returns with a muff and Mimi, lead on by Musetta, thinks that it's a present from Rodolfo. Marcello reports that the doctor will come soon. Musetta prays to the Madonna to save Mimi. But she is already dead, and the friends wait for Rodolfo to discover it.

### Vocabulary, Act IV

| addio | ah.dee.oh | good-by |
|---|---|---|

# TOSCA

Opera in three acts. First performed at Rome on January 14, 1900. Music by G. Puccini. Libretto by L. Illica, G. Giacosa and V. Sardou, after Sardou's play, *La Tosca.*

### PRINCIPAL CHARACTERS

| Angelotti | bass | an.jell.AH.tee |
|---|---|---|
| A Sacristan (the priest in charge of the church) | baritone | |
| Mario Cavaradossi, a painter | tenor | kah.vah.rah.DOS.see |
| Floria Tosca, a diva | soprano | |
| Scarpia, Chief of Police | baritone | SCAHR.pee.ah |
| Spoletta, a police agent | tenor | spol.EH.tah |
| A Shepherd Boy | (sings offstage) | |

The action takes place in Rome on June 17, 1800.

The political situation in Italy at the time of the opera is important. Rome in June, 1800, was a Papal State: the Pope was the political head of the city. For a few years after Napoleon's first invasion of Italy (1797–99) Rome had been a republic (1798–99). But when the French Army withdrew (1799), the Pope, aided by the Bourbons of Naples and by Austria, returned. The "republicans" in Rome hoped that Napoleon's second advance down the Italian peninsula (1800) would help them revive the republic and its short-lived reforms. The Church and the lay "conservatives" feared Napoleon and reform and suppressed "republicans" ruthlessly.

The opera is based on Sardou's five-act play, *La Tosca,* which he wrote for Sarah Bernhardt. Mosco Carner described the play as "sex, sadism, religion and art, mixed by 'the hands of a master-chef with the whole dish served on the platter of an important historical event." Bernhardt was particularly good at quick changes of facial expression, and the role of Tosca—with the flares of jealousy, ardor, fury and despair—was cut to order.

Cavaradossi is a "republican" in sympathy, which is why the Sacristan secretly dislikes him. In the play he wears French clothes and sports a goatee, which the Sacristan takes as a visible sign of aetheism.

Angelotti had been a consul of the Roman Republic. As a famous political prisoner, the Pope incarcerated him in the Castel Sant' Angelo, and in the play Scarpia's career hangs on his producing Angelotti.

Tosca is nonpolitical, pulled this way and that by her extreme pietism and her love for Cavaradossi. She began life as a goat girl, a wild savage. Some nuns took her into their convent and raised her. Cimarosa, the composer, heard her sing and arranged an audition before the Pope, who released her from her vows—to the disgust of the nuns. Since then, Tosca has thrilled audiences in Milan, Venice and Naples; at the time of the opera, she is singing at the Argentina in Rome.

The Queen (who does not appear) before whom Tosca sings the off-stage cantata in Act II is Queen Caroline of Naples, a sister of Marie Antoinette. As a friend and ally of the Pope she is visiting Rome.

The battle, which, only because of a famous last-minute decision, Napoleon won over the Austrians, is "Marengo." The first news to reach Rome was that the Austrians had triumphed, and Scarpia et al sing the Te Deum at the end of Act I. The true outcome is learned only in Act II, and then Cavaradossi (rather foolishly) sneers at Scarpia.

## ACT I (47 min.)

The Church of Sant' Andrea della Valle. On the right the Attavanti family chapel. On the left a scaffolding, a large picture covered by a cloth, a painter's brushes and palette, and a basket of food.

*Angelotti:* As the opera begins he has just escaped from the Castel Sant' Angelo and fled to the church. His sister, the Marchesa Attavanti, has hidden clothes for his disguise in the family chapel, which is always kept locked. He searches for the key at the foot of the statue of the Madonna: "Ecco la chiave" (here is the key). He lets himself into the chapel.

*Sacristan:* He shuffles in apologizing to Cavaradossi (whom he imagines is there painting) for not keeping the brushes clean. He has a nervous tic in his shoulder.

*Cavaradossi and Sacristan:* The painter enters and uncovers the picture. It is the Magdalene. The Sacristan recognizes the model as the strange lady, the Marchesa Attavanti, who prayed so devoutly near the chapel. Cavaradossi gazes first at the picture and then at a miniature of Tosca. The Magdalene combines the features of both ladies.

**aria**   He sings, "Recondit(a) armonia" (strange harmony . . . of Tosca's dark and the Marchesa's blonde coloring). The Sacristan grumbles throughout that the painter is irreverent and should be burned by the Inquisition. (Most singers make the Sacristan a purely comic figure and don't or can't suggest his pettiness.)

*Angelotti and Cavaradossi:* Angelotti hears the Sacristan go out and thinks the church is deserted. He stumbles from the chapel and is terrified to discover a man painting. Cavaradossi is equally surprised, but in a moment the men recognize each other and Cavaradossi promises help. Meanwhile, outside, Tosca calls "Mario, Mario." The side door to the church is locked, and she is irritated. Cavaradossi gives Angelotti his basket of food and pushes him back in the chapel. Then he admits Tosca.

*Tosca and Cavaradossi:* The locked door has fired her suspicions, and she accuses him of entertaining a lady. He protests but, only partly mollified, she refuses his embrace until she had made her offering to the Madonna. (The libretto insists that she arrange her flowers on the **aria**   statue "con arte.") Then, feeling better, she starts an aria describing his villa outside of Rome where all the garden scents and night air conspire for love. Her opera that night is short, and after it they can go to the villa. Cavaradossi agrees and, in the hope that she will go, tries to go on with his painting.

At once Tosca is suspicious, and she examines the picture. The face is familiar. "Aspetta, aspetta" (wait), she muses. Finally she recognizes the model: "È l'Attavanti" (it is the Attavanti woman). She accuses him of no longer loving her, of meeting the Marchesa in the chapel. Cavaradossi denies it, and she makes him swear to it: "Giura" (swear).

**duet** Cavaradossi then starts a duet in which he expands on his love for her. At first she is unconvinced but then she joins him.

Finally she leaves. Her parting quip is that he must make the Magdalene's eyes black like hers.

*Cavaradossi and Angelotti:* They plan the escape. Cavaradossi gives Angelotti a key to his villa, "ecco la chiave," and tells him to hide in a secret chamber, which can be reached only through a well in the garden. Suddenly a distant cannon booms. It is the Castel Sant' Angelo announcing the escape of a prisoner—Angelotti. Both men run out through the chapel.

*Sacristan:* He rushes in to twit Cavaradossi on Napoleon's rumored defeat at Marengo because "to grieve an unbeliever will gain me an indulgence." Choristers gather to hear the news. He tells them that there'll be a celebration cantata before the Queen with Tosca singing. Suddenly, in the midst of the hubbub, Scarpia enters with his agents. He knows where to search for Angelotti because he tortured a guard who aided the prisoner's escape.

*Scarpia and Sacristan:* He interrogates the Sacristan, who claims that he knows nothing; meanwhile, the chief agent, Spoletta, finds a fan in the chapel. It has a crest on it which Scarpia recognizes: "La Marchesa Attavanti . . . il suo stemma" (her coat of arms). Then he looks at the picture and links Cavaradossi to the Marchesa and Angelotti. Finally the empty lunch basket is produced, and he surmises that it was for Angelotti.

*Tosca and Scarpia:* She returns to tell Cavaradossi that the cantata will delay their departure for the villa. Scarpia quickly plans to use the fan to arouse her jealousy and thus make her lead him to Cavaradossi and Angelotti. He insinuates that Cavaradossi has been meeting the Marchesa and offers the fan as evidence. He claims he found it on the easel. Tosca looks at the picture, then at the fan: "La corona, lo stemma . . . È l'Attavanti" (her coronet, her arms . . . it is that Attavanti woman). Tosca works herself into a jealous rage, urged on by Scarpia, until finally she swears at the picture. Scarpia feigns shock, "in chiesa" (in church)! "Dio mi perdona" (God will forgive me), Tosca weeps.

*Scarpia:* He sees her politely out and then signals his agents to follow her. Cannon celebrating the victory boom in the background. Her beauty and passion have attracted him. "Va, Tosca," he sings (go . . .), there is room in your heart for Scarpia.

**Te Deum**     The church procession begins. Scarpia sings of his lust for Tosca. Then, as the choristers sing the Te Deum, he admits he'd renounce heaven to satisfy his desires. (The scoring of the Te Deum calls for bells, organ and twelve salutes on the cannon.)

Vocabulary, Act I

| | | |
|---|---|---|
| ecco la chiave | ek.koe la key.AH.veh | here is the key |
| recondita armonia | re.con.dee.t' ahr.moe. nee.ah | strange mixture |
| Mario | mah.ree.oh | Mario |
| aspetta | ah.SPET.ah | wait |
| è l'Attavanti | eh l'ah.tah.VAN.tee | it is the Attavanti woman |
| giura | JUR.rah | swear |
| il suo stemma | eel sue.oh stem.mah | her coat of arms |
| la corona | lah kor.own.ah | the coronet |
| in chiesa | in key.AY.zah | in church |
| Dio mi perdona | dio me pear.doan.ah | God will forgive me |
| va, Tosca | vah . . . | go |

## ACT II (41 min.)

(From the church Tosca, followed by Scarpia's agents, went straight to Cavaradossi's villa and, in a big scene, accused him of betraying her. To convince her otherwise, he finally produced Angelotti. She was overcome, cursed her jealous nature and, after a loving scene, returned to Rome for the command performance of the cantata. After she left, Scarpia's men, who had hid in the garden, broke into the villa and searched for Angelotti.)

This act is set in the Palazzo Farnese in Scarpia's apartment on an upper floor. A table is laid for two; a large window opens on the courtyard. It is night. Scarpia is alone.

*Scarpia:* He thinks of Tosca. On the floor below Queen Caroline is giving a party to celebrate the victory over Napoleon. The cantata has not yet begun. Scarpia sends out a man to bring Tosca up after she has sung. Meanwhile, the strains of a gavotte rise from the party.

**aria**     Alone, Scarpia sings of how he enjoys forcing women; there is no pleasure in love by consent.

*Spoletta and Scarpia:* Spoletta nervously reports that he had followed Tosca from the church to the villa, but that she had soon left to return to Rome. He had been unable to find Angelotti, although he had searched every room. In a rage Scarpia hits him. But he did find Cavaradossi, Spoletta cries, and brought him back in irons.

*Cavaradossi and Scarpia:* The cantata begins as Spoletta brings in Cavaradossi. Scarpia begins the questioning politely but, as Cavaradossi denies everything, begins to threaten. The cantata disturbs him and he slams the window. You fed Angelotti, you hid him, he insists. "Nego" (I deny it), Cavaradossi repeats; "non lo so" (I don't know).

Tosca is brought in. Cavaradossi whispers to her to tell nothing. Then he is led to the torture chamber in the next room.

*Tosca and Scarpia:* He starts off kindly: who was at the villa besides Cavaradossi? "Solo" (he was alone), she insists.

Then Scarpia describes the torture: a steel helmet is put on the head; it has three points, one on each temple and the third on the nape of the neck; at each unanswered question it is screwed tighter.

Tosca agrees to talk, but Cavaradossi calls to her to be silent.

Scarpia starts again. Spoletta holds open the door so she can hear Cavaradossi groan. Scarpia hounds her to speak. "Ah, non posso più" (I can no more), she gasps. But Cavaradossi calls, "No." Suddenly he gives a terrible shriek. She breaks down: "Nel pozzo nel giardino," she reveals (in the well in the garden).

*Tosca, Scarpia and Cavaradossi:* They bring in Cavaradossi, who thinks that he and Tosca have withstood the torture until he hears Scarpia tell Spoletta: "Nel pozzo del giardino. Va, Spoletta." Cavaradossi starts to berate Tosca as Spoletta comes back at once with the news that Napoleon in fact won the battle. "Vittoria, vittoria" (victory), Cavaradossi shouts. He turns on Scarpia, who directs the agents to take him out and hang him.

*Tosca and Scarpia:* Scarpia goes back to his dinner and insinuates that there may be a way to save Cavaradossi. "Quanto" (how much)? Tosca asks. "Il prezzo" (the price).

**aria**    Scarpia laughs. In an aria he explains that it isn't money he wants, but her body. "Mia" (to be mine).

Tosca refuses. He points out that she is free to leave at no cost but a life. She stays, and he tries to kiss her. A drum roll interrupts him. He explains it is the preparation for the hanging.

**Vissi d'arte**     Tosca breaks down. "Vissi d'arte, vissi d'amore," she sings (I have lived for art and love). "Perchè Signor . . ." she sobs (why, Heavenly Father . . .) have you forsaken me?

(This is a big soprano aria and some soar out on it as though it were a concert piece and Scarpia was not in the room. Others sing it brokenly. The latter draws less applause but is more dramatic. Puccini himself never liked the aria because he thought it stopped the action.)

Finally Tosca begs for pity. But Scarpia laughs and Tosca, enraged, again refuses him.

*Spoletta, Scarpia and Tosca:* Spoletta reports that Angelotti took poison and asks if Cavaradossi is to be hung. Scarpia looks at Tosca: "Aspetta," he says (wait). Tosca, broken, nods. But she insists that Cavaradossi be let free at once. Scarpia replies that for form he will have to have an execution, a fake one with a firing squad and blank bullets—as he did for Palmieri: "Simulata . . . come Palmieri" (simulated . . . just like Palmieri). Spoletta understands the bullets will be real; Tosca does not.

*Scarpia and Tosca:* He goes to the desk to write a safe-conduct pass for Tosca and Cavaradossi after the "execution." She sees the fruit knife on the table. He rises: "Tosca, finalmente mia" (finally mine). She stabs him. "Muori, muori, muori, muori" (die). Then, "È morto" (he's dead); "or glip erdono" (now I forgive him). And finally, "E avanti a lui tremava tutta Roma" (and before him trembled all Rome). She pulls the safe-conduct pass from his hand and, since she was raised in a convent, stops to put candles at his head and a crucifix on his chest.

## Vocabulary, Act II

| nego | nay.go | I deny it |
|---|---|---|
| non lo so | known lo so | I don't know |
| solo | so.lo | he was alone |
| non posso più | known poe.so p'you | I can no more |
| nel pozzo | nell poat.tso | in the well |
| nel giardino | nell jar.DEEN.oh | in the garden |
| Va, Spoletta | vah Spol.EH.tah | go, Spoletta |
| vittoria | vee.tor.ee.ah | victory |
| quanto | kwahn.toe | how much |
| il prezzo | eel prets.so | the price |
| mia | me.ah | mine |
| vissi d'arte | vee.see d'art.tay | I have lived for art |
| vissi d'amore | vee.see d'ah.MOR.eh | I have lived for love |

| | | |
|---|---|---|
| perchè Signor | pair.kay seen.yor | why, Heavenly Father (have you forsaken me) |
| aspetta | ah.SPET.ah | wait |
| simulata | see.MOO.lah.tah | simulated |
| come Palmieri | ko.may Palm.ee.air.ee | like for Palmieri |
| finalmente mia | fee.nal.MEN.tay me.ah | finally (you are) mine |
| muori | mwor.ee | die |
| è morto | eh more.toe | he is dead |
| or gli perdono | or lee pair.doe.no | now I forgive him |
| e avanti a lui tremava tutta Roma | eh ah.vahnt ah LOO.ee tray mah.vah TWO. TAH ROM.ah | and before him trembled all Rome |

## ACT III (27 min.)

Later the same night on an open terrace of the Castel Sant' Angelo. To the left, a casemate with a table, bench and stool; to the right, a trap door and steps leading up from below. In the background, the buildings of Rome with the Vatican and St. Peter's.

There is a short prelude followed by a mood scene of dawn over the city.

**aria** *Shepherd Boy:* He sings off stage as he drives his sheep into the city. In the distance, as dawn comes, church bells start to ring. *Jailer and Cavaradossi:* A jailer comes up followed by Cavaradossi. The jailer tells him that he has an hour to live. Cavaradossi refuses to see a priest and instead bribes the jailer for pen and paper to write to Tosca.

*Cavaradossi:* But words fail him as he remembers his happiness with Tosca and the nights of love at the villa. He has never loved her so **aria** much as now when he is about to die. (This is the tenor's great aria. His problem is to make it moving *and* virile. Some tenors turn Cavaradossi into a sniveling sister of the man who cried "vittoria." The aria is always called by its first line, "E lucevan le stelle . . ." [the stars were shining].)

*Tosca and Cavaradossi:* Spoletta brings her up and then leaves. She describes how she killed Scarpia, how he laughed at her, how evil he **aria** was. Cavaradossi wonders that her gentle hands could be the instrument of justice: "O dolci mani" (sweet hands). She tells him of the plan for escape and how he must pretend to be shot: "Simulato" **duet** (simulated). Then they will be free—"Liberi." They get more and more excited—how much they love each other, how lovely life will be—till finally they join in unison and without the orchestra: "Trionfal" (triumphant . . . a new life begins).

*The Execution:* The firing squad enters. Tosca whispers to Cavaradossi to act the part. He refuses the blindfold and is shot. The Captain of the squad raises his pistol to deliver the coup de grâce, but Spoletta waves him away. The soldiers go out slowly. She warns him to stay down a bit longer. Then, the last soldier gone, she tells him to get up, "Presto, su . . . su" (hurry, up . . . up), and discovers that he is dead.

A murmur of voices grows louder. Spoletta cries out that she has killed Scarpia. He comes back to find her. In despair and rage she climbs the parapet, shouting, "O, Scarpia, avanti a Dio" (we'll meet before God), and throws herself off.

### Vocabulary, Act III

| E lucevan le stelle | ay loo.chay.vahn lay stell.ay | and the stars were shining |
|---|---|---|
| oh, dolci mani | oh doll.chee mahn.ee | oh sweet hands |
| simulato | see.MOO.lah.toe | simulated |
| liberi | LEE.bear.ee | free |
| trionfal | tree.on.fa(1) | triumphant |
| presto, su | press.toe sue | hurry, up |
| avanti a Dio | ah.vahnt.ee ah dee.oh | we'll meet before God |

(In no other opera is the slaughter so terrific as here; every leading character is killed on stage and even Angelotti isn't allowed to escape. There is torture, attempted rape and a protracted execution. Most critics agree that the greatest spur to Puccini's genius was sadism. Certainly Verdi, who half considered the libretto, would have written a very different opera. But if the composer enjoyed sadism, what of the audience?)

# MADAMA BUTTERFLY

Opera in three acts. First performed at Brescia, Italy, on May 28, 1904, in a revised version. The original two-act version was performed once at Milan on February 17, 1904. Music by G. Puccini. Libretto by L. Illica and G. Giacosa, after D. Belasco's play from a story by J. L. Long.

## PRINCIPAL CHARACTERS

| | | |
|---|---|---|
| B. F. Pinkerton, Lieutenant in the United States Navy | tenor | |
| Goro, a marriage broker | tenor | GOR.oh |
| Suzuki, Butterfly's maid | mezzo-soprano | sue.ZOO.key |
| Sharpless, United States Consul at Nagasaki | baritone | |
| Madama Butterfly (her family name is Cio-cio-san) | soprano | cho.cho.san |
| The Bonze, Butterfly's uncle | bass | |
| Prince Yamadori, a rich suitor | baritone | yah.mah.DOR.ee |
| Kate, Pinkerton's wife | mezzo-soprano | |
| Butterfly's child | (mute) | |

The action takes place in a house on a hill overlooking Nagasaki in 1904.

Without doubt the greatest operatic fiasco of the century thus far was the première of *Madama Butterfly*. It was presented at La Scala on February 17, 1904. Three of Puccini's recent operas were tremendously popular, the cast was ideal, and the composer was confident that it was his best work. Yet the audience hissed, jeered, booed, whistled and even, it is reported, barked like dogs—and it, or at least most of it, left laughing and pleased with itself.

Clearly the debacle was organized. Even the piano scores of the opera which the publisher, Ricordi, had worked hard to have in every music shop window in Milan the day of the première had all disappeared the next morning. This could only have been accomplished by organized action.

Puccini had enemies among his fellow composers and the critics. Italian operatic life at the time was a vendetta, and there were many on whom each new Puccini success opened yet another sore. Even in far off England the contemporary articles pro and con Puccini today seem unbelievably shrill and un-British.

Probably the names of the organizers will never be known. Such action is not the sort men talk of with pride—especially in view of the opera's subsequent success. Nor is it likely that written documentation of it will ever turn up. Puccini never forgot that night—it was the first of his premières to which he had invited his family.

Puccini immediately withdrew the opera and revised it, and this revised version is the one given everywhere today. He also withdrew

the score of the first version, and his action, together with that of the clique, has made it almost impossible to find a copy of it.

Mosco Carner, a calm and disinterested critic, has carefully compared the two versions and suggests in *Of Men and Music* that the differences, although subtle, are considerable. The first version was in two acts of fifty-five and ninety minutes. The revised version is in three acts of forty-seven, forty-six and thirty-one minutes, or twenty-one minutes less. The original first act had far more atmospheric detail. Butterfly introduced each relative to Pinkerton. He commented on each. Japanese drinks were served. Her drunken uncle, Yokuside, had a scene. As Carner points out, the first act is fairly static without including an ethnographic description of a Nagasaki family wedding. In the other acts Puccini shortened the scenes in which Butterfly makes up for Pinkerton's arrival and prepares for her suicide. He also had Sharpless ask for the child instead of Kate, which had seemed particularly brutal. He added Pinkerton's arietta, "Addio fiorito asil," in Act III. In the original version the "waiting music" joined the present Acts II and III directly, forming an intermezzo with Butterfly, Suzuki and the child as a tableau on the stage. Now the curtain falls, and the "waiting music" is divided between the end of Act II and the beginning of Act III.

The changes were small but apparently sufficient to alter the balance and spacing of the scenes, particularly the first act. The opera in its revised version has, of course, been fantastically successful.

Of all of Puccini's operas *Butterfly* is the most truly tragic. Her death is not a question of disease or circumstance, but choice: she could return to her life as a geisha, marry Prince Yamadori or commit suicide. Puccini and the librettists successfully developed her character throughout the opera so that her decision is not stagy but inevitable and ennobling.

## ACT I (47 min.)

A Japanese house, terrace and garden overlooking the harbor of Nagasaki.

*Goro and Pinkerton:* Goro, the marriage broker, is showing Pinkerton the house. He introduces him to the servants. Suzuki starts a welcoming speech, but Goro sees that Pinkerton is bored and dismisses her. Pinkerton observes that all women talk too much. Goro describes the wedding and Butterfly's family.

*Sharpless and Pinkerton:* The consul arrives out of breath from the climb. He admires the house and view. Pinkerton explains that the lease is for 999 years with the right to cancel on a month's notice. **aria** Then he sings of how as a naval officer he cruises around the world trying to catch a girl in each country, "Dovunque al mondo . . ." (wherever in the world). Sharpless warns him that it is a poor philosophy. Pinkerton, however, continues being pleased with his "Japanese" marriage which, he claims, like the lease, he can cancel on a month's notice. He ends cynically in English: "America for ever."

**duet** Sharpless tries to warn him that Butterfly may not understand, that she is trusting. Pinkerton shrugs: the butterfly's wings may get torn in the chase.

*Butterfly's Entrance:* Goro runs in to announce that she is coming. **solo with chorus** In the distance there is a general hubbub of voices, and then Butterfly's voice is heard saying that there are only a few more steps to climb. Her friends exclaim over the view. Butterfly insists she is the happiest girl in Japan, for she is answering the call of love.

*Butterfly, Pinkerton and Sharpless:* She sees the two men and recognizes Pinkerton. Ceremoniously she kneels before him. Her friends imitate her. He is amused and a little derisive of such politeness. Sharpless interrupts to ask her about her family. They had been rich, she explains, but then she had to earn her living as a geisha. She has no sisters;

her mother is alive. "E vostro padre" (and your father)? Sharpless asks. "Morto" (dead), she replies. Then she makes them guess her age. She is fifteen, "quindici anni."

*Butterfly and Pinkerton:* Goro announces that the official registrar is coming, and the relatives begin to chatter: the bride is pretty; where's the food? Butterfly meanwhile shows Pinkerton her few possessions. One is a sword. Goro whispers to Pinkerton that her father received it from the Mikado with a message. He mimes hara-kiri. She also has some figurines, the souls of her ancestors. Pinkerton bows to them.

**arietta**  In an arietta she explains that to be a good wife to him she has gone secretly to the Mission and been baptized. She throws away the statues.

*The Wedding:* The ceremony is simple. After it, she corrects her friends: she is no longer "Madama Butterfly" but "Madama B. F. Pinkerton." Sharpless and the other officials leave together. The guests toast the couple by singing to a Japanese God: "O Kami, O Kami."

*The Bonze:* Angry cries from the hill interrupt the toasts. The guests are terrified. It is The Bonze, her uncle. He has discovered that Butterfly has gone to the Mission and curses her for renouncing her family and religion—"Rinnegato . . ." (renounced). He takes all the guests and relatives out with him. As they go, they all curse Butterfly for renouncing her religion and people.

*Pinkerton and Butterfly:* She is in tears. Pinkerton consoles her: "Bimba, non piangere" (dearest, don't cry). Butterfly observes, "Sola e rinnegata! Rinnegata e felice" (alone and renounced, renounced and

**duet**  happy)! The two then begin an extended love duet in which Pinkerton gets more and more impassioned—"Vieni, vieni" (come). He urges her towards the house. She sings of the lovely night and stars.

### Vocabulary, Act I

| | | |
|---|---|---|
| dovunque al mondo | doe.vunk qu'al mon.doe | wherever in the world |
| e vostro padre | eh vos.tro pah.dray | and your father |
| morto | MOR.toe | dead |
| quindici anni | kwin.dee.ch'on.knee | fifteen years |
| rinnegato | ree.nay.GAH.toe | renounced |
| bimba | beam.ba | dearest |
| non piangere | known p'yan.jair.eh | don't cry |
| sola e rinnegata | so.lah . . . eh . . . | alone and renounced, |
| rinnegata e felice | fay.LEE.chay | renounced and happy |
| vieni | v'YAY.nee | come |

## ACT II (46 min.)

Inside Butterfly's house. Three years have passed, although when he left, Pinkerton promised to return when the robins rebuilt their nests. *Butterfly and Suzuki:* Suzuki is praying to the Japanese Gods to end Butterfly's unhappiness. Butterfly asks how much money is left, and Suzuki can produce only a few coins. Butterfly announces calmly that soon Pinkerton will come. Suzuki is less sure, and Butterfly grows angry at her. "Tornerà" (he will come)! she states emphatically. She **aria** forces Suzuki to repeat it. Then, because Suzuki has so little faith, she describes to her how it will be: "Un bel dì vedremo . . ." (one fine day we shall see) . . . his ship sail into the harbor . . . I will wait for him here . . . he'll climb the hill . . . I know it will happen.

*Butterfly, Sharpless and Goro:* Goro and Sharpless appear in the garden. Sharpless enters, but Goro stays outside, although within earshot. Butterfly and Sharpless exchange pleasantries, and then he announces that he has a letter from Pinkerton. But she has a question first: when, in America, do robins nest? Sharpless doesn't understand, so she explains Pinkerton's promise. Goro laughs, but Butterfly treats him with contempt. Sharpless is embarrassed and replies that he is not an ornithologist. He tries to return to the letter, but she complains that Goro keeps producing suitors. Goro defends himself by pointing out that she has no money and has been deserted by her relatives.

*Butterfly, Sharpless, Goro and Yamadori:* At this moment, obviously by arrangement with Goro, Yamadori arrives to press his suit. Butterfly is scornful. She is already married. Goro advises her that desertion is a good ground for divorce. She denies that she's been deserted and rejects the Japanese law. She is the wife of an American. Goro whispers to Sharpless that Pinkerton's ship has already been sighted and she'll be even more difficult if she sees him again. Yamadori leaves followed by Goro.

*Sharpless and Butterfly:* He starts again on the letter. Pinkerton asks him "to find that lovely flower of a girl (Butterfly is pleased) and, now that three years have passed (again she's pleased because he's been counting, too), discover if she remembers me—'non mi ramenta più' (remembers me no more)." Butterfly is scandalized. Sharpless continues: "If she still cares for me (overcome, Butterfly kisses the letter), prepare her for the shock . . ." Butterfly does not hear him. She knows only that Pinkerton is coming. She leaps up: "Quando? Presto, presto" (when—quickly, quickly).

Sharpless cannot go on. Instead he asks her what she'd do if Pinkerton never returned. The thought staggers her. She stammers out the two choices: to go back to being a geisha or "meglio, morire" (better, to die). Sharpless urges her to marry Yamadori. She is deeply offended and asks him to leave. Then each apologizes to the other, and to explain her strong feelings, she shows him her son. She admits that Pinkerton does not know of the boy; but when Sharpless tells him, she says, he will come.

**aria**     She sings an aria addressed to the child: do you know what this man has suggested? That I take you with me back to town and become a geisha again. "Morta, morta, mai più danzar" (death, death, but never more dancing), she insists. (The act has two climaxes: the first and above, "Un bel dì vedremo," reveals Butterfly's faith; the second and here, "Che tua madre," her determination.)

Sharpless asks the child's name. She replies, "Today it is 'Dolore' but on Pinkerton's return it will be 'Gioia.' " Sharpless promises to tell Pinkerton and, deeply troubled, leaves. ("Dolore" means grief or sorrow; "gioia" is joy. Tradition in many librettos has insisted on calling the child "Trouble," an unfortunate translation of "dolore" as it suggests, at least to contemporary ears, that the child was a mistake or not wanted.)

*Suzuki, Goro and Butterfly:* Suzuki drags in Goro by the ear and complains that he is spreading rumors that the child's father is unknown. Goro claims that he was only saying that in America a child born under such circumstances would be an outcast. The innuendo infuriates Butterfly, who attacks him with a knife. Goro escapes quickly.

*Suzuki and Butterfly:* A cannon booms. Butterfly gets out the spyglass. It is Pinkerton's ship. He's come back; therefore, he loves her. Her faith has triumphed.

**duet**     She and Suzuki spread the house with flowers—"fiori" (flowers).

Then suddenly she thinks of how she looks. Now she is eighteen, three years older. Suzuki helps her to make up while she chatters of what her relatives will say and of Goro and Yamadori. Finally she puts

on her bridal cloak and places a red poppy in her hair. Then she, Su-
**waiting music**    zuki and the child go to the paper door to watch
and wait for Pinkerton to come up the hill.

(Puccini's stage directions require Butterfly to poke three holes in
the paper door through which they can watch the harbor. In the Metropolitan production of 1957–58, which was staged and designed by two
Japanese gentlemen, this was omitted as being wholly un-Japanese.)

### Vocabulary, Act II

| | | |
|---|---|---|
| tornerà | torn.air.AH | he will come |
| un bel dì vedremo | oon bell dee vay. DRAY.moe | one fine day we'll see him come |
| non mi rammenta più | known me rah.men.tah p'you | remembers me no more |
| quando, presto | kwan.doe  press.toe | when, quickly |
| meglio, morire | MAY.l'yo  more.rear. ay | better, to die |
| morta, morta, mai più danzar | MOR.tah . . . my p'you dance.are | death, never more to dance |
| dolore | doh.lor.ray | sorrow |
| gioia | je.OY.ah | joy |
| fiori | fee.OR.ee | flowers |

## ACT III (31 min.)

The same as before, early the following morning. Butterfly, Suzuki
and the child are in the same positions, waiting.

There is a prelude—part of the waiting music, which reflects Butterfly's thoughts through her vigil—and then from the harbor rises the
sound of sailors' voices.

*Butterfly and Suzuki:* Suzuki awakes with a start. "Verrà, verrà," But-
**arietta**    terfly says confidently (he will come). She carries the child
off to rest singing a lullaby: "Dormi amor mio . . ." (sleep my love).
Suzuki agrees to call her the moment Pinkerton comes.

*Sharpless, Pinkerton and Suzuki:* The men enter. Suzuki is about to
call Butterfly, but they stop her. Then she sees Kate in the garden.
Pinkerton stops in confusion, so Sharpless identifies the lady: "Sua
moglie" (his wife).

**trio**    Sharpless begins a trio in which he says that Kate will care for the child; Suzuki says that she can't urge Butterfly, a mother, to give up the boy; and remorse sweeps over Pinkerton. Sharpless sends Suzuki out to talk to Kate.

**duet**    The men continue. Pinkerton says good-by to the house, which will haunt him always: "Addio fiorita asil" (farewell, home of flowers); Sharpless urges him to go so that Butterfly can hear the truth alone.

*Suzuki, Kate, Butterfly and Sharpless:* Suzuki brings in Kate, who promises to raise the child as her own. At that moment Butterfly runs in looking for Pinkerton. "Dove, dove" (where)? she asks. Then she sees Sharpless and, finally, Kate.

But no one will answer her question. Suzuki weeps. Fearfully Butterfly says: "non ditemi nulla" (no, don't tell me anything). Then she turns to Suzuki: "Vive" (does he live)? Suzuki replies, "Si." "But he won't come any more?" She forces Suzuki to answer: "Mai più" (never more).

Then Butterfly looks at Kate and guesses: "Ah . . . sua moglie . . . tutto è finito" (all is finished).

"Coraggio" (courage), Sharpless urges. "Do you want the child also?" Butterfly asks. "Make the sacrifice for him," Sharpless pleads.

Butterfly is polite to Kate, but distant. She wishes her happiness. Finally she says she will give the child to Pinkerton if he will climb the hill and come for it in half an hour. Sharpless and Kate go out.

Butterfly then drives Suzuki from the room.

*Butterfly:* She gets out the dagger and reads the inscription: "To die with honor when one can no longer live with honor"—"onore."

Suzuki slips the child into the room. Butterfly bursts out passionately, "Tu, tu, piccolo Iddio, amore, amore, mio . . ." (you . . . my little idol . . . my love). For you I'm dying, she sings . . . remember my face. . . .

She blindfolds the child and retires behind a screen, where she kills herself.

(The staging of this last scene varies with each production. Puccini directed Butterfly to give the child an American flag and a doll, kill herself behind the screen, drag herself across the floor to the child and, when Sharpless and Pinkerton burst into the room, with a last feeble gesture point to the child. Others have Butterfly send the child out of the room and die alone. Pinkerton's last cries then come from the hill, and the curtain falis before he gets on stage.)

Vocabulary, Act III

| | | |
|---|---|---|
| verrà | ver.RAH | he will come |
| dormi amor mio | dor.m(e) ah.more me.oh | sleep, my love |
| sua moglie | sue.ah MOE.l'yay | his wife |
| addio fiorita asil | ah.DEE.oh f'yor.ee.t' ah.zeel | farewell, home (asylum) of flowers |
| dove | doe.veh | where |
| non ditemi nulla | known de.tay.me NUL. lah | don't tell me anything |
| vive | VEE.veh | does he live |
| si | see | yes |
| mai più | my p'you | never more |
| tutto è finito | toot.toe eh fee.NEE.toe | all is finished |
| coraggio | ko.rahd.joe | courage |
| onore | own.NOR.eh | honor |
| tu, tu | two | you |
| piccolo Iddio | pick.oh.1(o) id.DEE. oh | little idol |
| amore, amore, mio | ah.more.ay . . . me.oh | my love |

# IL TABARRO

## (The Cloak)

Opera in one act. First performed at New York on December 14, 1918. Music by G. Puccini. Libretto by G. Adami, after D. Gold's *Houppelande.*

### PRINCIPAL CHARACTERS

| | |
|---|---|
| Giorgetta, Michele's wife, 25 years old | soprano |
| Michele, skipper of a barge, 50 years old | baritone |
| Luigi, a stevedore and Giorgetta's lover, 20 years old | tenor |
| Tinca, a stevedore, 35 years old | tenor |
| Talpa, a stevedore, 55 years old | bass |
| La Frugola, Talpa's wife, 50 years old | mezzo-soprano |

The action takes place on a barge moored in the Seine within sight of Nôtre Dame about 1910.

This is the first of three one-act operas that Puccini presented as a single bill, *Il Trittico,* at their premières in 1918; the other two were *Suor Angelica* and *Gianni Schicchi. Il Tabarro* (The Cloak) concerns life on a barge and the search for happiness of the various persons connected with the barge. As the skipper's wife, Giorgetta, complains, "How hard it is to be happy." Her search leads her into being unfaithful to her husband; his into strangling the lover. Neither is an altogether sympathetic character: Giorgetta in her infidelity is unattractive, yet she is trapped and her small dreams are pathetic; Michele's awkward appeals for love are moving, yet his cruelty and frank enjoyment of murder are terrifying. Contrary to his practice, Puccini in this opera is impartial; he favors neither character. He simply presents what happens. This may be one reason the opera is not more popular, but it is also, possibly, one source of its strength.

## A SINGLE ACT (55 min.)

Michele is called "il padrone" by the men, Giorgetta "la padrona." *Giorgetta and Michele:* She takes down the wash. He sits, gazing into the sunset. She suggests that he give the men some wine, as they have worked hard. (Occasionally they can be heard in the background, groaning and straining.) So much concern for the men and, apparently, so little for himself hurts Michele's feelings, and he tries to kiss her. But she turns away.

*Luigi, Giorgetta, Tinca and Talpa:* They have a round of drinks and an organ-grinder appears on the dock. Giorgetta and Tinca dance. He is thrilled to dance with the padrona, but he steps on her foot, and Luigi pushes him aside. He and Giorgetta dance till Talpa suddenly announces that Michele is coming. The men start back to the hold.

*Giorgetta and Michele:* She fixes her hair and questions Michele about their plans. Will they stay another week? How many of the men will work? Michele replies, "all three." She is surprised, as he had not planned to keep on Luigi, the youngest. "I don't want him to starve," Michele explains. (A song peddler followed by some girls is heard, first in the distance and then onstage.) "I treat you well," Michele says to Giorgetta. She agrees but adds that she'd prefer rough handling to his dull silence. Then she asks what bothers him and he replies, "Ma nulla . . . nulla" (why nothing)! The song peddler sings a last chorus and leaves. La Frugola (the frugal woman), Talpa's wife, appears.

*Giorgetta and La Frugola:* While she waits for Talpa to finish, she shows Giorgetta the objects she has found. In another bag she has beef hearts for her cat, "Caporale." She describes him at home purring: "Ron Ron." The men come up. Michele asks Luigi to help load the next day.

*Giorgetta, La Frugola, Tinca, Talpa and Luigi:* La Frugola derides Tinca for drinking too much. Better to drink than stay sober and think, **aria** Tinca replies. Michele goes down into the hold. Luigi then starts an aria defending Tinca: "Hai ben ragione; meglio non pensare . . ." (you have good reasoning; it is better not to think). At the end Tinca, feeling vindicated, leaves for the tavern.

**arietta** La Frugola sings of her dream for life: a little home in the country, husband, "Caporale" the cat, all quietly waiting to die.

**duet** Giorgetta wants to live in the suburb where she was born— "Belleville." Luigi knows it well. She likes the shops, Paris close by, the sidewalks where you can hera your footfall—not like the river.

La Frugola and Talpa go off singing of the little house in the country. Luigi and Giorgetta swear to be true to each other: "E sempre uniti" (always together).

*Michele and Luigi:* Michele is surprised Luigi hasn't gone. Luigi asks to be dropped off at Rouen, where he may be able to find work. Michele urges him to stay in Paris; there is no work at Rouen. Luigi agrees. They say good night, "buona notte." Michele enters the cabin.

**duet** *Giorgetta and Luigi:* He explains that he was trying to get away; he can't bear to be so near her: "È la gioia rapita . . ." (it's a joy seized) with fear. They plan to meet that night. He has on his rope-soled, silent shoes. He asks if she will make the same signal, "Fai lo stesso signale?" She agrees that she will again light a match.

**aria** Luigi sings of his passion. For her he would kill and from the drops of blood he would make her a jewel. He goes.

Giorgetta, alone, remarks, "Come è difficile esser felice" (how hard it is to be happy).

*Michele and Giorgetta:* Michele lights the lanterns and they talk of the number of men they need. Giorgetta suggests that they fire Tinca, as he is always drunk. Michele explains that Tinca's wife is unfaithful and he drinks in order not to kill her. He turns to Giorgetta: "Perchè non m'ami più" (why don't you love me any more)?

Giorgetta says that she does. But it's stuffy in the cabin. He reminds her of how happy they were before the baby died, "nostro bimbo."

She begs him to stop. With her love, he continues, he was secure, warm and happy. He begs her to stay near him: "Resta vicino a me" (remain near me). Come back, he pleads: "Ritorna."

She fobs him off by saying they're older now and goes inside the cabin to bed.

*Michele:* "Sgualdrina," he cries (whore). On the boulevard a couple sing a popular song and say good night. In the distance at a barracks a trumpet sounds.

Michele listens at the cabin. "Nulla" (nothing). He peeks in. She is fully dressed, waiting. He doesn't know for whom. "Chi?" Who has changed her? He goes over the men: Talpa, to old; Tinca, too drunk; Luigi, wanted to leave for Rouen. He wants to crush the unknown, shouting at him "sei tu" (it's you). Finally in despair he collapses. Mechanically he lights his pipe.

At the flicker of the match, Luigi starts for the barge. Michele sees the shadow and is puzzled. Then he recognizes Luigi and grabs him.

*Luigi and Michele:* Luigi at first denies that he loves Giorgetta. But Michele forces him to admit and repeat, "ripeti," that he does— "L'amo" (I love her). Michele strangles him.

*Giorgetta and Michele:* She calls. Michele quickly sits, holding Luigi's body under his cloak. She comes out; she says she is afraid. Wouldn't Michele like her to sit with him. Wrapped in my cloak (tabarro)? he asks. She agrees, quoting his saying that every man's cloak hides joy and sorrow.

Michele rises. "And sometimes a crime," he adds savagely. Luigi's body rolls out at Giorgetta's feet, and Michele forces her down on the corpse.

## Vocabulary

| | | |
|---|---|---|
| il tabarro | eel tah.BAR.row | the cloak |
| il padrone | eel pah.DRO.nay | the boss |
| la padrona | lah pah.DRO.nah | the mistress |
| ma nulla | mah NUL.lah | why nothing |
| Caporale | cap.or.AHL.lay | Corporal (the cat's name) |
| ron, ron | ron | purr |
| hai ben ragione | hi ben ra.JOWN.nay | you're right |
| meglio non pensare | may.l'yo known pen. sahr.ray | it's better not to think |
| Belleville | Bell.veal | (a suburb of Paris) |
| e sempre uniti | eh sem.pray oon.nee. tee | always together |
| buona notte | bwahn.nah NOT.tay | good night |

| | | |
|---|---|---|
| è la gioia rapita | eh lah je.OY.ah rah. PEE.tah | it's a joy seized (with fear) |
| fai lo stesso signale | fie lo steh.so seen.ahl.lay | do you make the same signal |
| come è difficile esser felici | comb(e) eh dee.fee. cheel.ay(e) es.say fay.lee.chay | how hard it is to be happy |
| perchè non m'ami piu | pear.kay known m'ahm. ee p'you | why don't you love me any more |
| nostro bimbo | no.stro beam.bow | our baby |
| resta vicino a me | rest.ah vee.chee.n'(o) ah may | remain near me |
| ritorna | ree.TOR.nah | come back |
| sgualdrina | sgual.DREE.nah | whore |
| chi | key | who |
| sei tu | say two | it's you |
| ripeti | ree.PET.ee | repeat |
| l'amo | l'ah.moe | I love her |

# GIANNI SCHICCHI

Opera in one act. First performed at New York on December 14, 1918. Music by G. Puccini. Libretto by G. Forzano.

### PRINCIPAL CHARACTERS

The Relatives of Buoso Donati (nine in all), of whom the principal are:

| | | |
|---|---|---|
| Zita, the old woman | mezzo-soprano | |
| Rinuccio, Zita's nephew | tenor | ree.NEW.tcheo |
| Simone, the elder gentleman | bass | see.MOAN.nay |
| Gianni Schicchi | baritone | johnny skee.kee |
| Lauretta, Schicchi's daughter | soprano | |
| A Physician from Bologna | bass | |
| A Notary | bass | |

The action takes place in Florence in 1299.

This is the third of three one-act operas Puccini presented as single work, *Il Trittico,* at its première in 1918. They have no intrinsic connection except contrast, and any one can be given independently. *Gianni Schicchi* has been, thus far, the most popular. *Suor Angelica,* the middle one, has had no popular success, even in Italy. Its admirers talk of its mysticism and its great aria, "Senza Mamma." Its detractors complain of its cheap sentiment and monotony; it takes place in a nunnery, and no man's voice is heard throughout. *Il Tabarro,* the first, has had increasing success. It is somber and realistic.

*Gianni Schicchi* is Puccini's only comic opera. It mingles wit with farce and requires of the spectator the ability to look at himself honestly, if just for an hour, and laugh.

Gianni Schicchi, before the opera, was chiefly known because Dante mentioned him in the thirtieth Canto of *The Inferno,* where he appears with a lady named Myrrha. Dante disapproved of them because each pretended to be someone else to gain an end. Myrrha pretended in the dark to be her mother so that she could go to bed with her father. Schicchi pretended to be a rich old man named Buoso Donati and dictated a will in which he left the old man's property to himself. Gianni is short for Giovanni.

## A SINGLE ACT (50 min.)

Buoso Donati's bedroom. He is stretched out on a bed and has only just died.

*The Relatives:* They mumble and sob by the bedside: "I'll cry for days; me for months; me for years. . . ." "Povero Buoso" (poor Buoso). Then one mentions that in Signa, "a Signa," there is a rumor that the old man left everything to some monks. The relatives quickly abandon mourning in order to consider the problem. Simone, who had once been mayor of a suburb, points out that if the will is filed in court, nothing can be done. But if it is in the room. . . . All search for it.

**arietta** *The Will:* Rinuccio finds it. He demands as the price of giving it up that his aunt let him marry Lauretta, Schicchi's daughter. Zita grumbles but agrees, and Rinuccio sends out the boy to find Schicchi and his daughter.

They read the will, and the rumor is true: the monks. "I never thought I really would cry," says one. "We'll be laughed at," worries another, "for thinking we'd be heirs." They laugh bitterly.

Then they wonder if, maybe, they could change it. They appeal to Simone. But Rinuccio interrupts: only Schicchi can help them. All abuse Schicchi: a peasant, a nouveau. Rinuccio doesn't deny any of it but claims that Schicchi is smart and good-natured.

**aria** *Rinuccio:* He sings an aria in praise of Florence, a city to which men of all degree have contributed and which has grown strong and beautiful on the talents of such newcomers as Arnolfo, Giotto and the Medicis. Therefore, they should welcome Gianni Schicchi. At the end of it, Schicchi arrives.

(This aria and "O mio babbino caro," which follows, are the two daubs of sentiment in the opera. Purists object to them as hangovers from Puccini's earlier style and out of place in a swiftly paced opera buffa. Others argue that they are dramatically necessary for a change of pace and to give the audience a chance to collect its wits and catch up with the composer.)

*The Relatives and Schicchi:* Observing the sad faces as he enters, Schicchi remarks that Buoso's health must still be good. But on discovering that Buoso is dead, he urges them to cheer up, as now they have found an inheritance. Zita loses her temper and shrieks the truth at him: they've all been disinherited, and now she'll never let Rinuccio marry Lauretta.

Schicchi explodes with anger: "Brava, la vecchia . . ." (well done, old hag . . . that's the way to behave). This lets loose a babble, through which Rinuccio and Lauretta despair in a duet: "Addio, speranza bella . . ." (farewell, beautiful hope).

Rinuccio insists that they show Schicchi the will. But Schicchi flatly refuses to help that crowd—"Niente, niente" (never).

**aria**     *Lauretta:* She pleads with him. "O mio babbino caro . . ." (oh, my Daddy dear . . . for my sake). She'll just throw herself under the Ponte Vecchio if she can't marry Rinuccio. "Babbo, pietà, pietà" (Daddy, have pity).

(It is just possible that Puccini wrote this with tongue in cheek and wanted it sung with a suggestion of satire. No soprano, however, has been willing to forgo the sentiment.)

*Schicchi:* He hesitates and then refuses. The two lovers again despair, "Addio, speranza bella." But then Schicchi has an idea. He sends Lauretta out to the terrace to feed the birds some crumbs, and then he questions the relatives. Who has been in and out of the room? No one but themselves. Who outside the room knows that Buoso is dead? No one. He has them put the corpse in a closet and orders the ladies to remake the bed. Before he can explain, there is a knock on the door.

*The Doctor:* He has come to check on his patient. He talks with a Bolognese accent because during the Middle Ages the University was famous for its school of medicine. The relatives manage to keep him a good distance from the bed, and Schicchi from behind the curtains imitates the dead man's voice. He tells the doctor he is feeling better and wants to sleep. He suggests that the doctor return that evening, "a stasera" (till this evening). The doctor and the relatives agree, "a stasera," and the doctor departs.

*The Plan:* The masquerade a success, Schicchi then outlines for the **aria** slow-witted relatives his plan. In a long aria (to catlike-tread music) he describes how he will put on the nightcap, pull up the corner of the sheet, lie in Buoso's bed and dictate the will. His voice swells with pride in himself and his plan.

But the excited relatives haggle how the property is to be divided. The three best pieces are "la mula" (the mule), "la casa" (the house) and "i mulini di Signa" (the mills at Signa).

Schicchi suggests that the division be left to him. Suddenly in the ensuing disagreement the town bell tolls the death of someone. It is only the mayor's major-domo. But, frightened by it, all agree that Schicchi shall divide the property. Then one by one each relative manages to whisper a bribe to him in return for being left "la mula," "la casa" and "i mulini di Signa." To each Schicchi replies, "Sta bene" (agreed).

**trio** *The Costuming:* The women then sing a mock lullaby as they dress Schicchi in the bedclothes. He reminds everyone that the penalty for fixing a will or helping to do it is exile and amputation of the right hand. He reminds them again and again throughout the opera by the verse "Addio, Firenze, addio, cielo divino . . ." (good-by, Florence, good-by, heavenly sky . . .).

*Dictating the Will:* The notary and two witnesses enter. Schicchi whimpers that because of a paralysis he can't write himself and must dictate. The notary starts the will off in Latin: "In Dei nomini . . ." Schicchi adds, "revoking all wills heretofore made by me . . ." The relatives exclaim delightedly, "Che previdenza" (what foresight).

Schicchi then directs that his funeral is to cost only two florins. The relatives exclaim, "Che modestia" (what modesty). Schicchi leaves to the monks "cinque lire" (five lira). The relatives are thrilled, "Bravo." Then Schicchi makes, in order, a small bequest to each relative and finally has left to dispose of only "la mula," "la casa" and "i mulini di Signa."

Schicchi starts on the mule and leaves it to Gianni Schicchi. The relatives are incredulous. He leaves the house to Gianni Schicchi. They are furious. Through their suppressed growls of rage he reminds them of exile and no right hand by repeating "Addio, Firenze, addio, cielo divino . . ." Finally he bequeathes to himself "i mulini di Signa" while repeating the warning between each phrase. Then he directs Zita to pay the notary and witnesses out of her own pocket.

As soon as the notary and witnesses are gone, the relatives fall on Schicchi with abuse and revenge themselves by stealing all the silver, candlesticks and valuables. He chases them out and returns to see Rinuccio and Lauretta kissing. Then, as the curtain falls, he steps before it and asks what better use could be made of the money. He explains that his behavior has caused some good people to condemn him to the Inferno, but he hopes the audience, if it has enjoyed the evening, will excuse him, with all deference to "gran padre Dante," for extenuating circumstances.

### Vocabulary

| | | |
|---|---|---|
| povero Buoso | poe.vair.oh Bwoh.so | poor Buoso |
| a Signa | ah seen.ya | (they say) in Signa |
| brava, la vecchia | BRAH.vah la vek.ee.ah | well done, old hag |
| addio, speranza bella | ah.dee.oh spair.an.tsa bell.ah | farewell, beautiful hope |
| niente | nee.ENT.tay | never |
| oh, mio babbino caro | oh me.oh bah.BEEN.oh kar.oh | oh, my Daddy dear |
| babbo, pietà | bah.bo p'yay.tah | Daddy, have pity |
| a stasera | ah stah.SAY.rah | till this evening |
| la mula | lah MOOL.ah | the mule |
| la casa | lah kahs.sah | the house |
| i mulini di Signa | ee mool.ee.nee dee seen.ya | the mills at Signa |
| sta bene | stah bay.nay | agreed |
| addio, Firenze | ah.dee.oh fee.RENTS. ay | good-by, Florence |
| addio, cielo divino | . . . chell.low dee. VEE.no | good-by, heavenly sky |
| che previdenza | kay preh.vee.DEN.tsa | what foresight |
| che modestia | kay mode.DES.tee.ah | what modesty |
| cinque lire | chink.way lee.ray | five lira |
| gran padre Dante | gran pah.dray dahn.tay | old man Dante |

# TURANDOT

Lyric Drama in three acts. First performed at Milan on April 25, 1926. Music by G. Puccini, the last duet and final scene being completed by F. Alfano after Puccini's death. Libretto by G. Adami and R. Simoni, after Gozzi's play, "Turandote."

### PRINCIPAL CHARACTERS

| | | |
|---|---|---|
| Liu, a young slave girl | soprano | lee.oo |
| The Prince, whose name is Calaf | tenor | |
| Timur, his father and dethroned Tartar king | bass | tee.moor |
| Turandot, the Princess | soprano | TOUR.an.dot |
| Ping, the Grand Chancellor | baritone | |
| Pang, the General Purveyor | tenor | |
| Pong, the Chief Cook | tenor | |
| The Emperor | tenor | |

The action takes place in Peking in legendary times.

The opera is based at first remove on a Venetian play. But behind that and even behind Shakespeare's more gentle "Merchant of Venice" is the fairy tale, common to all countries, of the proud princess who slaughters her suitors. She despises men and is the personification of Anatole France's remark that of all the sexual aberrations chastity is the strangest. Always, finally, there comes a man who wins her, answers Turandot's riddles, chooses the casket concealing Portia's portrait and defeats Atalanta in the foot race.

The opera, like the myths and fairy tales, has a dreamlike unreality about it. Scenes of fantastic cruelty alternate with those of irrelevant beauty and comic silliness. None of the characters develops in any sense, and only one is even faintly human. Yet it has a barbaric validity; the sound, the color, the simple emotions are effective—when the opera is theatrically produced. Puccini, for example, sets the first scene "by the walls of the great Violet City: the City of the Celestial Empire. Massive bastions circle the stage. To the right the curve is broken by a high portico covered with sculptured monsters, unicorns, phoenix, and with pillars rising from the backs of huge tortoises.

"Near the portico a heavy bronze gong hangs from two arches.

"From the bastions spears suspend the heads of the unfortunate suitors. To the left three gigantic gates open from the walls. The curtain rises on a glorious sunset. In the distance, bathed in golden light, is Peking."

Obviously, this is easier to enjoy than to create on a stage.

There are two confusions about the opera. The first is how to pronounce the title, the name of the Princess. Properly the accent is strongly on the first syllable and the final "t" is sounded. But this is difficult to sing, and in performance most singers stress the three syllables equally and do not sound the final "t."

The other confusion is where Puccini stopped and Alfano began. Puccini completed all but the last scene (4 min.) and the duet preceding it (11 min.). These Alfano completed, using music sketched for them by Puccini. The break in style, however, is noticeable.

Puccini intended the final duet to be the crown of all his work, a glorification of love as the great ennobling, humanizing experience. One of the intriguing imponderables of opera is whether he could ever have done it, given his psychological make-up and his concept of love as guilt to be expiated by death. In none of his operas is he successful musically in presenting love as a liberating force. Mosco Carner in his biography of Puccini suggests that he could not have done it and points out that he conceived the music for the duet more than two years before his death and was never able to work it out.

## ACT I (35 min.)

A crowd fills the square of the Violet City. It listens, motionless, while a Mandarin reads a decree.

*Mandarin:* The law is that Turandot will be the bride of him who answers the three riddles; he who tries and fails dies. The Prince of Persia has just failed and will be decapitated when the moon rises.

*The Crowd:* It rushes to the palace calling for the executioner. The guards beat the crowd back. An old man falls and is nearly trampled.

*Liu, Timur and the Prince:* A young girl tries to protect the fallen man, and a stranger helps her. He recognizes his father, from whom he's been separated since a fearful battle in which they lost their kingdom. "Padre; mio figlio" (father; my son). Timur, the old man, explains that since the battle, the slave girl, Liu, has cared for him. The Prince asks her why she has been so good, and she replies that once in the old days in the palace the Prince had smiled at her.

*The Crowd:* As it watches the executioner's assistants grind the knife to a sharp edge, its excitement increases and it cries for blood and death. Finally the assistants are satisfied and they carry the knife off while the crowd settles down and softly invokes the moon, "la luna." When it rises, the crowd calls for the executioner, Pu Tin Pao, and the procession for the Prince of Persia, led by children, winds through the square. At the sight of the victim, the crowd's mood suddenly changes. It calls to the Princess, "Principessa," to have mercy, "grazia," and pity, "pietà." But Turandot from her balcony merely waves the procession on. The crowd follows it through the gates.

*Liu, Timur and the Prince:* The Prince is dazzled by the sight of Turandot and announces that he will try the riddles. Timur and Liu beg him to come away. But he insists and is about to hit the gong and present himself when Ping, Pang and Pong, three officers of the court, surround him.

*Ping, Pang and Pong:* They try to dissuade him with reasons: even if he saw Turandot naked—it's just flesh, not good to eat; and better to have two hundred other legs than her mere two, however fine. The Prince interrupts constantly with "lasciatemi passar" (let me pass).

Turandot's maids come out on the balcony and request "silenzio là" (silence there). Turandot is sleeping. Then the shadows of the previous suitors pass across the balcony. Softly they urge the Prince to sound the gong so that they may see Turandot again.

Ping, Pang and Pong try again. They say that Turandot is a phantom. She doesn't exist; only the executioner is real, and at that moment he appears on the wall holding the Prince of Persia's head.

**aria** *Liu:* Timur urges her to stop the Prince. She begs him, "Signore, ascolta. Liu non regge più" (listen, Liu can bear no more).

**aria** *The Prince:* He is kind but unmoved. "Non piangere, Liu" (don't weep). He tells her to take his father away and look after him.

*Liu, Timur, the Prince and Ping, Pang and Pong:* All of them urge him to abandon the idea. The crowd offstage sings quietly of death. The Prince sings of his passion for Turandot. Finally he breaks loose and bangs the gong. Liu and Timur sink in despair. Ping, Pang and Pong run off laughing.

### Vocabulary, Act I

| | | |
|---|---|---|
| padre | PAH.dray | father |
| mio figlio | me.oh FEEL.yo | my son |
| la luna | lah loo.rah | the moon |
| Principessa | prin.chee.PESS.ah | Princess |

| grazia | GRAH.tsee.ah | mercy |
| pietà | p'yay.tah | pity |
| lasciatemi passar | lah.SHAH.tay.mee pass. are | let me pass |
| silenzio là | see.lent.tsee.oh lah | silence there |
| signore, ascolta | seen.yor, ah.SCOLE. tah | signor, listen |
| Liu non regge più | lee.oo known red.jay p'you | Liu can bear no more |
| non piangere, Liu | known p'yahn.jere.ay | don't weep, Liu |

## ACT II (40 min.)

### SCENE 1 (8 min.)

A Pavilion, formed by a huge curtain curiously decorated with fantastic and symbolic figures.

In the privacy of their pavilion Ping, Pang and Pong discuss the situation. As usual, they have lanterns ready for either a wedding or **trio** funeral, but sadly they suspect that it will be the latter. Ping laments for China: "Oh China, where for centuries before Turandot life went on in the old way. Now life is just three bangs on a gong, three riddles, and one head off." They look up the statistics: in the year of the mouse, six; of the dog, eight; and now in the year of the tiger, they're already up to twenty. They're officials of no more than the knife.

**arietta** Ping longs for his little house on its lake of blue, surrounded by bamboo, "bambu." Pang has a garden, Pong forests. They never see them any more, just read sacred scrolls and behead crazy lovers. They remember each one—the one with earrings, the **trio** one dressed in fur. Overcome at the slaughter, they lament for China, "Addio amore, addio razza" (farewell love, farewell laughter).

They dream of the day they can prepare for a wedding with colored lanterns, flowers and serenades and of the night when Turandot surrenders to love when China will have peace again.

But trumpets interrupt their reverie. The trial is about to begin. The pavilion fades into the square in front of the palace, and the crowd gathers.

## SCENE 2 (32 min.)

The square in front of the Palace. An enormous marble staircase rises to a triple arch before which is the Emperor's ivory throne.

*The Crowd:* It comments softly on the officials as they arrive. First are the eight wise men, very tall and pompous: "They have the answers." Then come Ping, Pang and Pong. Incense burns on huge tripods. War flags pass in review. Lastly, through the incense, the Emperor appears like a vision at the top of the stairs. He is very old, tired and sacred.

*The Emperor and the Prince:* Only his oath makes the Emperor continue with the slaughter of suitors. Three times he begs the Prince to retire, but the Prince refuses, beginning each time, "Figlio del cielo" (Son of Heaven). Sadly the Emperor concedes his right to try.

*The Mandarin and the Crowd:* As in the first act, the Mandarin reads the law and the crowd calls quietly for the Princess. Turandot takes her place at the foot of the throne.

*Turandot:* In a long aria she explains her coldness. "In questa reg-**aria** gia . . ." (within this palace) an ancestor, the Princess Louling, had been captured, tortured and finally killed by a man, a Tartar Prince. Passionately Turandot insists, "Mai nessun m'avra" (but no man shall have me).

The crowd calls for the riddles, "enigmi," to begin. Turandot poses them. She addresses the Prince as "Straniero" (stranger).

*First Riddle:* What is that which everyone invokes and implores, which dies every dawn, and which, in the human heart, is reborn every night?

The Prince answers, "La Speranza" (hope). The wise men check their scrolls. The Prince is correct.

*Second Riddle:* What flares like a flame, burns like a fever, grows languorous if idle, grows cold if you die, hot if you love, and is red like a sunset?

The Prince answers, "Il Sangue" (blood). The crowd is now wholly for the Prince. Turandot turns furiously on them.

*Third Riddle:* What is that ice that fires you and yet from that fire harvests ice; the force that wants you free, yet makes you a slave, and in making you a slave, makes you a king?

The Prince answers, "Turandot." The crowd bursts into a hymn of praise.

*Turandot:* She turns to the Emperor. She insists—she begs not to be given to the Prince. The Emperor replies that he is bound by his oath. She rants that she is sacred; she won't go through with it; she taunts the Prince that she will lie in his arms like ice.

*The Prince:* He offers her a riddle. If she can answer it by dawn, she can kill him. His name is unknown. "Dimmi il mio nome" (give me my name). Turandot agrees; she has until dawn. The Emperor wishes the Prince luck, and everyone goes out as the crowd bursts out with the Peking national anthem.

### Vocabulary, Act II

| China | key.nah | China |
|---|---|---|
| bambu | bam.boo | bamboo |
| addio amore | ah.dee.oh ah.more.ray | farewell, love |
| addio razza | ah.dee.oh raht.tsa | farewell, laughter |
| figlio del cielo | feel.yo del chell.oh | Son of Heaven |
| in questa reggia | een ques.tah red.jah | within this palace |
| mai nessun m'avra | mynes.soon m'ah.vrah | but no man shall have me |
| enigmi | eh.nee.me | riddles |
| straniero | strahn.Y'ERE.oh | stranger |
| la speranza | lah spay.rahn.tsa | hope |
| il sangue | eel SAHNG.gway | blood |
| dimmi il mio nome | deem.(ee) eel m'yo no.may | give me my name |

## ACT III (40 min.)

---

### SCENE 1 (36 min.)

In the Palace garden, "very vast and undulating." Between the bushes bronze statues of the gods reflect the dim light cast by incense burners. It is night.

*The Heralds:* In the distance they repeat Turandot's edict, "Nessun dorma" (no one shall sleep) on pain of death until the Prince's name is discovered. All through the city the cry goes out.

**aria** *The Prince:* "Nessun dorma," he exults. Not even Turandot shall sleep, for tonight I shall triumph. "Vincerò" (I shall conquer). *Ping, Pang, Pong and the Crowd:* The three creep out of the bushes. They despair of learning the name. They beg him to save them from torture for failing. They offer him maidens, alluring and seminude. He refuses. They offer riches, jewels. He refuses. They offer to help him win glory—somewhere else. The crowd begs him to flee. He refuses. Pathetically they describe what they'll suffer—the knife, the wheel, the pincers—if he doesn't go. He replies that the whole world may die, but he will have Turandot. Furiously they threaten him.

Soldiers drag in Liu and Timur. The crowd turns on them. They were seen with the Prince. They know his name. The crowd calls for the Princess to begin the torture; she enters and indicates that the old man is to be first. But Liu steps forward; she alone knows the name, "il nome," and she will die before revealing it. The soldiers bind her, twist her arm, but she says nothing. Turandot asks her where she gets the strength to resist.

**aria**     *Liu:* From love, she says proudly. She loves the Prince so much that she will happily die for him. The crowd rages at her, and they torture her more. Finally she breaks down and agrees to speak.

**aria**     She tells Turandot that the Prince will melt her coldness, but that she, Liu, who also loves him, will never see him again. She snatches a soldier's dagger and kills herself. The crowd, balked of the name, is infuriated.

*Timur and the Crowd:* He is overcome at the crime against Liu. And as the crowd realizes the extent of her sacrifice, it is awed and forms a funeral procession for her. They march slowly off stage leaving the Prince and Turandot. (Here Puccini ended and Alfano began.)

*The Prince and Turandot:* He has won; but she remains imperious. Princess of death, of ice, he calls her. Roughly he tears her veil and tries to embrace her. She struggles, but finally he succeeds in kissing her. She feels that her glory is over; nothing but shame remains. She weeps; they are her first tears. She says that he is free to go. His name is unknown, and dawn is about to break. But he, confident in the tears and her trembling, reveals his name, "Calaf." She is triumphant. He insists that he has no life but in her.

## SCENE 2 (4 min.)

Outside the Imperial Palace, with its cold, white marble turning pink with the first streaks of dawn. The Emperor and the court are assembled, waiting for Turandot.

*Turandot:* Quickly she leads in Calaf. Proudly she mounts the stairs and announces to the Emperor that she knows the Prince's name. She turns and gazes at the Prince. "Il suo nome," she starts quietly, "è Amor" (his name is Love). Everyone rejoices. The opera ends.

### Vocabulary, Act III

| | | |
|---|---|---|
| nessun dorma | nes.soon dor.mah | no one shall sleep |
| vincerò | vin.CHAIR.row | I shall conquer |
| il suo nome è Amor | eel sue.oh no.may ay ah.MORE | his name is Love |

# PELLÉAS ET MÉLISANDE

Lyric drama in five acts. First performed at Paris on April 30, 1902. Music by C. A. Debussy. Libretto by Debussy, after the play by M. Maeterlinck first produced in 1892.

### PRINCIPAL CHARACTERS

| | | |
|---|---|---|
| Golaud, grandson of Arkel | baritone | go.low |
| Mélisande | soprano | may.lee.ZAWN.duh |
| Geneviève, daughter of Arkel and mother of Golaud and Pelléas by different husbands | contralto | |
| Arkel, King of Allemonde | bass | |
| Pelléas, half brother of Golaud | tenor | pel.lay.ahs |
| Yniold, son of Golaud by deceased first wife | soprano | EEN.yold |

The place and time of the drama are legendary.

*Pelléas et Mélisande* is a unique opera. Debussy took Maeterlinck's play of five acts and eighteen scenes and, with the exception of four scenes and a few lines, set it to music almost exactly word for word. Such an approach to opera is obviously different from the Italian, which generally rewrites the text to produce a libretto stressing the moments of lyrical effusion and cutting the moments of plot and plain talk. It also differs from Wagner who, writing his own librettos, tailored them exactly to fit the requirements of the music.

Debussy's technique emphasized the drama, and perhaps in no other opera is the word so important. But within the limitations he set himself, he made the music significant, and the opera has survived where the play has not. Because the music accompanies conversation rather than bursting into song, its sound is subtle and minutely varied. It is like a surface of water, nothing in and of itself, yet infinitely varied in color and texture as the light and air change above it. It is extraordinarily expressive and rewarding, but it requires work, for there is nothing obvious to grasp; the listener must read the libretto, not merely a synopsis.

DEBUSSY

The opera recounts how Golaud, a middle-aged man, married Mélisande, a girl he found one day in a forest. As time passed she continued to fascinate him, but he was aware that they had little in common and had failed to establish any real communication or relationship. He saw that his halfbrother Pelléas, considerably younger than he, was likewise charmed by the girl and that between them a bond was growing. Golaud grew jealous. The more he struggled not to know, the more he had to know till, the ultimate debasement, he used his child to spy on his wife and brother. Inevitably one night by a well he found them kissing, and he killed Pelléas. Mélisande died soon after, leaving him with a new child and a question of guilt, but whose, his or hers, he will never know.

The play and opera deliberately stripped from the characters everything that would make them unique rather than universal. They have no specified background of education, religion or culture; they have no dealings with the usual, everyday world. To the extent that characters can exist in a vacuum, these do; they are humans, merely and wholly human, struggling to communicate with each other and to express what they are and feel. This technique allows the drama to be infinitely symbolic, and while a certain number of symbols are clearly set forth in the drama itself, every listener must bring his own and contribute directly to the wealth or poverty of its meaning. There is even a group, small to be sure, that insists that the opera is really about the Partition of Poland, P for Pelléas, Poland, etc.

In the synopsis that follows the words stressed are those which can be most easily heard. Sometimes, but not always, these also stress the symbolic significance of the scene. It cannot be repeated too often that in this opera there is no substitute for reading the text itself.

The scenes are joined by links of music.

## ACT I (32 min.)
___

### SCENE 1 (A forest—11 min.)

*Golaud and Mélisande:* There is a short prelude (2 min.), and then Golaud is seen wandering through the forest. He has wounded a boar, but without purpose, for he has lost its track and himself in the forest. He comes upon Mélisande, weeping by a stream, and tries to comfort her. But she fears him: "Ne me touchez pas" (do not touch me). He asks what she is doing, why she is there, and she replies vaguely, admitting only that she is lost, "Je suis perdue." She has dropped a crown in the water, but she refuses to let him recover it, although it would be easy. She remarks on how gray his hair is. He urges her to come with him, but he cannot say exactly where, for he too is lost: "Je suis perdu aussi." At a distance she follows him. (Possible symbolism: we are all lost in the world and only with difficulty can communicate anything about ourselves to our fellows.)

### MUSICAL LINK (4 min.)

### SCENE 2 (A room in the castle—8 min.)

*Geneviève, Arkel and Pelléas:* Geneviève reads Arkel a letter from Golaud to Pelléas in which he tells of his marriage. He requests Pelléas to talk to their grandfather and, if Arkel approves of the marriage, to put a light in the tower. Then Golaud will return with his bride. Arkel is surprised and disappointed but approves. Pelléas enters and asks permission to visit a dying friend. This Arkel refuses because Pelléas' father also is sick and may not recover. (The man never appears onstage.) (Possible symbolism: Pelléas by an appeal to his best emotions and a duty imposed by society is trapped into staying, and his possible fates converge into one.)

## MUSICAL LINK (3 min.)

### SCENE 3 (The Gardens by the Castle Overlooking the Harbor— 6 min.)

*Mélisande, Geneviève and Pelléas:* Mélisande remarks on the gloom of the forest pressing in on the castle. Geneviève assures her that she will grow used to it. Pelléas joins them, and they watch the ship that brought Golaud and Mélisande depart. It begins to grow dark. Geneviève leaves to look after Yniold; Pelléas helps Mélisande down the path. (Possible symbolism: the departing ship is Mélisande's last chance to escape a fate entwined with Golaud and Pelléas.)

#### Vocabulary, Act I

The sign (n) indicates that the preceding syllable is to have a nasal twang.

| | | |
|---|---|---|
| ne me touchez pas | nuh muh too.shay pah | don't touch me |
| je suis perdue | shje swee pair.doo | I am lost |
| je suis perdu aussi | shje swee pair.doo oh. see | I am lost also |

## ACT II (29 min.)

### SCENE 1 (Near a well in the castle park—7 min.)

*Pelléas and Mélisande:* He has brought her to his favorite spot. The well, he explains, used to cure the blind, "aveugle," but no longer. She tries to see to the bottom, and her hair, longer than her arms, slips down and touches the water's surface. Pelléas asks if she didn't meet Golaud at a well. He wants to know what happened, what they said, and he is pleased when Mélisande murmurs that she did not want to kiss Golaud. She tosses the ring that Golaud gave her in a shaft of sunlight, and it falls in the well. "Elle est perdue" (it is lost), she exclaims. The loss agitates her greatly, and she wonders what to tell Golaud. The truth, "la vérité," Pelléas remarks. (Possible symbolism: hair is a symbol of physical attraction. Pelléas by his questions reveals a subconscious jealousy of Golaud; the loss of the ring reveals Mélisande's subconscious desire to be free of Golaud. The scene is at the "well of the blind" because neither "sees" what is happening.)

## MUSICAL LINK (3 min.)

## SCENE 2 (A room in the castle—12 min.)

*Golaud and Mélisande:* His horse threw him at the moment that the ring fell in the well, and he is in bed. He cannot understand why his horse, like "a blind fool," should have bolted. But he remarks that no harm has been done: "Mais mon coeur est solide" (my heart is solid). Mélisande offers to change the pillow, but he is comfortable. Then she begins to weep and confesses, "Je suis malade ici" (I am sick in this place). She explains that it is not so much being sick as unhappy. He asks who makes her so, mentioning Pelléas by name. But she denies that it is Pelléas or anyone. He comforts her and takes her hand. At once he notices the ring is gone. His agitation unnerves her; she lies that she lost it in a grotto by the sea. He insists she go at once to search for it. If she is afraid, she can ask Pelléas to accompany her. She leaves, weeping, "Je ne suis pas heureuse" (I am not happy).

## MUSICAL LINK (2 min.)

## SCENE 3 (Before a grotto by the sea—5 min.)

*Pelléas and Mélisande:* They have no torch, so at its mouth he describes the grotto to her, its beauties and its dangers. She is terrified. The moon uncovers and reveals three white-haired paupers asleep at the entrance of the grotto. She refuses to go in, and Pelléas promises that they will return another day. (Possible symbolism: there is disagreement over the grotto. To some it represents the only sort of love possible for the two, dark, terrifying, beautiful and inevitably in the end subject to the scrutiny and terrors of the world, the moon and the paupers. It is, of course, significant that neither Pelléas nor Mélisande attempted the impossible: to recover the ring from the well and thereby re-establish Mélisande's old relationship with Golaud.)

### Vocabulary, Act II

| | | |
|---|---|---|
| aveugle | ah.VER.gluh | blind |
| elle est perdue | ell ay PAIR.doo | it is lost |
| la vérité | lah ver.ee.tay | the truth |
| mais mon coeur est solide | may mon(n) ker ay so.lee.duh | my heart is solid |
| je suis malade ici | shje swee ma.lahd ee.cee | I am sick here |
| je ne suis pas heureuse | shje ne swee pah err.erse | I am not happy |

## ACT III (34 min.)

---

### SCENE 1 (A tower of the castle with a window above a path—12 min.)

*Mélisande, Pelléas and Golaud:* She sings a song at the window as she combs her hair. Pelléas enters, tells her that he is leaving in the morning and begs her to let him kiss her hand, "donne, donne, donne" (give . . . it). She consents, but only if he promises not to leave the next day. As she leans out, her hair spills over his face and shoulders. Rapturously he kisses it and declares his love for her. The time, the place and his passion make her nervous: "Laisse-moi, laisse-moi" (leave me). Some doves fly out of the tower, and she urges him to go or they will never return. Then she hears a step: "C'est Golaud" (it is Golaud). She cannot pull back, for her hair has caught in the vine, and he comes upon them. "Quels enfants" (what children), he laughs nervously, but takes Pelléas off with him. (Possible symbolism: it is her hair that arouses Pelléas to speak out and that traps her in spite of herself. The doves that can never return represent her innocence. At the grotto her hesitation was instinctive, but from this moment she recognizes what is happening.)

### MUSICAL LINK (3 min.)

### SCENE 2 (The vaults of the castle—2 min.)

*Golaud and Pelléas:* Golaud leads Pelléas down to the cisterns of the castle. Pelléas has visited them only once, long ago. Golaud points to the stagnating water and remarks on the smell of death. Pelléas gasps for fresh air, and they go out. (Possible symbolism: Golaud, reflecting a subconscious wish, shows Pelléas death. Some baritones make it more explicit by almost pushing Pelléas in.)

### MUSICAL LINK (1 min.)

### SCENE 3 (A terrace at the entrance to the vaults—4 min.)

*Pelléas and Golaud:* Pelléas breathes again and rejoices in the green leaves and sea air; in the distance he sees Geneviève and Mélisande. Golaud warns him that he heard everything the two said at the tower window; he advises Pelléas that Mélisande is pregnant and suggests that he avoid her as much as possible.

## MUSICAL LINK (1 min.)

## SCENE 4 (Under Mélisande's window at the tower—11 min.)

*Golaud and Yniold:* Golaud questions his son about Mélisande and Pelléas. What do they do when together? They argue, replies Yniold (he calls his father "petit-père"), as to whether the door should be open or shut. Golaud in his frustration twists Yniold's arm, and the boy weeps. Golaud, promising him a bow and arrow, asks what else they talk of. Yniold says of himself, how tall he'll grow someday and how he'll resemble his father. Do they ever kiss? Golaud presses. Once, when it rained, Yniold answers. Golaud is not satisfied. How? Yniold kisses his father on the mouth and laughs at his prickly, gray beard. Golaud insists, "Je crois que Pelléas est fou" (I believe Pelléas is mad), but the boy denies it. A light shines from Mélisande's window, and Golaud, lifting the child, asks what he can see. Uncle Pelléas and Mélisande, reports Yniold, sitting, just sitting, with their eyes open. Insistently Golaud asks what they do; do they come closer to each other? As Yniold begs to be put down, his father insists: "Regarde" (look). But Yniold in tears drops to the ground, and Golaud knows nothing. (Possible symbolism: for Golaud it would be easier to believe that Pelléas was mad and therefore not responsible for his actions. The worst is to have him responsible but the actions unknown.)

### Vocabulary, Act III

| | | |
|---|---|---|
| donne | dun.uh | give |
| laisse-moi | layss.mwa | leave me |
| c'est Golaud | say go.low | it is Golaud |
| quels enfants | kells en(n)fawn(n) | what children |
| petit-père | puh.tee PAIR.uh | little father |
| je crois que Pelléas est fou | shje crwa kuh...eh foo | I believe that Pelleas is mad |
| regarde | re.GAHR.duh | look |

## ACT IV (38 min.)

### SCENE 1 (A room in the castle—16 min.)

*Pelléas, Mélisande, Arkel and Golaud:* Pelléas has just seen his father, who has recovered sufficiently for Pelléas to depart. As he will leave in the morning, he begs Mélisande to meet him that night at the well. She consents. Arkel enters and rejoices at the return of health and happiness to the castle. He assures Mélisande that life will be happier now for all. Golaud enters with blood on his brow. He explains he has passed through a hedge of thorns. When she offers to wipe the blood away, he remarks that he does not want her to touch him. Sardonically he comments on her eyes, so proud of her beauty. Arkel sees only "une grande innocence" (a great innocence). Golaud repeats it contemptuously. He knows more of the secrets concealed in the other world than of those in her eyes. His anger against her builds till he rages that her flesh disgusts him. Seizing her hair, he pulls her on her knees "à droite, à gauche" (to the right, to the left). Arkel stops him, and Golaud, assuming a calm, says that he is too old to care, "je suis trop vieux," and will leave the rest to chance and custom. After he goes out, Arkel asks Mélisande if Golaud was drunk: "Il est ivre?" Mélisande weeps that he no longer loves her and adds, "je ne suis pas heureuse." (Possible symbolism: Golaud's fixation on her hair reveals that her flesh does not disgust him. His remarks about chance and custom mean that rather than assume personal responsibility for killing Pelléas, he will blame it on society which "demands" it in such circumstances. Arkel would like to believe that Golaud is drunk, for then he would not be responsible for his actions. Arkel's blindness is partly willful. The ultimate tragedy becomes certain as all refuse to "see" what is happening.)

### MUSICAL LINK (4 min.)

### SCENE 2 (A terrace in the twilight—3 min.)

(This scene is sometimes cut.) *Yniold:* He has lost his ball under a stone which he cannot move. A flock of sheep pass in the distance, bleating loudly. Suddenly they stop. Yniold calls to the shepherd and asks why they are silent. The shepherd (from offstage) explains that they have taken the road leading away from the fold. Yniold, who cannot imagine where the sheep will spend the night, runs off to tell someone about it. (Possible symbolism: the sheep are going to the slaughter house, and "all we, like sheep, have gone astray. . . .")

## MUSICAL LINK (1 min.)

## SCENE 3 (At the well in the park—14 min.)

*Pelléas and Mélisande:* He enters alone. He recognizes now that he loves her and wonders if he should leave alone without seeing her. But this will be the first time he has really seen her, fully aware of his love. She enters. Everything has contrived to make her late: Golaud had a nightmare, and her dress caught on the door. At first obliquely, then directly, they admit they love each other: "Je t'aime" and "Je t'aime aussi." He rhapsodizes over her beauty; she, with more foresight, has a touch of sadness. At the castle the doors clang shut for the night: "On ferme les portes" (they shut the doors). "Il est trop tard" (it is too late), Pelléas gasps. "Tant mieux" (so much the better), Mélisande responds. They embrace. Mélisande detects a figure in the bushes: it is Golaud with his sword. Pelléas urges her to flee, but she refuses. He'll kill us, Pelléas warns. "Tant mieux," she repeats. They kiss passionately. Golaud kills Pelléas, and Mélisande, bewailing her cowardice, flees. (The opera in general and this scene in particular are the French equivalent of *Tristan und Isolde,* in the second act of which King Mark surprises his wife with his nephew. Those who think they can certainly will expound on the national characteristics exhibited by Debussy and Wagner in handling the scene.)

### Vocabulary, Act IV

| | | |
|---|---|---|
| une grande innocence | oon grand in.oh. sonse(n) | a great innocence |
| à droite | ah drwhat | to the right |
| à gauche | ah gohsh | to the left |
| je suis trop vieux | shje swee troe v'yuh | I am too old |
| il est ivre | eel ay t'ee.vruh | he is drunk |
| je ne suis pas heureuse | shje ne swee pah err. erse | I am not happy |
| je t'aime | shje t'em.uh | I love you |
| je t'aime aussi | shje t'em.uh oh.see | I love you also |
| on ferme les portes | on(n) fairm lay por. tuh | they close the doors |
| il est trop tard | eel ay troe tahr | it is too late |
| tant mieux | tahn(n) m'yuh | so much the better |

ACT V (A room in the castle—26 min.)

*Physician, Arkel, Golaud and Mélisande:* After giving birth to her child, Mélisande now is dying. In his madness Golaud had wounded her slightly, but the physician assures him that he did not cause her death. Arkel observes that her soul seems to be forever cold. Golaud, however, first blames himself and then insists, "Je l'ai fait malgré moi" (I did it in spite of myself). Mélisande wakes and asks to have the window opened. The sun is sinking. Golaud asks to be alone with her. First he begs her pardon, which she quickly grants, remarking that there is nothing to forgive. Pleading that he will soon die, he asks if she loved Pelléas. Yes, "oui." With a guilty love? She denies it. But he cannot believe she understood the question. Again, this time saying that she is about to die, he begs her to tell the truth. But Mélisande passes over the question to a fact; she did not know she was going to die. "Vite, vite, la vérité, la vérité" (quick, the truth), Golaud pleads, using the same inadequate words as Pelléas when he urged her to tell the truth about the loss of the ring. "La vérité," she repeats. Golaud realizes he will never know; he will die blind, "comme un aveugle" (like a blindman). Arkel and the physician hurry in and reprove Golaud for killing her. She asks if it is true that winter is coming, and they try to distract her with the baby. Servants, as was the custom in Allemonde at a death, enter and line the wall, waiting. Golaud asks again to be alone with her, but this time Arkel refuses. In despair Golaud breaks out, "Ce n'est pas ma faute, ce n'est pas ma faute" (it is not my fault). Arkel orders him to be silent, and the servants suddenly fall on their knees. Mélisande has died. Arkel lifts the baby and, taking it and Golaud from the room, remarks that it is now the turn of the unfortunate little girl, "de la pauvre petite." (Literal minded persons frequently are bothered by Mélisande's vague answers to Golaud's questions, which seem so clear. Of course, the questions are not really clear at all. What is a guilty love? Quick! Only the church or society has a ready answer; the human heart does not. Golaud, with only inadequate words at hand, phrases the questions so that they cannot begin to encompass the events that have happened. Inevitably the answers are fragmentary and unsatisfactory. Thus any stage director who has Arkel, the physician, or the servants make the sign of the cross as Mélisande dies misunderstands Maeterlinck's purpose and suggests, quite incorrectly, a particular set of standards by which the events and motives of the characters are to be judged and the questions answered.)

### Vocabulary, Act V

| je l'ai fait malgré moi | shje lay fay mahl.gray mwa | I did it in spite of myself |
| vite, vite, la vérité | veet.uh . . . lah ver. ee.tay | quick, the truth |
| ce n'est pas ma faute | suh nay pah ma foe.tuh | it is not my fault |
| de la pauvre petite | de lah poh.vruh peh. teet.uh | of the unfortunate little one |

## CAVALLERIA RUSTICANA

Melodrama in one act. First performed at the Teatro Constanzi in Rome on May 17, 1890. Music by P. Mascagni. Libretto by G. Menasci and G. Targioni-Tozzetti, after the short story and play by G. Verga.

### PRINCIPAL CHARACTERS

| Santuzza | soprano | san.TOOT.tsa |
| Mamma Lucia, Turiddu's mother | contralto | |
| Alfio, a carter | baritone | |
| Turiddu | tenor | tour.REE.do |
| Lola | mezzo-soprano | |

The action takes place in a Sicilian village on Easter morning about 1880.

The fact everybody knows about *Cavalleria* is that it won a competition. In 1888 an Italian publishing house offered a prize for the best one-act opera. There were seventy-three entries, and *Cavalleria,* which Mascagni had composed in eight days, won. It was his first opera to be produced. He was only twenty-one, and although he composed fourteen more, he never improved on his first success.

The opera is a burst of passion. It runs just over an hour and yet unfolds its story without hurry or confusion. There is even time for Mascagni, in order to build color and atmosphere, to insert four choruses and the famous intermezzo. The libretto, based on a short story, is extremely terse, and so is Mascagni's music. His arias go right to the point. He does not linger on the choruses. He successfully characterizes Lola in a single aria—and even that is interrupted. Alfio, with three entrances, is on stage for a total of barely twelve minutes, yet musically he is rounded. Mamma Lucia, on the other hand, sings hardly at all, but she is continually on stage and, if well acted, can become a complex character.

These are three of the solo voices (there are only five). Each is developed beyond pasteboard and cliché, yet they sing only about a quarter of an hour in all and leave the stage free for the two main characters. This is part of the opera's success, for if *Cavalleria* ran an hour and a half, it would be too long.

It is almost always paired as a double bill with *Pagliacci,* and it is usual to remark how well the two go together. However, a disgruntled minority has always dissented. One argument is that the stories repeat each other and, the impact of each (more especially the second on the bill, usually *Pagliacci*) is blunted; another is that the soprano and tenor voices dominate each opera and tend to become monotonous; and finally the choruses are similar: villagers going home after work, gathering for a drink or the performance. The minority argues that the comparison of different composers on the same theme may be interesting for students but is not well-planned entertainment. It would prefer a ballet or comic opera as a curtain raiser for either tragedy and suggests, for example, *Gianni Schicchi,* in which a bass has the lead.

The opera begins "in media res" and, although Santuzza repeats it in her big aria, it is well to know *before* the curtain rises that before Turiddu entered the army, he and Lola had been engaged. However, she did not wait for him and instead married Alfio. When Turiddu returned, he took up with Santuzza. He has gotten her with child, which is why she is excommunicated. But he does not know this, nor does Mamma Lucia, though each may suspect it. Lola, meanwhile, has been dallying again with Turiddu to Santuzza's loss and frantic despair, for not only is she jealous but she has also the very practical problem of getting a father for the child. (It is not clear in the opera libretto or the original short story if Santuzza is pregnant. But it is clearly implied in the play that Verga made of his short story, and such an assumption seems necessary to explain some of the lines and actions in the opera.)

## PRELUDE (8 min.)

It consists of music from the opera except for the serenade, which Turiddu sings behind the closed curtains. It is to Lola, Alfio's wife, and heralds the tragedy. The solo singing during the prelude is unique to *Cavalleria* (unless, like the minority, you count the prologue to *Pagliacci*).

## A SINGLE ACT (57 min.)

The village square. On one side is the church, on the other Mamma Lucia's wineshop and home. The day is just beginning.

**chorus**      *Villagers:* They sing of spring, the season of love.

*Santuzza and Mamma Lucia:* Santuzza asks, "Dov'è Turiddu" (where is Turiddu)? Mamma Lucia nervously claims that she doesn't know. I don't want any trouble, she insists. Finally she states that Turiddu has gone to a neighboring town to buy wine. Santuzza denies it. He has been seen in the village. Lucia is startled. She asks Santuzza into her house, but Santuzza refuses: "Sono scomunicata" (I am excommunicated [and she must not enter by local moral law]). Mamma Lucia suspects the reason. At this moment Alfio drives in.

**aria and chorus**      *Alfio and Villagers:* Alfio is a carter. His aria describes his life, the horse, the harness bells and home after hard work. The villagers envy him his freedom and travel.

*Alfio and Mamma Lucia:* He asks for a special wine. She says that Turiddu has gone to buy more at the neighboring town. Not so, says Alfio, for he just saw Turiddu by his own house. Alfio goes off leaving Mamma Lucia upset.

**chorus**      *Villagers (in and outside the church):* They sing an Easter hymn, the refrain of which is "Il Signor non è morto" (the Lord is not dead). "Allelulia."

*Santuzza and Mamma Lucia:* Mamma Lucia questions Santuzza about

**aria**      Turiddu, and Santuzza reminds her, "Voi lo sapete" (you know it). Turiddu and Lola were once engaged, but when he returned from the army, Lola was married and he turned to Santuzza. Passionately she bursts out, "L'amai" (I love him). Then Lola lured him back, leaving Santuzza without love or honor: "Io piango" (I weep).

Mamma Lucia is horrified and would rather not listen. In despair Santuzza wails, "Io son dannata" (I am damned). She begs Mamma Lucia to pray for her at the service.

*Turiddu and Santuzza:* He asks her if she isn't going to church. She

**duet**      ignores the question and says that she as something to tell him. She tries to warn him that Alfio will get suspicious, but her warning strikes him as a jealous tirade, and he accuses her of spying on him. "Lasciami" (leave me), he spurns her. She insists that he loves Lola: "L'ami" (you love her). He denies it. Coldly he tells her to pull herself together. With anguish she pleads that she can't help herself: she loves him. They stop abruptly as they hear Lola in the distance.

**aria**    *Lola:* She sings a light, suggestive aria about a flower and a good-looking man. She stops when she sees them. She asks after Alfio and, when she discovers that he's not around, she asks Turiddu to go to church with her. Turiddu is confused and nervous. Santuzza begs him to stay. Lola enters the church alone with an amused shrug.

**duet**    *Turiddu and Santuzza:* Angrily he turns on Santuzza: "Va" (go). She begs him to stay: "Rimani, rimani ancora" (stay, stay yet). He accuses her again of spying on him—even at the church door. Furious now, she threatens him: "Bada" (enough). He throws her to the ground, and she curses him. He runs into the church after Lola. *Santuzza and Alfio:* He enters looking for Lola to go to church. Violently Santuzza tells him that Lola has gone in with Turriddu and

**aria**    that the two have been deceiving him. Alfio at first is incredulous but then believes her and swears vengeance on the lovers.

### INTERMEZZO (4 min.)

The intermezzo represents the passage of time as the church service concludes. Another composer might have lowered the curtain. Musically it is a distillation of the drama.

**chorus**    *Villagers:* The service is over and they sing of going home —"A casa" (to home).

**brindisi** (*See* Glossary)    *Turiddu and Villagers:* He starts a drinking song, and the villagers join him. It is Easter, a holiday.

*Alfio and Turiddu:* Turiddu offers him a glass. Alfio refuses because, as he says loudly, it might be poisoned. The women hurry Lola away. The challenge is implicit. Alfio merely asks if Turiddu is ready—"or ora" (now)?—and Turiddu replies instantly, "or ora," and, as Sicilian custom requires, bites Alfio on the right ear. Regretfully he wonders for a moment what will happen to Santuzza. Then he forgets her and snarls at Alfio, who goes off coldly remarking that he is waiting.

*Turiddu:* He calls Mamma Lucia. The wine, he says, is a little strong. He is going out for a walk. But if he doesn't return, she must be a mother to Santuzza, whom he promised to marry. Lucia can't under-

**aria**    stand why he speaks so strangely. Again he blames the wine. He asks for a kiss—"un bacio, un altro bacio" (a kiss, another kiss). She must look after Santuzza, he insists. He runs off calling "addio" (farewell).

Lucia begins to suspect the truth. Santuzza rushes in. Offstage a woman screams that Turiddu is killed.

Vocabulary

| | | |
|---|---|---|
| dov'è Turiddu | doe v'eh Tour.ree.do | where is Turiddu |
| sono scomunicata | so.no scoe.moon.ee.kah.tah | I am excommunicated |
| il Signor non è morto | eel seen.yor known eh more.toe | the Lord is not dead |
| voi lo sapete | voy low sah.pay.tay | you know it |
| l'amai | l'ah.meye | I loved him |
| io piango | yo p'yan.joe | I weep |
| io son dannata | yo sewn dah.nah.tah | I am damned |
| lasciami | lah.shah.me | leave me |
| va | vah | go, get away |
| rimani, rimani ancora | ree.mah.knee . . . an.core. ah | stay, stay yet |
| bada | bah.dah | enough |
| a casa | ah kah.sah | to home |
| or ora | oar oar.ah | now |
| un altro bacio | oon ahl.tro bah.choe | another kiss |
| addio | ah.dee.oh | farewell |

(Santuzza is frequently throughout the opera called and referred to as "Santa.")


# DER ROSENKAVALIER

Opera in three acts. First performed at Dresden on January 26, 1911. Music by Richard Strauss. Libretto by H. von Hofmannsthal.

## PRINCIPAL CHARACTERS

| | |
|---|---|
| Octavian, Count Rofrano | mezzo-soprano |
| The Marschallin, Princess von Werdenberg | soprano |
| Baron Ochs, a country cousin of The Marschallin | bass |
| Annina, an Italian intriguer | contralto |
| Valzacchi, her partner | tenor |
| Faninal, a rich merchant recently ennobled | baritone |
| Marianne, Sophie's maid | soprano |
| Sophie, Faninal's daughter | soprano |

The action takes place in Vienna in the early years of the reign of Maria Theresa, 1740–80.

Maria Theresa was the great Austrian Empress. She was, in her youth, beautiful. In her middle age she haggled with Prussia over Silesia, partitioned Poland with Catherine, gave away Italian duchies and produced sixteen children. Ten survived her. The youngest was Marie Antoinette. But whereas under the daughter, France collapsed, under Maria Theresa, Austria prospered. And in her old age, under her son's guidance, she instituted reforms that helped to keep Austria afloat in the wash of the French Revolution. During her reign, Vienna, center of the Holy Roman Empire, was the only rival in Europe to Versailles, and with Catherine the Great and the Sultan for neighbors it was, in some ways, even more cosmopolitan than Paris.

R. STRAUSS

At the time of the opera it was traditional that when two aristocratic families wished to ally by marriage, an ambassador from the groom's family would bear a silver rose to the bride as a pledge of love and a symbol that negotiations for the alliance had opened.

Purists sometimes object to the many waltz rhythms Strauss used in the opera. They argue that this type of waltz was unknown for another hundred years and cannot properly evoke Maria Theresa and that *they* in their knowledge are reminded of Franz Josef and the nineteenth century. Carried to its extreme, the theory becomes ludicrous. Yet the complaint has logic; but, of course, art has magic.

### ACT I (68 min.)

The bedroom of the Princess von Werdenberg, wife of one of Austria's two Field Marshals. She is known throughout as the Marschallin.

Strauss describes her as beautiful and in her early thirties. The Field Marshal (who never appears) is older by twenty or twenty-five years. At the moment, there being no war, he is off hunting. Octavian is seventeen. Throughout the act the Marschallin calls Octavian "Mein Bub" (my boy) when no one else is present; and he privately calls her "Bichette," a French endearment. She also sometimes calls him "Quinquin," another French endearment.

The act can be divided into six parts. There is a short prelude (4 min.).

*Octavian and the Marschallin* (13 min.): It is early morning. The Marschallin is still in her nightgown; Octavian is half dressed. It is the quiet after the storm. Octavian, stirred by his love, philosophizes passionately about reality—of words, of persons, of himself away from her and in her arms. Mildly the Marschallin remarks, "Ich hab dich lieb" (I love you so). He impetuously hates the day and pulls the shade.

A warning bell tinkles. But Octavian continues philosophizing until hastily he has to slip behind the screen as the Marshallin's breakfast is brought in. They nibble happily together until she remarks that she dreamt that her husband came home. Octavian is furious. Outside there is a noise of someone coming. Suddenly frightened, they rise: "Quinquin, es ist mein Mann!" (it's my husband). It is too late to get out, and he hides behind the screen.

After much scurrying in the hall as the servants try to stop the visitor, the Marschallin recognizes the voice of her cousin, Baron Ochs. Meanwhile, Octavian has disguised himself as a maid, hoping to get out before the Baron gets in. But he meets him face to face and has to stay.

*Ochs, Octavian and the Marschallin* (15 min.): The Baron, an aristocrat, is a country cousin and crude. Having burst into the Marschallin's bedroom, he begins to ogle the maid, whom the Marschallin calls, "Mariandel" (Mary-Ann). He explains, which the Marschallin had forgotten, that he is going to marry Sophie, the daughter of a very rich and recently ennobled burgher, Faninal. He wants the Marschallin to recommend some relative to bear the silver rose to Sophie and also to recommend a good attorney for drawing favorable settlements. But the maid so distracts him that he tries to make an assignation with her and launches into a coarse monologue on his sexual escapades past, present and hoped for. (In performance this is sometimes cut—which infuriated Strauss.)

The Marschallin brings him back to the point, however, by showing him a miniature of Octavian and suggesting that he bear the rose to Sophie. Ochs agrees but is more interested in her insinuation that the maid is really the illegitimate sister of Octavian. The Marschallin orders "Mariandel" to leave, and Octavian makes his escape.

*The Levée* (9 min.): Everyone comes in to the Marschallin, including her attorney, who discusses possible settlements with Ochs. The two begin to disagree when Ochs insists on a settlement by Sophie's father on him even before the wedding. Loudly he bangs the table and disrupts the Levée. The Marschallin dismisses everyone, and all go out except two Italian gossipmongers who recognize in Ochs a prospective employer.

*Annina, Valzacchi and Ochs* (3 min.): They offer their services, and Ochs hires them to arrange an assignation with the maid. Then he remarks to the Marschallin that his body servant is his own illegitimate son, and he leaves the rose with her.

*The Marschallin* (5 min.): The Marschallin, left alone, sighs for Sophie who is being married off to Ochs. But it is the way of the world. She herself years ago had been marched straight from the convent into marriage. The memory of it makes her feel old. No one can change the world—only bear it. And in the manner of bearing lies the only difference between this one and that. "Und in dem wie" (and in the "how").

*Octavian and the Marschallin* (19 min.): Octavian returns in his own clothes, elated at the masquerade and eager to pick up again the early morning mood. But the Marschallin now is pensive. She gently turns him away. "Don't be like all the others," she warns him. "Wie alle Manner" (how all men are). Octavian is suspicious, but she adds, "like the Marshall and Ochs." She warns him that things grasped tightly and emotions felt strongly pass and are lost. She and he will part, if not today then tomorrow—"heut oder morgen." She repeats it while he denies it: "Nicht heut, nicht morgen" (not today, not tomorrow). He refuses to think of it, to admit it. He at first is angry, then tender, then, not understanding, angry again. But she tells him that they must lightly meet their fate and lightly let their hands unclasp or suffer endless grief.

Then she dismisses him so that she can finish dressing to go to church and then to lunch with her old, bedridden uncle, who has no pleasures. Quietly he leaves. And she realizes that she has let him go without the rose—or a kiss. Quickly she sends the footman out to stop him. But they are too late. He ran out and galloped off, they say. She gives the silver rose to her servant to deliver to him.

Vocabulary, Act I

| Mein Bub | mine boob | my boy |
|----------|-----------|--------|
| ich hab dich lieb | ish hob dish leeb | I love you so |
| es ist mein Mann | es ist mine mahn | it is my husband |
| wie alle Manner | vee allah man.neh | how all men are |
| und in dem "wie" | oont in dem vee | and in the "how" |
| heut oder morgen | hoyt oh.der more.gen | today or tomorrow |

## ACT II (60 min.)

A room in the house of von Faninal.

*Sophie and Marianne* (5 min.): The major-domo insinuates to Faninal that it is not the custom for the father to be present when the Rosen-kavalier appears. Faninal withdraws, leaving Sophie alone with Marianne, her duenna. Sophie is nervous and hopeful. She tries to make up a little prayer but is too excited. Off stage Octavian's footmen cry "Rofrano," his family name, as he approaches. Marianne is frankly thrilled with the richness of it all.

*Octavian and Sophie* (12 min.): He enters and hands her the rose with a short speech. She tries to reply but breaks down in confusion. She takes refuge in smelling the rose, and he explains that it is a special Persian perfume. As they raise their heads, they start a duet in which each sings quietly of the wonder of the moment of falling in love. Gradually they manage to talk of commonplace things. She recites his names, his titles, even his nickname, "Quinquin," and naively confesses that she's been reading about his family and him in the Book of Nobility. He is overcome by her simplicity and beauty.

*Ochs and Sophie* (10 min.): Ochs enters and remarks, on kissing Sophie's hand, that it is rather delicate for a middle-class hand. Then he ostentatiously snubs Marianne and turns his back on Sophie while he tells Faninal about the illegitimate sister of Octavian and his own illegitimate son. Octavian is incensed at his behavior. Ochs then examines Sophie as though she were a filly and comments on her as such. She pushes him away. Marianne, however, greatly admires Ochs' "easy ways." Finally Ochs leaves with Faninal to discuss the marriage settlement.

*Sophie and Octavian* (7 min.): Sophie begs Octavian to help her. In the background one of Ochs' men chases a maid, and the major-domo and Marianne rush off to help her. Left alone, Sophie and Octavian admit they love each other, and in a duet he promises to protect her and she begs him to stay with her always.

*Discovery, Duel and Denunciation* (22 min.): Meanwhile, the two Italian gossipmongers, hoping Ochs will tip them well, have been spying on Sophie and Octavian. They call Ochs in to see the two lovers embracing. Ochs doesn't care except as it may affect the settlement. Octavian starts four times to help Sophie say that she will not marry him. He begins each time, "Die Fraulein" (the lady). But Sophie's courage each time fails and Ochs interrupts. Finally Octavian says that Sophie will not marry him. Ochs is not distressed; he simply tries to pull Sophie into the other room to talk to her father. She frees herself, and Octavian provokes a duel with Ochs in which he pinks him on the elbow. Ochs yells bloody murder—"Moerder"—and everyone comes in. Marianne is horrified; Faninal is furious; and the Italians want to get paid. Faninal berates Sophie: "Sie heirat ihn" (you will marry him). But Sophie refuses. She will throw herself from the carriage, be dragged to the altar, refuse to say "I do." She will not marry Ochs. Faninal threatens to put her in a convent "Auf Lebens zeit" (for all your life). She is adamant and Marianne takes her out.

> (The libretto is not clear on when the Italians start working for Octavian. Possibly for a while they work for both him and Ochs. But by the end of the act, when Ochs has refused to tip Annina for delivering the letter from "Mariandel," they are wholly for Octavian. Some productions have Octavian, in sight of the audience, hire them to deliver the letter on his way out. His plan is to have Annina make an assignation for Ochs with the Marschallin's maid and then expose him as an improper husband.)

Meanwhile, Faninal apologizes profusely to Ochs and promises that Sophie will come around. Ochs imperiously dismisses him to prepare a bed for him, as he is too wounded to leave at once.

*Ochs and Annina* (4 min.): Annina sneaks in behind him while he is alone and delivers the message from the supposed maid. Ochs is overjoyed and expands on his refrain: "Mit mir, mit mir" (with me time passes quickly, lucky girl).

Vocabulary, Act II

| Rofrano | row.FRAH.no | family name of Octavian |
|---|---|---|
| die Fraulein | dee.frow.line | the lady |
| Moerder | mer.der | murder |
| sie heirat ihn | zee hy.raht een | you will marry him |
| auf Lebens zeit | auf lay.ben tsite | for all your life |
| mit mir | mit meer | with me |

## ACT III (66 min.)

A private room in an inn.

*Prelude and Mime* (7 min.): There is a five-minute prelude, and then the curtains part to show Annina and Valzacchi setting up the private dinner on Octavian's instructions. Men are placed behind false windows, cupboards, under trap doors, and practice poking out on signal.

*Ochs and Octavian* (17 min.): Ochs arrives with Octavian masquerading as the maid, "Mariandel." The waiters and landlord suggest more candles and silver, but Ochs dismisses them all as too expensive. He puts out as many candles as he can and announces that he's brought his own waiter, his body servant.

He offers Octavian the wine. The maid replies coyly, "Nein, nein," and reminds Ochs that he's engaged. Ochs explains that to an aristocrat an engagement's no obstacle. He starts to kiss "Mariandel" when the facial resemblance to Octavian stops him. The man under the trap door pops out too soon and quickly disappears. Ochs is alarmed. "There's a man there," he insists. "Da is nix" (nothing's there), Octavian replies. Then he remarks, "Die schoene Musik" (the pretty music), and begins to weep. He begins to sentimentalize that life is nothing, nobody cares, and it's all fate. Ochs suggests that it's a tight girdle and reaches to loosen it. All the heads come out. Annina screams through a window. Ochs is terrified.

*Ensemble and Ochs* (10 min.): Annina leads the pack in. "Es ist mein Mann," she screams, pointing to Ochs. Four children run in screaming "Papa." Valzacchi reports to Octavian that a messenger, supposedly sent by Ochs, is bringing Faninal. In the midst of the uproar, the police arrive.

Ochs announces confidently that he's a Baron. But in his disarray the Commissary doesn't believe him. When questioned, Valzacchi denies knowing Ochs. The Commissary then asks Ochs to identify "Mariandel." It's Sophie Faninal, Ochs replies, portentously listing her father's title and address.

At that moment Faninal rushes in. Ochs is horrified and at first refuses to recognize him. Then he pretends he has a fever and can't see well. When asked to identify "Mariandel" as his daughter, Faninal is outraged and has Sophie brought in from his carriage. Annina and the children start up again and everyone begins to murmur about the scandal of it. Faninal turns on Ochs and is so angry that he has a seizure. Sophie assists him to an adjoining room to lie down.

The Commissary, determined to fathom the mystery, clears the room and questions Ochs; Octavian whispers his sex to the Commissary, who begins to laugh. This infuriates Ochs. Octavian goes behind a screen to change his clothes, and the landlord announces the Marschallin.

*Ensemble and Marschallin* (13 min.): Ochs at first is pleased: her rank will help him. He nods his satisfaction at his body servant, who ran out and asked her to come. But on second thought Ochs is less pleased. He tries to keep "Mariandel" out of sight and Sophie in the adjoining room. The Marschallin recognizes the Commissary as an old orderly of the Field Marshal, and he is complimented. She says nothing but waits for an explanation. Sophie steps out and delivers a message from her father: the marriage is off. Octavian, now in his own clothes, whispers to the Marschallin that it is the girl to whom he delivered the rose. The Marschallin never looks at Octavian; she already suspects why he undertook to expose Ochs to Sophie and her father.

Ochs refuses to call off the marriage and tries to force his way to Faninal. The Marschallin suggests to him that he leave. But Ochs won't give up.

The Marschallin then explains to the Commissary that the evening has been a joke that went awry—"eine Farce" (a farce). This is cruel news to Sophie, who now thinks that Octavian has been making fun of her. "Eine Farce," she repeats.

Ochs refuses to go and the Marschallin asks Octavian to explain it to him. This involves a recognition which Sophie doesn't quite understand and convinces her that she was nothing to Octavian. It also for the first time gives Ochs an advantage. For, if "Mariandel" in the inn was Octavian, so must she have been also in the Marschallin's bedroom.

The Marschallin warns him not to think too much. But Ochs insists and, having figured it out, suggests that he won't spoil her sport if she helps him with Faninal. Angrily she tells him to get out; she adds that any hopes for a marriage he must renounce—". . . vorbei" (renounce). Sophie, astounded, repeats it. The Marschallin moves to one side and sits, saying quietly to herself, "And I too must renounce" (vorbei). She avoids looking at Octavian.

Annina and all the waiters come in and demand payment. The only refuge is escape, and Ochs runs out.

*Sophie, Marschallin and Octavian* (11 min.): Sophie is in despair: "Mein Gott . . . eine farce." Octavian, standing behind the Marschallin, stammers his apologies for the situation. "Go to her," the Marschallin advises. She cannot bring herself to look at him.

But Sophie is hurt and Octavian can't find the right words. The Marschallin sees that Sophie is about to go to her father and leave Octavian. "Heut oder Morgen," she reminds herself (today or tomorrow), but she had not expected it would be so soon. Still she had promised to take it lightly.

She goes to Sophie and asks her if she loves Octavian. Sophie stammers that she has to go to her father, but her confusion reveals the answer. The Marschallin says that she herself will go to Faninal, talk with him and then take all four of them home in her own carriage.

Octavian recognizes how much the Marschallin is doing: "Marie Theres', Marie Theres' (her given names), he starts feelingly. This begins the trio. Octavian wonders first at the Marschallins goodness, but then all questions dissolve into his feeling for Sophie. Sophie wonders at the Marschallin, whom she doesn't understand and is not sure she likes. But all that matters is Octavian. The Marschallin sings, "I made a vow . . . to love his love . . . so soon redeemed . . . only the wounded can know the hurt . . . He will be happy . . . So be it." She goes to Faninal.

*Sophie and Octavian* (8 min.): Left alone, they sing a simple love duet. In the middle of it Faninal leads the Marschallin out. "Look at them," he says to her, not knowing how he hurts her. "Youth will be young," he clucks. She manages, "Ja, ja" (yes). They go out to the carriage.

Sophie and Octavian finish their duet and run out to join the others. Sophie has dropped her handkerchief and the Marschallin sends her Blackamoor back for it.

Vocabulary, Act III

| | | |
|---|---|---|
| nein | nine | no |
| da is nix | daw is nicks | nothing's there |
| die schoene musik | dee shern.uh mooz.eek | the pretty music |
| es ist mein Mann | es ist mine mahn | that's my husband |
| eine Farce | eye.neh farce | a joke |
| vorbei | for.by | renounce |
| heut oder Morgen | hoyt oh.der more.gen | today or tomorrow |
| ja, ja | yah, yah | yes, yes |

# APPENDIX A

This is in three parts. The first lists by title operas produced before 1940 and indicates for each its composer, librettist, date and city of première and, in some instances, the theater. The second part lists in the same style operas produced for the first time in the twenty years since 1939. This second list has a deliberate bias towards English and American operas and includes others only where they have acquired some international fame. The third part lists by date of production the complete works of Mozart, Verdi, Wagner and Puccini.

In both Parts 1 and 2 the operas are listed alphabetically, excluding the article, definite or indefinite, in any language. The composer is listed before the librettist—thus "Sullivan; Gilbert"—or, if the composer was his own librettist, his name stands alone. The theaters, where indicated, are abbreviated as follows:

| | |
|---|---|
| Berlin, | O, (Koenigliches) Opernhaus (later Staatsoper) |
| London, | CG, Covent Garden |
| | SW, Sadler's Wells |
| Milan, | Sc, La Scala |
| Moscow, | B, Bolshoi |
| Naples, | SC, San Carlo |
| New York, | M, Metropolitan |
| | CC, New York City Center |
| Paris, | O, Opéra (Académie Royale de Musique, etc.) |
| | OC, Opéra-Comique |
| Rome, | Ap, Apollo |
| | Arg, Argentina |
| | C, Costanzi |
| St. Petersburg, | Ma, Marinsky |
| Venice, | F, La Fenice |
| Vienna, | B, Burgtheater |
| | W, (Theater auf der) Wieden (later Theater an der Wien) |
| | O, Opernhaus (Hofoper, later Staatsoper) |

## 1.

## OPERAS PRODUCED FROM 1597 THROUGH 1939

| Opera | Composer; Librettist | Date | City |
|---|---|---|---|
| The Abduction from the Seraglio (*See* Die Entfuehrung aus dem Serail) | | | |
| Abu Hassan | Weber; Heimer | 6. 4.1811 | Munich |
| Adriana Lecouvreur | Cilea; Colautti | 11. 6.1902 | Milan |
| L'Africaine | Meyerbeer; Scribe | 4.28.1865 | Paris, O |
| Dei aegyptische Helena | R. Strauss; Hofmannsthal | 6. 6.1928 | Dresden |
| Aida | Verdi; Ghislanzoni | 12.24.1871 | Cairo |
| Alceste | Gluck; Calzabigi | 12.26.1767 | Vienna, B |
| Alessandro Stradella | Flotow; Friedrich | 12.30.1844 | Hamburg |
| Amelia al Ballo | Menotti | 4. 1.1937 | Philadelphia |
| Amelia goes to the Ball (*See* Amelia al Ballo) | | | |
| L'Amico Fritz | Mascagni; Daspuro | 10.31.1891 | Rome, C |
| L'Amore dei tre Re | Montemezzi; Benelli | 4.10.1913 | Milan, Sc |
| L'Amour des trois Oranges | Prokofiev | 12.30.1921 | Chicago |
| Andrea Chenier | Giordano; Illica | 3.28.1896 | Milan, Sc |
| Angelica vincitrice di Alcina | Fux; Pariati | 9.21.1716 | Vienna |
| Anna Bolena | Donizetti; Romani | 12.26.1830 | Milan |
| Arabella | R. Strauss; Hofmannsthal | 7. 1.1933 | Dresden |
| Ariadne auf Naxos | R. Strauss; Hofmannsthal | 10.25.1912 | Stuttgart |
| Arianna | Monteverdi; Rinuccini | 5.28.1608 | Mantua |
| L'Arlesiana | Cilea; Marenco | 11.27.1897 | Milan |
| Armide | Gluck; Quinault | 9.23.1777 | Paris, O |
| Artaserse | Hasse; Metastasio | 2. ?.1731 | Venice |
| Attila | Verdi; Solera | 3.17.1846 | Venice, F |
| Aureliano in Palmira | Rossini; Romani | 12.26.1813 | Milan, Sc |
| Der Bajazzo (*See* I Pagliacci) | | | |
| Un Ballo in Maschera | Verdi; Somma | 2.17.1859 | Rome, Ap |
| Bánk-Bán | Erkel; Egressy | 3. 9.1861 | Budapest |
| The Barber of Bagdad (*See* Der Barbier von Bagdad) | | | |
| The Barber of Seville (*See* Il Barbiere di Siviglia [by Rossini]) | | | |
| Der Barbier von Bagdad | Cornelius | 12.15.1858 | Weimar |
| Il Barbiere di Siviglia | Paisiello; Petrosellini | 9.26.1782 | St. Petersburg |
| Il Barbiere di Siviglia | Rossini; Sterbini | 2.20.1816 | Rome, Arg |
| The Bartered Bride (*See* Prodaná Nevěsta) | | | |
| La Battaglia di Legnano | Verdi; Cammarano | 1.27.1849 | Rome, Arg |
| Beatrice di Tenda | Bellini; Romani | 3.16.1833 | Venice, F |
| Béatrice et Bénédict | Berlioz | 8. 9.1862 | Baden-Baden |
| The Beggar's Opera | Pepusch; Gay | 2. 9.1728 | London |

| *Opera* | *Composer; Librettist* | *Date* | *City* |
|---|---|---|---|
| Belisario | Donizetti; Cammarano | 2. 4.1836 | Venice, F |
| La Belle Hélène | Offenbach; Meilhac, Halévy | 12.17.1864 | Paris |
| Benvenuto Cellini | Berlioz; Wailly, Barbier | 9.10.1838 | Paris, O |
| Der Bettelstudent | Milloecker; Zell, Genée | 12. 6.1882 | Vienna, W |
| Blue-Beard's Castle (*See* A Kékszakállú Herceg Vára) | | | |
| Boccaccio | Supée; Zell, Genée | 2. 1.1879 | Vienna |
| La Bohème | Puccini; Giacosa, Illica | 2. 1.1896 | Turin |
| La Bohème | Leoncavallo | 5. 6.1897 | Venice, F |
| The Bohemian Girl | Balfe; Bunn | 11.27.1843 | London |
| Boris Godunov | Mussorgsky | 2. 8.1874 | St. Petersburg, Ma |
| La Cambiale di Matrimonio | Rossini; Rossi | 11. 3.1810 | Venice |
| I Capuleti e i Montecchi | Bellini; Romani | 3.11.1830 | Venice, F |
| Carmen | Bizet; Meilhac, Halévy | 3. 3.1875 | Paris, OC |
| Cavalleria Rusticana | Mascagni; Menasci, Targioni-Tozzetti | 5.17.1890 | Rome, C |
| La Cena delle Beffe | Giordano; Benelli | 12.20.1924 | Milan, Sc |
| La Cenerentola | Rossini; Ferretti | 1.25.1817 | Rome |
| Chiara di Rosemberg | Ricci; Rossi | 10.11.1831 | Milan, Sc |
| The Chimes of Normandy (*See* Les Cloches de Corneville) | | | |
| Cinderella (*See* La Cenerentola) | | | |
| Clari | Bishop; Payne | 5. 8.1823 | London, CG |
| La Clemenza di Tito | Mozart; Metastasio | 9. 6.1791 | Prague |
| Les Cloches de Corneville | Planquette; Clairville, Gabet | 4.19.1877 | Paris |
| Le Comte Ory | Rossini; Scribe, Delestre-Poirson | 8.20.1828 | Paris, O |
| Les Contes d'Hoffmann | Offenbach; Barbier, Carré | 2.10.1881 | Paris, OC |
| Le Coq d'Or | Rimsky-Korsakov; Byelsky | 10. 7.1909 | Moscow |
| The Coronation of Poppea (*See* L'Incoronazione di Poppea) | | | |
| Der Corregidor | Wolf; Mayreder | 6. 7.1896 | Mannheim |
| Così fan tutte | Mozart; da Ponte | 1.26.1790 | Vienna, B |
| Cox and Box | Sullivan; Burnand | 5.11.1867 | London |
| Il Crociato in Egitto | Meyerbeer; Rossi | 3. 7.1824 | Venice, F |
| The Cunning Little Vixen (*See* Příhody Lišky Bystrovšky) | | | |
| Dafne | Peri; Rinuccini | 1597 | Florence |

OPERAS PRODUCED FROM 1597 THROUGH 1939 (*cont.*)

| Opera | Composer; Librettist | Date | City |
|---|---|---|---|
| Dafne | Schuetz; Opitz | 4.23.1627 | Torgau |
| La Dame Blanche | Boieldieu; Scribe | 12.10.1825 | Paris, OC |
| La Damnation de Faust | Berlioz; Berlioz, Gandonnière | 2.18.1893 | Monte Carlo |
| Daphne | R. Strauss; Gregor | 10.15.1938 | Dresden |
| The Demon | Rubinstein; Vis-kovatov | 1.25.1875 | St. Petersburg |
| The Desert Flower | Wallace; Harris, Williams | 10.12.1863 | London, CG |
| Dido and Aeneas | Purcell; Tate | 1689 | London |
| Dinorah (*See* Pardon de Ploeermel) | | | |
| Djamileh | Bizet; Gallet | 5.22.1872 | Paris, OC |
| Le Domino Noir | Auber; Scribe | 12. 2.1837 | Paris, OC |
| Don Carlo | Verdi; Mery, Du Locle | 3.11.1867 | Paris, O |
| Don Giovanni | Mozart; da Ponte | 10.29.1787 | Prague |
| La Donna del Lago | Rossini; Totola | 9.24.1819 | Naples, SC |
| Donna Juanita | Suppé; Zell, Genée | 2.21.1880 | Vienna |
| Le Donne curiose | Wolf-Ferrari; Sugano | 11.27.1903 | Munich |
| Don Pasquale | Donizetti; Donizetti, Ruffini | 1. 3.1843 | Paris |
| Die Dreigroschenoper | Weill; Brecht | 8.31.1928 | Berlin |
| Drot og Marsk | Heise; Richardt | 9.25.1878 | Copenhagen |
| I due Foscari | Verdi; Piave | 11. 3.1844 | Rome, Arg |
| Duke Blue-Beard's Castle (*See* A Kékszakállú Herceg Vára | | | |
| The Egyptian Helen (*See* Die aegyptische Helena) | | | |
| Elda (*See* Loreley) | | | |
| Elektra | R. Strauss; Hofmannsthal | 1.25.1909 | Dresden |
| Elisabetta Regina d'Inghil-terra | Rossini; Schmidt | 10. 4.1815 | Naples, SC |
| L'Elisir d'Amore | Donizetti; Romani | 5.12.1832 | Milan |
| The Elixir of Love (*See* L'Elisir d'Amore) | | | |
| Emperor Jones | Gruenberg; de Jaffa | 1. 7.1933 | New York, M |
| L'Enfant et les Sortileges | Ravel; Collete | 3.21.1925 | Monte Carlo |
| Die Entfuehrung aus dem Serail (The Abduction from the Seraglio) | Mozart; Bretzner, Stephanie | 7.16.1782 | Vienna, B |
| Ernani | Verdi; Piave | 3. 9.1844 | Venice, F |
| Ero s Onoga svijeta | Gotovac; Begovič | 11. 2.1935 | Zagreb |
| L'Étoile du Nord | Meyerbeer; Scribe | 2.16.1854 | Paris, OC |

| Opera | Composer; Librettist | Date | City |
|---|---|---|---|
| Eugene Onegin | Tchaikovsky; Tchaikovsky, Shilovsky | 3.29.1879 | Moscow |
| L'Euridice | Peri; Rinuccini | 10. 6.1600 | Florence |
| Euryanthe | Weber; Chezy | 10.25.1823 | Vienna |
| Der Evangelimann | Kienzl | 5. 4.1895 | Berlin, O |
| Ezio | Hasse; Metastasio | 1.20.1755 | Dresden |
| The Fair of Sorochinsty | Mussorgsky | 10.26.1917 | Petrograd (St. Petersburg) |
| The Fairy-Queen | Purcell; Anonymous | 4. ?.1692 | London |
| Falstaff | Verdi; Boito | 2. 9.1893 | Milan, Sc |
| La Fanciulla del West | Puccini; Civinini, Zangarini | 12.10.1910 | New York, M |
| Faust | Gounod; Barbier, Carré | 3.19.1859 | Paris |
| La Favola d'Orfeo | Monteverdi; Striggio | 1607 | Mantua |
| La Favorita (*See* La Favorite) | | | |
| La Favorite | Donizetti; Royer, Vaeez, Scribe | 12. 2.1840 | Paris, O |
| Fedora | Giordano; Colautti | 11.17.1898 | Milan |
| Die Feen | Wagner | 6.29.1888 | Munich |
| Fidelio | Beethoven; Sonnleithner | 11.20.1805 | Vienna, W |
| Figaro (*See* Le Nozze de Figaro) | | | |
| La Fille de Madame Angot | Lecocq; Clairville, Siraudin, Koning | 12. 4.1872 | Brussels |
| La Fille du Régiment | Donizetti; Vernoy de Saint-Georges, Bayard | 2.11.1840 | Paris, OC |
| La Figlia del Regimento (*See* La Fille du Regiment) | | | |
| Die Fledermaus | J. Strauss; Haffner, Genée | 4. 5.1874 | Vienna, W |
| Der fliegende Hollaender | Wagner | 1. 2.1843 | Dresden |
| La Forza del Destino | Verdi; Piave | 11.10.1862 | St. Petersburg |
| Four Saints in Three Acts | Thomson; Stein | 2. 7.1934 | Hartford, Conn. |
| Fra Diavolo | Auber; Scribe | 1.28.1830 | Paris, OC |
| Fra Gherardo | Pizzetti | 5.16.1928 | Milan, Sc |
| Francesca da Rimini | Zandonai; Ricordi | 2.19.1914 | Turin |
| Die Frau ohne Schatten | R. Strauss; Hofmannsthal | 10.10.1919 | Vienna, O |
| Der Freischuetz | Weber, Kind | 6.18.1821 | Berlin |
| Il Furioso nell' Isola di San Domingo | Donizetti; Ferretti | 1. 2.1833 | Rome |

OPERAS PRODUCED FROM 1597 THROUGH 1939 (*cont.*)

| Opera | Composer; Librettist | Date | City |
|---|---|---|---|
| La Gazza Ladra | Rossini; Gherardini | 5.31.1817 | Milan, Sc |
| Gemma di Vergy | Donizetti; Bidera | 12.26.1834 | Milan, Sc |
| Germania | Franchetti; Illica | 3.11.1902 | Milan, Sc |
| Gianni Schicchi | Puccini; Forzano | 12.14.1918 | New York, M |
| La Gioconda | Ponchielli; Boito | 4. 8.1876 | Milan, Sc |
| Giulio Cesare in Egitto | Handel; Haym | 3. 2.1724 | London |
| Goetterdaemmerung | Wagner | 8.17.1876 | Bayreuth |
| The Golden Cockerel (*See* Le Coq d'Or) | | | |
| The Gondoliers | Sullivan; Gilbert | 12. 7.1889 | London, Savoy |
| Gorenjski Slavček | Foerster; Pesjakova | 4.27.1872 | Ljublijana, Yugoslavia |
| Goyescas | Granados; Periquet y Zuaznabar | 1.28.1916 | New York, M |
| La Gran Via | Chucca, Valverde; Perez y Gonzalez | 7. 2.1886 | Madrid |
| La Grande-Duchesse de Gerolstein | Offenbach; Meilhac, Halévy | 4.12.1867 | Paris |
| Il Guarany | Gomes; Scalvini | 3.19.1870 | Milan, Sc |
| Guillaume Tell | Rossini; Etienne de Jouy, Bis | 8. 3.1829 | Paris, O |
| The Gypsy Baron (*See* Der Zigeunerbaron) | | | |
| H. M. S. Pinafore | Sullivan; Gilbert | 5.25.1878 | London |
| Halka | Moniuszko; Wolski | 2.16.1854 | Wilna |
| Hamlet | Thomas; Barbier, Carré | 3. 9.1868 | Paris, O |
| Hans Heiling | Marschner; Devrient | 5.24.1833 | Berlin, O |
| Haensel und Gretel | Humperdinck; Wette | 12.23.1893 | Weimar |
| Háry János | Kodály; Paulini, Harsányi | 10.16.1926 | Budapest |
| Haydée | Auber; Scribe | 12.28.1847 | Paris, OC |
| Hérodiade | Massenet; Milliet, Hartmann | 12.19.1881 | Brussels |
| L'Heure espagnole | Ravel; Franc-Nohain | 5.19.1911 | Paris, OC |
| Histoire du Soldat | Stravinsky; Ramuz | 9.28.1918 | Lausanne |
| Hoffmann (*See* Les Contes d'Hoffmann) | | | |
| Les Huguenots | Meyerbeer; Scribe, Deschamps | 2.29.1836 | Paris, O |
| Idomeneo | Mozart; Varesco | 1.29.1781 | Munich |
| L'Incoronazione di Poppea | Monteverdi; Busenello | 1642 | Venice |
| Les Indes galantes | Rameau; Fuzelier | 8.23.1735 | Paris, O |

| Opera | Composer; Librettist | Date | City |
|---|---|---|---|
| Indigo und die vierzig Raeuber (1,001 Nights) | J. Strauss; Steiner | 2.10.1871 | Vienna, W |
| Iolanta | P. Tchaikovsky; M. Tchaikovsky | 12.18.1892 | St. Petersburg, Ma |
| Iolanthe | Sullivan;,Gilbert | 11.25.1882 | Simultaneously, disregarding time differential, in London (Savoy) and New York |
| Iphigénie en Aulide | Gluck; Lebland du Roullet | 4.19.1774 | Paris, O |
| Iphigénie en Tauride | Gluck; Guillard | 5.18.1779 | Paris, O |
| Iris | Mascagni; Illica | 11.22.1898 | Rome, C |
| L'Italiana in Algeri | Rossini; Anelli | 5.22.1813 | Venice |
| Ivan Susanin (*See* A Life for the Tsar) | | | |
| Jeanne d'Arc au Bucher | Honegger; Claudel | 5.12.1938 | Basle |
| Jenufa | Janáček | 1.21.1904 | Brno |
| Jocelyn | Godard; Silvestre, Capoul | 2.25.1888 | Brussels |
| La jolie Fille de Perth | Bizet; Vernoy de Saint-Georges, Adenis | 12.26.1867 | Paris |
| Le Jongleur de Notre-Dame | Massenet; Lena | 2.18.1902 | Monte Carlo |
| Jonny spielt auf | Křenek | 2.10.1927 | Leipzig |
| La Juive | Halévy; Scribe | 2.23.1835 | Paris, O |
| Julius Caesar (Handel) (*See* Giulio Cesare) | | | |
| Káta Kabanová | Janáček; Cervinka | 10.23.1921 | Brno |
| A Kékszakállú Herceg Vára | Bartók; Balázs | 5.24.1918 | Budapest |
| Khovanshchina | Mussorgsky | 2.21.1886 | St. Petersburg |
| King and Marshall (*See* Drot og Marsk) | | | |
| King Arthur | Purcell; Dryden | 1691 | London |
| Kitezh | Rimsky-Korsakov; Byelsky | 2.20.1907 | St. Petersburg, Ma |
| Die Koenigin von Saba | Goldmark; Mosenthal | 3.10.1875 | Vienna, O |
| Koenigskinder | Humperdinck; Rosmer | 12.28.1910 | New York, M |
| Den kongelige Gast | Boerrsen; Leopold | 11.15.1919 | Copenhagen |
| Lady Macbeth of Mtsensk District | Shostakovich; Shostakovich; Preis | 1.22.1934 | Leningrad |
| Lakmé | Delibes; Gondinet, Gille | 4.14.1883 | Paris, OC |
| La Lanterna di Diogene | Draghi; Minato | 2. 5.1674 | Vienna |
| The Legend of the Invisible City of Kitezh and the Maiden Fevronia (*See* Kitezh) | | | |
| Liden Kirsten | Hartmann; Andersen | 5.12.1846 | Copenhagen |
| Das Liebesverbot | Wagner | 3.29.1836 | Magdeburg |
| A Life for the Tsar | Glinka; Rozen | 12. 9.1836 | St. Petersburg |

OPERAS PRODUCED FROM 1597 THROUGH 1939 (*cont.*)

| Opera | Composer; Librettist | Date | City |
|---|---|---|---|
| The Lily of Killarney | Benedict; Oxenford, Boucicault | 2. 8.1862 | London, CG |
| Little Kirsten (*See* Liden Kirsten) | | | |
| Linda di Chamounix | Donzetti; Rossi | 5.19.1842 | Vienna |
| Lodoletta | Mascagni; Forzano | 4.30.1917 | Rome, C |
| Lohengrin | Wagner | 8.28.1850 | Weimar |
| I Lombardi alla prima Crociata | Verdi; Solera | 2.11.1843 | Milan, Sc |
| Loreley | Catalini; d'Ormeville | 1.31.1880 | Turin |
| Louise | Charpentier | 2. 2.1900 | Paris, OC |
| The Love for Three Oranges (*See* L'Amour des trois Oranges) | | | |
| The Love of Three Kings (*See* L'Amore dei tre Re) | | | |
| Lucia di Lammermoor | Donizetti; Cammarano | 9.26.1835 | Naples, SC |
| Lucrezia Borgia | Donizetti; Romani | 12.26.1833 | Milan, Sc |
| Luisa Miller | Verdi; Cammarano | 12. 8.1849 | Naples, Sc |
| Lulu | Berg | 6. 2.1937 | Zurich |
| Lurline | Wallace; Fitzball | 2.23.1860 | London, CG |
| Der lustige Krieg | J. Strauss; Zell, Genée | 11.25.1881 | Vienna, W |
| Die lustige Witwe | Lehár; Leon, Stein | 12.30.1905 | Vienna, W |
| Die lustigen Weiber von Windsor | Nicolai; Mosenthal | 3. 9.1849 | Berlin, O |
| Macbeth | Verdi; Piave | 3.14.1847 | Florence |
| Macbeth | Bloch; Fleo | 11.30.1910 | Paris, OC |
| Madama Butterfly | Puccini; Giacosa, Illica | 2.17.1904 | Milan, Sc |
| The Maid of Pskov | Rimsky-Korsakov | 1.13.1873 | St. Petersburg, Ma |
| Madame Sans-Gêne | Giordano; Simoni | 1.25.1915 | New York, M |
| Les Malheurs d'Orphée | Milhaud; Lunel | 5. 7.1926 | Brussels |
| Manon | Massenet; Meilhac, Gille | 1.19.1884 | Paris, OC |
| Manon Lescaut | Puccini; Praga, Oliva, Illica | 2. 1.1893 | Turin |
| Margarethe (*See* Faust) | | | |
| Maria di Rohan | Donizetti; Cammarano | 6. 5.1843 | Vienna |
| Le Mariage aux Lanternes | Offenbach; Carré, Battu | 10.10.1857 | Paris |
| Maria Tudor | Gomes | 1879 | Milan |
| Maritana | Wallace; Fitzball | 11.15.1845 | London |

| Opera | Composer; Librettist | Date | City |
|---|---|---|---|
| Mârouf, Savetier du Caire | Rabaud; Népoty | 5.15.1914 | Paris, OC |
| Marta (*See* Martha) | | | |
| Martha | Flotow; Friedrich | 11.25.1847 | Vienna |
| Les Martyrs (*See* Poliuto) | | | |
| Masaniello (*See* La Muette de Portici) | | | |
| A Masked Ball (*See* Un Ballo in Maschera) | | | |
| Mathis der Maler | Hindemith | 5.28.1938 | Zurich |
| Il Matrimonio segreto | Cimarosa; Bertati | 2. 7.1792 | Vienna, B |
| Mavra | Stravinsky; Kochno | 6. 2.1922 | Paris, O |
| May Night | Rimsky-Korsakov | 1.21.1880 | St. Petersburg, Ma |
| Mazeppa | Tchaikovsky; Tchaikovsky, Burenin | 2.15.1884 | Moscow, B |
| Medea (*See* Médée) | | | |
| Médée | Cherubini; Hoffman | 3.13.1797 | Paris |
| Mefistofele | Boito | 3. 5.1868 | Milan, Sc |
| Die Meistersinger von Nuernberg | Wagner | 6.21.1868 | Munich |
| The Merry Widow (*See* Die lustige Witwe) | | | |
| The Merry Wives of Windsor (*See* Die lustigen Weiber von Windsor) | | | |
| Mignon | Thomas; Barbier, Carré | 11.17.1866 | Paris, OC |
| The Mikado | Sullivan; Gilbert | 3.14.1885 | London, Savoy |
| Mireille | Gounod; Carré | 3.19.1864 | Paris |
| Der Mond | Orff | 2. ?.1939 | Munich |
| Il Mondo della Luna | Haydn; Goldoni | 8. 3.1777 | Esterháza |
| Monsieur Beaucaire | Messager; Rivoire, Veber | 4. 7.1919 | Birmingham, England |
| Mosè in Egitto | Rossini; Tottola | 3. 5.1818 | Naples, SC |
| Les Mousquetaires au Couvent | Varney; Ferrier, Prével | 3.16.1880 | Paris |
| Mozart i Salieri | Rimsky-Korsakov; Pushkin | 12. 7.1898 | Moscow |
| La Muette de Portici | Auber; Scribe, Delavigne | 2.29.1828 | Paris, O |
| Nabucco (*See* Nabucodonosor) | | | |
| Nabucodonosor | Verdi; Solera | 3. 9.1842 | Milan, Sc |
| Eine Nacht in Venedig | J. Strauss; Zell, Genée | 10. 3.1883 | Berlin |
| Das Nachtlager von Granada | Kreutzer; Braun von Braunthal | 1.13.1834 | Vienna |
| La Navarraise | Massenet; Claretie, Cain | 6.20.1894 | London, CG |
| Nerone | Boito | 5. 1.1924 | Milan, Sc |

OPERAS PRODUCED FROM 1597 THROUGH 1939 (*cont.*)

| Opera | Composer; Librettist | Date | City |
|---|---|---|---|
| Die neugierigen Frauen (*See* Le Donne curiose) | | | |
| A Night in Venice (*See* Eine Nacht in Venedig) | | | |
| Nikola Šubic Zrinski | Zajc; Badalic | 11. 4.1876 | Zagreb, Yugoslavia |
| Les Noces de Jeannette | Massé; Barbier, Carré | 2. 4.1853 | Paris, OC |
| Norma | Bellini; Romani | 12.26.1831 | Milan, Sc |
| Le Nozze di Figaro | Mozart; da Ponte | 5. 1.1786 | Vienna, B |
| Oberon | Weber; Planché | 4.12.1826 | London, CG |
| Oedipus Rex | Stravinsky; Cocteau | 5.30.1927 | Paris |
| Der Opernball | Heuberger; Léon, Waldberg | 1. 5.1898 | Vienna, W |
| L'Oracolo | Leoni; Zanoni | 6.28.1905 | London, CG |
| Orfeo (Milhaud) (*See* Les Malheurs d'Orphée) | | | |
| Orfeo (Monteverdi) (*See* La Favola d'Orfeo) | | | |
| Orfeo, ed Euridice | Gluck; Calzabigi | 10. 5.1762 | Vienna, B |
| Orphée aux Enfers | Offenbach; Cremieux, Halévy | 10.21.1858 | Paris |
| Otello | Rossini; Berio di Salsa | 12. 4.1816 | Naples |
| Otello | Verdi; Boito | 2. 5.1887 | Milan, Sc |
| I Pagliacci | Leoncavallo | 5.21.1892 | Milan |
| Palestrina | Pfitzner | 6.12.1917 | Munich |
| Le Pardon de Ploeermel | Meyerbeer; Barbier, Carré | 4. 4.1859 | Paris, OC |
| Paride e Elena | Gluck; Calzabigi | 11. 3.1770 | Vienna, B |
| Parsifal | Wagner | 7.26.1882 | Bayreuth |
| Patience | Sullivan; Gilbert | 4.25.1881 | London |
| Le pauvre Matelot | Milhaud; Cocteau | 12.16.1927 | Paris, OC |
| Les Pêcheurs de Perles | Bizet; Cormon, Carré | 9.30.1863 | Paris |
| Pelléas et Mélisande | Debussy; Maeterlinck | 4.30.1902 | Paris, OC |
| La Périchole | Offenbach; Meilhac, Halévy | 10. 6.1868 | Paris |
| Philémon et Baucis | Gounod; Barbier, Carré | 2.18.1860 | Paris |
| Pinafore (*See* H. M. S. Pinafore) | | | |
| Pique Dame | P. Tchaikovsky; M. Tchaikovsky | 12.19.1890 | St. Petersburg, Ma |
| The Pirates of Penzance | Sullivan; Gilbert | 12.30.1879 | Paignton, England |
| Poliuto | Donizetti; Scribe | 4.10.1840 | Paris, O |

| Opera | Composer; Librettist | Date | City |
|---|---|---|---|
| Il Pomo d'Oro | Cesti; Sbarra | 1667 | Vienna |
| Pomone | Cambert; Perrin | 3. 3.1671 | Paris, O |
| Poppea (*See* L'Incoronazione di Poppea) | | | |
| Porgy and Bess | G. Gershwin; Heyward, I. Gershwin | 9.30.1935 | Boston, Mass. |
| Le Postillon de Longjumeau | Adam; de Leuven, Brunswick | 10.13.1836 | Paris, OC |
| Příhody Lišky Bystioušky | Janáček; Tešnohlídek | 11. 6.1924 | Brno |
| Prince Igor | Borodin | 11. 4.1890 | St. Petersburg |
| Princess Ida | Sullivan; Gilbert | 1. 5.1884 | London, Savoy |
| La Princesse Jaune | Saint-Saens; Gallet | 6.12.1872 | Paris, OC |
| Prodaná Nevěsta | Smetana; Sabina | 5.30.1866 | Prague |
| Le Prophète | Meyerbeer; Scribe | 4.16.1849 | Paris, O |
| I Puritani di Scozia | Bellini; Pepoli | 1.25.1835 | Paris |
| The Puritan's Daughter | Balfe; Bridgeman | 11.30.1861 | London, CG |
| I quattro Rusteghi | Wolf-Ferrari; Pizzolato | 3.19.1906 | Munich |
| The Queen of Sheba (*See* Die Koenigin von Saba) | | | |
| The Queen of Spades (*See* Pique Dame) | | | |
| The Quiet Don | Dzerzhinsky; Sholokhov | 10.22.1935 | Leningrad |
| Il Rapimento di Cefalo | Caccini; Chiabrera | 10. 9.1600 | Florence |
| Renard | Stravinsky | 6. 2.1922 | Paris, O |
| El Retablo de Maese Pedro | Falla | 3.23.1923 | Seville |
| Das Rheingold | Wagner | 9.22.1869 | Munich |
| Richard Coeur-de-Lion | Grétry; Sedaine | 10.21.1784 | Paris |
| Rienzi | Wagner | 10.20.1842 | Dresden |
| Rigoletto | Verdi; Piave | 3.11.1851 | Venice, F |
| The Ring (*See* Der Ring des Nibelungen) | | | |
| Der Ring des Nibelungen: A drama composed of four operas by Wagner: *Das Rheingold, Die Walkuere, Siegfried,* and *Goetterdaemmerung* | | | |
| Il Ritorno d'Ulisse in Patria | Monteverdi; Badoaro | 2. ?.1641 | Venice |
| Robert-le-Diable | Meyerbeer; Scribe, Delavigne | 11.21.1831 | Paris, O |
| Rodelinda | Handel; Salvi | 2.24.1725 | London |
| Le Roi d'Ys | Lalo; Blau | 5. 7.1888 | Paris, OC |
| Le Roi malgré lui | Chabrier; Najac, Burani | 5.18.1887 | Paris, OC |
| Roméo et Juliette | Gounod; Barbier, Carré | 4.27.1867 | Paris |
| La Rondine | Puccini; Adami | 3.27.1917 | Monte Carlo |
| Der Rosenkavalier | R. Strauss; Hofmannsthal | 1.26.1911 | Dresden |

OPERAS PRODUCED FROM 1597 THROUGH 1939 (*cont.*)

| Opera | Composer; Librettist | Date | City |
|---|---|---|---|
| The Rose of Castille | Balfe; Harris, Falconer | 10.29.1857 | London |
| Le Rossignol | Stravinsky; Stravinsky, Mitusov | 5.26.1914 | Paris, O |
| The Royal Guest (*See* Den kongelige Gast) | | | |
| Ruddigore | Sullivan; Gilbert | 1.22.1887 | London, Savoy |
| Rusalka | Dargomuizhsky | 5.16.1856 | St. Petersburg |
| Rusalka | Dvořák; Kvapil | 3.31.1901 | Prague |
| Russlan and Ludmilla | Glinka; Shirkof and others | 12. 9.1842 | St. Petersburg |
| Ruy Blas | Marchetti; d'Ormeville | 4. 3.1869 | Milan, Sc |
| Sadko | Rimsky-Korsakov; Byelsky | 1. 7.1898 | Moscow |
| Salome | R. Strauss; Lachmann, Wilde | 12. 9.1905 | Dresden |
| Samson et Dalila | Saint-Saens, Lemaire | 12. 2.1877 | Weimar |
| Satanella | Balfe; Harris, Falconer | 12.20.1858 | London, CG |
| La Scala di Seta | Rossini; Rossi | 5. 9.1812 | Venice |
| Der Schauspieldirektor | Mozart; Stephanie | 2. 7.1786 | Vienna |
| Lo Schiavo | Gomes; Paravicini | 9.27.1889 | Rio de Janeiro |
| Das Schlaue Fuechslein (The Cunning Little Vixen) (*See* Příhody Lišky Bystroušky) | | | |
| Die Schweigsame Frau (The Silent Woman) | R. Strauss; Zweig | 6.24.1935 | Dresden |
| The Secret Marriage (*See* Il Matrimonio segreto) | | | |
| Semiramide | Rossini; Rossi | 2. 3.1823 | Venice, F |
| Serse | Handel; Minato | 4.26.1738 | London |
| La Serva Padrona | Pergolesi; Federico | 8.28.1733 | Naples |
| Shwanda the Bagpiper (*See* Švanda Dudák) | | | |
| Siegfried | Wagner | 8.16.1876 | Bayreuth |
| Il Signor Bruschino | Rossini; Foppa | 1. ?.1813 | Venice |
| Simon Boccanegra | Verdi; Piave, Boito | 3.12.1857 | Venice, F |
| The Snow Maiden (*See* Snyegurochka) | | | |
| Snyegurochka | Rimsky-Korsakov | 2.10.1882 | St. Petersburg, Ma |
| Solimano | Hasse; Migliavacoa | 2. 5.1753 | Dresden |
| La Sonnambula | Bellini; Romani | 3. 6.1831 | Milan |
| The Sorcerer | Sullivan; Gilbert | 11.17.1877 | London |
| Suor Angelica | Puccini; Forzano | 12.14.1918 | New York, M |

| Opera | Composer; Librettist | Date | City |
|---|---|---|---|
| Švanda Dudák | Weinberger; Kareš | 4.27.1927 | Prague |
| Il Tabarro | Puccini; Adami | 12.14.1918 | New York, M |
| Tancredi | Rossini; Rossi | 2. 6.1813 | Venice, F |
| Tannhaeuser und der Saen-gerkrieg auf Wartburg | Wagner | 10.19.1845 | Dresden |
| Thais | Massenet; Gallet | 3.16.1894 | Paris, O |

Thousand and One Nights (*See* Indigo und die vierzig Raeuber)

The Threepenny Opera (*See* Die Dreigroschenoper)

| | | | |
|---|---|---|---|
| Tiefland. | d'Albert; Lothar | 11.15.1903 | Prague |
| Tosca | Puccini; Giacosa, Illica | 1.14.1900 | Rome, C |
| La Traviata | Verdi; Piave | 3. 6.1853 | Venice, F |
| Trial by Jury | Sullivan; Gilbert | 3.25.1875 | London |
| Tristan und Isolde | Wagner | 6.10.1865 | Munich |

Il Trittico (the title, when given together, of three one-act operas by Puccini: *Il Tabarro, Suor Angelica* and *Gianni Schicchi*)

| | | | |
|---|---|---|---|
| Der Trompeter von Saeck-ingen | Nessler; Bunge | 5. 4.1884 | Leipzig |
| Il Trovatore | Verdi; Cammarano, Bardare | 1.19.1853 | Rome, Ap |
| Les Troyens à Carthage (Part II of Les Troyens) | Berlioz· | 11. 4.1863 | Paris |
| Les Troyens | Berlioz | 12. 6.1890 | Carlsruhe |
| Tsar Saltan | Rimsky-Korsakov; Byelsky | 11. 3.1900 | Moscow |
| The Tsar's Bride | Rimsky-Korsakov; Mei | 11. 3.1899 | Moscow |
| Turandot | Puccini; Adami, Simoni | 4.25.1926 | Milan, Sc |
| Il Turco in Italia | Rossini; Romani | 8.14.1814 | Milan, Sc |
| Ungdom og Galskab (Youth and Folly) | Dupuy; Bruun | 5.19.1806 | Copenhagen |

Die Verkaufte Braut (The Bartered Bride) (*See* Prodaná Nevěsta)

| | | | |
|---|---|---|---|
| Véronique | Messager; Vanloo, Duval | 12.10.1898 | Paris |
| I Vespri Siciliani | Verdi; Scribe, Duveyrier | 6.13.1855 | Paris, O |
| La Vestale | Spontini; Etienne de Jouy | 12.16.1807 | Paris, O |
| Victorine | Mellon; Falconer | 12.19.1859 | London, CG |
| La Vida Breva | Falla; Shaw | 4. 1.1913 | Nice |
| La Vie Parisienne | Offenbach; Meilhac, Halévy | 10.31.1866 | Paris |
| Der Vogelhaendler | Zeller; West, Held | 1.10.1891 | Vienna, W |

## OPERAS FIRST PRODUCED AFTER 1939

| Opera | Composer; Librettist | Date | City |
|---|---|---|---|
| Der Waffenschmied | Lortzing | 5.31.1846 | Vienna, W |
| Die Walkuere | Wagner | 6.26.1870 | Munich |
| La Wally | Catalani; Illica | 1.20.1892 | Milan, Sc |
| Ein Walzertraum | O. Straus; Doermann, Jacobson | 3. 2.1907 | Vienna |
| Werther | Massenet; Blau, Milliet, Hartmann | 2.16.1892 | Vienna, O |
| Der Wildschuetz | Lortzing | 12.31.1842 | Leipzig |
| William Tell (*See* Guillaume Tell) | | | |
| Wozzeck | Berg; Buechner | 12.14.1925 | Berlin, O |
| The Yeomen of the Guard | Sullivan; Gilbert | 10. 3.1888 | London, Savoy |
| Youth and Folly (*See* Ungdom og Galskab) | | | |
| Zampa | Hérold; Melesville | 5. 3.1831 | Paris, OC |
| Zar und Zimmermann | Lortzing | 12.22.1837 | Leipzig |
| Die Zauberfloete (The Magic Flute) | Mozart; Schikaneder, Gieske | 9.30.1791 | Vienna, W |
| Zaza | Leoncavallo | 11.10.1900 | Milan |
| Der Zigeunerbaron | J. Strauss; Schnitzer | 10.24.1885 | Vienna, W |

## 2.

## OPERAS FIRST PRODUCED AFTER 1939

| Opera | Composer; Librettist | Date | City |
|---|---|---|---|
| Albert Herring | Britten; Crozier | 6.20.1947 | Glyndebourne |
| Amahl and the Night Visi-tors | Menotti (first performed on televison 12.24.1951) | 2.21.1952 | Bloomington, Ind. |
| Aniara | Blomdahl; Lindegren | 5.31.1959 | Stockholm |
| L'Assassinio nella Cat-tedrale | Pizzetti; Castelli | 3. 1.1958 | Milan, Sc |
| The Ballad of Baby Doe | Moore; Latouche | 7. 7.1956 | Central City, Colo. |
| Beatrice | Holby; Nardi (first performed on radio 10.23.1959) | 10.30.1959 | Louisville, Ky. |
| Billy Budd | Britten; Forster | 12. 6.1951 | London, CG |
| Capriccio | R. Strauss; R. Strauss, Krauss | 10.28.1942 | Munich |
| Catulli Carmina | Orff | 11. 6.1943 | Leipzig |

| *Opera* | *Composer; Librettist* | *Date* | *City* |
|---|---|---|---|
| The Consul | Menotti | 3. 1.1950 | Philadelphia |
| Dantons Tod | van Einem; Buechner | 8. 6.1947 | Salzburg |
| Les Dialogues des Carmé- lites | Poulenc; Bernanos | 1.26.1957 | Milan, Sc |
| Down in the Valley | Weill; Sundgaard | 7.15.1948 | Bloomington, Ind. |
| The Dybbuk | D. Tamkin; A. Tamkin | 10. 4.1951 | New York, CC |
| The Flaming Angel | Prokofiev | 9.29.1955 | Venice, F |
| Gloriana | Britten; Plomer | 6. 8.1953 | London, CG |
| The Good Soldier Schweik | Kurka; Allan | 4.23.1958 | New York, CC |
| He Who Gets Slapped (Pantaloon) | Ward; Stambler | 5.17.1956 | New York |
| The Island God | Menotti | 2.20.1942 | New York, M |
| Izaht | Villa Lobos; Azvedo, Fihlo | 12.13.1958 | Rio de Janeiro |
| Die Kluge | Orff | 2.18.1943 | Frankfurt-am- Main |
| Koenig Hirsch | Henze; Cramer | 9.23.1956 | Berlin, O |
| Die Liebe der Danae | R. Strauss; Gregor | 8.14.1952 | Salzburg |
| Lord Byron's Love Letter | de Banfield; Williams | 1.17.1955 | New Orleans |
| Les Mamelles de Tirésias | Poulenc; Appollinaire | 6. 3.1947 | Paris, OC |
| Maria Golovin | Menotti | 8.20.1958 | Brussels |
| The Medium | Menotti | 5. 8.1946 | New York |
| The Midsummer Marriage | Tippett | 1.27.1955 | London, CG |
| A Midsummer Night's Dream | Britten; Britten, Pears | 6.11.1960 | Aldeburgh, England |
| The Moon and Sixpence | Gardner; Terry | 5.24.1957 | London, SW |
| Moses und Aron | Schoenberg | 6. 6.1957 | Zurich |
| The Mother of Us All | Thomson; Stein | 5.12.1947 | New York |
| Murder in the Cathedral (*See* L'Assassinio nella Cattedrale) | | | |
| Nelson | Berkeley; Pryce-Jones | 9.22.1954 | London, SW |
| Peter Grimes | Britten; Slater | 6. 7.1945 | London, SW |
| Il Prigioniero (The Prisoner) | Dallapiccola | 5.20.1950 | Florence |
| The Rake's Progress | Stravinsky; Auden, Kallman | 9.11.1951 | Venice, F |
| The Rape of Lucretia | Britten; Duncan | 7.12.1946 | Glyndebourne |
| Regina | Blitzstein | 10.31.1949 | New York |
| Der Revisor (The Inspector General) | Egk | 5. 9.1957 | Schwetzingen |

OPERAS FIRST PRODUCED AFTER 1939 (*cont.*)

| Opera | Composer; Librettist | Date | City |
|---|---|---|---|
| The Ruby | Dello Joio | 5.13.1955 | Bloomington, Ind. |
| The Saint of Bleeker Street | Menotti | 12.27.1954 | New York |
| The Scarf | Hoiby; Duncan | 6.20.1958 | Spoleto |
| The School for Wives | Liebermann | 12. 3.1955 | Louisville, Ky. |
| Six Characters in Search of an Author | Weisgall; Johnston | 4.26.1959 | New York, CC |
| Der Sturm (The Tempest) | Martin | 6.17.1956 | Vienna, O |
| Susannah | Floyd | 9.27.1956 | New York, CC |
| A Tale of Two Cities | Benjamin; Cliffe | 7.23.1957 | London, SW |
| The Taming of the Shrew | Giannini; Fee | 1.31.1953 | Cincinnati |
| The Telephone | Menotti | 2.18.1947 | New York |
| The Tender Land | Copland; Everett | 4. 1.1954 | New York |
| Trionfo d'Afrodite | Orff; Catullus, Sappho,Euripides | 2.13.1953 | Milan, Sc |
| Troilus and Cressida | Walton; Hassall | 12. 3.1954 | London, CG |
| Trouble in Tahiti | Bernstein | 6.12.1952 | Waltham, Mass. |
| The Turn of the Screw | Britten; Piper | 9.14.1954 | Venice, F |
| Vanessa | Barber; Menotti | 1.15.1958 | New York, M |
| La Voix Humaine | Poulenc; Cocteau | 2. 6.1959 | Paris, OC |
| Volo di Notte | Dallapiccola | 5.18.1940 | Florence |
| War and Peace | Prokofiev; Mendelssohn | 4.18.1942 | Leningrad |
| West Side Story | Bernstein; Laurents, Sondheim | 9.26.1957 | New York |
| The Wife of Martin Guerre | Bergsma; Lewis | 2.15.1956 | New York |
| Wuthering Heights | Floyd | 7.16.1958 | Santa Fe, N.M. |

# 3.

# CATALOGUE OF THE OPERAS OF MOZART, VERDI, WAGNER AND PUCCINI

*With the year of the first production or if never produced the year of composition.*

## MOZART, Wolfgang Amadeus (1.27.1756–12.5.1791)

Die Schuldigkeit des ersten Gebotes, 1767
Apollo et Hyacinthus, 1767
Bastien und Bastienne, 1768
La Finta Semplice, 1769
Mitridate, Re di Ponto, 1770
Ascanio in Alba, 1771
Il Sogno di Scipione, 1772
Lucio Silla, 1772
La Finta Giardiniera, 1775
Il Re Pastore, 1775
Idomeneo, 1781
Die Entfuehrung aus dem Serail, 1782
Der Schauspieldirektor, 1786

Le Nozze di Figaro, 1786
Don Giovanni, 1787 (The true title is Il Dissoluto Punito, ossia Il Don Giovanni)
Così fan tutte, 1790
La Clemenza di Tito, 1791
Die Zauberfloete, 1791
Zaide (fragments), 1866
L'Oie du Caire (fragments), 1867
Thamos, Koenig in Aegypten, c. 1780
Lo Sposo Deluso, c. 1783, and unfinished. Libretto possibly by Da Ponte.

## VERDI, Giuseppe (10.10.1813–1.27.1901)

Oberto, Conte di Bonifacio, 1839
Un Giorno di Regno, 1840 (sometimes called Il Finto Stanislao)
Nabucodonosor, 1842 (usually called Nabucco)
I Lombardi alla Prima Crociata, 1843
Ernani, 1844
I Due Foscari, 1844
Giovanna d'Arco, 1845
Alzira, 1845
Attila, 1846
Macbeth, 1847
I Masnadieri, 1847
(I Lombardi revised as Jérusalem, 1847)
Il Corsaro, 1848
La Battaglia di Legnano, 1849
Luisa Miller, 1849

Stiffelio, 1850
Rigoletto, 1851
Il Trovatore, 1853
La Traviata, 1853
I Vespri Siciliani, 1855
Simon Boccanegra, 1857
(Stiffelio revised as Aroldo, 1857)
Un Ballo in Maschera, 1859
La Forza del Destino, 1862
(Macbeth revised, 1865)
Don Carlo, 1867
(La Forza del Destino revised, 1869)
Aida, 1871
(Simon Boccanegra revised, 1881)
(Don Carlo revised, 1884)
Otello, 1887
Falstaff, 1893

### MOZART, VERDI, WAGNER AND PUCCINI (*cont.*)

#### WAGNER, Richard (5.22.1813–2.13.1883)

Das Liebesverbot, 1836
Rienzi, 1842
Der Fliegende Hollaender, 1843
Tannhaeuser, 1845
Lohengrin, 1850
Tristan und Isolde, 1865
Die Meistersinger von Nuernberg, 1868

Das Rheingold, 1869
Die Walkuere, 1870
Siegfried, 1876
Goetterdaemmerung, 1876
Parsifal, 1882
Die Feen, 1888 (but composed from 1833–34)

#### PUCCINI, Giacomo (12.22.1858–11.29.1924)

Le Villi, 1884
Edgar, 1889
Manon Lescaut, 1893
La Bohème, 1896
Tosca, 1900
Madama Butterfly, 1904
La Fanciulla del West, 1910

La Rondine, 1917
Il Trittico, 1918
  Il Tabarro
  Suor Angelica
  Gianni Schicchi
Turandot, 1926

# APPENDIX B

## BASIC OPERATIC ITALIAN

Languages are a hurdle to the enjoyment of opera. But the hurdle sometimes looms larger than it really is. Most persons pick up some French on their way through school—enough, anyway, to recognize the construction and sound of it when they read a libretto. This seems to be less true of German and emphatically not true of Italian. Yet, of the three operatic languages, Italian is the most common and the easiest. First, all the Italian characters tend, rather rudely, to address each other in the imperative: die, be damned, flee; then, being good egocentrics, they tend to live almost entirely in the first person singular present with a few qualifying adjectives: I am happy.

The imperative is a fine mood, short and with few changes. Characters once ahold of it rarely let go. Pinkerton, for example, in his love duet with Butterfly, sticks cautiously to repeating twenty times, "Vieni" (come). Tosca breathes death to Scarpia four times, "Muori" (die), and then, more linguistically daring than Pinkerton, switches to "È morto" (he is dead).

For those who have never had any Italian, there follows a short outline of basic operatic Italian.

## *Verbs*

Of these the two most important (and on which much of all other action is merely variation) are:

| | | |
|---|---|---|
| va | VAH | go |
| vieni | v'YAY.nee | come |

Both are in the imperative mood. No one need, in operatic Italian, fuss over mood and tense; but, to keep it clear, the imperative is the mood used exclusively by Emperors, i.e. "I'm not asking you, I'm telling you: go."

Some of the variations, all imperative, on "va" and "vieni" are:

| | | |
|---|---|---|
| fuggi | FOOD.jee | flee |
| muori | MWORE.ee | die |
| lascia | LAH.shah | leave |
| sii | SEE | be (cursed) |
| aspetta | ah.SPET.tah | wait |
| ascolta | ah.SCOLE.tah | listen |
| dite | DEE.teh | tell, say |
| parla | PAR.lah | speak |
| aprite | ah.PREE.teh | open |
| credi | CRAY.dee | believe |
| taci | TAH.chee | be silent |

On some of these you can add the pronoun "mi," meaning "me." Thus, "credimi" means "believe me"; "lasciami," "leave me."

The verb "to go" has one form of the imperative that turns up so frequently that it deserves a paragraph to itself. It is the first person plural:

| | | |
|---|---|---|
| andiamo | an.D'YAH.moe | let's go |

The most important verb for forming sentences is the verb "to be." The present tense with the pronouns is:

| | | |
|---|---|---|
| io sono | ee.oh (or "yo") SO.no | I am |
| tu sei | two SAY'ee | you are |
| è | ay (sliding into "eh") | he she is it |
| noi siamo | noy see.AH.moe | we are |
| voi siete | voy see.AY.tay | you are |
| sono | SO.no | they are |

BASIC OPERATIC ITALIAN (*continued*)

The pronouns for "he," "she," "it" and "they" are almost never used in operatic Italian and were omitted. The other pronouns, too, are frequently dropped except where meter or emphasis requires them. For emphasis they frequently follow rather than precede.

The final vowels are frequently elided to fit the meter or because another vowel follows: son' io.

Simple sentences are put together just as in English:

| | | |
|---|---|---|
| son io | son EE.oh | it is I |
| sei tu | say'ee two | it is you (you are you!) |
| siamo soli | see.AH.moe SO.lee | we are alone |
| siamo due | see.AH.moe DEW.ay | we are two |
| sei perduto | say.e pear.DEW.two | you are lost |
| io son felice | ee.oh (yo) son fay.LEE.chay | I am happy |
| dov'è | doe.vay | where is he |
| é morto | eh MORE.toe | he is dead |
| sono poeta | so.no poe.EH.tah | I am a poet |

## Nouns

Most nouns are masculine. The plural of these is formed by changing the final vowel to "i." Most feminine nouns end in "a." The plural of these is formed by changing the final vowel to "e." Thus:

| | | | |
|---|---|---|---|
| dottore | dottori | doh.TOR.ee | doctors |
| ragazzo | ragazzi | rah.GAH.tsi | boys |
| uomo | uomini | oo.ALM.i.nee | men |
| tempo | tempi | TEM.pea | times |
| ragazza | ragazze | rah.GAH.tsay | girls |
| donna | donne | DUN.nay | women |
| ora | ore | OAR.ay | hours |

## The Definite Article

In the same manner, the definite article, "the," changes before singular and plural nouns of masculine and feminine gender.

| | | |
|---|---|---|
| il ragazzo | i ragazzi | eel, ee |
| la ragazza | le ragazze | lah,lay |

Thus, "I Pagliacci" is "The Clowns."

## The Indefinite Article

| | | |
|---|---|---|
| un ragazzo | oon | (there is no plural) |
| una ragazza | OON.ah | |

## The Prepositions

These are important, as they frequently are the start of key phrases which a composer repeats. When the prepositions precede the definite article, they merge with it. The principal prepositions with the contractions are:

| | | | contracted with | | |
|---|---|---|---|---|---|
| *prep.* | *meaning* | il | i | la | le |
| a | to, at | al | ai | alla | alle |
| da | from, by | dal | dai | dalla | dalle |
| di | of | del | dei | della | delle |
| in | in | nel | nei | nella | nelle |
| su | on | sul | sui | sulla | sulle |

Thus:

| | |
|---|---|
| nel giardino | in the garden |
| alla chiesa | to the church |
| sulla tomba | on the tomb |
| ai nostri monti | to our mountains |

One preposition is used constantly with certain pronouns. It is "con" (with) and, depending on the singer, it is pronounced somewhere between "kahn" and "cone."

| | | | | | |
|---|---|---|---|---|---|
| con me | kon MAY | with me | con noi | kon NOY | with us |
| con te | " TAY | " you | con voi | " VOY | " you |
| con lui | " LOO.ee | " him | | | |
| con lei | " LAY.ee | " her | | | |

## The Possessive

It is the same whether an adjective or pronoun and it takes the gender and number of the noun it qualifies or supplants.

## BASIC OPERATIC ITALIAN (*continued*)

| adjective | pronoun | masc. sing. | fem. sing. | masc. plural | fem. plural |
|---|---|---|---|---|---|
| my | mine | il mio | la mia | i miei | le mie |
| thy | thine | il tuo | la tua | i tuoi | le tue |
| his, her | his, her | il suo | la sua | i suoi | le sue |
| our | ours | il nostro | la nostra | i nostri | le nostre |
| your | yours | il vostro | la vostra | i vostri | le vostre |

Thus:

| | |
|---|---|
| il mio tesoro | my treasure |
| la sua casa | his or her house |

But, when talking about members of the family, the article is generally dropped. Thus:

| | | |
|---|---|---|
| suo marito | mah.REE.toe | her husband |
| sua moglie | MOE.l'yay | his wife |
| mia sorella | so.RELL.ah | my sister |
| suo fratello | frah.TELL.oh | his or her brother |
| mia figlia | FEEL.yah | my daughter |
| nostro figlio | FEEL.yo | our son |
| mio padre | PAH.dray | my father |
| sua madre | MAH.dray | his or her mother |

### Adjectives

| masc. | | fem. | masc. plural | fem. plural | |
|---|---|---|---|---|---|
| questo | QUEST.oh | questa | questi | queste | this |
| tutto | TOOT.toe | tutta | tutti | tutte | all |
| quello | QUAIL.oh | quella | quelli | quelle | that |
| bello | BELL.oh | bella | bei | belle | pretty |
| buono | BWAHN.oh | buona | buoni | buone | good |
| grande | GRAN.deh | grande | grandi | grandi | large |

Frequently the noun is left out if the meaning is clear, and the adjective does the work of a noun as well. Thus:

| | |
|---|---|
| quest(a) o quella | this girl or that girl |
| così fan tutte | thus do all women |

### Words and Phrases

Each opera, depending on its subject, develops a vocabulary of its own. Where there is a synopsis of the opera in this book, those words are set out at the end of each act. However, certain phrases, words, even sentences occur in almost every opera, and those not used as examples above are listed here:

| io t'amo | yo T'AH.moe | I love you |
| buon giorno | bwahn je.OR.no | good morning |
| buona sera | bwahn.ah SAY.rah | good evening |
| buona notte | bwahn.ah NOT.tay | good night |
| grazie | GRAH.tsee.ay | thank you |
| ecco | EK.koe | here, behold |
| pace | PAH.chay | peace |
| pietà | p'yay.TAH | have pity |
| mai più | p'eye p'you | no more, never more |
| dov' è | DOE.vay | where is |
| allora | ahl.LORE.ah | well then |
| ancora | ahn.KOR.ah | still, yet |
| amore | ah.MORE.ay | love |
| uno, due, tre | OON.o, DO.eh, tray | one, two, three |
| non è vero | known eh VAIR.oh | it is not true |
| sempre | SEM.pray | always |
| andiamo | an.D'YAH.moe | let's go |
| Signore | seen.YOR.ay | sir |
| Signorina | seen.yor.REEN.ah | miss |
| Signora | seen.YOR.ah | madam |
| gran Dio | gran DEE.oh | Great God! |
| oh gioja | oh je.OY.ah | oh joy |
| piangi | p'YAHN.jee | weep |
| si | see | yes |
| no | naw | no |

# INDEX

A cappella, 159-160
A tempo, 161
*Abduction from the Seraglio, see Ent-*
*fuehrung aus dem Serail, Die* under
Mozart
Absolute pitch, 159
Accent, agogic, 11; tonic, 11
Ad lib, 160
Adagio, defined, 160; 193
Adele (role), 191
*L'Africaine*, 28
*Aida, see* under Verdi
Albert, Eugene
*Tiefland*, 195
*Alceste, see* under Gluck
Alfredo (role), 26
Alfresco, 160
Allegro, defined, 160; 193
Almaviva, Count (role in *Il Barbiere di*
*Siviglia)*, 26
Amati, Nicolo, A., 74
American Ballet Co., 108-110
American Standards Association, 92
Amphora, about tenors, 160
Andante, defined, 160; 193
*Andrea Chenier*, 152, 166, 172, 176
Andrea Chenier (role), 26, 88
*Angelica vincitrice di Alcina*, 130
Antheil, George
*Ballet Mécanique*, 70
*Ariadne auf Naxos, see* under Strauss, R.
*Arianna*, 113-114, 115, 116
Arias, discussion of construction, 9-17; "da
Capo," 15, 168; in *Orfeo*, 47; to be sung
as written, 53; first popular aria, 113-
114; effect of lack of copyright, 133;
defined, 160-161
Arietta, 161
Arioso, 161
*L'Arlésienne, see* under Bizet
*Armide, see* under Gluck
*Artaserse*, 51
*L'Assassinio nella Cattedrale*, 20,
Attack, 161
Auber, Daniel F.E., 90

Auden, W. H., Quoted on librettos, 18-19;
on the Marschallin's monologue, 20
*Aureliano in Palmira, see* under Rossini
Ave Maria, 161
Azucena (role), 24

Baccelli, Giovanna Z., 161
"Bacchanal," 106
Bach, Johann S., 115; dies blind, 193
Balanchine, George, defines ballet, 102-103;
defines a "pas de deux," 105; at Metro-
politan, 108-110; concept of *Orfeo*, 109
"Balen, Il," 176
Ballabile, 161
*Ballad of Baby Doe, The*, 15, 21
Ballad opera, 161-162
*Ballet Mécanique*, 70
*Ballo in Maschera, Un, see* under Verdi
Band, 162; elastic, 170
*Barber of Seville, see Barbiere di Siviglia, Il*
under Rossini
Barbershop quartet, 162
*Barbiere di Siviglia, Il* (Paisiello), 52
*Barbiere di Siviglia, Il* Rossini), *see* under
Rossini
Barcarolle, 162
Baritone, 23; defined, 24; 26, 30, 32
Baroque operas, 130-131, 133
Barrel organ, 162
*Bartered Bride, The, see Prodaná Nevěsta*
Bartók, Béla
*Duke Blue-Beard's Castle*, 104
Bass, 23, defined, 24; 26, 30, 32, 33
Bass clarinet, 57; described, 63
Bass drum, *see* under Drum
Basso, 162
Basso buffo, 27, 139, 164
Basso cantante, 26-27, 139
Basso profundo, 27
Bassoon, 57, 58; described, 65-66; 196
Baton, picture, 149; described, 162
Bayreuth Festival, its creation, 144-150; 154
Beecham, Sir Thomas, 104

*682*